T0190483

Lecture Notes in Artificial Intelligence   12284

Subseries of Lecture Notes in Computer Science

Series Editors

Randy Goebel
University of Alberta, Edmonton, Canada
Yuzuru Tanaka
Hokkaido University, Sapporo, Japan
Wolfgang Wahlster
DFKI and Saarland University, Saarbrücken, Germany

Founding Editor

Jörg Siekmann
DFKI and Saarland University, Saarbrücken, Germany

More information about this series at http://www.springer.com/series/1244

Petr Sojka · Ivan Kopeček ·
Karel Pala · Aleš Horák (Eds.)

Text, Speech, and Dialogue

23rd International Conference, TSD 2020
Brno, Czech Republic, September 8–11, 2020
Proceedings

 Springer

Editors
Petr Sojka
Faculty of Informatics
Masaryk University
Brno, Czech Republic

Ivan Kopeček
Faculty of Informatics
Masaryk University
Brno, Czech Republic

Karel Pala
Faculty of Informatics
Masaryk University
Brno, Czech Republic

Aleš Horák
Faculty of Informatics
Masaryk University
Brno, Czech Republic

ISSN 0302-9743   ISSN 1611-3349   (electronic)
Lecture Notes in Artificial Intelligence
ISBN 978-3-030-58322-4   ISBN 978-3-030-58323-1   (eBook)
https://doi.org/10.1007/978-3-030-58323-1

LNCS Sublibrary: SL7 – Artificial Intelligence

This Springer imprint is published by the registered company Springer Nature Switzerland AG
The registered company address is: Gewerbestrasse 11, 6330 Cham, Switzerland

Preface

The annual Text, Speech and Dialogue Conference (TSD), which originated in 1998, is continuing its third decade. During this time, thousands of authors from all over the world have contributed to the proceedings. TSD constitutes a recognized platform for the presentation and discussion of state-of-the-art technology and recent achievements in the field of natural language processing (NLP). It has become an interdisciplinary forum, interweaving the themes of speech technology and language processing. The conference attracts researchers not only from Central and Eastern Europe but also from other parts of the world. Indeed, one of its goals has always been to bring together NLP researchers with different interests from different parts of the world and to promote their mutual cooperation.

One of the declared goals of the conference has always been, as its title suggests, twofold: not only to deal with language processing and dialogue systems as such, but also to stimulate dialogue between researchers in the two areas of NLP, i.e., between text and speech people. In our view, TSD 2020 was again successful in this respect. We had the pleasure to welcome three prominent invited speakers this year: Diana Maynard presented keynote titled "Combining Expert Knowledge with NLP for Specialised Applications" with insight on how to combine expert human knowledge with automated NLP technologies, Joakim Nivre showed how to combine multilingual parsing with deep learning techniques in "Multilingual Dependency Parsing from Universal Dependencies to Sesame Street," and Paolo Rosso reported on "Multimodal Fake News Detection with Textual, Visual and Semantic Information."

This volume contains the proceedings of the 23rd TSD conference, held in Brno, Czech Republic, in September 2020. In the review process, 54 papers were accepted out of 110 submitted, each based on three reviews, with an acceptance rate of 49%. Even though this year's organization was affected by the global epidemic of COVID-19, the scientific quality of the contributions was at the highest level.

We would like to thank all the authors for the efforts they put into their submissions, and the members of the Program Committee and reviewers who did a wonderful job selecting the best papers. We are also grateful to the invited speakers for their contributions. Their talks provided insight into important current issues, applications, and techniques related to the conference topics.

Special thanks are due to the members of Local Organizing Committee for their tireless effort in organizing the conference. The TEXpertise of Petr Sojka resulted in the production of the volume that you are holding in your hands.

We hope that the readers will benefit from the results of this event and disseminate the ideas of the TSD conference all over the world. Enjoy the proceedings!

July 2020

Aleš Horák
Ivan Kopeček
Karel Pala
Petr Sojka

Trmal, Jan, Czech Republic
Varadi, Tamas, Hungary
Vetulani, Zygmunt, Poland
Wawer, Aleksander, Poland
Wiggers, Pascal, The Netherlands

Wilks, Yorick, UK
Woliński, Marcin, Poland
Wróblewska, Alina, Poland
Zakharov, Victor, Russia
Žganec Gros, Jerneja, Slovenia

Additional Referees

Akhmetov, Iskander
Ayetiran, Eniafe Festus
Baisa, Vít
Beňuš, Štefan
Fedorov, Yevhen
Marciniak, Małgorzata
Matoušek, Jiří
Medveď, Marek
Michel, Wilfried

Nevěřilová, Zuzana
Rossenbach, Nick
Škvorc, Tadej
Tihelka, Dan
Ulčar, Matej
Vesnicer, Boštjan
Vieting, Peter
Zhou, Whei

Organizing Committee

Aleš Horák *(Co-chair)*, Ivan Kopeček, Karel Pala *(Co-chair)*, Adam Rambousek *(Web System)*, Pavel Rychlý, Petr Sojka *(Proceedings)*

Sponsors and Support

The TSD conference is regularly supported by International Speech Communication Association (ISCA). We would like to express our thanks to the Lexical Computing Ltd., IBM Česká republika, spol. s r. o., and Amazon Alexa for their kind sponsoring contribution to TSD 2020.

Organization

TSD 2020 was organized by the Faculty of Informatics, Masaryk University, in cooperation with the Faculty of Applied Sciences, University of West Bohemia in Plzeň. The conference webpage is located at http://www.tsdconference.org/tsd2020/.

Program Committee

Nöth, Elmar (General Chair), Germany
Agerri, Rodrigo, Spain
Agirre, Eneko, Spain
Benko, Vladimir, Slovakia
Bhatia, Archna, USA
Černocký, Jan, Czech Republic
Dobrisek, Simon, Slovenia
Ekstein, Kamil, Czech Republic
Evgrafova, Karina, Russia
Fedorov, Yevhen, Ukraine
Ferrer, Carlos, Cuba
Fischer, Volker, Germany
Fiser, Darja, Slovenia
Galiotou, Eleni, Greece
Gambäck, Björn, Norway
Garabík, Radovan, Slovakia
Gelbukh, Alexander, Mexico
Guthrie, Louise, UK
Haderlein, Tino, Germany
Hajič, Jan, Czech Republic
Hajičová, Eva, Czech Republic
Haralambous, Yannis, France
Hermansky, Hynek, USA
Hlaváčová, Jaroslava, Czech Republic
Horák, Aleš, Czech Republic
Hovy, Eduard, USA
Jouvet, Denis, France
Khokhlova, Maria, Russia
Khusainov, Aidar, Russia
Kocharov, Daniil, Russia
Konopík, Miloslav, Czech Republic
Kopeček, Ivan, Czech Republic
Kordoni, Valia, Germany

Kotelnikov, Evgeny, Russia
Král, Pavel, Czech Republic
Kunzmann, Siegfried, Germany
Ljubešić, Nikola, Croatia
Loukachevitch, Natalija, Russia
Magnini, Bernardo, Italy
Marchenko, Oleksandr, Ukraine
Matoušek, Václav, Czech Republic
Mihelić, France, Slovenia
Mouček, Roman, Czech Republic
Mykowiecka, Agnieszka, Poland
Ney, Hermann, Germany
Orozco-Arroyave, Juan Rafael, Colombia
Pala, Karel, Czech Republic
Pavesić, Nikola, Slovenia
Piasecki, Maciej, Poland
Psutka, Josef, Czech Republic
Pustejovsky, James, USA
Rigau, German, Spain
Rothkrantz, Leon, The Netherlands
Rumshinsky, Anna, USA
Rusko, Milan, Slovakia
Rychlý, Pavel, Czech Republic
Sazhok, Mykola, Ukraine
Scharenborg, Odette, The Netherlands
Skrelin, Pavel, Russia
Smrž, Pavel, Czech Republic
Sojka, Petr, Czech Republic
Stemmer, Georg, Germany
Šikonja, Marko Robnik, Slovenia
Stemmer, Georg, Germany
Štruc, Vitomir, Slovenia
Tadić, Marko, Croatia

Contents

Invited Papers

Combining Expert Knowledge with NLP for Specialised Applications   3
  Diana Maynard and Adam Funk

Multilingual Dependency Parsing from Universal Dependencies
to Sesame Street   11
  Joakim Nivre

Multimodal Fake News Detection with Textual, Visual
and Semantic Information   30
  Anastasia Giachanou, Guobiao Zhang, and Paolo Rosso

Text

A Twitter Political Corpus of the 2019 10N Spanish Election   41
  Javier Sánchez-Junquera, Simone Paolo Ponzetto, and Paolo Rosso

Mining Local Discourse Annotation for Features of Global
Discourse Structure   50
  Lucie Poláková and Jiří Mírovský

Diversification of Serbian-French-English-Spanish Parallel Corpus
ParCoLab with Spoken Language Data   61
  Dušica Terzić, Saša Marjanović, Dejan Stosic, and Aleksandra Miletic

Quantitative Analysis of the Morphological Complexity
of Malayalam Language.   71
  Kavya Manohar, A. R. Jayan, and Rajeev Rajan

Labeling Explicit Discourse Relations Using Pre-trained
Language Models   79
  Murathan Kurfalı

EPIE Dataset: A Corpus for Possible Idiomatic Expressions   87
  Prateek Saxena and Soma Paul

Experimenting with Different Machine Translation Models
in Medium-Resource Settings   95
  Haukur Páll Jónsson, Haukur Barri Símonarson,
  Vésteinn Snæbjarnarson, Steinþór Steingrímsson,
  and Hrafn Loftsson

FinEst BERT and CroSloEngual BERT: Less Is More
in Multilingual Models   104
Matej Ulčar and Marko Robnik-Šikonja

Employing Sentence Context in Czech Answer Selection   112
Marek Medveď, Radoslav Sabol, and Aleš Horák

Grammatical Parallelism of Russian Prepositional Localization
and Temporal Constructions   122
Victor Zakharov and Irina Azarova

Costra 1.1: An Inquiry into Geometric Properties of Sentence Spaces   135
Petra Barančíková and Ondřej Bojar

Next Step in Online Querying and Visualization of Word-Formation
Networks   144
Jonáš Vidra and Zdeněk Žabokrtský

Evaluating a Multi-sense Definition Generation Model
for Multiple Languages   153
Arman Kabiri and Paul Cook

Combining Cross-lingual and Cross-task Supervision
for Zero-Shot Learning   162
Matúš Pikuliak and Marián Šimko

Reading Comprehension in Czech via Machine Translation
and Cross-Lingual Transfer   171
Kateřina Macková and Milan Straka

Measuring Memorization Effect in Word-Level Neural Networks Probing . . .   180
Rudolf Rosa, Tomáš Musil, and David Mareček

Semi-supervised Induction of Morpheme Boundaries in Czech
Using a Word-Formation Network   189
Jan Bodnár, Zdeněk Žabokrtský, and Magda Ševčíková

Interpreting Word Embeddings Using a Distribution Agnostic Approach
Employing Hellinger Distance   197
Tamás Ficsor and Gábor Berend

Verb Focused Answering from CORD-19   206
Elizabeth Jasmi George

Adjusting BERT's Pooling Layer for Large-Scale Multi-Label
Text Classification.   214
Jan Lehečka, Jan Švec, Pavel Ircing, and Luboš Šmídl

Recognizing Preferred Grammatical Gender in Russian Anonymous
Online Confessions   222
    Anton Alekseev and Sergey Nikolenko

Attention to Emotions: Detecting Mental Disorders in Social Media   231
    Mario Ezra Aragón, A. Pastor López-Monroy, Luis C. González,
    and Manuel Montes-y-Gómez

Cross-Lingual Transfer for Hindi Discourse Relation Identification   240
    Anirudh Dahiya, Manish Shrivastava, and Dipti Misra Sharma

Authorship Verification with Personalized Language Models   248
    Milton King and Paul Cook

A Semantic Grammar for Augmentative and Alternative
Communication Systems   257
    Jayr Pereira, Natália Franco, and Robson Fidalgo

Assessing Unintended Memorization in Neural Discriminative
Sequence Models   265
    Mossad Helali, Thomas Kleinbauer, and Dietrich Klakow

Investigating the Impact of Pre-trained Word Embeddings on Memorization
in Neural Networks   273
    Aleena Thomas, David Ifeoluwa Adelani, Ali Davody, Aditya Mogadala,
    and Dietrich Klakow

Speech

Investigating the Corpus Independence of the
Bag-of-Audio-Words Approach.   285
    Mercedes Vetráb and Gábor Gosztolya

Developing Resources for Te Reo Māori Text To Speech
Synthesis System   294
    Jesin James, Isabella Shields, Rebekah Berriman,
    Peter J. Keegan, and Catherine I. Watson

Acoustic Characteristics of VOT in Plosive Consonants Produced
by Parkinson's Patients   303
    Patricia Argüello-Vélez, Tomas Arias-Vergara,
    María Claudia González-Rátiva, Juan Rafael Orozco-Arroyave,
    Elmar Nöth, and Maria Elke Schuster

A Systematic Study of Open Source and Commercial
Text-to-Speech (TTS) Engines 312
Jordan Hosier, Jordan Kalfen, Nikhita Sharma, and Vijay K. Gurbani

Automatic Correction of i/y Spelling in Czech ASR Output 321
Jan Švec, Jan Lehečka, Luboš Šmídl, and Pavel Ircing

Transfer Learning to Detect Parkinson's Disease from Speech In Different
Languages Using Convolutional Neural Networks with Layer Freezing 331
*Cristian David Rios-Urrego, Juan Camilo Vásquez-Correa,
Juan Rafael Orozco-Arroyave, and Elmar Nöth*

Speaker-Dependent BiLSTM-Based Phrasing 340
Markéta Jůzová and Daniel Tihelka

Phonetic Attrition in Vowels' Quality in L1 Speech of Late Czech-French
Bilinguals. 348
Marie Hévrová, Tomáš Bořil, and Barbara Köpke

Assessing the Dysarthria Level of Parkinson's Disease Patients
with GMM-UBM Supervectors Using Phonological Posteriors
and Diadochokinetic Exercises 356
Gabriel F. Miller, Juan Camilo Vásquez-Correa, and Elmar Nöth

Voice-Activity and Overlapped Speech Detection Using x-Vectors 366
Jiří Málek and Jindřich Žďánský

Introduction of Semantic Model to Help Speech Recognition 377
Stephane Level, Irina Illina, and Dominique Fohr

Towards Automated Assessment of Stuttering and Stuttering Therapy 386
*Sebastian P. Bayerl, Florian Hönig, Joëlle Reister,
and Korbinian Riedhammer*

Synthesising Expressive Speech – Which Synthesiser for VOCAs? 397
Jan-Oliver Wülfing, Chi Tai Dang, and Elisabeth André

Perceived Length of Czech High Vowels in Relation to Formant
Frequencies Evaluated by Automatic Speech Recognition. 409
Tomáš Bořil and Jitka Veroňková

Inserting Punctuation to ASR Output in a Real-Time Production
Environment. 418
Pavel Hlubík, Martin Španěl, Marek Boháč, and Lenka Weingartová

Very Fast Keyword Spotting System with Real Time Factor Below 0.01 426
Jan Nouza, Petr Červa, and Jindřich Žďánský

On the Effectiveness of Neural Text Generation Based Data Augmentation
for Recognition of Morphologically Rich Speech   437
  Balázs Tarján, György Szaszák, Tibor Fegyó, and Péter Mihajlik

Context-Aware XGBoost for Glottal Closure Instant Detection
in Speech Signal   446
  Jindřich Matoušek and Michal Vraštil

LSTM-Based Speech Segmentation Trained on Different
Foreign Languages   456
  Zdeněk Hanzlíček and Jakub Vít

Complexity of the TDNN Acoustic Model with Respect
to the HMM Topology   465
  Josef V. Psutka, Jan Vaněk, and Aleš Pražák

Dialogue

Leyzer: A Dataset for Multilingual Virtual Assistants   477
  Marcin Sowański and Artur Janicki

Registering Historical Context for Question Answering in a Blocks World
Dialogue System.   487
  Benjamin Kane, Georgiy Platonov, and Lenhart Schubert

At Home with Alexa: A Tale of Two Conversational Agents   495
  *Jennifer Ureta, Celina Iris Brito, Jilyan Bianca Dy, Kyle-Althea Santos,
  Winfred Villaluna, and Ethel Ong*

ConversIAmo: Improving Italian Question Answering Exploiting IBM
Watson Services   504
  Chiara Leoni, Ilaria Torre, and Gianni Vercelli

Modification of Pitch Parameters in Speech Coding
for Information Hiding.   513
  Adrian Radej and Artur Janicki

ConfNet2Seq: Full Length Answer Generation from Spoken Questions   524
  Vaishali Pal, Manish Shrivastava, and Laurent Besacier

Graph Convolutional Networks for Student Answers Assessment   532
  Nisrine Ait Khayi and Vasile Rus

Author Index   541

Invited Papers

Combining Expert Knowledge with NLP for Specialised Applications

Diana Maynard(✉) and Adam Funk

Department of Computer Science, University of Sheffield, Sheffield, UK
d.maynard@sheffield.ac.uk

Abstract. Traditionally, there has been a disconnect between custom-built applications used to solve real-world information extraction problems in industry, and automated learning-based approaches developed in academia. Despite approaches such as transfer-based learning, adapting these to more customised solutions where the task and data may be different, and where training data may be largely unavailable, is still hugely problematic, with the result that many systems still need to be custom-built using expert hand-crafted knowledge, and do not scale. In the legal domain, a traditional slow adopter of technology, black box machine learning-based systems are too untrustworthy to be widely used. In industrial settings, the fine-grained highly specialised knowledge of human experts is still critical, and it is not obvious how to integrate this into automated classification systems. In this paper, we examine two case studies from recent work combining this expert human knowledge with automated NLP technologies.

Keywords: Natural language processing · Ontologies · Information extraction

1 Introduction

Although machine learning, and more recently deep learning-based approaches, have shown enormous promise and success in Natural Language Processing (NLP), and more generally in the field of Artificial Intelligence (AI), there are nevertheless a number of drawbacks when applied to many real-world applications in industrial settings. The medical and legal domains have been traditionally slow to adopt automated technologies, due partly to the critical effect of mistakes. On the other hand, driverless cars and autonomous robots are fast becoming an everyday reality, despite the numerous ethical considerations. When a human driver hits the brakes in order to avoid hitting a child who runs in front of a car, they make a moral decision to shift the risk from the child to their passengers. How should an autonomous car react in such a situation? One piece of

This work was partially supported by European Union under grant agreement No.726992 KNOWMAK and No. 825091 RISIS; and by Innovate UK.

research [3] showed that in surveys, people preferred an autonomous vehicle to protect pedestrians even if it meant sacrificing its passengers, as most human drivers would do, but paradoxically, these people claimed that they would not want to buy one if it were programmed to do so.

The recent COVID-19 pandemic has driven a wealth of interest in automated AI technology such as call systems. While call centers have long been a forerunner in the use of such tools, the pandemic has accelerated their growth due to the combination of a shortage of workers and an enormous increase in calls. IBM witnessed a 40% increase in use of Watson Assistant between February and April 2020, and other technologies show a similar popularity rise.[1]

However, automated call systems only deal with part of the problem, and are still relatively simple. They are best at signposting users to sources of information and mostly rely on posing pre-set questions with simple answers that can be easily be processed (e.g. yes/no questions, or by spotting simple keywords). Adapting these kinds of conversational agents to the specific demands of individual businesses requires intensive labour and training materials, so is not a project to be undertaken lightly or urgently.

In this paper, we focus on two case studies in which we have investigated how expert human knowledge can be interlinked with the advantages of automated technologies. These enable traditional manual tasks to be carried out faster and more accurately by processing huge amounts of data, while still ensuring both the consistency and flexibility to deal with new data as it emerges. The first of these is in the legal domain, where we have developed tools to assist consultants to review collateral warranties - an expensive and time-consuming task which nevertheless demands high precision and intricate levels of linguistic detail. The second is in the wider field of European scientific and technological knowledge production and policy making, where tools are needed to assist policymakers in understanding the nature of this enormous, highly complex and fast-changing domain.

2   Legal IE

The reviewing of collateral warranties is an important legal and economic task in the construction industry. These warranties are a type of contract by which a member of the construction team (e.g. an architect) promises a third party (e.g. the project funder) that they have properly discharged their contract. For example, an architect of a new office development owes a duty of care to the occupier of the development, concerning any design defects that might show up later. Without a collateral warranty, the architect would typically not be liable. Collateral warranties may include 'step-in' rights which allow the beneficiary to step into the role of the main contractor. This can be important, for example to banks providing funding for a project, enabling them to ensure that the project is completed if that contractor becomes insolvent.

---

[1] https://www.technologyreview.com/2020/05/14/1001716/ai-chatbots-take-call-center-jobs-during-coronavirus-pandemic.

There are a number of standard forms of collateral warranty, but their specific terms can be disputed, with clients often claiming that industry standard warranties favour subcontractors and designers. There may also be complex wording or terminology in standard contracts which make them too risky because they are outside the scope of the warranty giver's insurance cover. Therefore, many collateral warranties are bespoke. However, completing collateral warranties to the satisfaction of all parties is incredibly difficult, especially for large projects with many consultants and sub-contractors, as well as multiple occupants, and it is legally complex and onerous for lawyers to review them. A single manual review typically takes 3 h, but is often not properly valued by clients, who see it as a sideline to the main construction contract.

We have therefore been developing prototype software to assist lawyers in reviewing collateral warranties. The legal industry typically does not make use of automated software for these kind of tasks. Existing contract review software is limited and based on machine learning, which tends to be inadequate because it neither analyses collateral warranties to the level of detail required, nor does it provide explanatory output. Furthermore, it is unclear how the highly specialised human expertise can be replicated in an automated approach. For this reason, our system uses a rule-based approach which automates some of the more straightforward parts of the review process and focuses on breaking the documents down into relevant sections pertaining to each kind of problem the human reviewer must address. It uses a traffic light system to check standard protocols and to flag possible problems that the lawyer should investigate, with explanations as to the nature of the problem.

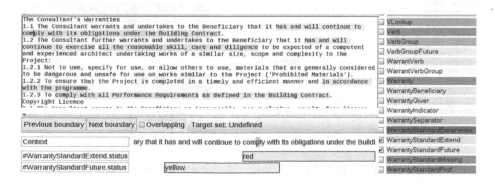

Fig. 1. Sample annotations in a collateral warranty in the GATE GUI (Color figure online)

The warranty annotation tool is based on the GATE architecture for NLP [4], an open source toolkit which has been in development at the University of Sheffield for more than 20 years. A rule-based approach is used to annotate different sections of the document and to recognise certain relevant entities (such as copyright issues, the warranty beneficiary, the warranty giver, and so on).

Figure 1 shows an example of a mocked-up warranty annotated in the GATE GUI.[2] Two annotations are highlighted here, which concern the extent of the warranty standard and the future warranty standard. In the bottom part of the picture, we see that these have features *red* and *yellow* respectively. This indicates that this part of the contract is something that a human reviewer needs to check manually.

The human reviewer does not see the GATE GUI at all; we show it only to explain the underlying technology. Instead, they use the reviewing interface also developed in the project, which enables them to upload a document, select some parameters, and run GATE on it via a web service. They can then view the contract in the interface and zoom in on different parts of the document to see the suggestions and highlights that GATE has made in an easily understandable way. The yellow and red flags ("translated" from the GATE features) indicate that they need to review these parts, and the review cannot be marked as completed until these are satisfactory. Figure 2 shows the same mocked-up document now in the reviewing interface. The reviewing process semi-automatically generates a final report (for the lawyer's client) based on the current human-written report, with warnings about the risky passages in the document.

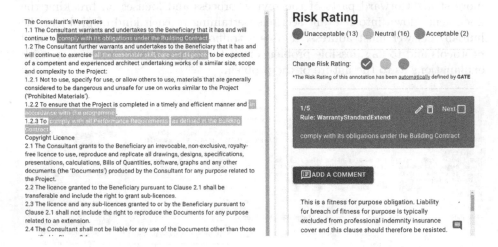

Fig. 2. Sample annotations in a mock-up collateral warranty in the GATE GUI

3   Understanding Scientific Knowledge Production in Europe

Understanding knowledge production and co-creation in key emerging areas of European research is critical for policy makers wishing to analyse impact and

---

[2] The warranty is not a real one, for legal reasons, but the annotation is genuine.

make strategic decisions. Essentially, they need to know who is doing research on what topic and in which country or region. The RISIS-KNOWMAK tool[3] is the result of a 3-year European project enabling the user to combine multiple data sources (publications, patents, and European projects), connect the dots by analysing knowledge production by topics and geography, and to pick from different kinds of visualisation options for the data they are interested in.

The tool generates aggregated indicators to characterise geographical spaces (countries or regions) and actors (public research organisations and companies) in terms of various dimensions of knowledge production. For each topic or combination of topics, the mapping of documents enables the generation of indicators such as the number of publications, EU-FP projects, and patents in a specific region, as well as various composite indicators combining dimensions, such as the aggregated knowledge production share and intensity, and the publication degree centrality.

Current methods for characterising and visualising the field have limitations concerning the changing nature of research, differences in language and topic structure between policies and scientific topics, and coverage of a broad range of scientific and political issues that have different characteristics. The kind of language used in patent descriptions is very different from that used in scientific publications, and even the terminology can be very different, so it is hard to develop tools which can classify both kinds of document in the same way.

In recent years, a priori classification systems for science and technology, such as the Field of Science Classification (OECD, 2002) and IPC codes for patents [6], have been increasingly replaced by data-driven approaches, relying on the automated treatment of large corpora, such as word co-occurrences in academic papers [2], clustering through co-citation analysis [9], and overlay maps to visualise knowledge domains [7]. These approaches have obvious advantages, since they are more flexible to accommodate the changing structures of science, and are able to discover latent structures of science rather than impose a pre-defined structure over the data [8]. Yet, when the goal is to produce indicators for policymakers, purely data-driven methods also display limitations. On the one hand, such methods provide very detailed views of specific knowledge domains, but are less suited to large-scale mapping across the whole science and technology landscape. On the other hand, lacking a common ontology of scientific and technological domains [5], such mappings are largely incommensurable across dimensions of knowledge production. Perhaps even more importantly, data-driven methods do not allow presumptions of categories used in the policy debate to be integrated in the classification process. These are largely implicit and subjective, implying that there is no gold standard against which to assess the quality and relevance of the indicators, but these are inherently debatable [1].

The RISIS-KNOWMAK classification tool is a GATE-based web service which classifies each document according to the relevant topics it is concerned with. This involves the novel use of ontologies and semantic technologies as a means to bridge the linguistic and conceptual gap between policy questions

---

[3] https://www.knowmak.eu/.

and (disparate) data sources. Our experience suggests that a proper interlinking between intellectual tasks and the use of advanced techniques for language processing is key for the success of this endeavour.

Our approach was based on two main elements: a) the design of an ontology of the Key Enabling Technologies and Societal Grand Challenges (KET and SGC) knowledge domains to make explicit their content and to provide a common structure across dimensions of knowledge production; and b) the integration between NLP techniques (to associate data sources with the ontology categories) and expert-based judgement (to make sensible choices for the matching process). This drove a recursive process where the ontology development and data annotation were successively refined based on expert assessment of the generated indicators.

Ontology development in our application involves three aspects: first, the design of the ontology structure, consisting of a set of related topics and subtopics in the relevant subject areas; second, populating the ontology with keywords; and third, classifying documents based on the weighted frequency of keywords. The mapping process can be seen as a problem of multi-class classification, with a large number of classes, and is achieved by relying on source-specific vocabularies and mapping techniques that also exploit (expert) knowledge about the structure of individual data sources. This is an iterative process, based on co-dependencies between data, topics, and the representation system.

Our initial ontology derived from policy documents was manually enriched and customised, based on the outcome of the matching process and expert assessment of the results. Eventually, the original ontology classes may also be adapted based on their distinctiveness in terms of data items. Such a staged approach, distinguishing between core elements that are stabilised (the ontology classes) and elements that are dynamic and can be revised (the assignment of data items to classes), is desirable from a design and user perspective. Therefore, the approach is flexible, for example to respond to changes in policy interests, and scalable since new data sources can be integrated within the process whenever required. All three steps require human intervention to define prior assumptions and to evaluate outcomes, but they integrate automatic processing through advanced NLP techniques. Consequently, if changes are deemed necessary, the process can easily be re-run and the data re-annotated within a reasonable period of time.

The ontology is freely available on the project web page[4]; we refer the interested reader also to the publications and documentation found there for full details of the technology. Our experience with this specialised ontology and classification shows that while NLP techniques are critical for linking ontologies with large datasets, some key design choices on the ontology and its application to data are of an intellectual nature and closely associated with specific user needs. This suggests that the design of interactions between expert-based a priori knowledge and the use of advanced data techniques is a key requirement for robust S&T ontologies.

---

[4] https://gate.ac.uk/projects/knowmak/.

We have also produced a number of case studies of how the tool could be used for policy making. In the field of genomics, we compared the technological and scientific knowledge production in Europe in the period 2010–2014. Technological production is measured by patents, while scientific production is measured by publications. These show different geographical distributions. The former is more concentrated in space: in terms of volume, Paris is the biggest cluster for both types. Within regions, production varies a lot: London is the biggest producer of both types, while Eindhoven is key in terms of technological knowledge (both for volume and intensity). These findings clearly reflect the different structure of public and private knowledge.

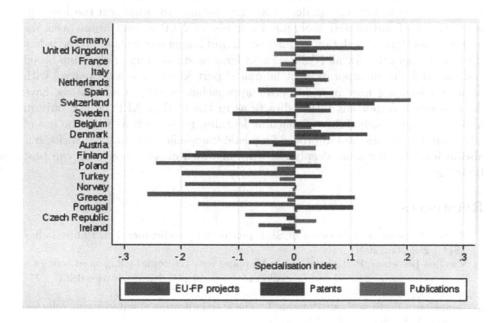

Fig. 3. Specialisation indexes in biotechnology around Europe

Another example is based on the topic of Industrial Biotechnology (IB), which offers new tools, products and technologies based on the exploitation of biological processes, organisms, cells or cellular components. Policymakers might like to know, for example, which European countries are (more) specialised in this field, and whether there are differences in the extent of specialisation when considering scientific and technological development. The tool provides ready-to-use indicators to answer these questions. Figure 3 indicates the country specialisation indexes in biotechnology for the three measures of knowledge production in the period 2010–2014. Values greater/lower than 0 in the specialisation indexes imply that a country is more/less specialised in IB compared with the average European country. Amongst larger countries in terms of knowledge production, Germany, France, Italy and the Netherlands exhibit no clear specialisation in

IB, with all indexes ranging at moderate levels from −0.09 to 0.07. The only exception is the UK, which is more specialised in terms of EU-FP projects (specialisation higher than 0.1).

4   Conclusions

This paper has focused on two case studies based around tools we have developed for specialised applications (in the legal and scientometrics domains) where standard NLP tools based on machine learning are unlikely to be satisfactory due to the kinds of knowledge and output required, and to other constraints such as explainability (in the legal case) and flexibility (in the scientometrics case). While new advances in deep learning continue to transform the levels of achievement of automated tools for a number of NLP classification tasks, as well as in machine translation and in speech and image recognition, nevertheless they are not suitable for all NLP tasks, at least as stand-alone tools. Rule-based systems and the incorporation of human expert knowledge interweaved with advanced learning may provide better approaches in some cases, as we have demonstrated. Important future directions in the field of NLP lie not only in improving the explainability of machine learning tools, such as with the use of adversarial examples, and improved linguistic knowledge in neural networks, but also in investigating more deeply the ways in which expert knowledge can best be integrated.

References

1. Barré, R.: Sense and nonsense of S&T productivity indicators. Sci. Public Policy **28**(4), 259–266 (2001)
2. Van den Besselaar, P., Heimeriks, G.: Mapping research topics using word-reference co-occurrences: a method and an exploratory case study. Scientometrics **68**(3), 377–393 (2006)
3. Bonnefon, J.F., Shariff, A., Rahwan, I.: The social dilemma of autonomous vehicles. Science **352**(6293), 1573–1576 (2016)
4. Cunningham, H.: GATE, a general architecture for text engineering. Comput. Humanit. **36**(2), 223–254 (2002). https://doi.org/10.1023/A:1014348124664
5. Daraio, C., et al.: Data integration for research and innovation policy: an ontology-based data management approach. Scientometrics **106**(2), 857–871 (2016)
6. Debackere, K., Luwel, M.: Patent data for monitoring S&T portfolios. In: Moed, H.F., Glänzel, W., Schmoch, U. (eds.) Handbook of Quantitative Science and Technology Research, pp. 569–585. Springer, Dordrecht (2004). https://doi.org/10.1007/1-4020-2755-9_27
7. Rafols, I., Porter, A.L., Leydesdorff, L.: Science overlay maps: a new tool for research policy and library management. J. Am. Soc. Inform. Sci. Technol. **61**(9), 1871–1887 (2010)
8. Shiffrin, R.M., Börner, K.: Mapping knowledge domains. PNAS **101**, 5183–5185 (2004)
9. Šubelj, L., van Eck, N.J., Waltman, L.: Clustering scientific publications based on citation relations: a systematic comparison of different methods. PloS ONE **11**(4), e0154404 (2016)

Multilingual Dependency Parsing from Universal Dependencies to Sesame Street

Joakim Nivre[✉]

Department of Linguistics and Philology, Uppsala University, Uppsala, Sweden
joakim.nivre@lingfil.uu.se

Abstract. Research on dependency parsing has always had a strong multilingual orientation, but the lack of standardized annotations for a long time made it difficult both to meaningfully compare results across languages and to develop truly multilingual systems. The Universal Dependencies project has during the last five years tried to overcome this obstacle by developing cross-linguistically consistent morphosyntactic annotation for many languages. During the same period, dependency parsing (like the rest of NLP) has been transformed by the adoption of continuous vector representations and neural network techniques. In this paper, I will introduce the framework and resources of Universal Dependencies, and discuss advances in dependency parsing enabled by these resources in combination with deep learning techniques, ranging from traditional word and character embeddings to deep contextualized word representations like ELMo and BERT.

Keywords: Dependency parsing · Multilingual · UD · Word representations

1 Introduction

Dependency parsing is arguably the dominant approach to syntactic analysis in NLP today, especially for languages other than English. Its increasing popularity over the last one and a half decade is undoubtedly due to several factors. First of all, a dependency tree provides a simple and transparent encoding of predicate-argument structure that has proven useful in many downstream applications, such as information extraction [37], often acting as a crude proxy for a semantic representation. Second, dependency parsing can be achieved with models that are both simple and efficient, sometimes with linear runtime guarantees [24,26], which facilitates the implementation and deployment of parsers for large-scale applications. Finally, dependency-based syntactic representations are compatible with many linguistic traditions around the world, and annotated corpora for a wide range of languages are therefore more readily available than for alternative representations. This is clearly reflected in the research on dependency parsing

© Springer Nature Switzerland AG 2020
P. Sojka et al. (Eds.): TSD 2020, LNAI 12284, pp. 11–29, 2020.
https://doi.org/10.1007/978-3-030-58323-1_2

in recent years, which has had a strongly multilingual orientation starting from the influential CoNLL shared tasks in 2006 and 2007 [2, 29].[1]

The first shared task on multilingual dependency parsing was held as part of the CoNLL-X conference in 2006 [2], and the community owes a huge debt to the organizing committee consisting of Sabine Buchholz, Amit Dubey, Yuval Krymolowski and Erwin Marsi, who not only managed to collect dependency treebanks from 13 different languages but also converted them to a single unified data format, the CoNLL-X format, which has been a de facto standard for dependency treebanks and dependency parsing ever since. In this way, they enabled a new line of multilingual research which has been very fruitful for the community. The first shared task was followed by a second edition in 2007 [29], this time involving 10 different languages, and the data sets thus created for 19 different languages[2] are still used as benchmarks.

One of the most striking observations in the multilingual evaluation of these shared tasks is the substantial variation in parsing accuracy across languages. In 2006, the highest labeled attachment score (LAS) achieved for any language was 91.7 for Japanese, while the lowest was a modest 65.7 for Turkish. In 2007, the corresponding extreme points were English (89.6) and Greek (76.3). While this variation clearly depends on multiple factors, including training set size and type of text, the organizers of the 2007 shared task in their error analysis found that one of the best predictors of accuracy level was language type [29]. High accuracy was mainly achieved for languages similar to English, with limited morphology and relatively fixed word order, while lower accuracy was attained for languages like Greek, with rich morphology and freer word order. This led to an increased interest in studying the challenges posed by different languages for syntactic parsing, in particular parsing of morphologically rich languages [41].[3]

However, efforts to disentangle the influence of language typology on parsing also encountered obstacles. In particular, while the CoNLL-X format imposes a uniform representation of dependency trees, it does not in any way standardize the content of the linguistic annotations. Thus, assumptions about what constitutes a syntactic head or what categories should be used to classify syntactic relations could (and did) vary almost without limit. This in turn meant that it was very hard to determine whether differences in parsing accuracy between languages were due to differences in language structure or differences in annotation schemes (or a combination of the two). Evidence that divergent annotations can be a confound came especially from studies that observed very different results for closely related languages, for example, Russian and Czech [28].

The desire to compare parsing results across languages in a more meaningful way was one of several motivations behind the Universal Dependencies

---

[1] A multilingual perspective is also prevalent in the theoretical tradition of dependency grammar, starting with the seminal work of Tesnière [38], and in earlier rule-based approaches to dependency parsing [34].

[2] There was an overlap of 4 languages between the two shared tasks.

[3] This research trend was not limited to dependency parsing, but also included groundbreaking work on constituency parsing.

(UD) initiative [27,30,31], which aims to create cross-linguistically consistent morphosyntactic annotation for as many languages as possible. Started as a small-scale project in 2014, UD has grown into a large community effort involving over 300 researchers around the world and has to date released over 150 treebanks in 90 languages. In addition to parsing research and benchmarking for individual languages [42,44], the treebanks are widely used in research on cross-lingual learning [7,9,40] as well as for linguistic research on word order typology [8,16,32], to mention only a few applications.

In this paper, I will first introduce the UD annotation framework and the resources that have been made available through the project. I will then review three recent studies that take a multilingual perspective on dependency parsing and uses data from UD to cast light on cross-linguistic similarities and differences. These studies explore different ways of representing words in neural dependency parsing, ranging from traditional word and character embeddings to deep contextualized word representations like ELMo [33] and BERT [4].

2   Universal Dependencies

The main goal of the UD project is to develop cross-linguistically consistent morphosyntactic annotation for as many languages as possible in order to facilitate multilingual research within NLP and linguistics. Ideally, the annotation should allow meaningful linguistic analysis across languages, enable research on syntactic parsing in multilingual settings, support the development of NLP systems for multiple languages, and facilitate resource-building for new languages. Since cross-linguistic consistency by necessity implies some abstraction over language-specific details, UD may not be ideal for in-depth analysis of a single language and should therefore be seen as a complement to language-specific annotation schemes, rather than as a replacement.

The UD project started in 2014, and the first version of the guidelines was released the same year together with an initial batch of ten treebanks [27,30]. A second version of the guidelines was launched in 2016, and treebanks have been released (roughly) every six months, with the latest release (v2.5) containing 157 treebanks representing 90 languages [31]. For more complete documentation, we refer to the UD website.[4]

2.1   Basic Principles of UD

The main idea underlying UD is to achieve cross-linguistically consistent annotation by focusing on grammatical relations between words, especially content words. This is illustrated in Fig. 1, which shows two parallel sentences in English and Finnish, two typologically rather different languages. The two sentences are similar in that they consist of a verbal predicate with a subject, an object and a locative modifier, but they differ in how the grammatical relations are

---

[4] https://universaldependencies.org.

morphosyntactically encoded. English relies on word order to distinguish the subject and the object, which are both realized as bare noun phrases, while the locative modifier is introduced by a preposition. Finnish instead uses different morphological cases to distinguish all three relations. In addition, the English noun phrases use an article to encode definiteness, a category that is not overtly marked at all in Finnish.

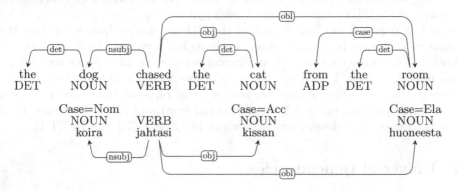

Fig. 1. Simplified UD annotation for equivalent sentences from English (top) and Finnish (bottom)

The goal is to bring out the similarities without obscuring the differences. Concretely, this is achieved by giving priority in the annotation to argument and modifier relations involving predicates and nominals – the three relations that are common to the English and Finnish sentences in Fig. 1. On top of these grammatical relations, we then capture concrete aspects of morphosyntactic realization in two different ways. On the one hand, we use part-of-speech tags and morphological features to describe words and their inflections, as exemplified by the nominal case-marking in Finnish.[5] On the other hand, we use special syntactic relations to link grammatical function words to their hosts, as shown by the articles and the preposition in English.

It is important to note that the notion of word that is relevant here is that of a syntactic word, which does not always coincide with orthographical or phonological units. For instance, clitics often need to be separated from their hosts and treated as independent words even if they are not recognized as such in conventional orthography, as in Spanish *dámelo* = *da me lo* (lit. give me it), and many contractions need to be split into several words, as in French *au* = *à le* (lit. at the). Conversely, compound words need a special treatment in languages where their written form may contain boundary markers such as whitespace. In fact, coming up with good criteria for determining word boundaries across languages with different writing systems and orthographic conventions has turned out to be one of the main challenges of the UD enterprise.

---

[5] The features displayed in Fig. 1 are only a small subset of the features that would appear in a complete annotation of the two sentences.

2.2   Morphological Annotation

The morphological annotation of a (syntactic) word in the UD scheme consists of three levels of representation:

1. A lemma representing the base form of the word.
2. A part-of-speech tag representing the grammatical category of the word.
3. A set of features representing lexical and grammatical properties associated with the particular word form.

The lemma is the canonical form of the word, which is the form typically found in dictionaries. The list of universal part-of-speech tags is a fixed list containing 17 tags, shown in Table 1. Languages are not required to use all tags, but the list cannot be extended to cover language-specific categories. Instead, more fine-grained classification of words can be achieved via the use of features, which specify additional information about morphosyntactic properties. We provide an inventory of features that are attested in multiple languages and need to be encoded in a uniform way, listed in Table 1. Users can extend this set of universal features and add language-specific features when necessary.

Table 1. PoS tags (left), morphological features (center) and syntactic relations (right).

			Syntactic Relations		
	Features		Clausal		
PoS Tags	Inflectional	Lexical	Core	Non-Core	Nominal
ADJ	Animacy	Abbr	nsubj	advcl	acl
ADP	Aspect	Foreign	csubj	advmod	amod
ADV	Case	NumType	ccomp	aux	appos
AUX	Clusivity	Poss	iobj	cop	case
CCONJ	Definite	PronType	obj	discourse	clf
DET	Degree	Reflex	xcomp	dislocated	det
INTJ	Evident	Typo		expl	nmod
NOUN	Gender			mark	nummod
NUM	Mood			obl	
PART	NounClass			vocative	
PRON	Number		**Linking**	**MWE**	**Special**
PROPN	Person		cc	compound	dep
PUNCT	Polarity		conj	fixed	goeswith
SCONJ	Polite		list	flat	orphan
SYM	Tense		parataxis		punct
VERB	VerbForm				reparandum
X	Voice				root

2.3 Syntactic Annotation

Syntactic annotation in the UD scheme consists of typed dependency relations between words, prioritizing predicate-argument and modifier relations that hold directly between content words, as opposed to being mediated by function words. As stated previously, the rationale is that this makes more transparent what grammatical relations are shared across languages, even when the languages differ in the way that they use word order, function words or morphological inflection to encode these relations. UD provides a taxonomy of 37 universal relation types to classify syntactic relations, as shown in Table 1. The taxonomy distinguishes between relations that occur at the clause level (linked to a predicate) and those that occur in noun phrases (linked to a nominal head). At the clause level, a distinction is made between core arguments (essentially subjects and objects) and all other dependents [1,39]. It is important to note that not all relations in the taxonomy are syntactic dependency relations in the narrow sense. First, there are special relations for function words like determiners, classifiers, adpositions, auxiliaries, copulas and subordinators, whose dependency status is controversial. In addition, there are a number of special relations for linking relations (including coordination), certain types of multiword expressions, and special phenomena like ellipsis, disfluencies, punctuation and typographical errors. Many of these relations cannot plausibly be interpreted as syntactic head-dependent relations, and should rather be thought of as technical devices for encoding flat structures in the form of a tree. The inventory of universal relation types is fixed, but subtypes can be added in individual languages to capture additional distinctions that are useful.

2.4 UD Treebanks

UD release v2.5[6] [43] contains 157 treebanks representing 90 languages. Table 2 specifies for each language the number of treebanks available, as well as the total number of annotated sentences and words in that language. It is worth noting that the amount of data varies considerably between languages, from Skolt Sámi with 36 sentences and 321 words, to German with over 200,000 sentences and nearly 4 million words. The majority of treebanks are small but it should be kept in mind that many of these treebanks are new initiatives and can be expected to grow substantially in the future. The languages in UD v2.5 represent 20 different language families (or equivalent). The selection is very heavily biased towards Indo-European languages (48 out of 90), and towards a few branches of this family – Germanic (10), Romance (8) and Slavic (13) – but it is worth noting that the bias is (slowly) becoming less extreme over time.[7]

---

[6] UD releases are numbered by letting the first digit (2) refer to the version of the guidelines and the second digit (5) to the number of releases under that version.

[7] The proportion of Indo-European languages has gone from 60% in v2.1 to 53% in v2.5.

Table 2. Languages in UD v2.5; number of treebanks (#), sentences (S) and words (W).

Language	#	S	W	Language	#	S	W	Language	#	S	W
Afrikaans	1	1,934	49,276	German	4	208,440	3,753,947	Old Russian	2	17,548	168,522
Akkadian	1	101	1,852	Gothic	1	5,401	55,336	Persian	1	5,997	152,920
Amharic	1	1,074	10,010	Greek	1	2,521	63,441	Polish	3	40,398	499,392
Ancient Greek	2	30,999	416,988	Hebrew	1	6,216	161,417	Portuguese	3	22,443	570,543
Arabic	3	28,402	1,042,024	Hindi	2	17,647	375,533	Romanian	3	25,858	551,932
Armenian	1	2502	52630	Hindi English	1	1,898	26,909	Russian	4	71,183	1,262,206
Assyrian	1	57	453	Hungarian	1	1,800	42,032	Sanskrit	1	230	1,843
Bambara	1	1,026	13,823	Indonesian	2	6,593	141,823	Scottish Gaelic	1	2,193	42,848
Basque	1	8,993	121,443	Irish	1	1,763	40,572	Serbian	1	4,384	97,673
Belarusian	1	637	13,325	Italian	6	35,481	811,522	Skolt Sámi	1	36	321
Bhojpuri	1	254	4,881	Japanese	4	67,117	1,498,560	Slovak	1	10,604	106,043
Breton	1	888	10,054	Karelian	1	228	3,094	Slovenian	2	11,188	170,158
Bulgarian	1	11,138	156,149	Kazakh	1	1,078	10,536	Spanish	3	34,693	1,004,443
Buryat	1	927	10,185	Komi Permyak	1	49	399	Swedish	3	12,269	206,855
Cantonese	1	1,004	13,918	Komi Zyrian	2	327	3,463	Swedish Sign Language	1	203	1,610
Catalan	1	16,678	531,971	Korean	3	34,702	446,996	Swiss German	1	100	1,444
Chinese	5	12,449	285,127	Kurmanji	1	754	1,0260	Tagalog	1	55	292
Classical Chinese	1	15,115	74,770	Latin	3	41,695	582,336	Tamil	1	600	9,581
Coptic	1	1,575	40,034	Latvian	1	13,643	219,955	Telugu	1	1,328	6,465
Croatian	1	9,010	199,409	Lithuanian	2	3,905	75,403	Thai	1	1,000	22,322
Czech	5	127,507	2,222,163	Livvi	1	125	1,632	Turkish	3	9,437	91,626
Danish	1	5,512	100,733	Maltese	1	2,074	44,162	Ukrainian	1	7,060	122,091
Dutch	2	20,916	306,503	Marathi	1	466	3,849	Upper Sorbian	1	646	11,196
English	7	35,791	620,509	Mbyá Guaraní	2	1,144	13,089	Urdu	1	5,130	138,077
Erzya	1	1,550	15,790	Moksha	1	65	561	Uyghur	1	3,456	40,236
Estonian	2	32,634	465,015	Naija	1	948	12,863	Vietnamese	1	3,000	43,754
Faroese	1	1,208	10,002	North Sámi	1	3,122	26,845	Warlpiri	1	55	314
Finnish	3	34,859	377,619	Norwegian	3	42,869	666,984	Welsh	1	956	16,989
French	7	45,074	1,157,171	Old Church Slavonic	1	6,338	57,563	Wolof	1	2,107	44,258
Galician	2	4,993	164,385	Old French	1	17,678	170,741	Yoruba	1	100	2,664

3   Studies in Dependency Parsing

The treebanks released by the UD project have been widely used in NLP research over the past five years and now constitute the natural benchmark data sets for dependency parsing in most languages. This tendency has been further reinforced by the CoNLL shared tasks on UD parsing organized in 2017 and 2018 [42,44]. These tasks are very similar in spirit to the old tasks from 2006 and 2007, designed to evaluate dependency parsing models on data from multiple languages, but there are two important differences. The first difference is that the new tasks focus on the entire task of mapping raw text to rich morphosyntactic representations with no prior segmentation or annotation of the input, whereas the old tasks used gold standard segmentation and morphological annotation as input to dependency parsing. The second difference is that annotations are now standardized across languages thanks to the UD framework, which facilitates cross-linguistic comparisons. In addition, the number of treebanks and languages has greatly increased since the pioneering efforts in 2006 and 2007. The CoNLL 2017 shared task featured 81 test sets from 49 languages (including 4 surprise languages), and the CoNLL 2018 shared task added 8 new languages. Figure 2 is an attempt to visualize the impact of these shared tasks on the languages appearing in both tasks. The x axis represents the amount of annotated data available and the y axis represents the top labeled attachment score (LAS). For each language, an orange dot and a red dot connected by an arrow represent the situation before and after the shared tasks, respectively. It is clear that the overwhelming majority of languages have seen an increase both in the amount of annotated resources and in parsing accuracy, sometimes very substantially so.

The CoNLL 2017 and 2018 shared tasks are only the tip of the iceberg when it comes to parsing research based on UD resources, which includes a wide range of studies of parsing models for individual languages, as well as work on cross- and multilingual parsing models. I will make no attempt at surveying this large body of literature here. Instead, I will present three specific studies by the Uppsala parsing group in order to illustrate how the availability of cross-linguistically consistent annotation for multiple languages enables us to study the interplay between parsing techniques and language structure in a more informed way.

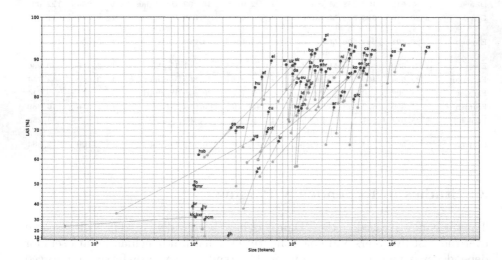

Fig. 2. Impact of the CoNLL 2017 and 2018 shared tasks on amount of data (x axis) and top LAS (y axis) for UD languages. Figure created by Filip Ginter and previously published in Nivre et al. [31].

3.1   Parsing Framework

Two of the three studies that will be discussed below make use of a generic framework for dependency parsing originally proposed by Kiperwasser and Goldberg [11]. The core component of the architecture is a BiLSTM encoder:

$$\text{BiLSTM}(x_1, \ldots, x_n) = v_1, \ldots, v_n$$

The input here is a sequence of vectors $x_1, \ldots, x_n$ representing the input words $w_1, \ldots, w_n$ of a sentence. The output is a corresponding sequence of vectors $v_1, \ldots, v_n$, where each v_i is a contextualized representation of the word w_i, that is, a representation that combines information from the input representation x_i with information from both the left context $x_1, \ldots, x_{i-1}$ and the right context $x_{i+1}, \ldots x_n$. These contextualized word representations are then fed into an MLP that scores alternative hypotheses about the dependency structure. If a graph-based parsing model is assumed, this may mean scoring a potential dependency arc $w_i \rightarrow w_j$:

$$S(w_i \rightarrow w_j) = \text{MLP}(v_i, v_j)$$

A full parse can then be computed by finding the maximum spanning tree over a complete score matrix [22].

If instead a transition-based parsing model is assumed, the model will score a potential transition t out of the current parser configuration c, represented by a small number of word vectors $v_i, \ldots v_k$ extracted from the parser's stack and buffer:

$$S(c, t) = \text{MLP}(v_i, \ldots v_k, t)$$

A parse tree can in this case be constructed by repeatedly applying the highest-scoring transition to the current configuration until a terminal configuration is reached, using a greedy deterministic parsing algorithm [25].

One of the main achievements of Kiperwasser and Goldberg was to show that this comparatively simple architecture can lead to state-of-the-art parsing accuracy for both graph-based and transition-based models if trained adequately [11]. This model has since been developed further by several researchers and currently underlie most of the state-of-the-art models for dependency parsing [3,5,6,12]. One of the evolved versions is UUParser [17], originally developed for the CoNLL 2017 and 2018 shared tasks [18,35], which involves two types of modifications. The first modification is the implementation of models that can handle non-projective dependency trees. In the transition-based case, this amounts to an extension of the arc-hybrid transition system [13] with a SWAP transition for online reordering [19,26]. In the graph-based case, this is achieved by using the Chu-Liu Edmonds maximum spanning tree algorithm [22]. The second modification concerns the input representations $x_1, \ldots, x_n$ and will be discussed in detail in the following sections.

3.2   Representing Word Types

Our first study, presented at EMNLP 2018 [36], concerns how neural transition-based dependency parsers benefit from different input representations, specifically pre-trained word embeddings, character-based representations, and part-of-speech tags. All of these techniques have previously been shown to be helpful, but there is a lack of systematic studies investigating how they compare to each other and whether the techniques are complementary or redundant. Another important goal, in line with the goals of this paper, is to find out how the usefulness of these techniques vary across languages.

For this study, we use the transition-based version of UUParser and only vary the way in which the input words $w_1, \ldots, w_n$ are represented. In the simplest model, the vector x_i representing input word w_i is simply a randomly initialized word embedding with a dimensionality of 100:

$$x_i = e^r(w_i)$$

In the most complex model, x_i is the concatenation of three vectors:

$$x_i = e^t(w_i) \circ \mathrm{BiLSTM}(c_{1:m}) \circ e(p_i)$$

The first vector $e^t(w_i)$ is a word embedding of the same dimensionality as $e^r(w_i)$, but initialized using the pre-trained word embeddings trained using word2vec [23] and released for the CoNLL 2017 shared task on universal dependency parsing [44]. The second vector $\mathrm{BiLSTM}(c_{1:m})$ is a character-based representation obtained by running a BiLSTM over the character sequence $c_1, \ldots, c_m$ of w_i, with a dimensionality of 100 for the output vector. The vector $e(p_i)$, finally, is an embedding of the part-of-speech tag p_i assigned to w_i by an independent part-of-speech tagger [6] (dimensionality 20, random initialization).

Table 3. Mean LAS across nine languages for a baseline system employing randomly initialised word embeddings only, compared to three separate systems using pre-trained word embeddings (+EXT), a character model (+CHAR), and part-of-speech tags (+POS). Scores are also shown for a combined system that utilises all three techniques and corresponding systems where one of the three techniques is ablated (−EXT, −CHAR and −POS).

BASELINE	67.7	COMBINED	81.0
+EXT	76.1	−EXT	79.9
+CHAR	78.3	−CHAR	79.2
+POS	75.9	−POS	80.3

In order to study the usefulness of pre-trained word embeddings, character representations, and part-of-speech tags across different languages, we train and evaluate the parser with different combinations of these input representations on a sample of nine languages, selected for diversity with respect to writing systems, character set sizes, and morphological complexity. Table 3 shows the labeled attachment score (LAS) for some of these systems when averaged over all nine languages. In the system +EXT, we *replace* the randomly initialized word embeddings of the BASELINE system with pre-trained word embeddings; in the systems +CHAR and +POS, we *concatenate* the random embeddings with character representations and part-of-speech tag embeddings, respectively. The results for these three systems show clearly that *either* of the three techniques by itself improves parsing accuracy by 8–10% points for our sample of languages, although the character representations appear to be a little more effective than the other two techniques. The COMBINED system, where we combine all three techniques (and omit random embeddings), adds another 5% points to the best score, which is a substantial improvement but far from what we should expect if the improvements were completely independent. Finally, omitting any of the three techniques from the COMBINED system, which gives us the systems −EXT, −CHAR and −POS, shows similar drops in accuracy of 1–2% points for all techniques (with the character representations again being slightly more important).

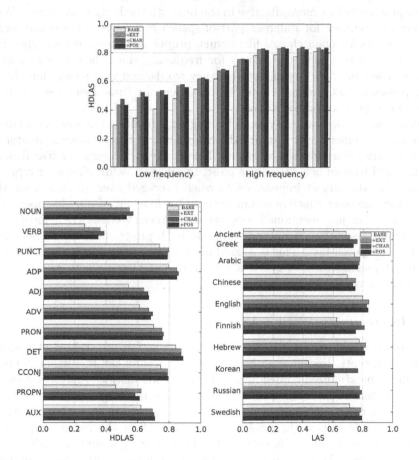

Fig. 3. Binned HDLAS by word frequency (top), HDLAS by part-of-speech categories (bottom left), and LAS per language (bottom right).

The conclusion so far is that all three techniques are helpful but their contributions somewhat redundant with diminishing returns when they are added on top of each other. However, these results are averaged over all words and sentences in all languages. In order to get a more fine-grained picture, Fig. 3 presents a breakdown of the results for the BASELINE, +EXT, +CHAR and +POS systems by word frequency (in equally sized bins), by part-of-speech category, and by language. The results per language are standard LAS scores; the other two diagrams plot HDLAS, a harsher metric that considers a word correctly analyzed only if its syntactic head and all its dependents are correct. The breakdown by frequency shows, not surprisingly, that all three techniques give the greatest improvements for low-frequency words, including unknown words, and that character representations are especially effective here. However, it is worth noting that we see improvements over the whole range of frequencies, and that character representations gradually lose their advantage, so that the other two techniques are in fact more effective in the bin with the highest frequency. When looking at accuracy for different part-of-speech categories, we see the largest improvements for open classes like nouns, proper nouns, verbs and adjectives, which is consistent with the results for frequency, since these classes contain the overwhelming majority of low-frequency words, and we also see that character representations give the largest improvement for these categories, with the notable exception of proper nouns.

When we break down the results by language, finally, some interesting differences start to emerge. First of all, the magnitude of the improvement over the baseline varies considerably, with morphologically rich languages like Russian, Finnish and Korean benefitting the most. In addition, while character representations give the largest improvements when averaged over all languages, they are in fact the most effective technique only for four out of nine languages (the three languages just mentioned together with Ancient Greek). For most of the other languages, they are outperformed by both pre-trained word embeddings and part-of-speech tags. This is a good illustration of the need to test hypotheses about parsing technology on a wide range of languages to guard against unfounded generalizations.

3.3 Representing Word Tokens

The word embeddings used in the first study, whether pre-trained or not, represent word types. Recent work has shown that results can be further improved by using contextualized embeddings, which provide distinct representations for different tokens of the same word type, and models like ELMo [33] and BERT [4] have quickly become ubiquitous in NLP. Our second study, presented at EMNLP 2019 [14], explores how these token embeddings affect the behavior of parsers belonging to the two main paradigms for dependency parsing: graph-based and transition-based. We knew from previous research that, although graph-based and transition-based parsers often achieve similar accuracy on average, they used to have distinct error profiles due to their inherent strengths and weaknesses [20, 21, 45]. Broadly speaking, transition-based parsers did better on local dependencies and short sentences, thanks to richer feature models, but struggled with non-local dependencies and longer sentences, due to greedy decoding and error propagation. Conversely, graph-based parsers were less accurate on local structures, because of lower structural sensitivity, but degraded less as dependencies and sentences get longer, thanks to exact decoding. However, this comparative error analysis was all done before the switch to neural network techniques, so we thought it was high time to replicate the old analysis in the new methodological framework with three main research questions:

1. Do the old error profiles persist after the switch to neural networks?
2. How do contextualized word embeddings change the picture?
3. Are the patterns consistent across different languages?

To answer these questions, we train and evaluate graph-based and transition-based versions of UUParser with three different input representations, yielding a total of six parsing models, each of which is applied to 13 different languages. The baseline parsers GR (graph-based) and TR (transition-based) use the same input representations as the −POS system in the first study, that is, a combination of pre-trained word embeddings and character representations (but no part-of-speech tags). For the other four models, we concatenate the baseline representation with a token embedding from either ELMo (GR+E and TR+E) or BERT (GR+B and TR+B). For ELMo, we make use of the pre-trained models provided by Che et al. [3], who train ELMo on 20 million words randomly sampled from raw WikiDump and Common Crawl datasets for 44 languages. For BERT, we employ the pretrained multilingual cased model provided by Google,[8] which is trained on the concatenation of WikiDumps for the top 104 languages with the largest Wikipedias.[9]

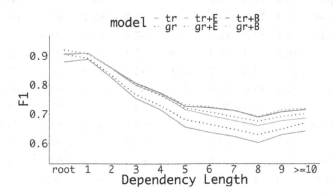

Fig. 4. Labeled F1 for six parsing models, averaged over 13 languages.

Figure 4 plots the labeled F1 of all six systems as a function of dependency length, one of the most striking dimensions previously for differentiating graph-

---

[8] Except for Chinese, for which we make use of a separate, pretrained model.
[9] https://github.com/google-research/bert.

based and transition-based parsers. Comparing first the two baseline models (GR and TR), we find that the old error profiles persist only partially. It is still true that the transition-based parser degrades more as dependencies get longer, but it no longer has an advantage for the shortest dependencies, because both models now benefit from an unbounded feature model thanks to the BiLSTM encoder. On the other hand, we see that the addition of contextualized word embeddings benefit the transition-based parser more than its graph-based counterpart, presumably because it mitigates error propagation by giving the parser a better representation of the global sentence structure. The effect is strongest for the BERT models (GR+B and TR+B), where the curves are virtually indistinguishable, showing that the two parsers do not only make a similar number of errors but also similar types of errors. The patterns observed both for the baseline models and their extended counterparts are remarkably consistent across languages, as can be seen from the first six columns of Table 4, which shows the LAS for all models and all languages. In particular, despite large variations in parsing accuracy across languages, the claim that transition-based parsers benefit more from contextualized word embeddings holds not only on average but for every single language with both ELMo and BERT embeddings.

Table 4. Column 1–6: LAS for parsing models with/without deep contextualized word representations [14]. Column 7–8: UAS for supervised parser and structural probe [15].

Language	LAS						UAS	
	TR	GR	TR+E	GR+E	TR+B	GR+B	GR+B	SP+B
Arabic	79.1	79.9	82.0	81.7	81.9	81.8	88.3	63.9
Basque	73.6	77.6	80.1	81.4	77.9	79.8	86.0	68.2
Chinese	75.3	76.7	79.8	80.4	83.7	83.4	87.0	61.9
English	82.7	83.3	87.0	86.5	87.8	87.6	92.0	73.9
Finnish	80.0	81.4	87.0	86.6	85.1	83.9	91.1	72.8
Hebrew	81.1	82.4	85.2	85.9	85.5	85.9	91.3	71.0
Hindi	88.4	89.6	91.0	91.2	89.5	90.8	95.0	80.0
Italian	88.0	88.2	90.9	90.6	92.0	91.7	95.1	80.4
Japanese	92.1	92.2	93.1	93.0	92.9	92.1	94.7	75.7
Korean	79.6	81.2	82.3	82.3	83.7	84.2	88.5	66.7
Russian	88.3	88.0	90.7	90.6	91.5	91.0	94.6	79.4
Swedish	80.5	81.6	86.9	86.2	87.6	86.9	90.9	74.9
Turkish	57.8	61.2	62.6	63.8	64.2	64.9	74.4	58.1
Average	**80.5**	**81.8**	**84.5**	**84.6**	**84.9**	**84.9**	**89.9**	**71.3**

3.4   Parserless Parsing?

The previous study shows a convergence in behavior of different parsing models when equipped with deep contextualized word representations, which suggests that the parsing model is less important than it used to be and that most of the work is done by the rich pre-trained input representations. This leads inevitably to the question of whether we need a dedicated parsing model at all, or whether we can extract syntactic representations directly from the contextualized word representations provided by models like ELMo and BERT. Our third study, presented at ACL 2020 [15], explores this question using the probing technique proposed by Hewitt and Manning [10]. The question asked in the original paper is whether the vector spaces of token embeddings encode parse trees implicitly, and the authors approach this question by trying to learn linear transforms of a vector space such that, given a sentence and its parse tree, the distance between two token vectors in the new space encodes their distance in the parse tree, on the one hand, and the norm of a token vector encodes the depth of the token in the parse tree, on the other. Information about distance and depth is sufficient to extract *undirected* dependency trees, and experiments on English shows that it is possible to reach an undirected unlabeled attachment score (UUAS) of over 80% when evaluating against existing treebanks.

In the new study, we extend this work in two directions. First, we propose a method for deriving *directed* dependency trees from the depth and distance measures, so that we can evaluate accuracy using the standard metric of unlabeled attachment score (UAS). We first derive scores for all possible directed dependency arcs $w_i \rightarrow w_j$:

$$S(w_i \rightarrow w_j) = \begin{cases} -\text{DIST}(w_i, w_j) & \text{if } \text{DEPTH}(w_i) < \text{DEPTH}(w_j) \\ -\infty & \text{otherwise} \end{cases}$$

The idea is that shorter distances correspond to higher arc scores, and that arcs from lower to higher nodes are excluded (by giving them a score of $-\infty$). Given the arc scores, a directed dependency tree can be obtained by extracted the maximum spanning tree over the complete score matrix [22]. Our second extension is to go beyond English and apply the method to the same 13 languages as in the previous study, to see whether there are interesting cross-linguistic differences.[10]

The last two columns of Table 4 show the UAS scores obtained for different languages when using a weighted average of the predictions from the 12 layers of the multilingual BERT model. For comparison, we include the UAS scores achieved by the GR+B parser from the previous study. On the one hand, it is impressive that we can achieve an average UAS of 71.3 using a simple linear model on top of a language model that has not been trained with a parsing objective and has not itself been exposed to parse trees. On the other hand,

---

[10] The published paper contains a third extension, which we omit here because of space constraints, where we investigate whether the models exhibit a preference for different syntactic frameworks.

we see that this result is still very far below the average UAS of 89.9 obtained with a dedicated parsing model that has access to the same language model representations. Finally, it is worth noticing that differences in accuracy across languages are strongly correlated between the two models, with a Pearson correlation coefficient of 0.88 ($p \leq 0.05$).

4 Conclusion

The use of deep neural language models that can be pre-trained on very large data sets and fine-tuned for particular tasks is prevalent in contemporary NLP, and dependency parsing is no exception. There is no question that models like ELMo and BERT learn aspects of syntax (although it is still far from clear exactly what they learn), which makes them very useful for the parsing task, although we are still not at the point where a dedicated parser is superfluous. The adoption of continuous representations and neural network techniques in general has led to a convergence across models and algorithms, where graph-based and transition-based dependency parsers now share most of their architecture and also exhibit very similar performance in terms of parsing errors. Thanks to research on multilingual parsing and initiatives like UD, there is also some convergence in parsing accuracy across languages, although we still see significant differences. It is therefore important to maintain a multilingual perspective going forward, and we hope that the resources provided by the UD community can continue to play a role as a touchstone for parsing and probing studies.

Acknowledgments. I want to thank (present and former) members of the Uppsala parsing group – Ali Basirat, Miryam de Lhoneux, Artur Kulmizev, Paola Merlo, Aaron Smith and Sara Stymne – colleagues in the core UD group – Marie de Marneffe, Filip Ginter, Yoav Goldberg, Jan Hajič, Chris Manning, Ryan McDonald, Slav Petrov, Sampo Pyysalo, Sebastian Schuster, Reut Tsarfaty, Francis Tyers and Dan Zeman – and all contributors in the UD community. I acknowledge the computational resources provided by CSC in Helsinki and Sigma2 in Oslo through NeIC-NLPL (www.nlpl.eu).

References

1. Andrews, A.D.: The major functions of the noun phrase. In: Shopen, T. (ed.) Language Typology and Syntactic Description. Volume I: Clause Structure, 2nd edn., pp. 132–223. Cambridge University Press, Cambridge (2007)
2. Buchholz, S., Marsi, E.: CoNLL-X shared task on multilingual dependency parsing. In: Proceedings of the 10th Conference on Computational Natural Language Learning (CoNLL), pp. 149–164 (2006)
3. Che, W., Liu, Y., Wang, Y., Zheng, B., Liu, T.: Towards better UD parsing: deep contextualized word embeddings, ensemble, and treebank concatenation. In: Proceedings of the CoNLL 2018 Shared Task: Multilingual Parsing from Raw Text to Universal Dependencies, pp. 55–64 (2018)

4. Devlin, J., Chang, M.W., Lee, K., Toutanova, K.: BERT: pre-training of deep bidirectional transformers for language understanding. In: Proceedings of the 2019 Conference of the North American Chapter of the Association for Computational Linguistics: Human Language Technologies (2019)

5. Dozat, T., Manning, C.D.: Deep biaffine attention for neural dependency parsing. In: Proceedings of the 5th International Conference on Learning Representations (2017)

6. Dozat, T., Qi, P., Manning, C.D.: Stanford's graph-based neural dependency parser at the CoNLL 2017 shared task. In: Proceedings of the CoNLL 2017 Shared Task: Multilingual Parsing from Raw Text to Universal Dependencies, pp. 20–30 (2017)

7. Duong, L., Cohn, T., Bird, S., Cook, P.: Low resource dependency parsing: cross-lingual parameter sharing in a neural network parser. In: Proceedings of the 53rd Annual Meeting of the Association for Computational Linguistics (ACL), pp. 845–850 (2015)

8. Futrell, R., Mahowald, K., Gibson, E.: Quantifying word order freedom in dependency corpora. In: Proceedings of the Third International Conference on Dependency Linguistics (Depling), pp. 91–100 (2015)

9. Guo, J., Che, W., Yarowsky, D., Wang, H., Liu, T.: Cross-lingual dependency parsing based on distributed representations. In: Proceedings of the 53rd Annual Meeting of the Association for Computational Linguistics (ACL), pp. 1234–1244 (2015)

10. Hewitt, J., Manning, C.D.: A structural probe for finding syntax in word representations. In: Proceedings of the 2019 Conference of the North American Chapter of the Association for Computational Linguistics: Human Language Technologies (2019)

11. Kiperwasser, E., Goldberg, Y.: Simple and accurate dependency parsing using bidirectional LSTM feature representations. Trans. Assoc. Comput. Linguist. **4**, 313–327 (2016)

12. Kondratyuk, D., Straka, M.: 75 languages, 1 model: parsing Universal Dependencies universally. In: Proceedings of the 2019 Conference on Empirical Methods in Natural Language Processing and the 9th International Joint Conference on Natural Language Processing (EMNLP-IJCNLP), pp. 2779–2795 (2019)

13. Kuhlmann, M., Gómez-Rodríguez, C., Satta, G.: Dynamic programming algorithms for transition-based dependency parsers. In: Proceedings of the 49th Annual Meeting of the Association for Computational Linguistics (ACL), pp. 673–682 (2011)

14. Kulmizev, A., de Lhoneux, M., Gontrum, J., Fano, E., Nivre, J.: Deep contextualized word embeddings in transition-based and graph-based dependency parsing - a tale of two parsers revisited. In: Proceedings of the 2019 Conference on Empirical Methods in Natural Language Processing and the 9th International Joint Conference on Natural Language Processing (EMNLP-IJCNLP), pp. 2755–2768 (2019)

15. Kulmizev, A., Ravishankar, V., Abdou, M., Nivre, J.: Do neural language models show preferences for syntactic formalisms? In: Proceedings of the 58th Annual Meeting of the Association for Computational Linguistics (ACL), pp. 4077–4091 (2020)

16. Levshina, N.: Token-based typology and word order entropy: a study based on Universal Dependencies. Linguist. Typology **23**, 533–572 (2019)

17. de Lhoneux, M.: Linguistically informed neural dependency parsing for typologically diverse languages. Ph.D. thesis, Uppsala University (2019)

18. de Lhoneux, M., et al.: From raw text to Universal Dependencies - look, no tags! In: Proceedings of the CoNLL 2017 Shared Task: Multilingual Parsing from Raw Text to Universal Dependencies, pp. 207–217 (2017)
19. de Lhoneux, M., Stymne, S., Nivre, J.: Arc-hybrid non-projective dependency parsing with a static-dynamic oracle. In: Proceedings of the 15th International Conference on Parsing Technologies, pp. 99–104 (2017)
20. McDonald, R., Nivre, J.: Characterizing the errors of data-driven dependency parsing models. In: Proceedings of the 2007 Joint Conference on Empirical Methods in Natural Language Processing and Computational Natural Language Learning (EMNLP-CoNLL), pp. 122–131 (2007)
21. McDonald, R., Nivre, J.: Analyzing and integrating dependency parsers. Comput. Linguist. **37**(1), 197–230 (2011)
22. McDonald, R., Pereira, F., Ribarov, K., Hajič, J.: Non-projective dependency parsing using spanning tree algorithms. In: Proceedings of the Human Language Technology Conference and the Conference on Empirical Methods in Natural Language Processing (HLT/EMNLP), pp. 523–530 (2005)
23. Mikolov, T., Chen, K., Corrado, G., Dean, J.: Efficient estimation of word representations in vector space. arXiv preprint arXiv:1301.3781 (2013)
24. Nivre, J.: An efficient algorithm for projective dependency parsing. In: Proceedings of the 8th International Workshop on Parsing Technologies (IWPT), pp. 149–160 (2003)
25. Nivre, J.: Algorithms for deterministic incremental dependency parsing. Comput. Linguist. **34**, 513–553 (2008)
26. Nivre, J.: Non-projective dependency parsing in expected linear time. In: Proceedings of the Joint Conference of the 47th Annual Meeting of the ACL and the 4th International Joint Conference on Natural Language Processing of the AFNLP (ACL-IJCNLP), pp. 351–359 (2009)
27. Nivre, J.: Towards a universal grammar for natural language processing. In: Gelbukh, A. (ed.) CICLing 2015. LNCS, vol. 9041, pp. 3–16. Springer, Cham (2015). https://doi.org/10.1007/978-3-319-18111-0_1
28. Nivre, J., Boguslavsky, I.M., Iomdin, L.L.: Parsing the SynTagRus treebank of Russian. In: Proceedings of the 22nd International Conference on Computational Linguistics (Coling 2008), pp. 641–648 (2008)
29. Nivre, J., et al.: The CoNLL 2007 shared task on dependency parsing. In: Proceedings of the CoNLL Shared Task of EMNLP-CoNLL 2007, pp. 915–932 (2007)
30. Nivre, J., et al.: Universal Dependencies v1: a multilingual treebank collection. In: Proceedings of the 10th International Conference on Language Resources and Evaluation (LREC) (2016)
31. Nivre, J., et al.: Universal Dependencies v2: an evergrowing multilingual treebank collection. In: Proceedings of the 12th International Conference on Language Resources and Evaluation (LREC) (2020)
32. Östling, R.: Word order typology through multilingual word alignment. In: Proceedings of the 53rd Annual Meeting of the Association for Computational Linguistics (Volume 2: Short Papers), pp. 205–211 (2015)
33. Peters, M.E., et al.: Deep contextualized word representations. In: Proceedings of the 2018 Conference of the North American Chapter of the Association for Computational Linguistics: Human Language Technologies, Volume 1 (Long Papers), pp. 2227–2237 (2018)
34. Schubert, K., Maxwell, D.: Metataxis in Practice: Dependency Syntax for Multilingual Machine Translation. Mouton de Gruyter, Berlin (1987)

35. Smith, A., Bohnet, B., de Lhoneux, M., Nivre, J., Shao, Y., Stymne, S.: 82 tree-banks, 34 models: universal dependency parsing with multi-treebank models. In: Proceedings of the 2018 CoNLL Shared Task: Multilingual Parsing from Raw Text to Universal Dependencies (2018)

36. Smith, A., de Lhoneux, M., Stymne, S., Nivre, J.: An investigation of the inter-actions between pre-trained word embeddings, character models and POS tags in dependency parsing. In: Proceedings of the 2018 Conference on Empirical Methods in Natural Language Processing (2018)

37. Stevenson, M., Greenwood, M.A.: Dependency pattern models for information extraction. Res. Lang. Comput. **7**, 13–39 (2009). https://doi.org/10.1007/s11168-009-9061-2

38. Tesnière, L.: Éléments de syntaxe structurale. Editions Klincksieck (1959)

39. Thompson, S.A.: Discourse motivations for the core-oblique distinction as a lan-guage universal. In: Kamio, A. (ed.) Directions in Functional Linguistics, pp. 59–82. John Benjamins, Amsterdam (1997)

40. Tiedemann, J.: Cross-lingual dependency parsing with Universal Dependencies and predicted PoS labels. In: Proceedings of the Third International Conference on Dependency Linguistics (Depling), pp. 340–349 (2015)

41. Tsarfaty, R., Seddah, D., Kübler, S., Nivre, J.: Parsing morphologically rich lan-guages: introduction to the special issue. Computat. Linguist. **39**, 15–22 (2013)

42. Zeman, D., et al.: CoNLL 2018 shared task: multilingual parsing from raw text to universal dependencies. In: Proceedings of the CoNLL 2018 Shared Task: Multi-lingual Parsing from Raw Text to Universal Dependencies (2018)

43. Zeman, D., et al.: Universal Dependencies 2.5 (2019). http://hdl.handle.net/11234/1-3105, LINDAT/CLARIN digital library at the Institute of Formal and Applied Linguistics (ÚFAL), Faculty of Mathematics and Physics, Charles University. http://hdl.handle.net/11234/1-3105

44. Zeman, D., et al.: CoNLL 2017 shared task: multilingual parsing from raw text to universal dependencies. In: Proceedings of the CoNLL 2017 Shared Task: Multi-lingual Parsing from Raw Text to Universal Dependencies, pp. 1–19 (2017)

45. Zhang, Y., Nivre, J.: Analyzing the effect of global learning and beam-search on transition-based dependency parsing. In: Proceedings of COLING 2012: Posters, pp. 1391–1400 (2012)

Multimodal Fake News Detection with Textual, Visual and Semantic Information

Anastasia Giachanou[1]([✉])[iD], Guobiao Zhang[1,2], and Paolo Rosso[1][iD]

[1] Universitat Politècnica de València, Valencia, Spain
angia9@upv.es, prosso@dsic.upv.es
[2] Wuhan University, Wuhan, China
zgb0537@whu.edu.cn

Abstract. Recent years have seen a rapid growth in the number of fake news that are posted online. Fake news detection is very challenging since they are usually created to contain a mixture of false and real information and images that have been manipulated that confuses the readers. In this paper, we propose a multimodal system with the aim to differentiate between fake and real posts. Our system is based on a neural network and combines textual, visual and semantic information. The textual information is extracted from the content of the post, the visual one from the image that is associated with the post and the semantic refers to the similarity between the image and the text of the post. We conduct our experiments on three standard real world collections and we show the importance of those features on detecting fake news.

Keywords: Multimodal fake news detection · Visual features · Textual features · Image-text similarity

1 Introduction

Recent years have seen a rapid growth in the amount of fake news that are published online. Although fake news is not a new phenomenon, the rise of social media has offered an easy platform for their fast propagation. A large amount of invalid claims, rumours and clickbaits are posted every day online with the aim to deceive people and to influence their opinions on different topics. For example, the outcome of Brexit[1] has been into question because of the amount of fake news that were posted before the referendum.

Fake news detection is not a trivial task since the content and the images are manipulated in many different ways which makes the development of an effective system difficult. Several researchers have tried to address the problem of fake news detection. Early works focused on using textual information extracted from the text of the document, such as statistical text features [2] and emotional

---

[1] https://www.theguardian.com/world/2017/nov/14/how-400-russia-run-fake-accounts-posted-bogus-brexit-tweets.

© Springer Nature Switzerland AG 2020
P. Sojka et al. (Eds.): TSD 2020, LNAI 12284, pp. 30–38, 2020.
https://doi.org/10.1007/978-3-030-58323-1_3

information [6,9]. Apart from the content, researchers have also explored the role of users [8,16] and the credibility of the source where the post is published [14].

Although content information is very important for the detection of fake news, it is not sufficient alone. Online articles and posts usually contain images that provide useful information for a classification system. Some researchers have proposed multimodal approaches for the detection of fake news [12,22]. The majority of those systems combine textual and visual information to address the problem. However, in addition to the visual information, the similarity between the image and the text is very important since it is possible that in some fake news the image to be contradictory to the content. Although text-image similarity can be an additional useful information, it still remains under-explored.

In this paper we propose a system that uses multimodal information to differentiate between fake and real news. To this end, we combine textual, visual and semantic information. Our main motivation is that information that comes from different sources complement each other in detecting fake news. In addition, some of the fake news contain manipulated images that do not correspond to the post's content. Therefore, we also incorporate semantic information that refers to the similarity between the text and the image. Our experimental results on three different collections show that combining textual, visual and semantic information can lead to an effective fake news detection.

2   Related Work

Early attempts on fake news detection were based on textual information. Castillo et al. [2] explored the effectiveness of various statistical text features, such as count of word and punctuation, whereas Rashkin et al. [15] incorporated various linguistic features extracted with the LIWC dictionary [20] into a Long Short Term Memory (LSTM) network to detect credible posts.

Some researchers explored the role of emotions on the area of fake news. Vosoughi et al. [21] investigated true and false rumours on Twitter and found that false rumours triggered fear, disgust and surprise in their replies, whereas the true rumours triggered joy, sadness, trust and anticipation. Giachanou et al. [9] proposed an LSTM-based neural network that leveraged emotions from text to address credibility detection, whereas Ghanem et al. [6] explored the impact of emotions regarding the detection of the different types of fake news.

Visual information complements the textual one and improve the effectiveness of systems on fake news detection. Wang et al. [22] proposed the Event Adversarial Neural Networks (EANN) model that consists of the textual component represented by word embeddings and the visual that was extracted using the VGG-19 model pre-trained on ImageNet. Khattar et al. [12] proposed the Multimodal Variational Autoencoder (MVAE) model based on bi-directional LSTMs and VGG-19 for the text and image representation respectively. Zlatkova et al. [24] explored the effectiveness of text-image similarity in addition to other visual information but on the task of claim factuality prediction with respect to an image.

Different to the previous work, not only we explore the effectiveness of a wider range of visual features on fake news detection but also of the similarity between the image and the text. Our visual features include image tags generated using five different models as well as LBP, whereas the similarity is calculated using the embeddings of the post's text and the image tags.

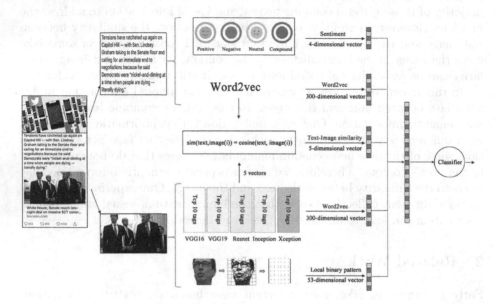

Fig. 1. Architecture of the multimodal fake news detection model.

3   Multimodal Fake News Detection

In this section, we present our multimodal system that aims to differentiate between fake and real news. Our system is based on a neural network and combines the following three different types of information: textual, visual and semantic. The architecture of our system is depicted in Fig. 1.

For the textual information, we combine word embeddings and sentiment. To extract the word embeddings, we use the public pre-trained words and phrase vectors GoogleNews-vectors-negative300 that contains 300-dimensional vectors for 3 million words and phrases.

In addition to the word embeddings, we also estimate the sentiment expressed in the posts. Sentiment analysis has in general attracted a lot of research attention and aims to annotate a text regarding to its polarity. Sentimental information has been shown to be useful for fake news detection as well as in other classification tasks [7]. To extract the sentiment score from the documents, we use the Valence Aware Dictionary for sEntiment Reasoning (VADER). VADER [4] is a sophisticated tool that in addition to the terms' sentiment, takes also into account factors such as negation and emoticon usage and predicts the normalized valence of positive or negative sentiment of the given text.

For the visual component, we combine image tags and Local Binary Patterns (LBP) [13]. The visual information can be very useful in case there are different patterns used in fake and real news or there are images that have been manipulated. To extract the image tags we use pre-trained CNN-based models. These models are the VGG16, VGG19 [18], Resnet [10], Inception [19], and Xception [3]. The models are pre-trained on the visual dataset ImageNet that contains over 14 million hand-annotated images [5]. We extract the top ten image tags using the pre-trained models, so every image has in total 50 tags. Then for each tag, we use the word2vec embeddings to estimate the 300-dimension vector by averaging the embeddings.

In addition to the image tags, we also explore the effectiveness of LBP. LBP is a very efficient texture operator which labels the pixels of an image by putting a threshold on the neighborhood of each pixel and considers the result as a binary number. LBP has been proved to be very effective in many visual tasks such as face recognition [11]. Similar to previous studies that have used LBP for other tasks such as multimodal sentiment analysis [23], we reduce the original 256-dimensional LBP feature histogram to a 53-dimensional vector.

Table 1. Label statistics of the collections

Collection	Real		Fake	
	Training	Test	Training	Test
MediaEval	4,997	1,202	6,742	2,483
PolitiFact	1,067	266	1,712	428
GossipCop	16,495	4,124	16,495	4,124

Finally, the semantic information refers to the text-image similarity. Estimating this similarity is very important since it is possible that fake news contain images that are not relevant to the text. To calculate the similarity we calculate the cosine similarity between the word embeddings of the text and the embeddings of the image tags extracted from the visual feature extraction. This feature provides a 5-dimensional vector, where each vector refers to one image tag model (e.g., VGG16) and is calculated based on the average similarity between the word embeddings of the text and the embeddings of the image tags.

4   Experimental Setup

In this section we describe the collections and the experimental settings used to run our experiments.

4.1 Collections

For our experiments we use MediaEval [1] and FakeNewsNet [17] that, to the best of our knowledge, are the only standard collections that contain tweets in English and that can be used for multimodal fake news detection. Table 1 shows the statistics regarding the labels of the collections.

– *MediaEval*: This collection was released as a part of the *Verifying Multimedia Use at MediaEval* challenge [1]. The aim of the task was to detect fake multimedia content on social media. The collection consists of tweets and each tweet is provided with textual content, image/video and social context information. After removing the tweets that did not have an image, we managed to have a training set of 11,739 tweets of which 4,997 are real and 6,742 are fake. Our test set contains 3,685 tweets of which 1,202 are real and 2,483 are fake.

– *PolitiFact*: This collection is based on tweets that have been collected with regards to the posts that are published in PolitiFact[2] and is part of the FakeNewsNet collection [17]. PolitiFact is a website that experts in journalism annotate news articles and political claims as fake or real. To create the FakeNewsNet collection Shu et al. used the headlines of those posts as queries to collect relevant tweets. We used the tweet_ids provided as part of the FakeNewsNet and the Twitter API to collect the tweets (text and image) that were available. In total, we managed to collect 2,140 fake and 1,333 real tweets posts.

Table 2. Neural network parameters

Layers	Neurons	Learning rate	Dropout	Activation	Optimiser	Epochs
4	1000, 500, 300, 100	0.001	0.6	Sigmoid	Adam	50

– *GossipCop*: Similar to PolitiFact, this collection is based on the FakeNewsNet collection [17]. This collection is based on tweets that were collected using the headlines of articles that were posted and annotated in GossipCop[3]. FakeNewsNet contains 5,323 fake and 16,817 real news posted in GossipCop. Due to the imbalance between the classes, we decided to use under-sampling and we randomly selected 5,323 real news posts. We used the tweet_ids and the Twitter API to collect the tweets (text and image) that were still available. In total, we managed to collect 20,619 tweets for each class.

4.2 Experimental Settings

For our experiments on the PolitiFact and the GossipCop collections, we use 20% of our corpus of tweets for test and 80% for training. For the MediaEval, we use the sets as provided in the original collection, that refer to 23% for

---

[2] https://www.politifact.com/.
[3] https://www.gossipcop.com/.

test and the rest for training. We initialize our embedding layer with the pre-trained GoogleNews-vectors-negative300 words and phrase vectors. It is worth to mention that at the beginning of our experiments, we tested also other classifiers including Support Vector Machines and Random Forest. The overall results showed that the neural network performed better for this particular task. Table 2 shows the parameters for the neural network. We have experimented with other hyperparameters, such as different hidden layer number, hidden units, learning rate and dropout. The dropout is applied to each layer. We used the same parameters for all the three different collections.

We used keras to build the neural network and the VGG16, VGG19, Resnet, Inception and Xception. Finally, opencv and scikit-image libraries were used to extract the LBP features[4].

5 Results

Table 3 shows the performance results of the experiments on PolitiFact, MediaEval and GossipCop with regards to F1-metric. First, we evaluate the system when one type of information is used. From the results, we observe that in this case the word embeddings achieve the best performance in all the three collections compared to the other types of information. This is expected given that word embeddings are usually a strong indicator in many text classification tasks. In addition, we notice that in MediaEval, text-image similarity manages to achieve a high performance as well. With regards to the visual information, we observe that image tags perform better than LBP on all the collections. This can be due to the fact that image tags represent a larger vector compared to LBP.

Table 3. Performance results of the different combinations of information and the different collections on the fake news detection task. The best result for every collection is emphasized in bold.

	PolitiFact	MediaEval	GossipCop
Embeddings	0.911	0.885	0.815
Sentiment	0.474	0.352	0.562
Tags	0.718	0.615	0.623
LBP	0.474	0.520	0.551
Similarity	0.474	0.875	0.538
Text-tags	0.924	0.637	0.825
Text-LBP	0.909	0.896	0.814
Text-tags-similarity	0.920	0.636	0.827
Text-LBP-similarity	0.910	**0.908**	0.816
Text-tags-LBP-similarity	**0.925**	0.622	**0.829**

---

[4] https://www.pyimagesearch.com/2015/12/07/local-binary-patterns-with-python-opencv/.

Next, we explore the effectiveness of our system when the text (embeddings + sentiment) is combined with the visual information. We observe that on Politi-Fact and GossipCop, the combination of text and image tags (*text-tags*) performs better than the combination of text and LBP, whereas in case of MediaEval, the text-LBP achieves a higher performance compared to text-tags. We believe that the poor performance of the image tags on MediaEval has to do with the images of the collection that refer to natural disasters and tend to be more complex than the images on PolitiFact and GossipCop.

Finally, we incorporate the text-image similarity into the system to evaluate its impact when it is combined with the rest of the information. From the results, we observe that incorporating text-image similarity improves the performance. With regards to GossipCop, the *text-tags-LBP-similarity* combination improves the performance by 1.72% and 1.84% compared to *word embeddings* and to *text-LBP* respectively. Similar, in case of PolitiFact, the *text-tags-LBP-similarity* combination achieves a 1.51% increase compared to word embeddings.

Finally, regarding MediaEval we observe that the best performance is achieved by the *text-LBP-similarity* combination, whereas the *text-tags-LBP-similarity* combination is not very effective. When with *text-LBP-similarity* the system combines the text, LBP and text-image similarity it manages to outperform word embeddings by 2.53%.

6   Conclusions and Future Work

In this paper, we proposed a multimodal system to address the problem of fake news detection. The proposed system is based on a neural network and combines textual, visual and semantic information. The textual information was based on the word embeddings and the sentiment expressed in the post, the visual information was based on image tags and LBP, whereas the semantic one referred to the text-image similarity. The experimental results showed that combining textual, visual and text-image similarity information is very useful for the task of fake news detection. Finally, our results showed that different visual information is effective for the different collections.

In future, we plan to investigate more visual features extracted from images such as the color histogram. In addition, we plan to explore the effectiveness of the multimodal information on fake news detection across different languages.

Acknowledgments. Anastasia Giachanou is supported by the SNSF Early Postdoc Mobility grant under the project Early Fake News Detection on Social Media, Switzerland (P2TIP2_181441). Guobiao Zhang is funded by China Scholarship Council (CSC) from the Ministry of Education of P.R. China. The work of Paolo Rosso is partially funded by the Spanish MICINN under the research project MISMIS-FAKEnHATE on Misinformation and Miscommunication in social media: FAKE news and HATE speech (PGC2018-096212-B-C31).

References

1. Boididou, C., et al.: Verifying multimedia use at MediaEval 2015. In: MediaEval 2015 Workshop, pp. 235–237 (2015)
2. Castillo, C., Mendoza, M., Poblete, B.: Information credibility on Twitter. In: WWW 2011, pp. 675–684 (2011)
3. Chollet, F.: Xception: deep learning with depthwise separable convolutions. In: CVPR 2017, pp. 1251–1258 (2017)
4. Davidson, T., Warmsley, D., Macy, M., Weber, I.: Automated hate speech detection and the problem of offensive language. In: ICWSM 2017 (2017)
5. Deng, J., Dong, W., Socher, R., Li, L.J., Li, K., Fei-Fei, L.: ImageNet: a large-scale hierarchical image database. In: CVPR 2009, pp. 248–255 (2009)
6. Ghanem, B., Rosso, P., Rangel, F.: An emotional analysis of false information in social media and news articles. ACM Trans. Internet Technol. (TOIT) 20(2), 1–18 (2020)
7. Giachanou, A., Gonzalo, J., Mele, I., Crestani, F.: Sentiment propagation for predicting reputation polarity. In: Jose, J.M., et al. (eds.) ECIR 2017. LNCS, vol. 10193, pp. 226–238. Springer, Cham (2017). https://doi.org/10.1007/978-3-319-56608-5_18
8. Giachanou, A., Ríssola, E.A., Ghanem, B., Crestani, F., Rosso, P.: The role of personality and linguistic patterns in discriminating between fake news spreaders and fact checkers. In: Métais, E., Meziane, F., Horacek, H., Cimiano, P. (eds.) NLDB 2020. LNCS, vol. 12089, pp. 181–192. Springer, Cham (2020). https://doi.org/10.1007/978-3-030-51310-8_17
9. Giachanou, A., Rosso, P., Crestani, F.: Leveraging emotional signals for credibility detection. In: SIGIR 2019, pp. 877–880 (2019)
10. He, K., Zhang, X., Ren, S., Sun, J.: Deep residual learning for image recognition. In: CVPR 2016, pp. 770–778 (2016)
11. Huang, D., Shan, C., Ardabilian, M., Wang, Y., Chen, L.: Local binary patterns and its application to facial image analysis: a survey. IEEE Trans. Syst. Man Cybern. Part C 41(6), 765–781 (2011)
12. Khattar, D., Goud, J.S., Gupta, M., Varma, V.: MVAE: multimodal variational autoencoder for fake news detection. In: WWW 2019, pp. 2915–2921 (2019)
13. Ojala, T., Pietikainen, M., Maenpaa, T.: Multiresolution gray-scale and rotation invariant texture classification with local binary patterns. IEEE Trans. Pattern Anal. Mach. Intell. 24(7), 971–987 (2002)
14. Popat, K., Mukherjee, S., Yates, A., Weikum, G.: DeClarE: debunking fake news and false claims using evidence-aware deep learning. In: EMNLP 2018, pp. 22–32 (2018)
15. Rashkin, H., Choi, E., Jang, J.Y., Volkova, S., Choi, Y.: Truth of varying shades: analyzing language in fake news and political fact-checking. In: EMNLP 2017, pp. 2931–2937 (2017)
16. Shu, K., Wang, S., Liu, H.: Understanding user profiles on social media for fake news detection. In: MIPR 2018, pp. 430–435 (2018)
17. Shu, K., Mahudeswaran, D., Wang, S., Lee, D., Liu, H.: FakeNewsNet: a data repository with news content, social context and spatialtemporal information for studying fake news on social media. arXiv:1809.01286 (2018)
18. Simonyan, K., Zisserman, A.: Very deep convolutional networks for large-scale image recognition. arXiv:1409.1556 (2014)

19. Szegedy, C., Vanhoucke, V., Ioffe, S., Shlens, J., Wojna, Z.: Rethinking the inception architecture for computer vision. In: CVPR 2016, pp. 2818–2826 (2016)
20. Tausczik, Y.R., Pennebaker, J.W.: The psychological meaning of words: LIWC and computerized text analysis methods. J. Lang. Soc. Psychol. **29**(1), 24–54 (2010)
21. Vosoughi, S., Roy, D., Aral, S.: The spread of true and false news online. Science **359**(6380), 1146–1151 (2018)
22. Wang, Y., et al.: EANN: event adversarial neural networks for multi-modal fake news detection. In: KDD 2018, pp. 849–857 (2018)
23. Zhao, Z., et al.: An image-text consistency driven multimodal sentiment analysis approach for social media. Inf. Process. Manag. **56**(6), 102097 (2019)
24. Zlatkova, D., Nakov, P., Koychev, I.: Fact-checking meets fauxtography: verifying claims about images. In: EMNLP-IJCNLP 2019, pp. 2099–2108 (2019)

Text

A Twitter Political Corpus of the 2019 10N Spanish Election

Javier Sánchez-Junquera[1]([✉]) [iD], Simone Paolo Ponzetto[2], and Paolo Rosso[1]

[1] Universitat Politècnica de València, Valencia, Spain
jjsjunquera@gmail.com
[2] Data and Web Science Group, University of Mannheim, Mannheim, Germany

Abstract. We present a corpus of Spanish tweets of 15 Twitter accounts of politicians of the main five parties (PSOE, PP, Cs, UP and VOX) covering the campaign of the Spanish election of 10th November 2019 (10N Spanish Election). We perform a semi-automatic annotation of domain-specific topics using a mixture of keyword-based and supervised techniques. In this preliminary study we extracted the tweets of few politicians of each party with the aim to analyse their official communication strategy. Moreover, we analyse sentiments and emotions employed in the tweets. Although the limited size of the Twitter corpus due to the very short time span, we hope to provide with some first insights on the communication dynamics of social network accounts of these five Spanish political parties.

Keywords: Twitter · Political text analysis · Topic detection · Sentiment and emotion analysis

1 Introduction

In recent years, automated text analysis has become central for work in social and political science that relies on a data-driven perspective. Political scientists, for instance, have used text for a wide range of problems, including inferring policy positions of actors [6], and detecting topics [13], to name a few. At the same time, researchers in Natural Language Processing (NLP) have addressed related tasks such as election prediction [11], stance detection towards legislative proposals [16], predicting roll calls [5], measuring agreement in electoral manifestos [8], and policy preference labelling [1] from a different, yet complementary perspective. Recent attempts to bring these two communities closer have focused on shared evaluation exercises [10] as well as bringing together the body of the scholarly literature of the two communities [4]. The effects of these two strands of research coming together can be seen in political scientists making use and leveraging major advances in NLP from the past years [12].

The contributions of this paper are the following ones: (i) we introduce a corpus of tweets from all major Spanish political parties during the autumn

© Springer Nature Switzerland AG 2020
P. Sojka et al. (Eds.): TSD 2020, LNAI 12284, pp. 41–49, 2020.
https://doi.org/10.1007/978-3-030-58323-1_4

2019 election; (ii) we present details on the semi-automated topic and senti-ment/emotion annotation process; and (iii) we provide a preliminary qualitative analysis of the dataset over different addressed topics of the election campaign. Building this preliminary resource of Spanish political tweets, we aim at provid-ing a first reference corpus of Spanish tweets in order to foster further research in political text analysis and forecasting with Twitter in languages other than English.

In the rest of the paper we will describe how each tweet was annotated with topic information together with sentiments and emotions. Moreover, we will illustrate the preliminary experiments we carried out on topic detection. Finally, we will present some insight about sentiment and emotion topic-related analyses.

2   Related Works

Twitter has been used as a source of texts for different NLP tasks like sentiment analysis [3,9]. One work that is very related to our study is [7]. They collected a dataset in English for topic identification and sentiment analysis. The authors used distant supervision for training, in which topic-related keywords were used to first obtain a collection of positive examples for the topic identification. Their results show that the obtained examples could serve as a training set for clas-sifying unlabelled instances more effectively than using only the keywords as the topic predictors. However, during our corpus development we noticed that keyword-based retrieval can produce noisy data, maybe because of the content and the topics of our tweets, and we then used a combination of both a keyword-based and a supervised approach.

3   Political Tweets in the 10N Spanish Election

In this paper, we focus on the Spanish election of November 10th, 2019 (10N Spanish Election, hereafter). For this, we analyse tweets between the short time span of October 10, 2019, and November 12, 2019. We focus on the tweets from 15 representative profiles of the five most important political parties (Table 1)[1]: i.e., Unidas Podemos (UP); Ciudadanos (Cs); Partido Socialista Obrero Español (PSOE); Partido Popular (PP); and VOX.

3.1   Topic Identification

Topic Categories. We first describe how we detect the topic of the tweets on the basis of a keyword-based and supervised approach. In the context of the 10N Spanish Election, we focused on the following topics that were mentioned in the political manifestos of the five main Spanish parties: *Immigration, Catalonia, Economy (and Employment), Education (together with Culture and Research), Feminism, Historical Memory, and Healthcare*. We additionally include a cate-gory label *Other* for the tweets that talk about any other topic.

---

[1] The dataset is available at https://github.com/jjsjunquera/10N-Spanish-Election.

Table 1. Number of tweets of the five political parties. For each party, we use its official Twitter account, its leader, and the female politician that took part in the 7N TV debate.

Parties	The main profiles	Tweets
UP	@ahorapodemos, @Irene_Montero_, @Pablo_Iglesias_	671
Cs	@CiudadanosCs, @InesArrimadas, @Albert_Rivera	789
PSOE	@PSOE, @mjmonteroc, @sanchezcastejon	527
PP	@populares, @anapastorjulian, @pablocasado_	684
Vox	@vox_es, @monasterior, @santi_abascal	749
Total		3582

Table 2. Total number of labelled tweets: the training set (i.e., manually annotated, and using keywords), and using automatic annotation. The last column has the total number of labelled tweets considering the training set and the classifier results.

Topic	Manual annotated	Keyword annotated	Automatically annotated	Total annotated
Catalonia	115	130	370	615
Economy	71	39	506	616
Education	2	19	23	44
Feminism	10	52	82	144
Healthcare	4	12	7	23
Historical Memory	12	16	30	58
Immigration	9	16	36	61
Other	541	153	1037	1731
Pensions	1	24	55	80
Total	765	461	2146	3372

Manual Topic Annotation. We first manually annotate 1,000 randomly sampled tweets using our topic labels.

Table 2 summarizes the label distribution across all parties. After removing the noisy tweets, we are left with only 765 posts. Many tweets in our corpus are not related to any of the topics of interest, and were assigned to the *Other* category. Moreover, during the annotation, we noticed in the manifestos of the five parties little information about topics such as research, corruption, renewable energy, and climate change.

Keyword-Based Topic Detection. Due to the manual annotation is time consuming, we complement it by using topic-related keywords to collect tweets about each topic. We ranked the words appearing in the sections corresponding to the topics of interest with the highest Pointwise Mutual Information (*PMI*). *PMI* makes it possible to select the most relevant words for each topic, and is computed as: $PMI(T, w) = \log \frac{p(T,w)}{p(T)p(w)}$. Where $p(T, w)$ is the probability of a word to appear in a topic, $p(T)$ is the probability of a topic (we assume the topic distribution to be uniform), and $p(w)$ is the probability of w. For each topic, we collect the top-10 highest ranked keywords and manually filter incorrect ones (Table 3).

Table 3. Keywords used for collecting training data for topic identification.

Topic	Keywords
Catalonia	*autonómica; cataluña; civil*
Economy	*bienestar; discapacidad; energía; fiscalidad; impuesto; innovación; inversión; tecnológico*
Education	*cultura; cultural; educación; lenguas; mecenazo*
Feminism	*conciliación; familia; machismo; madres; discriminación; mujeres; sexual; violencia*
Healthcare	*infantil; sanitario; salud; sanidad; sanitaria; universal*
Historical Memory	*historia; memoria; reparación; víctimas*
Immigration	*ceuta; extranjeros; inmigrantes; ilegalmente*
Pension	*pensiones; toledo*

Supervised Learning of Topics. For each topic, we collect all tweets in our corpus in which at least one of its keywords appears. All retrieved tweets are then manually checked to ensure that the annotated tweets have a ground-truth.

Inspired by the work of [7], we use the topic-related keywords to obtain a collection of "positive" examples to be used as a training set for a supervised classifier. However, in our dataset, we noticed that keyword-based retrieval can produce much noisy data. Therefore, the keyword-based collected tweets are manually checked before training the classifier.

While our solution still requires the mentioned manual checking, the advantage of using keywords is that the labelling is more focused on tweets that are likely to be in one of the topics of interest, thus reducing the annotation effort associated with tweets from the *Other* category.

Table 2 summarizes in the second and third columns the number of tweets that we used as a training set. The second column represents the results after manually evaluating the tweets labelled by using the keywords. It is interesting that the annotated data reveal most attention towards some topics such as *Catalonia*, *Feminism* and *Economy*. Finally, the dataset used for training is composed of all the labelled tweets. To avoid bias towards the most populated categories we reduce their number of examples to 100 for training, for which we balance the presence of manually annotated and keyword-based annotated tweets.

We employ a SVM[2] to classify the still unlabeled tweets and leave-one-out cross-validation because of the small size of the corpus. We represent the tweets

---

[2] We used the implementation from *sklearn* using default parameter values for with a linear kernel.

with unigrams, bigrams and trigrams, and use the *tf-idf* weighting scheme after removing the n-grams occurring only once.

Evaluation of Topic Detection. Table 4a shows the standard precision, recall, and F_1 scores. Table 2 shows in the fourth column the number of tweets annotated using our supervised model. The last column shows instead the total of labelled tweets for each of the topics – i.e., the overall number of labelled tweets obtained by combining manual, keyword-based annotations with the SVM classifier. We break down the numbers of these overall annotated tweets per party in Table 4b. The topic distributions seem to suggest that each party is biased towards specific topics. For instance, *Immigration* seems to be almost only mentioned by VOX, whereas parties like PP and Cs are mainly focused on *Catalonia* and *Economy*.

3.2 Sentiment Analysis

We next analyse the sentiment expressed by the parties about each topic. For this, we use SentiStrength to estimate the sentiment in tweets since it has been effectively used in short informal texts [15]. We compute a single scale with values from -4 (extremely negative) to 4 (extremely positive).

Table 4. Results on topic classification the total number of labelled tweets.

Results on topic classification

Topic	Precision	Recall	F1-score
Catalonia	0.72	0.86	0.78
Economy	0.56	0.7	0.62
Education	0.83	0.48	0.61
Feminism	0.8	0.73	0.77
Healthcare	1	0.38	0.55
Historical Memory	0.82	0.5	0.62
Immigration	0.92	0.44	0.59
Other	0.56	0.6	0.58
Pensions	0.85	0.68	0.76
Macro avg.	0.78	0.6	0.65

Total of labelled tweets

Topic	UP	Cs	PP	PSOE	VOX
Catalonia	40	198	110	50	72
Economy	114	117	203	84	88
Education	12	12	11	5	4
Feminism	44	30	8	29	31
Healthcare	10	2	3	6	2
Historical Memory	25	7	2	8	16
Immigration	4	1	–	7	49
Other	258	262	200	174	243
Pensions	17	2	14	37	10

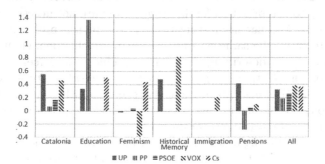

Fig. 1. Expressed sentiment for each topic and party.

In order to compare for each topic the sentiment expressed by a party, we compute the average of the scores for the party on that topic. Only the topics with a precision greater than 0.6 (Table 4a), and the parties that wrote more than 10 tweets on the corresponding topic, were considered in this comparison. It means that we ignore, for instance, the sentiment showed towards *Economy* (precision lower than 0.6), and *Healthcare* (only UP wrote 10 tweets, see Table 4b, and the sentiment that Cs showed towards *Pensions* (only two tweets, see Table 4b).

Figure 1 shows the expressed sentiment for the parties for each topic. Sentiment scores seem to reveal some common dynamics of political communication from political parties in social networks in that generally, even when the party is known to be negative or have a critical stance with respect to a certain topic (e.g., a populist party on immigration), tweets receive a positive score. Specifically, we see that VOX was the only party addressing the *Immigration* topic, and we observe that in general, its sentiment is positive (i.e., solutions were commented). Also, just two parties show mainly negative sentiments, they are VOX and PP towards *Feminism* and *Pensions* respectively.

3.3   Emotion Analysis

We finally analyse the emotions expressed by the parties for different topics using the Spanish Emotion Lexicon (SEL) [14]. SEL has 2,036 words associated with the measure of Probability Factor of Affective (PFA) concerning to at least one Ekman's emotions [2]: joy, anger, fear, sadness, surprise, and disgust. For each tweet, we compute the final measure for each of the five emotions by summing the PFA and dividing by the length of the tweet. We then compute the average PFA of all the emotions for each party and each topic.

Figure 2 (top image on the left) shows the emotions that the parties present in their tweets when talking about different topics. We analyse the emotions of the same pairs of parties and topics we analysed before in Sect. 3.2. Differently to the case of sentiment, there is a general trend shared in that joy and sadness are very much present across all parties. This could be due to several reasons. First, there is a bias in SEL towards joy (668 words related to joy vs. 391 for sadness, 382 for anger, 211 for fear, 209 for disgust, and 175 for surprise), and second, the terms that help to compute the SentiStrength score are not necessarily the same that are in SEL. Another interesting thing is the presence of joy and sadness in the same topic by the same parties. We attribute this behaviour to the fact that there are tweets describing the current problems and feelings present in the context of the election – e.g., using words like *sufrir* (to suffer), *muerte* (death), *triste* (sad), *grave* (grave), but also there are others with a propositive discourse about the problems – e.g., using words like *esperanza* (hope), *ánimo* (encouragement), *unión* (union), *fiesta* (party).

In Figure 2 we also highlight that PSOE shows contrasting emotions about Catalonia; and Cs shows high score of joy about topics related to feminism. The distribution of the emotions from VOX towards *Immigration* was omitted due

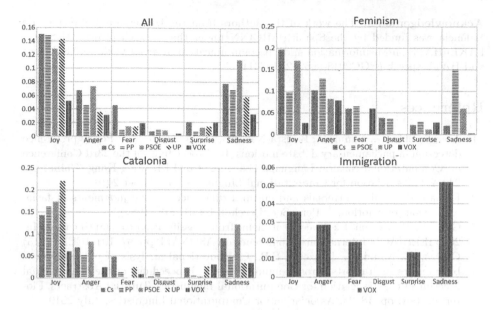

Fig. 2. Emotions distribution across topics.

to the space. However, despite the positive sentiment that VOX showed in this topic, the predominant expressed emotion was sadness.

4 Conclusions

In this paper we presented a first study about the most relevant topics that have been addressed in Twitter in the context of the 10N Spanish election for the five main political parties, together with their sentiments and emotions.

On the basis of the above analysis, we noticed that each party focused more on specific topics, expressing different sentiments and emotions. Our analysis, although preliminary, indicates potentially interesting dimensions of political communications on social networks such as the tendency towards positive tweets, as well the contrasted presence of problems vs. solutions. This work provides a first attempt towards analysing the political communication by the five main political parties in Spain on social networks using NLP techniques. Although we are aware of the limitations of this preliminary study due to the very short time span and the size of the corpus, we hope that this first analysis could contribute to understand how sentiments and emotions were expressed in Twitter by the politicians of the main five parties with respect to the topics mentioned in their manifestos during the political campaign of the 10N Election in Spain.

As future work we plan also to consider additional parties and languages (e.g. Catalan, Basque and Galician) to provide a more comprehensive resource as well as a comparative analysis.

Acknowledgements. The work of the authors from the Universitat Politècnica de València was funded by the Spanish MICINN under the research project MISMIS-FAKEnHATE on Misinformation and Miscommunication in social media: FAKE news and HATE speech (PGC2018-096212-B-C31).

References

1. Abercrombie, G., Nanni, F., Batista-Navarro, R., Ponzetto, S.P.: Policy preference detection in parliamentary debate motions. In: Proceedings of the 23rd Conference on Computational Natural Language Learning (CoNLL), Hong Kong, China, pp. 249–259. Association for Computational Linguistics, November 2019
2. Ekman, P., et al.: Universals and cultural differences in the judgments of facial expressions of emotion. J. Pers. Soc. Psychol. **53**(4), 712 (1987)
3. Gao, W., Sebastiani, F.: Tweet sentiment: from classification to quantification. In: 2015 IEEE/ACM International Conference on ASONAM, pp. 97–104. IEEE (2015)
4. Glavaš, G., Nanni, F., Ponzetto, S.P.: Computational analysis of political texts: bridging research efforts across communities. In: Proceedings of the 57th Annual Meeting of the Association for Computational Linguistics: Tutorial Abstracts, Florence, Italy, pp. 18–23. Association for Computational Linguistics, July 2019
5. Kornilova, A., Argyle, D., Eidelman, V.: Party matters: enhancing legislative embeddings with author attributes for vote prediction, pp. 510–515. Association for Computational Linguistics, July 2018
6. Lowe, W., Benoit, K., Mikhaylov, S., Laver, M.: Scaling policy preferences from coded political texts. Legis. Stud. Q. **36**(1), 123–155 (2011)
7. Marchetti-Bowick, M., Chambers, N.: Learning for microblogs with distant supervision: political forecasting with Twitter. In: Proceedings of the 13th Conference of the European Chapter of the Association for Computational Linguistics, Avignon, France, pp. 603–612. Association for Computational Linguistics, April 2012
8. Menini, S., Nanni, F., Ponzetto, S.P., Tonelli, S.: Topic-based agreement and disagreement in US electoral manifestos. In: Proceedings of the 2017 Conference on Empirical Methods in Natural Language Processing, Copenhagen, Denmark, pp. 2938–2944. Association for Computational Linguistics, September 2017
9. Nakov, P., Ritter, A., Rosenthal, S., Sebastiani, F., Stoyanov, V.: Semeval-2016 task 4: sentiment analysis in Twitter. arXiv preprint arXiv:1912.01973 (2019)
10. Nanni, F., et al.: Findings from the hackathon on understanding euroscepticism through the lens of textual data. European Language Resources Association (ELRA), May 2018
11. O'Connor, B., Balasubramanyan, R., Routledge, B.R., Smith, N.A.: From tweets to polls: linking text sentiment to public opinion time series. In: Proceedings of the Fourth International Conference on Weblogs and Social Media, ICWSM 2010, Washington, DC, USA, 23–26 May 2010 (2010)
12. Rheault, L., Cochrane, C.: Word embeddings for the analysis of ideological placement in parliamentary corpora. Polit. Anal. 1–22 (2019)
13. Roberts, M.E., et al.: Structural topic models for open-ended survey responses. Am. J. Polit. Sci. **58**(4), 1064–1082 (2014)
14. Sidorov, G., et al.: Empirical study of machine learning based approach for opinion mining in tweets. In: Batyrshin, I., González Mendoza, M. (eds.) MICAI 2012. LNCS (LNAI), vol. 7629, pp. 1–14. Springer, Heidelberg (2013). https://doi.org/10.1007/978-3-642-37807-2_1

15. Thelwall, M., Buckley, K., Paltoglou, G., Cai, D., Kappas, A.: Sentiment strength detection in short informal text. J. Am. Soc. Inform. Sci. Technol. **61**(12), 2544–2558 (2010)
16. Thomas, M., Pang, B., Lee, L.: Get out the vote: determining support or opposition from congressional floor-debate transcripts. In: Proceedings of the 2006 Conference on Empirical Methods in Natural Language Processing, pp. 327–335. Association for Computational Linguistics, July 2006

Mining Local Discourse Annotation
for Features of Global Discourse Structure

Lucie Poláková$^{(\boxtimes)}$ ⓘ and Jiří Mírovský ⓘ

Faculty of Mathematics and Physics, Charles University, Malostranské náměstí 25,
118 00 Prague, Czech Republic
{polakova,mirovsky}@ufal.mff.cuni.cz
http://ufal.mff.cuni.cz

Abstract. Descriptive approaches to discourse (text) structure and coherence typically proceed either in a bottom-up or a top-down analytic way. The former ones analyze how the smallest discourse units (clauses, sentences) are connected in their closest neighbourhood, locally, in a linear way. The latter ones postulate a hierarchical organization of smaller and larger units, sometimes also represent the whole text as a tree-like graph. In the present study, we mine a Czech corpus of 50k sentences annotated in the local coherence fashion (Penn Discourse Treebank style) for indices signalling higher discourse structure. We analyze patterns of overlapping discourse relations and look into hierarchies they form. The types and distributions of the detected patterns correspond to the results for English local annotation, with patterns not complying with the tree-like interpretation at very low numbers. We also detect hierarchical organization of local discourse relations of up to 5 levels in the Czech data.

Keywords: Local and global discourse coherence · Discourse relations · Hierarchy · Rhetorical Structure Theory · Penn Discourse Treebank · Prague Dependency Treebank

1   Introduction

Since the establishment of the discipline of text linguistics (and its equivalent discourse analysis), the various approaches to coherence and cohesion aiming at formalizable linguistic description can be characterized in terms of methodology as *local coherence models* and *global coherence models*.

Global coherence is connectivity between the main events of the text (scripts, plans and goals) and the global relations hold independently of the local coherence relations between discourse segments. In the NLP area and in particular in automatic discourse processing, the local and the global coherence models are also referred to as shallow and deep discourse analyses/parsing, respectively [13]. Both types of approaches deal with determination and description of semantic and pragmatic relations between individual text units; these relations are

© Springer Nature Switzerland AG 2020
P. Sojka et al. (Eds.): TSD 2020, LNAI 12284, pp. 50–60, 2020.
https://doi.org/10.1007/978-3-030-58323-1_5

typically called coherence relations, discourse relations or rhetorical relations, depending on the theoretical backgrounds and focus of the analyses.[1]

At present, there is a publicly available large corpus of local discourse annotation for Czech, the Prague Dependency Treebank 3.5 (PDT 3.5; [1], identification of discourse connectives and their scopes, see Sect. 2). However, there is so far no annotation of global coherence for Czech. Also internationally, the number of corpora annotated for local coherence cover a large range of languages – mostly following the first and most prominent Penn Discourse Treebank style (PDTB, [12]), whereas there are only few corpora with global annotations.[2] In spite of this, recent advances in discourse analysis show that global coherence modeling (often in addition to local coherence models), apart from its obvious application in automatic coherence evaluation [4,7] and global discourse parsing, can significantly contribute to complex NLP tasks, e.g. summarization, text generation, textual entailment, text mining and others.

The need to proceed further up from the local coherence analysis to the global one (more sentences as a separate unit, paragraphs, larger text blocks) became motivated not only by the applicability mentioned above. A zoomed-out look on a locally annotated discourse resource revealed even here some patterns typical for (some type of) global coherence analysis, i.e. *even the local annotation already displays features of global text structure:* we found hierarchical organization of smaller and larger discourse relations, connectives and other discourse cues operating between larger blocks of texts, long-distance relations, genre-related patterns and so on.

The goal of the present paper is to systematically exploit an existing local discourse annotation of Czech for possible signs or features of global discourse structure. As this includes a wide range of phenomena, we focus in this study on the issues of structure, or "the shape" of a text, in other words: we investigate mutual configurations of discourse relations (pairwise) and their complexity within locally annotated texts. We relate the detected settings to:

1. a similar research conducted on English Penn Discourse Treebank [5] - with the aim to compare the configurations of relations typical for discourse,
2. the principles of a global coherence analysis, namely, to those of Rhetorical Structure Theory, which represents any text document as a single tree-like structure (see below in Sect. 1.1). On these grounds we try to demonstrate where the local and global analytic perspectives meet and interact. We also contribute some empirical material to the burning scientific debate on whether projective trees are descriptively adequate to represent structure of texts (e.g. [3,6,9,17]).

---

[1] In this study, we use the term *discourse relations*, according to the Penn Discourse Treebank's terminology.

[2] Both ways of text analysis for the same data are rare, yet they exist, e.g. for English Wall Street Journal texts [2,13,18] and for German news commentaries [14]. For German, even a mapping procedure between the two annotation layers was introduced in [15].

1.1 Rhetorical Structure Theory, the Tree-Like Global Model

One of the most influential frameworks among the global models is the Rhetorical Structure Theory (RST, [8]). The main principle of RST is the assumption that coherent texts consist of minimal units, which are linked to each other, recursively, through rhetorical relations and that coherent texts do not exhibit gaps or non-sequiturs [16]. The RST represents the whole text document as a single (projective) tree structure. Basic features of these structures are the rhetorical relations between two textual units (smaller or larger blocks that are in the vast majority of cases adjacent) and the notion of nuclearity. For the classification of RST rhetorical relations, a set of labels was developed, which originally contained 24 relations. The RST has gained great attention, it was further developed and tested, language corpora were built with RST-like discourse annotation. On the other hand, the framework was criticized in some of its theoretical claims, above all, in the question of adequacy/sufficiency of representation of a discourse structure as a tree graph.[3] Linguistically, the strong constraints on the structure (no crossing edges, one root, all the units interconnected etc.) gave rise to a search for counter-examples in real-world texts. It was shown that not only adjacent text units exhibit coherence links and that there are even cue phrases, which connect non-adjacent units and thus support the claim that a tree graph is too restricted a structure for an adequate discourse representation [17] and others.

1.2 Complexity of Discourse Dependencies in PDTB

Lee et al. [5] studied various types of overlaps of discourse relations in the locally annotated Penn Discourse Treebank 2. They encountered a variety of patterns between pairs of discourse relations, including nested (hierarchical), crossed and other non-tree-like configurations. Nevertheless, they conclude that the types of discourse dependencies are highly restricted since the more complex cases can be factored out by appealing to discourse notions like anaphora and attribution, and argue that pure crossing dependencies, partially overlapping arguments and a subset of structures containing a properly contained argument should not be considered part of the discourse structure. The authors challenge Czech discourse researchers to introduce a similar study (footnote 1 in their paper) in order to observe and compare the complexity of discourse and syntax dependencies in two typologically different languages.[4] We take advantage of the fact that the corpora used in their and our studies are comparable in genre (journalism), size (50k sentences), discourse annotation style (PDTB vs. PDTB-like) and number of annotated explicit discourse relations (approx. 20 thousand).

---

[3] Basically a constituency tree, which is in its nature projective and does not allow crossing edges, in comparison to the basic mathematical definition of a tree graph.

[4] Due to the limited range of this paper, we only compare our results to theirs for discourse relations. The implications for syntax (level of complexity) is not explicitly discussed.

2 Data and Method

The data used in our study come from the Prague Dependency Treebank 3.5 (PDT 3.5; [1]), a corpus of approx. 50 thousand sentences of Czech journalistic texts manually annotated for morphology, surface syntax (analytics), deep syntax (tectogrammatics) and other phenomena. Discourse relations are annotated in the PDTB fashion, in a form of binary relations between two text spans (discourse arguments).[5] For explicit relations, all connectives in a given text were identified (there was no close list of connectives), then their two arguments were detected and a semantic/pragmatic relation between them assigned to the relation. Although the *minimality principle* [12] was taken into account like in the PDTB, the annotators could also mark large argument spans and non-adjacent arguments, if justified (compare Sect. 3.1). The discourse annotation of the PDT consists of 21 223 explicit discourse relations, i.e. relations signalled by explicit discourse connectives (both primary and secondary), and 361 list relations, i.e. relations between subsequent members of enumerative structures. For the present study, we only take into consideration the explicit discourse relations.

From the whole PDT, we first collected and classified close discourse relation pairs. We define a *close discourse relation pair* as pair of discourse relations that are either adjacent (the left argument of one relation immediately follows the right argument of the other relation), or they overlap, see Table 1 for various patterns. Second, we used pairs of nested relations where one of the relations is as a whole included in one argument of the other relation (lines 12 and 13 from Table 1) to recursively construct tree structures out of pairs of the nested relations, see Table 2. Based on the quantitative results, we inspected selected samples of the detected patterns manually, in order to check the script outcome and to provide a linguistic description and comparison.

3 Analysis

In this section, we first analyze the detected patterns for close relation pairs, next, a specific subsection is devoted to the description of the detected hierarchical structures (Sect. 3.1).

We were able to detect 17 628 close relation pairs and for each such pair, we investigated its pattern, the mutual arrangement of the two relations. In Table 1, these patterns are also graphically illustrated.[6] The table shows figures for all explicit relation pairs and, in brackets, only for inter-sentential relation pairs. The most common setting for all relations are "full embeddings", in other words **two-level hierarchies**, 7 134 in total (lines 12 and 13), which is even more than **pure adjacency** (succession) of two relations (6 572, line 1). These two

---

[5] Technically, the annotation is not carried out on raw texts, but on top of the syntactic trees.

[6] We have obtained so much data that we must only select certain aspects for this study. We therefore concentrate on the patterns studied by Lee et al., and on hierarchical structuring of discourse relations.

Table 1. Patterns of adjacent or overlapping pairs of discourse relations; the total number of such close relations was 17 628; 109 of them did not fit any of the listed patterns. (Numbers in brackets mean frequencies if only inter-sentential discourse relations were taken into account; in total, there were 2 984 such close relations, 85 of them did not fit the listed patterns.)

Line	Frequency	Pattern	Visualization
1	6 572 (983)	Adjacency	`<--------->  <--------->` `<--------->  <--------->`
2	1 923 (865)	Pprogress (shared argument)	`<--------->  <--------->` `<--------->  <--------->`
3	51 (21)	Total overlap	`<--------->  <--------->` `<--------->  <--------->`
4	266 (116)	Left overlap right adjacency	`<--------->  <--------->` `<--------->          <--------->`
5	25 (10)	Left overlap right contained	`<--------->  <--------->` `<--------->    <--->`
6	31 (10)	Right overlap left adjacency	`<--------->          <--------->` `<--------->  <--------->`
7	17 (8)	Right overlap left contained	`<--------->  <--------->` `<--->    <--------->`
8	250 (146)	Containment I	`<--------->  <--------->` `<--->  <--------->`
9	190 (150)	Containment II (opposite)	`<--------->    <--->` `<--------->  <--------->`
10	83 (14)	Both args contained I	`<--------->  <--------->` `<--->      <--->`
11	73 (8)	Both args contained II	`<--------->  <--->` `<--->  <--------->`
12	3 591 (299)	Left hierarchy	`<--------->  <--------->` `<---> <--->`
13	3 543 (56)	Right hierarchy	`<--------->  <--------->` `<---> <--->`
14	10 (10)	Crossing	`<--------->          <--------->` `<--------->          <--------->`
15	883 (196)	Envelopment	`<--------->                  <--------->` `<--------->  <--------->`

16	11 (7)	Partial overlap	`<--------->  <--------->`
			 `<--------->  <--------->`
			 `(<--------------->  <--------->)`

configurations represent together slightly more than 3/4 of all detected patterns. They are also referred to as *very "normal" structural relationships* in [5], (p. 82).

The next-largest group is **progress** (line 2), a shared argument in the PDTB terminology, with 1 923 instances or 10.9% of all patterns. Lee et. al. report 7.5% of this type, which is fairly comparable. Total overlap (line 3) is caused by the possibility to annotate two different relations between the same segments for cooccurring connectives, as in *because for example* or *but later*.

The **envelopment** pattern (line 15) concerns in vast majority a non-adjacent (long-distance) relation and a relation in between its arguments. Generally, the enveloped relation is a sentence with some inner syntactic structure annotated, which also explains the drastic difference between all detected envelopment patterns (883) and only the inter-sentential ones (196). Linguistically, some of these cases are sentences headed by two attribution spans (verbs of saying) and some structure in the reported content in between, also cases of two linked reporter's questions in an interview and the inner structuring of the interviewee's answer, but also texts with no striking structural reasons for such an arrangement. The pattern represents ca. 5% of all settings and it certainly needs further observation.

The patterns with **properly contained arguments**, either one of them (lines 5, 7, 8 and 9) or both (10 and 11), very often involve "skipping one level" in the syntactic tree of a sentence, see Example 1[7] of the type 8 (containment I), i.e. the exclusion of some governing clause from the argument, that makes its syntactically dependent clause (mostly a "reported-content-argument") to a subset of the other represented (mostly) by a whole sentence. Besides the discussed attribution (introductory statements), this is also the case of the annotation of some secondary connectives forming whole clauses (like *This means that ...*, Example 2, type 9, containment II). These verb phrases are not treated as parts of any of the arguments they relate to,[8] and pose a methodological issue. A third setting concerns multi-sentence arguments, where the contained argument is typically a single sentence. Patterns with properly contained arguments represent in total 3.6% (638) of all patterns.

(1) *The gap in the standard of living that appears between the qualified scientific elite and the business sphere, right now, at the beginning of the transformation of the society, will leave traces. It is <u>therefore</u> appropriate to pamper young researchers and not misuse the fact that* **a young researcher works with enthusiasm for science, regardless of salary.** <u>**But**</u> **a person who begins to find his mission in research also starts a family, wants to live at a good place and live with dignity.**

(2) *This brief overview essentially exhausts the areas of notarial activities within the framework of free competition between notaries.* **<u>This means that</u>** *in* **these notarial agendas, the client has the option of unlimited choice of notary at his own discretion**, <u>**as**</u> **the notary is not bound to the place of his work when providing these services.**

A (pure) **crossing** is a setting where the left-sided argument of the right relation comes in between the two arguments of the left relation, compare line 14 in Table 1. Pure crossings violate the RST constraints most visibly, with crossing edges, so the debate on tree adequacy often circles around the acceptability of crossings in discourse analysis. Lee et al. [5] identify only 24 cases (0.12%) of pure crossings in their corpus. We detected only 10 such cases, which is a

---

[7] Due to space limit we only present the English translations of the PDT Czech originals here. Relation 1 is highlighted in italics, relation 2 in bold. The connectives are underlined.

[8] In the representation in Example 2, the clause *This means that* is not in italics, not a part of any argument of the left relation.

negligible proportion. Manual inspection nevertheless revealed several different scenarios, from clearly incorrect annotation, more interpretations possible, across cases with attribution spans in between, to a few, in our opinion, perfectly sound analyses, as exemplified by Example 3.[9]

(3) (a) What can owners and tenants expect, what should they prepare for?
      (b) *The new legislation should allow all owners to sell apartments.* (c) **It is most urgent for flats owned by municipalities, as they manage about a quarter of the housing stock of the Czech Republic and some are - mainly for financial reasons - interested in monetizing a part of their apartments.** (d) *The law should also allow to complete transfers of housing association apartments and their sale to its members.* (e) **This is also not a "small portion", but a fifth of the total number of dwellings.**

If we accepted the possibility that not only (b), but a larger (b + c) unit to relates to (c) in the "also"-relation, which would be a completely fine interpretation in the Prague annotation, the relation of (e) – the "neither"-relation – cannot accept just (d) as its left-sided argument. We also think this case cannot be factored out due to anaphora. There is, for sure, room for different interpretations within different theories, we just offer our data, state our view and admit that crossing structures are extremely rare even in our empirical data.

Partial overlap is a type of structure that violates the RST tree constraint, too. In the PDTB, there were only 4 such cases. In the Czech data we detected 11 cases (line 16 of Table 1). They often include large arguments of untypical range (2,5 sentences etc.) which can be questioned. Some of the relations also include secondary connectives with strong anaphoric links (*in this respect, given the fact that etc.*). These relations can be factored out, yet, again, there was a small number of cases that are linguistically acceptable, compare Example 4.

(4) The responsibility of the future tenant of this 103,000-m^2 area will be to care for all properties, including their maintenance and repairs. *The tenant will also have to resolve the parking conditions for market visitors and to* **meet the conditions of the Prague Heritage Institute during construction changes due to the fact that the complex is a cultural monument.** The capital city at the same time envisages preserving the character of the Holešovice market.

3.1   Hierarchies

The results of applying the second step of the procedure to the whole PDT data are displayed in Table 2, arranged according to the scheme of such hierarchy trees (identical structures are summed and represented by the hierarchy scheme). We

---

[9] The "also-not" connective is originally in Czech *ani*, in the meaning of *neither*. Lit. translation: "Neither here is concerned a small portion...".

Table 2. Selected schemes of hierarchies of discourse relations. Numbers in brackets mean frequencies of hierarchy schemes if only inter-sentential discourse relations were taken into account (no other inter-sentential hierarchies were encountered in the data).

Line	Frequency	Depth	Hierarchy
1	381 (10)	3	A (B (C))
2	64 (1)	3	A (B (C) D)
3	50	3	A (B C (D))
4	23 (1)	3	A (B (C) D (E))
5	20	3	A (B (C D))
6	0 (1)	3	A (B (C) D E)
7	0 (1)	3	A (B C (D) E)
8	19	4	A (B (C (D)))
9	7	4	A (B (C (D)) E)
10	5	4	A (B C (D (E)))
11	5	4	A (B (C (D)) E (F (G)))
...			
12	2	5	A (B (C (D (E))) F)
13	1	5	A (B C (D (E (F))) G)
14	1	5	A (B (C (D) E (F (G))) H I J (K))
15	1	5	A (B (C (D (E))))
16	1	5	A (B (C (D E (F))))

only mention cases where there are at least three levels in the tree, as two-level hierarchies are part of Table 1.

For explanation: The scheme "A (B)" means that the whole relation B is included in one of the arguments of the relation A (this is, of course, only a two-level tree). The scheme "A (B C (D))" means that relations B and C are all included in the individual arguments of relation A (without specifying in which argument they are, so they can be both in one argument or each in a different argument) and the relation D is completely included in one of the arguments of relation C. It is a three-level hierarchy. Generally, we count the depth (number of levels) of a hierarchy tree as a number of nodes in the longest path from the root to a list.

There are many sub-hierarchies in a large/deep hierarchy, for example "B (C (D))" is a sub-hierarchy of "A (B (C (D)) E)", however such sub-hierarchies are not counted in Table 2, i.e., each hierarchy is only counted in the table in its largest and deepest form as it appeared in the PDT data.[10]

The purpose of looking for such hierarchical structures in the PDT data is to discover to what extent a local annotation shows signs of some structure, too.

---

[10] This also explains the zeros in Table 2.

We do not claim that the trees detected by us are the trees a global analysis like RST would discover, but we demonstrate the existence of some hierarchical text structure in local annotation. Some of it could perhaps partially match to RST-formed subtrees (and definitely there would be an intersection of separate relations, compare e.g. intersections in Wall Street Journal local and global annotations [10], but this is yet to be investigated. We are also aware, as pointed out in [3], that minimal, local annotations cannot form a connected graph.[11]

In the PDT data, local discourse relations form hierarchies up to five levels. We have identified 5 patterns of 5-level hierarchies (5-LH), with the total of 6 instances, see Table 2. There is also a number of 3- and 4-level hierarchies. An analysis of random samples (and of all the deepest ones) revealed, surprisingly, that there can be a 4-level hierarchy spanning 11 sentences, but also a 5-LH spanning only two sentences, from which one is typically a more complex compound sentence. The "longest" of the 5-LHs includes also 11 sentences (line 14) and it also exhibits branching (D, G and K as lists, where the G-path is the deepest). One of the 5-LHs should be in fact one level flatter (line 12), as the lowest two relations are three coordinated clauses with two *and*-connectives: *"the troops protected them and fed them and gave them the impression that they were invulnerable..."*. Such structures are notoriously hard to interpret for any framework, yet in Prague annotation, the annotation is incorrectly hierarchical where it should have been flat.

To find out how much structure is involved only within individual sentences, i.e. how much of sentential syntax forms the hierarchies, in a second phase we filtered out all intra-sentential relations. The numbers in brackets give counts for patterns of hierarchies, if only inter-sentential relations are accounted for. The hierarchies of this type are much less frequent and their maximum depth is just 3, which implies that beyond the sentence boundary, local annotation of explicit connectives does not represent hierarchical text structuring very often. A hypothesis for the lack of hierarchies build by only inter-sentential relations is that only some of the connectives operating at higher discourse levels were identified and annotated as such, some of them were assigned local coherence links due to the minimality principle. This issue was recently discussed in [11], where the annotated non-adjacency of left arguments of paragraph-initial connectives was partially interpretable as higher discourse structuring, and the relations in question were in fact adjacent. Moreover, there surely are other, non-connective cues operating between larger text blocks in our data.

4   Conclusion

In the present study, we have investigated configurations of pairs of discourse relations in a large corpus annotated for local discourse coherence of Czech, in order to detect possible features of global discourse structure (higher text structuring) and to describe the complexity of semantic/pragmatic relations in

---

[11] And the more so, as we do not include implicit and entity-based relations into our study.

discourse. We have identified patterns typical (adjacency, progress, hierarchy, etc.), less typical (argument containment patterns, envelopment) and quite rare (total overlap, crossing, partial overlaps etc.) in our data and analyzed them linguistically. We have compared our findings to those of a similar study conducted on English locally annotated texts [5], learning that the proportions of occurrence of individual patterns roughly correspond in both corpora, although our study distinguishes some more subtle configurations. Frequent patterns in our data comply with the RST tree structure rules. Less frequent patterns in the PDT mostly deal with attribution spans, but also with the annotation strategies for secondary connectives in cases where they form a whole clause (*It means that...*) or they are anaphoric (*in this respect*). In some rare patterns, where, in our opinion, there is a violation of the tree structure in the sense of RST, we have found a small number of linguistically defensible interpretations with no anaphora or attribution. Nevertheless, such specific settings would still need to be compared within a true RST interpretation. Second, we have investigated hierarchies built by the local relations and we have detected even 5-level hierarchies. On the other hand, much of the structure is intra-sentential: beyond the sentence boundary, local annotation of explicit connectives does not expose hierarchical text structuring very often. We believe that for a local annotation of the Penn Discourse Treebank type, hierarchical interpretation beyond the sentence structure may be advantageous, especially when prompted by connectives operating at higher levels. This perspective is particularly important, as a consistent application of the minimality principle can lead to a possible misinterpretation of such higher relations, which otherwise a local annotation scenario is perfectly fit to incorporate.

In the future, we plan to analyze especially paragraph-initial connectives and other signals collected during the implicit relation annotation, and, more importantly, in a RST-like pilot annotation we will compare and evaluate, whether the identified local and the global hierarchies actually match and represent the same types of relations.

Acknowledgments. The authors gratefully acknowledge support from the Grant Agency of the Czech Republic, project no. 20-09853S. The work described herein has been using resources provided by the LINDAT/CLARIAH-CZ Research Infrastructure, supported by the Ministry of Education, Youth and Sports of the Czech Republic (project no. LM2018101).

References

1. Hajič, J., et al.: Prague Dependency Treebank 3.5. Data/software. Institute of Formal and Applied Linguistics, Charles University, LINDAT/CLARIN PID (2018). http://hdl.handle.net/11234/1-2621
2. Carlson, L., Okurowski, M.E., Marcu, D.: RST Discourse Treebank. Linguistic Data Consortium, University of Pennsylvania (2002)
3. Egg, M., Redeker, G.: How complex is discourse structure? In: Proceedings of LREC 2010, Malta, pp. 619–1623 (2010)

4. Feng, V.W., Lin, Z., Hirst, G.: The impact of deep hierarchical discourse structures in the evaluation of text coherence. In: Proceedings of COLING, pp. 940–949 (2014)
5. Lee, A., Prasad, R., Joshi, A., Dinesh, N.: Complexity of dependencies in discourse: are dependencies in discourse more complex than in syntax? In: Proceedings of the TLT 2006, Prague, Czech Republic, pp. 79–90 (2006)
6. Lee, A., Prasad, R., Joshi, A., Webber, B.: Departures from tree structures in discourse: shared arguments in the Penn Discourse Treebank. In: Proceedings of the Constraints in Discourse III Workshop, pp. 61–68 (2008)
7. Lin, Z., Ng, H.T., Kan, M.Y.: Automatically evaluating text coherence using discourse relations. In: Proceedings of the 49th Annual Meeting of the ACL: Human Language Technologies-Volume 1, pp. 997–1006 (2011)
8. Mann, W.C., Thompson, S.A.: Rhetorical structure theory: toward a functional theory of text organization. Text-Interdiscip. J. Study Discourse 8(3), 243–281 (1988)
9. Marcu, D.: The Theory and Practice of Discourse Parsing and Summarization. MIT Press, Cambridge (2000)
10. Poláková, L., Mírovský, J., Synková, P.: Signalling implicit relations: a PDTB-RST comparison. Dialogue Discourse 8(2), 225–248 (2017)
11. Poláková, L., Mírovský, J.: Anaphoric connectives and long distance discourse relations in Czech. Computación y Sistemas 23(3), 711–717 (2019)
12. Prasad, R., Dinesh, N., Lee, A., et al.: The Penn discourse treebank 2.0. In: Proceedings of LREC 2008, Morocco, pp. 2961–2968 (2008)
13. Prasad, R., Joshi, A., Webber, B.: Exploiting scope for shallow discourse parsing. In: Proceedings of LREC 2010, Malta, pp. 2076–2083 (2010)
14. Stede, M., Neumann, A.: Potsdam commentary corpus 2.0: annotation for discourse research. In: Proceedings of LREC 2014, pp. 925–929 (2014)
15. Scheffler, T., Stede, M.: Mapping PDTB-style connective annotation to RST-style discourse annotation. In: Proceedings of KONVENS 2016, pp. 242–247 (2016)
16. Taboada, M., Mann, W.C.: Rhetorical structure theory: looking back and moving ahead. Discourse Stud. 8(3), 423–459 (2006)
17. Wolf, F., Gibson, E.: Representing discourse coherence: a corpus-based study. Comput. Linguist. 31(2), 249–287 (2005)
18. Wolf, F., Gibson, E., Fisher, A., Knight, M.: Discourse Graphbank, LDC2005T08 [Corpus]. Linguistic Data Consortium, Philadelphia (2005)

Diversification of Serbian-French-English-Spanish Parallel Corpus ParCoLab with Spoken Language Data

Dušica Terzić[1]([✉])[ID], Saša Marjanović[1][ID], Dejan Stosic[2][ID],
and Aleksandra Miletic[2]

[1] Faculty of Philology, University of Belgrade,
Studentski trg 3, 11000 Belgrade, Serbia
{dusica.terzic,sasa.marjanovic}@fil.bg.ac.rs
[2] CNRS and University of Toulouse,
5, Allées Antonio Machado, 31058 Toulouse, France
{dejan.stosic,aleksandra.miletic}@univ-tlse2.fr

Abstract. In this paper we present the efforts to diversify Serbian-French-English-Spanish corpus ParCoLab. ParCoLab is the project led by CLLE research unit (UMR 5263 CNRS) at the University of Toulouse, France, and the Romance Department at the University of Belgrade, Serbia. The main goal of the project is to create a freely searchable and widely applicable multilingual resource with Serbian as the pivot language. Initially, the majority of the corpus texts represented written language. Since diversity of text types contributes to the usefulness and applicability of a parallel corpus, a great deal of effort has been made to include spoken language data in the ParCoLab database. Transcripts and translations of TED talks, films and cartoons have been included so far, along with transcripts of original Serbian films. Thus, the 17.6M-word database of mainly literary texts has been extended with spoken language data and it now contains 32.9M words.

Keywords: Parallel corpus · Serbian · French · English · Spanish

1 Introduction

ParCoLab[1] is a Serbian-French-English-Spanish corpus developed by CLLE research unit (UMR 5263 CNRS) at the University of Toulouse, France, and the Department of Romance Studies at the University of Belgrade, Serbia. The primary goal of the ParCoLab project is to create a multilingual resource for the Serbian language, searchable via a user-friendly interface that can be used not only in NLP and contrastive linguistic research but also in comparative literature studies, second language learning and teaching, and applied lexicography [14,17].

---

[1] http://parcolab.univ-tlse2.fr. Last access to URLs in the paper: 20 Apr 2020.

© Springer Nature Switzerland AG 2020
P. Sojka et al. (Eds.): TSD 2020, LNAI 12284, pp. 61–70, 2020.
https://doi.org/10.1007/978-3-030-58323-1_6

Another goal of the ParCoLab project is to add several layers of annotation to the corpus text, such as lemmas, morphosyntactic descriptions (MSDs) and syntactic relations [10,13,14,17]. Currently, two portions of the Serbian subcorpus are annotated – a 150K-token literary subcorpus, ParCoTrain-Synt [12], and a 30K-token journalistic subcorpus, ParCoJour [18].[2]

In the composition of the ParCoLab corpus, quality of the collected data and the processing of the texts is prioritized over quantity, which requires a significant implication of the human factor in the process [17]. The creation of the ParCoLab corpus started with written literary texts which, in general, come with high quality translations. The result, a useful, high-quality corpus was created based on literary classics and a careful selection of good translations. However, uniformity of the corpus has an important impact on NLP applications. For instance, the annotation models trained on a single domain corpus are not particularly robust when used to process the texts of another domain [1,2,6,15]. This was confirmed in a parsing experiment in which a parsing model was trained on the ParCoTrain-Synt literary treebank and used to parse the ParCoJour journalistic corpus (see [18]).

It is not only the uniformity of the data that has an impact on the NLP applications but also the type of that data. It was shown that the differences between spoken and written language have a significant impact on machine translation. Ruiz and Federico [16] compared 2M words from 2 English-German corpora, one of which contained TED talks and the other newspaper articles. They found that TED talks consisted of shorter sentences with less reordering behavior and stronger predictability through language model perplexity and lexical translation entropy. Moreover, there were over three times as many pronouns in TED corpus than in news corpus and twice as many third person occurrences, as well as a considerable amount of polysemy through common verbs and nouns [16].

It is therefore necessary to diversify corpus data in order to make them useful for the development of good and robust NLP models. The expansion and diversification of the ParCoLab database represents an important task for Serbian corpus linguistics, considering that Serbian is one of the under-resourced European languages in terms of both NLP resources and corpora for other specialists (teachers, translators, lexicographers, etc.). In order to accomplish the goals of the ParCoLab project, the corpus should be diversified especially by adding spoken language data.

However, collecting, transcribing, and translating an authentic spontaneous speech corpus requires considerable financial and human resources. We were therefore constrained to search for the data closest to the spontaneous speech that could be collected more efficiently. It was decided to introduce TED talks and film and cartoon transcripts and subtitles and the term "spoken language data" is used to refer to this type of data. We are aware that TED talks are written and edited to be spoken in a limited time frame and thus do not represent spontaneous speech. Film and cartoon transcripts, on the other hand, are more

---

[2] Both corpora can be queried via the ParCoLab search engine and are available for the download at http://parcolab.univ-tlse2.fr/about/ressources.

likely to resemble transcribed natural speech although they are also written and edited beforehand. Another possible downside to using this type of documents is the questionable quality of the available transcripts and translations of TED talks and films, which may compromise the quality of the corpus material and its usefulness (cf. [7]). The method used to include transcripts and translations of films in the ParCoLab corpus tries to palliate the shortcomings of massive inclusion of unverified data and we present it in this paper. In Sect. 2, we introduce similar corpora in order to demonstrate the position of the ParCoLab corpus amongst other parallel resources containing Serbian. In Sect. 3, we describe the state of the ParCoLab database before the inclusion of the spoken data. The ongoing work on including spoken data in the ParCoLab corpus is detailed in Sect. 4. Finally, we draw conclusions in Sect. 5, and present plans for future work.

2   Related Work

In this section, we present other corpora containing the Serbian language and one of three other languages of the project – French, English or Spanish. We also discuss the share of spoken data in those corpora. There are two bilingual parallel corpora[3] developed at the Faculty of Mathematics, University of Belgrade – SrpEngKor and SrpFranKor. SrpEngKor [8] is a 4.4M token Serbian-English corpus consisting of legal and literary texts, news articles, and film subtitles. There are subtitles of only three English films containing approximately 20 K tokens. SrpFranKor [21] is a Serbian-French corpus of 1.7M tokens from literary works and general news with no spoken data. Texts in both corpora are automatically aligned on the sentence level and alignment was manually verified.

Texts in the Serbian language also appear in multilingual corpora. "1984" [9] of MULTEXT-East project contains George Orwell's *1984* and its translation into several languages including 150K-token Serbian translation. SETimes is a parallel corpus of news articles in eight Balkan languages, including Serbian, and English [20]. Its English-Serbian subcorpus contains 9.1M tokens. ParaSol (Parallel Corpus of Slavic and Other Languages), a corpus originally developed under the name RPC as a parallel corpus of Slavic languages [22], was subsequently extended with texts in other languages [23]. The Serbian part of the corpus contains 1.3M tokens of literary texts, of which only one novel is originally written in Serbian. These corpora either do not include spoken data in Serbian language or the film subtitles they contain are neither relevant in size nor originally produced in the Serbian language.

There are, however, two multilingual corpora, each containing a Serbian subcorpus with film subtitles – InterCorp and OPUS. InterCorp[4] [5], contains 31M tokens in Serbian. Texts from literary domain contain 11M tokens, whereas another 20M tokens come from film subtitles. Given that the pivot language is Czech, sentences in Serbian are paired with their Czech counterparts. It is

---

[3] Consultable at: http://www.korpus.matf.bg.ac.rs/korpus/login.php. It is necessary to demand authorization to access the interface.

[4] The official website of the project is: https://intercorp.korpus.cz.

unclear which portion of the Serbian subcorpus can be paired with the subcorpora in languages of the ParCoLab project. According to the information[5] on the official website, subtitles are downloaded from the OpenSubtitles[6] database. OPUS[7] [19] also contains subtitles from this database. The Serbian subcorpus contains 572.1M tokens. Neither alignment nor the quality of the translations are manually verified in these two corpora, leading to a significant amount of misaligned sentences and questionable quality of the translations. It is highly unlikely that these corpora contain films originally produced in Serbian.

Serbian spoken data can also be found in several multilingual corpora of TED talks. TED talks are lectures presented at non-profit events in more than 130 countries [24]. They are filmed and stored in a free online database at https://www.ted.com/talks. TED provides English transcripts which are translated by volunteer translators. The translation is then reviewed by another TED translator, who has subtitled more than 90 min of talk content. Finally, the reviewed translation is approved by a TED Language Coordinator or staff member [24]. Hence, the TED talks are supposed to be of higher quality than the subtitles from OpenSubtitles database, which are not verified. Free access to hours of spoken data translated into more than 100 languages has generated works on collecting corpora based on TED talks. WIT[8] [4], is an inventory that offers access to a collection of TED talks in 109 languages. All the texts for one language are stored in a single XML file. There are 5.3M tokens in the Serbian file. In order to obtain parallel corpus, it is necessary to extract TEDs by their ID and to use alignment tools since the subcorpus for each language is stored separately [4]. MulTed [24] is a parallel corpus of TED talks which contains an important amount of material in under-resourced languages such as Serbian. The Serbian subcorpus comprises 871 talks containing 1.4M tokens. All the translations are sentence-aligned automatically. Only the English-Arabic alignment was manually verified [24]. According to the official website[9] of the project, the corpus will be available for download soon.

As already mentioned in Introduction, the goal of the ParCoLab project is to create a parallel corpus of high quality. Even though it is clear that ParCoLab is not the largest available parallel corpus containing the Serbian language, an important effort is devoted to ensuring the quality of the alignment. Besides prioritizing quality over quantity, we pay special attention to including original Serbian documents. This is also true for film subtitles, whose translation we improve. Another advantage of the ParCoLab corpus is that it contains transcripts of Serbian films, providing original Serbian content. In comparison to other corpora destined to NLP users, ParCoLab is accessible and freely available to general public via the user-friendly interface, which widens its applicability.

---

[5] https://wiki.korpus.cz/doku.php/en:cnk:intercorp:verze12.
[6] https://www.opensubtitles.org/en/search/subs.
[7] http://opus.nlpl.eu/OpenSubtitles2016.php.
[8] https://wit3.fbk.eu/#releases.
[9] http://oujda-nlp-team.net/en/corpora/multed-corpus.

Since 2018, it has been possible to use ParCoLab search engine directly online without creating an account.

3   ParCoLab Content

The texts included in ParCoLab database are aligned with their translations using an algorithm integrated in the corpus platform. The alignment process starts with 1:1 pairing of chapters. It then continues on the level of paragraphs and, finally, of sentences. Possible errors are pointed out by the algorithm and corrected manually afterwards [10,11,17]. Corpus material is stored in XML format in compliance with TEI P5 (https://tei-c.org/guidelines/p5). XML files include standardized metadata – title, subtitle, author, translator, publisher, publication place and date, creation date, source, language of the text, language of the original work, domain, genre, number of tokens, etc. [17].

ParCoLab has been growing steadily since its inception. Initially, it contained 2M tokens [17]. Before the work on diversification presented in this paper, it contained 17.6M tokens, with 5.9M tokens in Serbian, 7.4M in French, 3.9M in English and 286K in Spanish. All the languages except for Spanish were represented through both original works and translations. In Spanish, there were only fiction translations. Its low representation is due to the fact that it has been incorporated recently in order to palliate the lack of existing Serbian-Spanish corpora. There is ongoing work on including more Spanish texts, both original and translated.

Regarding the type of texts, the corpus content came from predominantly literary works [3]. A small portion of the corpus was characterized as web content, legal and political texts and spoken data, but they were not significant in size – ∼30K tokens of film and TV show subtitles and ∼60K tokens from TED talks [14]. There were some efforts to diversify the corpus by including domain specific texts from biology, politics, and cinematography, but this material remained secondary. The original number of tokens per type of data and per language is shown in Table 1.

Table 1. Token distribution per language and text type before including spoken data.

Text type	Serbian	French	English	Spanish	Total	%
Literary texts	5,535,926	6,542,014	3,301,397	286,948	15,666,285	88.77
Non-literary written texts	340,060	761,595	566,656	0	1,668,311	9.45
Spoken data	104,935	125,919	82,504	0	313,358	1.78
Total	5,980,921	7,429,528	3,950,557	286,948	17,647,954	
% of corpus	33.89	42.10	22.39	1.63		

Even though there were some diversification efforts, the literary works remained dominant and represented 88.7% of the corpus. ParCoLab corpus consisted mainly of written texts, apart from only 1.78% of spoken data [11]. As mentioned in Introduction, linguistic differences between written and spoken corpus influence the performance of NLP tools. Therefore, we put in a great deal of effort to overcome the main shortcoming of the corpus, which we discuss in the next section.

4   Spoken Language Data in ParCoLab

As we have already discussed in Introduction, one of the easiest way to diversify a corpus by adding spoken language data is to include TED talks and film subtitles even though this material is written and edited before oral production. This method presents a number of other shortcomings. For instance, some of the subtitles are translated automatically or by amateur translators without subsequent verification by professional translators. In addition, transcripts and translations are influenced by the number of characters that can appear on the screen. Moreover, the subtitles usually do not represent the translation of the speech in the film, but the translation of the transcripts of that speech, which are edited to fit the character number limit (see [7]). In what follows, we describe how these downsides were overcome in the present work.

Although the quality of TED talks translations cannot be guaranteed, they are reviewed by experienced translators and are supposed to be of higher quality then subtitle translations downloaded from the OpenSubtitles database. Therefore, we downloaded TED talks from the official TED site in a batch. We did not use the transcripts existing in other corpora (cf. Sect. 2). Transcripts of original TED talks are included in the database alongside their translations into three languages of the project – Serbian, French, Spanish. At the time of writing this paper, 2000 TED talks have been included in the ParCoLab database for a total of 13,458,193 tokens. A TED talk in ParCoLab corpus contains 1,652 words on average. The shortest TEDs contain only brief introductions or explanations of musical or art performances of about 200 words, whereas the longest contain around 8,000 words. They date from 1984 to 2019.

As for the film subtitles, the methodology is slightly different. Original English and French transcripts are downloaded from the OpenSubtitles database. The Serbian films were manually transcribed since it was not possible to download original transcripts or to find open source speech-to-text tools for Serbian. The inclusion of the Serbian film transcripts makes the ParCoLab corpus unique. The film subtitles translations are downloaded from the OpenSubtitles database and then improved by students who are translators in training and by the members of the ParCoLab team who work as professional translators as well. Moreover, the subtitles are compared to the actual speech in the film and corrected accordingly. That way, the limit on the number of characters to appear on screen does not affect the quality of the transcript and translation.

Apart from film transcripts, the transcripts of a large collection of cartoons are being included in the ParCoLab corpus. The data is collected from the Smurfs official Youtube channels[10] in all four languages of the corpus. The transcripts

---

[10] https://www.youtube.com/channel/UCeY4C8Sbx8B4bIyREPSvORQ/videos.

of popular children's stories produced by Jetlag Productions[11] are also included in the corpus in all four languages. One of the advantages of this approach is the fact that the cartoons are dubbed. That way, transcripts in all languages are transcripts of the speech in that language and not the translations of the edited transcripts of that speech. There are currently 19 The Smurfs cartoons and 19 children stories from the Jetlag productions in all four languages.

All the spoken language data is stored in XML files in compliance with the TEI P5 guidelines and included in the ParCoLab database using the same methodology as for the rest of the corpus (see Sect. 3). Apart from standardized metadata, the name of the TED editor is included. Time spans are omitted. Additional metadata for film and cartoon transcripts represent names of characters, gender, and age in order to make it useful for linguistic analysis.

There are now 32.9M tokens in ParCoLab database. The Serbian subcorpus currently contains 9.6M tokens, French 11.5M, English 7.7M, whereas the Spanish portion contains 4.06M. The current percentage of spoken data is listed in Table 2.

Table 2. Token distribution per language after adding spoken data.

Text type	Serbian	French	English	Spanish	Total	% of corpus
TED talks	3,215,129	3,592,230	3,304,572	3,346,261	13,458,193	40.88
Films	292,916	356,749	252,355	0	902,020	2.74
Cartoons	110,865	68,516	173,865	23,324	376,570	1.14
Spoken data	3,618,910	4,017,495	3,730,792	3,369,585	**14,736,783**	44.77
Written data	5,989,500	7,475,463	4,030,951	687,127	**18,183,041**	55.23
Total	9,608,410	11,492,958	7,761,743	4,056,712	**32,919,824**	
% of corpus	29.19	34.91	23.58	12.32		

The percentage of literary works dropped from 88.7% to 55.23% whereas the spoken data represent 44.77% instead of 1.78% of the corpus before the diversification. We can conclude that the inclusion of, what is called here, spoken data has already demonstrated a substantial progress in diversifying ParCoLab corpus. All the spoken material can be queried via the user-friendly interface which makes this corpus accessible not only to researchers but also to the translators, lexicographers, teachers, etc. The Spanish section of the corpus rose from 1.63% to 12.32%.

When it comes to the qualitative evaluation of the corpus, this diversification helped to cover certain senses and contexts of specific words. For instance, the Serbian adjective *domaći* (Eng. domestic) mostly occurred with the sense 'related to the home' in the original corpus [11]. Currently, its dominant sense is 'not foreign', which is in accordance with the monolingual Serbian corpora. Furthermore, as was supposed previously [10], film transcripts contributed to

---

[11] https://en.wikipedia.org/wiki/Jetlag_Productions.

augmenting the number of the examples in which French adjective *sale* (Eng. dirty) is 'used to emphasize one's disgust for someone or something'.

5 Conclusion and Future Work

The quadrilingual corpus ParCoLab is one of rare parallel resources containing a Serbian subcorpus, especially when it comes to original Serbian texts. In the expansion of the corpus, priority was given to quality over quantity. In addition to continuing work on enlarging the corpus, a great deal of effort has also been devoted to the diversification of the predominantly literary content. This paper describes the method that allowed us to include transcripts and translations of 2000 TED talks containing 13.5M tokens in ParCoLab. Apart from TED talks, there are film subtitles, among which are those originally produced in Serbian, as well as the transcripts of dubbed cartoons that are included in the ParCoLab database. By including additional 73 film and cartoon transcripts alongside the aforementioned TED talks, ParCoLab corpus database surpasses 32.9M. Thus we created the material not only for the development of NLP tools (especially machine translation) but also for teaching and learning French, English, Serbian, and Spanish as foreign languages and for lexicography.

While the ParCoLab content is being diversified more and more, the annotated portion of the corpus still comes from written documents. Given that the training corpus for the annotation tools needs to be built on the in-domain data to perform well, it is necessary to improve the training corpus. A new spoken language data subcorpus provides us with material to pursue this goal. Therefore, our next steps in annotating the corpus would be to tag, lemmatize, and parse added spoken subcorpus.

References

1. Agić, Ž., Ljubešić, N.: Universal dependencies for Croatian (that work for Serbian, too). In: Piskorski, J. (ed.) Proceedings of the 5th Workshop on Balto-Slavic Natural Language Processing (BSNLP 2015), pp. 1–8. INCOMA, Hissar (2015)
2. Agić, Ž., Ljubešić, N., Merkler, D.: Lemmatization and morphosyntactic tagging of Croatian and Serbian. In: Piskorski, J. (ed.) Proceedings of the 4th Biennial International Workshop on Balto-Slavic Natural Language Processing (BSNLP 2013), pp. 48–57. Association for Computational Linguistics, Sofia (2013)
3. Balvet, A., Stosic, D., Miletic, A.: TALC-sef a manually-revised POS-tagged literary corpus in Serbian, English and French. In: LREC 2014, pp. 4105–4110. European Language Resources Association, Reykjavik (2014)
4. Cettolo, M., Girardi, C., Federico, M.: WIT3: web inventory of transcribed and translated talks. In: Proceedings of the 16th EAMT Conference, pp. 261–268 (2012)
5. Čermák, F., Rosen, A.: The case of interCorp, a multilingual parallel corpus. Int. J. Corpus Linguist. **13**(3), 411–427 (2012)
6. Gildea, D.: Corpus variation and parser performance. In: Proceedings of the 2001 Conference on Empirical Methods in Natural Language Processing (2001). https://www.aclweb.org/anthology/W01-0521

7. van der Klis, M., Le Bruyn, B., de Swart, H.: Temporal reference in discourse and dialogue (Forth)
8. Krstev, C., Vitas, D.: An aligned English-Serbian corpus. In: Tomović, N., Vujić, J. (eds.) ELLSIIR Proceedings (English Language and Literature Studies: Image, Identity, Reality), vol. 1, pp. 495–508. Faculty of Philology, Belgrade (2011)
9. Krstev, C., Vitas, D., Erjavec, T.: MULTEXT-East resources for Serbian. In: Erjavec, T., Gros, J.Z. (eds.) Zbornik 7. mednarodne multikonference "Informacijska druzba IS 2004", Jezikovne tehnologije, Ljubljana, Slovenija, 9–15 Oktober 2004. Institut "Jožef Stefan", Ljubljana (2004)
10. Marjanović, S., Stosic, D., Miletic, A.: A sample French-Serbian dictionary entry based on the ParCoLab parallel corpus. In: Krek, S., et al. (eds.) Proceedings of the XVIII EURALEX International Congress: Lexicography in Global Contexts, pp. 423–435. Faculty of Arts, Ljubljana (2018)
11. Marjanović, S., Stošić, D., Miletić, A.: Paralelni korpus ParCoLab u službi srpsko-francuske leksikografije. In: Novaković, J., Srebro, M. (eds.) Srpsko-francuske književne i kulturne veze u evropskom kontekstu I, pp. 279–307. Matica srpska, Novi Sad (2019)
12. Miletic, A.: Un treebank pour le serbe: constitution et exploitations. Ph.D. thesis. Université Toulouse Jean Jaurès, Toulouse (2018)
13. Miletic, A., Fabre, C., Stosic, D.: De la constitution d'un corpus arboré á l'analyse syntaxique du serbe. Traitement Automatique des Langues **59**(3), 15–39 (2018)
14. Miletic, A., Stosic, D., Marjanović, S.: ParCoLab: a parallel corpus for Serbian, French and English. In: Ekštein, K., Matoušek, V. (eds.) TSD 2017. LNCS (LNAI), vol. 10415, pp. 156–164. Springer, Cham (2017). https://doi.org/10.1007/978-3-319-64206-2_18
15. Nivre, J., et al.: The CoNLL 2007 shared task on dependency parsing. In: Proceedings of the CoNLL Shared Task Session of EMNLP-CoNLL, pp. 915–932. Association for Computational Linguistics, Prague (2007)
16. Ruiz, N., Federico, M.: Complexity of spoken versus written language for machine translation. In: Proceedings of the 17th Annual Conference of the European Association for Machine Translation (EAMT), pp. 173–180. Hrvatsko društvo za jezične tehnologije, Zagreb (2014)
17. Stosic, D., Marjanović, S., Miletic, A.: Corpus parallèle ParCoLab et lexicographie bilingue français-serbe: recherches et applications. In: Srebro, M., Novaković, J. (eds.) Serbica (2019). https://serbica.u-bordeaux-montaigne.fr/index.php/revues
18. Terzic, D.: Parsing des textes journalistiques en serbe par le logiciel Talismane. In: Proceedings of TALN-RECITAL, PFIA 2019, pp. 591–604. AfIA, Toulouse (2019)
19. Tiedemann, J.: Parallel data, tools and interfaces in OPUS. In: Calzolari, N. (eds.) Proceedings of the 8th International Conference on Language Resources and Evaluation (LREC 2012). European Language Resources Association, Istanbul (2014)
20. Tyers, F.M., Alperen, M.S.: South-East European times: a parallel corpus of Balkan languages. In: Proceedings of the LREC Workshop on Exploitation of Multilingual Resources and Tools for Central and (South-) Eastern European Languages, pp. 49–53 (2010)
21. Vitas, D., Krstev, C.: Literature and aligned texts. In: Slavcheva, M., et al. (eds.) Readings in Multilinguality, pp. 148–155. Institute for Parallel Processing, Bulgarian Academy of Sciences, Sofia (2006)
22. von Waldenfels, R.: Compiling a parallel corpus of Slavic languages. Text strategies, tools and the question of lemmatization in alignment. In: Brehmer, B., Zdanova, V., Zimny, R. (eds.) Beiträge der Europäischen Slavistischen Linguistik (POLYSLAV) 9, pp. 123–138. Verlag Otto Sagner, München (2006)

23. von Waldenfels, R.: Recent developments in ParaSol: breadth for depth and XSLT based web concordancing with CWB. In: Daniela, M., Garabík, R. (eds.) Natural Language Processing, Multilinguality, Proceedings of Slovko 2011, Modra, Slovakia, 20–21 October 2011, pp. 156–162. Tribun EU, Bratislava (2011)
24. Zeroual, I., Lakhouaja, A.: MulTed: a multilingual aligned and tagged parallel corpus. Appl. Comput. Inform. (2018). https://doi.org/10.1016/j.aci.2018.12.003

Quantitative Analysis of the Morphological Complexity of Malayalam Language

Kavya Manohar[1,3]([✉]) [ID], A. R. Jayan[2,3] [ID], and Rajeev Rajan[1,3]

[1] College of Engineering Trivandrum, Thiruvananthapuram, Kerala, India
sakhi.kavya@gmail.com
[2] Government Engineering College Palakkad, Palakkad, Kerala, India
[3] APJ Abdul Kalam Technological University, Thiruvananthapuram, Kerala, India

Abstract. This paper presents a quantitative analysis on the morphological complexity of Malayalam language. Malayalam is a Dravidian language spoken in India, predominantly in the state of Kerala with about 38 million native speakers. Malayalam words undergo inflections, derivations and compounding leading to an infinitely extending lexicon. In this work, morphological complexity of Malayalam is quantitatively analyzed on a text corpus containing 8 million words. The analysis is based on the parameters type-token growth rate (TTGR), type-token ratio (TTR) and moving average type-token ratio (MATTR). The values of the parameters obtained in the current study is compared to that of the values of other morphologically complex languages.

Keywords: Morphological complexity · Types and tokens · TTR · Malayalam language

1 Introduction

Malayalam[1] is a language with complex word morphology. Malayalam words undergo inflections, derivations and compounding producing an infinite vocabulary [19]. As a language with high morphological complexity it has a large number of wordforms derived from a single root word (such as the English words *houses* and *housing*, which stem from the same root word *house*). Morphological complexity can be measured either in terms of the average number of grammatical features getting encoded into a word or in terms of the diversity of word forms occurring in the text corpus of a language. The former approach is called typological analysis and the latter one is called corpus based analysis of morphological complexity [5]. Morphological complexity of a language has its impact on applications like automatic speech recognition (ASR) where speech to text conversion depends largely on the underlying language model. A measure of the

---

[1] https://en.wikipedia.org/wiki/Malayalam.

© Springer Nature Switzerland AG 2020
P. Sojka et al. (Eds.): TSD 2020, LNAI 12284, pp. 71–78, 2020.
https://doi.org/10.1007/978-3-030-58323-1_7

complexity is important for improving and adapting the existing methods of natural language processing (NLP) [10].

This paper analyses the morphological complexity of Malayalam in terms of corpus based parameters namely, type-token growth rate (TTGR), type-token ratio (TTR) and moving average type-token ratio (MATTR). These parameters are formally defined in Sect. 5. The study is conducted on a Malayalam text corpus of 8 million words.

2 Literature Review

Complexity of a natural language can be in terms of morphology, phonology and syntax [3]. Morphological level complexity of a language implies a large possibility of inflections (by grammatical tense, mood, aspect and case forms) and agglutinations (of different wordforms). The number of possible inflection points in a typical sentence, the number of inflectional categories, and the number of morpheme types are all morphological complexity indicators [4]. It requires a strict linguistic supervision to analyze each word in terms of its morpheme types to quantify complexity in this manner. Bentz et al. performed typological analysis of morphological complexity involving human expert judgement and compared it with corpus based analysis of morphological complexity and drew strong correlation between the two [5].

Covington et al. suggested the use of MATTR as a reliable measure of linguistic complexity independent of the total corpus length and suggested an efficient algorithm for computing MATTR [6]. Kettunen [13] compared corpus based parameters like TTR and MATTR with other methods of complexity measures as defined by Patrick Juola [12] and concluded both TTR and MATTR give a reliable approximation of the morphological complexity of languages. Ximena Gutierrez-Vasques et al. suggested estimating the morphological complexity of a language directly from the diverse wordforms over a corpus is relatively easy and reproducible way to quantify complexity without the strict need of linguistic annotated data [10].

3 Problem Statement

Malayalam has seven nominal case forms (nominative, accusative, dative, sociative, locative, instrumental and genitive), two nominal number forms (singular and plural) and three gender forms (masculine, feminine and neutral). These forms are indicated as suffixes to the nouns. Verbs in Malayalam get inflected based on tense (present, past and future), mood (imperative, compulsive, promissive, optative, abilitative, purposive, permissive, precative, irrealis, monitory, quotative, conditional and satisfactive), voice (active and passive) and aspect (habitual, iterative, perfect) [16,19]. The inflecting suffix forms vary depending on the final phonemes of the root words. Words agglutinate to form new words depending on the context [2]. Table 1 gives examples of a few complex word formation in Malayalam.

Table 1. Complex morphological word formation in Malayalam

Malayalam Word	Translation to English	Remark
പെട്ടിയിൽ (peṭṭijil)	in the box	Nominal locative suffix to the word പെട്ടി (peṭṭi, box)
കുട്ടിയോട് (kuṭṭijoːṭ)	to the child	Nominal sociative suffix to the word കുട്ടി (kuṭṭi, child)
ആനക്കുട്ടി (aː-nakkuṭṭi)	baby elephant	Compound word formed by agglutination of nouns ആന (aːna, elephant) and കുട്ടി (kuṭṭi, baby)
ആനക്കുട്ടികളോട് (aːnakkuṭṭikaloːṭ)	to the baby elephants	Nominal sociative suffix to the plural form of the compound word ആനക്കുട്ടി (aːnakkuṭṭi, baby elephant)
ഉണർന്നിരിക്കണ്ട (uṇarṉṉirikkaṇṭa)	do not stay awake	Negative imperative mood of the verb ഉണരുക (uṇaruka, be awake)
പാടിക്കൊണ്ടിരിക്കും (paːṭikkoṉṭirikkum)	will be singing	Future tense iterative aspect of the verb പാടുക (paːṭuka, to sing)

The productive word formation and morphological complexity of Malayalam are documented qualitatively in the domain of grammatical studies. However a quantitative study on the same is not yet available for Malayalam language. Adoption of general NLP solutions of high resource languages like English is not feasible in the setting of morphologically complex languages. A functional morphology anlayzer, *mlmorph* addresses the morphological complexity of Malayalam applying grammatical rules over root word lexicon [19]. Quantification of linguistic complexity is important to adapt and improve various NLP applications like automatic speech recognition, parts of speech (POS) tagging and spell checking [9,14,17,18]. This study aims at quantifying the morphological complexity of Malayalam in terms of corpus parameters.

4   Material

This study is performed on Malayalam running text from Wikipedia articles. The Malayalam Wikipedia dump is curated and published by Swathanthra Malayalam Computing (SMC) as *SMC Corpus* [1]. It consists of 62302 articles. The Malayalam running text often has foreign words, punctuation and numerals present in it. The corpus is first cleaned up to eliminate non Malayalam content and punctuations. It is then unicode normalized [7]. The cleaned up corpus contained 8.14 million Malayalam words. The nature of the text is formal encyclopedic Malayalam.

5   Method

An element of the set of distinct wordforms in a running text is called a *type*. Every instance of a type in the running text is called a *token*. For example, in the sentence, *To be or not to be is the question*, there are 7 types and 9 tokens. The types *to* and *be* repeat two times each. The relationship between the count of types and tokens is an indicator of vocabulary richness, morphological complexity and information flow [10]. The type-token ratio (TTR) is a simple baseline measure of morphological complexity [13]. TTR is calculated by the formula defined in Eq. (1), where V is the count of types and N is the count of tokens.

$$TTR = \frac{V}{N} \tag{1}$$

The type count gets expanded due to productive morphology and higher values of TTR correspond to higher morphological complexity [5]. However TTR is affected by the token count, N [6]. Longer the corpus, it is more likely that the new tokens belong to the types that have occurred already. The value of TTR gets smaller with the increase in token count. Computing TTR over incrementally larger corpus can indicate how the TTR varies with the token count. In this study, TTR is computed with different token counts starting with 1000 and increasing upto the entire corpus size. This has enabled comparison of Malayalam with the morphological complexity of other languages whose TTR values are available in literature for different token counts.

The type-token growth rate (TTGR) curve is obtained by plotting the graph of token count vs. type count. It indicates how many new types appear with the increase in the token count. If the slope of the growth rate curve reduces and approaches horizontal at a lower value of token count, it indicates a simple morphology [15]. For a morphologically complex language, the type count continues to grow with the token count [11].

The moving average type-token ratio (MATTR) computes the relationship between types and tokens that is independent of the text length. Its efficient implementation by Covington et al. has been used by Kettunen to compare the morphological complexity of different European languages [6,13]. The algorithm to compute MATTR is as follows [8]:

Algorithm 1: Computation of MATTR

Data: A text Corpus
Result: MATTR
1   N ← length of corpus;
2   L ← length of window (L¡N);
3   start ← initial position of window ;
4   i = start ← index of window position;
5   **while** $i \leq (N - L + 1)$ **do**
6      $V_i = $ *type count in the window* $[i, i + L - 1]$;
7      $TTR(i) = \frac{V_i}{L}$;
8      $i = i + 1$;
9   **end**
10   $MATTR(L) = \frac{\sum_{i=1}^{N-L+1} TTR(i)}{N-L+1}$

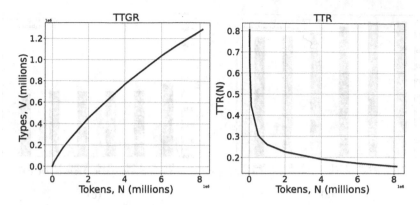

Fig. 1. TTGR and TTR plot of Malayalam for *SMC Corpus* of Wikipedia text

The corpus with N tokens is divided into the overlapped subtexts of the same length, say L, the window length. Window moves forward one token at a time and TTR is computed for every window. MATTR is defined as the mean of the entire set of TTRs [6]. In this work L is chosen as 500, enabling comparison with other languages in the study by Kettunen, where the window length is 500 [13].

6 Result and Discussion

Counting the types and tokens on *SMC Corpus*, TTGR and TTR curves are plotted. Figure 1 shows the TTGR curve on the left and the TTR on the right. TTGR curve shows a steep rise initially. As the token count reaches 8 million, the type count is around 1.2 million. But the curve does not flatten even at that token count. This pattern is a common property of Dravidian languages as many unseen wordforms appear as the corpus size is increased [15]. TTR is very high at around 0.82 when the token count is 1000. TTR reduces to around 0.44 when the token count is 0.1 million and finally saturates at around 0.16 for the full corpus of 8 million tokens.

To compare the TTR obtained for Malayalam with that of other languages, we have used the data reported for European languages by Kettunen and for Indian languages by Kumar et al. [13,15]. Figures 2a and 2b illustrates the comparison. Only those languages with the highest reported TTRs in the respective papers and English are used for comparison. The token size (in millions) used for computing TTRs used in the comparisons is indicated for each language. Malayalam clearly shows more morphological complexity than the European languages, Finnish, Estonian, Czech, Slovak, English and Spanish in terms of TTR values. Values of TTR obtained for Malayalam when compared with other Indian languages Marathi, Hindi, Tamil, Kannada and Telugu indicate a higher level of morphological complexity for Malayalam.

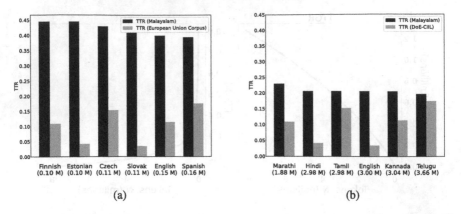

(a)   (b)

Fig. 2. Comparison of Malayalam TTR with that of *European Union Constitution Corpus* [13] and *DoE-CIIL Corpus* [15]

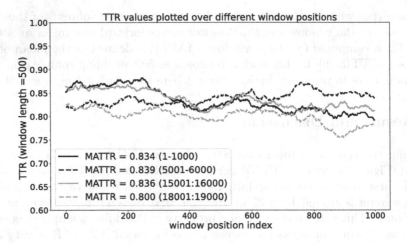

Fig. 3. TTR plotted at different segments of the SMC corpus for 1000 window positions

MATTR is computed with window length, L = 500 over different segments of the *SMC corpus*. TTR values for the segments with window position index 1–1000, 5001–6000, 15001–16000 and 18001–19000 are plotted in Fig. 3. These segments gave MATTR values 0.834, 0.839, 0.836 and 0.800 respectively. Computing MATTR with 0.1 million tokens of *SMC corpus* resulted in a value 0.806 for Malayalam. Kettunen has reported MATTR values on *European Union constitution corpus* with each language having a token count slightly above 0.1 million [13]. A comparative graph of the MATTR values reported by Kettunen with the values obtained for Malayalam is plotted in Fig. 4. It clearly indicates a higher degree of morphological complexity for Malayalam in terms of MATTR on a formal text corpus. An equivalent comparison with other Indian languages could not be done due to non availability of reported studies.

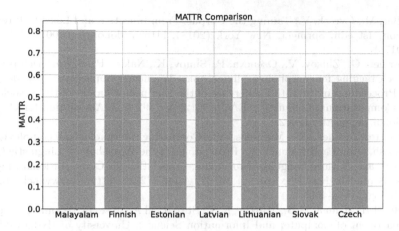

Fig. 4. Comparison of MATTR values computed for Malayalam on *SMC Corpus* with that of *European Union Constitution Corpus* [13]

7 Conclusion

In this paper we have reported a quantitative analysis of the morphological complexity of Malayalam language on a formal text corpus of 8 million words. The corpus based analysis has revealed high degrees of morphological complexity of Malayalam in terms of TTR and MATTR. It is important that this aspect of morphological complexity be considered while developing natural language processing applications like automatic speech recognition, spell checking and POS tagging for Malayalam. This involves preparing morpheme based language models and phonetic lexicons for ASR and performing a morphological analysis of words for POS tagging and spelling correction.

References

1. Malayalam Corpus, by Swathanthra Malayalam Computing, April 2020. https://gitlab.com/smc/corpus
2. Asher, R.E., Kumari, T.: Malayalam. Psychology Press, London (1997)
3. Baerman, M., Brown, D., Corbett, G.G.: Understanding and Measuring Morphological Complexity. Oxford University Press, Oxford (2015)
4. Bane, M.: Quantifying and measuring morphological complexity. In: Proceedings of the 26th West Coast Conference on Formal Linguistics, Cascadilla Proceedings Project Somerville, MA, pp. 69–76 (2008)
5. Bentz, C., Ruzsics, T., Koplenig, A., Samardzic, T.: A comparison between morphological complexity measures: typological data vs. language corpora. In: Proceedings of the Workshop on Computational Linguistics for Linguistic Complexity (CL4LC), pp. 142–153 (2016)
6. Covington, M.A., McFall, J.D.: Cutting the gordian knot: the moving-average type-token ratio (MATTR). J. Quant. Linguist. **17**(2), 94–100 (2010)
7. Davis, M., Dürst, M.: Unicode normalization forms (2001)

8. Fidler, M., Cvrček, V.: Taming the Corpus: From Inflection and Lexis to Interpretation, 1st edn. Springer, New York (2018). https://doi.org/10.1007/978-3-319-98017-1

9. Georgiev, G., Zhikov, V., Osenova, P., Simov, K., Nakov, P.: Feature-rich part-of-speech tagging for morphologically complex languages: application to Bulgarian. In: Proceedings of the 13th Conference of the European Chapter of the Association for Computational Linguistics, EACL 2012, pp. 492–502. Association for Computational Linguistics (2012)

10. Gutierrez-Vasques, X., Mijangos, V.: Comparing morphological complexity of Spanish, Otomi and Nahuatl. In: Proceedings of the Workshop on Linguistic Complexity and Natural Language Processing, Association for Computational Linguistics, Santa Fe, New-Mexico, pp. 30–37, August 2018. https://www.aclweb.org/anthology/W18-4604

11. Htay, H.H., Kumar, G.B., Murthy, K.N.: Statistical Analyses of Myanmar Corpora. Department of Computer and Information Sciences, University of Hyderabad pp, Hyderabad, pp. 1–15 (2007)

12. Juola, P.: Measuring linguistic complexity: the morphological tier. J. Quant. Linguist. **5**(3), 206–213 (1998)

13. Kettunen, K.: Can type-token ratio be used to show morphological complexity of languages? J. Quant. Linguist. **21**(3), 223–245 (2014)

14. Kipyatkova, I., Karpov, A.: Study of morphological factors of factored language models for Russian ASR. In: Ronzhin, A., Potapova, R., Delic, V. (eds.) SPECOM 2014. LNCS (LNAI), vol. 8773, pp. 451–458. Springer, Cham (2014). https://doi.org/10.1007/978-3-319-11581-8_56

15. Kumar, G.B., Murthy, K.N., Chaudhuri, B.: Statistical analyses of Telugu text corpora. IJDL. Int. J. Dravidian Linguist. **36**(2), 71–99 (2007)

16. Nair, R.S.S.: A grammar of Malayalam. Lang. Ind. **12**, 1–135 (2012)

17. Pakoci, E., Popović, B., Pekar, D.: Using morphological data in language modeling for Serbian large vocabulary speech recognition. Comput. Intell. Neurosci. **2019**, 8 (2019)

18. Pirinen, T.: Weighted Finite-State Methods for Spell-Checking and Correction. University of Helsinki, Helsinki (2014)

19. Thottingal, S.: Finite state transducer based morphology analysis for Malayalam language. In: Proceedings of the 2nd Workshop on Technologies for MT of Low Resource Languages, European Association for Machine Translation, Dublin, Ireland, pp. 1–5, August 2019. https://www.aclweb.org/anthology/W19-6801

Labeling Explicit Discourse Relations Using Pre-trained Language Models

Murathan Kurfalı(✉) (iD)

Linguistics Department, Stockholm University, Stockholm, Sweden
murathan.kurfali@ling.su.se

Abstract. Labeling explicit discourse relations is one of the most challenging sub-tasks of the shallow discourse parsing where the goal is to identify the discourse connectives and the boundaries of their arguments. The state-of-the-art models achieve slightly above 45% of F-score by using hand-crafted features. The current paper investigates the efficacy of the pre-trained language models in this task. We find that the pre-trained language models, when finetuned, are powerful enough to replace the linguistic features. We evaluate our model on PDTB 2.0 and report the state-of-the-art results in extraction of the full relation. This is the first time when a model outperforms the knowledge intensive models without employing any linguistic features.

Keywords: Explicit discourse relations · Shallow discourse parsing · Argument labeling

1 Introduction

Shallow discourse parsing (SDP) refers to the task of segmenting a text into a set of discourse relations. A typical discourse relation consists of two arguments and a discourse connective accompanied with a sense reflecting the semantic relation between the arguments (e.g. cause, precedence). Within the Penn Discourse Treebank (PDTB), discourse connectives are assumed to be the lexical items which connect two abstract objects such as events, states, and propositions following the definition of [8]. There are two main types of discourse relations, *explicit* and *implicit*, where the difference is the presence of an overt discourse connective. Parsing explicit and implicit relations are often treated as separate tasks, and implicit discourse relations have received much of the attention due to the challenges brought by a lack of an overt signal. In this work, we instead focus on the less studied task of identifying explicit discourse relations. This consists of identifying discourse connectives and their arguments in text.

Labeling explicit relations is a challenging task due to three main reasons: (i) connectives do not always assume a discursive role (ii) the arguments can consist of discontinuous text spans (iii) the same text span can have different

© Springer Nature Switzerland AG 2020
P. Sojka et al. (Eds.): TSD 2020, LNAI 12284, pp. 79–86, 2020.
https://doi.org/10.1007/978-3-030-58323-1_8

roles in different relations. All three challenges are illustrated in the Example 1 and 2[1].

(1) *Although Dr. Warshaw points out that stress and anxiety have their positive uses, 'stress perceived to be threatening implies a component of fear and anxiety that may contribute to burnout.'* **He** <u>also</u> **noted that various work environments, such as night work, have their own stressors**.

(2) <u>Although</u> Dr. Warshaw points out that **stress and anxiety have their positive uses**, *"stress perceived to be threatening implies a component of fear and anxiety that may contribute to burnout"*

Example 1 presents a case where a complete discourse relation, which is provided in Example 2, is embedded within another relation. Therefore, the text span 'stress and ... uses' assumes two different roles in two different relations; it is part of the first argument in the first relation, whereas it is the second argument in Example 2. Additionally, the second argument in Example 1 consists of an discontinuous text span as it is interrupted by the connective. Similarly, the text span ('Dr. Warshaw ... that') creates discontinuity between the connective and the second argument in Example 2 as it does not belong to the relation at all. Finally, the lexical item *and*, which is the most common discourse connective, in Example 2 do not assume any discursive role in this case as it only connects two noun phrases rather than abstract objects.

Most existing literature heavily relies on feature engineering to deal with these issues, with [2] and [3] being the only notable exceptions. The current work follows the latter studies in performing explicit discourse relation labeling without resorting to any linguistic features. Specifically, we try to answer the following question: can pre-trained language models, which have shown significant gains in a wide variety of natural language tasks, replace the rich feature sets used in a standard parser? To this end, we model explicit discourse relation labeling as a pipeline of two tasks, namely connective identification and argument labeling. Each sub-task is regarded as a token-level sequence prediction problem and modeled as a simple neural architecture employing BERT [1].

We evaluated our system on the PDTB 2.0 corpus. Experimental results show that contextual embeddings are indeed powerful enough to replace the linguistics features used in previous work. Unlike the previous feature-independent models, the proposed system manages to improve over the existing systems by achieving 8% increase in the extraction of the both arguments[2]. Besides the performance gain, the proposed system has the benefit of being directly applicable to any raw text as it does not require any pre-processing and can straightforwardly be extended to other languages with available training data and a pre-trained language model.

---

[1] In the examples, unless otherwise stated, Arg2 is shown in bold, Arg1 is in italics and the discourse connective is underlined.

[2] The source code is available at: https://github.com/MurathanKurfali/shallowdisc.

2 Background

Shallow discourse parsing (SDP) aims to uncover the local coherence relations within text without assuming any tree/graph structure between the relations, hence the name *shallow*. It started with the release of PDTB 2.0 [8] and, lately, it attracted attention thanks to the two subsequent shared tasks at CoNLL 2015 [12] and 2016 [13]. Most of the participating systems treat SDP as a pipeline of sub-tasks following [5] which is the first full end-to-end PDTB-style discourse parser. A standard pipeline starts with labeling explicit discourse relations which is followed by sense classification and labeling Implicit discourse relations. Labeling explicit relations are further decomposed into a set of sub-tasks which are connective identification, argument position identification, extraction of each argument. Each sub-task is addressed by employing a rich set of linguistics features, including dependency trees, part-of-speech tags, Brown clusters and Verbnet classes [12, 13].

[2] marks the beginning of a new line of research which is to perform shallow discourse parsing without any feature engineering. The authors address labeling of explicit discourse relations task in a simplified setting where the task is reduced to determining the role of each token within a pre-extracted relation span. The authors train a LSTM on those spans which takes Glove embeddings as its input and classifies each token with one of the four labels which are *Conn, Arg1, Arg2, None*. The network achieves F-score of 23.05% which is significantly lower than the state-of-the-art models. Nevertheless, the study is of great importance as it shows that argument labeling is possible without any feature engineering. [3] extends the idea of [2] to full shallow discourse parsing on raw texts. They employ a BiLSTM and a sliding window approach, according to which the text is split into overlapping windows. In each window the system tries to capture the parts which belong to a discourse relation. The predicted relation spans are later assembled using a novel aggregation method based on Jaccard distance. The proposed hierarchy performs considerably better than [2] but still falls short of matching the state-of-the-art methods.

Method-wise, the closest work to the current paper is that of [6] (ToNy) which employs contextual embeddings to perform multilingual RST-style discourse segmentation. Instead of directly finetuning BERT, ToNy uses a simplified sequence prediction architecture which consists of an LSTM conditioned on the concatenation of the contextual embeddings (either Elmo or BERT) and the character embeddings obtained by convolution filters.

3 Method

Unlike previous studies which realize labeling explicit discourse relations as a long pipeline of tasks which usually consists of 4 to 6 sub-components [9, 11], we propose a simplified pipeline consisting of only two steps, namely connective identification and argument extraction.

The connective identification step helps us to exploit the lexicalized approach of the PDTB. In the PDTB framework, the discourse connectives function as anchor points and without them, determining the number of relations in a text become highly problematic, especially when the arguments of multiple relations overlap as in Example 1 and 2. Bypassing connective identification would require an extra post-processing step to sort different relations with common arguments out which is not a trivial task. In order to avoid those problem, we perform connective identification as the first task, mimicking the original annotation schema.

Following the previous studies of [2,3], we approach explicit discourse relation labeling as an N-way token classification problem. To this end, we follow the standard token classification architecture used in sequence prediction tasks, e.g. named entity recognition, employing BERT [1]. The architecture consists of a BERT model with a linear layer on top. The linear layer is connected to the hidden-states of the BERT and outputs the label probabilities for each token based on the sub-task it is trained on.

3.1   Connective Identification

The aim of this component is to identify the lexical items which assume a discursive role in the text. Although connective identification seems to be the easiest step among the other sub-tasks of shallow discourse parsing [4,9], it has its own challenges. One problem is that discourse connectives in PDTB can be multiword expressions such as lexically frozen phrases, e.g. *on the other hand*, or as modified connectives which co-occur with an adverb e.g. *partly because, particularly since*. Such multi-word connectives pose a challenge because different connectives may also appear in the text consecutively without forming a longer connective, as illustrated in Example 3 and 4.

(3)   a.   *Typically, developers option property,* <u>and</u> **then once they get the administrative approvals, they buy it** (Conjunction)
   b.   *Typically, developers option property,* **and** <u>then</u> **once they get the administrative approvals, they buy it** (Precedence)
   c.   Typically, developers option property, *and then* <u>once</u> **they get the administrative approvals,** *they buy it* (Succession) (WSJ_2313)
(4)   *Consider the experience of Satoko Kitada, a 30-year-old designer of vehicle interiors who joined Nissan in 1982.* <u>At that time</u>, **tasks were assigned strictly on the basis of seniority** (Synchrony) (WSJ_0286)

Both Example 3 and 4 involve a three word sequence annotated as connectives but in Example 3 each token signals a different relation whereas in the latter example they are part of the same connective, hence signal only one relation. Therefore, correct prediction of the boundaries of the connectives is as crucial as identifying them as such because failing to do so may cause whole system to miss existing relations or add artificial ones. To this end, unlike previous studies [2,3], we assign different labels to single and multi token connectives (#Conn and #MWconn respectively) so at the time of inference, we can decide whether consecutive tokens predicted as connective is a part of a multiword connective or signal different relations.

Table 1. Number of annotations with various span lengths, in terms of the number of words in the relation, in the training set which consists of 14722 relations in total.

# of Annotations (%)	Span length
6231 (42.32%)	<25
12243 (83.16%)	<50
13810 (93.81%)	<75
14240 (96.73%)	<100
14617 (99.29%)	<250
Average	36.79

One drawback of using the publicly available BERT model is that text spans longer than 512 wordpieces cannot be encoded [1]. Therefore, we decided to split the text into paragraphs to ensure the coherence of the text segments as splitting into an arbitrary number of sentences would risk having incoherent segments. Manual inspection of the training data reveals that majority of the relations (84.94%) have both of their arguments in the same paragraph which further support our decision.

3.2 Argument Extraction

The argument extractor needs to identify the Arg1 and Arg2 spans of each predicted connective. The extractor searches for the arguments of the relation within a window of 100 words centered around the discourse connective[3]. Following the IOB2 format, the first word of each argument is tagged as #ARGX-B while other words within the argument spans are simply labeled as #ARGX where X is the argument number (1 or 2). The words outside of the relations are labeled as #NONE.

The window size is determined by considering the number of relations that can be covered and the label distribution in the extracted spans as longer windows sizes introduce a high of number of #NONE labels which negatively affect the training. Based on the span lengths of the relations in the training data (Table 1), window size of 100 presents itself as the best candidate since longer windows only minimally increase the coverage.

4   Experiments

Following the CoNLL 2015 setting, we use the PDTB Sections 2–21, 22 and 23 as the training, development and test set respectively. We use the cased BERT$_{base}$ model in our experiments[4] and the classifiers are implemented using the Huggingface's Transformer library[5]. The maximum sequence length is set to 400

---

[3] For multiword connectives, we center the window around the first token.
[4] https://github.com/google-research/bert.
[5] https://github.com/huggingface/transformers.

for connective identification and 250 for argument extraction. We use AdamW optimizer with the learning rate of 5×10^{-5} and $\epsilon = 10^{-8}$. Both classifiers are fine-tuned for 3 epochs. We train each classifier for 4 runs in order to estimate the variance and report the average performance.

5   Results and Discussion

We evaluate our model using the official evaluation script of the CoNLL 2016 shared task[6]. The script calculates the exact match scores of the identified connectives, extracted spans of the first and the second argument separately as well as the identification of the both arguments together (Arg1+Arg2).

Table 2. Exact match results (precision, recall, F-score) of explicit discourse relation labeling on PDTB test set. The models within horizontal lines are the best performing systems of CoNLL 2015, CoNLL 2016 and the feature independent systems respectively. *refers to the results when the gold connectives are provided to the model.

	Conn			Arg1			Arg2			Arg1+Arg2		
	P	R	F	P	R	F	P	R	F	P	R	F
[11]	94.83	93.49	94.16	51.05	50.33	50.68	77.89	76.79	77.33	45.54	44.90	45.22
[10]	–	–	92.77	–	–	50.05	–	–	76.23	–	–	44.58
[14]	91.8	86.6	89.1	47.5	44.8	46.1	70.5	66.4	68.4	40.0	37.7	38.8
[7]	83.42	92.22	87.6	51.25	56.65	53.81	68.36	75.57	71.79	43.12	47.66	45.28
[9]	92.42	94.88	93.63	49.73	51.06	50.38	75.73	77.75	76.73	44.31	45.49	44.9
[4]	**99.67**	**98.19**	**98.92**	42.47	41.84	42.15	76.06	74.92	75.48	36.51	35.97	36.24
[3]	71.35	62.73	66.76	33.16	29.15	31.03	52.47	46.13	49.09	37.25	32.75	34.86
[3]*	–	–	–	46.69	44.59	45.62	68.94	65.83	67.35	48.16	45.99	47.05
Ours	96.62	96.93	96.77	**60.02**	**60.22**	**60.12**	**80.37**	**80.63**	**80.50**	**53.20**	**53.37**	**53.28**

We compare our results with the top performing systems of CoNLL 2015/16 Shared tasks as well as with [3] which is the only feature-independent study that can run on raw texts (Table 2). We selected the top systems in each sub-task from CoNLL 2016 whereas for CoNLL 2015 we chose the top 3 ranked systems as [11] single-handedly achieved the best score in each sub-task that year.

Connective Identification: In line with the previous work, connective identification is the easiest step where our model achieves almost 97% F-score. Since the standard deviation among different runs is pretty low (<0.5), we randomly selected one run and manually checked the predicted connectives. In total, 16 unique text spans are incorrectly predicted as discourse connective for a total of 28 times where most of them are *and* tokens (30.6%). Similarly, *and* also constitutes the 30% of the false negatives (the connectives which are *not* labeled as

---

[6] https://github.com/attapol/conll16st.

such by the classifier), suggesting that *and* is more challenging to disambiguate in term of its discursive role than other connectives. Finally, of all predictions, only two of them (*10 min* and *end*) are not valid connective candidates which further proves the model's success on connective identification. However, since there is not any unseen connective in the test set, we cannot draw any conclusions regarding the generalization capabilities of the proposed model which will be further examined in a future study.

Argument Extraction: The proposed model achieves the state-of-the-art results in separate extraction of the arguments as well as the full relation extraction. The increase in the extraction of the first argument is of special importance because the first argument is the most challenging component to automatically predict as it can reside anywhere in the text and do not have any syntactic bounds with the connective, unlike the second argument.

Manual analysis of the predicted first argument spans reveals that 20% of all mismatches are only by one or two words and mostly occur in the beginning of the argument. Several cherry-picked examples are provided in Example 5 where the predicted spans are underlined and the gold spans are shown in bold.

(5)   a. I expect **the market to open weaker Monday**
      b. crumbled. **Arbitragers couldn't dump their UAL stock**
      c. **This has both made investors uneasy and the corporations more vulnerable**

To further investigate the performance of the argument extraction, we ran two additional evaluations. Firstly, we evaluated the performance on the relations where the second argument precedes the first one in the text (e.g. Example 2) which is quite infrequent (less than 10% the relations have this structure in the test set). However, the proposed model turned out to be quite successful in those relations and achieves 75.6% F-score in full relation extraction, suggesting that it learned the argument structure of the discourse connectives considerably well.

In the second evaluation, we focused on the relations with discontinuous spans where there are at least a five word sequence which do not belong to the any part of the relation between the first argument and the connective. There are 93 such relations in the test set and they are the most challenging ones spreading over a text span of 91 words on average. Unfortunately, the proposed model fails to extract the arguments of those relations by achieving only 14.7% F-score in the extraction of the full relation, hence extraction of the arguments which are not located in the immediate vicinity of the connective still remains a challenge. Yet, it should also be noted that some of these relations falls outside of the argument extractor's scope due to its window size (see Sect. 3.2).

6   Conclusion

We have shown that labeling explicit discourse relations is possible without any feature engineering. We achieve state-of-the-art results by finetuning a pre-trained language model on PDTB 2.0 which is the first time that a feature-independent system outperforms the existing knowledge intensive systems on this task. However, detailed evaluations reveal that there is much room for improvement, especially in identifying the discontinuous relations where the arguments are interrupted by various text spans. We see the proposed system as a first step towards a high-performance shallow discourse parser that can be extended to any language with a sufficient annotated data and a pre-trained language model.

Acknowledgments. I would like to thank Robert Östling and Ahmet Üstün for their useful comments and NVIDIA for their GPU grant.

References

1. Devlin, J., Chang, M.W., Lee, K., Toutanova, K.: Bert: pre-training of deep bidirectional transformers for language understanding. arXiv preprint arXiv:1810.04805 (2018)
2. Hooda, S., Kosseim, L.: Argument labeling of explicit discourse relations using LSTM neural networks. arXiv preprint arXiv:1708.03425 (2017)
3. Knaebel, R., Stede, M., Stober, S.: Window-based neural tagging for shallow discourse argument labeling. In: Proceedings of the 23rd Conference on Computational Natural Language Learning (CoNLL), pp. 768–777 (2019)
4. Li, Z., Zhao, H., Pang, C., Wang, L., Wang, H.: A constituent syntactic parse tree based discourse parser. In: Proceedings of the CoNLL-16 Shared Task, pp. 60–64 (2016)
5. Lin, Z., Ng, H.T., Kan, M.Y.: A PDTB-styled end-to-end discourse parser. Nat. Lang. Eng. **20**(2), 151–184 (2014)
6. Muller, P., Braud, C., Morey, M.: ToNy: contextual embeddings for accurate multilingual discourse segmentation of full documents (2019)
7. Nguyen, M.: SDP-JAIST: a shallow discourse parsing system @ CoNLL 2016 shared task. In: Proceedings of the CoNLL-16 Shared Task, pp. 143–149 (2016)
8. Prasad, R., et al.: The Penn discourse TreeBank 2.0. In: LREC. Citeseer (2008)
9. Qin, L., Zhang, Z., Zhao, H.: Shallow discourse parsing using convolutional neural network. In: Proceedings of the CoNLL-16 Shared Task, pp. 70–77 (2016)
10. Stepanov, E., Riccardi, G., Bayer, A.O.: The UniTN discourse parser in CoNLL 2015 shared task: token-level sequence labeling with argument-specific models. In: Proceedings of the Nineteenth Conference on Computational Natural Language Learning-Shared Task, pp. 25–31 (2015)
11. Wang, J., Lan, M.: A refined end-to-end discourse parser. In: Proceedings of the Nineteenth Conference on Computational Natural Language Learning-Shared Task, pp. 17–24 (2015)
12. Xue, N., Ng, H.T., Pradhan, S., Prasad, R., Bryant, C., Rutherford, A.: The CoNLL-2015 shared task on shallow discourse parsing. In: Proceedings of the Nineteenth Conference on Computational Natural Language Learning-Shared Task, pp. 1–16 (2015)
13. Xue, N., et al.: CoNLL 2016 shared task on multilingual shallow discourse parsing. In: Proceedings of the CoNLL-16 Shared Task, pp. 1–19 (2016)
14. Yoshida, Y., Hayashi, K., Hirao, T., Nagata, M.: Hybrid approach to PDTB-styled discourse parsing for CoNLL-2015. In: Proceedings of the Nineteenth Conference on Computational Natural Language Learning-Shared Task, pp. 95–99 (2015)

EPIE Dataset: A Corpus for Possible Idiomatic Expressions

Prateek Saxena[✉][iD] and Soma Paul[iD]

International Institute of Information Technology, Hyderabad, India
prateek.saxena@research.iiit.ac.in, soma@iiit.ac.in

Abstract. Idiomatic expressions have always been a bottleneck for language comprehension and natural language understanding, specifically for tasks like Machine Translation (MT). MT systems predominantly produce literal translations of idiomatic expressions as they do not exhibit generic and linguistically deterministic patterns which can be exploited for comprehension of the non-compositional meaning of the expressions. These expressions occur in parallel corpora used for training, but due to the comparatively high occurrences of the constituent words of idiomatic expressions in literal context, the idiomatic meaning gets overpowered by the compositional meaning of the expression. State of the art Metaphor Detection Systems are able to detect non-compositional usage at word level but miss out on idiosyncratic phrasal idiomatic expressions. This creates a dire need for a dataset with a wider coverage and higher occurrence of commonly occurring idiomatic expressions, the spans of which can be used for Metaphor Detection. With this in mind, we present our English Possible Idiomatic Expressions (EPIE) corpus containing 25,206 sentences labelled with lexical instances of 717 idiomatic expressions. These spans also cover literal usages for the given set of idiomatic expressions. We also present the utility of our dataset by using it to train a sequence labelling module and testing on three independent datasets with high accuracy, precision and recall scores.

Keywords: Idioms · Idiomatic expressions · Multiword expressions

1 Introduction

Natural language understanding of idiomatic expressions embedded in sentences has been a complex problem to solve for some time. Idiom handling has been a problematic area for a variety of NLP tasks. [2,11,14] have discussed the magnified complexity of this problem with respect to linguistic precision. [12] provides empirical evidence that state-of-the-art machine translation systems may achieve only half of the BLEU score on sentences that contain idiomatic expressions as compared to the ones that do not. This drop in the score occurs not only due to the comparatively low frequency of the idiomatic phrase with respect to the frequency of the constituent words, but also due to the lack of

© Springer Nature Switzerland AG 2020
P. Sojka et al. (Eds.): TSD 2020, LNAI 12284, pp. 87–94, 2020.
https://doi.org/10.1007/978-3-030-58323-1_9

automatically determinable clear patterns in the wide and varied instances of idioms in data [4]. This makes a regular monolingual training dataset sparse with respect to idiomatic expressions. The absence of a dataset rich in idiomatic expressions hampers the possibility of modelling the problem into a machine learning task.

Any attempt on handling these idiomatic expressions has to follow certain predefined steps as discussed in [9]. The first step is to detect lexical occurrences of idiomatic expressions in a given text. The subsequent steps constitute identifying the underlying semantics and learning a simpler representation for any downstream task. In this paper, we attempt the first step from the aforementioned steps i.e. detection of possible idiomatic expressions in a given text. These lexical variations can have a literal occurrence as our purpose is to capture the span of the phrase in order to identify a metaphorical usage as the next step. We present a dataset of 25,206 sentences which contain lexical occurrences of 717 idiomatic expressions from the IMIL dataset [1]. We identify the detection of idiomatic expressions as a sequence labelling task and present a two pronged approach for detection of two different kinds of idioms: Static and Formal. Static idioms do not undergo lexical changes, therefore labelling them can be as simple as a string search in the text. Formal idioms, on the other hand, undergo various lexical modifications, therefore labelling them can be modelled as a supervised task. We test a model trained on our dataset and test on three datasets, "all words" and "lex sample" training datasets of SemEval-2013 Task 5b Dataset [7], and PIE Corpus [5]. All tests give results with high accuracy, precision and recall scores.

The major contributions of this work can be summarized as follows:

- We publically release a dataset of 25,206 sentences labelled with lexical occurrences of 717 idioms. These labels are done by automatic systems with high accuracy. Of these, 21,891 sentences contain occurrences of Static idioms which are 359 in number and 3,135 sentences contain occurrences of Formal idioms which are 358 in number.[1]
- An analysis of the distribution (Mean and Standard Deviation) of idioms over the dataset.

2   Related Work

[4] created a distinction in idioms i.e. Formal and Static. Static idioms are the kind of idioms which do not exhibit internal or morphosyntactic variation. For example, *As soon as possible, no comment*, etc. Formal idioms, on the other hand, undergo inflectional changes, pronominal and determiner modifications, and internal qualitative modifiers (adjectival and adverbial). For example, *keep eye on, race against time* etc. StringNet [15] identified that mapping base forms of phrases is necessary in order to extract their surface realization. StringNet used hybrid ngrams and cross indexing to create a resource to extract idiomatic

---

[1] Dataset available at: https://github.com/prateeksaxena2809/EPIE_Corpus.

sentences from the British National Corpus [8]. We use StringNet for the first level extraction of sentences for our work. [1] has created the IMIL dataset which maps 2000 of the highly occurring English idioms to their counterparts in different Indian languages. We use their idiom list as a starting point for our sentence extraction.

There have been some attempts to extract idiomatic expressions. The VNC-Tokens Dataset [3], IDIX Corpus [13], PIE Corpus [5] and SemEval-2013 Task 5 Dataset [7] all contain around 3,000 to 4,500 potential idiomatic expressions instances of 53 to 65 candidate idioms. These datasets, though thorough for their respective candidate idioms, are small in size and limited in coverage. Our dataset attempts to provide a wider coverage over a larger dataset.

3 Data

Our aim is to create a dataset only containing sentences with lexical occurrences of idioms for the IMIL dataset. This requires multiple data filtering steps. These steps are explained in the subsequent subsections.

3.1 StringNet Extraction

Variations in Idiomatic Expressions occurs in the following forms:

- Inflectional Modifications (tense, gender, number, etc):

  Bite the dust
    - The visiting team *bit the dust* in the football game yesterday.
- Determiner/Pronominal Replacement:

  Keep up the good work
    - *Keep up your good work* and the promotion will follow.
- Named Entities and Qualitative Modifiers inclusions (Adjectival and Adverbial)

  Keep an eye on
    - *Keep a keen eye on* the child while he plays.

  Behind his back
    - People say a lot *behind James' back*.

In order to extract all instances of an idiomatic expression, it is important to account for all the variation in the expression. We use StringNet for this task. Stringnet contains two billion connected hybrid ngrams cross-indexed with lexeme information, parts of speech information and various word forms. This matches an idiomatic expression like *keep your eye on* to its inflectional modifications like *kept your eye on* and *keeps your eye on*. We also utilize StringNet's unique feature of vertical pruning and horizontal pruning. Vertical pruning refers to generalization of lexemes in a given search entry in order to search occurrence of parent ngrams and child ngrams of the entry in the corpus. For example, a parent ngram of the entry *Keep your eye on* is *keep [pron] eye on* as [pron] constitutes all pronouns. Vertical Pruning helps in extraction of pronominal and determiner variation. Horizontal pruning refers to connecting an ngram with another ngram which differs by one unit or type of ngram. For example, the entry *keep [det] eye on* can be connected to *keep eye on* and *keep [det] keen eye on* using horizontal pruning because it differs from these ngrams by a length of 1. But the entry *keep your eye on* can also be connected to *keep an eye on* using horizontal pruning because both entries differ by 1 ngram type. Horizontal pruning helps in extraction of determiner-pronoun interchangeability and internal qualitative modifiers.

We take the 2,000 idioms present in the IMIL dataset and process them automatically in order to be used as search entries into StringNet. The processing involves two features; lemmatization, and generalization of pronouns and determiners into generic entries *[pron]* and *[det]* respectively. An entry *keep an eye on* becomes *keep [det] eye on*. In addition to searching the term, we also search the idiom in both directions through one level each of vertical and horizontal pruning. This results in the extraction of 81562 sentences containing instances from 758 of the 2,000 idioms.

3.2 Candidate Idioms Selection

In this step, we filter out redundant idioms from our idioms list Redundant idioms constitute similar idiom entries in the 758 idioms list like *music to my ears* and *music to my ear* are clubbed into a single entry, removing duplicate entries of instances from the sentences. This step results in filtering 749 idioms and 77,894 sentences. The idioms that remain are unique and have idiomatic usages.

3.3 Candidate Instances Selection

Idiomatic Expressions are also idiosyncratic in the kind of lexical variations they allow. In this step, we filter out those lexical variations of idioms, which will never occur idiomatically. This requires extraction of specific patterns which are relevant exclusively to particular idioms. For example, the idiom *keep an eye on* can occur as *keep your eye on* but *give me a hand* cannot occur as *give me your hand.* In order to efficiently extract correct patterns, we manually divide the idioms list into two categories based on [4].

Static Idioms. Static idioms are idioms which do not undergo any lexical modification. We identify 388 idioms as Static in our idioms list. These idioms have 45,955 instances in the data. We filter out sentences which did not have an exact occurrence of the idiom. If no exact occurrence of an idiom is found, we reject the idiom altogether. At the end of this step, 21,891 sentences with 359 Static idioms are left.

Formal Idioms. Formal Idioms are idioms which occur in sentences with various lexical modifications. We identify 361 idioms from our idioms list as Formal idioms based on their occurrences. These idioms have 31,939 instances in the data. As this task requires more flexibility and complexity than Static idioms, an completely automatic approach is not feasible. At the same time, going through the whole dataset sentence by sentence is quite inefficient. Thus, in order to efficiently sift through the data, we extract the unique variations of each idiom and then manually remove the irrelevant occurrence patterns, thus removing all sentences with those occurrences. This reduces our load by a scale factor of 1/3 as the unique occurrences are around 10,000 in number. This process does not reduce the number of idioms to large extent (358) but we do filter out a considerable number of patterns, resulting in only 3,135 remaining sentences.

3.4   Final Result

Finally we create a dataset of 717 idioms in 25,026 sentences/instances. We separate the data into two groups; Static and Formal idioms. We create this distinction in our data because detection of both categories of idioms require separate steps. Static idioms can be detected by treating them like words-with-spaces and simply finding their exact matches in the sentence. Formal idioms detection requires a more complex approach which can identify the similarities between instances of the same idiom and their difference from other phrases. Number of sentences and idioms left after each step are given in Table 1. The first three rows show the results for the total data extraction while the subsequent rows show extraction results for Formal and Static idioms separately.

Table 1. Number of Sentences and Idioms left after each extraction step

Extraction step	Sentences	Idioms
StringNet Extraction	81,562	758
Candidate Idioms Selection (Total)	77,894	749
Candidate Instances Selection (Total)	**25,206**	**717**
Candidate Idioms Selection (Static Idioms)	45,955	388
Candidate Instances Selection (Static Idioms)	**21,891**	**359**
Candidate Idioms Selection (Formal Idioms)	31,939	361
Candidate Instances Selection (Formal Idioms)	**3,135**	**358**

We are also interested in finding the spread of each idiom in our idioms list. In this effort, we calculate the total instances of each idiom and calculate the mean

Table 2. Test Results from the model trained on Formal Idioms Training Dataset. Formal Idioms Test Dataset is 25% split from the Formal Idioms Dataset. All datasets have been tested separately for *All Usages* and *Only Idiomatic usages* of potentially idiomatic expressions in sentences

Test dataset	Accuracy	Precision	Recall
Formal Idioms Test Dataset	**0.98**	**0.95**	**0.91**
SemEval All Words Dataset (all usages)	0.84	0.90	0.85
SemEval All Words Dataset (idiomatic usages)	0.86	0.93	0.86
SemEval Lex Sample Dataset (all usages)	0.89	0.90	0.90
SemEval Lex Sample Dataset (idiomatic usages)	0.92	0.95	0.92
PIE Corpus (all usages)	0.69	0.60	0.69
PIE Corpus (idiomatic usages)	0.88	0.94	0.88

Table 3. Mean and standard deviations of final datasets

Idiom type	Sentences	Mean	Std Dev
Formal	3,135	8.75	8.61
Static	21,891	60.9	160

and standard deviation on the resultant counts respectively for Formal idioms and Static idioms. Table 3 shows the mean and standard deviation of both the Formal idioms dataset and Static idioms dataset with respect to their number of occurrences in data. The mean and standard deviation for Formal idioms are very close which suggests an exponential distribution whereas the Static idioms show a skewed distribution.

4   Experiments

We use our Formal idioms dataset containing 3,135 sentences to train on a typical sequence labelling neural network. We do a 75–25 train-eval split on our dataset for our training and evaluation. In addition to the Formal idioms test dataset, we use three independent datasets for testing mentioned as follows:

- "All words" training dataset from [7] containing 1,143 sentences. All sentences contain potentially idiomatic phrases, each usage is labelled with *idiomatic,literal* or *both* usage.
- "Lex sample" training dataset from [7] containing 1,423 sentences. All sentences contain potentially idiomatic phrases, each usage is labelled with *idiomatic,literal* or *both* usage.
- PIE corpus[5] containing 2,239 sentences. All sentences contain potentially idiomatic phrases, each usage labelled with a sense label, "y" meaning idiomatic usage and "n" meaning literal usage.

We evaluate our models on two versions of each of the three datasets: All samples and samples labelled with idiomatic usages.

We use a BiLSTM-CRF [6] module for our task. We use 300 dimensional glove embeddings [10] as our embedding input. We use LSTM hidden representation of dimension 100 and batch size of 20. We train the model for 25 epochs.

5 Results

The Results can be seen in Table 2. We see that the Formal idioms test dataset gives the best results because of similarity with the training dataset. However, the model also gives good results with other independent datasets.

6 Conclusion

In this paper, we present a semi-automatic approach to create a new dataset of labelled potentially idiomatic expressions in 25,206 English Sentences extracted from the BNC corpus [8] with high accuracy. We segregate our dataset into two categories, Formal and Static. This we do because of the difference in the potentially idiomatic span detection mechanisms of these categories.

References

1. Agrawal, R., Kumar, V.C., Muralidaran, V., Sharma, D.: No more beating about the bush: a step towards idiom handling for Indian language NLP. In: Proceedings of the Eleventh International Conference on Language Resources and Evaluation (LREC-2018) (2018)
2. Cap, F., Nirmal, M., Weller, M., Im Walde, S.S.: How to account for idiomatic German support verb constructions in statistical machine translation. In: Proceedings of the 11th Workshop on Multiword Expressions, pp. 19–28 (2015)
3. Cook, P., Fazly, A., Stevenson, S.: The VNC-tokens dataset. In: Proceedings of the LREC Workshop Towards a Shared Task for Multiword Expressions (MWE 2008), pp. 19–22 (2008)
4. Fillmore, C.J., Kay, P., O'connor, M.C.: Regularity and idiomaticity in grammatical constructions: the case of let alone. Language **64**, 501–538 (1988)
5. Haagsma, H., Nissim, M., Bos, J.: Casting a wide net: robust extraction of potentially idiomatic expressions. arXiv preprint arXiv:1911.08829 (2019)
6. Huang, Z., Xu, W., Yu, K.: Bidirectional LSTM-CRF models for sequence tagging. CoRR abs/1508.01991 (2015). http://arxiv.org/abs/1508.01991
7. Korkontzelos, I., Zesch, T., Zanzotto, F.M., Biemann, C.: SemEval-2013 task 5: evaluating phrasal semantics. In: Second Joint Conference on Lexical and Computational Semantics (* SEM), Volume 2: Proceedings of the Seventh International Workshop on Semantic Evaluation (SemEval 2013), pp. 39–47 (2013)
8. Leech, G.N.: 100 million words of English: the British national corpus (BNC) (1992)
9. Liu, C., Hwa, R.: Phrasal substitution of idiomatic expressions. In: Proceedings of the 2016 Conference of the North American Chapter of the Association for Computational Linguistics: Human Language Technologies, pp. 363–373 (2016)

10. Pennington, J., Socher, R., Manning, C.: Glove: global vectors for word representation. In: Proceedings of the 2014 Conference on Empirical Methods in Natural Language Processing (EMNLP), pp. 1532–1543 (2014)
11. Sag, I.A., Baldwin, T., Bond, F., Copestake, A., Flickinger, D.: Multiword expressions: a pain in the neck for NLP. In: Gelbukh, A. (ed.) CICLing 2002. LNCS, vol. 2276, pp. 1–15. Springer, Heidelberg (2002). https://doi.org/10.1007/3-540-45715-1_1
12. Salton, G., Ross, R., Kelleher, J.: An empirical study of the impact of idioms on phrase based statistical machine translation of English to Brazilian-Portuguese (2014)
13. Sporleder, C., Li, L., Gorinski, P., Koch, X.: Idioms in context: the IDIX corpus. In: LREC. Citeseer (2010)
14. Volk, M., Weber, N.: The automatic translation of idioms. machine translation vs. translation memory systems. Sprachwissenschaft, Computerlinguistik und neue Medien (1), 167–192 (1998)
15. Wible, D., Tsao, N.L.: Stringnet as a computational resource for discovering and investigating linguistic constructions. In: Proceedings of the NAACL HLT Workshop on Extracting and Using Constructions in Computational Linguistics, pp. 25–31. Association for Computational Linguistics (2010)

Experimenting with Different Machine Translation Models in Medium-Resource Settings

Haukur Páll Jónsson[1] , Haukur Barri Símonarson[2] ,
Vésteinn Snæbjarnarson[2] , Steinþór Steingrímsson[1] ,
and Hrafn Loftsson[1(✉)]

[1] Language and Voice Lab, Reykjavik University, Reykjavik, Iceland
{haukurpj,steinthor18,hrafn}@ru.is
[2] Mieind ehf., Reykjavik, Iceland
{haukur,vesteinn}@mideind.is

Abstract. State-of-the-art machine translation (MT) systems rely on the availability of large parallel corpora, containing millions of sentence pairs. For the Icelandic language, the parallel corpus ParIce exists, consisting of about 3.6 million English-Icelandic sentence pairs. Given that parallel corpora for low-resource languages typically contain sentence pairs in the tens or hundreds of thousands, we classify Icelandic as a medium-resource language for MT purposes. In this paper, we present on-going experiments with different MT models, both statistical and neural, for translating English to Icelandic based on ParIce. We describe the corpus and the filtering process used for removing noisy segments, the different models used for training, and the preliminary automatic and human evaluation. We find that, while using an aggressive filtering approach, the most recent neural MT system (Transformer) performs best, obtaining the highest BLEU score and the highest fluency and adequacy scores from human evaluation for in-domain translation. Our work could be beneficial to other languages for which a similar amount of parallel data is available.

Keywords: Machine translation · Parallel data · Evaluation

1 Introduction

Most work in Machine Translation (MT) through the years has mainly either focused on high-resource or low-resource language pairs. Usually, a language pair is considered high-resource if a parallel corpus exists consisting of millions of sentence pairs. In contrast, a language pair is considered low-resource if either no parallel corpus exists, or the corpus only consists of a few tens or hundreds of thousands of sentence pairs.

H. P. Jónsson, H. B. Símonarson, V. Snæbjarnarson, S. Steingrímsson—Equal contribution.

© Springer Nature Switzerland AG 2020
P. Sojka et al. (Eds.): TSD 2020, LNAI 12284, pp. 95–103, 2020.
https://doi.org/10.1007/978-3-030-58323-1_10

Neural Machine Translation (NMT), in particular sequence-to-sequence models based on attention mechanisms, e.g. the Transformer [22], has in recent years become the dominant paradigm in high-resource settings, replacing the previously long-standing dominance of Statistical Machine Translation (SMT) [10].

One parallel corpus, ParIce [2], containing about 3.6 million English-Icelandic (*en-is*) sentence pairs, currently exists for Icelandic. Given the size of ParIce, and the fact that we have only been able to use about 1.6 million of its sentence pairs for training (see Sect. 3.2), we currently categorize the *en-is* pair as a medium-resource language pair.

In this paper, we present on-going work of experimenting with different MT systems, both based on SMT and NMT, for translating in the *en → is* direction. We describe the ParIce corpus and the filtering process used for removing noisy segments, the different models used for training, and the preliminary evaluation – both with regard to BLEU scores and human evaluation. We find that, while using an aggressive filtering approach, the most recent NMT system, based on the Transformer, performs best in our setting, obtaining a BLEU score of 54.71 (6.11 points higher than the next best performing system, Moses). Furthermore, the Transformer system also obtained the highest fluency and adequacy scores from human evaluation, in the in-domain setting. Our work could be beneficial to other languages for which a similar amount of parallel data is available.

2   Related Work

In the last few years, research has shown that the NMT approach has significantly pushed ahead the state-of-the-art in MT, which before belonged to phrase-based SMT (PBSMT) systems. For example, [3] compared and analysed the output of three PBSMT systems and one NMT system for English → German and found, *inter alia*, that *i)* the overall post-edit effort needed on the output from the NMT system is considerably lower compared to the best PBSMT system; *ii)* that the NMT system outperforms the PBSMT on all sentence lengths; and *iii)* that the NMT output contains less morphological errors, less lexical errors and less word order errors.

Even though NMT has emerged as the dominant MT approach, there have also been reports of poor performance when using NMT under low-resource conditions. Compared to SMT, [11] found that NMT systems have lower quality on out-of-domain texts, sacrificing adequacy (how much of the meaning is transferred between the source and the generated target) for the sake of fluency (a rating of how fluent the generated target language is). They also found that the NMT systems performed worse in low-resource settings, but better in high-resource settings.

[5] discuss the quality of NMT vs. SMT. They argue that "so far it would appear that NMT has not fully reached the quality of SMT", based on automatic and human evaluations for three use cases, and that the results depend on the different domains and on the various language pairs.

In a study, using the medium-resource language pair English-Polish, [8] found that an SMT model achieves a slightly better BLEU score than an NMT model based on an attention mechanism. On the other hand, human evaluation carried out on a sizeable sample of translations (2,000 pairs) revealed the superiority of the NMT approach, particularly in the aspect of output fluency.

Given the mixed findings in the literature regarding comparison between NMT and PBSMT, especially in low or medium-resource settings, we decided to include SMT in our experiments.

The only previously published MT results regarding Icelandic are [4,9], although Icelandic has been included in massively multilingual settings [6]. The results rely either on rule-based systems or variants of transfer learning. In contrast, our work constitutes the first published MT and NMT results for Icelandic based on direct supervised learning.

3 Corpus and Filtering

In this section, we describe the ParIce corpus and explain which parts of it are used for training/testing as well as the filtering process for removing segments not suited for training.

3.1 ParIce

For training, we used ParIce [2], an *en-is* parallel corpus consisting of roughly 3.6 million translation segments. The corpus data is aligned with hunalign [21] and filtered using a sentence scoring algorithm based on a bilingual lexicon bag-of-words method and a comparison between an MT generated translation of a segment and the original segment.

ParIce is a collection of data from different sources, the largest being a collection of EEA regulatory texts (48%), data from OpenSubtitles (37%), published on OPUS [20] but refiltered in the ParIce corpus, and translation segments from the European Medicines Agency (EMA; 11%) published in the Tilde MODEL corpus [17] (other sources amount to 4% of the data). From each of these three corpora, we sampled roughly 2000 segments to serve as test sets.

3.2 Filtering

Starting from the 3.6 million segments compiled in ParIce, we filtered the corpus before training any models. Among the filters we used, many were adapted from the suggestions of [15]. Most of the filters are proxies for alignment errors, OCR errors, encoding errors and general text quality.

Primarily, the filters and post-editing consist of: *1)* empty sentence filter; *2)* identical or approximately identical source and target sequence, measured by absolute and relative edit distance; *3)* sentence length ratio filter, in characters and tokens; *4)* maximum and minimum sequence length filter, in characters and tokens; *5)* maximum token length; *6)* minimum average token length; *7)* character whitelist; *8)* digit mismatch: both sides should have the same set of number sequences; *9)* unique sequence pair, after removing whitespace, punctuation, capitalization and normalizing all numbers to 0 (all number sequences are equivalent); *10)* case mismatches where one side is all uppercase and the other not; *11)* corrupt symbols, e.g. weird punctuation like ? and " inside words; *12)* many other ad-hoc regular expressions for Icelandic and dataset specific OCR artifacts and encoding errors (e.g. common words where b replaces, i replaces l, missing accents); *13)* normalizing of quotes, bullets, hyphens and other punctuation; *14)* fixing line splits where a word was split due to text reflow.

When applicable, we use the numbers provided in [15]. Otherwise the filters were tuned to fit Icelandic and ParIce specifically. Roughly half of ParIce was filtered out with this approach, leaving 1.6 million translation segments for training, consisting of around 29 million Icelandic tokens and 32 million English tokens.

4 Models

In this section, we describe the key characteristics of PBSMT and NMT models and the three different systems/models we have experimented with: the SMT system Moses, and two NMT models, the first one based on BiLSTM and the second one on the Transformer. Each model attempts to estimate the probability $p(t|s)$, the probability of a sentence t in the target language given a sentence s in the source language.

4.1 PBSMT

In PBSMT, $p(t|s)$ is not modelled explicitly, rather Bayes' theorem is applied and t is reached via a translation model $p(s|t)$ and a language model $p(t)$ by estimating $\mathrm{argmax}_t\, p(s|t)p(t)$. Furthermore, s and t are segmented into smaller phrases, upon which the translation model is defined. The phrases are extracted and their probabilities estimated during training using the underlying parallel corpus. The language model ensures the fluidity of t and can be derived from the training data and/or from a separate monolingual corpus. For further details see [10].

Moses. We used the standard open source implementation of PBSMT, the Moses system[1]. We created a number of different Moses models in order to deal with the morphological richness of Icelandic. For example, we used a large out-of-domain monolingual corpus and tokenizers including subword tokenizers such as SentencePiece [13] with Byte Pair Encoding (BPE) and Unigram for both *is* and *en*, with a 30k vocabulary for each language. For all models we used the default alignment heuristic, the default distortion model, and a 5-gram KenLM [7] language model trained on additional monolingual data, i.e. 6.5 million sentences from the Icelandic Gigaword Corpus [18]. The best performing model, which uses the Moses tokenizer for both *en* and *is*, is evaluated against the NMT based systems in Sect. 5.

---

[1] http://www.statmt.org/moses/.

4.2   NMT

An NMT system attempts to model $p(t|s)$ directly using a large modular neural network that reads s and outputs t, token by token. Instead of representing the tokens symbolically, like PBSMT systems, the tokens are represented using vectors (embeddings). The typical NMT system is based on sequence-to-sequence learning, and consists of two components: an encoder and a decoder. The system is trained to maximize $p(t|s)$ by updating the parameters of the network using stochastic gradient descent to back-propagate the errors from the output layer to the previous layers. The two dominant NMT architectures over the last few years are based on 1) LSTM, and 2) self-attention networks (Transformer).

BiLSTM. The general LSTM model for NMT is described in [19]. In this model, the encoder is an LSTM that converts an input sequence s to a fixed-sized vector v from which the decoder, another LSTM, generates t. Given the embedded tokens of s, $(x_1, \ldots, x_T)$ and v, the model estimates the conditional probability $p(y_1, \ldots, y_{T'}|x_1, \ldots, x_T)$ as follows:

$$p(y_1, \ldots, y_{T'}|x_1, \ldots, x_T) = \prod_{t=1}^{T'} p(y_t|v, y_1, \ldots, y_{t-1}) \tag{1}$$

where $(y_1, \ldots, y_{T'})$ represents the target sentence t, and where T' may be different from T. In other words, the prediction of each target token depends on the encoded version of the whole input sequence, as well as on the previously predicted target words.

The model is further improved by adding an additional LSTM to the encoder which reads the input in the reverse order, i.e. the encoder is bidirectional. Additionally, during decoding, these networks can be augmented with attention [1,14] where alignments between target and source tokens can be modeled more explicitly. We used the standard BiLSTM implementation from OpenNMT[2], medium and large NMT models with Luong attention [14] (4-layer 256 hidden unit encoder, 4 layer 512 hidden unit decoder; large model has 6 layers and double the number of hidden units). We used a 16k joint BPE vocabulary.

Transformer. The Transformer, proposed by [22], builds on previous models in various ways. Its design provides for much better parallelization, and it leverages GPU architecture more so than LSTMs. In general, it achieves better machine translation performance for the same training time and data as compared to LSTMs.

The Transformer consists of stacked transformer blocks, each of which comprises 2–3 sublayers, self-attention, decoder-to-encoder attention, and a fully connected layer. The block operates independently over a sequence of hidden

---

[2] https://opennmt.net/.

vectors h_i whereby each vector in the sequence can attend to (i.e. receive information from) all other hidden vectors in the sequence before being transformed by the fully connected sublayer. The decoder block has an added attention sublayer that allows it to attend to the encoder in addition to itself. Finally, the last decoder block has a softmax output layer for token probabilties.

The implementation we use is the reference implementation from [22] of the transformer-base architecture which is part of the Tensor2Tensor package[3]. It has 6 layers each for its encoder and decoder with attention head count of 8. We used shared source and target embeddings. The included subword tokenizer provided by Tensor2Tensor was used to build a 16k joint subword vocabulary.

5 Evaluation

In this section, we present the results of automatic and human evaluation of the individual models, Moses, BiLSTM and Transformer, for translating in the $en \rightarrow is$ direction.

Neither NMT model was fine-tuned before evaluation, and the Transformer used checkpoint-averaging (a gain of about 0.5 BLEU). The batch sizes for the Transformer and the BiLSTM were 1700 (subword) tokens and 32 sequences, respectively. No other hyperparameter tuning was performed due to computational restraints.

5.1 BLEU Scores

We use BLEU for automatic evaluation. It is the most widely used MT quality metric and it has reasonably high correlation with human evaluations. Due to possible biases that may be "unfair" to some technologies [16], the BLEU scores cannot be the primary evidence of the quality of our systems. Therefore, we also rely on human evaluation.

As discussed in Sect. 3.1, the test sets consists of about 2000 segments sampled from three parts of the ParIce corpus: EEA, EMA, and OpenSubtitles. Table 1 shows the results for the three system and the different test sets, as well as the combined sets.

Table 1. BLEU scores for the three systems and the different test sets.

Model	EES	EMA	OpenSubtitles	Combined
BiLSTM	38.68	41.60	23.32	38.12
Moses	49.70	54.93	26.11	48.60
Transformer	**56.31**	**58.37**	**34.71**	**54.71**

---

[3] https://github.com/tensorflow/tensor2tensor

Table 2. Fluency and adequacy scores from human evaluation.

Test set	Model	Fluency	Adequacy
In-domain	BiLSTM	2.49	2.01
	Moses	3.64	3.84
	Transformer	**4.30**	**4.33**
	Google	3.80	4.16
Out-of-domain	BiLSTM	1.85	1.30
	Moses	2.54	2.32
	Transformer	3.20	2.86
	Google	**3.40**	**3.80**

In [22] it was shown that the Transformer is the dominant model in high-resource settings. Our results indicate that the Transformer also performs best in medium-resource settings. It is, however, noteworthy that the Moses systems performs significantly better than the BiLSTM model.

5.2 Human Evaluation

We recruited three people with translation experience for adequacy evaluation and three Icelandic linguists for fluency evaluation. We randomly chose 100 sentences from our test set for in-domain evaluation, and 100 sentences from news for out-of-domain evaluation. The sentence lengths varied substantially, averaging 18.2 words per sentence, with a standard deviation of 13.7. Each sentence was translated by our three systems as well as by Google Translate, for reference. We used Keops[4] for the evaluation.

The fluency group was given the following instructions: Is the sentence good fluent Icelandic? Rate the sentence on the following scale from 1 to 5. 1 – incomprehensible; 2 – disfluent Icelandic; 3 – non-native Icelandic; 4 – good Icelandic; 5 – flawless Icelandic. The adequacy group was given the following instructions: Does the output convey the same meaning as the input sentence? Rate the sentence on the following scale from 1 to 5. 1 – none; 2 – little meaning; 3 – much meaning; 4 – most meaning; 5 – all meaning.

We calculated the Intraclass Correlation Coefficient (ICC) for both groups. This resulted in ICC of 0.749, with 95% confidence interval (CI) in the range 0.718–0.777 for the fluency group, and ICC of 0.734 and 95% CI in the range 0.705–0.760 for the adequacy group. According to [12], this suggests that inter-rater agreement is moderate to good for both groups.

We calculated adequacy and fluency on our original scale resulting in the values shown in Table 2. The results show that the Transformer is perceived to give more adequate and more fluent translations than our other two systems, both for out-of-domain translations and in-domain, where it even outperforms Google

---

[4] https://github.com/paracrawl/keops.

Translate, although that may of course be because our in-domain translations are not in Google Translate's domain. Our SMT system performs decently, not as good as the Transformer or Google Translate, but outperforms the BiLSTM system by far.

6   Conclusion

We have described experiments in using three different architectures (Moses, BiLSTM and Transformer) for translating in the $en \rightarrow is$ direction. Automatic and human evaluation shows that the Transformer architecture performs best, followed by Moses and BiLSTM (in that order).

In future work, we intend to experiment with larger model sizes, backtranslation, and bilingual language model pre-training. Explicit handling of named entities is also a problematic issue, as the available parallel data contains very few Icelandic names.

Acknowledgments. This project was funded by the Language Technology Programme for Icelandic 2019–2023. The programme, which is managed and coordinated by Almannarómur, is funded by the Icelandic Ministry of Education, Science and Culture.

References

1. Bahdanau, D., Cho, K., Bengio, Y.: Neural machine translation by jointly learning to align and translate. In: Bengio, Y., LeCun, Y. (eds.) Proceedings of the 3rd International Conference on Learning Representations, ICLR, San Diego (2015)
2. Barkarson, S., Steingrímsson, S.: Compiling and filtering ParIce: an English-icelandic parallel corpus. In: Proceedings of the 22nd Nordic Conference on Computational Linguistics, NODALIDA, Turku, Finland (2019)
3. Bentivogli, L., Bisazza, A., Cettolo, M., Federico, M.: Neural versus phrase-based machine translation quality: a case study. In: Proceedings of the Conference on Empirical Methods in Natural Language Processing, EMNLP, Austin, TX, USA (2016)
4. Brandt, M.D., Loftsson, H., Sigurþórsson, H., Tyers, F.M.: Apertium-IceNLP: a rule-based Icelandic to English machine translation system. In: Proceedings of the 15th Annual Conference of the European Association for Machine Translation, EAMT, Leuven, Belgium (2011)
5. Castilho, S., Moorkens, J., Gaspari, F., Calixto, I., Tinsley, J., Way, A.: Is neural machine translation the new state of the art? Prague Bull. Math. Linguist. **108**(1), 109–120 (2017)
6. Defauw, A., Vanallemeersch, T., Van Winckel, K., Szoc, S., Van den Bogaert, J.: Being generous with sub-words towards small NMT children. In: Proceedings of the 12th Language Resources and Evaluation Conference, LREC, Marseille, France (2020)
7. Heafield, K., Pouzyrevsky, I., Clark, J.H., Koehn, P.: Scalable modified Kneser-Ney language model estimation. In: Proceedings of 51st Annual Meeting of the Association for Computational Linguistics, ACL, Sofia, Bulgaria (2013)

8. Jassem, K., Dwojak, T.: Statistical versus neural machine translation - a case study for a medium size domain-specific bilingual corpus. Poznan Stud. Contemp. Linguist. **55**(2), 491–515 (2019)
9. Johnson, M., Firat, O., Aharoni, R.: Massively multilingual neural machine translation. In: Proceedings of the Conference of the North American Chapter of the Association for Computational Linguistics: Human Language Technologies, Volume 1 (Long and Short Papers), NAACL, Minneapolis, MN, USA (2019)
10. Koehn, P.: Statistical Machine Translation. Cambridge University Press, Cambridge (2009)
11. Koehn, P., Knowles, R.: Six challenges for neural machine translation. In: Proceedings of the First Workshop on Neural Machine Translation, Vancouver, Canada (2017)
12. Koo, T., Li, M.: A guideline of selecting and reporting intraclass correlation coefficients for reliability research. J. Chiropractic Med. **15**, 155–163 (2016)
13. Kudo, T., Richardson, J.: SentencePiece: a simple and language independent subword tokenizer and detokenizer for Neural Text Processing. In: Proceedings of the Conference on Empirical Methods in Natural Language Processing: System Demonstrations, EMNLP, Brussels, Belgium (2018)
14. Luong, T., Pham, H., Manning, C.D.: Effective approaches to attention-based neural machine translation. In: Proceedings of the Conference on Empirical Methods in Natural Language Processing, EMNLP, Lisbon, Portugal (2015)
15. Pinnis, M.: Tilde's parallel corpus filtering methods for WMT 2018. In: Proceedings of the Third Conference on Machine Translation: Shared Task Papers, Brussels, Belgium (2018)
16. Reiter, E.: A structured review of the validity of BLEU. Comput. Linguist. **44**(3), 393–401 (2018)
17. Rozis, R., Skadiņš, R.: Tilde MODEL - multilingual open data for EU languages. In: Proceedings of the 21st Nordic Conference on Computational Linguistics, NODAL-IDA, Gothenburg, Sweden (2017)
18. Steingrímsson, S., Helgadóttir, S., Rögnvaldsson, E., Barkarson, S., Gunason, J.: Risamálheild: a very large icelandic text corpus. In: Proceedings of the 11th International Conference on Language Resources and Evaluation, LREC, Miyazaki, Japan, May 2018
19. Sutskever, I., Vinyals, O., Le, Q.V.: Sequence to sequence learning with neural networks. In: Proceedings of the 27th International Conference on Neural Information Processing Systems - Volume 2, NIPS, Montreal, Canada (2014)
20. Tiedemann, J.: Parallel data, tools and interfaces in OPUS. In: Proceedings of the 8th International Conference on Language Resources and Evaluation, LREC 2012, Istanbul, Turkey (2012)
21. Varga, D., Németh, L., Halácsy, P., Kornai, A., Viktor Trón, V.N.: Parallel corpora for medium density languages. In: Proceedings of Recent Advances in Natural Language Processing, RANLP, Borovets, Bulgaria (2005)
22. Vaswani, A., et al.: Attention is all you need. In: Guyon, I., et al. (eds.) Advances in Neural Information Processing Systems, vol. 30, pp. 5998–6008. Curran Associates, Inc. (2017)

FinEst BERT and CroSloEngual BERT
Less Is More in Multilingual Models

Matej Ulčar[✉] and Marko Robnik-Šikonja

Faculty of Computer and Information Science, University of Ljubljana,
Večna pot 113, Ljubljana, Slovenia
{matej.ulcar,marko.robnik}@fri.uni-lj.si

Abstract. Large pretrained masked language models have become
state-of-the-art solutions for many NLP problems. The research has been
mostly focused on English language, though. While massively multilingual models exist, studies have shown that monolingual models produce much better results. We train two trilingual BERT-like models,
one for Finnish, Estonian, and English, the other for Croatian, Slovenian, and English. We evaluate their performance on several downstream
tasks, NER, POS-tagging, and dependency parsing, using the multilingual BERT and XLM-R as baselines. The newly created FinEst BERT
and CroSloEngual BERT improve the results on all tasks in most monolingual and cross-lingual situations.

Keywords: Contextual embeddings · BERT model · Less-resourced
languages · NLP

1 Introduction

In natural language processing (NLP), a lot of research focuses on numeric
word representations. Static pretrained word embeddings like word2vec [12] are
recently replaced by dynamic, contextual embeddings, such as ELMo [14] and
BERT [4]. These generate a word vector based on the context the word appears
in, mostly using the sentence as the context.

Large pretrained masked language models like BERT [4] and its derivatives
achieve state-of-the-art performance when fine-tuned for specific NLP tasks. The
research into these models has been mostly limited to English and a few other
well-resourced languages, such as Chinese Mandarin, French, German, and Spanish. However, two massively multilingual masked language models have been
released: a multilingual BERT (mBERT) [4], trained on 104 languages, and
newer even larger XLM-RoBERTa (XLM-R) [3], trained on 100 languages. While
both, mBERT and XLM-R, achieve good results, it has been shown that monolingual models significantly outperform multilingual models [11,20]. Arkhipov et
al. (2019) [2] trained a four language (Russian, Bulgarian, Polish, Czech) BERT
model by bootstrapping mBERT. They reported improvements over mBERT on
named entity recognition task.

© Springer Nature Switzerland AG 2020
P. Sojka et al. (Eds.): TSD 2020, LNAI 12284, pp. 104–111, 2020.
https://doi.org/10.1007/978-3-030-58323-1_11

In our work, we reduced the number of languages in multilingual models to three, two similar less-resourced languages from the same language family, and English. The main reasons for this choice are to better represent each language, and keep sensible sub-word vocabulary, as shown by Virtanen et al. (2019) [20]. We decided against production of monolingual models, because we are interested in using the models in multilingual sense and for cross-lingual knowledge transfer. By including English in each of the two models, we expect to better transfer existing prediction models from English to involved less-resourced languages. Additional reason against purely monolingual models for less-resourced languages is the size of training corpora, i.e. BERT-like models use transformer architecture which is known to be data hungry.

We thus trained two multilingual BERT models: FinEst BERT was trained on Finnish, Estonian, and English, while CroSloEngual BERT was trained on Croatian, Slovenian, and English. In the paper, we present the creation and evaluation of these models, which required considerable computational resources, unavailable to most NLP researchers. We make the models which are valuable resources for the involved less-resourced languages publicly available[1].

2   Training Data and Preprocessing

BERT models require large quantities of monolingual data. In Sect. 2.1 we first describe the corpora used, followed by a short description of their preprocessing in Sect. 2.2.

2.1   Datasets

To obtain high-quality models, we used large monolingual corpora for each language, some of them unavailable to the general public. High-quality English language models already exist and English is not the main focus of this research, we therefore did not use all available English corpora in order to prevent English from overwhelming the other languages in our models. Some corpora are available online under permissive licences, others are available only for research purposes or have limited availability. The corpora used in training are a mix of news articles and general web crawl, which we preprocessed and deduplicated. Details about the training set sizes are presented in Table 1, while their description can be found in works on the involved less-resourced languages, e,g., [18].

2.2   Preprocessing

Before using the corpora, we deduplicated them for each language separately, using the Onion (ONe Instance ONly) tool[2]. We applied the tool on sentence

---

[1] CroSloEngual BERT: http://hdl.handle.net/11356/1317

   FinEst BERT: http://urn.fi/urn:nbn:fi:lb-2020061201.

[2] http://corpus.tools/wiki/Onion.

Table 1. The training corpora sizes in number of tokens and the ratios for each language.

Model	CroSloEngual	FinEst
Croatian	31%	0%
Slovenian	23%	0%
English	47%	63%
Estonian	0%	13%
Finnish	0%	25%
Tokens	$5.9 \cdot 10^9$	$3.7 \cdot 10^9$

Table 2. The sizes of corpora subsets in millions of tokens used to create wordpiece vocabularies.

Language	FinEst	CroSloEngual
Croatian	/	27
Slovenian	/	28
English	157	23
Estonian	75	/
Finnish	97	/

level for those corpora that did have sentences shuffled, and on paragraph level for the rest. As parameters, we used 9-grams with duplicate content threshold of 0.9.

BERT models are trained on subword (wordpiece) tokens. We created a wordpiece vocabulary using bert-vocab-builder tool[3], which is built upon tensor2tensor library [19]. We did not process the whole corpora in creating the wordpiece vocabulary, but only a smaller subset. To balance the language representation in vocabulary, we used samples from each language. The sizes of corpora subsets are shown in Table 2. The created wordpiece vocabularies contain 74,986 tokens for FinEst and 49,601 tokens for CroSloEngual model.

3   Architecture and Training

We trained two BERT multilingual models. FinEst BERT was trained on Finnish, Estonian, and English corpora, with altogether 3.7 billion tokens. CroSloEngual BERT was trained on Croatian, Slovenian, and English corpora with together 5.9 billion tokens.

Both models use bert-base architecture [4], which is a 12-layer bidirectional transformer encoder with the hidden layer size of 768 and altogether 110 million parameters. We used the whole word masking for the masked language model training task. Both models are cased, i.e. the case information was preserved. We followed the hyper-parameters settings of Devlin et al. (2018) [4], except for the batch size and total number of steps. We trained the models for approximately 40 epochs with maximum sequence length of 128 tokens, followed by approximately 4 epochs with maximum sequence length of 512 tokens. The exact number of steps was calculated using the expression $s = \frac{N_{tok} \cdot E}{b \cdot \lambda}$, where s is the number of steps the models were trained for, N_{tok} is the number of tokens in the train corpora, E is the desired number of epochs (in our case 40 and 4), b is the batch size, and λ is the maximum sequence length.

We trained FinEst BERT on a single Google Cloud TPU v3 for a total of 1.24 million steps where the first 1.13 million steps used the batch size of 1024

---

[3] https://github.com/kwonmha/bert-vocab-builder.

and sequence length 128, and the last 113 thousand steps used the batch size 256 and sequence length 512. Similarly, CroSloEngual BERT was trained on a single Google Cloud TPU v2 for a total of 3.96 million steps, where the first 3.6 million steps used the batch size of 512 and sequence length 128, and the last 360 thousand steps were trained with the batch size 128 and sequence length 512. Training took approximately 2 weeks for FinEst BERT and approximately 3 weeks for CroSloEngual BERT.

4   Evaluation

We evaluated the two new BERT models on sensible languages and three down-stream evaluation tasks available for the four involved less-resourced languages: named entity recognition (NER), part-of-speech tagging (POS), and dependency parsing (DP). We compared both models with BERT-base-multilingual-cased model (mBERT). On the NER task we compared also XLM-RoBERTa (XLM-R) and Finnish BERT (FinBERT).

4.1   Named Entity Recognition

NER is a sequence labeling task, which tries to correctly identify and classify each token from an unstructured text into one of the predefined named entity (NE) classes, or as not NE. The publicly available NER datasets for the involved languages that we used have only three NE classes in common. To allow a more direct comparison between languages, we reduced them to the four labels in common: *person*, *location*, *organization*, and *other*. All tokens, which are not NE or belong to any other NE class were labeled as *other*.

For Croatian and Slovenian, we used NER data from hr500k [10] and ssj500k [8], respectively. Not all sentences in Slovenian ssj500k are annotated, so we excluded those that are not annotated. The English dataset comes from the CoNLL 2013 shared task [17]. For Finnish we used the Finnish News Corpus for NER [15], and as the Estonian dataset we used the Nimeüksuste korpus [9].

The implementation uses the Huggingface's Transformer library v2.8, and our code is based on its NER example[4]. We fine-tuned each of our BERT models with an added token classification head for 3 epochs on the NER data. We compared the results with mBERT, XLM-R and FinBERT models, which we fine-tuned with exactly the same parameters on the same data. We used maximum sequence length of 512 and batch size of 6 for all models and languages.

We evaluated the models in a monolingual setting (training and testing on the same language), and cross-lingual setting (training on one language, testing on another). We present the results as macro average F_1 scores of the three NE classes, excluding *other* label. Results are shown in Table 3.

In monolingual setting, the differences in performance of tested models on English data is negligible. In other languages, our models outperform both the

---

[4] https://github.com/huggingface/transformers/tree/v2.8.0/examples/ner.

Table 3. The results of NER evaluation task. The scores are macro average F_1 scores of the three NE classes. NER models were fine-tuned from mBERT(mB), CroSloEngual BERT (CSE), FinEst BERT (FE), XLM-RoBERTa (XR), and FinBERT (FB).

Train	Test	mB	CSE	XR		Train	Test	mB	FE	XR	FB
Croatian	Croatian	0.790	0.884	0.817		Finnish	Finnish	0.933	0.957	0.930	0.954
Slovenian	Slovenian	0.897	0.920	0.914		Estonian	Estonian	0.898	0.927	0.908	0.876
English	English	0.939	0.944	0.937		English	English	0.939	0.945	0.937	0.922
Croatian	English	0.807	0.868	0.773		Finnish	English	0.688	0.812	0.722	0.573
English	Croatian	0.602	0.799	0.641		English	Finnish	0.764	0.900	0.823	0.817
Slovenian	English	0.745	0.845	0.747		Estonian	English	0.774	0.816	0.755	0.641
English	Slovenian	0.708	0.833	0.739		English	Estonian	0.783	0.832	0.794	0.523
Croatian	Slovenian	0.810	0.891	0.855		Finnish	Estonian	0.798	0.880	0.825	0.529
Slovenian	Croatian	0.765	0.849	0.786		Estonian	Finnish	0.819	0.914	0.869	0.823

mBERT and XLM-R, the difference is especially large in Croatian. FinEst BERT performs on par with FinBERT on Finnish. In cross-lingual setting, both FinEst and CroSloEngual BERT show a significant improvement over both mBERT and XLM-R. This leads us to believe that multilingual BERT models with fewer languages are more suitable for cross-lingual knowledge transfer.

4.2   Part-of-Speech Tagging and Dependency Parsing

Next, we evaluated the created BERT models on two more syntactic classification tasks: POS-tagging and DP. In the POS-tagging task, we predict the grammatical category of each token (verb, adjective, punctuation, adverb, noun, etc). DP models predict the tree structure, representing the syntactic relations between words in a given sentence.

We trained classifiers on universal dependencies (UD) treebank datasets, using universal part-of-speech (UPOS) tag set. For Croatian, we used the dataset of Agic and Ljubesic (2015) [1]; for English, we used A Gold Standard Dependency Corpus [16], and for Estonian we used Estonian Dependency Treebank [13], converted to UD. The Finnish treebank used is based on the Turku Dependency Treebank [6]. Slovenian treebank [5] is based on the ssj500k corpus [8].

We used Udify tool [7] to train both POS tagger and DP classifiers at the same time. We fine-tuned each BERT model for 80 epochs on the treebank data, keeping the tool parameters at default values, except for "warmup_steps" and "start_step" values, which we changed to the number of training batches in one epoch.

We present the results of POS tagging as UPOS accuracy in Table 4. In the monolingual setting, the differences in performance between different BERT models are small for this task. FinEst and CroSloEngual BERTs perform slightly better than mBERT on all languages, except Croatian, where mBERT and CroSloEngual BERT are equal. On Finnish, FinBERT (acc = 0.984) slightly outperforms FinEst BERT (acc = 0.981). The differences are more pronounced in cross-lingual setting. When training on Slovenian, Finnish, or Estonian and

Table 4. The performance on the UD POS-tagging task, using UPOS accuracy for CroSloEngual BERT (CSE), FinEst BERT, and mBERT.

Train	Test	mBERT	CSE		Train	Test	mBERT	FinEst
Croatian	Croatian	0.983	0.983		English	English	0.969	0.970
English	English	0.969	0.972		Estonian	Estonian	0.972	0.978
Slovenian	Slovenian	0.987	0.991		Finnish	Finnish	0.970	0.981
English	Croatian	0.876	0.869		English	Estonian	0.852	0.878
English	Slovenian	0.857	0.859		English	Finnish	0.847	0.872
Croatian	English	0.750	0.756		Estonian	English	0.688	0.808
Croatian	Slovenian	0.917	0.934		Estonian	Finnish	0.872	0.913
Slovenian	English	0.686	0.723		Finnish	English	0.535	0.701
Slovenian	Croatian	0.920	0.935		Finnish	Estonian	0.888	0.919

testing on English, CroSloEngual and FinEst BERT significantly outperform mBERT. The exception is training on English and testing on Croatian, where mBERT outperforms CroSloEngual BERT.

We present the results of DP task with two metrics, the unlabeled attachement score (UAS) and labeled attachment score (LAS). In the monolingual setting, CroSloEngual BERT shows improvement over mBERT on all three languages (Table 5) with the highest improvement on Slovenian and only a marginal improvement on English. FinEst BERT outperforms mBERT on Estonian and Finnish, with the biggest margin being on the Finnish data, while the two models perform equally on English data. FinBERT again outperforms FinEst on Finnish, scoring UAS = 0.946 and LAS = 0.930.

In the cross-lingual setting, the results are similar to those seen on the POS tagging task. Major improvements of FinEst and CroSloEngual BERT over mBERT are observed in English-Estonian, English-Finnish and English-Slovenian pairs, minor improvements in Estonian-Finnish and Croatian-Slovenian pairs, while on English-Croatian pair mBERT outperformed CroSloEngual BERT.

Table 5. The results on the DP task presented with UAS and LAS scores for CroSloEngual BERT, FinEst BERT, and mBERT.

Train	Test	mBERT		CroSloEngual		Train	Test	mBERT		FinEst	
		UAS	LAS	UAS	LAS			UAS	LAS	UAS	LAS
Croatian	Croatian	0.930	0.891	0.940	0.903	English	English	0.917	0.894	0.918	0.895
English	English	0.917	0.894	0.922	0.899	Estonian	Estonian	0.880	0.848	0.909	0.882
Slovenian	Slovenian	0.938	0.922	0.957	0.947	Finnish	Finnish	0.898	0.867	0.933	0.915
English	Croatian	0.824	0.724	0.822	0.725	English	Estonian	0.697	0.531	0.768	0.591
English	Slovenian	0.830	0.719	0.848	0.736	English	Finnish	0.706	0.561	0.781	0.624
Croatian	English	0.759	0.627	0.782	0.657	Estonian	English	0.633	0.492	0.726	0.567
Croatian	Slovenian	0.880	0.802	0.912	0.840	Estonian	Finnish	0.784	0.695	0.864	0.801
Slovenian	English	0.741	0.578	0.794	0.648	Finnish	English	0.543	0.433	0.684	0.558
Slovenian	Croatian	0.861	0.773	0.891	0.810	Finnish	Estonian	0.782	0.691	0.852	0.778

5   Conclusion

We built two large pretrained trilingual BERT-based masked language models, Croatian-Slovenian-English and Finnish-Estonian-English. We showed that the new CroSloEngual and FinEst BERTs perform substantially better than massively multilingual mBERT on the NER task in both monolingual and cross-lingual setting. The results on POS tagging and DP tasks show considerable improvement of the proposed models for several monolingual and cross-lingual pairs, while they are never worse than mBERT.

In future, we plan to investigate different combinations and proportions of less-resourced languages in creation of pretrained BERT-like models, and use the newly trained BERT models on the problems of news media industry.

Acknowledgments. The work was partially supported by the Slovenian Research Agency (ARRS) core research programme P6-0411. This paper is supported by European Union's Horizon 2020 research and innovation programme under grant agreement No 825153, project EMBEDDIA (Cross-Lingual Embeddings for Less-Represented Languages in European News Media). Research was supported with Cloud TPUs from Google's TensorFlow Research Cloud (TFRC).

References

1. Agić, Ž., Ljubešić, N.: Universal dependencies for Croatian (that work for Serbian, too). In: The 5th Workshop on Balto-Slavic Natural Language Processing, pp. 1–8 (2015)
2. Arkhipov, M., Trofimova, M., Kuratov, Y., Sorokin, A.: Tuning multilingual transformers for language-specific named entity recognition. In: Proceedings of the 7th Workshop on Balto-Slavic Natural Language Processing, pp. 89–93. Association for Computational Linguistics, Florence, August 2019. https://doi.org/10.18653/v1/W19-3712
3. Conneau, A., et al.: Unsupervised cross-lingual representation learning at scale. arXiv preprint arXiv:1911.02116 (2019)
4. Devlin, J., Chang, M.W., Lee, K., Toutanova, K.: BERT: pre-training of deep bidirectional transformers for language understanding. arXiv preprint arXiv:1810.04805 (2018)
5. Dobrovoljc, K., Erjavec, T., Krek, S.: The universal dependencies treebank for Slovenian. In: Proceeding of the 6th Workshop on Balto-Slavic Natural Language Processing (BSNLP 2017) (2017)
6. Haverinen, K., et al.: Building the essential resources for Finnish: the Turku dependency treebank. LREC **48**, 493–531 (2013)
7. Kondratyuk, D., Straka, M.: 75 languages, 1 model: parsing universal dependencies universally. In: Proceedings of the 2019 EMNLP-IJCNLP, pp. 2779–2795 (2019)
8. Krek, S., et al.: Training corpus ssj500k 2.2 (2019). Slovenian language resource repository CLARIN.SI
9. Laur, S.: Nimeüksuste korpus. Center of Estonian Language Resources (2013)
10. Ljubešić, N., Klubička, F., Agić, Ž., Jazbec, I.P.: New inflectional lexicons and training corpora for improved morphosyntactic annotation of Croatian and Serbian. In: Proceedings of the LREC 2016 (2016)

11. Martin, L., et al.: CamemBERT: a tasty French language model. arXiv preprint arXiv:1911.03894 (2019)
12. Mikolov, T., Le, Q.V., Sutskever, I.: Exploiting similarities among languages for machine translation. arXiv preprint 1309.4168 (2013)
13. Muischnek, K., Müürisep, K., Puolakainen, T.: Estonian dependency treebank: from constraint grammar tagset to universal dependencies. In: Proceedings of LREC 2016 (2016)
14. Peters, M.E., et al.: Deep contextualized word representations. arXiv preprint arXiv:1802.05365 (2018)
15. Ruokolainen, T., Kauppinen, P., Silfverberg, M., Lindén, K.: A Finnish news corpus for named entity recognition. Lang. Res. Eval. **54**(1), 247–272 (2020)
16. Silveira, N., et al.: A gold standard dependency corpus for English. In: Proceedings of LREC-2014 (2014)
17. Tjong Kim Sang, E.F., De Meulder, F.: Introduction to the CoNLL-2003 shared task: language-independent named entity recognition. In: Daelemans, W., Osborne, M. (eds.) Proceedings of CoNLL-2003, Edmonton, Canada, pp. 142–147 (2003)
18. Ulčar, M., Robnik-Šikonja, M.: High quality ELMo embeddings for seven less-resourced languages. In: Proceedings of the 12th Language Resources and Evaluation Conference, pp. 4731–4738. European Language Resources Association, Marseille, May 2020
19. Vaswani, A., et al.: Tensor2tensor for neural machine translation. In: Proceedings of the AMT, pp. 193–199 (2018)
20. Virtanen, A., et al.: Multilingual is not enough: BERT for Finnish. arXiv preprint arXiv:1912.07076 (2019)

Employing Sentence Context in Czech Answer Selection

Marek Medveď[(✉)], Radoslav Sabol, and Aleš Horák[iD]

Natural Language Processing Centre, Faculty of Informatics, Masaryk University,
Botanická 68a, 602 00 Brno, Czech Republic
{xmedved1,xsabol,hales}@fi.muni.cz

Abstract. Question answering (QA) of non-mainstream languages requires specific adaptations of the current methods tested primarily with very large English resources. In this paper, we present the results of improving the QA answer selection task by extending the input candidate sentence with selected information from preceding sentence context. The described model represents the best published answer selection model for the Czech language as an example of a morphologically rich language. The text contains thorough evaluation of the new method including model hyperparameter combinations and detailed error discussion. The winning models have improved the previous best results by 4% reaching the mean average precision of 82.91%.

Keywords: Question answering · Answer selection · Czech · Answer context · Morphologically rich languages

1 Introduction

The state-of-the-art results in question answering (QA) methods have already surpassed the estimated human performance[1] when trained on very large word-based datasets of more than 100,000 questions such as SQuAD [12], RACE [4] or GLUE [18]. This allows for very wide benchmarking and comparison of new deep learning techniques but straightforward application in non-mainstream languages is difficult.

Nowadays, the answer selection subtask, i.e. identification of the one sentence containing the exact answer to a given question, has advanced from the early works based on measuring sentence similarity according to string overlapping [17] to complex deep neural network architectures first introduced in [19] and later improved and refined [13,16,20]. The latest approaches prevalently lean on employing advanced language models such as BERT/ALBERT [3,5] or GPT-2 [10].

In this paper, we show the details of a method adaptation and a new technique evaluated with Czech as a representative of a small but lexically and

---

[1] The human performance with the SQuAD database is 86.8% exact match [11] while the current best results reach more than 90.7% [20].

© Springer Nature Switzerland AG 2020
P. Sojka et al. (Eds.): TSD 2020, LNAI 12284, pp. 112–121, 2020.
https://doi.org/10.1007/978-3-030-58323-1_12

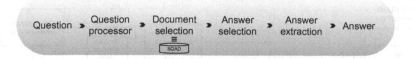

Fig. 1. AQA pipeline schema

morphologically rich language. All methods are evaluated with a published QA benchmark dataset SQAD 3.0 [9] which contains more than 13,000 question-answer pairs with detailed metadata related to the morphology and question answer typology. The current improvements of the QA answer selection task lie in extending the input candidate sentence with selected information from preceding sentence context. The following text contains thorough evaluation of all model hyperparameter combinations and detailed error discussion. The winning models have improved the previous best results by 4% reaching mean average precision of 82.91%.

2 AQA Modules for the Czech Language

The Automatic Question Answering system (AQA) is designed to answer questions in Slavonic languages with the Czech language selected as their representative for testing and developing purposes. The whole AQA system consists of multiple modules organised in one pipeline. The pipeline structure is as follows (see Fig. 1):

1. The first module, triggered after the question input, is the *question type analysis* module. This part of the system provides information about what type of question the system receives and what type of answer it should look for. This information is exploited later in the pipeline where the system searches for the final answer. The core of this module uses pre-trained bi-LSTM network that was trained with the training subset of the SQAD database of manually annotated question and answer types. For in-depth information see [8].
2. The second module in the pipeline is the *document selection* module. Its main purpose it to pick up a document (or top k documents) from the underlying document collection to be searched for sentences with expected answers. This module is based on weighted TF-IDF scoring with syntax-based similarity measures between the question and the document content. The result is a list of documents ranked according to document relevance to the given question. For detailed design and evaluation see [9].
3. After a part of the document collection is selected for further analysis, the *answer selection* module is employed to select a candidate answer sentence. The answer selection module is based on attentive bi-directional gated recurrent unit architecture that is trained on question-answer pairs and yields a list of candidate sentences ranked by their relevance to the input question.

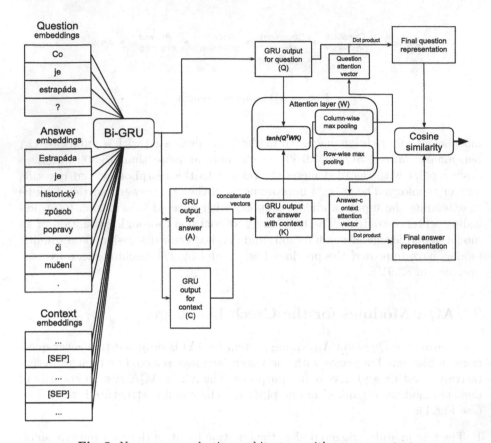

Fig. 2. New answer selection architecture with answer context.

For detailed description see [9]. In the following section, we present new developments of this module with concentration on adding the answer context to the network input.

4. From the best scored sentence of the answer selection module, the last *answer extraction* module selects the smallest part containing enough information to answer the input question. The extraction is based on rules based on the question-answer type information for identifying the boundaries of the exact answer. Detailed description of this module can be found in [6].

3 Neural Answer Selection Architecture with Context

The AQA answer selection module is based on a specific Siamese neural network [2,15] which exploits a bi-GRU attentive recurrent network to learn the question-answer similarities of correct answers and dissimilarities of related incorrect answers [9]. In this paper, we present the latest results of both new network hyperparameter setup with improved answer selection and an extension of the technique with answer contexts as another network input.

The extended network architecture requires three sequences as an input. Besides the question and a candidate answer, the network takes the answer context as its third input sequence. Currently, the context is presented in the form of selected noun phrases from the preceding two sentences in the input document separated by a new "[SEP]" token.[2]

The new architecture is presented in Fig. 2. A shared Bidirectional Gated Recurrent Unit (bi-GRU) layer is applied to all three input sequences, each sequence using its individual hidden state. Subsequently, the bi-GRU representation of context is concatenated with the candidate answer representation forming a single sequence for the question-answer attention matrix.

In the following step, a two-way attention mechanism is applied to the question (Q) and answer-context (K) representations, producing their respective attention vectors. The question vector contains importance scores of each word with regard to the answer, while the answer attention vector consists of importance scores for all words of the answer and the context, potentially improving the final ranking in case the target entity was mentioned in the previous sentence(s). Using the dot product with the corresponding bi-GRU output makes the final representations to be compared using the vector cosine similarity measure.

4 Experiments and Results

The SQADv3 [14] dataset consists of almost 13,500 richly annotated question-answer pairs with full texts of 6,500 Wikipedia articles used as the underlying

Table 1. The answer selection results for various hyperparameter settings with a comparison of context and non-context model.

Embedding size	Hidden size	Optimizer	Learning rate	Non-context		Context	
				MAP	MRR	MAP	MRR
500	400	Adagrad	0.005	**81.78**	**88.07**	**82.91**	88.75
500	300	Adagrad	0.005	81.65	87.98	82.81	**88.86**
500	200	Adagrad	0.005	81.33	87.66	82.38	88.51
300	300	Adagrad	0.005	80.99	87.55	82.33	88.53
300	200	Adagrad	0.005	80.8	87.37	82.26	88.38
100	300	Adagrad	0.005	78.97	86.02	80.42	87.21
100	200	Adagrad	0.005	78.54	85.67	80.24	87.04
100	300	SGD	0.6	78.87	85.94	79.39	86.35
100	200	SGD	0.9	79.13	86.13	79.35	86.23

---

[2] Similar approach is frequently used in sequence to sequence machine translation neural architectures.

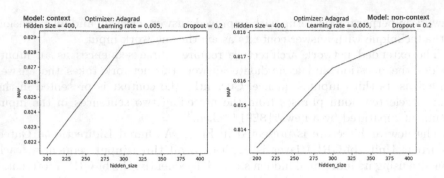

Fig. 3. Hyperparameter sensitivity comparison for both architectures via the hidden layer size.

document collection. The dataset is partitioned into training, validation and test set in the ratio of 60:10:30. The validation set is used as an evaluation of the current model state after each training epoch. The best validated epoch is then chosen for the final evaluation using the test set. The content of the partitions is the same as in previous experiments with answer contexts added. Current experiments were run for both the models with and without context to produce comparable results.

For each question, the training algorithm randomly samples 20 negative candidate answers along with the positive run. The input vectors use pre-trained FastText [1] word embeddings which are prepared in 100- and 300-dimensional vectors. A dropout layer is applied to the input data to support generalization. In previous experiments, the dropout probability of 0.2 was the most prominent while other values were degrading the precision with every single setup [7]. Therefore, the dropout probability was kept at this value for all the following runs.

Table 2. The answer selection accuracy per question and answer types

Question Type	Count	Context MAP (%)	Non-ctx MAP (%)	Diff. (%)	Answer Type	Count	Context MAP (%)	Non-ctx MAP (%)	Diff. (%)
ABBR.	97	88.66	91.75	−3.09	ABBR.	95	88.42	91.58	**−2.16**
LOC.	498	84.94	83.13	1.81	DENOT.	53	88.68	86.79	1.89
DTTIME	592	84.63	83.95	0.68	LOC.	494	88.68	83.20	**5.48**
ADJ_P.	449	83.07	82.63	0.44	DTTIME	589	84.55	83.87	0.67
VERB_P.	678	83.63	82.74	0.89	YES_NO	675	83.56	82.81	0.75
PERSON	526	83.65	83.84	−0.19	ENTITY	527	82.35	79.70	**2.65**
ENTITY	738	81.71	79.54	**2.17**	OTHER	668	80.39	78.44	1.95
NUM.	293	79.52	78.84	0.68	NUM.	298	79.53	79.19	0.34
CLAUSE	139	71.94	68.35	**3.59**	ORG.	83	74.70	78.31	**−3.61**

The size of the bi-GRU layer (*hidden size*) also corresponds to the dimensionality of the attention layer weights thus affecting multiple internal layers of the network. The following experiments primarily focus on hidden size values from 100 to 500. Models were trained using multiple optimizers, ranging from the Stochastic Gradient Descent (SGD) with a learning rate scheduler[3] to Adagrad, Adadelta and Adam.

Overall 423 new models were produced while optimizing the parameters for the non-context model. The best performing models have achieved a Mean Average Precision (MAP) of *81.78%* using the 300-dimensional embeddings which is a *2.91% increase* when compared to the older result [9] with the MAP of 78.87%. The reason behind this increase is a fine-grained optimization of model parameters along with larger embedding size. The best model setups are summarized in Table 1.

In experiments optimizing the new context architecture, 125 models were produced. The number of parameter combinations was reduced to the ones which had achieved reasonable accuracy with the non-context architecture. The best setup has reached the MAP of **82.91%**, outperforming the best configuration of the non-context architecture by **1.13%** (and the previous best result by **4.04%**) using the same parameters. As can be seen in Fig. 3, the hyperparameter sensitivity remains more or less the same but with an increase in the overall precision.

The parameter combinations affect also the running times of the training and testing process. The non-context model used an average running time of 242 min for 100-dimensional word embeddings.[4] For 300-dimensional embeddings, the running times increased to 497 min on average, raising to 1,100 min

Table 3. A comparison of Precision at k for the best performing context and non-context models.

k	Context			Non-context			Sum
	Num	P@k	Sum	Num	P@k	Sum	Diff.
1	3327	82.91	82.91	3287	81.91	81.91	1.00
2	319	7.95	90.85	351	8.75	90.66	0.19
3	105	2.62	93.47	117	2.92	93.66	−0.19
4	65	1.62	95.09	65	1.62	95.19	−0.10
5	39	0.97	96.06	39	0.97	96.16	−0.10
6	29	0.72	96.79	21	0.52	96.69	0.10
7	21	0.52	97.31	16	0.4	97.08	0.23
8	12	0.3	97.61	16	0.4	97.48	0.13
9	17	0.42	98.03	16	0.4	97.88	0.15
≥10	79	1.97	100.00	85	2.11	100.00	

---

[3] For each epoch, the new learning rate is computed by dividing the initial learning rate by the current epoch.

[4] Including all 25 epochs with their respective validation and the final evaluation.

with 500-dimensional input. The context models required more complex data preparation with larger input sequences. This is reflected in the increase of running times, where 100-dimensional embeddings raised the time to 550 min on average, 990 min for 300-dimensional word embeddings, and 1,800 min for 500-dimensional input.

4.1 Discussion and Error Analysis

The context model proved to be superior to the standard (non-context) model in almost all types of questions and exact answers, see Table 2 for details. Major improvements can be seen with *clause* question types (more than 3%) and with answers of type *location* (more than 5%). Most other categories are improved except the *abbreviations* category which shows a decrease of 2–3% and with answers that provide a name of an *organization* (decrease of more than 3%).

If we analyze the system improvements regarding the position of the correct answer denoted as the *Precision at k* (or P@k) we can see that the context model specifically helps to improve the position of the top 3 answers. Since these are the frequent positions, such step is very important in improving the system as a whole. See the list of P@k values for the first 10 positions in Table 3.

Record ID:	003189
Question (Q)	Jaké kapely patří do tzv. Velké thrashové čtyřky ? (Which bands belong to the "Big Four of Thrash"?)
Non-context answer with attention	Thrash zpopularizovala tzv.$_{0.81}$ " Velká$_{0.64}$ thrashová$_{0.57}$ čtyřka$_{0.62}$ " : Anthrax, Megadeth, Metallica a Slayer. (The subgenre was popularized by the "Big Four of Thrash": Anthrax, Megadeth, Metallica, and Slayer.)
Q with att. score: position:	Jaké kapely patří$_{0.51}$ do$_{0.53}$ tzv.$_{1.0}$ Velké$_{0.68}$ thrashové$_{0.58}$ čtyřky ? 0.587 1st
Context answer with attention	Tyto$_{1.0}$ dvě$_{0.39}$ kapely, spolu s Death a Obituary, patří mezi nejvýznamnější$_{0.38}$ skupiny na hlavní deathmetalové scéně, která povstala na Floridě v polovině 80. let. (These two bands, along with Death and Obituary, were leaders of the major death metal scene that emerged in Florida in the mid-1980s)
Q with att. context phrases: score: position:	Jaké$_{0.86}$ kapely patří$_{0.53}$ do tzv.$_{1.0}$ Velké$_{0.73}$ thrashové čtyřky ? Morbid Angel; neofašistickou symboliku (neo-fascist symbolism); z výjimek (of exceptions); Glen Benton; z kapely (from band); Deicide; při vystoupeních (on stage) 0.569 1st
corr. answer with attention score: position:	Thrash zpopularizovala$_{1.0}$ tzv.$_{0.37}$ " Velká thrashová čtyřka " : Anthrax, Megadeth, Metallica a Slayer. 0.469 7th

Fig. 4. An example QA pair which is better analyzed with the standard non-context model.

Detailed error analysis of the achieved results showed that not all question analyses are improved with the context network model. For example, Fig. 4 shows a QA example where the standard non-context model ranks the correct answer as the first one of possible answers whereas the context model places the correct answer at the 7th position. If we compare the normalized attention scores between the two models, we can see that the standard model puts an emphasis on the words $patří_{\text{belongs}}$, do_{to}, $tzv_{\text{so\_called}}$, $Velké_{\text{Big}}$, and $thrashové_{\text{of\_Trash}}$ in the question and $tzv_{\text{so\_called}}$, $Velká_{\text{Big}}$, $thrashová_{\text{of\_Trash}}$, and $čtyřka_{\text{Four}}$ in the answer. On the other hand, the context model significantly emphasizes the words $Jaké_{\text{which}}$, $patří_{\text{belongs}}$, $tzv_{\text{so\_called}}$, and $Velké_{\text{Big}}$ of the question and $Tyto_{\text{These}}$, $dvě_{\text{two}}$, and $nejvýznamnější_{\text{most\_important}}$ in the first (incorrect) answer and $zpopularizovala_{\text{popularized}}$ and $tzv_{\text{so\_called}}$ in the correct answer at the 7th position. This information leads us to conclusion that in the case of more names in the context, the context phrases confused the attention layer and the model focused on incorrect words.

On the other hand, the context model obviously helps to identify the answer in candidate sentences that refer to an entity from the question via anaphoric reference (pronoun) to a preceding sentence. However, even in non-anaphoric cases, the context model can increase the attentive score of a key phrase, for example in a question of *Kdo dal dohromady koncept výstroje?* (Who put together the equipment concept?) the context model assigns a higher combined score to the phrase $koncept\ výstroje_{\text{equipment\_score}}$ which allowed to improve the rank of the correct answer sentence.

5   Conclusions

In this paper, we have presented a new method of the answer selection task based on employing broader answer context in the input of the recurrent neural network model. The new model is consistently better than the model without context using the same network hyperparameters. Overall, the best context model offers an improvement of 4% when compared to the previous best published result (from 78.87% to 82.91%).

Since the non-context and context models are (partly) supplemental to each other, one of the main future directions lies in testing ensemble model architectures building on top of these two models.

References

1. Bojanowski, P., Grave, E., Joulin, A., Mikolov, T.: Enriching word vectors with subword information. Trans. Assoc. Comput. Linguist. 5, 135–146 (2017)
2. Bromley, J., Guyon, I., LeCun, Y., Säckinger, E., Shah, R.: Signature verification using a "Siamese" time delay neural network. In: Advances in Neural Information Processing Systems, pp. 737–744 (1994)
3. Devlin, J., Chang, M.W., Lee, K., Toutanova, K.: BERT: pre-training of deep bidirectional transformers for language understanding. In: Proceedings of the NAACL 2019, Volume 1 (Long and Short Papers), pp. 4171–4186 (2019)

4. Lai, G., Xie, Q., Liu, H., Yang, Y., Hovy, E.: Race: large-scale reading comprehension dataset from examinations. arXiv preprint arXiv:1704.04683 (2017)
5. Lan, Z., Chen, M., Goodman, S., Gimpel, K., Sharma, P., Soricut, R.: Albert: a lite bert for self-supervised learning of language representations. arXiv preprint arXiv:1909.11942 (2019)
6. Medveď, M., Horák, A.: AQA: automatic question answering system for Czech. In: Sojka, P., Horák, A., Kopeček, I., Pala, K. (eds.) TSD 2016. LNCS (LNAI), vol. 9924, pp. 270–278. Springer, Cham (2016). https://doi.org/10.1007/978-3-319-45510-5_31
7. Medveď, M., Horák, A.: Sentence and word embedding employed in open question-answering. In: Proceedings of the 10th International Conference on Agents and Artificial Intelligence (ICAART 2018), Setúbal, Portugal, pp. 486–492. SCITEPRESS - Science and Technology Publications (2018)
8. Medveď, M., Horák, A., Kušniráková, D.: Question and answer classification in czech question answering benchmark dataset. In: Proceedings of the 11th International Conference on Agents and Artificial Intelligence, Prague, Czech Republic, vol. 2, pp. 701–706. SCITEPRESS (2019)
9. Medveď, M., Sabol, R., Horák, A.: Improving RNN-based answer selection for morphologically rich languages. In: Proceedings of the 12th International Conference on Agents and Artificial Intelligence (ICAART 2020), Valleta, Malta, pp. 644–651. SCITEPRESS - Science and Technology Publications (2020)
10. Radford, A., Wu, J., Child, R., Luan, D., Amodei, D., Sutskever, I.: Language models are unsupervised multitask learners. OpenAI Blog 1(8), 9 (2019)
11. Rajpurkar, P., Jia, R., Liang, P.: Know what you don't know: unanswerable questions for SQuAD. In: Proceedings of the ACL 2018 (Volume 2: Short Papers), Melbourne, Australia, pp. 784–789. Association for Computational Linguistics (2018)
12. Rajpurkar, P., Zhang, J., Lopyrev, K., Liang, P.: Squad: 100, 000+ questions for machine comprehension of text. CoRR abs/1606.05250 (2016)
13. Rao, J., Liu, L., Tay, Y., Yang, W., Shi, P., Lin, J.: Bridging the gap between relevance matching and semantic matching for short text similarity modeling. In: Proceedings of the 2019 Conference on Empirical Methods in Natural Language Processing and the 9th International Joint Conference on Natural Language Processing (EMNLP-IJCNLP), pp. 5373–5384 (2019)
14. Sabol, R., Medveď, M., Horák, A.: Czech question answering with extended SQAD v3.0 benchmark dataset. In: Proceedings of Recent Advances in Slavonic Natural Language Processing, RASLAN 2019, pp. 99–108 (2019)
15. dos Santos, C., Tan, M., Xiang, B., Zhou, B.: Attentive pooling networks. arXiv preprint arXiv:1602.03609 (2016)
16. Shen, Y., et al.: Knowledge-aware attentive neural network for ranking question answer pairs. In: The 41st International ACM SIGIR Conference on Research & Development in Information Retrieval, pp. 901–904 (2018)
17. Wang, M., Smith, N.A., Mitamura, T.: What is the jeopardy model? A quasi-synchronous grammar for QA. In: Proceedings of the 2007 Joint Conference on Empirical Methods in Natural Language Processing and Computational Natural Language Learning (EMNLP-CoNLL), pp. 22–32 (2007)
18. Warstadt, A., Singh, A., Bowman, S.R.: Neural network acceptability judgments. Trans. Assoc. Comput. Linguist. 7, 625–641 (2019)

19. Yih, S.W., Chang, M.W., Meek, C., Pastusiak, A.: Question answering using enhanced lexical semantic models. In: Proceedings of the 51st Annual Meeting of the Association for Computational Linguistics. ACL - Association for Computational Linguistics, August 2013
20. Zhang, Z., Yang, J., Zhao, H.: Retrospective reader for machine reading comprehension. arXiv preprint arXiv:2001.09694 (2020)

Grammatical Parallelism of Russian Prepositional Localization and Temporal Constructions

Victor Zakharov[⊠] and Irina Azarova

Saint-Petersburg State University, 199034 Saint-Petersburg, Russia
{v.zakharov,i.azarova}@spbu.ru

Abstract. In this paper we present a part of corpus-driven semantico-grammatical ontological description of Russian prepositional constructions. The main problem of a prepositional ontology is its inner controversy because the ontological structure presupposes logical analysis of concepts, however, prepositions are usually interpreted as non-lexical grammatical language elements. In our understanding, this is an ontology of lexico-grammatical relations that are implemented in prepositional constructions. We demonstrate the ontological structure for semantic rubrics of temporal and locative syntaxemes extracted through the elaborated technique for processing corpus statistics of prepositional constructions in modern Russian texts. Common and contrastive traits between this two topmost semantic domains are shown.

Keywords: Russian prepositional constructions · Preposition meaning · Corpus statistics · Locative constructions · Temporal constructions · Semantic rubrics

1 Introduction

The paper presents the next stage of corpus-driven semantic-grammatical description of Russian prepositional constructions. The collected statistics from various contemporary corpora for pairs "preposition – its meaning", their scholarly description [1, 2] and existing schemes of lexical and syntactic structuring [3] led us to the conception of the prepositional ontology. We consider this notion as a semi-grammatical language component linking fuzzy lexico-semantic word classes by the hierarchical set of grammatical relations. These relations are established by a combination of the particular preposition, a semantic type of the lexeme attaching the prepositional construction, and a semantic class and a grammatical form of the dependent noun.

The main problem of such an ontology is its inner controversy since the ontological structure presupposes logical analysis of concepts. Prepositions, however, are usually interpreted as non-lexical or not fully lexical language elements. Currently, there is an understanding that the meaning of prepositions should be considered as a special type of relationship inside prepositional constructions. A prepositional ontology has a significant difference from a classic one. Our understanding is, that it is an ontology of lexico-grammatical relations which are implied in prepositional constructions. We

© Springer Nature Switzerland AG 2020
P. Sojka et al. (Eds.): TSD 2020, LNAI 12284, pp. 122–134, 2020.
https://doi.org/10.1007/978-3-030-58323-1_13

believe that such an ontology cannot be built from the top down. We advocate a data-driven corpus approach from the bottom up and focus on patterns of usage. The similar approach one can see in the building the Pattern Dictionary of English Prepositions (PDEP) [4]. The links and relations between objects of our ontology (syntaxemes), in turn, can also be identified on the basis of corpus-based approach. The relations of this kind are usually calculated by the vector space model [5]. Our approach is closer to [6]. But unlike [6], where machine learning is used, we rely on corpus statistics.

We ground our research on two observations by M.I. Steblin-Kamenskiy [7]: (1) an incomplete awareness of the motivation for grammatical meanings, which is expressed, for example, in the attribution of animateness to obviously inanimate nominations such as *покойник*, *мертвец* ('dead person') or *кукла* ('a doll') and the like, and (2) the particular type of binary grammatical opposition, where one member, so called characteristic category, expresses a grammatical meaning "A", and its counterpart is not a simple opposite of "non A" but some sort of a merger between "non A" and "A" [8]. For our approach, this is a fairly clear principle of distinguishing grammatical oppositions on the basis of corpus statistics. We will use this idea of the characteristic category as a guideline for distinguishing grammatical oppositions since purely logical comparisons of prepositional meanings lead to the so-called "inconsistency" in the use of prepositional-case constructions due to their grammatical nature.

This corpus-based semantic and grammatical description of Russian prepositional constructions uses empiric data from various contemporary Russian corpora in order to identify and then formalize the basic ontological semantic patterns of "prepositional grammar".

2 Prepositional Ontology

It is claimed in [9] that a prepositional ontology has a hierarchical structure. The most abstract concepts are semantic rubrics, which are realized as syntaxemes. This term was proposed by G.A. Zolotova [3] as a designation of the minimal syntactic-morphological prepositional constructions having particular meanings. Syntaxemes may be divided into subtypes (subsyntaxemes) which convey lexico-grammatical meanings and may be expressed by primary or secondary prepositions in a variety of textual forms. Notions from ontological levels have grammatical nature that requires a special quantitative grammatical approach for further structuring.

Quantitative grammatical description is carried out on morphological annotated corpora using corpus searching tools. Besides, we developed own software to extract prepositional phrases from the syntactically annotated corpus Taiga [10]. Frequencies of prepositional meanings obtained from various corpora differ for a variety of reasons, the most important being the balance of stylistic and thematic text characteristics. Frequencies in this paper are derived from a balanced corpus of Russian developed at the Saint-Petersburg University.

The crucial point of our methodology [11] is a compilation of a random sample of contexts with prepositional constructions from corpora. The sample contexts are annotated at the first stage by linguists. Prepositional meanings are ranked according to the percentage of a particular meaning of a preposition. The top ranks demonstrate the regular use of prepositional constructions, and the bottom ranks show their irregular use. The meanings from the top ranks are extrapolated due to the total frequency of a preposition in the corpus and normalized to a number of millions of tokens presented in the corpus and processed as an ipm frequency measure of prepositional meanings. They may be used for aligning the pairs "preposition – its meaning" according to the similarity of meanings to subsyntaxemes, syntaxemes, and rubrics of prepositional constructions.

A prepositional syntaxeme is characterized by a morphological arrangement (a preposition plus a noun case form) which has a unity of the form and the meaning functioning as a constructive and significant component of a phrase or a sentence. Syntaxemes in the original Zolotova's description look like semantic roles or argument specification: locative, temporative, directive, destinative, correlative, quantitative, mediative, qualitative. A typical syntaxeme is expressed by several prepositional phrases, some of them are synonyms and some are not.

The prepositional semantic rubrics, as well as syntaxemes and subsyntaxemes are arranged into cortege sets, that manifest the conceding corpus frequencies. Ratio enumeration of rubrics according to [9] includes localization (.35); temporative (.22); objective (.14); derivative (.09); qualificative (.05); partitive (.03); quantificative (.02). Two topmost semantic rubrics of prepositional meanings are localization and temporative.

In [11] the structure of the localization semantic rubric with appropriate syntaxemes and subsyntaxemes is outlined. It is build on the context analysis for 10 topmost Russian prepositions, that are common for all functional styles and periods from Russian National Corpus [12]: "в" ('in'), "на" ('on'), "с" ('with'), "по" ('by'), "к" ('to'), "из" ('from'), "у" ('at'), "за" ('behind'), "от" ('from'), "о" ('about').

We verify the alleged structure of the localization rubric incorporating more frequent prepositions from the list in [12]: "до" ('to'), "при" ('at'), "под" ('under'), "после" ('after'), "без" ('without'), "через" ('through'), "перед" ('before'), "между" ('between'), "над" ('over'), "из-за" (out of'), "из-под" ('from under'). The verified structure of the localization rubric is described in the next section.

3   The Grammatical Structure of the Localization Rubric

This rubric is informative due to its frequency domination (about 14000 ipm) in text corpora, thus various grammatical "characteristic categories" are presented in its types and subtypes. The framework of this rubric is – in some way – reproduced by other semantic rubrics conforming the localization grammatical oppositions to their particular nature. This correspondence is illustrated by the structure of the prepositional temporative rubric. In [11] 4 syntaxemes are set up: locative, directive, departive, and transitive. Distribution of ipm frequencies for them and their subtypes (subsyntaxemes) is shown below in Table 1.

3.1 Locative Syntaxeme

The general meaning of the *locative syntaxeme* is the designation of the point or extent in space. Its 6 subtypes are opposed in corpus frequencies, the case form of the governee noun, and particularities referring to lexico-semantic classes of governor words and governee nouns. Governor words in general for all subtypes have verbal nature designating actions, states and processes. Concrete nouns are used also but with minor corpus frequencies. The locative_1 formed by "в" ('in') and locative_2 formed by "на" ('on') are combined with nouns in the same case form. This case is placed at the sixth position in the standard Russian case paradigm, and called "prepositional". Governee nouns in these subsyntaxemes are artificial and natural objects which form the human environment. They are classified into two intersecting groups: Place_1 and Place_2. Usually difference between these groups is associated with the idea of "inclusion" for the former in the contrast to "support" and "contiguity" for the latter [13]. This opposition is supported in examples *сидеть в саду* ('to sit in the garden'), *сидеть на стуле* ('to sit on the chair'). The locative_2 subsyntaxeme with "на" ('on') concedes the locative_1 with "в" ('in') greatly: 1800 ipm to 3700 ipm. It is a part of Russian grammatical structure, that reflects statistical and combinatory characteristics of modern Russian grammatical usage.

The most frequent variant of the locative_3 involves the genitive case of the governee noun from both groups Place_1 and Place_2 and designates immediate proximity. The core preposition is "у" ('at') [250 ipm], other synonymous secondary prepositions designating 'near' are "возле" [66 ipm], "около" [16 ipm], "неподалеку от" [8 ipm], "вблизи от" [1 ipm]: *сидеть у (возле/около) моря* ('to sit by (near/about) the sea'); *занять место у окна* ('to take a seat by the window'). There is another variant including the ablative case form: "рядом с" [73 ipm], "под" [35 ipm]: *воевать рядом с/под Москвой* ('to fight near Moscow').

The preposition "за" ('behind') with the ablative case [260 ipm] denotes the locative_4 designating a dividing limit (*кричать за домом* 'to scream behind the house'; *стоять за спиной* 'to stand behind'), which can simultaneously be a marker of the offered services (*стоять за прилавком* 'to stand behind the counter', *скучать за барной стойкой* 'to be bored behind the bar counter'), the latter construction leads to an "active" interpretation of the locative_4 (*быть продавцом, барменом* 'to be a seller, a bartender'). Prepositions are often included in various idioms. In this case they lose their primary grammatical meaning. In this article, the problem of identifying and describing such "prepositional" idioms is not discussed. The object standing as a governee after "за" ('behind') may be a real obstacle, hiding from the sight of a person what is behind it *стоять за дверью/воротами* 'to stand behind the door/gate', *находиться за забором* 'to be behind the fence'. The locative_4 tends to lexicalize: *быть за городом* (= *на природе*) 'to be in the country', *находиться за рубежом* 'to be abroad'. This phenomenon indicates the starting point of the threshold range dividing grammatical and lexical characteristics of a prepositional construction. The preposition "перед" ('in front of', 'before') with the ablative case denotes a opposite variant of the locative_4 designating being on this side of a dividing limit from the sight of a observing person.

The locative_5 is formed by the preposition "под" ('under') with the ablative case [145 ipm]. It designates the position below some marked location: *лежать под столом* ('to lie under the table'), *стоять под навесом* ('to stand under an awning').

Another subsyntaxeme locative_6 represents the peripheral usage of the frequent preposition "по" ('over') taking the dative case [110 ipm]. This preposition is considered by G.A. Zolotova predominantly as a transitive syntaxeme (see below), although it is also used for a localization specification denoting the boundaries of non-directional or chaotic movement: *бродить по городу/улицам* ('to wander around the city/the streets'), *путешествовать по стране* ('to travel around the country'). This subtype signals the end of the grammatical threshold range. Less frequent prepositional constructions are structured according the principles of lexical organization, as a lexico-semantic group. Plenty examples are given in [9].

Different subtypes of a grammatical syntaxeme may co-occur in the text at the same time: *сидеть в кресле на веранде* ('to sit in a chair on the veranda'), *грабить на открытых дорогах за городом* ('to rob on open roads outside the city'). This fact is usually considered an evidence that these prepositional constructions have different semantic roles.

3.2   Directive, Departive, and Transitive Syntaxemes

The next type of localization prepositional groups reflects the trajectory of object or subject movement which is compatible with verbal governors denoting self-propelled movement or changing object location. Three aspects of this trajectory are usually specified in corpus texts: (a) the end point of the trajectory, that is, the goal; (b) the initial or starting point of the trajectory; (c) the space traversed.

The **directive syntaxeme** [4575 ipm] specifies the end point of the movement. It shows the conformity with subtypes of the locative syntaxeme. The topmost frequent prepositions "в" ('in') and "на" ('on') have impressive parallelism in their grammatical specificity. They require the accusative case of nouns and have the identical selectional preferences for governee nouns as locative_1 and locative_2. Thus, we can introduce two syntaxeme subtypes: the directive_1 [2500 ipm] and the directive_2 [1250 ipm]: *положить в шкаф* ('to put in the closet'), *поставить на стол* ('to put on the table'). The same grammatical shift is valid for less frequent directive_4 with the preposition "за" (in this sense 'over') [115 ipm] and directive_5 with the preposition "под" ('under') [70 ipm]: *бросить за ограду* ('to throw over the fence'), *выйти за ограду* ('to go over the fence'), *прыгнуть под вагон* ('to jump under the wagon'), *положить под кровать* ('to put under the bed').

The novelty in this group is the preposition "к" ('to') taking the dative case [650 ipm] which is analogous to locative_3 with preposition "у" ('at') as regards lexical nature of governee nouns: *устремиться к веранде* ('to rush to the veranda'), *подвинуть к окну* ('to move to the window'). The enumeration of this syntaxeme subtype is directive_3. Another variant of this subtype is preposition "до" ('to') taking the genitive case [65 ipm]: *плыть до острова* ('to sail to the island'). This variant is used with the prefixal verbal derivatives coinciding with the preposition: *добраться до острова* ('to get to the island').

The **departive syntaxeme** specifies the starting point of the movement trajectory. It does not look sustainable because these constructions have corpus frequencies comparable with those of the directive group, and follow the similar type of lexical preferences for governee nouns. Its subtypes match straightforwardly enumeration of the directive syntaxeme. Departive subtypes attach governee nouns in the genitive case form. The departive_1 uses the preposition "из" ('from') [660 ipm] and denotes the movement of an object or a subject opposite to that of directive_1: *уйти из сада* ('to leave the garden'), *вытащить из шкафа* ('to pull out of the closet'). The same opposition can be seen in the departive_2 with the preposition "с" ('from') [410 ipm]: *убрать со стола* ('to clear the table'), *уйти с веранды* ('to leave the veranda'). The departive_3 expressed by the preposition "от" ('from') [300 ipm] is an opposite to the directive_3: *отодвинуть от окна* ('to move away from the window'), *уйти от стола* ('to get away from the table'). The departive_4 is expressed by the preposition "из-за" (in this sense 'from') [40 ipm]. It is the counterpoise of the directive_4: *вытащить из-за пазухи* ('to pull out from the bosom'), *встать из-за стола* ('to get up from the table'). Similarly the departive_5 with "из-под" ('from under') [22 ipm] is the counteraction of the directive_5: *вытащить из-под стола* ('to pull out from under the table'), *торчать из-под снега* ('to stick out of the snow').

The **transitive syntaxeme** forms the peripheral syntaxeme in the localization rubric due to lesser corpus frequency and more intricate subtype oppositions. The transitive_1 is formed by the only core preposition "по" (in this sense 'along') with the dative case [360 ipm]: *пройти по коридору/полю* ('to walk along the corridor/field'), *спускаться по лестнице* ('to go down the stairs'). The secondary synonym is peripheral "вдоль по" ('along') [2 ipm]. The primary preposition "через" ('through' or 'across') with the accusative case of the governee noun [135 ipm] forms the transitive_2 subtype: *пройти через холл* ('to go through the hall'), *провозить через переезд* ('to transport across highway crossing'). The secondary preposition "сквозь" ('through') [38 ipm] is usually considered to belong to the transitive_2 subtype.

Table 1. Distribution of ipm frequencies of syntaxemes from the localization rubric in a balanced corpus (the superscript following the preposition designates the case form as its position in the standard case paradigm)

Locative			Directive			Departive			Transitive		
Locative_1	$в_6$	4000	Directive_1	$в_4$	2500	Departive_1	$из_2$	660	Transitive_1	$по_3$	360
Locative_2	$на_6$	2500	Directive_2	$на_4$	1250	Departive_2	$с_2$	410	Transitive_2	$через_4$	135
Locative_3	$у_2 ...$	449	Directive_3	$к_5 до_2$	640	Departive_3	$от_2$	300	Transitive_2	$сквозь_4$	38
Locative_4	$за_5$	260	Directive_4	$за_4$	115	Departive_4	$из$-$за_2$	40			
Locative_5	$под_5$	145	Directive_5	$под_4$	70	Departive_5	$из$-$под_2$	22			
Locative_6	$по_3$	110									
ipm		7464	ipm		4575	ipm		1432	ipm		533

The distribution of the frequencies of localization syntaxemes illustrates the quantitative realization of grammatical oppositions in the ontological structure of prepositional meanings. Jacobson's characteristic categories can be seen in the syntaxeme group: the locative_1 prevails over the locative_2, and so forth, and this ratio is recurrent in every syntaxeme group. This structure is transformed subsequently into other semantic rubrics, though the fundamental cognitive traits of the localization rubric are quite clear. The significant feature of the localization syntaxeme structure is the fact that they are predominantly unambiguous: they involve different prepositions, and if they coincide, attached case forms vary. This leads to a situation in which the juxtaposition of Russian localization syntaxemes cannot be translated into English as a valid phrase due to the repetition of the same preposition. Therefore, we may consider enumerated syntaxemes to be a joint form of grammatical expression of the localization ontological system. English translations of the localization syntaxemes reflect the fact that in some parts the ontological structures in two languages overlap, and partially they are totally different.

Contextual examples of Russian localization syntaxemes show the correlation between prefix verbal derivatives and localization syntaxemes in use. The usual interpretation of this correlation is formulated as follows: prefixal verbal derivatives create constituents of "governed" prepositional constructions, the prefix regularly matching the preposition in such a constituent. However, the investigation of this phenomenon with a help of corpus statistics analysis in [11] shows that realization of derivative, departive and transitive syntaxemes for prefixed verbal derivatives is higher than for those without prefixes. The distribution of substantial frequencies of localization syntaxemes over prefixal verbal derivatives illustrates that the appearance of localization syntaxemes to a considerable extent depends on the semantic type of the governee noun. Localization subsyntaxemes tend to substitute one another, the formal repetition of the prefix by its matching preposition is possible, but not obligatory and predominant.

4   The Grammatical Structure of the Temporative Rubric

The temporative rubric [6140 ipm] concedes to the localization one in frequency. Naturally, there is no complete isomorphism of spatial and temporal relations, nevertheless, the loose specification of governor words enlarges the number of verbal derivatives comparing with the localization rubric. The topmost syntaxeme [2765 ipm] in the temporative rubric is the *temporal* specification of some event. The grammatical opposition in corpus frequencies holds between the principal preposition in the localization rubric "в" ('in') in combination with the prepositional (locative) case [1150 ipm] and accusative case [920 ipm] in the same manner as the locative_1 versus the directive_1. However, these prepositional constructions in the temporative rubric even at the highest level of the structure exploit specific lexical preferences. The first subtype temporal_1 attaches nouns denoting months, years, and longer time intervals, these time specifications may be loaded with an additional meaning component: *в 1999 году* ('in 1999'), *в августе* ('in August'), *в 19 веке* ('in the 19th century'), *в неолите* ('in the Neolithic'), *в детстве* ('in childhood'). The second subtype temporal_2 with nouns in the accusative case is used to indicate the day of the week or the time of the day: *в пятницу* ('on Friday'), *в пять часов утра* ('at five in the morning'). The difference between temporal_1 and temporal_2 reflects the distinction between governee nouns denoting time intervals (Time_1) and moments of time (Time_2), and this linguistic classification appears to be as latent as the locative division into Place_1 and Place_2.

The opposition between two groups of governee nouns (Time_1 and Time_2) is nullified in the construction temporal_3 similar to directive_4 "за" ('during') attaching the accusative case [230 ipm]: *уничтожить за секунду* ('to destroy in a second'), *поставки за год* ('deliveries per year'). The secondary preposition "в течение" ('during') with genitive case [120 ipm] is widely used supporting this group: *действовать в течение декабря* ('to act during December'), *заезд в течение пятницы* ('a check in during Friday').

The next subsyntaxeme temporal_4 is formed according the model of the locative_4: "за" ('during') attaching the ablative case [110 ipm]. It provides the temporal reference by mentioning some action: *сидеть рядом за обедом* ('to sit nearby at dinner'), *сказать за завтраком* ('to say at breakfast'). This subsyntaxeme is supported by the secondary preposition "во время" ('during')[138 ipm] with nouns in the genitive case: *во время беседы* ('during the conversation').

The last subtype temporal_5 in this group is formed on the pattern of the directive_2: "на" (in this sense 'at') with the accusative case, the governee noun phrase denotes the date of some event [55 ipm]: *готовить вторжение на 12 мая* ('to prepare the invasion for May 12'), *положение дел на 6 февраля* ('the state of affairs on February 6'). Distribution of ipm frequencies for the syntaxemes from the temporative rubric is shown in the Table 2.

The co-occurence of temporal subsyntaxemes is possible. There are two basic types. The standard one: nouns appropriate for temporal_1 stands in genitive after various subtypes: *произойти в октябре 1995 г.* ('to happen in October, 1995'); the second type is the sequence of several temporal_2 constructions: *арестовать в воскресенье в девять часов утра* ('to arrest on Sunday at nine in the morning').

The second syntaxeme in the temporative rubric **aspective** specifies a trajectory projected on the limits of some time interval: its beginning, accomplishing, duration, and repetition. In this syntaxeme the opposition of intervals and moments turns in twofold aspects. The first predominant method presents direct time designation and indirect nomination by reference to the event as a point without proper duration, this is a metaphorical transfer of the space trajectory. They are represented as time "marks": the beginning happens after this mark as a point of departure, the accomplishment – before that mark as a point of arrival. The second method presents time as a time duration in which it is possible to specify logically the beginning and the end. Secondary prepositions incorporating the preposition "в" ('in') designate these boundaries of the time interval: *в начале* [27 ipm] *июня* ('at the beginning of June'), *в конце* [41 ipm] *1995 года* ('at the end of 1995'), *в период* [24 ipm] *нереста* ('during spawning'). We divide propositional constructions compatible with aspects of temporal variation into 4 subtypes: the terminative, the intervallum, the inchoative, and the repetitive. The description of these subtypes is focused primarily on usage of primary prepositions, because secondary ones include them as a part attaching lexical items overtly presenting the subsyntaxeme meaning.

The topmost subtype of the aspective syntaxeme is the **terminative** [504 ipm], it designates the time of event accomplishment, it is usually the point-wise method of time specification. Its first variant transforms the second variant of the directive_3 with the preposition "до" (in this sense 'by') with the genitive case [236 ipm]: *закончить до осени* ('to finish by fall'), *наладить до 15 мая* ('to set up by may 15'). This subsyntaxeme may be included into a sequence with the inchoative producing the intervallum subsyntaxeme: "с… до" [22 ipm]: бегать *с утра до позднего вечера* ('to run <u>from</u> morning <u>till</u> late evening'), "от… до" [14 ipm] *длиться от нескольких минут до часа*, ('to last <u>from</u> a few minutes <u>to</u> an hour'). The second variant is the modification of directive_3 "к" (in this sense 'by') with dative case [122 ipm]: *закончить к осени* ('to finish by fall'). Another variant looks like the directive_5: the preposition "под" (in this sense 'before') attaching the accusative case [25 ipm] with lexical restrictions: *уйти под вечер* ('to leave in the evening'), *приехать под Новый Год* ('to come on New Year's Eve'). The secondary preposition "в конце" ('at the end') [41 ipm] presents the extended view to the time interval: *получить аттестат в конце года* ('to get a certificate at the end of the year').

The ***inchoative*** subsyntaxeme [367 ipm] is opposed to the terminative in the point-wise system of time representation and specifies the time of event beginning. The topmost variant is the transformed departive_2, the preposition "с" ('from') with the genitive case [170 ipm]: *пить чай с утра* ('to drink tea in the morning'), *начать работать с 13 лет* ('to start working from 13 years old'). The second variant is the transformed departive_3, the preposition "от" ('from') with the genitive case [110 ipm]: *в возрасте от 7 лет* ('from the age of 7'), *слепой от рождения* ('blind from birth'), *указ от 12 мая* ('Decree of May 12'). Both variants are combined with the terminatives, and form the intervallum ("с… до"). The frequent extended inchoative is formed by the secondary preposition "в начале" ('at the beginning').

The ***intervallum*** syntaxemes [467 ipm] overlaps with the inchoative and the terminative presented in a sequence in the time. The topmost variant is "за" (in this sense 'in') with the accusative case [230 ipm] (it coincides with the directive_4 in the localization rubric): *просмотреть текст за 10 минут* ('to look through the text in 10 min'). The second variant is a new construction "по" (in this sense 'till') with the accusative case [180 ipm], it expresses a quantificative time period: *жить по два месяца в деревне* ('to live two months in the village'). This construction may be used as binary expression of the time period: "с… по" [24 ipm] *работать с марта по май* ('to work from March till May'). The third variant of this subtype is the transformed directive_2, the preposition "на" (in this sense 'for') with the accusative case [24 ipm]: *оставить на ночь* ('to leave overnight'), *освободить на два-три дня* ('to free for two-three days'). The secondary prepositions "в период" and "за период" ('during the period') present lexically the intervallum subtype.

Table 2. Distribution of ipm frequencies of syntaxemes from the temporative rubric in a balanced corpus (the superscript following the preposition designates the case form as its position in the standard case paradigm)

Temporal			Aspective			Taxis		
Temporal_1	$в^6$	1150	Terminative	$до^2\ к^3$	504	Consequent	$после^2$	857
Temporal_2	$в^4$	920		$в\ конце^2$			$через^4$	
				$под^5$			$спустя^2$	
Temporal_3	$за^4$	350	Intervallum	$за^4\ по^4$	467	Concurrent	$при^6$	675
	$в\ течение^2$			$на^4$				
Temporal_4	$за^6$	290		$в\ период^2$		Antecedent	$до^2$	340
	$во\ время^2$		Inchoative	$с^2\ от^2$	367		$перед^5$	
				$в\ начале^2$				
Temporal_5	$на^4$	55	Repetitive	$по^5$	180			
ipm	2765		ipm	1518		ipm	1872	

The **repetitive** subsyntaxeme [180 ipm] is expressed by the transformed locative_6 "по" ('on') with the ablative case: *играть в карты по пятницам* ('to play cards on Fridays'). Distribution of ipm frequencies for the aspective syntaxeme and its subtypes from the temporative rubric is shown in Table 2.

The time definition in texts may reffer to the time of some event. In this case the time specification turnes out to be relative, such prepositional constructions form the third syntaxeme **taxis** (after R. Jacobson's terminology for verbal relative time). Specification of taxis is straightforward: the time interval preceding some event – antecedent, following it – consequent, simultaneous – concurrent.

The topmost subtype of this syntaxeme is **consequent** [857 ipm]. The first variant is formed with the secondary preposition "после" ('after') [500 ipm] attaching the genitive case.: *произойти после оказания помощи* ('to happen after assisting'), *заметить после обыска на квартире* ('to notice after searching the apartment'). The second variant is the transformed transitive_2 "через" (in this sense 'after') [300 ipm] with the accusative case, the governee noun phrase is usually designation of standard time measurements potentially quantified: *прийти через день* ('to come in a day'), *произойти через 2 столетия* ('to happen after 2 centuries'). The secondary preposition "спустя" ('later') with the accusative case [57 ipm] forms the equivalent construction: *возглавить министерство спустя 20 лет* ('to head the ministry 20 years later'). This preposition in small number of contexts (5%) stands after the governee noun phrase in a postposition: *найти несколько лет спустя* ('to find a few years later'). The first and the second variants can be used in a sequence with a first variant: *вернуться спустя| через год после рождения малыша* ('to come back a year after the birth of the baby').

The next subtype is **concurrent**, although there is the only primary preposition "при" ('during') [675 ipm]: *использовать при оказании помощи* ('to use in assisting' = to use when assist).

The third subtype is **antecedent** [340 ipm] which attaches governee nouns, designating actions, events, and so on. The topmost variant transforms the second variant of the directive_3: "до" ('before') with the genitive case [266 ipm]: *оценивать* *сотрудника до его появления* ('to evaluate an employee before he appears'). The second variant is formed by the preposition "перед" ('before') with the ablative case [74 ipm]: *выскочить перед закрытием дверей* ('to pop out before closing the doors'), *осмотреться перед выходом* ('to look around before going out'). A great number of secondary prepositions for this syntaxeme are listed in [9].

5   Semantico-Grammatical Parallelism of Localization and Temporative Rubrics

Semantic rubrics are abstract semantic classes divided into syntaxemes by which we describe the meaning of prepositional constructions. The localization and temporative semantic rubrics are two topmost rubrics of prepositional meanings. As shown above, their framework, division into subtypes, and specification of subtypes are sometimes similar. Let's illustrate this parallelism in a compressed form (Table 3). We suppose that it is a result of an associative transfer of spatial relations into the realm of imaginary location and movement on the timeline of events.

Table 3. Proximity between subsyntaxemes of temporative and localization rubrics

Temporative			Localization		
Syntaxeme	Subsyntaxeme	Example	Syntaxeme	Subsyntaxeme	Example
Temporative	Temporal_1	*в августе*	Locative	Locative_1	*в саду*
Temporative	Temporal_3	*за год, в течение декабря*	Locative	Locative_6	*в пределах поля, на протяжении пути*
Temporative	Temporal_4	*за завтраком, во время беседы*	Locative	Locative_1	*в комнате, на веранде*
Aspective	Terminative	*закончить к осени, до осени*	Directive	Directive_3	*подойти к веранде, плыть до острова*
Aspective	Inchoative	*пить чай с утра, начать с 13 лет*	Departive	Departive_2/Departive_3	*уйти с веранды, уйти от стола*
Aspective	Intervallum	*дойти за 5минут, с марта по май*	Directive/Departive	Directive3/Departive3	*от дома до реки*
Taxis	Consequent	*после обыска, через день*	Locative	Locative_4	*через 3 километра, за городом*
Taxis	Concurrent	*при оказании помощи*	Locative	Locative_3	*сидеть у моря*
Taxis	Antecedent	*до появления, перед закрытием*	Locative	Locative_4	*стоять перед дверью*

We would like to note that there are not only hierarchical relationships between syntaxemes and subsyntaxemes in our ontology, but horizontal relations between units from different semantic rubrics, too.

6 Conclusion and Further Work

The semantic rubrics presented in our approach help to organize rather vague prepositional meanings. Their affinity and difference may be explicated through the overlap of semantic classes of governing and subordinate words. The whole structure of prepositional frequencies that so far have not been in any study and neighbor semantic distributions are resources for the compilation of the quantitative prepositional grammar for Russian.

We proceed to compile the structure of other semantic rubrics on the basis of outlined technique. The frame of grammatical oppositions are organized by dispersion of primary prepositional meanings. Secondary prepositions are attached to this system appending their particular lexical connotation. Occasionally they gain the appropriate position in the grammatical framework, thus shifting to another level of balance between grammatical and lexical components of meaning.

Further stages of investigation include:

- to finalize the set of syntaxemes and subsyntaxemes of prepositional semantic rubrics referring to governers and governees semantic types;
- to compare sets of prepositional constructions (grammatical syntaxemes and their lexicalized versions with secondary prepositions) from corpora of different genres in order to discover the significant variation of statistical parameters;
- to investigate the combinatory potential of the extracted grammatical syntaxemes in order to separate their subtypes and synonymic variants;
- to compile rules of the hybrid generative grammar showing the use and interpretation of syntaxemes for the corpus text.

Acknowledgements. This paper has been supported by the Russian Foundation for Basic Research, project No. 17-29-09159.

References

1. Solonitskiy, A.V.: Problems of semantics of Russian primitive prepositions. 125 p. (in Rus) [Problemy semantiki russkikh pervoobraznykh predlogov]. Vladivostok (2003)
2. Filipenko, M.V.: Problems of the description of prepositions in modern linguistic theories [Problemy opisaniya predlogov v sovremennykh lingvisticheskikh teoriyakh]. In: Research on the semantics of prepositions. Moscow: Russkie slovari, pp. 12–54 (2000)
3. Zolotova, G.A.: Syntactical Dictionary: a Set of Elementary Units of Russian Syntax. 440 p. (in Rus) [Sintaksicheskiy slovar': repertuar elementarnykh edinits russkogo sintaksisa], 4th edn. Moscow (2011)
4. Litkowski, K.: Notes on grilled Opakapaka: ontology in preposition patterns. Technical report 15–01. Damascus, MD: CL Research (2015)
5. Zwarts, J., Winter, Y.S.: A semantic characterization of locative PPs. In: Lawson, A. (ed.) Proceedings of Semantics and Linguistic Theory, pp. 294–311 (1998)
6. Lassen, T.: An ontology-based view on prepositional senses. In: Proceedings of the Third ACL-SIGSEM Workshop on Prepositions, pp. 45–50. ACM (2006)

7. Steblin-Kamenskiy, M.I.: Controversial in Linguistics. Leningrad: Leningrad University Publishing House. 144 p. (in Rus.) [Spornoye v yazykoznanii. Leningrad: Izd-vo Leningradskogo universiteta] (1974)
8. Jakobson, R.O.: Selected Works, Moscow, 1985. 460 p. (In Rus.) Izbrannyye raboty. Moskva: Progress. 460 s. (1985)
9. Zakharov, V., Azarova, I.: Semantic structure of Russian prepositional constructions. In: Ekštein, K. (ed.) TSD 2019. LNCS (LNAI), vol. 11697, pp. 224–235. Springer, Cham (2019). https://doi.org/10.1007/978-3-030-27947-9_19
10. Gudkov, V., Golovina, A., Mitrofanova, O., Zakharov, V.: Russian prepositional phrase semantic labelling with word embedding-based classifier. In: CEUR Workshop Proceedings, vol. 2552, pp. 272–284 (2020)
11. Azarova, I., Zakharov, V., Khokhlova, M., Petkevič, V.: Ontological description of Russian prepositions. In: CEUR Workshop Proceedings, vol. 2552, pp. 245–257 (2020)
12. Lyashevskaya, O.N., Sharoff, S.A.: Frequency dictionary of the modern Russian language, vol. XXII, 1087 p. (in Rus.). Moscow: Azbukovnik [Novyj chastotnyj slovar' russkoj leksiki] (2009). http://dict.ruslang.ru/freq.php?act=show&dic=freq_freq&title=%D7%E0% F1%F2%ED%FB%E9%20%F1%EF%E8%F1%EE%EA%20%EB%E5%EC%EC
13. Herskovits, A.: Semantics and pragmatics of locative expressions. Cogn. Sci. **9**, 341–378 (1985)

Costra 1.1: An Inquiry into Geometric Properties of Sentence Spaces

Petra Barančíková[(✉)] [ID] and Ondřej Bojar [ID]

Charles University, MFF ÚFAL, Prague, Czech Republic
{barancikova,bojar}@ufal.mff.cuni.cz

Abstract. In this paper, we present a new dataset for testing geometric properties of sentence embeddings spaces. In particular, we concentrate on examining how well sentence embeddings capture complex phenomena such paraphrases, tense or generalization. The dataset is a direct expansion of Costra 1.0 [7], which we extended with more sentences and sentence comparisons. We show that available off-the-shelf embeddings do not possess essential attributes such as having synonymous sentences embedded closer to each other than sentences with a significantly different meaning. On the other hand, some embeddings appear to capture the linear order of sentence aspects such as style (formality and simplicity of the language) or time (past to future).

Keywords: Sentence embeddings · Sentence transformations · Paraphrasing · Semantic relations

1 Introduction

Trained vector representations of words and sentences, known as embeddings, have become ubiquitous throughout natural language processing (NLP). Since their popularity took off with the introduction of word2vec word embeddings [15], numerous different methods with different properties have emerged, highlighting the importance of estimating their quality. However, it is not entirely clear in which way the embeddings should be evaluated, aside from the performance in the task they originate in. Two main classes, *extrinsic evaluation* and *intrinsic evaluation*, are considered [17].

Extrinsic evaluation utilizes word embeddings as feature vectors for machine learning algorithms in downstream NLP tasks. It serves well in choosing the best method for a particular task but not as an absolute metric of embedding quality as the performances of embeddings do not correlate across different tasks [5].

This research was supported by the grants 19-26934X (NEUREM3) of the Czech Science Foundation, 825303 (Bergamot) of the EU, and SVV project 260 575. This work has been using language resources stored and distributed by the project No. LM2015071, *LINDAT-CLARIN*, of the Ministry of Education, Youth and Sports of the Czech Republic.

© Springer Nature Switzerland AG 2020
P. Sojka et al. (Eds.): TSD 2020, LNAI 12284, pp. 135–143, 2020.
https://doi.org/10.1007/978-3-030-58323-1_14

[16] demonstrate the presence of linguistic regularities in the word2vec embedding space. Namely, they show that various word analogy tasks can be solved by simple vector arithmetic in the embedding space, e.g. finding correct word D for words A, B, C and their respective embeddings v_A, v_B, v_C by optimizing:

$$\arg \max_{D \in V \backslash \{A,B,C\}} \operatorname{sim}_C(v_D, v_A - v_B + v_C), \tag{1}$$

where sim_C represent cosine similarity between two vectors. This works for various semantic and syntactic relationships, like for example:

A	B	C	D
king	man	woman	queen
Russia	Moscow	Paris	France
walked	walk	tell	told
bigger	big	small	smaller

This lead to a novel approach—intrinsic evaluation—in which word embeddings are compared with human judgment on word relations. There is a large number of available datasets for syntactic and semantic intrinsic evaluation, word analogy task [15,16] belongs among the most popular methods.

For sentence embeddings this is a different story. When Kiros et al. [12] introduced Skip-Thought vectors, they evaluated their quality in eight supervised tasks such as paraphrase detection or sentiment polarity. This extrinsic evaluation or 'transfer tasks' became the de facto standard for evaluation and comparison of sentence embeddings, despite the fact that even simple bag-of-words (BOW) approaches often achieve competitive results on transfer tasks [18].

[1,11] introduce intrinsic evaluation of sentence embeddings, however, most of the research in interpretation of sentence embeddings consists of probing for surface linguistic features of the sentence such as its length, verb tense, word order, etc. Furthermore, [4,14] indicate that strong performance in these tasks might be caused by test flaws—the test sentences are grammatically too simple.

However, any geometric properties of an embedding space remain a largely uncharted territory. We attempt to fill this gap, examining whether sentence representation spaces exhibit regularities with regard to certain kinds of relationships, in a way similar to the linear relations observed in word vector spaces.

To this end, we devise a new dataset on the basis of Costra 1.0 [7], which we extend with information on linear ordering of embedded sentences with regard to certain kinds of relationships. These allow us to test empirically whether existing sentence embedding models reflect analogical relationships between sentences.

The paper is structured as follows: Sect. 2 presents existing methods of semantic evaluation of sentence embeddings and available off-the-shelf embeddings. Section 3 describes the methodology for constructing our dataset. Section 4 details the evaluation of embeddings and Sect. 5 presents the results.

2   Related Work

2.1   Sentence Embedding Space Evaluation

Zhu et al. [21] compare sentence embeddings from a relational perspective using automatically generated triplets of sentence variations and explore how syntactic or semantics changes of a given sentence affect the similarities among their sentence embeddings. The following example sentences illustrate this point:

S1: A pig is eating goulash.
S2: A pig is feeding on goulash.
S3: A pig is not eating goulash.

Synonyms (S1, S2) should be embedded closer to each other in a vector space than sentences with similar wording but different meaning (S1, S3) and (S2, S3). They discover that several embeddings perform surprisingly well in these tasks.

A sentence analogy task was recently introduced in [21]: in template sentences they substitute a pair of words such as state/capital, man/woman or plural/singular. To test, whether the embeddings are really able to find the analogy correctly, they create incorrect sentences similar in wording to the correct ones and examine whether Eq. (1) finds the 'correct' sentence.

Similarly, [6] examined sentences that are close in wording but differ in one key aspect (e.g. change of gender, adding an adjective, removing a numeral) and show that the changes form meaningful clusters in the sentence vector space.

In Costra 1.0 [7], we attempted to move to more sophisticated types of sentence relations, beyond those in [6,20]. We present a dataset of complex sentence transformations in Czech. It is created manually with the aim to thoroughly test how well sentence embeddings capture the meaning and style of sentences. The dataset contains sentences very different in wording with a similar meaning as well as sentences similar on the surface level but very different in meaning.

However, the dataset has certain limitations. For instance, it contains several generalizations of a sentence but their mutual relations are no further studied. In other words, we do not know, which ones are more general and should be embedded closer to the original sentence. Our work directly builds upon [7]. We decided to make the dataset more robust by extending it with more sentences and also to ensure that sentences are related to each other whenever possible. We also created a tool to automatically evaluate the quality of embeddings using our dataset and used it to compare several off-the-shelf Czech embeddings.

2.2   Sentence Embedding Methods

Since we extend the Costra dataset, we stick to the Czech language. Our goal is to test as many off-the-shelf Czech sentence embeddings as possible. Unfortunately, to our best knowledge there is only one directly learned representation for entire sentences available for the Czech language: LASER [3].

However, there are available pretrained language models such as multilingual BERT (mBERT) [10] or Flair [2]. Despite neglecting the word order, these methods yield surprisingly strong results in many downstream tasks. In order to move from word vector representations towards representations for entire sentences, we simply average embeddings of hidden states of all tokens in a sentence. For BERT, we also consider the CLS token as a sentence embedding.

Sentence multilingual BERT[1] (SentBERT) is a sentence encoder initialized with multilingual BERT and fine-tuned using MultiNLI [19] and XNLI [9] datasets. The recommended sentence representations are mean-pooled token embeddings, we use the CLS token too.

3   Annotation

We acquired the data in two rounds of annotation. In the first one, we were concentrating on adding more related sentences, i.e., making the sentence space denser. In order to project sentence transformation to a linear scale, we decided to collect *interpolations* and *extrapolations*. In the second round, we collected pairwise comparisons of sentences from both Costra 1.0 and our first round.

3.1   First Round: Collecting Interpolations and Extrapolations

In the first round of annotation, we present annotators with a seed sentence and its transformation and ask them to write the following two new sentences: **interpolation** – a sentence with meaning/style between the two sentences, and **extrapolation** – a sentence with meaning/style even further away from the seed sentence than the transformation in the suggested direction. An example of one annotation is presented in Fig. 1.

From the 14 transformation types available in Costra 1.0, we did not select all types of transformation for the first round.[2] The reason was straightforward: it does not make sense to collect interpolations or extrapolations for some of them. For example, meaning of *paraphrases* should be identical or very close to original sentences and searching for interpolation would be a waste of annotators' time. Similarly, there is the *non-sense* transformation, which is created by shuffling content words of a seed sentence, so the final sentence is grammatically correct but has no meaning. There are no interpolations or extrapolations of nonsense.

We manually examined all transformation types and selected only 6 of them that look most linearly scalable: *formal sentence, future, generalization, nonstandard sentence, opposite meaning* and *past*. We do not introduce any new type of transformations.

We collected almost 1,500 annotations from 7 annotators, containing 2,749 unique sentences. Total volume of Costra 1.1 is 6,968 sentences.

---

[1] http://docs.deeppavlov.ai/en/master/features/models/bert.html.

[2] Costra 1.0 contains the following 14 different transformation types: *paraphrase, different meaning, opposite meaning, nonsense, minimal change, generalization, gossip, formal sentence, non-standard sentence, simple sentence, possibility, ban, future, past.*

seed	*"Občas se mi na hlavě málo prokrvuje kůže."*
	The skin on my head sometimes fills with little blood.
interpolation	*"Kůže na hlavě se mi prokrvuje tak akorát"*
	The skin on my head fills with just the right amount of blood.
transformation	*"Občas se mi na hlavě hodně prokrvuje kůže"*
	The skin on my head sometimes fills with too much blood.
extrapolation	*"Nemám žádnou kůži na hlavě"*
	There is no skin on my head.

Fig. 1. Example from the first round of annotations. The annotator filled the interpolation and extrapolation to the seed and its transformation with *opposite meaning*.

Implied Sentence Comparison. In the second round of annotations, the annotators are sorting sentence pairs. We however know that an interpolation is closer in meaning or style to the seed sentence than its pre-existing transformation or the extrapolation. These implied relations provide us with almost 7,000 sentence comparisons.

3.2   Second Round: Sentence Comparison

Again, we have manually chosen transformation categories to be compared. We selected those that are linearly comparable, i.e. changes in tense (*future, past*), changes in style (*formal sentence, gossip, nonstandard sentence, simple sentence*) and significant changes in meaning (*generalization, opposite meaning*). We merged two categories (*non-standard* and *gossip*) because the actual sentences in the collection often realized 'gossipping' via non-standard language and vice versa.

The annotators were presented with a pair of sentences and criteria, how to compare them.[3] Of course, not always are the sentences comparable. Their meaning might be either very close or very far from each other, both making them hard to compare. For every pair of sentences S_1 and S_2, the annotators had the following four options:

1. S_1 is more general/formal/in the past/non-standard/... than S_2.
2. S_2 is more general/formal/in the past/non-standard/... than S_1
3. S_1 and S_2 are **too similar**, for example: *"Byl rozčilený a hodně mluvil."* (He was upset and talked a lot.) and *"Ovlivněn silnými emocemi říkal ledacos."* (Influenced by strong emotions, he said all kind of things.) are so close in their meaning that it is almost impossible to select the more general one.
4. S_1 and S_2 **too dissimilar**, for example: neither of the sentences *"Všechno zlé je pro něco dobré."* (Every cloud has a silver lining; lit. All bad is good for something.) and *"V Asii jsou různá období."* (There are different seasons

---

[3] Only for *opposite meaning* the annotators were presented with three sentences: two candidates and a source sentence. The annotators were then supposed to say which of the candidates is closer to meaning of the source sentence.

in Asia.) is generalization of the other sentence, even though they both were created as generalizations of the sentence "*Bangladéšská monzunová sezóna přináší radost, problémy i pozoruhodné fotografie*" (Bangladesh's monsoon season brings joy, problems and remarkable photos.)

We collected more than 25k sentence pairwise comparisons from 7 annotators. We compute inter and intra-annotator agreement using average pairwise Kohen's kappa [8]. The scores are generally good, not lower than other types of linguistic annotation. Our inter-annotator agreement is 0.62 ($\kappa = 0.49$) and our intra-annotator agreement is 0.77 ($\kappa = 0.7$).

4   Vector Evaluation

4.1   Sentence Comparison

We combine sentence comparisons obtained in the first and second round of the annotation. A pair of sentences can have multiple annotations in the collection. We trust the annotation only if there is an option with the majority of votes.

We keep 16,385 sentence pairs with human comparison and 1,620 were disregarded because of a disagreement in annotators' judgments.

4.2   Sentence Evaluation

We evaluate sentence embeddings in 12 scales grouped into 6 classes for conciseness. Two focus on transformations without an assumed linear scale behind: **basic**: paraphrases should be closer to their seed than any transformation, which significantly changed the meaning of the seed (*different meaning, nonsense, minimal change*), **modality**: paraphrases should be closer to their seed than any transformation, which changes modality of the seed (*possibility, ban*).

The remaining four classes evaluate whether sentence space reflects the ordering implied by the collected comparisons: **time** (how often the mutual ordering of all transformation towards *future* matches the relative distances in the embedding space; similarly but separately for *past*), **style** (*formal sentence, nonstandard sentence, simple sentence*), **generalization**, and **opposite**.

For categories in the first two classes, we compute the accuracy of sentence embeddings, i.e., how often $\text{sim}_C(v_{\text{seed}}, v_P) > \text{sim}_C(v_{\text{seed}}, v_T)$ for every paraphrase P and every transformation T of the particular category and in the examined sentence embeddings $v_\bullet$.

For categories in the latter four classes, the evaluation is based on collected judgments. So if the annotators judge that sentences A, B and C satisfy A < B and B < C, we test how often $\text{sim}_C(v_A, v_B) > \text{sim}_C(v_A, v_C)$ and $\text{sim}_C(v_B, v_C) > \text{sim}_C(v_A, v_C)$. To make use of the options *too similar* and *too dissimilar*, we check whether $\text{sim}_C(v_A, v_B) > \text{sim}_C(v_B, v_C)$ for all sentences A, B, C where the annotations indicate that A and B are too similar to each other and B and C are too dissimilar.

Table 1. Experimental results: geometric relations in sentence embedding spaces

	Basic	Modality	Time	Style	Gener.	Opposite	Avg
SentBERT - mean	0.150	0.251	0.667	0.588	**0.718**	0.685	0.510
SentBERT - CLS	0.172	**0.303**	0.654	0.577	0.690	0.654	0.508
Flair - mean	0.145	0.157	**0.682**	**0.627**	0.695	**0.728**	0.506
mBERT - CLS	**0.262**	0.274	0.616	0.579	0.603	0.640	0.496
mBERT - mean	0.103	0.115	0.674	0.621	0.691	0.727	0.489
LASER	0.255	0.244	0.583	0.533	0.667	0.636	0.486

5   Results

As Table 1 shows, none of the examined sentence embeddings are particularly good in the basic requirement of paraphrases being embedded closer to each other than sentences with a significantly different meaning. The best performing method mBERT-CLS reach the accuracy of 26%. This contrasts with [13], which shows that LASER is particularly good at identifying related sentences in Polish. However, we must emphasize that transformations in the **basic** class were purposefully selected to pose a difficult challenge[4] – only very sophisticated embedding method can achieve high accuracy, which is precisely the purpose of this testing dataset.

As one can expect, the first two tasks turned out too hard for all BOW embeddings that use mean to calculate the final vector. On the other hand, LASER and mBert-CLS perform surprisingly well with more than one-fourth of paraphrases embedded close to their seeds.

The linearity of time, style, level of generality or the level of opposition are reflected considerably better: 63–74% of tested sentence triples satisfy the expectation. Mean-based embeddings (Flair and mBert in particular) achieve the best performance in this evaluation of linear relations.

6   Conclusion

We presented an extension of COSTRA 1.0, a corpus of sentence transformations, providing new transformations and relations in order to examine to what extent embedding spaces reflect linear ordering with regard to certain kinds of sentence relationships.

We find that paraphrases are often embedded too far from each other and many meaning-altering transformations lie in a closer range. This confirms that the selected transformations are not easy to capture since all BOW methods perform very poorly on them. The natural ordering of sentences with respect to

---

[4] *Different meaning, nonsense* and *minimal change* are all very similar in wording to a seed sentence unlike its paraphrases, which must use different words to express similar meaning. For more details see [7].

time, style and level of generalization or opposition is embedded considerably better.

Interestingly, the only directly learned sentence embedding LASER shows on average the worst results from all tested methods. However, the differences between all methods are very small.

Our hope is that Costra 1.1 will help to develop new better sentence embedding for the Czech language. It is freely available at the following link:

http://hdl.handle.net/11234/1-3248

Easy-to-use Czech sentence embeddings quality evaluator is available here:

https://github.com/barancik/costra

References

1. Adi, Y., et al.: Fine-grained analysis of sentence embeddings using auxiliary prediction tasks. CoRR abs/1608.04207 (2016)
2. Akbik, A., Blythe, D., Vollgraf, R.: Contextual string embeddings for sequence labeling. In: COLING (2018)
3. Artetxe, M., Schwenk, H.: Massively multilingual sentence embeddings for zeroshot cross-lingual transfer and beyond. CoRR abs/1812.10464 (2018)
4. Bacon, G., Regier, T.: Probing sentence embeddings for structure-dependent tense. In: EMNLP BlackboxNLP (2018)
5. Bakarov, A.: A survey of word embeddings evaluation methods. CoRR abs/1801.09536 (2018)
6. Barančíková, P., Bojar, O.: In search for linear relations in sentence embedding spaces. In: ITAT SloNLP (2019)
7. Barančíková, P., Bojar, O.: COSTRA 1.0: a dataset of complex sentence transformations. In: LREC (2020)
8. Carletta, J.: Assessing agreement on classification tasks: the kappa statistic. Comput. Linguist. 22(2), 249–254 (1996)
9. Conneau, A., et al.: XNLI: evaluating cross-lingual sentence representations. In: EMNLP (2018)
10. Devlin, J., et al.: BERT: pre-training of deep bidirectional transformers for language understanding. CoRR abs/1810.04805 (2018)
11. Ettinger, A., Elgohary, A., Resnik, P.: Probing for semantic evidence of composition by means of simple classification tasks. In: ACL RepEval (2016)
12. Kiros, R., et al.: Skip-thought vectors. In: NIPS (2015)
13. Krasnowska-Kieraś, K., Wróblewska, A.: Empirical linguistic study of sentence embeddings. In: ACL (2019)
14. Linzen, T., Dupoux, E., Goldberg, Y.: Assessing the ability of LSTMs to learn syntax-sensitive dependencies. In: TACL, vol. 4 (2016)
15. Mikolov, T., Chen, K., Corrado, G.S., Dean, J.: Efficient estimation of word representations in vector space (2013)
16. Mikolov, T., Yih, W.T., Zweig, G.: Linguistic regularities in continuous space word representations. In: NAACL/HLT (2013)
17. Schnabel, T., Labutov, I., Mimno, D., Joachims, T.: Evaluation methods for unsupervised word embeddings. In: EMNLP (2015)

18. Wieting, J., Bansal, M., Gimpel, K., Livescu, K.: Towards universal paraphrastic sentence embeddings. CoRR abs/1511.08198 (2015)
19. Williams, A., Nangia, N., Bowman, S.R.: A broad-coverage challenge corpus for sentence understanding through inference. In: NAACL-HLT (2018)
20. Zhu, X., Li, T., de Melo, G.: Exploring semantic properties of sentence embeddings. In: ACL (2018)
21. Zhu, X., de Melo, G.: Sentence analogies: exploring linguistic relationships and regularities in sentence embeddings (2020)

Next Step in Online Querying and Visualization of Word-Formation Networks

Jonáš Vidra(✉) and Zdeněk Žabokrtský

Faculty of Mathematics and Physics, Institute of Formal and Applied Linguistics,
Charles University, Malostranské náměstí 25, 118 00 Prague 1, Czech Republic
{vidra,zabokrtsky}@ufal.mff.cuni.cz

Abstract. In this paper, we introduce a new and improved version of
DeriSearch, a search engine and visualizer for word-formation networks.

Word-formation networks are datasets that express derivational, compounding and other word-formation relations between words. They are
usually expressed as directed graphs, in which nodes correspond to words
and edges to the relations between them. Some networks also add other
linguistic information, such as morphological segmentation of the words
or identification of the processes expressed by the relations.

Networks for morphologically rich languages with productive derivation or compounding have large connected components, which are difficult to visualize. For example, in the network for Czech, DeriNet 2.0,
connected components over 500 words large contain ⅛ of the vocabulary, including its most common parts. In the network for Latin, Word
Formation Latin, over 10 000 words (⅓ of the vocabulary) are in a single
connected component.

With the recent release of the Universal Derivations collection of word-
formation networks for several languages, there is a need for a searching
and visualization tool that would allow browsing such complex data.

Keywords: Derivational morphology · Word formation · Graph
visualization · Search engine

1 Introduction

A word-formation network is a dataset capturing information about derivational,
compounding, conversional and other processes, through which words can be
created. The networks come in many forms [4], but a typical one we focus on in
this paper is a directed graph structure in which the nodes represent individual
lexemes (generally represented by a lemma, which stands for a set of inflectional
forms) and edges represent the word-formation relations between them.

Both the lexemes and the relations can be further annotated in the dataset.
Lexemes are typically listed with their part of speech and morphological information such as nominal gender or verbal conjugation paradigm, while relations

© Springer Nature Switzerland AG 2020
P. Sojka et al. (Eds.): TSD 2020, LNAI 12284, pp. 144–152, 2020.
https://doi.org/10.1007/978-3-030-58323-1_15

Fig. 1. An excerpt from a word-formational family of the word *vraždit* ("to murder"), as present in DeriNet 2.0 in UDer [5]. It shows morph segmentation (roots delimited by dots), relation labels and compounding. Rendering was made by the presented tool.

can be annotated with the type of the represented process (e.g. derivation, compounding, conversion or clipping) or with the change occurring between the related words (e.g. addition of the *-er* suffix). An example of a graph structure from DeriNet 2.0, a word-formation network for Czech [14], is given in Fig. 1.

A collection of 10 word-formation networks for 10 different languages has been published recently under the name Universal Derivations 0.5 (UDer) [5]. Several resources in the collection contain large and complex graphs that are difficult to browse and visualize without specialized tools. For example, the largest connected component from DeriNet 2.0 contains 56 362 lexemes and over 12% of the vocabulary is found in components over 500 lexemes large. Similarly, the largest component in Word Formation Latin [6] contains 10 514 lexemes.

The aim of this article is to present a search engine that is capable of processing and visualizing the graphs in a user-friendly manner. A demo of the search engine runs at https://quest.ms.mff.cuni.cz/derisearch2/v2/databases/.

2   Related Work

Visualization and searching methods are useful when developing any linguistic resources whose annotations specify structured data, and word-formation networks are no exception. A good visualization tool, which allows its users to gain insights into the structure and find interesting phenomena in both the annotations and the raw data, helps prevent annotation errors and inconsistencies and discover more annotation possibilities. Such tools are in use for a long time in syntactic analysis or in Wordnet creation.

2.1   Comparison with Visualization of Syntactic Trees

Both the syntactic annotation and the word-formation annotation are graph-based in nature. The practical difference is the size of the trees. The number of nodes in syntactic trees corresponds to the number of tokens in the annotated sentence - very closely for dependency trees, but even in theories that have many nonterminal nodes in the structure, the number of nonterminals generally doesn't grow too much. Although sentences can be arbitrarily long, typical ones are usually shorter than a couple dozen tokens. Longer sentences, whether created with artist's intent or as a result of stylistic clumsiness, are atypical. In contrast, languages with rich derivation, such as Russian or Czech, have many derivational families that contain several thousands of lexemes.

For example, many toponyms in Czech have corresponding compound adjectives with north-, east-, south- and west-, such as *jihoamerický* ("South American") or *západolondýnský* ("of west London"), which makes them all members of a single huge connected component through the words *jih* ("the south"), *západ* ("the west") etc. This difference in sizes requires different approaches to visualization and therefore different tools.

2.2   Comparison with Visualization of Wordnets

Wordnet creation is another field similar to word-formation networks, perhaps more so than syntactic analysis. The authors of various wordnets have, too, created tools to support browsing and searching their datasets.

One example is the VisDic/DEBVisDic/DEBGrid family of tools [3]. Here, we can again see differences in requirements - word-formation networks have a bigger focus on the overall structure and connections between the lexemes, while DEBVisDic was created to support dictionary editing and browsing (hence the DEB in the name), which focuses more on the individual dictionary entries. As a result, for a long time, the tool only visually showed the tree of the hypero- and hyponyms, other relations had to be browsed a single node at a time, with hyperlinks pointing to the node's neighbors. A way of showing the structure of the synsets as a graph was added recently [9], but even this visualization only shows neighboring synsets and their member words, not transitive relations to further synsets and members.

2.3   Visualizers of Word-Formation Networks

As noted by creators of the Word Formation Latin resource a few years ago, visualization tools for word-formation networks are still in their infancy [2]. The six searching and visualization tools from five projects, which we list below in alphabetical order, are known to us:

The creators of CroDeriV [10] have a public search engine that allows looking a word up by its morphological composition, for example, by its root, part of speech or prefixes, and an unpublished version that also shows its derivational family as a graph. It doesn't allow searching by lemma.

DeriNet [14] has two different browsers and visualizers. Both can only process and display trees, not more complex graphs with e.g. compounding. DeriNet Viewer is more limited in its searching abilities, only allowing browsing by lemma. It has two modes: Either a display of a complete derivational tree for a given

size, or statistical overviews of tree shapes. DeriSearch allows searching by any
conjunction of regular expressions over lemmas and parts of speech, but doesn't
allow querying other attributes [12]. It is also able to search for structures,
allowing queries like "all nouns ending in -ti derived from verbs". Its visualization
capabilities include several graph layouts optimized for large trees [13].

Another search engine was created for another Czech resource, Derivancze [7].
It allows searching by lemma and shows the immediate derivational neighbors
of the found word, annotated with their logarithmic frequency in a corpus and a
tag specifying the type of relation between the found word and the neighbor. The
neighbors are hyperlinked, allowing the user to explore the whole derivational
family one word at a time by clicking on the links.

A basic search engine is provided by the DerIvaTario project [11]. It allows
querying by part-of-speech and by affix and various affixal properties, but not by
word form or lemma. The output is a textual listing of the matching lexemes with
their properties and base words, and tables of statistics of the word-formational
processes visible in the set of results. Since the base words are not hyperlinked
and derived words are not listed, browsing the dataset as a graph is difficult.

The last search engine known to us was made for the Word Formation Latin
project [6]. The search engine [2] allows lookup by lemma (using a regular expression), part of speech, affix (chosen from a list) and word-formational rule. The
results can be further trimmed down: for example, when looking a word up by
lemma, one can view only derivational roots (words without a base word) or
only derived words, and in affix search, include or exclude words that contain
the affix internally, not as the last word-formational step. Visualization is done
using graphs and the user can choose whether to only show the derivational
family, or compounding relations as well.

The tool we introduce in this paper is a reimplementation of DeriSearch, with
an extended query language and improved visualizations aimed at large graphs.

3   Query Language

DeriSearch uses a query language called DCQL [12]. As the name suggests, it is
based on the Corpus Query Language (CQL) used by Manatee, SketchEngine
and other text corpora query engines and descended from a common root in
the IMS Corpus Workbench [1]. The original DCQL used in previous versions of
DeriSearch (called DCQL-1 for the purposes of this paper) had to be extended to
support querying the kinds of information not found in DeriNet versions up to
1.7, such as compounding, morpheme segmentation or relation labels. In the
following two sections, we first give a tutorial on DCQL-1 and then introduce
our extensions as DCQL-2.

3.1   Original Query Language: DCQL-1

The DCQL-1 query language was designed with accessibility to new users in
mind. You can search for a lexeme by typing its lemma into the search box, no

syntax needed. The result shows you an excerpt of the lexeme's word-formational family, with the lexeme itself highlighted. More complex queries need syntactic constructions, which are expressed in a language similar to CQL. An overview of the syntax and a discussion of its limits are given below.

Individual lexemes are queried using their attributes. In DCQL-1, these are the "lemma", "pos" (the part-of-speech tag) and several resource-specific ones, such as "techlemma" used for storing bits of extra morphological and semantic annotations in the DeriNet network. A bare-word query means exact string matching against the "default attribute" (selectable in the graphical user interface, defaulting to lemma).

To query other attributes, or several of them at once, a square bracket notation familiar from CQL, "[*attribute*="*regex*"]", is used. It searches for all lexemes in which the value of "*attribute*" matches the regular expression "*regex*". Multiple queries in conjunction can be connected with "and". For example, to search for all nouns ending in -er, one would write "[pos="NOUN" and lemma=".*er"]". As a special case, the empty brackets "[]" match any lexeme.

DCQL-1 only allows to specify each attribute at most once and connect the individual properties with logical AND. This makes some queries more awkward to express - e.g. a query for all nouns or adjectives must be expressed as "[pos="NOUN|ADJ"]" instead of the, perhaps more natural, "[pos="NOUN" or pos="ADJ"]" - and other queries inexpressible, such as "all nouns ending in -ater or verbs ending in -at". Approximating this query as "[pos="NOUN|VERB" and lemma=".*ater|.*at"]" would erroneously include e.g. the noun *seat*.

Derivational structure can be queried by assembling a tree-shaped query out of individual lexeme queries using concatenation, similar to how one searches for consecutive words in CQL, and parentheses with commas. Neighboring lexeme queries correspond to base-derivative relations between the lexemes. For example, to search for lexeme B derived from lexeme A, one would write "A B", e.g. "[pos="VERB"] [lemma=".*er"]" ("words ending in -er derived from a verb"). Several derivatives at the same level of the tree are written in parentheses separated by commas, e.g. "[pos="VERB"] ([pos="NOUN"], [pos="NOUN"])" ("a verb with at least two nouns immediately derived from it").

DCQL-1 limits queries to tree-shaped ones, because it was designed for use with DeriNet 0.9, which only contained tree-shaped derivational families. Other networks and newer versions of DeriNet can contain non-tree-shaped subgraphs.

3.2   Extended DCQL Language: DCQL-2

To support the increased variety and complexity found in the UDer collection, we extended the DCQL-1 language in several ways, described below. We refer to the extended language as DCQL-2

We extended the set of queryable attributes of lexemes by all attributes stored in UDer databases, such as nominal gender (for Czech, French, German and Latin), verbal aspect (for Czech) or nominal declension (for Latin). Any attributes present in the resources can be queried by string comparison and regular expressions without requiring specific code support in the search engine.

A second extension is the ability to query relations. The UDer collection has introduced relations as an explicit object in the database, which can carry annotation such as semantic labels or word-formation process type. The query syntax is similar to lexeme queries, but with angle brackets instead of square ones. The relation query must occur between two lexeme queries, like this: "[] <SemanticLabel="Possessive"> []" ("all derived possessives").

A third extension is the ability to query general contiguous graphs instead of just trees. To facilitate this, we introduced *labeled nodes* with references and allowed the user to search for several interlinked trees at once by coindexing the nodes. The user can label an arbitrary node by prepending a user-selected textual label and a colon before the node or relation definition.

Nodes and relations are coindexed if they are labeled by the same string. A node can't be coindexed with a relation and labeling a relation identically as a node is an error. Coindexed nodes or relations only match if they can point to the same lexeme or relation in the search results. For example, the query "a: [] [] a: []" matches all nodes (labeled a) that are in a bi-directional relation with another node (the middle unlabeled one). This currently does not happen in any dataset from UDer, but it can occur when two lexemes are derivationally related, but the direction of derivation is unclear, as with some neoclassical formations [8], and the annotators decide to include both directions of derivation in the dataset. When coindexing nodes with constraints in them, the resulting query must match all of them, as if they were connected by logical "and".

Not all directed structures can be described by a single tree that loops back on itself using labels. For example, querying compounding requires specifying two independent parents that needn't be connected by a cycle. Any general graph can be, however, described as a union of several directed trees. The user can specify such a union by connecting several tree queries with "&", e.g. "[lemma=="week"] weekday:[lemma=="weekday"] & [lemma=="day"] weekday:[]".

A final extension is the ability to query morphological segmentation under the attribute "morfeman". This is done with regular expressions over a string representing the segmentation using vertical bars and colons. Each segment is specified as *morph:morpheme:type*, where type is R for root, P for prefix, S for suffix, I for infix, X for interfix and U for unknown. The segments are separated by vertical bars, with extra bars at the start and end of the whole string. For example, the word *revalidation* could be expressed as "|re:re:P|valid:valid:R|at:ate:S|ion:ion:S|".

We've also made a single backwards-incompatible change: The meaning of regular expressions was changed to match the whole string, instead of a substring. This means that e.g. the expression ""er$"" from DCQL-1 should be written as "".*er"" in DCQL-2. The change makes the search engine behavior identical to the behavior of popular corpus managers using CQL. All examples in this paper are given in the new format. Otherwise, the regular expressions of DCQL-2 conform to the specification of Java's util.regex.Pattern.

4   Visualization of Results

Since DCQL-1 worked with tree-shaped derivational data only, the search engine could use algorithms for display of trees that produce tidy, readable layout. It allowed the user to choose from four different ways of displaying the trees [13]. DCQL-2 can be used to search arbitrary graphs, limiting our choice of visualization methods. Therefore, we decided to use a force-directed 2D physics simulation, in which word-formation links correspond to springs of preset length and stiffness and lexemes repel one another with an electromagnetic force.

The challenge with large connected components found in recent versions of several word-formation networks is that we want to allow users to explore the whole component at their leisure, but at the same time focus at the results of their query. With huge graphs, this means showing only the part of the graph with the result, but allowing the user to view other parts on demand easily.

When there are multiple results in a single connected component, which can easily happen with general queries such as "all adjectives derived from words ending in -at", we have several options:

1. unroll enough of the cluster to show them all at the same time,
2. show a limited selection, possibly indicating that there are more results that are hidden and giving the user an option to view them on demand,
3. display multiple independent views of the same cluster, each focusing on a different part.

Each of these options has its drawbacks and each can be confusing in some situations. Option 1 leads to too much data being displayed at once, particularly for queries such as "[]" ("all lexemes"). With option 2, it can become unclear how many results there are and how to see them. With very deep clusters, giving the user an option to quickly show enough of the cluster to see multiple results reverts to option 1. Option 3 is overwhelming in another way - for queries such as "[morfeman=".*\|slav:[^:]*:R\|.*"]" ("words with root morph 'slav'") it shows many result panels, all showing the same cluster, just focusing on a different part.

In the current implementation, we chose method 2, with the option to hide or show neighbors of arbitrary lexemes by clicking on them. By default, we show all nodes up to the root of the derivational family of the result and the immediate neighbors of nodes in the result.

The notions of "neighbors" and "root of derivational family" are, however, somewhat complicated here. The result may contain nodes belonging to multiple families, and simply hiding the children of a lexeme on click is not sufficient, nor is transitively showing all the parents by default, because the graphs may contain cycles and in those cases it is unclear what to hide, and the default view may have too many nodes visible. Therefore, we use the following algorithm: We pick one of the nodes of the selected result as its anchor. For results that happen to be trees, this is its root; otherwise the selection is arbitrary. We consider the result to belong to the derivational family given by this anchor, and on click, we show or hide nodes further away from the anchor than the clicked node.

By doing all operations relative to a single node, they become well defined, because the graph can be converted to a tree via breadth-first search from this node.

5   Conclusions

We presented a new search engine and visualizer for word-formation networks. It extends the query language of an existing tool to support querying non-tree structures and attributes found in many existing resources, and adds an improved visualization that allows for browsing even very large graphs.

Acknowledgments. This work was supported by the Grant No. GA19-14534S of the Czech Science Foundation, by the Charles University Grant Agency project No. 1176219 and by the SVV project No. 260 575. It uses language resources developed, stored, and distributed by the LINDAT/CLARIAH CZ project (LM2015071, LM2018101).

References

1. Christ, O., Schulze, B.M., Hofmann, A., König, E.: The IMS Corpus Workbench: Corpus Query Processor (CQP) User's Manual. University of Stuttgart, Germany (1999)
2. Culy, C., Litta, E., Passarotti, M.: Visual exploration of Latin derivational morphology. In: Proceedings of FLAIRS 2017, pp. 601–606 (2017)
3. Horák, A., Pala, K., Rambousek, A., Povolný, M.: DEBVisDic - first version of new client-server Wordnet browsing and editing tool. In: Proceedings of the Third International WordNet Conference (GWC 2006), pp. 325–328 (2005)
4. Kyjánek, L.: Morphological resources of derivational word-formation relations. Technical report ÚFAL TR-2018-61, ÚFAL MFF UK, Prague, Czechia (2018)
5. Kyjánek, L., Žabokrtský, Z., Ševčíková, M., Vidra, J.: Universal derivations kickoff: a collection of harmonized derivational resources for eleven languages. In: Proceedings of DeriMo 2019, Prague, Czechia, pp. 101–110 (2019)
6. Litta, E., Passarotti, M., Culy, C.: Formatio formosa est. Building a word formation lexicon for Latin. In: Proceedings of CLiC-IT 2016, pp. 185–189 (2016)
7. Pala, K., Šmerk, P.: Derivancze — derivational analyzer of Czech. In: Král, P., Matoušek, V. (eds.) TSD 2015. LNCS (LNAI), vol. 9302, pp. 515–523. Springer, Cham (2015). https://doi.org/10.1007/978-3-319-24033-6_58
8. Panocová, R.: Internationalisms with the suffix -ácia and their adaptation in Slovak. In: Proceedings of DeriMo 2017, Milano, Italy, pp. 129–139 (2017)
9. Rambousek, A., Horák, A., Klement, D., Kletečka, J.: New features in DEBVisDic for WordNet visualization and user feedback. In: Proceedings of RASLAN 2017 (2017)
10. Šojat, K., Srebačić, M., Tadić, M., Pavelić, T.: CroDeriV: a new resource for processing Croatian morphology. In: Proceedings of LREC 2014 (2014)
11. Talamo, L., Celata, C., Bertinetto, P.M.: DerIvaTario: an annotated lexicon of Italian derivatives. Word Struct. **9**(1), 72–102 (2016)
12. Vidra, J.: Implementation of a search engine for DeriNet. In: Proceedings of ITAT 2015, Prague, Czechia, pp. 100–106 (2015)

13. Vidra, J., Žabokrtský, Z.: Online software components for accessing derivational networks. In: Proceedings of DeriMo 2017, Milano, Italy, pp. 129–139 (2017)
14. Vidra, J., Žabokrtský, Z., Ševčíková, M., Kyjánek, L.: Derinet 2.0: towards an all-in-one word-formation resource. In: Proceedings of DeriMo 2019, Prague, Czechia (2019)

Evaluating a Multi-sense Definition Generation Model for Multiple Languages

Arman Kabiri[✉] [iD] and Paul Cook

Faculty of Computer Science, University of New Brunswick,
Fredericton, NB E3B 5A3, Canada
{arman.kabiri,paul.cook}@unb.ca

Abstract. Most prior work on definition modelling has not accounted for polysemy, or has done so by considering definition modelling for a target word in a given context. In contrast, in this study, we propose a context-agnostic approach to definition modelling, based on multi-sense word embeddings, that is capable of generating multiple definitions for a target word. In further contrast to most prior work, which has primarily focused on English, we evaluate our proposed approach on fifteen different datasets covering nine languages from several language families. To evaluate our approach we consider several variations of BLEU. Our results demonstrate that our proposed multi-sense model outperforms a single-sense model on all fifteen datasets.

Keywords: Definition modelling · Multi-sense embeddings · Polysemy

1 Introduction

The advent of pre-trained distributed word representations, such as [12], led to improvements in a wide range of natural language processing (NLP) tasks. One limitation of such word embeddings, however, is that they conflate all of a word's senses into a single vector. Subsequent work has considered approaches to learn multi-sense embeddings, in which a word is represented by multiple vectors, each corresponding to a sense [3,10]. More recent work has considered contextualized word embeddings, such as [5], which provide a representation of the meaning of a word in a given context.

Definition modelling, recently introduced by [16], is a specific type of language modelling which aims to generate dictionary-style definitions for a given word. Definition modelling can provide a transparent interpretation of the information represented in word embeddings, and has the potential to be applied to generate definitions for newly-emerged words that are not yet recorded in dictionaries.

The approach to definition modelling of [16] is based on a recurrent neural network (RNN) language model, which is conditioned on a word embedding for the target word to be defined, specifically pre-trained word2vec [12] embeddings. As such, this model does not account for polysemy. To address this limitation,

© Springer Nature Switzerland AG 2020
P. Sojka et al. (Eds.): TSD 2020, LNAI 12284, pp. 153–161, 2020.
https://doi.org/10.1007/978-3-030-58323-1_16

a number of studies have proposed context-aware definition generation models [4,7,9,11,15]. In all of these approaches, the models generate a definition corresponding to the usage of a given target word in a given context.

In contrast, in this paper we propose a context-agnostic multi-sense definition generation model. Given a target word type (i.e., without its usage in a specific context) the proposed model generates multiple definitions corresponding to different senses of that word. Our proposed model is an extension of [16] that incorporates pre-trained multi-sense embeddings. As such, the definitions that are generated are based on the senses learned by the embedding model on a background corpus, and reflect the usage of words in that corpus. Under this setup—i.e., generating multiple definitions for each word corresponding to senses present in a corpus—the proposed definition generation model has the potential to generate partial dictionary entries. In order to train the proposed model, pre-trained sense vectors for a word need to be matched to reference definitions for that word. We consider two approaches to this matching based on cosine similarity between sense vectors and reference definitions.

Recently, [20] propose a multi-sense model for generating definitions for the various senses of a target word. This model utilizes word embeddings and coarse-grained atom embeddings to represent senses [1], in which atoms are shared across words. In contrast, we only rely on fine-grained multi-sense embeddings. To match sense vectors to reference definitions during training, [20] propose a neural approach, and also consider a heuristic-based approach that incorporates cosine similarity between senses and definitions. Our proposed approach to this matching is similar to their heuristic-based approach, although we explore two variations of this method. Furthermore, [20] only consider English for evaluation, whereas we consider fifteen datasets covering nine languages.

Following [20] we evaluate our proposed model using variations of BLEU [17]. We evaluate our model on fifteen datasets covering nine languages from several families. Our experimental results show that, for every language and dataset considered, our proposed approach outperforms the benchmark approach of [16] which does not model polysemy.

2   Proposed Model

Here we briefly describe the model of [16], referred to as the base model, and then present our proposed multi-sense model which builds on the base model.

The base model is an RNN-based language model which, given a target word to be defined (w^*), predicts the target word's definition ($D = [w_1, \ldots, w_T]$). The probability of the tth word of the definition sequence, w_t, is calculated based on the previous words in the definition as well as the word being defined, as shown in Eq. 1.

$$P(D|w^*) = \prod_{t=1}^{T} p(w_t|w_1, \ldots, w_t - 1, w^*) \tag{1}$$

The probability distribution is estimated by a softmax function. The model further incorporates a character-level CNN to capture knowledge of affixes. A full explanation of this model is in [16].

In the base model, the target word being defined (w^*) is represented by its word2vec word embedding. This reliance on single-sense embeddings limits the model's ability to generate definitions for different senses of polysemous target words. To address this limitation, we propose to extend the base model by incorporating multi-sense embeddings, in which each word is represented by multiple vectors which correspond to different meanings or senses for that word. Specifically, we replace w^* in Eq. 1 by a sense of the target word, represented as a sense vector.

Most prior work on definition modelling has considered polysemy through context-aware approaches [4,7,9,11,15] that require an example of the target word in context for definition generation. In contrast, the model we propose is context agnostic (as is the base model) and is able to generate multiple definitions for a target word without requiring that specific contexts of the target word be given in order to generate definitions.

The base model is trained on instances consisting of pairs of a word—represented by a word2vec embedding—and one of its definitions, i.e., from a dictionary. Our proposed approach is trained on pairs of a word sense—represented as a sense vector—and one of the corresponding word's definitions. In order to train our proposed approach, we require a way to associate pre-trained sense vectors with dictionary definitions, where the number of sense vectors and definitions is often different for a given word.

We consider two approaches to associating sense vectors with definitions: definition-to-sense and sense-to-definition. For both approaches we require a representation of definitions. We represent a definition as the average of its word embeddings, after removing stopwords. For each word in the training data, we then calculate the pairwise cosine similarity between its sense vectors and definitions. For definition-to-sense, each definition is associated with the most similar sense vector for the corresponding word. For sense-to-definition, on the other hand, each sense is associated with the most similar definition. For both approaches, the selected sense–definition pairs form the training data.

These approaches to pairing senses and definitions are only used to create training instances. At test time, to generate definitions for a given target word, each sense vector for the target word is fed to the definition generation model, which then generates one definition for each of the target word's sense vectors.

3 Materials and Methods

In this section, we describe the datasets, word and sense embeddings, and evaluation metrics used in our experiments.

Table 1. The number of words, and proportion of polysemous words (PPW) in each dataset.

Language	Omega		Wiktionary		WordNet	
	#Words	PPW	#Words	PPW	#Words	PPW
Dutch	13093	0.18	–	–	–	–
English	17000	0.20	17000	0.27	20000	0.18
French	15869	0.17	20000	0.26	–	–
German	13338	0.12	16000	0.26	–	–
Greek	–	–	–	–	11517	0.26
Italian	18351	0.21	–	–	16290	0.22
Japanese	–	–	–	–	20000	0.30
Russian	–	–	15000	0.17	–	–
Spanish	17000	0.19	–	–	18934	0.12

3.1 Datasets

In this work, we conduct a multi-lingual study of definition modelling. We extract monolingual dictionaries for nine languages covering several language families, from three different sources: Wiktionary,[1] OmegaWiki,[2] and WordNet [13].

Wiktionary is a free collaboratively-constructed online dictionary for many languages. The structure of Wiktionary pages is not consistent across languages. Extracting word–definitions pairs from Wiktionary pages for a given language requires a carefully-designed language-specific parser, which moreover requires some knowledge of that language to build. We therefore use publicly-available Wiktionary parsers. We use WikiParsec for English, French, and German,[3] and Wikokit for Russian,[4] to extract word–definition pairs for these languages.

OmegaWiki, like Wiktionary, is a free collaborative multilingual dictionary. In OmegaWiki data is stored in a relational database, and so language-specific parsers are not required to automatically extract words and definitions. We extract the word–definition pairs from OmegaWiki for English, Dutch, French, German, Italian, and Spanish—the six languages with the largest vocabulary size in OmegaWiki—using the BabelNet Java API [14].

Finally, we consider WordNets. We only use WordNets for which the words and definitions are in the same language. We again use the BabelNet Java API to extract the word–definition entries from English [13], Italian [2], and Spanish [6] WordNets. We separately extract word–definition pairs from Greek [19] and Japanese [8] WordNets.

Properties of the extracted datasets are shown in Table 1. Each dataset is partitioned into train (80%), dev (10%), and test (10%) sets. We ensure that,

---

[1] https://en.wiktionary.org.
[2] http://www.omegawiki.org.
[3] https://github.com/LuminosoInsight/wikiparsec.
[4] https://github.com/componavt/wikokit.

for each word in each dataset, all of its definitions are included in only one of the train, dev, or test sets, so that models are only evaluated on words that were not seen during training.

3.2 Word and Sense Embeddings

Following [16], we use word2vec embeddings in the singe-sense definition generation model (i.e., the base model). For the proposed multi-sense models, we utilize AdaGram embeddings [3]. AdaGram is a non-parametric Bayesian extension of Skip-gram which learns a variable number of sense vectors for each word, unlike many multi-sense embedding models which learn a fixed number of senses for every word. Note that although here we use AdaGram, any multi-sense embedding method could potentially be used.[5]

For each language, word2vec and AdaGram embeddings are trained on the most recent Wikipedia dumps as of January 2020.[6] We extract plain text from these dumps, and then pre-process and tokenize the corpora using tools from AdaGram,[7] modified for multilingual support, except in the case of Japanese where we use the Mecab tokenizer.[8] The resulting corpora range in size from roughly 86 million tokens for Greek to 3.7 billion tokens for English. The same pre-processing and tokenization is also applied to the datasets of words and definitions extracted from dictionaries.

We train word2vec embeddings using Gensim [18] with its default parameters. We also use the default parameter settings for AdaGram. To obtain representations for words, as opposed to senses, from AdaGram sense embeddings, as required to form representations for definitions (Sect. 2), we take the most frequent sense vector of each word (as indicated by Adagram) as the representation of the word itself.

3.3 Evaluation Metrics

BLEU [17] has been widely used for evaluation in prior work on definition modelling [9,15,16]. BLEU is a precision-based metric that measures the overlap of a generated sequence (here a definition) with respect to one or more references. For multi-sense models, we calculate BLEU as the average BLEU score over each generated definition.

While BLEU is appropriate for evaluation of single-sense definition generation models, it does not capture the ability of a model to produce multiple definitions corresponding to different senses of a polysemous word. We therefore also consider a recall-based variation of BLEU, known as rBLEU, in which the generated and reference definitions are swapped [20], i.e., the overlap of a

---

[5] In preliminary experiments with MUSE embeddings [10] we found MUSE to perform poorly compared to AdaGram, and so only report results for AdaGram here.

[6] https://dumps.wikimedia.org.

[7] https://github.com/sbos/AdaGram.jl/blob/master/utils/tokenize.sh.

[8] https://github.com/jordwest/mecab-docs-en.

reference definition is measured with respect to the generated definition(s). For each target word, we calculate rBLEU as the average rBLEU score for each of its reference definitions (for both single and multi-sense models).

In addition to precision-based BLEU, and recall-based rBLEU, we report the harmonic mean of BLEU and rBLEU, referred to as fBLEU.

Table 2. BLEU, rBLEU, and fBLEU for the single-sense definition generation model (base) and the proposed multi-sense models using sense-to-definition (S2D) and definition-to-sense (D2S) for each dataset. The best result for each evaluation metric and dataset is shown in boldface.

Lang.	Model	OmegaWiki			Wiktionary			WordNet		
		BLEU	rBLEU	fBLEU	BLEU	rBLEU	fBLEU	BLEU	rBLEU	fBLEU
DE	Base	12.12	11.55	11.83	11.35	08.80	09.91	–	–	–
	S2D	12.43	16.26	14.09	**15.00**	15.82	**15.40**	–	–	–
	D2S	**12.44**	**16.83**	**14.31**	14.07	**16.54**	15.21	–	–	–
EL	Base	–	–	–	–	–	–	**13.21**	12.06	12.61
	S2D	–	–	–	–	–	–	12.44	12.85	12.64
	D2S	–	–	–	–	–	–	13.08	**13.63**	**13.35**
EN	Base	14.74	14.32	14.53	20.21	16.88	18.40	13.78	12.77	13.26
	S2D	14.23	16.02	15.07	18.88	16.99	17.89	12.85	13.09	12.97
	D2S	**15.22**	**17.80**	**16.41**	**21.49**	**19.78**	**20.60**	**13.84**	**14.84**	**14.32**
ES	Base	**17.68**	17.70	17.69	–	–	–	**26.46**	24.69	25.54
	S2D	16.52	19.00	17.67	–	–	–	25.80	**28.14**	**26.92**
	D2S	17.54	**20.28**	**18.81**	–	–	–	25.68	27.97	26.78
FR	Base	**12.58**	12.66	12.62	63.48	59.87	61.62	–	–	–
	S2D	11.70	14.26	12.85	63.56	60.00	61.73	–	–	–
	D2S	11.94	**14.82**	**13.23**	**64.12**	**60.41**	**62.21**	–	–	–
IT	Base	**12.29**	11.93	12.11	–	–	–	21.33	20.65	20.98
	S2D	11.43	13.61	12.43	–	–	–	20.35	23.67	21.88
	D2S	11.74	**13.95**	**12.75**	–	–	–	**21.96**	**25.10**	**23.43**
JA	Base	–	–	–	–	–	–	10.13	08.50	09.24
	S2D	–	–	–	–	–	–	**11.53**	**11.96**	**11.74**
	D2S	–	–	–	–	–	–	09.42	09.37	09.39
NL	Base	14.37	14.04	14.20	–	–	–	–	–	–
	S2D	13.49	15.88	14.59	–	–	–	–	–	–
	D2S	**14.46**	**17.07**	**15.66**	–	–	–	–	–	–
RU	Base	–	–	–	47.04	46.04	46.53	–	–	–
	S2D	–	–	–	46.24	46.69	46.46	–	–	–
	D2S	–	–	–	**47.52**	**48.09**	**47.80**	–	–	–

4   Results

In this section, we present experimental results comparing the proposed multi-sense definition generation models against the single-sense base model [16]. All models are trained using parameter settings from [16], i.e., a two-layer LSTM as the RNN component with 300 units in each level; a character-level CNN with kernels of length 2–6 and size $\{10, 30, 40, 40, 40\}$ with a stride of 1; and Adam optimization with a learning rate of 0.001.

To generate definitions at test time, for each word and sense for the single-sense and multi-sense models, respectively, we sample tokens at each time step from the predicted probability distribution with a temperature of 0.1. We compute BLEU, rBLEU, and fBLEU for each word, and then the average of these measures over all words in a dataset. We repeat this process 10 times, and report the average scores over these 10 runs.

Results are shown in Table 2. Focusing on fBLEU, for every dataset, the best results are obtained using a multi-sense model—i.e., sense-to-definition (S2D), or definition-to-sense (D2S). Moreover, for every dataset, D2S improves over the base model. These results show that definition modelling can be improved by accounting for polysemy through the incorporation of multi-sense embeddings.

To qualitatively compare the base model and the proposed model, we consider the definitions generated for the word *state*. The following three definitions are generated for this word by the base model: (1) *a state of a government*, (2) *to make a certain or permanent power*, and (3) *to make a certain or administrative power*. In contrast, the proposed multi-sense model using D2S generates the following three definitions, which appear to capture a wider range of the usages of the word *state*: (1) *a place of government*, (2) *a particular region of a country*, and (3) *a particular place of time*.

Comparing S2D and D2S in terms of fBLEU, we observe that D2S often performs better. The number of sense vectors learned by Adagram for a given word is on average higher than the number of reference definitions available for that word, for every dataset. We hypothesize that the poor performance of S2D relative to D2S could therefore be due to sense vectors being associated with inappropriate definitions.

rBLEU is a recall-based evaluation metric that indicates the extent to which the reference definitions are covered by the generated definitions. A multi-sense definition generation model—which produces multiple definitions for a target word—is therefore particularly advantaged compared to a single-sense model—such as the base model—which produces only one, with respect to this metric. Indeed, we see that for every dataset, both S2D and D2S, outperform the base model in terms of rBLEU. BLEU, on the other hand, is a precision-based metric that indicates whether a generated definition contains material present in the reference definitions. The improvements of the multi-sense models over the base model with respect to rBLEU do not substantially impact BLEU—as observed by the overall higher fBLEU obtained by the multi-sense models. Overall, these results indicate that a multi-sense model is able to generate definitions that better reflect the various senses of polysemous words than a single-sense model, without substantially impacting the quality of the individual generated definitions.

5   Conclusions

Definition modelling is a recently-introduced language modelling task in which the aim is to generate dictionary-style definitions for a given word. In this paper, we proposed a multi-sense context-agnostic definition generation model which employed multi-sense embeddings to generate multiple senses for polysemous words. In contrast to most prior work on definition modelling which focuses on English, we conducted a multi-lingual study including nine languages from several language families. Our experimental results demonstrate that our proposed multi-sense model outperforms a single-sense baseline model. Code and datasets for these experiments is available.[9] In future work, we intend to consider incorporating alternative approaches to learning multi-sense embeddings into our model, as well as alternative approaches to associating sense vectors to definitions for constructing training instances.

References

1. Arora, S., Li, Y., Liang, Y., Ma, T., Risteski, A.: Linear algebraic structure of word senses, with applications to polysemy. TACL **6**, 483–495 (2018)
2. Artale, A., Magnini, B., Strapparava, C.: Wordnet for Italian and its use for lexical discrimination. In: Lenzerini, M. (ed.) AI*IA 97: Advances in Artificial Intelligence, pp. 346–356. Springer, Berlin, Heidelberg (1997)
3. Bartunov, S., Kondrashkin, D., Osokin, A., Vetrov, D.: Breaking sticks and ambiguities with adaptive skip-gram. In: Proceedings of AISTATS 2016. pp. 130–138. Cadiz, Spain (2016)
4. Chang, T.Y., Chen, Y.N.: What does this word mean? Explaining contextualized embeddings with natural language definition. In: Proceedings EMNLP-IJCNLP 2019. pp. 6064–6070. Hong Kong, China (2019)
5. Devlin, J., Chang, M.W., Lee, K., Toutanova, K.: BERT: Pre-training of deep bidirectional transformers for language understanding. In: Proceedings of NAACL 2019. pp. 4171–4186. Minneapolis, Minnesota (2019)
6. Fernández-Montraveta, A., Vázquez, G., Fellbaum, C.: The Spanish version of WordNet 3.0. In: Text Resources and Lexical Knowledge. Selected Papers from KONENS 2008. pp. 175–182. Mouton de Gruyter (2008)
7. Gadetsky, A., Yakubovskiy, I., Vetrov, D.: Conditional generators of words definitions. In: Proceedings of ACL 2018. pp. 266–271. Melbourne, Australia (2018)
8. Isahara, H., Bond, F., Uchimoto, K., Utiyama, M., Kanzaki, K.: Development of the Japanese WordNet. In: Proceedings of LREC 2008. Marrakech, Morocco (2008)
9. Ishiwatari, S., Hayashi, H., Yoshinaga, N., Neubig, G., Sato, S., Toyoda, M., Kitsuregawa, M.: Learning to describe unknown phrases with local and global contexts. In: Proceedings of NAACL 2019. pp. 3467–3476. Minneapolis, Minnesota (2019)

---

[9] https://github.com/ArmanKabiri/Multi-sense-Multi-lingual-Definition-Modeling.

10. Lee, G.H., Chen, Y.N.: MUSE: modularizing unsupervised sense embeddings. In: Proceedings EMNLP 2017. pp. 327–337. Copenhagen, Denmark (2017)
11. Mickus, T., Paperno, D., Constant, M.: Mark my word: A sequence-to-sequence approach to definition modeling. In: Proceedings of the First NLPL Workshop on Deep Learning for Natural Language Processing. pp. 1–11. Turku, Finland (2019)
12. Mikolov, T., Sutskever, I., Chen, K., Corrado, G.S., Dean, J.: Distributed representations of words and phrases and their compositionality. Advances in Neural Information Processing Systems **26**, 3111–3119 (2013)
13. Miller, G.A.: WordNet: An electronic lexical database. MIT press (1998)
14. Navigli, R., Ponzetto, S.P.: Babelnet: The automatic construction, evaluation and application of a wide-coverage multilingual semantic network. Artificial Intelligence **193**, 217–250 (2012)
15. Ni, K., Wang, W.Y.: Learning to explain non-standard English words and phrases. In: Proceedings of IJCNLP 2017. pp. 413–417. Taipei, Taiwan (2017)
16. Noraset, T., Liang, C., Birnbaum, L., Downey, D.: Definition modeling: Learning to define word embeddings in natural language. AAAI **2017**, 3259–3266 (2017)
17. Papineni, K., Roukos, S., Ward, T., Zhu, W.J.: Bleu: a method for automatic evaluation of machine translation. In: Proceedings of ACL 2002. pp. 311–318. Philadelphia, Pennsylvania, USA (2002)
18. Řehůřek, R., Sojka, P.: Software Framework for Topic Modelling with Large Corpora. In: Proceedings of the LREC 2010 Workshop on New Challenges for NLP Frameworks. pp. 45–50. ELRA, Valletta, Malta (May 2010), https://is.muni.cz/publication/884893/en
19. Stamou, S., Nenadic, G., Christodoulakis, D.: Exploring balkanet shared ontology for multilingual conceptual indexing. In: Proceedings of LREC 2004. Lisbon, Portugal (2004)
20. Zhu, R., Noraset, T., Liu, A., Jiang, W., Downey, D.: Multi-sense definition modeling using word sense decompositions. arXiv preprint arXiv:1909.09483 (2019)

Combining Cross-lingual and Cross-task Supervision for Zero-Shot Learning

Matúš Pikuliak[⊠] and Marián Šimko

Slovak University of Technology in Bratislava, Bratislava, Slovakia
{matus.pikuliak,marian.simko}@stuba.sk

Abstract. In this work we combine cross-lingual and cross-task supervision for zero-shot learning. Our main contribution is that we discovered that coupling models, i.e. models that share neither a task nor a language with the zero-shot target model, can improve the results significantly. Coupling models serve as a regularization for the other auxiliary models that provide direct cross-lingual and cross-task supervision. We conducted a series of experiments with four Indo-European languages and four tasks (dependency parsing, language modeling, named entity recognition and part-of-speech tagging) in various settings. We were able to achieve 32% error reduction compared to using cross-lingual supervision only.

Keywords: Transfer learning · Cross-lingual learning · Parameter sharing · Zero-shot learning

1 Introduction

Despite the recent advances in neural methods for NLP, we can not realistically train deep models for many low resource languages, mainly because we lack the annotated data [20]. This inspired researchers to use transfer learning [16] to bootstrap the learning from auxiliary sources. We can use either *cross-lingual supervision*, with data from other languages annotated for the same task, or we can use *cross-task supervision*, with data in the same language, but annotated for other tasks. However, various forms of supervision are currently only rarely combined. We believe that this is unfortunate, since various combinations might complement each others and improve the results even further.

In this work, we combine these two approaches for *zero-shot learning*, i.e. for a situation when we do not have *any* annotated data for the target model and we need to rely only on the transfer supervision from auxiliary sources. As confirmed previously [13], a combination of cross-lingual and cross-task supervision is quite viable. However, unlike previous works, we supervise the zero-shot target model with a full grid of models, as depicted in Fig. 1.

This work was partially supported by the Scientific Grant Agency of the Slovak Republic, grants No. VG 1/0725/19 and VG 1/0667/18 and by the Slovak Research and Development Agency under the contracts No. APVV-15-0508, APVV-17-0267 and APVV SK-IL-RD-18-0004.

© Springer Nature Switzerland AG 2020
P. Sojka et al. (Eds.): TSD 2020, LNAI 12284, pp. 162–170, 2020.
https://doi.org/10.1007/978-3-030-58323-1_17

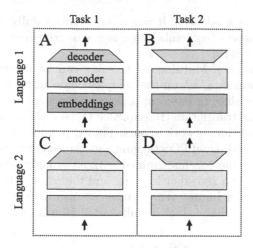

Fig. 1. A grid of models. Each model solves a specific task in a specific language. If model A is our target model, we can use cross-task supervision from model B and/or cross-lingual supervision from model C. Model D does not share neither a task nor a language with A. Instead it serves as a regularization connecting models B and C. We call models like D *coupling models*. Color coded is the parameter sharing strategy described in Sect. 3 - layers with the same color have identical parameters.

We can provide each model with both cross-lingual and cross-task supervision. On top of that, we also have models that share neither a task nor a language with the zero-shot target. We found out that these "unrelated" models significantly improve the performance in zero-shot setting. We hypothesize, that these models – we call them the *coupling models* – serve mainly as a regularization for the other auxiliary models that provide direct cross-lingual or cross-task supervision. Coupling models enable a communication between the other models and help them find a common ground that can be then exploited by the zero-shot target model.

This work is a step towards understanding how to use cross-lingual and cross-task supervision at the same time. The main contribution of our work is that we are to the best of our knowledge the first to describe the regularization power of the *coupling models* and show that they improve performance for zero-shot learning. We evaluate this claim with a full grid of 16 models (4 tasks and 4 languages). We contrast these results with a low resource scenario, where only a limited amount of training data is available for the target model. We also release our code and data, that can be used as a benchmark for future research[1].

2   Related Work

Parameter Sharing. Parameter sharing is a technique for multitask learning that is based on an idea of having the same parameter values (and thus the same

---

[1] https://github.com/matus-pikuliak/crosslingual-parameter-sharing.

behavior) for different models [4]. It was recently successfully used in deep NLP. Most often, whole layers (e.g. embedding layers or recurrent layers) are shared across the models [5, 8, 19].

Multilingual Learning. Multilingual learning can be perceived as a specific type of multitask learning, where the samples come from different languages. Recently, parameter sharing based approaches were used to solve dependency parsing [14], machine translation [1], sequence tagging [21] as well as other NLP tasks. [13] is the most similar work to ours. They explore various parameter sharing strategies for cross-lingual POS tagging and named entity recognition (NER) and are able to beat the baseline trained without transfer learning. Compared to this work we focus on zero-shot learning and the concept of coupling models, which proved to further improve the results. We also work with more tasks and languages at the same time using the full grid of 16 models.

3   Transfer Learning Model

Here we propose a neural model that will be used to test various forms of transfer learning. We need a model that is able to solve word-level tasks and that can use similar encoder architecture for all the tasks, i.e. dependency parsing, language modeling, NER and POS tagging. Based on these requirements we propose an LSTM-based model with following parts:

1. *Word embeddings.* We use multilingual word embeddings [17] as word representations.
2. *Bi-directional LSTM encoder.* We use an LSTM encoder [9] to get a contextualized representation for each word. This part contains the main bulk of trainable parameters.
3. *Task-specific decoders.* We designed a task-specific decoder for each task. We use *conditional random fields* [12] based decoders for POS tagging and NER. Parsing is done via graph-based parser [22]. For language modeling we predict the word from the previous states of both forward and backward pass of the encoder, i.e. we do a leave-one-out language modeling.

To implement parameter sharing, we create a model for each task-language pair, e.g. Spanish NER has its own model. One of the models is then designed to be the *target model*. Our goal is to get the best possible performance for this model. During training we use supervision from other *auxiliary* models via parameter sharing. For each learning step we sample a model from all the models in the grid, we update its parameters with one training batch and then we propagate the updated parameters to all the other models which are bound to this model. Each epoch consists of a fixed number of these steps.

Word embeddings are naturally shared across models with the same language and they are fixed during the training, i.e. their parameters are not changing. Encoder parameters are shared across all the models. This is where most of the transfer learning happens. Finally, decoder parameters are shared across models with the same task. With this setup, we can transfer the parameters to each layer of the target model from some auxiliary model(s). This schema is depicted in Fig. 1 with color-coded blocks representing the layers of the models. Layers with the same color effectively have the same parameters.

4 Experiments

We have done a series of experiments with various forms of supervision. Our goal is to find out how well do the coupling models work compared to and combined with the other forms. We evaluate their performance in zero-shot and low resource setting on four tasks and four languages.

4.1 Data

We have a dataset for each task in each language (Czech, English, German and Spanish). Table 1 shows the size of the training sets.

Table 1. Number of sentences in training datasets.

	Czech	German	English	Spanish
DP & POS	67.9k	13.8k	12.0k	14.0k
NER	7.1k	24.8k	38.4k	6.9k
LM	6.2M	7.3M	7.4M	6.3M

Dependency Parsing and Part-of-speech Tagging. We use *Universal Dependencies* [15] dataset for these two tasks. Data from all languages are annotated with universal tagging schemata for both tasks. POS tagset contains 17 word tags, tagset for dependency parsing contains 37 syntactic relation tags.

Named Entity Recognition. We combined several datasets: *Groningen Meaning Bank* [3] for English, *GermEval 2014* [2] for German, *CoNLL 2002* [18] for Spanish and *Czech Named Entity Corpus* [11] for Czech. We unified the tagging schemata to the standard IOB schema with four types of named entities: persons, locations, organizations and miscellaneous.

Language Modeling. We use dumps from *Wikipedia* as corpora for language modeling.

Word Embeddings. We use pre-trained multilingual *MUSE* [6] word embeddings that are available online[2].

---

[2] https://github.com/facebookresearch/MUSE.

4.2 Evaluation Measures

We use accuracy for POS tagging, chunk F1 score for NER and LAS (labeled attachment score) for dependency parsing as evaluation metrics. Language modeling was used as an auxiliary task only.

We consider two training settings: (1) 4×4 *setting*, in which case we designate one model to be the target model and the 15 remaining models are auxiliary (three models provide cross-lingual supervision, three models provide cross-task supervision and 9 models are coupling). (2) 2×2 *setting*, where we randomly sampled 20 target models and with random auxiliary task and language. In this case we have one model for each kind of supervision.

We show the performance either for a specific task and setting, e.g. POS_4 is an average POS performance in 4×4 setting. Or we show the overall performance across multiple tasks by calculating the *average error reduction* (AER), which is calculated as $AER = \frac{M-B}{U-B}$, where M is the method being compared to the baseline B and U is the upper bound of the performance. We calculate U as a performance of the model trained on its training data without any form of transfer supervision. AER shows how much error are we able to remove compared to the baseline. We report the performance on a test set during the epoch with the highest validation set performance. Validation set is also used for early stopping.

Tuning hyperparameters for each training run we have done would be too expensive for us. Instead we opted out for fixed hyperparameters tuned beforehand using several models (Czech NER, German POS, English parsing) without any form of auxiliary supervision. All the hyperparameters we use will be published alongside the code.

4.3 Results

We divided the auxiliary models into three categories: models providing cross-lingual supervision (CL), models providing cross-task supervision (CT) and coupling models (Co) as illustrated in Fig. 1. The left part of Table 2 shows the results for zero-shot learning approach, i.e. when we did not use any data for the target model and all we use was auxiliary supervision.

Note, that cross-lingual supervision is used in all zero-shot learning experiments, since we need it to train the decoder parameters. Having only cross-lingual supervision is therefore our baseline in zero-shot learning. Combining cross-lingual and cross-task supervision improves the results, as previously shown in [13]. Adding coupling tasks to the baseline did not help very much, on contrary, the results even deteriorated for 4×4 setting. However, using both cross-task supervision and coupling tasks had an interesting synergic effect. Even though the coupling tasks proved to be ineffective by themselves (CL-Co), when combined with cross-task supervision (CL-CT-Co) the resulting performance improvement is even greater than the performance improvement gained by adding cross-task supervision alone. We were able to remove almost one third of the error rate simply by adding additional auxiliary sources.

Table 2. Performance for transfer learning with various auxiliary models: cross-lingual (CL), cross-task (CT) and coupling models (Co).

	Zero-shot					Low resource				
	DP_4	NER_4	POS_4	AER_4	AER_2	DP_4	NER_4	POS_4	AER_4	AER_2
No transfer	–	–	–	–	–	57.26	53.91	87.35	0.00	0.00
CL	38.75	49.30	69.05	0.00	0.00	64.30	60.16	90.10	29.54	17.32
CT	–	–	–	–	–	65.56	61.91	91.64	41.35	29.28
CL-CT	37.38	53.13	77.34	12.62	7.01	70.78	**64.82**	92.23	**54.29**	37.89
CL-Co	36.70	47.84	68.95	−3.47	0.28	–	–	–	–	–
CL-CT-Co	**46.25**	**56.62**	**84.09**	**32.40**	**18.11**	**71.05**	63.02	**92.51**	53.63	**39.17**

The right side of Table 2 shows the results for low resource target model. In this case, we provided 200 training samples for the target model. The target model is being used during the training, along with all the other models. The baseline in this case is a model trained with these 200 samples and without any auxiliary supervision. We can see that both cross-lingual and cross-task supervision improve the performance, and their combination even more so. We were able to remove more than 50% of the error in 4×4 setting compared to the baseline. However, note that the coupling tasks hardly provide any improvement (from 54.29 to 53.63 AER_4). The performance seems to be on par with the training without them. Compare this to the huge performance improvement that coupling models brought for zero-shot learning (from 12.62 to 32.40 AER_4).

Based on this behavior of coupling tasks supervision, we hypothesize that their role in actually to perform as a sort of regularization between models providing cross-lingual and cross-task supervision. By using coupling tasks we force these two types of models to find a common ground. This common ground can then be exploited during the target model evaluation. Even with little target model data, this external regularization is no longer needed. The target model by itself is able to couple cross-lingual and cross-task models and perhaps even better so, considering that it directly optimizes the evaluation objective.

5   Discussion and Conclusions

The conducted experiments are limited by the tasks and language we have selected. We used high resource language for which we could gather significant datasets for both training and evaluation. This might have posed unrealistic performance expectation [10]. We mainly focus on the basic research of NLP supervision types and their combination. The application of these techniques to truly low resource languages is left to future work. We are working mainly with low-level syntactic tasks here. We believe that it is possible to extend our app-roach to other, more semantics oriented tasks, e.g. natural language inference, question answering, etc. It is also possible that this method could be used in other domains than NLP, where there are multiple tasks being solved for mul-tiple domains, e.g. in computer vision various tasks can be solved on real-life photography data and rendered 3D images. In that case, a grid similar to ours could be constructed.

It is practically impossible to compare our results to the previous state-of-the-art, because we work with unique data requirements. Previous work is mainly focused on either cross-lingual or cross-task supervision. Using the same auxiliary datasets is necessary for the comparability of the results. We believe that it is an important future work to create a standardized benchmark to better compare results combining various forms of supervision. The data we plan to release might be a step towards this goal. As far as supervision techniques go, our cross-lingual supervision baseline used for zero-shot learning is similar to what is currently being used as state-of-the-art methods and our comparison with this baseline should be sufficient to prove the merit of our approach. The only work that combines cross-lingual and cross-task supervision in similar fashion to ours is [13]. We confirm their results and extend their work by using coupling models.

We show in this work that it is possible to efficiently combine various forms of supervision for zero-shot learning. We also show that previously overlooked coupling models provide in many cases a significant performance boost. Discovering their regularizational power is the main contribution of our work.

We plan to extend our work with evaluation on additional text representation techniques. Right now we use multilingual word embeddings, but we believe that our method would still apply even if we used non-aligned monolingual word embeddings or even if we used pre-trained large-scale language models [7]. It would be also interesting to explore how well our method works with various data requirements, e.g. with low-level target languages or target tasks. In the future, it might be possible to construct a large-scale repository of many NLP datasets that can form a supervision grid similar to the 4×4 grid that we used in our experiments. Training a new task in a new language could be relatively easy, even if this grid would be sparse. We believe that constructing such grids and working on methods of training with them is an interesting research direction.

References

1. Arivazhagan, N., et al.: Massively multilingual neural machine translation in the wild: findings and challenges. CoRR abs/1907.05019 (2019)
2. Benikova, D., Biemann, C., Reznicek, M.: NoSta-D named entity annotation for German: guidelines and dataset. In: Proceedings of the Ninth International Conference on Language Resources and Evaluation, LREC 2014, Reykjavik, Iceland, 26–31 May 2014, pp. 2524–2531. ELRA (2014)
3. Bos, J., Basile, V., Evang, K., Venhuizen, N.J., Bjerva, J.: The groningen meaning bank. In: Ide, N., Pustejovsky, J. (eds.) Handbook of Linguistic Annotation, pp. 463–496. Springer, Dordrecht (2017). https://doi.org/10.1007/978-94-024-0881-2_18
4. Caruana, R.: Multitask learning: a knowledge-based source of inductive bias. In: Proceedings of the Tenth International Conference Machine Learning, University of Massachusetts, Amherst, MA, USA, 27–29 June 1993, pp. 41–48 (1993)

5. Collobert, R., Weston, J., Bottou, L., Karlen, M., Kavukcuoglu, K., Kuksa, P.P.: Natural language processing (almost) from scratch. J. Mach. Learn. Res. **12**, 2493–2537 (2011)
6. Conneau, A., Lample, G., Ranzato, M., Denoyer, L., Jégou, H.: Word translation without parallel data. In: 6th International Conference on Learning Representations, Vancouver, Canada (2018)
7. Devlin, J., Petrov, S.: Multilingual bert (2019). https://github.com/google-research/bert/blob/master/multilingual.md. Accessed 14 Mar 2020
8. Hashimoto, K., Xiong, C., Tsuruoka, Y., Socher, R.: A joint many-task model: growing a neural network for multiple NLP tasks. In: Proceedings of the 2017 Conference on Empirical Methods in Natural Language Processing, Copenhagen, Denmark, pp. 1923–1933. ACL, September 2017
9. Hochreiter, S., Schmidhuber, J.: Long short-term memory. Neural Comput. **9**(8), 1735–1780 (1997)
10. Kann, K., Cho, K., Bowman, S.R.: Towards realistic practices in low-resource natural language processing: the development set. In: Proceedings of the 2019 Conference on Empirical Methods in Natural Language Processing and the 9th International Joint Conference on Natural Language Processing (EMNLP-IJCNLP), Hong Kong, China, pp. 3340–3347. ACL, November 2019
11. Kravalova, J., Zabokrtsky, Z.: Czech named entity corpus and SVM-based recognizer. In: Proceedings of the 2009 Named Entities Workshop: Shared Task on Transliteration (NEWS 2009), pp. 194–201. ACL (2009)
12. Lample, G., Ballesteros, M., Subramanian, S., Kawakami, K., Dyer, C.: Neural architectures for named entity recognition. In: Proceedings of the 2016 Conference of the North American Chapter of the ACL: Human Language Technologies, San Diego, California, pp. 260–270. ACL, June 2016
13. Lin, Y., Yang, S., Stoyanov, V., Ji, H.: A multi-lingual multi-task architecture for low-resource sequence labeling. In: Proceedings of the 56th Annual Meeting of the ACL, Melbourne, Australia, vol. 1, pp. 799–809. ACL (2018)
14. McDonald, R., Petrov, S., Hall, K.: Multi-source transfer of delexicalized dependency parsers. In: Proceedings of the 2011 Conference on Empirical Methods in Natural Language Processing, Edinburgh, Scotland, UK, pp. 62–72. ACL (2011)
15. Nivre, J., et al.: Universal dependencies v1: a multilingual treebank collection. In: Proceedings of the Tenth International Conference on Language Resources and Evaluation LREC 2016, Portorož, Slovenia. ELRA (2016)
16. Pan, S.J., Yang, Q.: A survey on transfer learning. IEEE Trans. Knowl. Data Eng. **22**(10), 1345–1359 (2010)
17. Ruder, S., Vulic, I., Søgaard, A.: A survey of cross-lingual word embedding models. J. Artif. Intell. Res. **65**, 569–631 (2019)
18. Sang, E.F.T.K.: Introduction to the CoNLL-2002 shared task: language-independent named entity recognition. CoRR cs.CL/0209010 (2002)
19. Søgaard, A., Goldberg, Y.: Deep multi-task learning with low level tasks supervised at lower layers. In: Proceedings of the 54th Annual Meeting of the ACL, Berlin, Germany, vol. 2, pp. 231–235. ACL (2016)
20. Tsvetkov, Y.: Opportunities and Challenges in Working with Low-Resource Languages. Carnegie Mellon University (2017), lecture notes

21. Yang, Z., Salakhutdinov, R., Cohen, W.W.: Transfer learning for sequence tagging with hierarchical recurrent networks. In: 5th International Conference on Learning Representations (2017)
22. Zhang, X., Cheng, J., Lapata, M.: Dependency parsing as head selection. In: Proceedings of the 15th Conference of the EACL, Valencia, Spain, vol. 1, pp. 665–676. ACL (2017)

Reading Comprehension in Czech via Machine Translation and Cross-Lingual Transfer

Kateřina Macková[ID] and Milan Straka[(✉)][ID]

Faculty of Mathematics and Physics, Charles University,
Malostranské náměstí 25, 118 00 Prague 1, Czech Republic
katerina.mackova@mff.cuni.cz, straka@ufal.mff.cuni.cz

Abstract. Reading comprehension is a well studied task, with huge training datasets in English. This work focuses on building reading comprehension systems for Czech, without requiring any manually annotated Czech training data. First of all, we automatically translated SQuAD 1.1 and SQuAD 2.0 datasets to Czech to create training and development data, which we release at http://hdl.handle.net/11234/1-3249. We then trained and evaluated several BERT and XLM-RoBERTa baseline models. However, our main focus lies in cross-lingual transfer models. We report that a XLM-RoBERTa model trained on English data and evaluated on Czech achieves very competitive performance, only approximately 2% points worse than a model trained on the translated Czech data. This result is extremely good, considering the fact that the model has not seen any Czech data during training. The cross-lingual transfer approach is very flexible and provides a reading comprehension in any language, for which we have enough monolingual raw texts.

Keywords: Reading comprehension · Czech · SQuAD · BERT · Cross-lingual transfer

1 Introduction

The goal of a reading comprehension system is to understand given text and return answers in response to questions about the text. In English, there exist many datasets for this task, some of them very large. In this work, we consider the frequently used SQuAD 1.1 dataset [12], an English reading comprehension dataset with around 100,000 question-answer pairs, which is widely used to train many different models with relatively good accuracy. We also utilize SQuAD 2.0 dataset [11], which combines SQuAD 1.1 dataset with 50,000 unanswerable questions linked to already existing paragraphs, making this dataset more challenging for reading comprehension systems.

In this paper, we pursue construction of a reading comprehension system for Czech without having any manually annotated Czech training data, by reusing English models and English datasets. Our contributions are:

© Springer Nature Switzerland AG 2020
P. Sojka et al. (Eds.): TSD 2020, LNAI 12284, pp. 171–179, 2020.
https://doi.org/10.1007/978-3-030-58323-1_18

- We translated both SQuAD 1.1 and SQuAD 2.0 to Czech by state-of-the-art machine translation system [10] and located the answers in the translated text using MorphoDiTa [13] and DeriNet [14], and released the dataset.
- We trained several baseline systems using BERT and XLM-RoBERTa architectures, notably a system trained on the translated Czech data, and a system which first translates a text and a question to English, uses an English model, and translates the answer back to Czech.
- We train and evaluate cross-lingual systems based on BERT and XLM-RoBERTa, which are trained on English and then evaluated directly on Czech. We report that such systems have very strong performance despite not using any Czech data nor Czech translation systems.

2 Related Work

There exist many English datasets for reading comprehension and question answering, the readers are referred for example to [12] for a nice overview.

Currently, the best models for solving reading comprehension are based on BERT architecture [4] (which is a method of unsupervised pre-training of contextualized word embeddings from raw texts), or on some follow-up models like ALBERT [7] or RoBERTa [9].

Most BERT-like models are trained on English, with two notable exceptions. Multilingual BERT (mBERT), released by [4], is a single language model pre-trained on monolingual corpora in 104 languages including Czech; XLM-RoBERTa (XLM-R) [2] is a similar model pre-trained on 100 languages, and is available in both *base* and *large* sizes, while only *base* mBERT is available.

Cross-lingual transfer capability of mBERT has been mentioned in 2019 by many authors, for example by Kondratyuk et al. [6] for morphosyntactic analysis or by Hsu et al. [5] for reading comprehension.

Very similar to our paper is the parallel independent work of Lewis et al. [8], who perform cross-lingual transfer evaluation of reading comprehension models on six non-English languages (neither of them being Czech).

3 Constructing Czech Reading Comprehension Dataset

The SQuAD 1.1 dataset consists of 23,215 paragraphs belonging to 536 articles. Attached to every paragraph is a set of questions, each with several possible answers, resulting in more than 100,000 questions. While the train and the development datasets are public, the test set is hidden. We refer the readers to [12] for details about the dataset construction, types of answers and reasoning required to answer the questions.

The SQuAD 2.0 dataset [11] extends SQuAD 1.1 with more than 50,000 unanswerable questions linked to the existing paragraphs.

3.1 Translating the Data and Locating the Answers

We employed the English-Czech state-of-the-art machine translation system [10] to translate the SQuAD data.[1] Translation of all texts, questions and answers of SQuAD 2.0 took 3 days.

Because the answers are subsequences of the given text in SQuAD, we also needed to locate the translated answers in the text. We considered several alternatives:

- Estimate the alignment of the source and target tokens using attention of the machine translation system, and choose the words aligned to the source answer. Unfortunately, we could not reliably extract alignment from the attention heads of a Transformer-based machine translation system.
- Mark the answer in the text before the translation, using for example quotation marks, similarly to [8]. Such an approach would however result in a dataset with every question linked to a custom text, which would deviate from the SQuAD structure.
- Locate the answer in the given text after the translation, without relying on the assistance from the machine translation system.

We chose the third alternative and located the translated answers in the texts as follows:

1. We lemmatized the translated text and answer using MorphoDiTa [13].
2. We replaced the lemmas by roots of their word-formation relation trees according to the DeriNet 2.0 lexicon [14].
3. Then we found all continuous subsequences of the text with the same DeriNet roots as the answer, but with any word order.
4. Finally, if several occurrences were located, we chose the one with the relative position in the text being the most similar to the relative position of the original answer in the original text.

We believe the proposed algorithm has substantially high precision (after manually verifying many of the located answers), and we also find its recall satisfactory. Notably, in the SQuAD 2.0 training dataset, we have preserved 107,088 questions (which is 82.2% of the English ones) and in the development dataset we kept 10,845 questions, 91.3% of the original dataset. The detailed sizes of the created Czech datasets are presented in Table 1. Note that the ratio of the kept data in SQuAD 1.1 is lower, because unanswerable questions of SQuAD 2.0 are always preserved.

The dataset is available for download at http://hdl.handle.net/11234/1-3249.

3.2 Evaluation Metrics

The SQuAD dataset is usually evaluated using two metrics: **exact match**, which is the accuracy of exactly predicted answers, and **F1-score** computed over individual words of the answers.

---

[1] Available on-line at https://lindat.mff.cuni.cz/services/translation/.

Table 1. Size of the translated Czech variant of SQuAD 1.1 and SQuAD 2.0.

Dataset		English questions	Czech questions	Percentage kept
SQuAD 1.1	Train	87,599	64,164	73.2%
	Test	10,570	8,739	82.7%
SQuAD 2.0	Train	130,319	107,088	82.2%
	Test	11,873	10,845	91.3%

Given that Czech is a morphologically rich language, we performed lemmatization and then replaced lemmas by DeriNet roots (as in Sect. 3.1) prior to evaluation with the official evaluation script.

4   Model Training and Evaluation

Considering that the current best SQuAD models are all BERT based, we also employ a BERT-like architecture. We refer readers to [4] for detailed description of the model and the fine-tuning phase.

Because our main goal is Czech reading comprehension, we consider such BERT models which included Czech in their pre-training, notably Multilingual BERT (mBERT), released by [4], both cased and uncased, and also XLM-RoBERTa (XLM-R) [2], both *base* and *large*. As a reference, we also include English BERT *base*, both cased and uncased.

We finetuned all models using the 🤗 transformers library [15]. For all *base* models, we used two training epochs, learning rate 2e−5 with linear warm-up of 256 steps and batch size 16; for XLM-RoBERTa we increased batch size to 32 and for XLM-RoBERTa *large* we decreased learning rate to 1.5e−5 and increased warm-up to 500.

All our results are presented in Table 2 and also graphically in Fig. 1.

English. For reference, we trained and evaluated all above models on English SQuAD 1.1 and SQuAD 2.0. The results are consistent with the published results. It is worth noting that the only *large* model reaches considerably better performance, and that mBERT achieves better results than English BERT.

Czech Training, Czech Evaluation. Our first baseline model is trained directly on the Czech training data and then evaluated on the development set. The relative performance of the BERT variants is very similar to English, but the absolute performance is considerably lower. Several facts could contribute to the performance decrease – a smaller training set, noise introduced by the translation system and morphological richness of the Czech language.

Table 2. Development performance of English and Czech models on SQuAD 1.1, 2.0.

Model	Train	Dev	SQuAD 1.1		SQuAD 2.0	
			EM	F1	EM	F1
BERT cased	EN	EN	81.43%	88.88%	72.85%	76.03%
BERT uncased	EN	EN	80.92%	88.59%	73.35%	76.59%
mBERT cased	EN	EN	81.99%	89.10%	75.79%	78.76%
mBERT uncased	EN	EN	81.98%	89.27%	74.88%	77.98%
XLM-R base	EN	EN	80.91%	88.11%	74.07%	76.97%
XLM-R large	EN	EN	87.27%	93.24%	83.21%	86.23%
BERT cased	EN	CZ	9.53%	21.62%	53.48%	53.84%
BERT uncased	EN	CZ	6.16%	21.75%	54.78%	54.83%
mBERT cased	EN	CZ	59.49%	70.62%	58.28%	62.76%
mBERT uncased	EN	CZ	62.09%	73.89%	59.59%	63.89%
XLM-R base	EN	CZ	64.63%	75.85%	62.09%	65.93%
XLM-R large	EN	CZ	73.64%	84.07%	73.50%	77.58%
BERT cased	EN	CZ-EN-CZ	64.06%	76.78%	64.35%	69.11%
BERT uncased	EN	CZ-EN-CZ	63.57%	76.61%	65.26%	69.86%
mBERT cased	EN	CZ-EN-CZ	65.09%	77.47%	67.40%	71.96%
mBERT uncased	EN	CZ-EN-CZ	65.00%	77.38%	66.20%	70.72%
XLM-R base	EN	CZ-EN-CZ	64.52%	76.91%	65.62%	70.00%
XLM-R large	EN	CZ-EN-CZ	69.04%	81.33%	72.82%	78.04%
mBERT cased	CZ	CZ	59.49%	70.62%	66.60%	69.61%
mBERT uncased	CZ	CZ	62.11%	73.94%	64.96%	68.14%
XLM-R base	CZ	CZ	69.18%	78.71%	64.98%	68.15%
XLM-R large	CZ	CZ	76.39%	85.62%	75.57%	79.19%

English Models, Czech Evaluation via Machine Translation. Our second baseline system (denoted CS-EN-CS in the results) reuses English models to perform Czech reading comprehension – the Czech development set is first translated to English, the answers are then generated using English models, and finally translated back to Czech.

The translation-based approach has slightly higher performance for *base* models, which may be caused by the smaller size of the Czech training data. However, for the *large* model, the direct approach seems more beneficial.

Cross-Lingual Transfer Models. The most interesting experiment is the cross-lingual transfer of the English models, evaluated directly on Czech (without using any Czech data for training). Astonishingly, the results are very competitive with the other models evaluated on Czech, especially for XLM-R *large*, where there are within 1.6% points in F1 score and 2.75% points in exact match of the best Czech model.

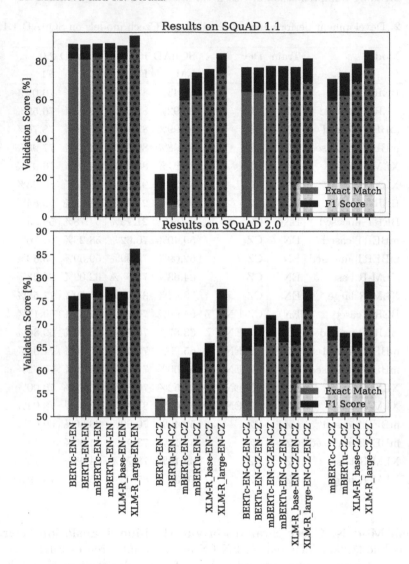

Fig. 1. Development set performance of all models for English and Czech SQuAD 1.1 and SQuAD 2.0 datasets.

4.1   Main Findings

Why Does Cross-Lingual Transfer Work. The performance of the cross-lingual transfer model is striking. Even if the model never saw any Czech reading comprehension data and it never saw any parallel Czech-English data, it reaches nearly the best results among all evaluated models.

This strong performance is an indication that mBERT and XLM-R represent different languages in the same shared space, without getting an explicit training signal in form of parallel data. Instead, we hypothesise that if there is a large-enough similarity among languages, the model exploits it by reusing the same part of the network to handle this phenomenon across multiple languages. This in turn saves capacity of the model and allows reaching higher likelihood, improving the quality of the model. In other words, greedy decrease of a loss function performed by SGD is good enough motivation for representing similarities in a shared way across languages.

Furthermore, word embeddings for different languages demonstrate a remarkable amount of similarity even after a simple linear transformation, as demonstrated for example by [1] or [3]. Such similarities are definitely exploitable (and as indicated by the results also exploited) by BERT-like models to achieve shared representation of multiple languages.

Pre-training on Czech Is Required. The strong performance of cross-lingual models does not necessarily mean the models can "understand" Czech – the named entities could be similar enough in Czech and English, and the model could be capable of answering without understanding the question.

Therefore, we also considered an English reading comprehension model based on English BERT, which did not encounter any other language but English during pre-training. Evaluating such a model directly on Czech delivers surprisingly good performance on SQuAD 2.0 – the model is unexpectedly good in recognizing unanswerable questions. However, the performance of such model on SQuAD 1.1 is rudimentary – 9.53% exact match and 21.62% F1-score, compared to 62.90% exact match and 73.89% F1-score of an mBERT uncased model.

Cased Versus Uncased. Consistently with intuition, cased models seem to perform generally better than uncased. However, in the context of cross-lingual transfer, we repeatedly observed uncased models surpassing the cased ones. We hypothesise that this result could be caused by larger intersection of Czech and English subwords of the uncased models (which discard not only casing information, but also diacritical marks), because larger shared vocabulary could make the cross-lingual transfer easier.

5   Conclusion

In this paper, we have explored Czech reading comprehension without any manually annotated Czech training data. We trained several baseline BERT-like models using translated data, but most importantly we evaluated a cross-lingual transfer model trained on English and then evaluated directly on Czech. The performance of this model is exceptionally good, despite the fact that no Czech training data nor Czech translation system was needed to train it.

Acknowledgements. The work was supported by the Grant Agency of the Czech Republic, project EXPRO LUSyD (GX20-16819X) and by the SVV 260 575 grant of Charles University. This research has also been using data and services provided by the LINDAT/CLARIAH-CZ Research Infrastructure (https://lindat.cz), supported by the Ministry of Education, Youth and Sports of the Czech Republic (Project No. LM2018101).

References

1. Artetxe, M., Labaka, G., Agirre, E.: A robust self-learning method for fully unsupervised cross-lingual mappings of word embeddings. In: Proceedings of the 56th Annual Meeting of the Association for Computational Linguistics (Volume 1: Long Papers), Melbourne, Australia, pp. 789–798. Association for Computational Linguistics, July 2018
2. Conneau, A., et al.: Unsupervised cross-lingual representation learning at scale. arXiv e-prints arXiv:1911.02116, November 2019
3. Conneau, A., Lample, G., Ranzato, M., Denoyer, L., Jégou, H.: Word translation without parallel data. arXiv e-prints arXiv:1710.04087, October 2017
4. Devlin, J., Chang, M.W., Lee, K., Toutanova, K.: BERT: pre-training of deep bidirectional transformers for language understanding. In: Proceedings of the 2019 Conference of the North American Chapter of the Association for Computational Linguistics: Human Language Technologies, Minneapolis, Minnesota, vol. 1, pp. 4171–4186. Association for Computational Linguistics, June 2019
5. Hsu, T.Y., Liu, C.L., Lee, H.Y.: Zero-shot reading comprehension by cross-lingual transfer learning with multi-lingual language representation model. arXiv e-prints arXiv:1909.09587, September 2019
6. Kondratyuk, D., Straka, M.: 75 languages, 1 model: parsing universal dependencies universally. In: Proceedings of the 2019 Conference on Empirical Methods in Natural Language Processing and the 9th International Joint Conference on Natural Language Processing (EMNLP-IJCNLP), Hong Kong, China, pp. 2779–2795. Association for Computational Linguistics, November 2019
7. Lan, Z., Chen, M., Goodman, S., Gimpel, K., Sharma, P., Soricut, R.: ALBERT: a lite BERT for self-supervised learning of language representations. arXiv e-prints arXiv:1909.11942, September 2019
8. Lewis, P., Oğuz, B., Rinott, R., Riedel, S., Schwenk, H.: MLQA: evaluating cross-lingual extractive question answering. arXiv e-prints arXiv:1910.07475, October 2019
9. Liu, Y., et al.: RoBERTa: a robustly optimized BERT pretraining approach. arXiv e-prints arXiv:1907.11692, July 2019
10. Popel, M.: CUNI transformer neural MT system for WMT18. In: Proceedings of the Third Conference on Machine Translation: Shared Task Papers, Belgium, Brussels, pp. 482–487. Association for Computational Linguistics, October 2018
11. Rajpurkar, P., Jia, R., Liang, P.: Know what you don't know: unanswerable questions for SQuAD. In: Proceedings of the 56th Annual Meeting of the Association for Computational Linguistics (Volume 2: Short Papers), Melbourne, Australia, pp. 784–789. Association for Computational Linguistics, July 2018
12. Rajpurkar, P., Zhang, J., Lopyrev, K., Liang, P.: SQuAD: 100,000+ questions for machine comprehension of text. In: Proceedings of the 2016 Conference on Empirical Methods in Natural Language Processing, Austin, Texas, pp. 2383–2392. Association for Computational Linguistics, November 2016

13. Straková, J., Straka, M., Hajič, J.: Open-source tools for morphology, lemmatization, POS tagging and named entity recognition. In: Proceedings of 52nd Annual Meeting of the Association for Computational Linguistics: System Demonstrations. Johns Hopkins University, USA, pp. 13–18. Association for Computational Linguistics, Stroudsburg (2014)
14. Vidra, J., Žabokrtský, Z., Ševčíková, M., Kyjánek, L.: DeriNet 2.0: towards an all-in-one word-formation resource. In: Proceedings of the Second International Workshop on Resources and Tools for Derivational Morphology, Charles University, Faculty of Mathematics and Physics, Institute of Formal and Applied Linguistics, Prague, Czechia, pp. 81–89, September 2019
15. Wolf, T., et al.: HuggingFace's transformers: state-of-the-art natural language processing. arXiv e-prints arXiv:1910.03771, October 2019

Measuring Memorization Effect
in Word-Level Neural Networks Probing

Rudolf Rosa[✉][iD], Tomáš Musil[iD], and David Mareček[iD]

Faculty of Mathematics and Physics, Institute of Formal and Applied Linguistics,
Charles University, Malostranské náměstí 25, 118 00 Praha, Czechia
{rosa,musil,marecek}@ufal.mff.cuni.cz
https://ufal.mff.cuni.cz/

Abstract. Multiple studies have probed representations emerging in
neural networks trained for end-to-end NLP tasks and examined what
word-level linguistic information may be encoded in the representations.
In classical probing, a classifier is trained on the representations to
extract the target linguistic information. However, there is a threat of
the classifier simply memorizing the linguistic labels for individual words,
instead of extracting the linguistic abstractions from the representations,
thus reporting false positive results. While considerable efforts have been
made to minimize the memorization problem, the task of actually measuring the amount of memorization happening in the classifier has been
understudied so far. In our work, we propose a simple general method
for measuring the memorization effect, based on a symmetric selection of
comparable sets of test words seen versus unseen in training. Our method
can be used to explicitly quantify the amount of memorization happening in a probing setup, so that an adequate setup can be chosen and the
results of the probing can be interpreted with a reliability estimate. We
exemplify this by showcasing our method on a case study of probing for
part of speech in a trained neural machine translation encoder.

Keywords: Probing · Memorization · Neural networks

1 Introduction

In recent years, there has been a considerable amount of research into linguistic
abstractions emerging in neural networks trained for various natural language
processing (NLP) tasks. It has been found that, to some degree, neural networks often capture abstractions which seem to correspond to classical linguistic
notions known from the linguistic studies of morphology, syntax or semantics,
even if they were not explicitly trained to do so. The common hypothesis is

This work has been supported by grant 18-02196S of the Czech Science Foundation.
It has been using language resources and tools developed, stored and distributed by
the LINDAT/CLARIAH-CZ project of the Ministry of Education, Youth and Sports
of the Czech Republic (project LM2018101).

P. Sojka et al. (Eds.): TSD 2020, LNAI 12284, pp. 180–188, 2020.
https://doi.org/10.1007/978-3-030-58323-1_19

that modern neural networks are sufficiently powerful to unravel many linguistic properties and regularities of language, and that they do so if this is useful for solving the task for which they are trained.

In this work, we focus on the subfield of identifying word-level linguistic abstractions, such as part-of-speech (POS) labels, in word-level representations, such as static or contextual word embeddings.

The usual method of assessing the amount to which linguistic abstractions are captured by a neural network is to use *probing*, which we review in Sect. 2. In word-level probing, we take representations of words from a trained neural network (such as word embeddings or hidden states from an encoder) and train a classifier to predict linguistic labels (such as POS) from the representations corresponding to the words, using linguistically annotated data (such as a tagged corpus). The common assumption is that if the classifier learns to predict the linguistic labels with a high accuracy, it is an indication that the neural word representations contain a latent abstraction similar to the linguistic notion (e.g. that contextual word embeddings encode POS of the words).

1.1 The Memorization Problem

A major threat associated with the probing approach is that of *memorization*. As the probing classifier learns to assign labels to words, it can succeed in two ways. Either, it learns to extract an abstraction from the word representation which corresponds to the label to assign; this is the intended case, which we refer to as *generalization*. Or, it simply memorizes the label associated with each word; we refer to this as *memorization*. If memorization occurs, the result of the probing can be misinterpreted as the representations capturing some linguistic abstractions, while the actual underlying mechanism is that the representations simply capture the word identity. The probing classifier thus only learns to extract the word identity from the representation and memorizes the label for the word.[1] A crucial problem is that, without taking additional measures, there is no way of distinguishing the true positive result from the false positive result.

With context-independent word representations (static word embeddings), it is of course possible to avoid the problem by splitting the vocabulary into two disjoint sets of words, training the classifier on a train set and testing it on a test set. However, for contextual representations, this cannot be done easily, as the representations need to be computed for whole sentences, not for individual words, and the train and test sets thus need to be composed of full sentences, which unavoidably have a large word overlap. While we might evaluate the probe only on test set words unseen in the training data, these are not representative of the language, as such a set of test words will be biased towards low-frequency words. We argue that we rather need to evaluate on the full test set while measuring and minimizing the memorization effect.

---

[1] Unlike static word embeddings, contextual representations of the same word in different sentences are different, which makes memorization harder, but not impossible: the identity of the word is still strongly encoded in the contextual representation and can be extracted from it, especially when a stronger classifier is used.

1.2   Measuring Memorization

In this paper, we suggest a general method of measuring the amount of memorization occurring in word-level probing of neural network representations, based on comparing the probing classifier accuracy on sets of *seen* and *unseen* words. Although a standard test set contains both words seen and unseen in training data, the seen words tend to be frequent while the unseen ones are typically rare words; we thus regard an approach of comparing accuracies on these sets of words as inadequate and uninformative. Instead, we propose a method which samples the seen and unseen words in a symmetric way to ensure their comparability.

We do not present a new method for probing itself; our method is designed to complement existing probing approaches by explicitly measuring their reliability with respect to the memorization problem. This can help the researcher to select an adequate probing setup by providing means for quantifying the magnitude of the memorization problem, allowing for a trustworthy interpretation of the probing results.

As a case study, we apply our method to measure the amount of memorization in probing for POS in word representations from a neural machine translation system.

2   Related Work

A comprehensive survey of word embeddings evaluation methods was compiled by Bakarov [2]. An overview can also be found in the survey of methodology for analysis of deep learning models for NLP by Belinkov and Glass [4]. Another overview [12] mentions "[n]o standardized splits & overfitting" as one of the problems of evaluating word embeddings with similarity tasks.

There are various strategies when it comes to the train/dev/test splitting in probing.

When it is possible to predict the probed property from the word type itself, the vocabulary may be split into train/test sets. This strategy is used e.g. in [19,21] to evaluate POS tag and other morphological features prediction.

Some works split the dataset into train/dev/test sets, without regard to the same words occuring in both. These include predicting syntactic and semantic labels (including POS) from hidden states on sentences [3,5,11,18,22] or treebanks [7,15].

Bisazza and Tump [6] address the problem with the overlap. They observe that even a dummy random feature can be predicted with high accuracy when the same words occur both in the train and the test data. They extract one vector per token from the NMT encoder. They randomly split the vocabulary into two parts and use one to filter the training data and the other to filter the test data. They repeat the experiments several times and report mean accuracies.

Another approach to evaluating words in context of sentences is presented by [10]. They propose the word content task that tests whether it is possible to recover information about the original words in the sentence from its embedding.

They pick 1000 mid-frequency words from the source corpus vocabulary and sample equal numbers of sentences that contain one and only one of these words. The words can then be partitioned into train and test sets without the risk of their overlapping.

The ability of deep neural networks to memorize is a challenge for the theory of deep learning [1]. It also has implications for the applications of neural networks, because it may be problematic if a portion of the training data can be reconstructed from the trained model [9].

In connection with probing neural networks, memorization was addressed by Hewitt and Liang [14], who propose control tasks to complement the linguistics tasks. A control task associates word types with random labels. If the classifier performs well on the control task, this means that it is able to memorize the training set. However, the data distribution affects the generalization ability of deep neural networks and they tend to learn simple patterns when possible [16]. Our approach differs from [14] by using the original data to measure the memorization effect, evading the problem created by altering the distribution in a control task.

3 Method

In the usual probing approach, we operate with two sets of sentences, a training set and a test set, both labelled with the word-level labels corresponding to the linguistic abstraction for which we are probing the neural word representations (e.g. POS). The training set is used to train a probing classifier to predict the labels from the word representations. The classifier is then evaluated on the test set, and its accuracy, compared to a baseline, is used to estimate to what extent the given linguistic abstraction is encoded in the word representations.

The goal of our method is to measure to what extent the probing classifier only memorizes word identities instead of measuring the generalization captured by the word representations. The main idea is to compare the probing classifier accuracies on words that are part of the training data (*seen* words) and on words that are not (*unseen* words), while keeping the sets of seen and unseen words otherwise comparable (as discussed in Sect. 1), which we ensure by a symmetric way of creating these sets.

We propose the following approach:

1. Randomly split the training set into two halves, which we will refer to as *seen sentences* and *unseen sentences*.
2. Train the probing classifier only on the seen sentences.
3. Apply the probing classifier to the test set.
4. Define the set of *seen words* as words that are contained in the seen sentences but not in the unseen sentences.
5. Define the set of *unseen words* as words that are contained in the unseen sentences but not in the seen sentences.

6. Evaluate the accuracy of the probing classifier separately on seen words and on unseen words, ignoring words that are neither seen nor unseen.[2]

Using this approach, we can now quantify the magnitude of the memorization effect occurring in the probing setup as the difference between the classifier accuracy on seen and on unseen words. If the memorization problem is not present, these accuracies should be identical, as the classifier only extracts the linguistic abstraction from the representation, regardless of the word identity; in this case, the classifier accuracy reliably measures the amount of linguistic information encoded by the representation. On the other hand, a higher accuracy on seen words than on unseen words signalizes that the classifier memorized some of the seen words' identities to some extent, instead of extracting the linguistic abstractions from them.

To stabilize the evaluation, we propose to sample the seen and unseen sentences and train the classifier multiple times, and to compute the microaverage accuracy.

We define our method as operating on words and word representations, as this makes the subsequent word-level probing straightforward. Our method is in principle applicable even for setups using subwords. However, in such cases, it is up to the researcher to decide whether for the given language and setup, subword-level memorization is a problem or not, as our method only deals with word-level memorization.

3.1 Which Words Are Selected for Evaluation?

It is important to note that the distribution of words selected for evaluation by our method is strongly biased towards lower-frequency words. Very frequent words are never selected for evaluation, and medium-frequency words are rarely selected, as they always or nearly always appear in both seen and unseen sentences, and our method is thus unable to measure the memorization effect for such words.

Specifically, the probability $P_{sel}(w)$ of a word w being selected as *unseen* (or *seen*) follows a hypergeometric distribution: $P_{sel}(w) \sim$ Hypergeometric $\left(|S|, \frac{|S|}{2}, |S_w|\right)$, where S is the set of training sentences, out of which its subset S_w contains the word w. For most words,[3] it is similar to the binomial distribution $\mathrm{Bi}(|S_w|, 0.5)$, and $P_{sel}(w)$ is thus inversely exponentially proportional to $|S_w|$: $P_{sel}(w) \approx \left(\frac{1}{2}\right)^{|S_w|}$.

---

[2] Note that words which occur in both seen and unseen sentences are neither seen words nor unseen words. We also need to remove words that are part of the development set if one is used for training the probing classifier. Technically, words that do not appear in the test set can also be removed from the sets of seen and unseen words as they do not influence the results.

[3] For frequent words, the actual probability is even lower than the (already negligible) approximated value; for words that appear in more than half of the training sentences, the probability is 0. The probability is also technically 0 for words that do not appear in the test set.

We believe that for **very frequent words** (especially function words such as common prepositions, pronouns, determiners and punctuation), avoiding memorization is hard – a set of sentences constructed not to contain a given word from this class would typically not be very representative of the language. Moreover, the probed neural network is typically not very likely to meaningfully abstract over such words, as it is usually more economical for the network to simply memorize the most frequent words and treat them as special cases.[4,5]

For **medium-frequency words**, such as common nouns and verbs, we see their underrepresentation as a shortcoming of our method which we intend to focus on in future work. We specifically plan to further investigate the approach of Bisazza and Tump [6], reviewed in Sect. 2, who train the probing classifier on representations of only some words in the training sentences and regard the other words as *unseen*. We appreciate the approach, but we believe that it must be analyzed to what degree it may be influenced by the contextual representations of the *seen* words containing information about surrounding words regarded as *unseen*.[6]

Our method mostly focuses on **lower-frequency words**, which we believe to be reasonable, as the lower the frequency of the word, the stronger is the network forced to abstract over the word. We are thus mostly interested in such words in probing, as if the network captures the abstractions that we are probing for, they should be most prominent in representations of lower-frequency words.

Still, we also omit **very rare words**, which either do not appear in the test sentences or in the training sentences (or, obviously, in none of those). For these words, the memorization effect is very unlikely to occur.

4   Case Study

As a case study, we apply our method to probing representations from a neural machine translation model for POS. We study the memorization phenomenon along three dimensions, varying the train set size, the contextuality of the representation (static word embeddings versus encoder output states), and the power of the probing classifier, using either a linear classifier or a multi-layer perceptron classifier (MLP).

We analyze a Transformer model [24] implemented within the Neural Monkey framework[7] [13], trained for the task of machine translation from Czech to

---

[4] Which they often are, as frequent words tend to behave irregularly in language [23, p. 116].

[5] Arguably, it is sane to memorize very frequent words rather than abstracting over them. Nevertheless, we should be able to measure this reliably, not mistaking one for the other.

[6] In their method, *unseen* words are part of the training sentences and can thus influence the contextual representations of the *seen* words which are used for training the probing classifier, whereas in our method, the training sentences do not contain the *unseen* words at all.

[7] https://github.com/ufal/neuralmonkey.

Table 1. Case study evaluation on POS prediction, varying the number of training sentences, the probed representations, and the probing classifier. The difference between the accuracy of the probe on seen versus unseen words represents the magnitude of the memorization problem. Micro-average over 10 repetitions, in percentage points, with standard deviations.

Train sent.	Accuracy			Stand. dev.		Train sent.	Accuracy			Stand. dev.	
	seen	unseen	diff	seen	unseen		seen	unseen	diff	seen	unseen
Encoder output states, linear classifier						Encoder word embeddings, linear classifier					
50	90.5	87.3	3.3	3.4	5.6	50	98.5	74.3	24.1	0.9	7.6
100	89.1	86.8	2.3	1.8	2.0	100	97.0	78.0	19.0	0.8	2.3
500	93.9	92.8	1.1	0.9	1.1	500	97.6	80.5	17.1	0.7	3.2
1,000	94.7	93.9	0.8	0.9	0.8	1,000	97.0	82.8	14.2	1.0	1.5
5,000	95.5	94.9	0.7	0.5	0.6	5,000	96.2	84.7	11.4	0.5	1.7
10,000	95.7	95.5	0.2	0.8	0.8	10,000	95.2	85.3	10.0	0.8	1.0
30,000	95.8	95.9	0.0	0.4	0.4	30,000	93.5	88.0	5.4	0.6	1.3
Encoder output states, MLP						Encoder word embeddings, MLP					
50	97.7	93.3	4.4	1.5	3.2	50	98.5	76.6	21.8	0.9	6.9
100	96.2	93.6	2.7	1.0	1.4	100	97.0	81.4	15.6	0.7	3.0
500	97.2	94.5	2.7	0.3	0.9	500	97.8	87.4	10.3	0.4	1.9
1,000	96.8	94.9	1.9	0.7	0.7	1,000	97.7	89.8	7.9	0.5	1.4
5,000	97.6	95.7	1.9	0.4	0.5	5,000	98.4	92.7	5.6	0.2	1.0
10,000	98.0	96.2	1.8	0.7	0.7	10,000	98.7	93.5	5.2	0.2	1.0
30,000	97.7	96.1	1.6	0.6	0.7	30,000	98.4	94.2	4.1	0.6	1.2

English on the CzEng dataset[8] [8]. The setup is based on [17], with the exception of splitting the sentences into words instead of subwords, as explained in Sect. 3; we use a vocabulary of 25,000 words that are most frequent in the parallel training data.

We probe the source word embeddings and source encoder output states for Universal POS with a linear classifier (softmax) or a MLP with one hidden layer of dimension 512, using the Universal Dependencies 1.4 version of the Czech Prague Dependency Treebank [20]. We use the first 500 sentences from the treebank training data as tuning data for the probing classifier, the rest of the training data is used to create the seen and unseen sentence sets, using either the full data or subsampling smaller subsets. The probing classifier is then evaluated using the development part of the treebank using token-based evaluation. For each setup, we repeat the experiment 10 times with different samples of the seen and unseen sentences and report micro-average results.

By comparing the accuracies of the probing classifier on seen and unseen words in Table 1, we can see that the memorization problem is clearly most pronounced with static word embeddings, where the magnitude of the effect (the difference in the accuracies) ranges from 4 points for the full training set up to 24 points for a training set of 50 sentences, while for the contextual representations,

---

[8] http://ufal.mff.cuni.cz/czeng.

the effect does not surpass 5 points. The memorization effect is more pronounced with the stronger classifier, and disappears only with the linear classifier applied to contextual representations when trained with the largest train set.

5 Conclusion

We presented a method for measuring the memorization effect in word-level prob- ing of neural representations of words, based on a comparison of the accuracy of the probing classifier on symmetrically sampled comparable sets of *seen* and *unseen* words. As we showed in a case study on probing for POS, our method can measure the magnitude of the memorization problem and can thus serve as a means for selecting an appropriate probing setup, as well as for estimating the reliability of the findings of the probing experiment with respect to the threat of mistaking memorization for generalization.

In future, we intend to tackle the shortcoming of our method of underrepre- senting medium-frequency words. We also plan to apply the method to a wider range of word-based probing tasks, as well as to measure the memorization effect for existing previous probing works and reassess results reported by their authors from this perspective.

References

1. Arpit, D., Jastrzebski, S., Ballas, N., Krueger, D., Bengio, E., Kanwal, M.S., et al.: A closer look at memorization in deep networks. In: Proceedings of ICML, pp. 233–242 (2017)
2. Bakarov, A.: A survey of word embeddings evaluation methods. arXiv preprint arXiv:1801.09536 (2018)
3. Belinkov, Y., Durrani, N., Dalvi, F., Sajjad, H., Glass, J.: What do neural machine translation models learn about morphology? In: Proceedings of ACL, Vancouver, Canada, pp. 861–872 (2017)
4. Belinkov, Y., Glass, J.: Analysis methods in neural language processing: a survey. In: TACL, vol. 7, pp. 49–72 (2019)
5. Belinkov, Y., Màrquez, L., Sajjad, H., Durrani, N., Dalvi, F., Glass, J.: Evaluating layers of representation in neural machine translation on part-of-speech and seman- tic tagging tasks. In: Proceedings of IJCNLP, Taipei, Taiwan, pp. 1–10 (2017)
6. Bisazza, A., Tump, C.: The lazy encoder: a fine-grained analysis of the role of morphology in neural machine translation. In: Proceedings of EMNLP, Brussels, Belgium, pp. 2871–2876 (2018)
7. Blevins, T., Levy, O., Zettlemoyer, L.: Deep RNNs encode soft hierarchical syntax. In: Proceedings of ACL, Melbourne, Australia, pp. 14–19 (2018)
8. Bojar, O., et al.: CzEng 1.6: enlarged Czech-English parallel corpus with process- ing tools dockered. In: Sojka, P., Horák, A., Kopeček, I., Pala, K. (eds.) TSD 2016. LNCS (LNAI), vol. 9924, pp. 231–238. Springer, Cham (2016). https://doi.org/10. 1007/978-3-319-45510-5_27
9. Carlini, N., Liu, C., Erlingsson, Ú., Kos, J., Song, D.: The secret sharer: evaluating and testing unintended memorization in neural networks. In: USENIX Security. Santa Clara, CA, pp. 267–284 (2019)

10. Conneau, A., Kruszewski, G., Lample, G., Barrault, L., Baroni, M.: What you can cram into a single vector: probing sentence embeddings for linguistic properties. arXiv preprint arXiv:1805.01070 (2018)
11. Dalvi, F., Durrani, N., Sajjad, H., Belinkov, Y., Vogel, S.: Understanding and improving morphological learning in the neural machine translation decoder. In: Proceedings of IJCNLP, Taipei, Taiwan, pp. 142–151 (2017)
12. Faruqui, M., Tsvetkov, Y., Rastogi, P., Dyer, C.: Problems with evaluation of word embeddings using word similarity tasks. arXiv preprint arXiv:1605.02276 (2016)
13. Helcl, J., Libovický, J., Kocmi, T., Musil, T., Cífka, O., Variš, D., et al.: Neural monkey: the current state and beyond. In: Proceedings of AMTA, Boston, MA, pp. 168–176 (2018)
14. Hewitt, J., Liang, P.: Designing and interpreting probes with control tasks. In: Proceedings of EMNLP-IJCNLP, Hong Kong, China, pp. 2733–2743 (2019)
15. Köhn, A.: What's in an embedding? Analyzing word embeddings through multilingual evaluation. In: Proceedings of EMNLP, pp. 2067–2073 (2015)
16. Krueger, D., Ballas, N., Jastrzebski, S., Arpit, D., Kanwal, M.S., Maharaj, T., et al.: Deep nets don't learn via memorization. In: Proceedings of ICLR, p. 4 (2017)
17. Libovický, J., Rosa, R., Helcl, J., Popel, M.: Solving three Czech NLP tasks end-to-end with neural models. In: Proceedings of SloNLP (2018)
18. Linzen, T., Dupoux, E., Goldberg, Y.: Assessing the ability of LSTMs to learn syntax-sensitive dependencies. In: TACL, vol. 4, pp. 521–535 (2016)
19. Musil, T.: Examining structure of word embeddings with PCA. In: Ekštein, K. (ed.) TSD 2019. LNCS (LNAI), vol. 11697, pp. 211–223. Springer, Cham (2019). https://doi.org/10.1007/978-3-030-27947-9_18
20. Nivre, J., et al.: Universal dependencies 1.4, LINDAT/CLARIAH-CZ digital library at ÚFAL MFF UK, Charles University (2016)
21. Qian, P., Qiu, X., Huang, X.: Investigating language universal and specific properties in word embeddings. In: Proceedings of ACL, pp. 1478–1488 (2016)
22. Shi, X., Padhi, I., Knight, K.: Does string-based neural MT learn source syntax? In: Proceedings of EMNLP, Austin, Texas, pp. 1526–1534 (2016)
23. Stubbs, M.: Language corpora. In: Davies, A., Elder, C. (eds.) The Handbook of Applied Linguistics, Chap. 4, pp. 106–132. Blackwell Publishing, Malden (2004)
24. Vaswani, A., Shazeer, N., Parmar, N., Uszkoreit, J., Jones, L., Gomez, A.N., et al.: Attention is all you need. In: Guyon, I., et al. (eds.) NeurIPS 30, pp. 6000–6010. Curran Ass (2017)

Semi-supervised Induction of Morpheme Boundaries in Czech Using a Word-Formation Network

Jan Bodnár$^{(\boxtimes)}$ ⓘ, Zdeněk Žabokrtský ⓘ, and Magda Ševčíková ⓘ

Faculty of Mathematics and Physics, Institute of Formal and Applied Linguistics, Charles University, Prague, Czech Republic
jan.bodnar@seznam.cz, {zabokrtsky,sevcikova}@ufal.mff.cuni.cz

Abstract. This paper deals with automatic morphological segmentation of Czech lemmas contained in the word-formation network DeriNet. Capturing derivational relations between base and derived lemmas, and segmenting lemmas into sequences of morphemes are two closely related formal models of how words come into existence. Thus we propose a novel segmentation method that benefits from the existence of the network; our solution constitutes new state-of-the-art for the Czech language.

Keywords: Morphological segmentation · Morpheme · Word formation

1 Introduction

Morphological segmentation in a standard task in NLP, whose aim is to decompose a word into a sequence of minimal meaning-bearing units called morphemes (e.g., *unreachable* → *un-reach-able*). It has been tackled by a variety of approaches (ranging from rule-based methods to modern machine learning methods), and several shared tasks focused on it.

In this paper, we report a work in progress focused on morphological segmentation of Czech lemmas. Czech is a morphologically rich language, both in inflection and derivation. Large-coverage NLP tools for Czech inflection have been developed since the 1990s (such as the MorfFlex CZ dictionary, currently covering around 1M lemmas [3]), and data resources for derivation are available, too; cf. the word-formation network DeriNet [15]. However, to our knowledge, there is no publicly available large-scale machine-tractable segmentation lexicon for Czech. We aim to build one.

The task of modeling inflection and derivation of a natural language and the task of morphological segmentation are closely connected. Thus we hypothesize that the information stored in derivational trees of DeriNet (see Fig. 1 (a) for a sample) could be used – in combination with deep learning methods – for improving performance in morphological segmentation.

Relying on the existence of a derivational resource might look as a rather exotic bottleneck, as derivational data are much scarcer than, e.g., data resources

© Springer Nature Switzerland AG 2020
P. Sojka et al. (Eds.): TSD 2020, LNAI 12284, pp. 189–196, 2020.
https://doi.org/10.1007/978-3-030-58323-1_20

for inflection. However, according to [7] there are at least 22 languages for which reasonably-scaled derivational databases exist, out of which data for 11 languages are available in the tree-shaped scheme used in our approach [6]. Thus our approach could be viable also for several languages other than Czech.

2   Related Work

2.1   Morphological Segmentation as a Linguistic Task

Even if a morpheme is defined simply as a phoneme/grapheme sequence associated with a particular meaning that cannot be further subdivided, i.e., as the smallest linguistic sign, delimitation of morphemes in Czech is difficult especially because individual morphemes are often attested in multiple variants (morphs) due to allomorphy; cf. the morphs of the morpheme *br* (as in the verb *br-á-t* 'to take') in *vy-bír-a-t* 'to choose', *ví-běr* 'choice', and *vý-bor* 'committee'.

In the linguistic description of Czech, morphological segmentation as identification of all morphemes within the word structure is considered a task of morphology; e.g., *lod'-k-a* 'small boat' is cut into the root morpheme *lod'*, the (derivational) suffix *k* and the (inflectional) ending *a*. A related task of delimiting morphemes that distinguish a word from an immediately simpler word (e.g. *lod'-ka* 'small boat' from *lod'* 'boat') falls under derivation as part of word-formation, which is subsumed under lexicology in the Czech linguistic tradition.

These two perspectives are documented in existing NLP accounts and data resources, too. Slavíčková's retrograde dictionary [13], Weisheitelová et al. [16], Osolsobě and Pala [9], or Skoumalová [12] aim at providing complete morphological segmentation, whereas Šiška's dictionary of root allomorphs [11] and Šimandl's dictionary of affixes [10] focus rather on word-formation analysis.

2.2   Approaches to Automatic Morphological Segmentation

The task of morphological segmentation is recognized in NLP for a long time, and solutions have been proposed as early as in the 1950s. Diverse approaches have been developed since, based, e.g., on (i) lists of affixes and grammar rules, (ii) supervised machine learning models, (iii) unsupervised models that optimize heuristic criteria such as minimal description length, or (iv) unsupervised models that optimize probability such as Bayesian models (see [1] for references).

One can find empirical performance comparisons of various approaches in publications related to shared tasks on morphological segmentation, such as [8] or [5], but Czech is not among the studied languages. As shown in [14], even the modern models considered as state-of-the-art in these shared tasks, do not reach reasonable accuracy for Czech.

3 Our Annotated Data

3.1 Sample of Completely Segmented Lemmas

For training and evaluation purposes, we selected 2,100 lemmas from the Der-iNet lemma set as follows: (1) 1,000 lemmas were sampled randomly with uniform probabilities, (2) additional 1,100 lemmas were sampled randomly with probabilities proportional to their frequencies in the Czech National Corpus [4].

Morpheme boundaries in both sets were manually annotated. The basic principle of delimiting morphemes through their recurrence in words is challenged by allomorphy, in particular, of root morphemes. In Czech, roots often start and end in consonants, having a CVC (consonant-vowel-consonant), CC and other structures, with the final consonant alternated due to some suffixes (*hák* 'hook' > *háč-ek* 'small hook') and the middle vowel (if present) dropped or alternated in individual allomorphs (cf. the allomorphy of the *br* root above).

While segmentation of prefixes is rather easy due to their limited number and relatively regular patterns documented across the part-of-speech boundaries (e.g., prefix vowel lengthening in verb-to-noun derivation *vy-br-a-t* 'to choose' > *vý-běr* 'choice'), suffix parts of many lemmas allow for multiple analyses based on different analogies. For instance, the *ova* suffix is delimited in *kup-ova-t* 'to buy.imperf' in contrast to *koup-i-t* 'to buy.perf'; if propagated to *kup-ová-va-t* 'to buy.imperf-iter', one obtains a lengthened variant (*ová*), which is not found in other iteratives. An alternative, more subtle segmentation (*kup-ov-a-t* > *kup-ov-áv-a-t*) which is applicable also to other iteratives (*plav-a-t* 'to swim.imperf' > *plav-áv-a-t* 'to swim.imperf-iter') was thus preferred in the annotation.

The resulting set of completely segmented lemmas was randomly divided into a training portion (1,050 lemmas), a development test portion (525 lemmas), and an evaluation test portion (525 lemmas).

3.2 Sets of Root Allomorphs for Selected DeriNet Trees

The complete manual segmentation drew our attention to native, high frequent roots with individual allomorphy, which is hard to capture (cf. the analysis *dá-t* 'to give.perfective' vs. *d-á-v-a-t* 'to give.imperfective' provided by [13]).

In order to annotate these lemmas as consistently as possible, a simple method was proposed on how to detect root morpheme boundaries in groups of derivationally related words gathered in individual derivational trees in the DeriNet network, still with minimal annotation effort. First, 1,760 biggest derivational trees were selected in DeriNet. Then an annotator added a list of all root morpheme variants to each tree as a whole (actually the list was pre-generated, in order to make the annotation even faster), without annotating individual lemmas in the tree. Then the longest-matching root allomorph was marked as the root morpheme in each lemma. This resulted in 240k lemmas with highly reliable root-morpheme boundaries.

4   Morphological Segmentation Procedure

In general, our segmentation approach is constructed as a combination of rule-based and machine learning methods operating on separate words, with methods that detect and propagate morpheme-boundaries along derivational edges in the DeriNet 2.0 derivational trees.

Our algorithm consists of four main parts, detection, propagation, pruning, and post-processing. In the detection phase, the morpheme boundaries are detected separately on each word, with use of simple rules and neural classifiers. In this phase, we also add manually annotated root morphemes. In the propagation phase, we operate on DeriNet 2.0 derivational trees, and use them to induce new morphological boundaries, as well as to propagate already known boundaries to other words. The following pruning phase uses two neural classifiers for removing wrong boundaries. In the final post-processing phase, a small set of rules is used to correct systematic errors of the classifiers, and we once again use the manual root annotations, this time to add the annotated boundaries which may have been removed, and to remove any further segmentation of annotated roots.

4.1   Inducing Morpheme Boundaries from Derivational Trees

This approach consists of two techniques, boundary detection and boundary propagation. Boundary detection tries to detect new morpheme boundaries by examining the changes along derivational edges. For instance, the change in the parent–child pair *lod'ka* 'small boat' > *lodička* 'tiny boat' can be used to reveal the child's internal structure. We first use the edit-distance measure to find the most likely way how the words are aligned, and then examine the difference between them. We see that *lodička* was created as [*"lod'"*, *"+ič"*, *"ka"*], i.e., *lod'* remained the same, *ič* was inserted, and *ka* was repeated. The most likely scenario is that *ič* is either a morpheme or a group of morphemes, and that it was inserted between two morphemes, i.e., where a morpheme boundary is assumed to be located. The induced segmentations are *lod'-ka* and *lod-ič-ka*.

The boundary propagation propagates the known boundaries (be it from the previous algorithm or, e.g., from neural networks), between two words connected with a derivational edge. For instance, if we have an edge between *roz-dělit* 'to distribute' > *přerozdělit* 'to redistribute', we would like to transfer the boundary *roz-* into the second word. For this, we create the exact same mapping between two words as above: *přerozdělit* = [*"+pře"*, *"rozdělit"*]. We can conclude from this mapping that the boundary can safely be translated into the second word since the subword *rozdělit*, which contains our boundary, remained unchanged. The boundary just needs to be shifted inside the word because three letters were added in front of the boundary. This way, we get the boundary *přeroz-dělit*.

The actual algorithm applies both rules at the same time, while iterating trough edges in a specific order: We start with leaves and create and propagate boundaries to their parents. Once all children of a node are processed, boundaries are propagated from this node to its parent. When the tree root is reached, the second phase starts and boundaries are propagated in the opposite direction, i.e., from parents to their children. This approach ensures that the whole propagation is handled in $\mathcal{O}(N)$, where N is the number of words in the tree.

This method helps us to find boundaries that would otherwise remain undetected, but it also leads to a relatively high number of false positives. For this reason, the differences caused by changes in letter accents are ignored, while comparing two words. This may cause some false negatives but the overall impact is highly positive. Boundaries in the final output are further pruned by classifiers to increase precision.

4.2 Deep Learning Component

We use two neural network classifiers. Both of them are convolutional networks with character level embeddings trained altogether with the classifiers.[1] For each position of the input word, they return values 0 to 1 signalizing whether there is a morpheme-boundary on a given position of the word. The first network was trained on the manually annotated dataset mentioned in Sect. 3.1, whereas the second one was trained in a semi-supervised manner using a combination of the manually annotated and of a synthetically generated dataset. The synthetic dataset was generated by the complete algorithm as described in this paper, without the final post-processing, and cleanup phase. The goal was to make the second classifier learn from the tree-based algorithm and to smooth its outputs. Both classifiers are used with two thresholds, one for the addition of new boundaries and the second one for removal of suspicious boundaries.

4.3 Adding Further Information on Morphemes

Our procedure also attempts to classify the identified morphemes as prefixes, suffixes, or roots. Given a derivational tree with segmented lemmas, the root morpheme of the lemma is identified in the root node of the tree, and the information about the root morpheme is then propagated down the tree. With the root being identified in all nodes, we distinguish prefix and suffix morphemes (simply by their relative position with respect to the root morpheme), which is certainly an oversimplification that completely disregards the existence of interfix morphemes in compounds and other issues.

In the last step, a representative allomorph is assigned to each morpheme, which could be considered "allomorph lemmatization". We align morpheme sequences of a parent lemma and a child lemma, allowing only links 1-1, 1-0, and 0-1. Aligned morphemes are either written identically, or they are allomorphs. For each group of allomorphs, we chose their representative as the topmost-appearing allomorph (the one that appears closest to the root node of the derivational tree).

---

[1] TensorFlow, http://tensorflow.org/.

Table 1. Comparison of our method with other approaches on the dictionary data [13]

Method	Morphemes			Boundaries			Words
	Precision	Recall	F1	Precision	Recall	F1	Accuracy
Our method	58.94%	62.62%	63.74%	96.11%	91.63%	93.81%	72.15%
EMmh, i1	64.82%	66.54%	65.67%	91.38%	87.42%	89.36%	35.45%
FlatCat unsup.	37.19%	21.57%	27.31%	97.98%	64.92%	78.10%	1.17%
FlatCat sup.	66.20%	57.72%	61.67%	92.59%	81.15%	86.49%	31.10%

5   Experiments and Evaluation

5.1   Evaluated Setups

Similarly to [14], we use three measures to evaluate the quality of generated segmentations by comparing them to manually annotated data: (1) *lemma correctness* – the percentage (accuracy) of lemmas whose segmentation is completely correct, (2) *morpheme correctness* – the precision, recall, and f-measure of correctly recognized morphemes, and (3) *boundary correctness* – precision, recall, and f-measure of correctly recognized boundaries between adjacent morphemes.

We have experimented with various sets of rules as well as with multiple neural network architectures based on recurrent, convolutional and deconvolutional networks with various hyper-parameters. Only the configuration that achieved the best results on the development set is presented here. In general, recurrent neural networks did not work, probably due to the small training set, while the best results were achieved by convolutional networks with 2 convolutional layers (400 filters, kernel size 4, stride 1, ReLU activation) and a single fully connected layer with one output (sigmoid activation). However, this architecture is more of an example, since slightly different architectures had comparable results. With the deconvolutions we expected to help spreading information about morphemes through the word, but it did not yield any improvements.

The pipeline required certain structural optimization: we have experimented with omitting various layers and also with using the same layer on multiple places. Special care was needed to set-up the classifiers. Each of them has two thresholds – one for adding a new boundary, and one for removing a boundary from a place where it likely should not be. The first threshold was set independently for each classifier in such a way that classifier has the highest possible recall, while not dropping bellow 95% precision. The second – removal – thresholds were configured together on both classifiers. The performance of the pipeline was evaluated for various combinations of thresholds, and the values which have sufficient precision and a reasonable precision-recall balance were chosen. The architecture of the classifiers was chosen on the basis of the maximum recall at 95% precision too, which resulted in choosing a simple CNN with two hidden convolutional layers.

5.2   Results

The performance of our algorithm was evaluated on the part of our manually annotated dataset which was not used during previous development. We evaluated the performance in three ways: We measured how accurately the algorithm marks boundaries (Precision 93.3%, Recall 81.5%) and morphemes (Prec. 64.5%, Rec. 58.6%), and how big a percentage of words was correctly segmented (58.9%). In comparison, semisupervised Morfessor Flatcat achieved results: Boundaries - P:83.7%, R:35.7%; Morphemes - P:36.4%, R:21.2%, Words 26.7%. To compare our method with Czech state of the art we evaluate it also on the retrograde dictionary data. [13], on which we can compare it with EMmh method [14] as well as with Morfessor FlatCat [2], as also evaluated in [14]; see Table 1.

Figure 1 (b) shows how precision and recall change as data passes through the layers of the pipeline. Interestingly, classifier 2 during its training learned to partially mimic the behavior of the Tree Propagation. Because of this, it looks as if all the work was done by the classifiers, and the Tree Propagation was not useful at all. The plot was evaluated on our manually segmented dataset.

The outputs of the previous versions of the algorithm have undergone a linguistic inspection, and most of the observed systematic errors have been fixed by adding specialized rules into the post-processing phase. Yet there are still some known sources of errors remaining, such as compounds, which we are unable to handle in standard ways, and therefore will need a specialized approach. There is also an issue with clean-up done by classifiers. As can be seen in Fig. 1 (b), their presence is essential, yet they tend to remove many correct segments.

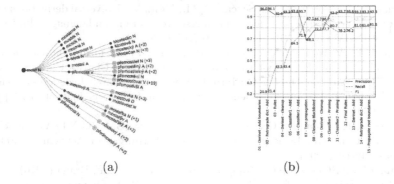

(a)   (b)

Fig. 1. (a) The derivational tree with the base noun *most* 'bridge' from DeriNet 2.0. (b) The changes of precision, recall and F1 on different layers of the pipeline.

6   Conclusions

We have presented a novel approach to morphological segmentation, which benefits from the availability of derivational trees and uses deep learning components. Our system outperforms previous solutions developed for the Czech language. A natural extension of the task would be to segment also inflected word forms.

Acknowledgments. This work was supported by the Grant No. GA19-14534S of the Czech Science Foundation. It uses language resources developed, stored, and distributed by the LINDAT/CLARIAH CZ project (LM2015071, LM2018101). We thank Michal Křen for helping us query morpheme segmentation patterns in the Czech National Corpus.

References

1. Goldsmith, J.A., Lee, J.L., Xanthos, A.: Computational learning of morphology. Ann. Rev. Linguist. **3**, 85–106 (2017)
2. Grönroos, S.A., Virpioja, S., Smit, P., Kurimo, M.: Morfessor FlatCat: an HMM-based method for unsupervised and semi-supervised learning of morphology. In: Proceedings of COLING 2014, the 25th International Conference on Computational Linguistics: Technical Papers. pp. 1177–1185. Dublin City University and Association for Computational Linguistics, Dublin, August 2014
3. Hajič, J., Hlaváčová, J.: MorfFlex CZ. LINDAT/CLARIN digital library at Institute of Formal and Applied Linguistics, Charles University in Prague (2016). http://hdl.handle.net/11234/1-1673
4. Křen, M., et al.: SYN2015: representative corpus of written Czech (2015). http://hdl.handle.net/11234/1-1593, LINDAT/CLARIAH-CZ digital library at the Institute of Formal and Applied Linguistics (ÚFAL). Faculty of Mathematics and Physics, Charles University
5. Kurimo, M., Virpioja, S., Turunen, V.T., Blackwood, G.W., Byrne, W.: Overview and results of morpho challenge 2009. In: Peters, C., et al. (eds.) CLEF 2009. LNCS, vol. 6241, pp. 578–597. Springer, Heidelberg (2010). https://doi.org/10.1007/978-3-642-15754-7_71
6. Kyjánek, L., Žabokrtský, Z., Ševčíková, M., Vidra, J.: Universal derivations kickoff: a collection of harmonized derivational resources for eleven languages. In: Proceedings of DeriMo, vol. 2019, pp. 101–110 (2019)
7. Kyjnek, L.: Morphological resources of derivational word-formation relations. Tech. rep. TR-2018-61, Faculty of Mathematics and Physics, Charles University (2018)
8. Liu, C.H., Liu, Q., Dublin, G.: Introduction to the shared tasks on cross-lingual word segmentation and morpheme segmentation. In: Proceedings of MLP, pp. 71–74 (2017)
9. Osolsobě, K., Pala, K.: Czech stem dictionary for IBM PC XT/AT. In: Conference on Computer Lexicography, pp. 163–172. Hungarian Academy of Sciences, Balatonfüred (1991)
10. Šimandl, J.: Slovník afixů užívaných v češtině. Karolinum, Praha (2016)
11. Šiška, Z.: Bázový morfematický slovník češtiny. UPOL, Olomouc (2005)
12. Skoumalová, H.: A Czech morphological lexicon. In: Proceedings of the Third Meeting of the ACL Special Interest Group in Computational Phonology, Madrid, pp. 41–47. ACL (1997)
13. Slavíčková, E.: Retrográdní morfematický slovník češtiny. Academia, Praha (1975)
14. Vidra, J.: Morphological segmentation of Czech words. Master Thesis (2018)
15. Vidra, J., Žabokrtský, Z., Kyjánek, L., Ševčíková, M., Dohnalová, Š.: DeriNet 2.0. LINDAT/CLARIN digital library at Institute of Formal and Applied Linguistics, Charles University in Prague (2019). http://hdl.handle.net/11234/1-2995
16. Weisheitelová, J., Králíková, K., Sgall, P.: Morphemic Analysis of Czech. MFF UK, Prague (1982)

Interpreting Word Embeddings Using a Distribution Agnostic Approach Employing Hellinger Distance

Tamás Ficsor[1]([⊠])(iD) and Gábor Berend[1,2](iD)

[1] Institute of Informatics, University of Szeged, Szeged, Hungary
{ficsort,berendg}@inf.u-szeged.hu
[2] MTA-SZTE Research Group on Artificial Intelligence, Szeged, Hungary

Abstract. Word embeddings can encode semantic and syntactic features and have achieved many recent successes in solving NLP tasks. Despite their successes, it is not trivial to directly extract lexical information out of them. In this paper, we propose a transformation of the embedding space to a more interpretable one using the Hellinger distance. We additionally suggest a distribution-agnostic approach using Kernel Density Estimation. A method is introduced to measure the interpretability of the word embeddings. Our results suggest that Hellinger based calculation gives a 1.35% improvement on average over the Bhattacharyya distance in terms of interpretability and adapts better to unknown words.

Keywords: Word embeddings · Interpretability · Computational semantics

1 Introduction

There have been many successes in the field of NLP due to the application of word embeddings [3]. There is a new forefront as well called contextual embeddings (e.g., BERT), which further increases the complexity of models to gain better performance. [2] showed there is only a small performance increase on average regard to complexity, but this performance varies on each employed task. Thus static embeddings still serve a good ground for initial investigations about the interpretability.

Prior research by [12] has investigated the issue of semantic encoding in word embeddings by assuming that the coefficients across each dimensions of the embedding space are distributed normally. This assumption may or may nor hold for a particular embedding space (e.g. the normality assumption is unlikely to hold for sparse word representations), hence we argue for the necessity of similar algorithms that operate in an distribution-agnostic manner. We introduce such a model that allows the word embedding coefficients to follow arbitrary distributions by relying on Kernel Density Estimation (KDE). A further novelty

© Springer Nature Switzerland AG 2020
P. Sojka et al. (Eds.): TSD 2020, LNAI 12284, pp. 197–205, 2020.
https://doi.org/10.1007/978-3-030-58323-1_21

of our work is that we propose the application of the Hellinger distance – as opposed to the Bhattacharyya distance – which could be a more suitable choice due to its bounded nature. We also make our source code publicly available[1] in order to foster the reproducibility of our experiments.

2   Related Work

Word embeddings can capture the semantic and syntactic relationships among words [9]. [15] was one of the first providing a comparison of several word embedding methods and showed that incorporating them into established NLP pipelines can also boost their performance.

There are several ways to incorporate external knowledge into NLP models. Related methods include the application of auto-encoders [16], embedding information during training [1] or after the training phase, called retrofitting [5]. One way to understand the semantic encoding of a dimension in embedding spaces is to link them to human interpretable features. [12] introduced the SEMCAT dataset and a method that relies on the Bhattacharyya distance for doing so. Their proposed method can produce a more interpretable space where each dimension encodes a predefined semantic category from the SEMCAT dataset, which was tested on GloVe [11] word embedding. There have been various approaches to nd these semantic categories. Such an approach is to construct datasets in a way which involves human participants only [8], or in a semi-automated manner where the construction is based on statistics to make the connections between the members of semantic categories and curated later by human participants [13].

Our proposed approach relies on the application of the Hellinger distance, which has already been used in NLP for constructing word embeddings [7]. Note that the way we rely on the Hellinger distance is different from prior work in that we use it for improving the interpretability of some arbitrarily trained embedding, whereas in [7] the Hellinger distance served as the basis for constructing the embeddings.

3   Our Approach

In this paper we follow a process to produce interpretable word vectors which is similar to [12]. Unlike [12], who trained their own GloVe embeddings, in order to mitigate the variability due to training, we are using the pre-trained GloVe with 6 billion token as our embedding space with 300 dimensions. Furthermore the SEMCAT dataset is going to serve as the definition of the semantic categories. Instead of GloVe and SEMCAT other kinds of embeddings (e.g., fastText) and datasets incorporating semantic relations (e.g., the McRae dataset [8]) can be integrated into our framework.

---

[1] https://github.com/ficstamas/word_embedding_interpretability.

3.1 Information Encoding of Dimensions

The assumption of normality of the embedding dimensions is statistically a convenient, however, empirically not necessarily a valid approach. As the normal distribution is simple and well-understood, it is also frequently used in predictive models, however, assuming normality could have its own flaws [14]. The assumption of normality plays an essential role in the method proposed by [12], that we relax in this paper.

If we try to express the information gain from a dimension regarding some concept, we can do so by measuring the distance between the concept's and dimension's distribution. In order to investigate the semantic distribution of semantic categories across all dimensions, we define $\mathcal{W_D} \in \mathbb{R}_{\geq 0}^{|d| \times |c|}$, with $|d|$ and $|c|$ denoting the number of dimensions of the embedding space and the number of semantic categories, respectively.

In this paper, we rely on two metrics, Bhattacharyya and Hellinger distances. The suggestion of Hellinger distance is an important step, as it is more sensitive to small distributional differences when the fidelity (overlap) of the two distributions is close to 1, which can be utilized in case of dense embeddings. Furthermore it is bounded on interval $[0, 1]$, which could be beneficial for sparse embeddings where the fidelity has a higher chance of being close to 0 (causing the Bhattacharrya distance to approach infinity).

First we separate the ith dimension's coefficients into category ($P_{i,j}$) and out-of-category ($Q_{i,j}$) vectors. A coefficient belongs to the $P_{i,j}$ vector if the associated word to that coefficient is an element of the jth semantic category, and it belongs to the $Q_{i,j}$ otherwise. It is going to be denoted for P and Q for short.

By assuming that P and Q are normally distributed, we can derive the closed form definitions for the Bhattacharyya and Hellinger distances as included in Eqs. (1) and (2), respectively. In the below formulas μ and σ denote the mean and standard deviation of the respective distributions.

$$D_B(P,Q) = \frac{1}{4}\ln\left(\frac{1}{4}\left(\frac{\sigma_p^2}{\sigma_q^2} + \frac{\sigma_q^2}{\sigma_p^2} + 2\right)\right) + \frac{1}{4}\left(\frac{(\mu_p - \mu_q)^2}{\sigma_p^2 + \sigma_q^2}\right) \tag{1}$$

$$D_H(P,Q) = \sqrt{1 - \sqrt{\frac{2\sigma_p\sigma_q}{\sigma_p^2 + \sigma_q^2}}e^{-\frac{1}{4}\cdot\frac{(\mu_p - \mu_q)^2}{\sigma_p^2 + \sigma_q^2}}} \tag{2}$$

By discarding the assumption that P and Q are distributed normally, the more general formulas are included in Eqs. (3) and (4) for the Bhattacharyya and Hellinger distances

$$D_B(p,q) = -\ln\int_{-\infty}^{\infty}\sqrt{p(x)q(x)}\,dx \tag{3}$$

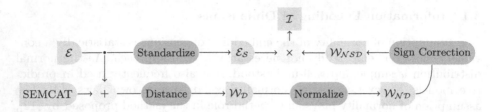

Fig. 1. The flowchart of the generation of the interpretable space $\mathcal{I}$. $\mathcal{E}$ refers to the input word embeddings, whereas $\mathcal{W_D}$ denotes the matrix describing the semantic distribution of the embedding. $\mathcal{W_D}$ constructed from the distances of distributions of semantic category (from SEMCAT) - dimension pairs.

$$D_H(p,q) = \sqrt{1 - \int_{-\infty}^{\infty} \sqrt{p(x)q(x)}\, dx} \qquad (4)$$

with the integrand being the Bhattacharyya coefficient, also called fidelity. In order to calculate the fidelity, we can apply Kernel Density Estimation (KDE) [6] for turning the empirical distributions of coefficients P and Q into continuous (and not necessarily normally distributed) probability density functions p and q.

By calculating either the closed or the continuous form of distances, we can calculate $\mathcal{W_D}(i,j) = D(P_{i,j}, Q_{i,j})$, where D is any of the above defined distances.

3.2   Interpretable Word Vector Generation

We normalize $\mathcal{W_D}$ so, that each semantic category vector in $\mathcal{W_{ND}}$ sum up to 1 (ℓ_1 norm). This step is important because otherwise the dominance of certain semantic categories could cause an undesired bias. Additionally, $\mathcal{W_{NSD}}(i,j) = sgn(\Delta_{i,j})\mathcal{W_{ND}}(i,j)$, where $\Delta_{i,j} = \mu_{p_{i,j}} - \mu_{q_{i,j}}$ and sgn is the signum function. This form of sign correction is useful as a dimension can encode a semantic category in negative or positive direction and we have to keep the mapping of the words in each dimension.

We standardize the input word embeddings in a way that each dimension has zero mean and unit variance. We denote the standardized embeddings as $\mathcal{E_S}$ and obtain the interpretable space of embeddings $\mathcal{I}$ as the product of $\mathcal{E_S}$ and $\mathcal{W_{NSD}}$.

3.3   Word Retrieval Test

In order to measure the semantic quality of $\mathcal{I}$, we used 60% of the words from each semantic category for training and 40% for validation. By using the training words, we are calculating the distance matrix $\mathcal{W_D}$ using either one of the Bhattacharyya or the Hellinger distance. We select the largest k weights ($k \in \{15, 18, 30, 37, 62, 75, 125, 150, 250, 300\}$) for each category and replace the other weights with 0 ($\mathcal{W_D^S}$). We are doing that, so we can inspect the strongest encoding dimensions generalization ability. Then in the calculation pipeline (Fig. 1) we are going to use $\mathcal{W}_D^S$ instead of $\mathcal{W}_D$, and we continue the rest of the calculations as it was defined earlier, by that we are going to obtain the interpretable space $\mathcal{I}_S$. We are going to rely on the validation set and see whether the words of a semantic category are seen among the top n, $3n$ or $5n$ words in the corresponding dimension in $\mathcal{I}_S$, where n is the number of the test words varying across the semantic categories. The final accuracy is the weighted mean of the accuracy of the dimensions, where the weight is the number of words in each category for the corresponding dimension.

3.4 Measuring Interpretability

To measure the interpretability of the model, we are going to use a functionally-grounded evaluation method [4], which means it does not involve humans in the process of quantification. Furthermore we use continuous values to express the level of interpretability [10]. The metric we rely on is an adaptation of the one proposed in [12]. We desire to have a metric that is independent from the dimensionality of the embedding space, so models with different number of dimensions can be easily compared.

$$IS_{i,j}^+ = \frac{|S_j \cap V_i^+(\lambda \times n_j)|}{n_j} \tag{5}$$

$$IS_{i,j}^- = \frac{|S_j \cap V_i^-(\lambda \times n_j)|}{n_j} \tag{6}$$

In the same way we defined the interpretability score for the positive (5) and negative (6) directions. In both equations i represents the dimension ($i \in \{1, 2, 3, \ldots, |d|\}$) and j the semantic categories ($j \in \{1, 2, 3, \ldots, |c|\}$). S_j represents the set of words belonging to the jth semantic category, n_j the number of words in that semantic category. V_i^+ and V_i^- gives us the top and bottom words selected by the magnitude of their coordinate respectively in the ith dimension. $\lambda \times n_j$ is the number words selected from the top and bottom words, hence $\lambda \in \mathbb{N}$ is the relaxation coefficient, as it controls how strict we measure the interpretability. As the interpretability of a dimension-category pair, we take the maximum of the positive and negative direction, i.e. $IS_{i,j} = \max\{IS_{i,j}^+, IS_{i,j}^-\}$.

Once we have the overall interpretability ($IS_{i,j}$), we are going to calculate the categorical interpretability Eq. (7). We thought that it is a too optimistic method to decide the interpretability level based on the maximum value in each selection. It is apparent from $IS_i = \max_j IS_{i,j}$, taking the max for every dimension would overestimate the true interpretability, because it would take the best-case scenario. Instead, we calculate Eq. (7), where we have a condition on the selected i which is defined by Eq. (8). We are going to select from the given interpretability scores provided by $IS_{i,j}$ (where j is fixed) the ith value where i is the maximum in the jth concept in $\mathcal{W}_D(i, j)$. This condition Eq. (8) ensures that we are going to obtain the interpretability score from the dimensions where the semantic category is encoded. This method is more suitable to obtain the interpretability scores, because it is relying on the distribution of the semantic categories, instead of the interpretability score from each dimension.

$$IS_j = IS_{i_j^*,j} \times 100 \tag{7}$$

$$i_j^* = _{i'} \; \mathcal{W}_\mathcal{D}(i',j). \tag{8}$$

Finally, to get the overall interpretability of the embedding space, we have to calculate the average of the interpretability scores across the semantic categories, where C is the number of categories.

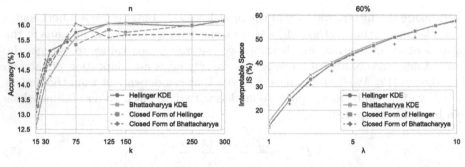

Accuracy of the word embedding
a

Interpetability of the word embedding
b

Fig. 2. Values from Table 1 with n test words in word retrieval test in a and Table 2 with 60% of the categories used in b.

4   Results

We load the most frequent 50,000 words from the pre-trained embeddings similar to [12] and tested for their normality using the Bonferroni corrected Kolmogorov-Smirnov test for multiple comparisons. Our test showed that 183 of the dimensions are normally distributed ($p > 0.05$). [12] reported more dimensions to behave normally, which could be explained by the fact that the authors trained their own GloVe embeddings. We deem this as an indication for the need towards the kind of distribution agnostic approaches we propose by relying on KDE. During the application of KDE, we utilized a Gaussian kernel and a bandwidth of 0.2 throughout all experiments.

4.1   Accuracy and Interpretability

Table 1 and Table 2 contains the quantitative performance of the embeddings from two complementary angles, i.e. their accuracy and interpretability. These

Table 1. Performance of the model on word category retrieval test for the top $n, 3n$ and $5n$ where n is the number of test words varying across the categories. $k (\in \{15, 18, 30, 37, 62, 75, 125, 150, 250, 300\})$ is the number of top weight kept from $\mathcal{W}_\mathcal{D}$ in each category. The method was discussed in Sect. 3.3

k	15	18	30	37	62	75	125	150	250	300
					n					
Closed form of Bhattacharyya	13.18	13.85	14.84	14.67	15.61	16.05	15.58	15.66	15.69	15.64
Closed form of Hellinger	13.44	13.27	14.46	14.85	15.55	15.34	15.84	15.75	15.99	16.13
Bhattacharyya KDE	12.54	12.86	14.06	14.29	15.23	15.58	16.05	16.08	16.10	16.13
Hellinger KDE	13.09	13.71	14.55	15.14	15.43	15.75	16.04	16.04	15.96	16.16
					$3n$					
Closed form of Bhattacharyya	25.76	27.25	29.53	30.61	32.92	33.71	34.15	34.30	33.39	33.18
Closed form of Hellinger	25.35	26.87	29.74	30.73	32.36	33.77	34.03	34.56	34.82	34.73
Bhattacharyya KDE	24.76	26.20	29.06	29.82	31.72	32.16	33.59	33.48	33.63	33.57
Hellinger KDE	25.32	27.39	29.88	30.38	32.54	33.27	34.27	34.38	34.50	34.41
					$5n$					
Closed form of Bhattacharyya	34.53	36.43	39.65	40.56	43.24	43.51	44.21	45.03	44.68	44.30
Closed form of Hellinger	33.92	36.05	39.15	40.41	42.87	43.30	44.59	44.15	45.00	44.94
Bhattacharyya KDE	33.07	34.41	37.90	39.15	42.55	43.01	44.30	44.68	45.18	45.27
Hellinger KDE	34.10	35.79	39.33	40.21	42.87	43.39	44.73	44.65	45.00	45.12

Table 2. Interpretability scores for the interpretable space $\mathcal{I}$ with different λ parameter values ($\lambda = 1$ the most strict and $\lambda = 10$ the most relaxed) using different distances. The $r \in \{100, 80, 60\}$ percentage of the words kept from the semantic categories relative to category centers

λ	1	2	3	4	5	6	7	8	9	10
					100% of the words					
GloVe	2.82	4.84	6.83	8.72	10.37	12.08	13.34	14.55	15.79	16.87
Closed form of Bhattacharyya.	35.34	48.84	56.47	61.35	65.01	68.21	70.81	72.42	73.88	75.45
Closed form of Hellinger	36.32	49.94	57.64	62.75	66.72	69.52	72.08	74.09	75.54	76.72
Bhattacharyya KDE	35.47	49.05	56.69	61.60	65.35	68.37	70.57	72.53	74.02	75.31
Hellinger KDE	36.24	49.49	57.35	62.73	66.63	69.56	71.92	74.04	75.42	76.78
					80% of the words					
GloVe	1.85	3.42	4.91	6.33	7.69	9.00	10.21	11.34	12.20	13.07
Closed form of Bhattacharyya	23.96	36.99	45.70	51.66	55.37	59.13	61.96	64.50	66.40	67.91
Closed form of Hellinger	24.36	38.36	47.18	53.32	57.49	61.09	63.35	65.89	67.91	69.48
Bhattacharyya KDE	25.08	39.04	46.80	52.70	57.10	60.73	63.18	65.26	67.16	68.62
Hellinger KDE	24.57	38.34	47.16	53.09	57.22	60.54	63.38	65.70	67.82	69.38
					60% of the words					
GloVe	1.05	1.87	2.62	3.71	4.71	5.67	6.59	7.47	8.20	9.08
Closed form of Bhattacharyya	12.44	22.76	30.72	36.61	41.38	45.00	47.89	50.64	52.78	55.02
Closed form of Hellinger	13.12	24.36	33.14	39.24	43.66	47.25	50.76	53.42	55.69	57.57
Bhattacharyya KDE	15.01	26.44	34.92	40.22	44.66	48.10	51.01	53.45	55.87	57.56
Hellinger KDE	13.37	24.36	32.74	39.51	43.94	47.36	50.65	53.30	55.82	57.95

results are better to be observed jointly (Fig. 2) since it is possible to have a high score for interpretability but a low value for accuracy suggests that the original embedding has a high variance regarding to the probed semantic categories. Figure 2a illustrates a small sample of the results where we can observe that a word's semantic information is encoded in few dimensions, since relying on a reduced number of coefficients from $\mathcal{W}_D$ achieves similar performance to the application of all the coefficients. Our results tend to have close values, which can be caused by the high number of normally distributed dimensions. The results show that the proposed method is at least as good as [12]'s method, but it can be applied to any embedding space without restrictions.

5   Conclusions

The proposed method can transform any non-contextual embedding into an interpretable one, which can be used to analyze the semantic distribution which can have a potential application in knowledge base completion.

We suggested the usage of Hellinger distance, which shows better results in terms of interpretability when we have more words per semantic categories. Furthermore, easier to analyze the Hellinger distance due to its bounded nature. By relying on KDE, our proposed method can be applied even in cases when the normality for the coefficients of the dimensions is not necessarily met. This allows our approach a broader range of input embeddings to be applicable over (e.g., sparse embeddings).

The proposed modification on interpretability calculation, opened another dimension of freedom. It let us compare the interpretability of word embeddings with different dimensionality. So for every embedding space, the compression of semantic categories can be observed and the modification gives us a better look at the encoding of semantic categories, because we probe the category words from dimensions where they are deemed to be most likely encoded.

Acknowledgements. This research was supported by the European Union and co-funded by the European Social Fund through the project "Integrated program for training new generation of scientists in the fields of computer science" (EFOP-3.6.3-VEKOP-16-2017-0002) and by the National Research, Development and Innovation Office of Hungary through the Artificial Intelligence National Excellence Program (2018-1.2.1-NKP-2018-00008).

References

1. Alishahi, A., Barking, M., Chrupała, G.: Encoding of phonology in a recurrent neural model of grounded speech. In: Proceedings of the 21st Conference on Computational Natural Language Learning (CoNLL 2017), pp. 368–378 (2017)
2. Arora, S., May, A., Zhang, J., Ré, C.: Contextual embeddings: when are they worth it? arXiv preprint arXiv:2005.09117 (2020)
3. Chen, Y., Perozzi, B., Al-Rfou, R., Skiena, S.: The expressive power of word embeddings (2013)

4. Doshi-Velez, F., Kim, B.: Towards a rigorous science of interpretable machine learning (2017)
5. Faruqui, M., Dodge, J., Jauhar, S.K., Dyer, C., Hovy, E., Smith, N.A.: Retrofitting word vectors to semantic lexicons. In: Proceedings of NAACL (2015)
6. Hwang, J.N., Lay, S.R., Lippman, A.: Nonparametric multivariate density estimation: a comparative study. Trans. Sig. Proc. **42**(10), 2795–2810 (1994)
7. Lebret, R., Collobert, R.: Word embeddings through hellinger PCA. In: Proceedings of the 14th Conference of the European Chapter of the Association for Computational Linguistics (2014)
8. McRae, K., Cree, G., Seidenberg, M., Mcnorgan, C.: Semantic feature production norms for a large set of living and nonliving things. Behav. Res. Methods **37**, 547–59 (2005)
9. Mikolov, T., Sutskever, I., Chen, K., Corrado, G., Dean, J.: Distributed representations of words and phrases and their compositionality (2013)
10. Murdoch, W.J., Singh, C., Kumbier, K., Abbasi-Asl, R., Yu, B.: Definitions, methods, and applications in interpretable machine learning. Proc. Natl. Acad. Sci. **116**(44), 22071–22080 (2019)
11. Pennington, J., Socher, R., Manning, C.: Glove: global vectors for word representation. In: Proceedings of the 2014 Conference on Empirical Methods in Natural Language Processing (EMNLP), pp. 1532–1543 (2014)
12. Senel, L.K., Utlu, I., Yucesoy, V., Koc, A., Cukur, T.: Semantic structure and interpretability of word embeddings. IEEE/ACM Trans. Audio Speech Lang. Proc. **26**(10), 1769–1779 (2018)
13. Speer, R., Chin, J., Havasi, C.: Conceptnet 5.5: an open multilingual graph of general knowledge (2016)
14. Taleb, N.N.: The Black Swan: The Impact of the Highly Improbable, 1st edn. Random House, London (2008)
15. Turian, J., Ratinov, L.A., Bengio, Y.: Word representations: a simple and general method for semi-supervised learning. In: Proceedings of the 48th Annual Meeting of the Association for Computational Linguistics, pp. 384–394 (2010)
16. Yin, P., Zhou, C., He, J., Neubig, G.: StructVAE: tree-structured latent variable models for semi-supervised semantic parsing. In: Proceedings of the 56th Annual Meeting of the Association for Computational Linguistics (Volume 1: Long Papers), pp. 754–765 (2018)

Verb Focused Answering from CORD-19

Elizabeth Jasmi George[✉][iD]

MT-NLP Lab, LTRC, International Institute of Information Technology, Hyderabad, Hyderabad, India
elizabeth.george@research.iiit.ac.in

Abstract. At this time of a pandemic turning into an infodemic, it is significant to answer questions asked on the research related to that. This paper discusses a method of answering questions leveraging the syntactic structure of the sentences to find the verb of action in the context corresponding to the action in the question. This method generates correct answers for many factoid questions on descriptive context passages. The proposed method finds all the sentences in the passage, which has the same or synonymous verb as the verb in the question, processes the dependencies of the verbs obtained from the dependency parser and proceeds with further rule-based filtering for matching the other attributes of the answer span. We demonstrate this method on CORD-19 data [3] evaluated with free form natural language questions.

1 Introduction

Machine reading comprehension (MRC) is the essential task of textual question answering, in which each question is given a related context from which the answer should be inferred. This paper presents a method for answering a natural language question from a single descriptive passage, in which the verb describing the action in the question is identified, and the passage is analyzed for candidate sentences having verbs synonymous with the verb in the question out of which the answer can be deduced. Machine comprehension systems are particularly suited to high-volume, rapidly changing information sources. The most effective way of understanding a passage is by answering multiple questions on the passage, and it requires domain knowledge [8].

The human reader starts to comprehend by skimming the passage to get a general idea about the text, followed by scanning the passage to get some specific information. We speculate that one of the approaches during scanning is attempting to identify the verb in the question and finding a similar verb in the passage. A question will often have a main verb in it. Our machine reader focuses on pruning the passage text based on the required action comparable to the one mentioned in the question.

Supported by organization Advainet Solutions Private Limited.

P. Sojka et al. (Eds.): TSD 2020, LNAI 12284, pp. 206–213, 2020.
https://doi.org/10.1007/978-3-030-58323-1_22

2   Related Work

The different datasets, their comparison [23], and approaches for MRC are described by [25]. The methods and trends for MRC are explained by [15] and an investigation on the popular benchmarks in MRC is done by [12]. There are popular non-neural methods used in MRC, such as the bag of words [9], sliding window, logistic regression, TF-IDF boosted method, and integrated triaging [7]. The neural methods include mLSTM+Ptr, DCN, GA [4], BiDAF, FastQA [5], and QAnet [24]. There are methods incorporating reading strategies [19] and discourse relations [11].

Some syntax-based comprehension methods like [22] replace the options from the multiple-choice answers in the question and compare it with the sentences in the context passage. While the state-of-the-art results are obtained by neural models relying on embeddings such as Bert [2] and Electra [6], they hugely depend on the quality and quantity of training data and the fine-tuning of the hyper-parameters. While the majority of question answering systems on CORD-19 [3] depend on BioBERT [14] or SciBERT [10] language models explicitly trained on biomedical texts and scholarly articles, we present a syntax-based method which can produce significant answers. Our approach can be applied successfully to multiple datasets, supports free form questions, and does not require any training with a specific dataset.

3   Proposed Method

We propose a method for answering free form natural language English questions on any passage given as context. Our approach begins with dependency parsing the question and the passage using StanfordCoreNLP [17] to obtain the typed dependency relations existing in them. The question word is identified, and all the nouns and verbs in the question are filtered along with their corresponding dependencies. Structural connections establish dependency relations between words [20]. The Stanford parser [18] converts the parse into a dependency tree. For every element that one has in the utterance at hand, there is exactly one node in the syntactic structure that corresponds to that element. One of the advantages of dependency parsers for NLP is that the parse can be easily encoded in a table. The output obtained from Stanford CoreNLP parser [17] consists of tuples like { *'dep': 'nsubj', 'governor': 6, 'governorGloss': 'celebrated', 'dependent': 5, 'dependentGloss': 'Koch'*}[1] which mainly consist of a *governorGloss*, *dependentGloss* and a dependency relation existing between them. In the dependency tree obtained for a sentence, there will be edges labeled with the dependency relation from the governorGlosses to the dependentGlosses.

The modules in our syntax-based MRC is shown in Fig. 1. The *Question handler* does all the processing, such as POS tagging, verb and noun filtering, finding the dependency relation associated with verbs, and question word identification

---

[1] This is one of the tuples obtained for the sentence "Christina Koch celebrated with a thumbs up as she got out of the Souyz capsule".

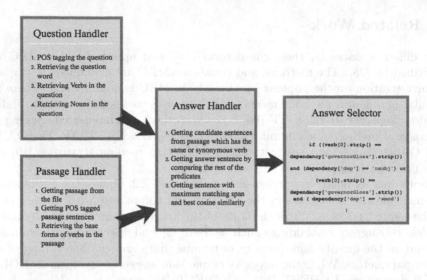

Fig. 1. Modules in this syntax-based MRC

on the question utterance. The *Passage handler* processes the passage by preprocessing and separating the sentences. Finding the dependency relations of verbs in it, getting the list of lemmatized verbs and POS tagging the sentences in the passage. The *Answer handler* identifies candidate answers, which either matches the verb in the question or has a synonymous verb as that in the question or otherwise, has the maximum text span matching with the question. The *Answer selector* module pinpoints the answer to the question by iterating through the dependency tuples obtained from the dependency parser. For the named entities that could not be filtered from the candidate answer, the whole candidate sentence is output as the answer. The following section outlines the answering strategy.

3.1   Strategy for Answering Questions

The context passage is a scholarly article from the CORD-19 dataset UID: br33p9xd, titled *"Preventive Behaviors Conveyed on YouTube to Mitigate Transmission of COVID-19"*. The question asked is, *"Does COVID spread by contact?"*.

The algorithm selects the article whose title and abstract contain the named entities which significantly overlap with the list of named entities of the question asked. The answering strategy is explained in the following sections.

Identify the Question Word, Verbs and Nouns. Question word is identified from the question, and all the nouns and all the verbs in the question are filtered with their corresponding dependencies. The dependency parsed question is given in Fig. 2. The parts-of-speech tagged question is *[('does', 'VBZ'), ('COVID', 'NN'), ('spread', 'VBN'), ('by', 'IN'), ('contact', 'NN'), ('?', '.')]*

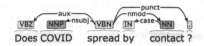

Does COVID   spread by   contact ?

Fig. 2. Dependency parsed question

Preprocess the Question and the Passage. The question and the passage sentences are converted to lowercase and preprocessed by converting the verbs in the question to their lemmatized form. WordNet Lemmatizer in NLTK [16] is used for lemmatizing the verbs. The question word is *Does*, which is a polar question. The nouns in the question are *'COVID': 'NN', 'contact': 'NN'*, and the verbs in the question are *[('do', 'VBZ', 0), ('spread', 'VBN', 2)]*.

The 141 sentences in the article given as context contain 185 verbs and 160 nouns as follows: *[('cross-sectional', 'NNP'), ('study', 'NNP'), ('monitoring', 'VBG')], [('travis', 'NNP'), ('sanchez', 'NNP'), ('reviewed', 'VBN')], [('author', 'NN'), ('information', 'NN'), ('article', 'NNP'), ('notes', 'VBZ')], [('coronavirus', 'NN'), ('spreads', 'VBZ')], [('system', 'NN'), ('meet', 'VBP')],..... [('surveillance', 'NNP'), ('are', 'VBP'), ('provided', 'VBN')]*

Find the Candidate Sentences by Matching the Verbs. The verbs in the question are compared with the verbs in the passage, by iterating through the dependency tuples and comparing the V.+ nodes. If they match, then that sentence from the passage is added to the candidate sentence list. The auxiliary verbs such as *'am', 'are', 'is', 'was', 'were', 'can', 'could', 'may', 'might', 'must', 'shall', 'should', 'will', 'would', 'do', 'does', 'did', 'has', 'have'* can frequently occur in most English passages and they can often overshadow the main verbs. So the auxiliary verbs are deprioritized while considering the passage to identify the presence of the verb from the question. The auxiliary verbs are considered only when there is no main verb. In the question "Does COVID spread by contact?", the main verb 'spread' is considered instead of 'does' for comparison with verbs in context passage sentences. The possible answer from the original passage is obtained as *'COVID-19 is largely spread by contact with respiratory droplets from an infected individual'*. The dependency structure of the sentence with a matching verb is given in Fig. 3.

Find the Candidate Sentences if Synonymous Verbs Match. If a sentence contains a verb that is synonymous with the verb in the question, then that sentence is added to the candidate sentence list. Thesaurus and Synonyms are generated using NLPCompromise packages [13]. The sense of the word is also included while finding synonyms to avoid confusion between noun and verb senses. If candidate sentences are not obtained on the exact verb match, they are retrieved through the synonymous verb match by replacing the question verbs with each verb in the synonym list and rechecking the passage for a match. For the verb, 'spread', the synonyms 'grow, increase, escalate, advance, develop, broaden, proliferate' are also considered.

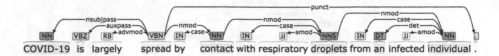

Fig. 3. Dependency parsed matching sentence from the passage

Select Sentences with the Highest Cosine Similarity and Longest Matching Span. Out of the candidate sentences collected, those with the longest matching span, and the best cosine similarity are selected to be the answer sentence. For passages describing many actors doing the same action in different contexts, all the passage sentences with the action verb will be matching. The order of their occurrence in the passage is not significant for deciding their candidature for being the answer to the question. So, in that case, the cosine similarity of the matching passage sentence with the question is evaluated for making the best choice. The longest matching span is also evaluated for reinforcing the decision.

Find the Candidate Sentences with Matching Predicates. If there is no matching verb in the passage, then the predicate of the question is matched with the sentences in the passage, to get the answer. The nouns in the best-matched sentences are compared with the nouns in question to get the most suitable candidate sentence as the answer sentence.

Obtain Answer Phrase from the Answer Sentence. Once the answer sentence is identified, the answer to a 'Who' question is found out by iterating through the dependency relation tuples obtained from the dependency parser and matching *'governorGloss'* of the dependency tuple with the verb in the question and the having *'dep'* as *'nSubj'* or *'amod'*. The sentence with the verbs converted to their lemmatized form is used to identify the answers. If the answer is a noun compound, the chain of nouns in the answer is obtained by following the dependency relation 'compound' until it reaches the last modifier from the head noun. To find the answer to 'How' questions, 'dependentGloss' of dependencies 'advmod' and 'amod' are found out. For answering 'What' questions, the matching verb's dependent 'dependentGloss' with a dependency relation 'dobj' is found out.

4   Results and Evaluation

This approach of utilizing the syntactic structure and matching the verbs is efficient in the cases where the passage is action-oriented. However, this method is not suitable if inference calculation, paraphrase understanding, or coreference resolution is required for finding the answer. This approach shows lesser efficiency when a chain of verbs is embedded in the sentence. Comparing to the deep learning methods in MRC requiring long passages as training data, this approach using syntax obtains answers with fewer data.

Table 1. Evaluation results of our machine reader

Data source	#Documents considered	#Questions	Genre	EM	p@1	p@3	Hit@3
CORD-19	2	14	Scholarly Articles	–	0.64	0.71	0.71
NewsQA	4	4	Crowd sourced questions on news articles	25%	0.5	0.75	0.75

Table 2. Context passages, questions and computed answers

Context passage	Question	Computed answer
CORD-19 UID: 41jqgsv0	What are the precautions needed while using hydroxychloroquine as a drug?	caution and contraindication with chloroquine and hydroxychloroquine expectedly, some precautions will be need while use both these drugs that include frequent monitoring of hematological parameters (rbc, wbc and platelet counts), measurement of serum electrolytes, blood glucose (because of hypoglycemic potential of hcq) and hepatic as well as renal functions
CORD-19 UID: cpu3q9o6	What is the recommended dose?	retinopathy be a dose-limiting adverse effect of hydroxychloroquine, and a safe daily dose appear to correspond to 6.5 mg/kg of ideal body weight and 5.0 mg/kg of actual body weight [8]

For evaluating our system, we use some extractive metrics mentioned in a survey on machine reading comprehension systems [1]. The metrics applied are (i) Exact Match (EM) or Accuracy - the percentage of answers that exactly match with the correct answers (ii) Precision@K - the number of correct answers in the first K returned answers without considering the position of these correct answers (iii) Hit@K - count of the number of samples where their first K returned answers include the correct answer. The evaluation results of our reader on a few samples from CORD-19 [3] and NewsQA [21] are given in Table 1, and the context passages, questions, and computed answers are given in Table 2.

5   Conclusion and Future Work

Finding out the answer span is the first step in reading comprehension, which is attained in this work. Even when the verb in the question is not present in the passage, the matching span congruence and similarity calculations identify the best candidate answer if the question is answerable. The future work would incorporate paraphrasing, inferences, and sentence reduction techniques to answer questions from the syntactic structure obtained as dependency tuples with enhanced results from Stanza [26].

References

1. Baradaran, R., Ghiasi, R., Amirkhani, H.:. A Survey on Machine Reading Comprehension Systems. arXiv preprint arXiv:2001.01582 (2020)
2. Devlin, J., Chang, M.-W., Lee, K., Toutanova, K.: Bert: Pre-training of deep bidirectional transformers for language understanding. arXiv preprint arXiv:1810.04805 (2018)
3. COVID-19 Open Research Dataset (CORD-19) (2020). Version 2020-03-20. https://pages.semanticscholar.org/coronavirus-research. https://doi.org/10.5281/zenodo.3715505. Accessed 11 Apr 2020
4. Dhingra, B., Liu, H., Cohen, W.W., Salakhutdinov, R.: Gated-Attention Readers for Text Comprehension. ACL (2016). https://arxiv.org/pdf/1606.01549.pdf
5. Weissenborn, D., Wiese, G., Seiffe, L.: FastQA: A Simple and Efficient Neural Architecture for Question Answering. ArXiv abs/1703.04816: n. pag (2017)
6. Clark, K., Luong, M.-T., Le, Q.V., Manning, C.D.: Electra: Pre-training text encoders as discriminators rather than generators. arXiv preprint arXiv:2003.10555 (2020)
7. Wu, F., Li, B., Wang, L., Lao, N., Blitzer, J., Weinberger, K.Q.: Integrated triaging for fast reading comprehension. In: WWW 2018, Lyon, France, 23–27 April, 2018. ArXiv abs/1909.13128: n. pag (2019)
8. Hirsch, E.: Reading Comprehension Requires Knowledge-of Words and the World (2003)
9. Hirschman, L., Light, M., Breck, E., Burger, J.D.: Deep read: a reading comprehension system. ACL In: Proceedings of the 37th Annual Meeting of the Association for Computational Linguistics (1999). https://doi.org/10.3115/1034678.1034731
10. Beltagy, I., Lo, K., Cohan, A.: SciBERT: a pretrained language model for scientific text. In: Proceedings of the 2019 Conference on Empirical Methods in Natural Language Processing and the 9th International Joint Conference on Natural Language Processing (EMNLP-IJCNLP), pp. 3606–3611 (2019)
11. Narasimhan, K., Barzilay, R.: Machine comprehension with discourse relations. In: Proceedings of the 53rd Annual Meeting of the Association for Computational Linguistics and the 7th International Joint Conference on Natural Language Processing (Volume 1: Long Papers), pp. 1253–1262 (2015). https://doi.org/10.3115/v1/p15-1121

12. Kaushik, D., Lipton, Z.C.: How Much Reading Does Reading Comprehension Require? A Critical Investigation of Popular Benchmarks. EMNLP (2018). https://doi.org/10.18653/v1/d18-1546
13. Kelly, S., et al.:. Compromise- modest natural-language processing in Javascript. https://www.npmjs.com/package/compromise. Accessed 2019/11/09
14. Lee, J., et al.: BioBERT: a pre-trained biomedical language representation model for biomedical text mining, Bioinformatics **36**(4), 1234–1240 (2020). https://doi.org/10.1093/bioinformatics/btz682
15. Liu, S., Zhang, X., Zhang, S., Wang, H., Zhang, W.: Neural machine reading comprehension: methods and trends. Appl. Sci. **9**(18), 3698 (2019). https://doi.org/10.3390/app9183698, ArXiv abs/1907.01118 (2019): n. pag
16. Loper, E., Bird, S.: NLTK: The Natural Language Toolkit (2002). https://doi.org/10.3115/1118108.1118117. ArXiv cs.CL/0205028: n. pag
17. Manning, C.D., Surdeanu, M., Bauer, J., Finkel, J., Bethard, S.J., McClosky, D.: The stanford CoreNLP natural language processing toolkit. In: Proceedings of the 52nd Annual Meeting of the Association for Computational Linguistics: System Demonstrations, pp. 55–60 (2014). https://doi.org/10.3115/v1/p14-5010
18. de Marneffe, M.-C., MacCartney, B., Manning, C.D.: Generating Typed Dependency Parses from Phrase Structure Parses. LREC (2006)
19. Sun, K., Yu, D., Yu, D., Cardie, C.: Improving Machine Reading Comprehension with General Reading Strategies. NAACL-HLT (2018). https://doi.org/10.18653/v1/n19-1270
20. Tesnière, L.: Elements of Structural Syntax (2015). https://www.jbe-platform.com/content/books/9789027269997
21. Trischler, A., et al.: NewsQA: a machine comprehension dataset. Rep4NLP@ACL (2016). https://doi.org/10.18653/v1/w17-2623
22. Wang, H., Bansal, M., Gimpel, K., McAllester, D.: Machine comprehension with syntax, frames, and semantics. In: Proceedings of the 53rd Annual Meeting of the Association for Computational Linguistics and the 7th International Joint Conference on Natural Language Processing (Volume 2: Short Papers), pp. 700–706 (2015)
23. Yatskar, M.: A qualitative comparison of CoQA, SQuAD 2.0 and QuAC. In: Proceedings of the 2019 Conference of the North American Chapter of the Association for Computational Linguistics: Human Language Technologies, Volume 1 (Long and Short Papers), Minneapolis, MN, USA, 3–5 June 2019, pp. 2318–2323 (2019). https://arxiv.org/abs/1809.10735
24. Yu, A.W., et al.: QANet: Combining Local Convolution with Global Self-Attention for Reading Comprehension. ArXiv abs/1804.09541 (2018). n. pag
25. Zhang, X., Yang, A., Li, S., Wang, Y.: Machine Reading Comprehension: a Literature Review (2019). https://arxiv.org/abs/1907.01686
26. Qi, P., Zhang, Y., Zhang, Y., Bolton, J., Manning, C.D.: Stanza: a python natural language processing toolkit for many human languages (2020). https://arxiv.org/abs/2003.07082

Adjusting BERT's Pooling Layer for Large-Scale Multi-Label Text Classification

Jan Lehečka[✉][ID], Jan Švec[ID], Pavel Ircing[ID], and Luboš Šmídl[ID]

Department of Cybernetics, University of West Bohemia in Pilsen,
Pilsen, Czech Republic
{jlehecka,honzas,ircing,smidl}@kky.zcu.cz

Abstract. In this paper, we present our experiments with BERT models in the task of Large-scale Multi-label Text Classification (LMTC). In the LMTC task, each text document can have multiple class labels, while the total number of classes is in the order of thousands. We propose a pooling layer architecture on top of BERT models, which improves the quality of classification by using information from the standard [CLS] token in combination with pooled sequence output. We demonstrate the improvements on Wikipedia datasets in three different languages using public pre-trained BERT models.

Keywords: Text classification · BERT model

1 Introduction

In present days, text classification task plays a very important role among Natural Language Processing (NLP) problems. With increasing amounts of available electronic texts, there is a natural need to classify those texts automatically into predefined classes. In many real-world problems, however, a text can belong to more than one class (e.g. news article about hurricane can be classified into both weather and disaster classes). The NLP task where one text document can belong to more than one class, is known as *Multi-label Text Classification*.

When the number of classes the text can possibly belong to reaches the order of thousands, it is known as *Large-scale Multi-label Text Classification* problem (LMTC) [2].

In the last few years, deep neural networks based on Transformers [4] has dominated the research field of NLP and NLU (Natural Language Understanding). Self-attention [13] Transformers, known as BERT (Bidirectional Encoder Representations from Transformers), has achieved amazing results in many tasks, including multi-label text classification [1,11], sentiment analysis [9], language modeling [15] or text summarization [7].

BERT-based classification models typically use the feature vector generated for a special classification token (denoted as [CLS]), which was used during pre-training for *next sentence prediction*. In this task, the classification token was

© Springer Nature Switzerland AG 2020
P. Sojka et al. (Eds.): TSD 2020, LNAI 12284, pp. 214–221, 2020.
https://doi.org/10.1007/978-3-030-58323-1_23

used to distinguish between inputs with two consequent sentences and inputs with two randomly chosen sentences from a corpus, i.e. it was pre-trained to a classification problem with two classes.

When using only output from the [CLS] token, the information about the document's classification must be encoded in a single vector, which in the case of BERT-base architecture has 768 elements. In this paper, we hypothesize that for LMTC tasks where the number of labels is in the order of thousands, the classification could be inaccurate due to information compression. Another motivation for our proposed solution was the fact that the text classification result is often based on a presence or absence of a strong keyword in the documents. In our solution, the information about such strong keywords can be easily pooled out from the sequence of output features (one feature vector per input token) and thus it can contribute to the classification results more directly. We call the top layer which converts BERT's output into classification a *Pooling Layer*.

The paper is organized as follows. Section 2 describes related work we are aware of. In Sect. 3, we propose novel architecture of BERT's pooling layer and Sect. 4 offers details about experimental setup. Results are summarized in Sect. 5 and in the final Sect. 6, we discuss achieved results.

2 Related Work

The automatic text classification problem has been studied intensively during the last decades with significant improvements scored recently by models based on Transformers [4]. Since text classification tasks are also part of GLUE benchmark [14], it attracts the most successful researchers in NLU field in present days to compete[1].

BERT model was successfully applied to document classification tasks for example in [1], while an exhaustive set of experiments concerning fine-tuning methods of BERT models for text classification was published in [11]. In both mentioned papers, the number of target classes was rather small (in the order of tens).

Large-scale multi-label text classification with thousands of labels has been studied in [2]. In this paper, BERT model was used to classify legislative documents into a set of 4.3 thousand of labels. It was shown that fine-tuned BERT model significantly outperforms all previously published attention-based deep neural networks models in a LMTC task.

Moreover, when the number of labels raises to extreme values (e.g. order of millions), the standard approaches using one neuron per label in the output layer easily reach hardware limitations. This task is known as XMC (extreme multi-label text classification) and BERT-based solution was presented in [3]. The paper proposes X-BERT, a scalable solution to fine-tune BERT models on the XMC problem by building label representations.

The majority of published works use BERT with default pooling layer, i.e. the classification is based only on the final hidden state of the [CLS] token. In

---

[1] https://gluebenchmark.com/leaderboard.

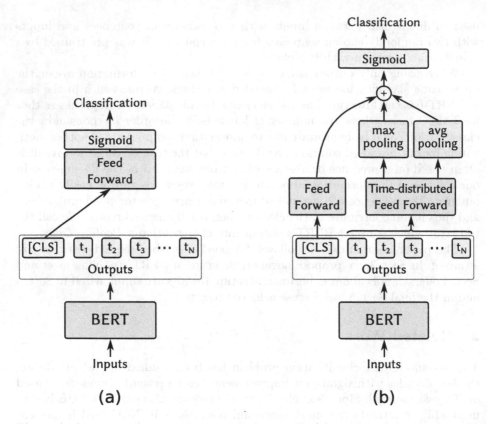

Fig. 1. Architecture of pooling layer in baseline model (a) and in our proposed model (b).

[8], the effect of different pooling layers on top of BERT models was studied. The mean-pooling of hidden states performed the best in this paper experiments. In [10], another two effective pooling strategies have been proposed. The idea here was to pool all intermediate representations of the [CLS] token. In this paper, we propose a pooling layer which combines [CLS] token with pooled sequence output. As far as we know, there is no published work similar to our proposed solution for LMTC task.

3   Proposed Solution

We propose a model where the classification result is based not only on the information from the final hidden state of the first token (i.e. [CLS] token) but also on the information from the full output sequence. The difference between the standard use of BERT models in classification tasks and our proposed solution is depicted in Fig. 1.

As a baseline approach, we took a standard pooling layer used on top of BERT models for classification tasks (model (a) in Fig. 1). In this model, the classification is based only on the information encoded in the final hidden state of [CLS] token, which is fully connected to a feed forward layer with as many neurons as the number of different labels in the dataset. In this final classification layer, each neuron computes output for one label. The output is then squeezed between 0 and 1 by a sigmoid activation function.

Our proposed model (model (b) in Fig. 1) uses additional information from final hidden states of input tokens $t_1, t_2, \ldots t_N$. The BERT's sequence output is fetched into time-distributed fully connected dense layer with the number of neurons equal to the number of labels. The output of this layer is pooled in two different ways using the max-pooling and the average-pooling. Max-pooling outputs the maximum of each feature across all tokens, thus it reacts on strong class-related keywords. The average-pooling, on the other hand, outputs the average of each feature over the sequence and thus attends to all tokens in the sequence evenly. To compute average-pooling, we clipped all features into interval $[-1, 1]$ to intentionally suppress the influence of strong keywords. When computing pooled values, we ignored all padding tokens (denoted as [PAD]). Finally, the features generated from the pooled output and the output for the [CLS] token are summed together. The sigmoid functions predict the output of the model in the form of class probabilities.

As we involved one extra time-distributed dense layer into our solution, we slightly increased the number of trainable parameters (by BERT's hidden size times the number of labels). However, we did not observe any slowdown of the fine-tuning.

4 Experimental Setup

Since the first paragraph of Wikipedia pages typically contains short text summary (which should be enough to classify the whole text), we limited input sequences to the first 128 tokens.

The output for each classified document is a vector of per-label scores (soft predictions), which must be converted into binary hard prediction. We used the following thresholding strategy:

Given a vector of per-label scores $s = (s_1, s_2, \ldots, s_K)$, assign i-th label, if

$$\frac{s_i}{\max(s_1, s_2, \ldots, s_K)} \geq p \tag{1}$$

with threshold p optimized on development data. This simple yet effective strategy was used for example by two winning teams in WISE 2014 Challenge [12].

For each experiment, we used the training dataset to fine-tune the BERT model, the development dataset for early stopping and to estimate optimal thresholds and the test dataset to evaluate models. As an evaluation metric, we used sample-averaged F1 score, which is the harmonic mean of precision P and recall R:

$$F1 = \frac{2PR}{P + R}, \tag{2}$$

$$P = \frac{tp}{tp + fp}, \qquad (3)$$

$$R = \frac{tp}{tp + fn}, \qquad (4)$$

where tp are true positives (number of correctly assigned labels), fp false positives (incorrectly assigned labels) and fn false negatives (missed labels).

4.1 BERT Models

For all our experiments, we used BERT-base model architecture, i.e. all models had 12 transformation blocks, 12 attention heads, 110 million trainable parameters and the hidden size of 768 neurons.

For English dataset, we used uncased variants of published pretrained BERT-base model[2]. For Czech and Slovak, we used recommended cased variant of published pretrained multi-lingual model[3].

Fine-Tuning. We run fine-tuning on a single GPUs using the `keras-bert` library[4]. During the fine-tuning, we used adapters [5] and updated only about 2% of the model's parameters, namely self-attention normalization layers, feed forward normalization layers and the adapter layers.

All models were fine-tuned with the same setup: learning rate $1e - 4$ with RAdam [6] and categorical entropy loss, maximum sequence length 128 tokens, batch size 32 and maximum 50 epochs with early stopping after 3 non-improving epochs. The improvement in the mean of the loss function was measured on the development data after each epoch. Most of the time, the model converged after approximately 10 epochs, which took about 7 h of fine-tuning on a single Tesla T4 GPU.

4.2 Datasets

We tested the proposed approach on Wikipedia datasets. We used individual Wikipedia pages as documents (instances) and associated categories as labels (classes). We chose 3 languages: Czech and Slovak, which are at our main focus, and English to incorporate also one widely-studied dataset.

To keep the problem in the limits of a LSMC, which typically contains thousands of labels (classes), we randomly selected an appropriate subset of each dataset. This was especially important for English dataset, which has about 6 million of pages associated with more than 1.35 million different categories in total. Classifying documents into such a large collection of classes is a different task known as XMC (extreme multi-label text classification), which cannot

---

[2] https://storage.googleapis.com/bert_models/2018_10_18/uncased_L-12_H-768_A-12.zip.

[3] https://storage.googleapis.com/bert_models/2018_11_23/multi_cased_L-12_H-768_A-12.zip.

[4] https://github.com/CyberZHG/keras-bert.

Table 1. Datasets statistics. For each dataset, we are showing the total number of documents (split into train, development and test subsets) and a total number of different labels. Since we are dealing with the multi-label problem, we are also showing average per-document label count and average per-label document count.

Dataset	#trainDocs	#devDocs	#testDocs	#labels	#labels/doc	#docs/label
English	44 651	14 884	14 884	1 212	2.7	165.7
Czech	63 631	21 211	21 211	2 720	3.9	153.6
Slovak	75 523	25 175	25 175	1 268	1.5	147.2

be solved by standard pooling layer on top of BERT model due to extreme computational complexity [3].

Since the XMC task is not in the focus of this paper, we restricted Wikipedia dataset for each language by following these steps:

1. Extract all pages and associated categories from the latest Wikipedia dump.
2. Randomly select subcorpus containing 200 thousand pages.
3. To avoid rare labels, keep only categories with at least $N = 50$ pages in selected subcorpus.
4. Remove pages without any associated label from selected subcorpus.
5. Split dataset into train-dev-test in ratio 60:20:20.

In this way, we created a dataset for each of three selected languages with the number of labels suitable for LSMC task. The details about created datasets are shown in Table 1.

5 Results

Our achieved results are summarized in Table 2. For each dataset, we fine-tuned the pre-trained BERT model with four different output layers. We run each experiment five times and report mean results with standard deviations.

The baseline uses only information encoded in the final hidden state of [CLS] token, which is the standard approach of how to use BERT model in classification tasks. The other three tested pooling layers combine information from [CLS] token with pooled sequence output as depicted in Fig. 1(b). In all three variants of the proposed pooling layer, the final classification is based on a simple element-wise vector addition of information from [CLS] token and pooled information. To make the addition possible, vectors [CLS], AVG and MAX must have the same size (one feature per label), which is ensured by setting a corresponding number of neurons in the preceding feed forward layers.

As can be seen from the results, adding only the output from the average-pooling ([CLS]+AVG rows) is not beneficial. On the contrary, this pooling layer adjustment harmed the classification performance in all of our experiments. On the other hand, for all tested datasets, adding information from max-pooling

Table 2. Results table. The abbreviations used for the pooling layer are following: [CLS] stands for using information encoded in the final hidden state of [CLS] token, AVG is average-pooled information from BERT's sequence output, MAX is max-pooled information from BERT's sequence output and the "+" symbol stands for element-wise addition of vectors.

Dataset	BERT-model	Pooling layer	F1[%]
English	public English (uncased)	[CLS] (baseline)	81.64 ± 0.13
		[CLS]+AVG	81.05 ± 0.10
		[CLS]+MAX	82.10 ± 0.12
		[CLS]+MAX+AVG	82.26 ± 0.14
Czech	public multi-lingual (cased)	[CLS] (baseline)	77.41 ± 0.38
		[CLS]+AVG	77.07 ± 0.31
		[CLS]+MAX	77.92 ± 0.25
		[CLS]+MAX+AVG	79.86 ± 0.17
Slovak	public multi-lingual (cased)	[CLS] (baseline)	88.70 ± 0.14
		[CLS]+AVG	88.54 ± 0.03
		[CLS]+MAX	89.07 ± 0.08
		[CLS]+MAX+AVG	89.15 ± 0.12

([CLS]+MAX rows) improved F1 score and additional adding of AVG vector leads to further improvement.

To summarize the achieved results, adding the max-pooled information from BERT's output always improved F1 score while average-pooled information is only advantageous in combination with max-pooling. A simple two-sided t-test confirmed that our improvements are statistically significant with $p < 0.005$ for all tested datasets.

6 Conclusion

In this paper, we have presented our experiments with BERT models in the task of Large-scale Multi-label Text Classification (LMTC) in three languages (English, Czech and Slovak). We proposed pooling layer adjustment leading to an improvement in terms of F1 score. Results of our experiments confirmed that using pooled information from BERT's sequence output can be used as additional information in order to enhance the quality of multi-label text classification with thousands of labels.

We obtained the best results when the document classification was based on the combined information of the classification token with both max- and average-pooled information from BERT's sequence output. The absolute improvement of F1 varies between 0.3% for Slovak dataset and 3.3% for Czech dataset with more than two times more labels.

For future research, it would be interesting to investigate in detail the relation between the total number of labels and improvement gained from the proposed solution.

Acknowledgments. This research was supported by the Ministry of Culture of the Czech Republic, project No. DG18P02OVV016.

References

1. Adhikari, A., Ram, A., Tang, R., Lin, J.: DocBERT: BERT for document classification. arXiv preprint arXiv:1904.08398 (2019)
2. Chalkidis, I., Fergadiotis, M., Malakasiotis, P., Androutsopoulos, I.: Large-scale multi-label text classification on EU legislation. arXiv preprint arXiv:1906.02192 (2019)
3. Chang, W.C., Yu, H.F., Zhong, K., Yang, Y., Dhillon, I.: X-BERT: extreme multi-label text classification using bidirectional encoder representations from transformers. arXiv preprint arXiv:1905.02331 (2019)
4. Devlin, J., Chang, M.W., Lee, K., Toutanova, K.: BERT: pre-training of deep bidirectional transformers for language understanding. arXiv preprint arXiv:1810.04805 (2018)
5. Houlsby, N., et al.: Parameter-efficient transfer learning for NLP. arXiv preprint arXiv:1902.00751 (2019)
6. Liu, L., et al.: On the variance of the adaptive learning rate and beyond. arXiv preprint arXiv:1908.03265 (2019)
7. Liu, Y., Lapata, M.: Text summarization with pretrained encoders. arXiv preprint arXiv:1908.08345 (2019)
8. Ma, X., Xu, P., Wang, Z., Nallapati, R., Xiang, B.: Universal text representation from BERT: an empirical study. arXiv preprint arXiv:1910.07973 (2019)
9. Rietzler, A., Stabinger, S., Opitz, P., Engl, S.: Adapt or get left behind: domain adaptation through BERT language model finetuning for aspect-target sentiment classification. arXiv preprint arXiv:1908.11860 (2019)
10. Song, Y., Wang, J., Liang, Z., Liu, Z., Jiang, T.: Utilizing BERT intermediate layers for aspect based sentiment analysis and natural language inference. arXiv preprint arXiv:2002.04815 (2020)
11. Sun, C., Qiu, X., Xu, Y., Huang, X.: How to fine-tune BERT for text classification? In: Sun, M., Huang, X., Ji, H., Liu, Z., Liu, Y. (eds.) CCL 2019. LNCS (LNAI), vol. 11856, pp. 194–206. Springer, Cham (2019). https://doi.org/10.1007/978-3-030-32381-3_16
12. Tsoumakas, G., et al.: WISE 2014 challenge: multi-label classification of print media articles to topics. In: Benatallah, B., Bestavros, A., Manolopoulos, Y., Vakali, A., Zhang, Y. (eds.) WISE 2014. LNCS, vol. 8787, pp. 541–548. Springer, Cham (2014). https://doi.org/10.1007/978-3-319-11746-1_40
13. Vaswani, A., et al.: Attention is all you need. In: Advances in Neural Information Processing Systems, pp. 5998–6008 (2017)
14. Wang, A., Singh, A., Michael, J., Hill, F., Levy, O., Bowman, S.R.: Glue: a multi-task benchmark and analysis platform for natural language understanding. arXiv preprint arXiv:1804.07461 (2018)
15. Wang, C., Li, M., Smola, A.J.: Language models with transformers. arXiv preprint arXiv:1904.09408 (2019)

Recognizing Preferred Grammatical Gender
in Russian Anonymous Online Confessions

Anton Alekseev[1](✉) and Sergey Nikolenko[1,2]

[1] Samsung-PDMI Joint AI Center, Steklov Mathematical Institute at St. Petersburg,
St. Petersburg 191023, Russia
anton.m.alexeyev@gmail.com
[2] Neuromation OU, 10111 Tallinn, Estonia

Abstract. We present annotation results for a dataset of public anonymous online confessions in Russian ("Overheard/Podslushano" group in *VKontakte*, posts tagged #family). Unlike many other cases with online social network data, intentionally anonymous posts do not contain any explicit metadata such as age or gender. We consider the problem of predicting the author's preferred grammatical gender for self-reference, a problem that proved to be surprisingly hard and not reducible to simple morphological analysis. We describe an expert labeling of a dataset for this problem, show the findings of predictive analysis, and introduce rule-based and machine learning approaches.

Keywords: Anonymous data · User profiling · Russian NLP

1 Introduction

The Web 2.0 era has brought an abundance of user-generated content (UGC) in popular social online services, both general-purpose such as *Facebook*, *MySpace*, *VKontakte*, or *Odnoklassniki*, and specialized such as *Instagram* for images, *Last.FM* for music etc. Some portals add a certain degree of anonymity, e.g., *4chan* allows completely anonymous responses, *ask.fm* allows to ask registered users anonymous questions, etc., and an important recent trend is the rise in the desirable level of anonymity; see also, e.g., [5,7]. Anonymous texts lack important metadata usually available in social network profiles such as age, gender, location, etc. Previous studies that had aimed to predict, e.g., demographic information given user-generated texts [3,9,12], tried to mine for clues that come up in an anonymous text: e.g., a mention of "my wife" strongly suggests the marital status of the author. Or, if a user refers to themselves in the feminine grammatical gender, this does not lead to strong conclusions but still can be used as a feature for various author profiling tasks (though actual usefulness is yet to be studied) or generating correct automatic responses for the user.

In this work, we have focused on the analysis of anonymous texts written by *VKontakte* social network users in the *Overheard* ("*Podslushano*") group[1]. A typical post in

---

[1] https://vk.com/overhear, with more than 3,987,000 users reading the community as of February 20, 2020.

P. Sojka et al. (Eds.): TSD 2020, LNAI 12284, pp. 222–230, 2020.
https://doi.org/10.1007/978-3-030-58323-1_24

this community is a short text; the editors claim that "people share their secrets, rev-elations and real-life situations anonymously in front of a massive audience". Judging by the hashtags (special tokens usually starting with #) provided by moderators, one of the most popular topics in *Overheard* is *family*. Many posts touch upon serious cases of adverse childhood experiences, home abuse, sex-related problems, etc. We consider the problem of detecting the grammatical gender of the author in short Russian texts; e.g., the author of the sentence *Я лето целое всё пела* ("I **was singing** all through the summer") clearly prefers the feminine gender, and the author of the sentence *Ах, я чем виноват* ("But why am I to blame?") prefers the masculine gender. Russian speakers can easily recognize the gender of verbs, but there are many cases where the speaker does not refer to themselves and the grammatical gender remains unclear. Note that we are talking strictly about *grammatical* gender: sometimes people change their gender in writing, and we are not suggesting a one-to-one correspondence.

The contribution of this work is twofold: first, we introduce the dataset of 2603 *Overheard* posts in Russian annotated with the authors' preferred grammatical gender (PGG); second, we develop and compare several models for PGG prediction. In the paper, Sect. 2 reviews related work, Sect. 3 describes the original dataset, Sect. 4 introduces the baseline models, in Sect. 5 we report and discuss the problem and our results, and Sect. 6 concludes the paper.

2 Related Work

Anonymity on the Web has been studied and discussed in numerous research works, e.g., [5,7]. We have found one study analyzing the *Overheard* community data: the thesis [6] measures the dynamics of topics in the posts dynamics and reports that large UGC-driven communities inevitably shift towards family, health issues, midlife crises etc. A large number of works have used *VKontakte* data; e.g., the work [13] claims to have constructed the largest so far Russian-language sentiment analysis dataset based on *VKontakte* posts.

To the best of our knowledge, this is the first study of text author's preferred gram-matical gender prediction for Russian or any other Slavic languages.

3 Data

We have collected all anonymous posts in the *Overheard* (*Podslushano*) *VKontakte* community from January 4th, 2014 to November 27th, 2019 that were annotated with #family (#семья) hashtags by the moderators. The texts are usually free of mis-spellings and grammatical errors. We have collected 6,803 #family posts (latest at the moment of collection), removed the hashtags, and annotated a random sample of 2,631 of them.

The annotation task follows the proposed research question: each text is assigned a label of "femn" (feminine grammatical gender), "masc" (masculine), or "unk" (unknown). We took a formal approach, instructing the annotators to use only *grammat-ical* clues, overlooking, e.g., the mention of a "wife" unless there is a masculine self-reference[2]. Based on the experience of several unsuccessful attempts at crowdsourcing, we have asked annotators to pay special attention to reported speech and quotations. If the quote was related to the author (someone addressing them using some grammatical gender), this was a valid clue, but if the quote was about a different person one obviously could not use it to derive PGG. The annotators were also asked to be careful with potentially gender-specific job names, roles etc.; e.g. the word "юрист" ("lawyer", masc.) does not necessarily imply a masculine PGG; judging by the data, both "юрист" and "юристка" might be used by a user that refers to themselves in feminine.

Basic text statistics of the prepared dataset are the following: "femn", 1539 (58.4%) posts, 11129 sentences; "unk", 878 (33.4%) posts, 4743 sentences; "masc", 214 (8.1%) posts, 1574 sentences. To evaluate the approaches described in Sect. 4, we have split the data into training (80%), development (10%), and test (20%) sets, keeping the shares of classes ("femn", "masc", "unk") approximately the same as in the whole dataset.

4   Prediction

In this section we introduce the baseline models.

Bag-of-Words. In the bag-of-words (BoW) approach, the text is treated as a multiset of its tokens. Clearly, BoW-based models will not be able to distinguish which person a given gendered verb refers to. Still, we use this as the simplest baseline possible, training a logistic regression on tokens and token bigrams as features[3], with and without lemmatization (done with the RNNMorph analyzer [4]).

Syntax-Aware Rule-Based Approach. In Russian, PGG prediction can be solved (up to a point) with a few simple syntax-based rules, for example:

- a sentence with a gendered verb in the past tense referring to the pronoun "я" ("I/me") is an almost certain indication of PGG; e.g., *я прочитала руководство* (*I've read a manual*) has an arc "прочитала$_{verb}$ → я$_{pron}$" that implies feminine PGG;
- in a "sequence" of verbs with conjunct relations, e.g. *я делаю тесто и нашла для этого яйца* (*I'm making dough and have found eggs for it*), it suffices to have at least one gendered verb (only *нашла* in the example above);
- if a sentence has no nominal subject, and the root of a syntax tree is a verb (singular, past tense), then the verb's grammatical gender in many cases corresponds to the PGG: *Сел и поехал.* (*Mounted [it] and moved away.*)

These rules clearly do not cover all cases, e.g., the feminine PGG in *обернусь я, бедная, кукушкой* (*I will turn poor me into a cuckoo*) will be missed, but can be used as a baseline.

---

[2] We have made several attempts to tackle the annotation task via crowdsourcing platforms, updating the instructions and adding more advanced qualification tests. However, most annotators still derived the gender based on stereotypes, so we had to ask our own experts to label the data, which explains the modest size of the corpus.

[3] We have used tokens and bigrams available in the training set with the minimum document frequency of 3; scikit-learn's [11] default TF-IDF weighting scheme was employed.

Algorithm 1: Rule-based PGG Prediction

---

1 **function** IsGender(v_{from}, gen, conjAllow)
2   isVerb $\leftarrow$ IsVerb(v_{from}), isConj $\leftarrow$ IsConj(v_{from})
3   isRoot $\leftarrow$ IsRoot(v_{from}) **or** conjAllow **and** isConj
4   **if** $\exists v' : (v_{\text{from}} \rightarrow v') \in E$ **then**
5   selfNSubj $\leftarrow$ **false**, nSubj $\leftarrow$ **false**, chlnResult $\leftarrow \emptyset$ **for** $(v_{\text{from}} \rightarrow v_{\text{to}}) \in E$ **do**
6   nSubj $\leftarrow$ nSubj **or** IsNSubj(v_{to})
7   selfNSubj $\leftarrow$ selfNSubj **or** IsNSubj(v_{to}) **and** v_{to} = 'я'
8   **if** isVerb **then**
9   **if** IsRoot(v_{from}) **and** selfNSubj = **true then**
10   conjAllow $\leftarrow$ **true**
11   **if** HasGender(v_{from},gender) **then**
12   **if** selfNSubj = **true then**
13   **return** CertainlyYes
14   **if** isRoot **and** nSubj = **false then**
15   **return** MaybeYes
16   **for** $(v_{\text{from}} \rightarrow v_{\text{to}}) \in E$ **do**
17   chlnResult $\leftarrow$ chlnResult $\cup$ IsGender(v_{to}, gen, conjAllow)
18   **return** AggChildren(chlnResult)
19   **else if** isVerb **and** isRoot **and** HasGender(v_{from}, gen) **then**
20   **return** MaybeYes
21   **return** MaybeNo

The algorithm is shown in Listing 1. The input of the algorithm is a dependency grammar syntax tree with set of vertices V and set of arcs E. The recursive function IsGender checks whether the given subtree of a vertex v_{from} allows to make a conclusion that author prefers grammatical gender gen. conjAllow is a parameter that helps to work with verb "sequences" mentioned above. The function IsGender returns MaybeNo, MaybeYes or CertainlyYes. Having applied the function to all sentences in a text, we aggregate the outputs, ordering these values by "strength" for each gender: CertainlyYes $\succ$ MaybeYes $\succ$ MaybeNo. A similar procedure is performed in function AggChildren computer after the recursive calls of IsGender on all subtrees of v_{from}.

To preprocess the data for syntax-based methods, we have used the UDPipe [14] pretrained model for Russian "russian-syntagrus-ud-2.5-191206.udpipe"[4] [15].

"Bag-of-Arcs" Gradient Boosted Decision Trees Approach. The relative efficiency of the previous approach (at least compared to bag-of-words) leads to the idea of allowing a machine learning model to construct syntax-based rules by itself. We

---

[4] As of June 11, 2020, the model is available at: https://lindat.mff.cuni.cz/repository/xmlui/handle/11234/1-3131.

Table 1. PGG prediction results (Pr — precision, Re — recall).

Method	macro $F1$	femn Pr	Re	masc Pr	Re	unk Pr	Re
Bag-of-words, lemmatized	0.4923	0.682	0.695	0.278	0.233	0.534	0.537
Bag-of-words, tokenized	0.6148	0.762	0.750	0.526	0.465	0.578	0.611
Syntax-based rules	0.7474	**0.897**	0.796	0.597	**0.861**	0.665	0.726
Bag-of-arcs, GBDT	**0.7733**	0.895	**0.854**	**0.923**	0.558	**0.694**	**0.817**

have again parsed all the sentences, and converted each text into a multiset ("counts-preserving set") of the items using the following feature engineering algorithm:

1. for every childless vertex v, generate $(\mathrm{DepRel}(v), \mathrm{Gender}(v), 'no\_children')$;
2. for every v without outgoing $nsubj$ arcs, generate $(\mathrm{DepRel}(v), \mathrm{Gender}(v), \mathrm{Case}(v),' \to no\_nsubj')$;
3. for every arc $v_{from} \to v_{to}$, where v_{to} is not a punctuation mark, generate $(\mathrm{DepRel}(v_{from}), \mathrm{Gender}(v_{from}), \mathrm{Case}(v_{from}), \mathrm{DepRel}(v_{to}), \mathrm{IsMe}(v_{to}))$, where $\mathrm{IsMe}(x)$ returns $True$ iff x = "я" ("me" in Russian).

We collect such items for every sentence and merge them for every text into a single multiset that we call bag-of-arcs (BoA). The only weakness of this approach compared to the previous one is that BoA-based models cannot make predictions taking sentence splitting into account. We have trained a Gradient Boosted Decision Trees model (Light-GBM [8, 10]), finding the best hyperparameters on training and validation sets via the *Optuna* framework [2]. We have run a hyperparameters search based on tree-structured Parzen estimators, maximizing the mean of on 10 last $F1_{macro}$ values in 4-fold validation. In a one-vs-all multiclass setting, one of the strategies leading to the achieved score was to run 863 boosters, each of them being a decision tree of depth ≤ 2, with minimal number of samples to create a "child" equal to 18 and feature sampling rate equal to 0.43.

5 Results and Discussion

For evaluation, we have used the macro-averaged F1-measure. The results are presented in Table 1. As expected, BoW-based approaches are relatively weak. Using **eli5** [1], we have built a table (see Fig. 1) showing which logistic regression weights "favor"/"disfavor" which classes. It clearly demonstrates that word-based representations make the models encode non-grammatical properties of the texts. E.g. for class "femn", the top feature in terms of regression model weight is the word "муж" ("husband") rather than any grammatical feature. We believe that a more sophisticated approach could yield better results in terms of classification performance. However, this bias-encoding behaviour is inescapable in word/n-gram models, from BoW-based linear models to the best-performing text classification ones such as e.g. [16]. This is why the main focus of this work are syntax-aware approaches that perform clearly better.

y=femn top features		y=masc top features		y=unk top features	
Weight?	Feature	Weight?	Feature	Weight?	Feature
+1.978	муж	+3.467	жена	+1.428	нас
+1.672	была	+2.187	решил	... 2712 more positive ...	
+1.543	сама	+2.158	женой	... 3576 more negative ...	
+1.453	мне	+2.028	девушкой	-0.989	мной
+1.289	думала	+1.924	видел	-1.074	сделать
+1.201	поняла	+1.534	понял	-1.077	решил
... 3460 more positive ...		+1.458	увидел	-1.227	бы
... 2828 more negative ...		+1.453	жену	-1.446	не
-1.110	решил	+1.448	понял что	-1.601	было
-1.186	девушкой	... 2501 more positive ...		-1.844	что
-1.553	женой	... 3787 more negative ...		-1.847	мне
-2.496	жена	-2.556	муж	-1.881	меня

Fig. 1. Largest logistic regression weights in the BoW-based setting. "муж", "жена", "девушка" are relationship roles. This bias-encoding behaviour is inescapable in word/n-gram models, being our motivation to propose bias-free syntax-based models described in this paper.

The rule-based method's results are a challenging benchmark, at least for the bag-of-arcs approach, which showed similar or superior performance when compared to other models, except for "masculine" class recall. The label imbalance in the dataset shown in Sect. 3 might be the reason why rule-based approach might favor the "masculine" class in a larger number of cases than an essentially statistical GBDT model. The natural question is why are the results so weak on so simple a task? It turns out that there are several important problems that leave this problem open for further research, including the more fine-grained error analysis by testing the impact of each of the challenges listed below.

1. **Quotations and reported speech**. It is hard to say who is being quoted, while simply skipping quotations corrupts the data, degrading parsing performance, and might miss important hints on the author's PGG, e.g., when the quotation refers to the author. For example, in <...> *А муж недавно заявил: "А ведь все это время, пока ты работала на дому, я был как султан из восточной сказки <...>"* (<...> *My husband said recently: "All this time, while you were working from home, I lived like a sultan from an oriental tale <...>"*) the models predict masculine PGG, while in reality the quoted person refers to the author in feminine and to himself in masculine.

2. **Coreferences and ellipsis**. Simple pattern-matching rules applied at the sentence level can fail when the referents are in another sentence or omitted. E.g., in *Сыну 4 года. Вчера вечером требовал привезти ему зажигалку, пиво и девочек.* (*[My] son is 4 years old. Demanded cigar-lighters, beer and ladies last night.*) the rule-based system interpreted the lack of nominal subject in the second sentence as referring to the author while in reality it refers to the son mentioned in the first sentence.

3. **Insufficient syntactic analysis**. Many other errors could be detected with a deeper syntactic analysis on the sentence level; e.g., *статуи помнят меня молодой* (*statues remember me youthful*).

6   Conclusion

In this work, we have introduced a new dataset of texts annotated with preferred grammatical gender of their authors: "feminine", "masculine", and "unknown". We have established several baselines: a BoW-based model, a rule-based algorithm, and a feature engineered "bag-of-arcs" predictive model. The latter showed the best performance in terms of macro-averaged F-score: 0.773. The results show that in spite of the seeming simplicity of the task, there is still a lot of room for improvement, and we suggest this as an interesting problem for further research.

Acknowledgement. This work was carried out at the Samsung-PDMI Joint AI Center at Steklov Mathematical Institute at St. Petersburg and supported by Samsung Research. We would like to thank anonymous reviewers for insightful comments that helped us to improve the paper.

Appendix: instructions for annotation

Which grammatical gender do authors use when talking about themselves?[5]

Short description: We ask you to carefully read the short text and report in what grammatical gender the authors refer to themselves, based on grammatical evidence/clues.

It is usually clear which grammatical gender (feminine/masculine/etc.) the users prefer when speaking about themselves in their posts. However, sometimes it may be impossible. **Not all cases are obvious, please do read the instructions.**

Task: to determine the grammatical gender (or make sure it is impossible to determine one) and choose the corresponding option. Sample text with feminine PGG: «Я младше его, живу **одна** за границей, никогда у мамы ничего не **просила**» ("I am younger than him, I live alone and abroad, never asked my mom to do anything for me"). This is indicated by the word forms in bold. Sample text with masculine PGG: «Сына **воспитывал** в строгости, но и не **препятствовал** общению с бывшей женой и ее родителями» ("Raised my son in a strict way, but never got in the way of his communication with my ex-wife and her parents").
Sample text without any clues: «Моя мама работает воспитателем в детском саду. Её уважают взрослые, и любят дети» ("My mother works as a teacher in a kindergarten. Adults respect her, and children love her".).

IMPORTANT: only grammatical features and clues can be used to determine the gender. The task is not to guess whether a man or a woman wrote the text. The task is to determine with confidence which grammatical gender they prefer when talking about themselves.

Sample cases with possible errors.

«У моего мужа две дочери от другого брака» ("My husband has two daughters from another marriage"). Having a husband does not necessarily mean that the person refers to themselves in feminine, so here the PGG should be labeled as unknown.

---

[5] Originally in Russian, translated into English.

«Я, как **двоечница**, сижу на родительском собрании за последней партой» ("I sit at the parents-teacher meeting at the last desk as if I'm a slacker"). Here the word «двоечница» clearly indicates feminine PGG.

«Моя мечта – стать юристом» ("My dream is to become a lawyer"). This does not mean that the authors refer to themselves using the masculine gender. The following is possible: «Моя мечта – стать юристом. Всегда **хотела** быть **похожей** на Сола из сериала» ("My dream is to become a lawyer. I have always wanted to be like Sol from the series"). Feminine PGG here is guaranteed to us by words «хотела» ("wanted") and «похожей» ("like").

In the texts, people do not always use feminitives ("feminine" variants of the names of professions, etc.) when appropriate; therefore, the masculine gender of nouns such as *юрист* (*lawyer*) are not a strong evidence of the author's PGG.

Therefore, please (1) read the text carefully to the end, (2) make sure that grammatical clues do not belong to another person's direct/reported speech or a quote, (3) do not be guided by words such as *юрист* (*lawyer*), please look for other grammatical evidence in the text.

References

1. ELI5: a Python package to debug machine learning classifiers and explain their predictions (2016). https://github.com/TeamHG-Memex/eli5/
2. Akiba, T., Sano, S., Yanase, T., Ohta, T., Koyama, M.: Optuna: a next-generation hyperparameter optimization framework. In: Proceedings of the 25rd ACM SIGKDD International Conference on Knowledge Discovery and Data Mining (2019)
3. Alekseev, A., Nikolenko, S.: Word embeddings for user profiling in online social networks. Computación y Sistemas **21**(2), 203–226 (2017)
4. Anastasyev, D., Gusev, I., Indenbom, E.: Improving part-of-speech tagging via multi-task learning and character-level word representations. arXiv preprint arXiv:1807.00818 (2018)
5. Christopherson, K.M.: The positive and negative implications of anonymity in internet social interactions: "on the internet, nobody knows you're a dog". Comput. Hum. Behav. **23**(6), 3038–3056 (2007)
6. Ефимов, А.М., Павлова, А.Д.: Социальная динамика в сообществах пользовательского контента (на примере сообществ социальной сети «Вконтакте»). In: Солидарность и конфликты в современном обществе. pp. 88–89 (2018)
7. Kang, R., Brown, S., Kiesler, S.: Why do people seek anonymity on the internet? informing policy and design. In: Proceedings of the SIGCHI Conference on Human Factors in Computing Systems, pp. 2657–2666 (2013)
8. Ke, G., et al.: Lightgbm: a highly efficient gradient boosting decision tree. In: Advances in Neural Information Processing Systems, pp. 3146–3154 (2017)
9. Kestemont, M., et al.: Overview of the author identification task at pan-2018: cross-domain authorship attribution and style change detection. In: Working Notes Papers of the CLEF 2018 Evaluation Labs. Avignon, France, 10–14 September, 2018/Cappellato, Linda [edit.] et al, pp. 1–25 (2018)
10. Meng, Q., et al.: A communication-efficient parallel algorithm for decision tree. In: Advances in Neural Information Processing Systems, pp. 1279–1287 (2016)
11. Pedregosa, F., Varoquaux, G., Gramfort, A., Michel, V., Thirion, B., Grisel, O., Blondel, M., Prettenhofer, P., Weiss, R., Dubourg, V., Vanderplas, J., Passos, A., Cournapeau, D., Brucher, M., Perrot, M., Duchesnay, E.: Scikit-learn: machine learning in Python. J. Mach. Learn. Res. **12**, 2825–2830 (2011)

12. Rangel, F., Rosso, P., Potthast, M., Stein, B.: Overview of the 5th author profiling task at pan 2017: Gender and language variety identification in twitter. Working Notes Papers of the CLEF, pp. 1613–0073 (2017)

13. Rogers, A., Romanov, A., Rumshisky, A., Volkova, S., Gronas, M., Gribov, A.: Rusentiment: an enriched sentiment analysis dataset for social media in Russian. In: Proceedings of the 27th International Conference on Computational Linguistics, pp. 755–763 (2018)

14. Straka, M., Straková, J.: Tokenizing, POS tagging, lemmatizing and parsing UD 2.0 with udpipe. In: Proceedings of the CoNLL 2017 Shared Task: Multilingual Parsing from Raw Text to Universal Dependencies, pp. 88–99. Association for Computational Linguistics, Vancouver, Canada, August 2017

15. Straka, M., Straková, J.: Universal dependencies 2.5 models for UDPipe (2019–12-06) (2019), http://hdl.handle.net/11234/1-3131, LINDAT/CLARIAH-CZ digital library at the Institute of Formal and Applied Linguistics (ÚFAL), Faculty of Mathematics and Physics, Charles University

16. Yang, Z., Dai, Z., Yang, Y., Carbonell, J., Salakhutdinov, R.R., Le, Q.V.: XLNET: generalized autoregressive pretraining for language understanding. In: Advances in Neural Information Processing Systems, pp. 5754–5764 (2019)

Attention to Emotions: Detecting Mental Disorders in Social Media

Mario Ezra Aragón[1] , A. Pastor López-Monroy[2], Luis C. González[3],
and Manuel Montes-y-Gómez[1($\boxtimes$)]

[1] Instituto Nacional de Astrofísica, Óptica y Electrónica (INAOE),
San Andrés Cholula, Mexico
{mearagon,mmontesg}@inaoep.mx
[2] Centro de Investigación en Matemáticas (CIMAT), Guanajuato, Mexico
pastor.lopez@cimat.mx
[3] Facultad de Ingeniería, Universidad Autónoma de Chihuahua, Chihuahua, Mexico
lcgonzalez@uach.mx

Abstract. Different mental disorders affect millions of people around the world, causing significant distress and interference to their daily life. Currently, the increased usage of social media platforms, where people share personal information about their day and problems, opens up new opportunities to actively detect these problems. We present a new approach inspired in the modeling of fine-grained emotions expressed by the users and deep learning architectures with attention mechanisms for the detection of depression and anorexia. With this approach, we improved the results over traditional and deep learning techniques. The use of attention mechanisms helps to capture the important sequences of fine-grained emotions that represent users with mental disorders.

Keywords: Mental disorders · Emotional patterns · Deep learning

1 Introduction

There are many different mental disorders characterized by abnormal behaviors, thoughts, and perceptions that affect the relationships and daily activities of people [1]. Mental disorders continue to grow in all countries of the world and provoke significant impacts on health, social environments, and big expenses to maintain hospitals. The causes of mental disorders are related to different risk factors like stressful environments, including abuse, neglect, traumatic events, etc. [2]. Mental disorders increase in countries over time, some studies reveal that one person in five suffers a mental disorder, and one in four will be damaged with these problems at least once in their life.

Living in a modern world implies that social life is developed in the physical world and also in a virtual world created by social media platforms. Around 45% of the worldwide population has an active social media account, where they share personal information about their daily life [3]. This presents an opportunity to

P. Sojka et al. (Eds.): TSD 2020, LNAI 12284, pp. 231–239, 2020.
https://doi.org/10.1007/978-3-030-58323-1_25

analyze this information and actively detect people that present signs of a mental disorder. With this in mind, the main focus of this research is to analyze social media texts and detect people with depression or anorexia.

Several studies for the detection of depression and anorexia have used linguistic and sentiment analysis [4]. For example, [5] proposed the use of emotions as features, such as "anger", "disgust" or "joy" instead of only positive or negative sentiments. Making a step forward with emotions, [6] introduced a new representation built using information extracted from emotion lexicons combined with word embeddings, creating sub-groups of emotions for a flexible representation of users with depression; this approach creates emotions in a fine-grained way, thus being called, sub-emotions. In this study, we extend this preceding work by evaluating a deep learning architecture that incorporates an attention mechanism to try to exploit sub-emotions to capture their relevance in the context. To test the robustness of the approach we also add the analysis of another important mental disorder, anorexia. Results suggest that the proposed approach outperforms traditional and other deep learning methods.

2   Related Work

Depression is a common mental disorder that is characterized by recurrent sadness, loss of interest in daily activities, feelings of guilt, low self-esteem, loss of appetite, tiredness, among others symptoms. On the other hand, Anorexia Nervosa is a mental disorder mainly characterized by weight loss. People that suffer anorexia have difficulties maintaining an appropriate weight, as a consequence of unusual habits of eating and a distorted body image. Recently, several works have focused on detecting users with these mental disorders in social media platforms. One of the most common strategies consists in using the frequency of words and words sequences to create an encoded language of the users [4] and build a rule-based classifier. The results are still modest with this strategy; an analysis showed an overlap in the language between healthy people and people with a mental disorder. It is also common to apply sentiment analysis techniques to look for the positive and negative charge in the users' posts [4].

Other strategies focus on the usage of LIWC [9] to extract different categories of words at a psychological level and analyze their relation depression or anorexia common topics [7]. Another approach proposed the creation of lexicons related to mental disorders, for example, in [8] the authors designed a method to exploit a micro-blog platform for detecting psychological pressures from teenagers.

Finally, in [10] the authors employed and combined multiple strategies based on four machine learning models. They considered a wide range of features to build their models, e.g., they used models based on LSTM neural networks and convolutional neural networks for the extraction of local features, and then extract readability features, LIWC features, user-level linguistic metadata, and specific terms related to depression and anorexia. Although in that work it was shown that neural models were useful to determine if a person suffers from depression and anorexia, the interpretability of the models were limited; this presents an opportunity to create a model that extracts important information using a neural model with attention mechanism to help ameliorate this issue.

3   Modeling Text by Sub-emotions

As previously mentioned, in [6] the authors proposed the use of sub-emotions instead of words for representing the users' posts. In this section, we briefly describe the creation of the sub-emotions and how to convert the posts' content into sub-emotions sequences.

Creation of Sub-emotions. The creation of sub-emotions, as proposed in [6], is based on the lexical resource from [13]. This lexical resource consists of eight recognized emotions [15] and two sentiments: Anger, Anticipation, Disgust, Fear, Joy, Sadness, Surprise, Trust, Positive and Negative, respectively. Each of these emotions is defined by a set of words associated to it. The process to create the sub-emotions consists of two steps. Given the set of words associated to each emotion, first we obtain a word vector for each word using pre-trained word embeddings from FastText [14]. Then, we generate sub-groups of words using the *Affinity Propagation* clustering algorithm [16]. The centroids of each sub-group represent the new sub-emotions. The main idea of this approach is to separate the words of each emotion in different topics. With the help of these topics, we can capture more specific emotions that users expressed in their posts. For example, if the lexicon associated to the emotion *Surprise* contains the words: accident, art, crash, disaster, museum, magician, gallery and wizard, then, after this process it will be generated three subgroups, each one representing a different sub-emotion or type of surprise, such as Surprise1 = [accident, crash, disaster], Surprise2 = [art, museum, gallery] and Surprise3 = [magician, wizard].

Text to Sub-emotions. Once generated the sub-emotions, we mask the users' posts by replacing each word with the label of its closest sub-emotion. To do this, we calculate for each word in the vocabulary their embedding vector using FastText. Then, we use the set of sub-emotions to measure the cosine similarity between each word vector and all sub-emotions (i.e., their centroid vector). Once we obtain these similarities, each word is replaced by the label of the closest sub-emotion. For example, the text *"The most important thing is to try and inspire people."*, will be masked as *"anticipation27 joy27 positive5 negative62 anticipation10 anticipation29 positive20 negative80 trust23 joy16"*.

4   Deep Emotion Attention Model

To detect users that suffer from a mental health disorder, particularly depression or anorexia, our proposal consists on processing their posts masked with sub-emotions using a deep learning model with an attention mechanism. Figure 1 represents the whole process step by step. The intuition of using attention models is that not all sub-emotions contribute equally to the representation of the sentence in the post history. Using the attention mechanism, we can extract the sub-emotions that are more important to the meaning of the sentence and aggregate this importance to the representation. In the following lines we described the architecture in detail.

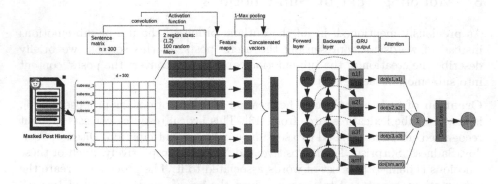

Fig. 1. Diagram of the deep attention model.

Feature Extraction. Given an input text masked with its sub-emotions, first, we represent each sub-emotion with an embedding vector, which corresponds to the centroid of the vectors from their associated words, and then, we use a Convolutional Neural Network (CNN) architecture for feature extraction of the sub-emotions [17]. The intuition about this network is to see the post history as images, that is, we look for the convolution taking one or two sub-emotions at once since our filters size are 1 and 2. We can think of filter sizes as unigrams and bigrams. We obtain different feature maps for each region and concatenate together to form a single feature vector.

Sequence Learning. After we obtained the feature vectors with the CNN, we capture the context provided for the sequence of sub-emotions using a BiDirectional Gated Recurrent Unit (GRU). GRU helps us to remember previous information learning the sequential structure of the sub-emotions, where every sub-emotion is dependent on the previous one. Furthermore, the BiDirectional GRU keeps the contextual information in both directions.

Attention Mechanism. With the CNN extracting the feature vectors and the GRU taking care of the sequence structure, we add the ability to give higher weight to more important sub-emotions using an attention mechanism. This mechanism extracts sub-emotions that are important in the sentence and add the information of those sub-emotions. Then, we multiplied each sub-emotion score with their GRU output obtaining a weight according to their importance. Finally, the summed outputs use dense layers with a softmax for the classification.

5   Evaluation

5.1   Data Collections

We use the datasets from eRisk 2018 and 2019 evaluation tasks [11,12]. They contain the post's history and comments of several users from Reddit. For each task, we have two categories of users, users that are affected by depression or anorexia, and control users that are not affected by any mental disorder. The positive class is composed of people that explicitly mentioned that they were diagnosed by a medical specialist with depression or anorexia. Users with vague expressions like "I think I have anorexia/depression" were discarded. The negative class of users is composed of random users from the Reddit platform, but including users who often interact in the depression or anorexia threads to add more realism to the data. Table 1 shows some numbers from these data sets.

Table 1. Mental disorders datasets. Each dataset have two classes (No Control (have mental disorder) = NC, Control (do not have mental disorder) = C).

Data set	Training		Test	
	NC	C	NC	C
dep eRisk'18	135	752	79	741
anor eRisk'19	61	411	73	742

5.2   Experimental Settings

Preprocessing: For the experiments, we normalized all words with lowercase and removed special characters. After preprocessing, we masked the posts' words with the created sub-emotions (refer to Sect. 3 for details).

Classification: Once the post history of each user is masked, we separate it in parts of N sub-emotions[1]. We process each part of the post history as an individual input and then we average the results from all their parts. If the majority of the posts are positive the user is classified as showing a mental disorder. The main idea is to detect consistent and major signs of depression or anorexia through all the posts of the users. In the training part, we used the weighted class parameter for the imbalance present in the collections.

Baselines: We considered methods using well-known representations based on the occurrences of words (BoW) and word sequences (N-grams). We also included some deep learning approaches for text classification: CNN and RNN networks with Glove and word2vec word embeddings. Furthermore, RNN networks with

---

[1] We select N empirically, testing recommended sizes of sequences in the literature of 25, 35, 50 and 100.

attention mechanisms that use words and general emotions are also considered using FastText embeddings (we named these approaches as Deep Attention and Deep Emotion Attention with emotions respectively).

Evaluation Measure: We expressed the results using the f1-measure over the positive class, as done in the eRisk shared task [11].

5.3 Results of the Deep Emotion Attention Model

Table 2 presents the evaluation results of our approach and the different baselines in the two tasks. The first thing to notice is that our approach, using sub-emotions as well as emotions as text representation, achieves the best results, outperforming traditional and deep learning approaches. This result proves that the attention mechanism helps to improve the detection of both depression and anorexia. These results also indicate that the use of sub-emotions allow obtaining better performance than the use of broad emotions, demonstrating that sub-emotions helps to capture more specific topics of interest and moods from social media users. On the other hand, it is surprising to observe that traditional approaches based on a BOW representation in combination with a SVM classifier were able to achieve better results than deep learning models based on standard CNN and RNN architectures. We presume that these results could be due to the small size of the data collections as well as to the diversity of their vocabularies.

Table 2. F1 results over the positive class in the two collections.

	Method	Anorexia	Depression
Baselines	BoW	0.67	0.54
	N-grams	0.66	0.54
	RNN-Glove	0.65	0.46
	RNN-word2vec	0.65	0.48
	CNN-Glove	0.67	0.51
	CNN-word2vec	0.66	0.48
	Deep-Attention (with FastText)	0.66	0.50
eRisk results	First place	**0.71**	**0.64**
	Second place	0.68	0.60
	Third place	0.68	0.58
Our methods	Deep Emotion Attention (broad emotions)	0.71	0.46
	Deep Emotion Attention (sub-emotions)	**0.79**	**0.58**

5.4   Analysis of the Results

For the analysis of what is captured by the attention model, we extracted the weights given to each sub-emotion on different sequences. For this, we selected examples of sequences with a high probability of being positive cases of a mental disorder and extracted the weights for each sub-emotion. Figure 2 presents some examples of these sequences, the shading represents the weight given to the sub-emotion, a darker shade means a higher weight. In these examples, it is possible to appreciate that the weight of sub-emotions depend on their surrounding context. For example, take the sub-emotion "anticipation16" related to life, experience, and events. In the first sequence, the weight is high because it is close to sub-emotions related to worries, afraid, mistakes, and incidents. But, its weight is lower in the second and third sequence because it is close to gain, growth, home, and place. With the attention model, we can capture the importance of the sub-emotions in the post history taking into account the context and the sub-emotions help the model to learn these patterns.

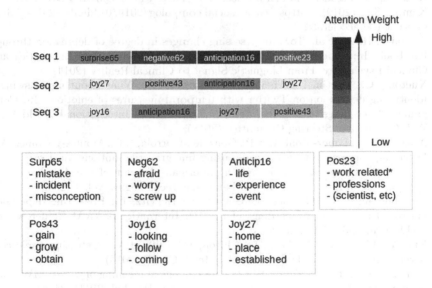

Fig. 2. Examples of weighted sequences of sub-emotions, each sequence in this Figure corresponds to the label of sub-emotion assigned to each word in a sequence of words. The lower part shows the topics related to each sub-emotion.

6   Conclusions

In this paper we considered the representation of social media posts as a sequence of emotion and sub-emotion labels, and proposed using a deep neural architecture with an attention mechanism to learn *emotional patterns* useful for the automatic detection of users that suffer from mental health issues, particularly depression and anorexia. Our experiments showed that this approach outperformed traditional and other deep learning methods, and confirmed that representing the posts' content by means of fine-grained emotions is particularly pertinent for these kind of tasks, since they help capturing specific topics of interest and moods from social media users. Because the attention model allowed learning the importance of the sub-emotions depending on their context in the post history, its inclusion improved the interpretability and analysis of results.

Acknowledgments. This research was supported by CONACyT-Mexico (Scholarship 654803 and Project CB-2015-01-257383).

References

1. Kessler, R., Bromet, E., Jonge, P., Shahly, V., Wilcox, M.: The burden of depressive illness. In: Public Health Perspectives on Depressive Disorders (2017)
2. Ocampo, M.: Salud mental en Mexico. NOTA-INCyTU NÚMERO 007 (2018)
3. Kemp, S.: (2019). https://wearesocial.com/blog/2019/01/digital-2019-global-internet-use-accelerates
4. Schwartz, H.A., et al.: Towards assessing changes in degree of depression through Facebook. In: Proceedings of the Workshop on Computational Linguistics and Clinical Psychology: From Linguistic Signal to Clinical Reality (2014)
5. Xuetong, C., Martin, D., Thomas, W., Suzanne, E.: What about mood swings? Identifying depression on Twitter with temporal measures of emotions. In: Companion Proceedings of the The Web Conference 2018, International World Wide Web Conferences Steering Committee (2018)
6. Aragón, M.E., López-Monroy, A.P., González-Gurrola, L.C., Montes-y-Gómez, M.: Detecting depression in social media using fine-grained emotions. In: Proceedings of the 2019 Conference of the North American Chapter of the Association for Computational Linguistics: Human Language Technologies, vol. 1 (2019)
7. De Choudhury, M., Gamon, M., Counts, S., Horvitz, E.: Predicting depression via social media. In: Proceedings of the 7th International AAAI Conference on Weblogs and Social Media (2013)
8. Xue, Y., Li, Q., Jin, L., Feng, L., Clifton, D., Clifford, G.: Detecting adolescent psychological pressures from micro-blog. In: IJCNLP (2013)
9. Tausczik, Y.R., Pennebaker, J.W.: The psychological meaning of words: LIWC and computerized text analysis methods. J. Lang. Soc. Psychol. **29**(1), 24–54 (2010)
10. Trotzek, M., Koitka, S., Friedrich, C.M.: Word embeddings and linguistic metadata at the CLEF 2018 tasks for early detection of depression and anorexia. In: Proceedings of the 9th International Conference of the CLEF Association, CLEF 2018, Avignon, France (2018)
11. Losada, D.E., Crestani, F., Parapar, J.: Overview of eRisk 2018: early risk prediction on the internet (extended lab overview). In: Proceedings of the 9th International Conference of the CLEF Association, CLEF 2018, Avignon, France (2018)
12. Losada, D.E., Crestani, F., Parapar, J.: Overview of eRisk 2019 early risk prediction on the internet. In: Crestani, F., et al. (eds.) CLEF 2019. LNCS, vol. 11696, pp. 340–357. Springer, Cham (2019). https://doi.org/10.1007/978-3-030-28577-7_27
13. Mohammad, S.M., Turney, P.D.: Crowdsourcing a word-emotion association lexicon. Comput. Intell. **29**(3), 436–465 (2013)

14. Bojanowski, P., Grave, E., Joulin, A., Mikolov, T.: Enriching word vectors with subword information. Trans. Assoc. Comput. Linguist. **5**, 135–146 (2016)
15. Ekman, P.E., Davidson, R.J.: The Nature of Emotion: Fundamental Questions. Oxford University Press, New York (1994)
16. Thavikulwat, P.: Affinity propagation: a clustering algorithm for computer-assisted business simulation and experimental exercises. In: Developments in Business Simulation and Experiential Learning (2008)
17. Kim, Y.: Convolutional neural networks for sentence classification. In: Proceedings of the 2014 Conference on Empirical Methods in Natural Language Processing (EMNLP) (2014)

Cross-Lingual Transfer for Hindi Discourse Relation Identification

Anirudh Dahiya[✉], Manish Shrivastava, and Dipti Misra Sharma

Language Technologies Research Center, IIIT, Hyderabad, India
anirudh.dahiya@research.iiit.ac.in, {m.shrivastava,dipti}@iiit.ac.in

Abstract. Discourse relations between two textual spans in a document attempt to capture the coherent structure which emerges in language use. Automatic classification of these relations remains a challenging task especially in case of implicit discourse relations, where there is no explicit textual cue which marks the discourse relation. In low resource languages, this motivates the exploration of transfer learning approaches, more particularly the cross-lingual techniques towards discourse relation classification. In this work, we explore various cross-lingual transfer techniques on Hindi Discourse Relation Bank (HDRB), a Penn Discourse Treebank styled dataset for discourse analysis in Hindi and observe performance gains in both zero shot and finetuning settings on the Hindi Discourse Relation Classification task. This is the first effort towards exploring transfer learning for Hindi Discourse relation classification to the best of our knowledge.

Keywords: Discourse relation classification · Cross-lingual transfer learning

1 Introduction

Linguistic units such as clauses and sentences are stitched together to form a wider and consistent semantic context than just the individual meaning immediately represented by them. Discourse Analysis forms the study of how such linguistic units come together to present a coherent semantic structure in language. Various frameworks such as Rhetorical Structure Theory [10] and Tree Adjoining Grammar for discourse [16] aim to understand and formalise the underlying structure and semantics of these discourse units in language.

The Penn Discourse Treebank (PDTB) takes a theory neutral approach to annotate the argument structure, semantics and attribution of discourse units in text following [15]. Two adjacent spans of text (eg. clauses, sentences) called the discourse arguments, may be related to each other by a discourse relation. As shown in Example 1.1, this discourse relation may be explicitly established by lexical items (called discourse connective) and thus called a explicit discourse relation, or implied by the discourse arguments and thus called implicit discourse relation.

© Springer Nature Switzerland AG 2020
P. Sojka et al. (Eds.): TSD 2020, LNAI 12284, pp. 240–247, 2020.
https://doi.org/10.1007/978-3-030-58323-1_26

Explicit Relation: *The game was cancelled* <u>because</u> **it started to rain heavily.**
Implicit Relation: *Encouragement is fine,* [Implicit but] **compulsion is not.**

Example 1.1: Examples for Explicit and Implicit Discourse relations. The *argument 1*, <u>connective</u> and **argument 2** have been formatted for clarity.

Following the lines of PDTB annotations, discourse treebanks were developed for several other languages like Hindi, Turkish, Chinese etc [11,18]. While the development of discourse treebanks in other languages has fostered research into discourse parsers for these languages, the scarcity of annotated data has limited their performance and hindered the adoption of recently proposed deep learning methods in low resource settings. With this purview, we explore various cross-lingual transfer learning approaches for implicit discourse relation classification in Hindi.

Implicit Discourse Relation Classification is one of the most challenging parts of a discourse parser owing to the absence of any explicit discourse connective to mark the relation [17]. Infact during the development of PDTB, annotators proceeded by first inserting an implicit discourse connective along the arguments, and then proceeding to mark the implicit discourse relation type. In this work, we investigate both, the zero shot and the finetuning performance of Implicit Discourse relation classification for Hindi via cross-lingual transfer learning from English. We evaluate the cross transferability across 3 different model types, namely the MUSE multilingual embeddings encoder, the pretrained multilingual sentence encoder LASER, and the transformer based cross-lingual Masked Language Model XLM. We also evaluate the performance on the relatively easier task of explicit discourse relation classification. Our results suggest that discourse relation classification can gain performance from both zero shot and finetuning on small amount of available training data for the resource scarce discourse treebanks like Hindi.

2 Related Work

Implicit Discourse relation identification has received considerable interest due to the challenging nature of the task. Traditional methods used linguistic feature based approaches using dependency and syntactic parse, lexical and polarity based features, often requiring extensive feature engineering to see performance gains [12,13].

More recently, end to end neural network based approaches have led to increase in performance, with word vector based feedforward network [3], latent variable recurrent and recursive neural networks [6,7]. [14] perform a comprehensive set of experiments to show the efficacy of simple bag of words feedforward networks at implicit discourse classification, in comparison to various recurrent and recursive architectures. [2] encode multiple layers of information in arguments, including character, subword, word, sentence and sentence pair level information to push the state of the art performance on the PDTB2 test set.

[8] for the first time explore the cross-lingual transfer of implicit discourse classification in zero-shot setting from English to Turkish and the TED multilingual discourse corpus. They employ a simple feedforward network proposed in [14] to evaluate the cross lingual transferability of implicit discourse classification.

Table 1. Data distribution across relation types for PDTB2 and HDRB

Sense	PDTB2			HDRB		
	Train	Dev	Test	Train	Dev	Test
Comparison	1884	398	146	169	14	10
Contiguity	3263	622	276	262	13	9
Expansion	6756	1240	556	472	73	87
Temporal	659	93	68	62	14	8

3 Approach

As seen in the example in Example 1.1, the Implicit Discourse relations are characterised by an implied discourse connective which is absent in the surface form in text. Owing to this lack of an explicit connective marking the relation, the Implicit Discourse relation classification is a challenging part of discourse parsing, even more so in comparison to its explicit relation classification counterpart.

As shown in Table 1, the Hindi Discourse Relation Treebank is a low resource dataset for the task in comparison to its English counterpart, the Penn Discourse Treebank. The datasets are annotated with textual spans marking the *discourse_relation_type (Implicit or Explicit)*, *arg_1 span*, *arg_2 span*, *lexical connective* and various levels of *discourse relation senses*, as illustrated in the examples in Example 1.1. The discourse relation senses are annotated with multiple levels of granularity with the four senses at the top level, namely *Comparison, Contingency, Expansion and Temporal*. Since the discourse relation classification is a semantic task and the annotations used in the two datasets largely follow similar guidelines, we propose to investigate the cross-lingual transferability of the task from English to Hindi.

We formulate the task as follows: Given the *arg_1* and *arg_2* for an implicit discourse relation, we want to predict the relation sense for this discourse relation. For our study, since the amount of data was limited, we choose to predict among the 4 top level relation types. We explore 3 neural network models for the relation classification task, which take a pair of arguments as inputs to predict the discourse relation among them. To work with the high class imbalance and to allow a comparison of results with previous work [8], we train the models in a one vs all manner, thus resulting in a model for each relation sense. The model approaches are described below:

LASER Based Feedforward Neural Network: Following [8], we explore a simple feedforward neural network for relation classification. The input to the model is a pair of multilingual sentence representations generated by the LASER encoder [1], which is multilingual sentence encoder trained on 93 languages for the translation objective. The LASER encoder performs well on the zero-shot cross-lingual NLI (XNLI), a task similar to the implicit discourse relation classification as both are multiclass classification tasks which expect a pair of texts as input. Given V_1 and V_2 as the LASER representation for *arg_1* and *arg_2* respectively, the input to the feedforward model is $[V_1; V_2; (V_1 + V_2)/2; V_1 - V_2; V_1 \times V_2]$, where; represents concatenation. The resulting vector is followed by a 100 dimensional hidden layer and ReLU activation, and finally to 2 dimensions followed by Softmax function to output the distribution for the relation sense. Since the pretrained LASER encoder generates the semantic sentence representations aligned across languages, we keep the incoming representations from the encoder fixed.

Multilingual Word Embeddings Based Model: We also propose a multilingual word embedding based LSTM encoder pair model. We employ two bidirectional LSTMs [5] to encode *arg_1* and *arg_2* using the multilingual word embeddings for Hindi and English (we use 100 dimensional glove vectors aligned in the same space using the MUSE library [4]). The terminal hidden states of the bidirectional LSTM (128 dims in each direction) are concatenated to represent the argument encoding, which are further concatenated to form the input to a 128 dimensional multilayer perceptron similar to the LASER based feedforward neural network described above.

Cross-Lingual Language Models (XLM): Since pretrained masked language models have demonstrated their efficiency at a variety of language understanding tasks, we propose to employ a pretrained cross lingual language model (XLM) [9] for discourse relation classification. It is a transformer based masked language model which is characterised by deep bidirectional multihead self attention to generate token and sequence representations trained on both masked LM and masked translation LM objective. The XLM has proven its efficacy on the similar cross lingual natural language inference task (XNLI), and is pretrained on both English and Hindi, further motivating its efficacy for relation classification task. We segment the arguments using the BPE vocabulary for the pretrained model, concatenate them as a single input sequence with a delimiter token, and add [CLS] symbol as the first token to represent the whole sequence. The resulting sequence is input to the pretrained XLM model and the resulting vector representation corresponding to the [CLS] token is followed by a linear layer and Softmax function to predict the relation.

4   Experiments

The above described models are evaluated in both the zero-shot and finetuning setup by training them first on the Penn Discourse Treebank (PDTB2), and then evaluating and finetuning them on the Hindi Discourse Relation Treebank (HDRB) data. To compare results with previous work, we split the PDTB2 data into the following respective splits: Training (Section 2–20), Validation (Section 0–1 and 23–24) and Test (Section 21–22). For HDRB, we split the Section_11 into validation and test portion, and Section_16 and Section_17 as the training portion. To deal with the high class imbalance among the relation types, we train each model in a one-vs-all manner for each relation type, and randomly oversample from other classes at each epoch to balance the positive and negative samples. We train the models using Cross Entropy loss, and use Adam optimizer for gradient updates. For finetuning, the learning rate was reduced by a factor of 0.8. For XLM model, we also use a linear schedule with warmup for the first 10% training steps. For LASER and MUSE model, we report the average of 25 runs to account for variance in performance.

Table 2. Results for implicit discourse classification.

Training mode	Test set	
	PDTB2	HDRB
LASER model		
HDRB training only	39.31	29.60
Zero Shot	40.68	31.95
Finetuning	42.76	34.56
MUSE model		
HDRB training only	35.90	30.55
Zero Shot	41.79	28.82
Finetuning	39.65	31.98
XLM model		
HDRB training only	38.28	33.88
Zero Shot	43.15	37.06
Finetuning	43.05	36.75

In the zero-shot learning setup, we train our model on the PDTB2 training set for upto 100 epochs with early stopping criteria on the validation f-score for 15 epochs. We then evaluate the best validation model on the test set of both PDTB2 and HDRB. To evaluate the gain posed by further training the best English model on the limited available Hindi data, we finetune the model on HDRB training data with the same early stopping condition, and evaluate on the HDRB test set.

To draw parallel with the easier explicit connective counterpart, we run the same set of experiments for the explicit relation classification. Since the explicit connective is syntactically tied to *arg_2*, we append the discourse connective to beginning or end of the *arg_2* span corresponding to their relative position. The rest of the preprocessing and modelling procedure for the explicit case follows the implicit relation classification setting.

Table 3. Results for explicit discourse classification.

Training mode	Test set	
	PDTB2	HDRB
LASER model		
HDRB training only	44.04	41.33
PDTB pretraining	44.14	39.30
HDRB Finetuning	38.64	31.55
MUSE model		
HDRB training only	57.68	59.60
PDTB pretraining	88.73	28.68
HDRB Finetuning	54.25	63.15
XLM model		
HDRB training only	64.25	57.53
PDTB pretraining	88.25	59.30
HDRB Finetuning	73.85	58.23

5   Results and Discussion

Table 2 and Table 3 report the results of experiments on implicit and explicit discourse relation classification respectively. All reported results are macro-averaged F1 scores across the relation categories. We report the the performance on both PDTB2 and HDRB test set in the columns of the tables. For each model class, we report the result of training the model only on the HDRB training set (*HDRB training only*), which serves as a non-transfer learning baseline for that model class, training the model only on PDBT2 training set (*Zero Shot*), and finetuning the PDTB2 pretrained models on the HDRB training set (*Finetuning*). We primarily focus on the results corresponding to the HDRB test set to measure the efficacy of our experiments towards zero shot and finetuning mode of cross-lingual transfer learning.

For the implicit case, we observe that pretraining on the larger PDTB2 helps in both zero shot and finetuning settings for HDRB, when compared to training on HDRB alone. We also observe that while zero shot leads to considerable gain for both LASER and XLM model, it leads to a decrease in performance in case of MUSE model. One explanation to this decrease is that while the encoders for LASER and XLM model have already been pretrained on Hindi data in their encoder specific pretraining objective (i.e. translation and masked language modelling), the MUSE model encoder needs finetuning on the Hindi sequences to be able to perform well, and its efficacy is observable when finetuned on the limited HDRB training data. We also observe that in most cases, the models perform better as the training data increases (due to both PDTB2 pretraining and follow-up HDRB finetuning.) This is true even on the PDTB2 test data for LASER model, where the sentence encodings are unperturbed by training on discourse classification.

For the explicit case, we observe that the model performances are considerably higher compared to the implicit case. For the LASER model, we observe that the HDRB deteriorates with increasing data. This could be explained by the fact that the *arg_2* when concatenated with the discourse connective forms a clause with a connective, thus forming a half sentence which is not seen in the encoder-specific pretraining, and thus leads to poorly aligned representations for such inputs. On the other hand, both MUSE and XLM perform well as they are trained on HDRB data in both HDRB only as well as Finetuning settings. The high performance of zero shot on PDTB2 test set indicates that the models learn the corresponding task well.

6   Conclusion

In this work, we present the first set of experiments towards the efficacy of cross-lingual transfer learning for Hindi Discourse Relation Classification. We investigate both zero shot and finetuning transfer learning across 3 different modelling approaches and show consistent gains in performance for both explicit and implicit discourse relation classification. Our proposed methods can plug into existing discourse parsers to improve relation identification module, and can also be further extended to develop end-to-end discourse parsers for low resource languages.

References

1. Artetxe, M., Schwenk, H.: Massively multilingual sentence embeddings for zero-shot cross-lingual transfer and beyond. Trans. Assoc. Comput. Linguist. **7**, 597–610 (2019)
2. Bai, H., Zhao, H.: Deep enhanced representation for implicit discourse relation recognition. arXiv preprint arXiv:1807.05154 (2018)
3. Braud, C., Denis, P.: Comparing word representations for implicit discourse relation classification (2015)
4. Conneau, A., Lample, G., Ranzato, M., Denoyer, L., Jégou, H.: Word translation without parallel data. arXiv preprint arXiv:1710.04087 (2017)
5. Hochreiter, S., Schmidhuber, J.: Long short-term memory. Neural Comput. **9**(8), 1735–1780 (1997)
6. Ji, Y., Eisenstein, J.: One vector is not enough: entity-augmented distributed semantics for discourse relations. Trans. Assoc. Comput. Linguist. **3**, 329–344 (2015)
7. Ji, Y., Haffari, G., Eisenstein, J.: A latent variable recurrent neural network for discourse relation language models. arXiv preprint arXiv:1603.01913 (2016)

8. Kurfalı, M., Östling, R.: Zero-shot transfer for implicit discourse relation classification. arXiv preprint arXiv:1907.12885 (2019)
9. Lample, G., Conneau, A.: Cross-lingual language model pretraining. arXiv preprint arXiv:1901.07291 (2019)
10. Mann, W.C., Thompson, S.A.: Rhetorical structure theory: A theory of text organization. University of Southern California, Information Sciences Institute Los Angeles (1987)
11. Oza, U., Prasad, R., Kolachina, S., Sharma, D.M., Joshi, A.: The hindi discourse relation bank. In: Proceedings of the Third Linguistic Annotation Workshop (LAW III), pp. 158–161 (2009)
12. Park, J., Cardie, C.: Improving implicit discourse relation recognition through feature set optimization. In: Proceedings of the 13th Annual Meeting of the Special Interest Group on Discourse and Dialogue, pp. 108–112. Association for Computational Linguistics (2012)
13. Pitler, E., Louis, A., Nenkova, A.: Automatic sense prediction for implicit discourse relations in text. In: Proceedings of the Joint Conference of the 47th Annual Meeting of the ACL and the 4th International Joint Conference on Natural Language Processing of the AFNLP: volume 2, pp. 683–691. Association for Computational Linguistics (2009)
14. Rutherford, A., Demberg, V., Xue, N.: A systematic study of neural discourse models for implicit discourse relation. In: Proceedings of the 15th Conference of the European Chapter of the Association for Computational Linguistics: Volume 1, Long Papers, pp. 281–291 (2017)
15. Webber, B.: D-ltag: extending lexicalized tag to discourse. Cogn. Sci. **28**(5), 751–779 (2004)
16. Webber, B.L., Joshi, A.K.: Anchoring a lexicalized tree-adjoining grammar for discourse. arXiv preprint cmp-lg/9806017 (1998)
17. Xue, N., Ng, H.T., Pradhan, S., Prasad, R., Bryant, C., Rutherford, A.: The conll-2015 shared task on shallow discourse parsing. In: Proceedings of the Nineteenth Conference on Computational Natural Language Learning-Shared Task, pp. 1–16 (2015)
18. Zeyrek, D., Webber, B.: A discourse resource for Turkish: annotating discourse connectives in the metu corpus. In: Proceedings of the 6th workshop on Asian language resources (2008)

Authorship Verification with Personalized Language Models

Milton King$^{(\boxtimes)}$ (iD) and Paul Cook

Faculty of Computer Science, University of New Brunswick,
Fredericton, NB E3B 5A3, Canada
{milton.king,paul.cook}@unb.ca

Abstract. Malicious posts from a social media account by an unauthorized user could have severe effects for the account holder, such as the loss of a job or damage to their reputation. In this work, we consider an authorship verification task to detect unauthorized malicious social media posts. We propose a novel approach for authorship verification based on personalized, i.e., user-tailored, language models. We evaluate our proposed approach against a previous approach based on word embeddings and a one-class SVM. A large amount of text might not necessarily be available for an individual social media user. We therefore demonstrate that our proposed approach out-performs previous approaches, while requiring orders of magnitude less user-specific training text.

Keywords: Authorship verification · Language models · Personalized NLP

1 Introduction

Malicious posts from a social media account by an unauthorized user could have severe effects for the account holder such as the loss of a job or a negative impact on their reputation. Authorship verification is the task of determining if a given text is written by a particular author. One potential application of authorship verification is to determine if a social media post is indeed written by the account holder, or whether it is a malicious post by an unauthorized user. In this work, we propose the use of personalized (user-tailored) language models for authorship verification. In our experiments, we simulate malicious posts from an unauthorized user with text from three sources that would typically not be appropriate if posted from a professional social media account, specifically erotic stories, hate speech, and email spam.

[5] approached authorship verification by averaging word embeddings to represent a document and recruited a one-class SVM for classification. Their method outperformed the method used by [3], which was one of the best performing

© Springer Nature Switzerland AG 2020
P. Sojka et al. (Eds.): TSD 2020, LNAI 12284, pp. 248–256, 2020.
https://doi.org/10.1007/978-3-030-58323-1_27

models in the PAN-2013 authorship verification task[1] and used as the benchmark in the PAN-2014 authorship verification task.[2]

Language models can be used to generate probability distributions over text after training on a background corpus. Tuning language models to text from people sharing demographic characteristics with an author, such as age or gender, has outperformed untuned language models [7]. [6] found that tuning a language model to a single author can outperform models that were tuned to texts written by people sharing demographic characteristics with that author. They tuned an LSTM language model using a priming technique, which involves exposing the LSTM to text from the author to update its state without updating the hidden layers (which are usually tuned during training). This priming approach required relatively little text from the author to outperform untuned models, as well as models tuned on text from authors from the same demographic.

We propose and evaluate two different types of methods for authorship verification. The first method involves representing a document by embedding it, and then using a one-class SVM for classification. The second method involves personalizing a language model by tuning it on text from an author, and comparing its probabilities to a non-personalized language model. We compare our models across different amounts of author-specific text available for model training and tuning, and different sized test documents. We show that our proposed personalized language model-based method outperforms embedding-based methods, while requiring orders of magnitude fewer tokens from the user for tuning.

2   Dataset and Evaluation

Here we discuss the creation of our dataset, and the evaluation measures used.

2.1   Dataset

In this subsection, we describe the sources of positive and negative instances used to create our dataset, and then the structure of the dataset. Here, positive instances are texts from a specific author, while negative instances are texts from one of the three malicious text types.

Sources of Text. The positive instances in our dataset consist of blog posts from a corpus containing 19,320 authors [12]. We select all authors who have at least 300 posts with at least 100 tokens in them, giving us 103 authors for experiments. For each of these 103 authors, we ignore their 10% smallest and 10% largest documents to avoid outlier documents.

The texts belonging to the remaining authors are used as a background corpus for training our language models, which consists of approximately $143M$ tokens. The text from any one author is limited to 30k tokens to avoid text from any

---

[1] http://pan.webis.de/clef13/pan13-web/author-identification.html.
[2] http://pan.webis.de/clef14/pan14-web/author-identification.html.

one author strongly biasing the corpus to represent their text. We replace each word in the background corpus that has a frequency less than 10 with a special token (UNK). We do this to reduce the cost of training language models.

The negative instances were gathered from three different sources, specifically erotic stories, hate speech, and email spam. We use several types of malicious documents to avoid the task being framed as document classification for a specific (malicious) text type. For example, if we only used hate speech, then the task could be approached as identifying hate speech, as opposed to the broader authorship verification task that we consider.

All erotic stories are gathered from textfiles.com/sex/EROTICA. We arbitrarily selected all plaintext documents with titles starting with "A" or "B", which resulted in a relatively large amount of text. We removed lines containing metadata from each document. We then selected all documents that contain at least 200 tokens, giving us 1463 documents.

We gathered hate speech documents from a white supremacy forum from the dataset of [2]. The dataset originally contained individual sentences from the documents with information about which sentences are from the same document and the order in which they appear. We reconstructed the documents using this information. We selected all documents that contain more than 50 tokens. This resulted in 172 documents in total.

We gathered spam from the Enron-Spam dataset [9]. We removed lines containing the text "subject:" and removed paragraph boundaries. We then selected all documents containing at least 200 tokens, resulting in 6230 documents.

All documents—positive and negative instances—were casefolded and tokenized using the Stanford Core NLP toolkit [8], except for the hate speech texts, which were pre-tokenized. All training and testing documents are prepended with a start-of-sentence token and appended with an end-of-sentence token.

Dataset Structure. We split our dataset into a development set (*DEV*) and a testing set (*TEST*). We randomly select 10 authors from the 103 blog post authors for *DEV* for preliminary experiments, and we use the remaining 93 authors for *TEST*. The authors in *TEST* include 48 males and 45 females, with an average age of 27 years, ranging from 14 to 48 years old.

The following design is used for both *DEV* and *TEST*. For each author, we create user-specific training (*DEV_train* and *TEST_train*) and testing (*DEV_test* and *TEST_test*) datasets. For each author, we randomly select 45 of their documents for testing, which make up the positive instances in *DEV_test* and *TEST_test*. The remaining documents for each author are put into *DEV_train* and *TEST_train*. For each author, we then select 15 erotica, 15 hate speech, and 15 spam documents as negative test instances, and add them to the user-specific testing sets (i.e., *DEV_test* and *TEST_test*). A given malicious document is never included in both *DEV* and *TEST*. For each author, this gives 45 malicious documents that do not belong to them. We repeat this 5 times, to create 5 different test sets for each author. All test documents (positive and negative instances) are selected without replacement for an individual author. As such, a given document will only occur in *TEST_test* at most once for a given author.

We limit negative instances to approximately the first 1000 tokens. This reduces computational cost. Moreover, we control the number of tokens used from test documents in our experiments, and none of the authorship verification approaches considered use document length as a feature.

In *TEST*, the average amount of text from an author is approximately $200\,k$ tokens, with a minimum and maximum of $97\,k$ and $526\,k$, tokens respectively.

2.2 Evaluation

We evaluate our models on the 93 authors from *TEST* over 5 iterations. In each iteration, we select documents for training/tuning by concatenating documents from *TEST_train* until we have at least x tokens, where x is a parameter that controls the amount of text available for training. We then give the model y tokens of running text from a test document from *TEST_test* for classification, where y is a parameter that controls the amount of text used from a test document. Limiting the amount of text from training documents simulates having only a small amount of text from the user available for building the model; limiting the amount of text from test documents simulates documents of various lengths, e.g., microblogs vs longer documents, such as blogs.

We evaluate our models using accuracy and F_1 score. Our test sets contain a 50/50 split of positive and negative instances, which makes accuracy an appropriate metric.

3 Methods

In this section, we describe our two methods for authorship verification based on embeddings and language models. We frame the authorship verification task as predicting whether an unknown document belongs to a given author or not, while crucially only observing documents from that author during training, i.e., the model does not see negative instances during training. This resembles the real-world scenario where we do not know in advance what kinds of malicious documents an unauthorized user of a social media account would attempt to post. The lack of negative instances during training means that standard supervised approaches to binary document classification are not applicable.

3.1 Embeddings

In this method, we represent documents as embeddings, using either word2vec [10] or DistilBERT [11], and then use a one-class SVM for classification. For word2vec, following [5], we train skipgram [10] on a snapshot of English Wikipedia with an embedding size of 300 and a window size of ± 8, and then represent a document as the average of its word embeddings.

DistilBERT [11] is a lighter-weight version of the BERT transformer model with 6 layers, an embedding size of 768, and 12 attention heads. These are the default parameters for the DistilBERT implementation from [13] which we use. We embed a document by using the document as input to the model, which generates an embedding for the document as part of its output layer.

We represent training documents using these approaches to document representation—i.e., either word2vec or DistilBERT—and then train a one-class SVM. Given a test document, we use the same approach to representing it, and then input it into the trained one-class SVM to classify the document as belonging to the author or not. We use the one-class SVM implementation from scikit-learn.[3] We use the default parameters for this model, which include a radial basis function kernel.[4] We refer to these approaches which use a one-class SVM along with document representations based on either word2vec or DistilBERT as *W2V* and *BERT*, respectively.

3.2 Language Models

In this method, we require two language models. The first language model, referred to as the background language model, is trained on a background corpus of blog posts (described in Sect. 2.1). The second language model is a personalized language model that is generated by copying the first language model, and then tuning it using the training text from a single author. Our language models consist of an LSTM with a single hidden layer with 1024 units, an embedding size of 128, and are trained for 1 epoch with a batch size of 45.

We personalize language models—i.e., tune language models to a specific author—using the priming technique from [6], which has performed relatively well when only a small amount of author-specific text is available for tuning. To prime our model, we expose the language model to text from the author's training documents to modify the LSTM's state without altering the hidden layer of the network that is tuned during standard training.

Given a test document, each language model—i.e., the background and personalized language model—outputs a probability for every token in the document. We score each model by counting the number of tokens for which that model assigns a higher probability than the other language model. We classify the document as belonging to the author (i.e., a positive instance) if the personalized language model scored higher than the non-personalized background language model, and classify the document as not belonging to the author (i.e., a negative instance) if the background model achieved a higher score.[5] We refer to this method as *LM* from hereon.

In preliminary experiments on *DEV*, we found *LM* performed well on shorter test documents, but performed poorly as the length of the test documents

---

[3] https://scikit-learn.org.

[4] These parameter settings could be tuned on *DEV*. We leave this for future work.

[5] In preliminary experiments on *DEV* we considered alternative approaches, including comparing the perplexity of the two language models, and thresholds for differences in probability. None of these approaches performed as well as our proposed approach.

increased. We believe this was due to the fact that the state of the LSTM changes fairly quickly as a test document is processed. As such, for longer documents, the state of the personalized language model becomes similar to the state of the background language model, and the effect of personalization is lost. To address this, we sentence tokenized the test documents,[6] and reinitialized the personalized language model's state to its original primed state at the beginning of each sentence.[7] We found that this sentence-level re-initialization always led to improvements, and so only report results for this approach.

4   Experimental Results

In this section, we evaluate our proposed models using accuracy and F_1 score. We consider different amounts of user-specific training text, to simulate having varying amounts of user-specific data available. We further consider different cut-off lengths for test documents, to simulate different test document sizes.

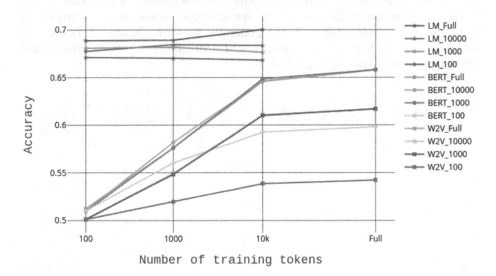

Fig. 1. Accuracy for each method, using different amounts of training text, and different test document sizes.

Figure 1 shows the accuracy of our models when using different amounts of user-specific training data, and differing cut-offs for test document sizes;[8]

---

[6] We used NLTK's sentence tokenizer [1].

[7] Each sentence had the beginning-of-sentence and end-of-sentence tokens appended to the start and end of the sentence, respectively.

[8] We do not report results for *LM* using all available user-specific training data. These experiments are computationally expensive, and preliminary experiments indicated that this approach performed very well with only modest amounts of training data.

the number appended to each model's name in the legend indicates the cut-off length for the number of tokens used from the test documents; i.e., *BERT_100* indicates *BERT* with test documents cut-off after the first 100 tokens. *LM* outperforms both embedding-based models—i.e., *W2V* and *BERT*—regardless of the amount of training text or test document size. Remarkably, *LM* achieves an accuracy of 0.69 with only 100 tokens of user-specific training text when using the full test documents. The embedding-based models perform relatively poorly when only a small amount of user-specific training data is available, but perform better as more training text is used. For every amount of training data, and test document length, considered, *BERT* always outperforms W2V. The highest accuracies achieved by *BERT* and *W2V* are 0.66 and 0.62, respectively. Unlike the embedding-based models, *LM* does not always perform better when more training text is available, which could be because the state of the LSTM does not retain much information from tokens that are far away [4].

Figure 1 also shows that the embedding-based models achieve close to their highest values when using only 1000 tokens from the test documents, and do not perform substantially better on longer test documents. This could be due to the construction of the dataset, where malicious documents are truncated to approximately 1000 tokens.[9] *LM* generally performs better on larger test documents, and achieves its best accuracy of 0.70 using full test documents and 10k tokens of user-specific training text.

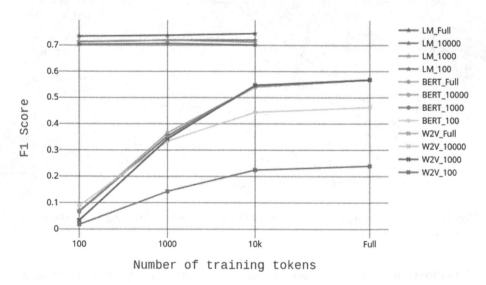

Fig. 2. F_1 score for each method, using different amounts of training text, and different test document sizes.

Figure 2 shows the F_1 score of our models for different amounts of training data and test document sizes. The findings are overall similar to those in Fig. 1,

---

[9] We do not apply the same document size limitation to documents from the user.

with *LM* outperforming the embedding-based models, and achieving a highest F_1 score of 0.74, and an F_1 score of 0.73 when trained on only 100 tokens of user-specific text. The best F_1 score of an embedding-based model is 0.57. Interestingly, here the performance of *LM* is not overly affected by the test document length. One difference here is that *BERT* no longer outperforms *W2V* for the same amount of training text and test document size.

5 Conclusions

Malicious posts from an unauthorized user on a social media account could be damaging to the account holder. We proposed a novel approach to authorship verification using personalized language models, and evaluated it in an experimental setup motivated by this scenario. We compared our proposed approach against a previous embedding-based model, and showed that it outperformed embedding-based models while requiring orders of magnitude less user-specific training data, and shorter test documents. Our proposed language model-based approach, trained on just 100 tokens of user-specific text, achieved an accuracy and F_1 score of 0.69 and 0.73, respectively, compared to the best embedding-based model which achieved an accuracy and F_1 score of 0.66 and 0.57, respectively, while requiring much more user-specific training text. In future work, we intend to consider language models based on transformers, and further sources of malicious documents.

References

1. Bird, S., Loper, E., Klein, E.: Natural Language Processing with Python. O'Reilly Media Inc., Sebastopol (2009)
2. de Gibert, O., Perez, N., García-Pablos, A., Cuadros, M.: Hate speech dataset from a white supremacy forum. In: Proceedings of the 2nd Workshop on Abusive Language Online (ALW2), Brussels, Belgium, pp. 11–20 (2018)
3. Jankowska, M., Milios, E., Keselj, V.: Author verification using common n-gram profiles of text documents. In: Proceedings of COLING 2014, Dublin, Ireland, pp. 387–397 (2014)
4. Khandelwal, U., He, H., Qi, P., Jurafsky, D.: Sharp nearby, fuzzy far away: How neural language models use context. In: Proceedings of ACL 2018, Melbourne, Australia, pp. 284–294 (2018)
5. King, M., Alhadidi, D., Cook, P.: Text-based detection of unauthorized users of social media accounts. In: Bagheri, E., Cheung, J.C.K. (eds.) Canadian AI 2018. LNCS (LNAI), vol. 10832, pp. 292–297. Springer, Cham (2018). https://doi.org/10.1007/978-3-319-89656-4_29
6. King, M., Cook, P.: Building personalized language models through language model interpolation. In: CICLING 2019, La Rochelle, France (2019)
7. Lynn, V., Son, Y., Kulkarni, V., Balasubramanian, N., Schwartz, H.A.: Human centered NLP with user-factor adaptation. In: Proceedings of EMNLP 2017, Copenhagen, Denmark, pp. 1157–1166 (2017)

8. Manning, C., Surdeanu, M., Bauer, J., Finkel, J., Bethard, S., McClosky, D.: The stanford CoreNLP natural language processing toolkit. In: Proceedings of ACL 2014, Baltimore, USA, pp. 55–60 (2014)
9. Metsis, V., Androutsopoulos, I., Paliouras, G.: Spam filtering with Naive Bayes-which Naive Bayes? In: Proceedings of the Third Conference on Email and Anti-Spam 2006, vol. 17, pp. 28–69 (2006)
10. Mikolov, T., Chen, K., Corrado, G., Dean, J.: Efficient estimation of word representations in vector space. In: Proceedings of Workshop at the International Conference on Learning Representations, 2013, Scottsdale, USA (2013)
11. Sanh, V., Debut, L., Chaumond, J., Wolf, T.: DistilBERT, a distilled version of BERT: smaller, faster, cheaper and lighter. In: NeurIPS EMC^2 Workshop, Vancouver, Canada (2019)
12. Schler, J., Koppel, M., Argamon, S., Pennebaker, J.W.: Effects of age and gender on blogging. In: AAAI Spring Symposium: Computational Approaches to Analyzing Weblogs, vol. 6, pp. 199–205 (2006)
13. Wolf, T., et al.: Huggingface's transformers: state-of-the-art natural language processing. ArXiv abs/1910.03771 (2019)

A Semantic Grammar for Augmentative and Alternative Communication Systems

Jayr Pereira[✉][iD], Natália Franco[✉][iD], and Robson Fidalgo[✉][iD]

Center of Informatics, Federal University of Pernambuco, Recife, Brazil
{jap2,nmf,rdnf}@cin.ufpe.br

Abstract. The authoring of meaningful sentences is an essential requirement for AAC systems aimed at the education of children with complex communication needs. Some studies propose the use of linguistic knowledge databases to meet that requirement. In this paper, we propose and present a Semantic Grammar (SG) for AAC systems based on visual and semantic clues. The proposed SG was acquired using an automatic process based on Natural Language Processing (NLP) techniques for the extraction of semantic relations from text samples. We assessed the SG precision on suggesting the correct words on reconstructing telegraphic sentences and obtained a precision average of 90%.

Keywords: Semantic Grammar · Augmentative and Alternative Communication · Ontology.

1 Introduction

Augmentative and Alternative Communication (AAC) [2] systems are essential tools for supporting the inclusion of children with complex communication needs in the educational process. In this context, these systems must be intuitive and may work with images (e.g., photos or pictograms) that represent an object, person, place, or concept. Figure 1 shows a telegraphic message created with a set of pictograms. Notice that the telegraphic message is formed only by keywords (i.e., nouns, verbs, adjectives, and adverbs), without connecting words (i.e., conjunctions, prepositions, and articles) and verb conjugation. According to [9], an AAC system should provide clues to help the authoring of telegraphic phrases with syntactic and semantic correctness. These clues can be visual (e.g., colors and arrows) or semantic (e.g., questions and sample words). For this, these systems must rely on linguistic knowledge bases, which provide information on how words relate in natural language.

Some studies [12–14] propose the use of Semantic Grammars (SGs) as a basis to support the construction of understandable sentences in AAC systems. In this type of base, lexical semantics relations of hierarchy and predicate-argument

This research was supported by the Coordination of Improvement of Higher Education Personnel (CAPES) [88882.347547/2019-01 and 88887.481522/2020-00].

P. Sojka et al. (Eds.): TSD 2020, LNAI 12284, pp. 257–264, 2020.
https://doi.org/10.1007/978-3-030-58323-1_28

Fig. 1. Example of a telegraphic sentence with pictograms.

connect the lexical concepts that make up a controlled vocabulary, facilitating the text's automatic analysis and construction [6]. However, the SGs used in these works do not take into account visual and semantic cues for helping the users on structuring sentences and founding words. Besides, the construction of the proposed SGs does not take into account AAC vocabulary or grammar, or even corpus evidence on how words are semantically related to each other in natural language. To overcome these weaknesses, we propose an SG for AAC systems based on three resources: (i) an AAC controlled vocabulary, (ii) text samples extracted from an extensive corpus, and (iii) a grammar extracted from a therapeutic tool for teaching deaf children to construct and read well-formed sentences. Besides, in this paper, we report how the proposed SG was automatically generated by using NLP techniques for semantic role labeling, dependency parsing, word sense disambiguation, and named entity recognition; and report how it was evaluated.

2   Background and Related Work

A Semantic Grammar (SG) [6] is a linguistic knowledge base in which lexical-semantic properties of hierarchy (e.g., cat *isA* animal) and predicate-argument (e.g., cat *hasDescriptor* color) connect the words and concepts they denote. Its theoretical foundation comes from the Frame Semantics theory [8], which states that understanding the meaning of a word requires access to all the essential knowledge related to that word. Thus, each word evokes a semantic frame that represents the specific concept to which it refers. Each semantic frame is a set of statements that provide characteristics, attributes, and functions of a concept, and their interactions with things necessary or typically associated with it [1]. For example, in the sentence *"He ate the fish quickly"*, the word *ate* denotes the frame *eat* that carries its meaning and its attributes defined by semantic roles: the agent (*He*), the theme (*the fish*), and the manner (*quickly*).

In an SG, others semantic frames fill the semantic roles of each semantic frame with predicative characteristics. For example, for the frame *eat* a frame of *persons* may fill the semantic role agent. According to [6], this allows the usage of the lexical-semantic knowledge of hierarchy (e.g., man *isA* person) in the process of analyzing and constructing sentences in natural language, avoiding the grammatical ambiguity that can exist when using only grammatical classes (e.g., noun).

Some AAC proposals use SGs, or similar linguistic bases, for supporting the authoring of meaningful sentences. The COMPANSION system [13], for example, uses an ontology as a basis for expanding telegraphic sentences to complete and correctness sentences. In this system, the users input keywords of a pretended sentence, not necessarily well ordered, and the system finds the best order and the word relations through semantic parsing, based on the ontology. According to [14], the main issue regarding this approach is how efficient a semantic parser can be, given the existing gaps in the telegraphic text (e.g., absence of prepositions, conjunctions, and verb conjugation). For this reason, the authors proposed a AAC system based on a controlled process for creating sentences. In this system, a set of specifications made by a surface realizer[1], which uses an ontology as a basis, controls the sentence construction by suggesting words. [12] adopted a similar method on proposing the Simple Upper Ontology (SUpO), described as a semantic grammar for beginning communicators. SUpO is an extension of a subset of FrameNet [4] combined with grammar rules for text realisation.

The central gap of these solutions is the absence of the use of SGs based on visual and semantic clues to support sentences authoring. Besides, these bases construction was not based on evidence extracted from text samples, and, except for SUpO, they do not use vocabularies aimed at AAC users.

3   Semantic Grammar

3.1   Construction

Figure 2 shows an overview of the method used to build the proposed SG, which is divided into three steps and takes three materials as input. The following sub-sections present both, the inputs and the steps.

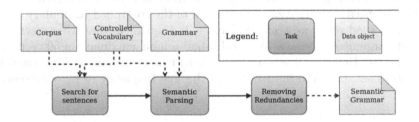

Fig. 2. Overview of the method for constructing semantic grammar

Input Materials. The three materials taken as input are: a controlled vocabulary, a text corpus, and a grammar. The controlled vocabulary consists of a list of the 621 words that have the best accumulated-recall over children's statements extracted from CHILDES corpora [11] and its corresponding WordNet

---

[1] A module of natural language generation systems, that convert an abstract semantic representation into a linguistic utterance.

synsets[2] organized in a taxonomy. It is a result produced by a research project started in [10]. The text corpus is the British National Corpus (BNC) [7], which is extensive, has well-formed sentences, and is widely used in the field of NLP. The grammar is based on the Colourful Semantic (CS) [5], which is a therapeutic tool used for teaching children with complex communication needs to create and read meaningful well-formed sentences. As shown in Fig. 3, this tool uses a simple grammatical structure in which the slots are assigned by semantic roles associated with colors and questions. According to [5], this association (i) establishes a significant relationship between the question and the semantic role, (ii) associates each type of phrase with a visual sequence of colors, and (iii) serves to alert children when they omit a semantic role. The input grammar consists of a mapping of Colourful Semantics roles to PropBank-like [3] labels, and of rules that determines what class of synset can fill each role. For example, only synsets of adverbs can fill the manner role, and no verbs, adverbs, or adjectives synsets can fill the agent role.

Who?	What Doing?	What?	To Whom?	What Like?	Where?	When?
Agent	Verb	Theme	Recipient	Manner/ Description	Location	Time

Fig. 3. Colourful semantics

Sentence Searching. The first step of the method consists of searching in the corpus sentences in which each verb or noun of the controlled vocabulary occurs. These are called reference sentences, and it is from there that we extracted the predicate-argument relations. We established a limit maximum of 500 sentences for each word. However, it was not possible to reach this number for some words (e.g., breakfast, out, and lunch), due to the low frequency of its occurrence in BNC.

Semantic Parsing. This step consists of extracting the semantic structures (e.g., eat *hasAgent* person) from the reference sentences. For this, for each sentence, two sub-tasks are performed. The first one has the objective of identifying the arguments (e.g, *hasAgent*, *hasTheme*) presents in the sentences. For doing that, we use (i) Semantic Role Labeling (SRL) when the target word is a verb, or (ii) Dependency Parsing (DP) when it is a noun. For SRL, we use the SLING framework [17], which can identify verbal predicates in text and label its arguments with ProbBank-like [3] labels. In this work, these labels are mapped to VerbNet labels using SemLink [15] and then mapped to the roles used by CS.

---

[2] A synset is a set of cognitive synonyms expressing a concept.

For DP, we use spaCy dependency parser[3] for identifying adjectival modifiers of nouns and label it as Descriptor in CS labels. This process generates a semantic structure for each sentence, in which the arguments are labeled with the CS semantic roles, and its complements are words.

The second sub-task of semantic parsing consists of identifying the synsets evoked by each of these words. For this, we use Named Entity Recognition (NER) and Word Sense Disambiguation (WSD). For NER, we use SLING, which labels named entities with OntoNotes classes (e.g., PERSON, LOCATION, ORG) that we mapped to WordNet synsets based on their meanings (e.g., PERSON is mapped to *person.n.*01). For WSD, we use a structure-based agent based on Wu & Palmer similarity [18], with labels ambiguous words with WordNet synsets. However, the synsets identified by NER and WSD may not necessarily be part of the set of synsets of the input controlled vocabulary. Therefore, we use Wu & Palmer similarity to identify its most similar in the input set.

The execution of these two sub-tasks generates a semantic structure in which each word has the arguments that were identified in the text samples, the synsets that fill those arguments, and the frequencies with which each of these synsets occurs. For example, the verb *eat* has the argument *hasAgent* that filled by the synsets *person.n.*01 and *pronou.n.*01 with their respective frequencies: 10 and 8.

Removing Redundancies. There may be redundancy in synsets that fill a given argument of a given verb or noun. It happens when two or more synsets of the same taxonomy branch (i.e., they have some level of inheritance relation) fill an argument. These redundancies can have adverse effects when performing queries on the SG, so they must be removed.

For removing the redundancies, the synsets filling a given argument are organized in a tree according to their hyperonymy relationships from WordNet. Then, the tree is analyzed from the lowest to the highest nodes, removing those that are less frequent than their nearest hyperonym. Next, a cut by importance is made by establishing a cut-off threshold based on the frequency of occurrence of the synsets. This cut-off threshold is established empirically, using Z-score when the frequency distribution follows the normal distribution, and T-score when not. Finally, the remaining synsets tree is analyzed, keeping only the highest nodes of each branch. This way, the redundant and insignificant synsets are removed. The remaining are inserted as complements to that argument in the SG.

3.2 Overview

The proposed SG consists of an ontology that is composed by a structure of concepts (synsets) with relations of hierarchy and predicate-argument. The hierarchy relations are inherited from WordNet, and the predicate-argument relations are inserted by the procedure described in the previous section. The proposed SG has a total of 4295 predicate-argument relationships, which can be used

---

[3] https://spacy.io/.

to perform searches in the prediction and suggestion of words during the creation of sentences. The properties used for these relations are based on CS (i.e., *hasAgent*, *hasTheme*, *hasRecipient*, *hasManner*, *hasLocation*, *hasTime*, and *hasDescriptor*), and connects the predicates to its arguments, as shown in Fig. 4.

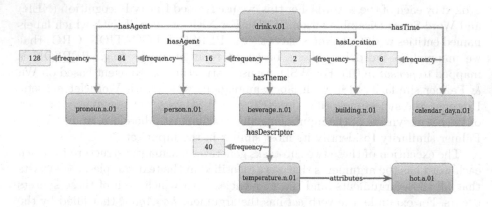

Fig. 4. Excerpt from the semantic grammar

4   Evaluation

As the proposed SG consists of an ontology, it is evaluated following an ontology assessment approach. It is a task-based assessment, which consists of assessing how efficient an ontology is in fulfilling the task for which it is directed [16]. In our case, SG's task is to support the construction of meaningful telegraphic sentences. For this reason, we evaluated the precision the SG has on suggesting the correct words in the reconstruction of telegraphic phrases extracted from CHILDES [11]. For this, the sentences of CHILDES were preprocessed to become telegraphic, and its reconstruction was simulated.

Table 1 shows the summary of evaluation results, with the total number of sentences for each sentence type, the average precision, the number of sentences that were wholly reconstructed (100%), and the number of those in which the reconstruction precision was higher than or less than 50%. The results show that the proposed SG can support the reconstruction of understandable telegraphic phrases with an average accuracy of 90%, considering a total of 1246 sentences. This means that the probability of a user of an AAC system using the SG as a database to find the correct arguments for verbal predicates during sentence construction is 90%. In addition, 71.9% of the sentences were fully reconstructed. This number indicates the level of coverage that the predicate-argument relationships present in the SG have over children's statements extracted from CHILDES. 26.6% of the sentences were not fully reconstructed but had a precision greater than or equal to 50%, and 1.4% (18) had precision less than 50%.

The low score of some sentences is caused by errors in the annotation of CHILDES sentences (e.g., blackbirds lemmatized as black), or by semantic

Table 1. Summary of evaluation results

Sentence type	n	Average precision	100%	>50%	<50%
Agent + Verb + Theme	1162	0,91	864	285	13
Agent + Verb + Location	42	0,80	22	13	5
Agent + Verb + Theme + Location	23	0,86	10	13	0
Theme + Verb + Description	19	0,67	0	19	0
TOTAL	1246	0,90	896	332	18

errors, as in the telegraphic sentence *"bed sit bed"*. However, it is also the result of the absence of predicate-argument relationships between some concepts in the SG. For example, in the sentence *"I sit in the chair"*, no one of the arguments of the verb *sit* was filled, given to the absence of relations between the concept evoked by this verb and the concepts *pronoun.n.01* (for *I*) and *chair.n.01* (for *chair*).

5   Conclusions

This paper proposes a Semantic Grammar (SG) as a basis for supporting well-formed and semantic correct telegraphic sentences authoring in AAC systems. It was acquired by an automatic process that extracted predicate-argument relations from text corpus using NLP techniques. For this, we used three main resources: 1) an AAC domain controlled vocabulary, 2) a corpus, and 3) a grammar based on visual and semantic clues. We evaluated the proposed SG using a task-based ontology assessment approach. For this, we extracted a total of 1246 sentences from CHILDES corpora and simulated its reconstructions using the knowledge represented in the SG. We compared the reconstructed sentences with its references extracted from CHIELDS by assessing a modified precision score and obtained a precision average of 90%. Besides, the SG supported the full reconstruction of 71,9% of the sentences.

These results demonstrate that the proposed SG can provide the necessary support for the construction of meaningful sentences. However, there are still aspects that need to be addressed better. Besides, the proposed SG has not been evaluated by humans or tested in real contexts of AAC use. As future work, we intend to gather resources to replicate the SG construction method to build a similar base for the Portuguese language.

References

1. Allan, K.: Natural language semantics (2001)
2. ASHA: Augmentative and alternative communication (2019). https://www.asha. org/PRPSpecificTopic.aspx?folderid=8589942773xion

3. Babko-Malaya, O.: Propbank annotation guidelines (2005). http://verbs.colorado.edu

4. Baker, C.F., Fillmore, C.J., Lowe, J.B.: The Berkeley framenet project. In: Proceedings of the 17th International Conference on Computational Linguistics-Volume 1, pp. 86–90. Association for Computational Linguistics (1998)

5. Bryan, A.: Colourful semantics: thematic role therapy. In: Language Disorders in Children and Adults: Psycholinguistic Approaches to Therapy, pp. 143–161 (1997)

6. Burton, R.R.: Semantic grammar: an engineering technique for constructing natural language understanding systems (1976)

7. Consortium, B., et al.: The British national corpus, version 3 (BNC xml edition). Distributed by Oxford University Computing Services on behalf of the BNC Consortium 5(65), p. 6 (2007)

8. Fillmore, C.J.: Frame semantics. Linguistics in the Morning Calm, pp. 111–138 (1982)

9. Franco, N., Silva, E., Lima, R., Fidalgo, R.: Towards a reference architecture for augmentative and alternative communication systems. In: Brazilian Symposium on Computers in Education (Simpósio Brasileiro de Informática na Educação-SBIE), vol. 29, p. 1073 (2018)

10. Franco, N.M., de Lima, A.L., Lima, T.P., da Silva, E.A., de Lima, R.J., do Nascimento Fidalgo, R.: A recall analysis of core word lists over children's utterances for augmentative and alternative communication. In: 2017 IEEE 30th International Symposium on Computer-Based Medical Systems (CBMS), pp. 278–283. IEEE (2017)

11. MacWhinney, B.: The CHILDES Project: Tools for Analyzing Talk, Volume II: The Database. Psychology Press, New York (2014)

12. Martínez-Santiago, F., Díaz-Galiano, M.C., Ureña-López, L.A., Mitkov, R.: A semantic grammar for beginning communicators. Knowl.-Based Syst. **86**, 158–172 (2015)

13. McCoy, K.F., Pennington, C.A., Badman, A.L.: Compansion: from research prototype to practical integration. Nat. Lang. Eng. 4(1), 73–95 (1998)

14. Netzer, Y., Elhadad, M.: Using semantic authoring for blissymbols communication boards. In: Proceedings of the Human Language Technology Conference of the NAACL, Companion Volume: Short Papers, pp. 105–108. Association for Computational Linguistics (2006)

15. Palmer, M.: Semlink: linking propbank, verbnet and framenet. In: Proceedings of the Generative Lexicon Conference, GenLex 2009, Pisa, Italy, pp. 9–15 (2009)

16. Raad, J., Cruz, C.: A survey on ontology evaluation methods. In: International Conference on Knowledge Engineering and Ontology Development, part of the 7th International Joint Conference on Knowledge Discovery, Knowledge Engineering and Knowledge Management (2015)

17. Ringgaard, M., Gupta, R., Pereira, F.C.: Sling: a framework for frame semantic parsing. arXiv preprint arXiv:1710.07032 (2017)

18. Wu, Z., Palmer, M.: Verbs semantics and lexical selection. In: Proceedings of the 32nd Annual Meeting on Association for Computational Linguistics, pp. 133–138. Association for Computational Linguistics (1994)

Assessing Unintended Memorization in Neural Discriminative Sequence Models

Mossad Helali$^{(\boxtimes)}$ (iD), Thomas Kleinbauer, and Dietrich Klakow

Spoken Language Systems Group, Saarland Informatics Campus,
Saarland University, Saarbrücken, Germany
{mhelali,thomas.kleinbauer,dietrich.klakow}@lsv.uni-saarland.de

Abstract. Despite their success in a multitude of tasks, neural models trained on natural language have been shown to memorize the intricacies of their training data, posing a potential privacy threat. In this work, we propose a metric to quantify unintended memorization in neural discriminative sequence models. The proposed metric, named d-exposure (discriminative exposure), utilizes language ambiguity and classification confidence to elicit the model's propensity to memorization. Through experimental work on a named entity recognition task, we show the validity of d-exposure to measure memorization. In addition, we show that d-exposure is not a measure of overfitting as it does not increase when the model overfits.

Keywords: Named entity recognition · Natural language understanding · Privacy

1 Introduction

Neural networks have become prevalent in numerous machine learning tasks in general and in natural language processing in particular. An issue that has been identified with neural models, however, is that they tend to memorize their training data [2,7,10]. Memorization raises severe privacy concerns in cases where such models are trained on datasets that contain sensitive information such as credit card numbers, passwords, etc. If such models are deployed e.g. on smartphones [5] or as a service [4], they give attackers access to the memorized sensitive information.

The focus of this paper is on *unintended* memorization, which occurs when models retain information that are orthogonal to the learning task. For example, for the task of named entity recognition (NER) on a dataset of emails, memorizing passwords that appear in the dataset is unintended. Existing work focuses on neural generative sequence models, such as language models and machine translation models, and uses model perplexity to quantify unintended memorization

This research has received funding by the European Union's Horizon 2020 research and innovation programme under grant agreement No. 3081705 – COMPRISE (https://www.compriseh2020.eu/).

P. Sojka et al. (Eds.): TSD 2020, LNAI 12284, pp. 265–272, 2020.
https://doi.org/10.1007/978-3-030-58323-1_29

[2]. In this paper, we propose a metric for discriminative models where perplexity cannot be utilized. The idea is to give practitioners the means to assess the degree of memorization in models intended for deployment, allowing them, e.g., to choose hyper-parameter settings that minimize privacy-threatening information leakage.

Our main contributions are:

- A method for quantifying memorization in discriminative models. This involves inserting specifically designed ambiguous phrases into the training set of the model and analyzing the model's confidence with respect to the created phrases. The proposed metric is named *d-exposure* (for discriminative exposure).
- An experimental validation of the proposed definition on a competitive neural NER model and benchmark dataset. As in previous work, we find that exposure increases with the number of repetitions of inserted phrases in the training set. In addition, we confirm that d-exposure is not a measure of overfitting as unintended memorization does not increase when the model starts to overfit.

2   Related Work

In one of the earliest studies on memorization in neural networks, Zhang et al. [10] show that neural networks have the capability to fit data with random labels, meaning that state-of-the-art models are at risk of memorization. Song et al. [7] present a method to create neural models that memorizes the training data with no noticeable difference in utility. This raises concerns because utility is often the main criterion for deciding which model to deploy. In their analysis of memorization, Arpit et al. [1] show that memorization is not only dependent on the model, but also on the dataset. While these works are important in the analysis of memorization, they do not provide a quantitative method for gauging the depth of the problem.

The first work on assessing *unintended* memorization in neural models on language tasks was by Carlini et al. [2]. To assess unintended memorization, they define a metric, named *exposure*, that is based on comparing the perplexity $Px(s)$ of a random phrase s inserted into the training set with the perplexities of other phrases from the same random space. The basic tenet is that a significantly lower perplexity of the inserted phrase vs. those of the other random phrases signals that the neural model has unintentionally memorized that phrase. Specifically, for a random phrase s inserted into the training set of a model θ, exposure is defined as:

$$\mathbf{exposure}_\theta(s) = -log_2 \Pr_{r \in \mathcal{R}}[Px_\theta(r) \leq Px_\theta(s)] \tag{1}$$

where $\mathcal{R}$ is the random space of all such phrases. Note that high memorization, i.e., low perplexity, is reflected by high exposure values. The authors test their definition empirically and conclude that memorization is not directly linked to overfitting but rather to the learning process itself, making memorization a prevalent issue in state-of-the-art neural models. However, the authors' approach is limited to generative sequence models because the definition of exposure is based on perplexity. We show below how a similar line of reasoning can be utilized for an exposure measure on discriminative models.

Another related notion to the problem of memorization is membership inference attacks, where an attacker tries to infer whether a set of samples belong to the dataset of a trained model. Truex et al. [9] have done an extensive analysis on how such attacks can be carried out and on the vulnerability of the models under attack. Though membership inference is related to our work, there are notable differences between the approaches. First, the goal of our work is to measure the model's propensity to leaking information, not analyzing whether the model can be attacked. For example, for an overfit model, membership inference probability increases [6], while memorization is not correlated with overfitting. Moreover, calculating exposure is a simpler procedure that does not involve building shadow datasets and attack models as in membership inference.

3   Approach

The existing definition of exposure in [2] is inapplicable to discriminative models because it is based on perplexity, which is not supplied by discriminative models. Instead, such models output for each class a level of confidence that the input word belongs to that class. This motivates a definition of exposure *per class* as it can behave differently for each class. While exhaustive enumeration of perplexity is inefficient [2], it is feasible to enumerate the model's confidence for all words in each class because these are in the magnitude of only a few thousands, depending on the dataset.

Intuitively, memorizing is the opposite of generalizing. A good model will classify an unambiguous sentence with high confidence. For example, in the sentence "I prefer Germany", the last word should clearly be labeled as a location in an NER task. Polysemous words, however, may constitute different named entities depending on the context. For instance, the word "Jordan" could refer to a person (e.g., Michael Jordan), a location (e.g. the country of the same name), or an organization (e.g. The Jordan Company). If some of these cases appear with roughly the same frequency in the training data, an ambiguous test sentence, such as "I prefer Jordan", should thus be classified with low confidence. Even adding the same sentence to the training data should not change this – unless the model tends to memorize sentences. In other words, an unexpected high confidence in the classification of an ambiguous sentence hints at the possibility of unintended memorization in a given model. We base our definition of d-exposure on this notion and follow the general procedure given by Carlini et al. [2].

3.1   d-exposure for Discriminative Models

Given a fixed phrase that has a word s with multiple possible class labels, we insert the phrase in the training set with s labeled as C_i and train the model θ.

d-exposure for class C_i is then given by:

$$\text{d-exposure}_{\theta, C_i}(s) = -log_2 \Pr_{w \in C_i}[\text{conf}(w) \geq \text{conf}(s)] \qquad (2)$$

where $\text{conf}(s)$ is the confidence returned by the model when labeling s. Therefore, d-exposure has a value $\in [0, log_2|C_i|]$ with $|C_i|$ denoting the number of words that are labeled only as C_i. Maximum d-exposure is obtained when s has the highest confidence (high memorization) and vice versa. Note that this is the case if all words are assigned the correct class. If s is labeled incorrectly, however, d-exposure is defined to be zero. On the other hand, if other words in C_i are incorrectly labeled, they are treated as having lower confidence than s, because the model classified the ambiguous phrase correctly while failing to correctly classify the clear one. We apply the same process for other entity classes in the dataset and calculate d-exposure of the model as:

$$\text{d-exposure}_{\theta}(s) = \frac{1}{N} \sum_{C_i} \text{d-exposure}_{\theta, C_i}(s) \qquad (3)$$

where N is the number of classes. This definition allows one to ignore classes that are considered irrelevant for the task at hand. For example, if one is interested in measuring the memorization of their model on the names of persons and locations only, one could simply compute d-exposure for these two classes. Recall that the purpose of the metric is to guide the choice of model settings before deployment. Which phrases and classes to consider are choices made by the user.

4   Experimental Validation

In this section, we experimentally test the proposed definition of d-exposure in order to: (1) show its validity as a measure of unintended memorization in discriminative models, and (2) demonstrate that d-exposure is not linked to overfitting. We show our results on a named entity recognition task as an example of discriminative models.

4.1   Setup

We conduct our experiments on CoNLL-2003 [8], a popular NER dataset in English. In our experiments, we focus on the tags: S-PER, S-ORG, and S-LOC. We discard S-MISC to decrease the variability as including it would lead to the inserted phrase having multiple correct labels (based on the definition of S-MISC). Table 1 shows statistics of these classes in CoNLL-2003 dataset. The first column is the number of unique entities that belong only to the respective class ($|C_i|$); the second column is the number of unique entities that have more than one possible label (i.e. candidates for s); the third column is the frequency of each class in the training set.

For the inserted phrase, we choose the ambiguous format: "There are many people who like _____", which allows entities of the three types to fill the blank.

Table 1. Statistics of the chosen classes in the training set of CoNLL-2003.

Label	Exclusive	Overlapped	Frequency
S-ORG	1001	101	3836
S-PER	949	19	2316
S-LOC	937	97	6101

Table 2. Number of occurrences of the chosen entities in the training set of CoNLL-2003.

Word	S-PER	S-ORG	S-LOC
Williams	7	8	0
Chelsea	5	6	0
Melbourne	0	4	5

For the chosen entities, "Williams" was inserted as S-ORG, "Chelsea" as S-PER and "Melbourne" as S-LOC. We chose these entities because their occurrences in the training set are more balanced than others. Table 2 shows the number of occurrences of these entities as each class. That said, we found out that the general behavior of d-exposure does not change based on the chosen entities, as long as they are not highly imbalanced towards one class, nor does it change based on the format, as long as it is ambiguous.

For the model, we use a BiLSTM with GloVe embeddings, SGD optimizer, dropout (50%) and learning rate decay, implemented with Targer[1], a neural tagging library [3]. This model achieves an F1 of 90.0 on CoNLL-2003 dataset.

4.2   Repeated Occurrences in the Training Set

In this experiment, we test whether d-exposure increases with the number of times the chosen phrase appears in the training set. The intuition is that the more the model sees the sentence, the higher the incentive to memorize it. For this matter, we insert the chosen sentences 4, 16, 64, 128 and 256 times and observe d-exposure for each category. Figure 1 shows the effect of the number of repetitions of the inserted sentence on d-exposure. As expected, d-exposure generally increases with the number of repetitions, implying that repeated occurrence of a sentence in the training set tends to produce higher memorization. Another observation is that d-exposure does not behave the same in all classes. Rather, it is much lower for S-LOC than the other two. This validates our claim that exposure is to be measured per-class as different classes occur in different contexts but the exact reasons for the differing behavior require further investigation. In additional experiments with other model architectures not detailed here, we found the same general trend in the curves but the behavior of S-PER and S-LOC reversed. Table 3 shows d-exposure evaluated at different epochs (columns) and number of repetitions (rows) for the three classes. The first row is the value of d-exposure when the phrase is not inserted in the training set.

---

[1] https://github.com/achernodub/targer.

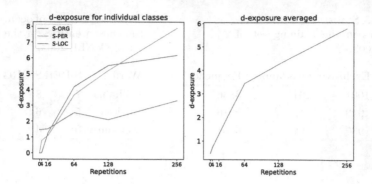

Fig. 1. d-exposure vs. repetitions for individual classes and averaged on CoNLL-2003 at 150 epochs.

4.3 Overfitting

In this experiment, we observe the behavior of d-exposure against overfitting. We conduct this analysis to confirm that exposure is not a measure of overfitting but rather of memorization. If it was so, we expect it to reach its maximum value for all classes when overfitting begins or to keep increasing while the model is overfitting. To make the model overfit, we train it only on 10% of the training data, increase the number of epochs to 250 and disable learning rate decay and dropout. Figure 2 shows the results when the phrases are repeated 16 times. d-exposure increases as the model is learning and stops increasing when overfitting begins. In addition, maximum d-exposure for S-LOC (8.0) or S-ORG (8.1) is not reached at any point. Recall that the maximum d-exposure for a class C_i is $log_2|C_i|$, where $|C_i|$ is the number of entities belonging only to that class. For S-PER, however, maximum d-exposure (7.5) is reached only at stages where the model has not yet overfit. Therefore, we conclude that d-exposure is not correlated with overfitting and for the case of S-PER, the model has higher memorization. Similar results were found for different numbers of repetitions.

Table 3. d-exposure for the classes S-LOC, S-PER, and S-ORG for different numbers of repetitions (rows) and epochs (columns).

	S-LOC						S-PER						S-ORG					
	25	50	75	100	125	150	25	50	75	100	125	150	25	50	75	100	125	150
0	1.76	1.42	1.51	1.33	1.55	1.46	0.00	0.00	0.00	0.31	0.34	0.00	0.00	0.00	0.00	0.00	0.00	0.00
4	1.87	1.68	1.47	1.71	1.57	1.46	0.00	0.43	0.48	0.59	0.72	0.78	0.00	0.00	0.00	0.82	0.00	0.00
16	1.87	1.74	1.72	2.00	1.78	1.51	0.49	0.58	0.82	0.98	0.79	1.10	0.00	1.12	0.67	1.28	1.28	1.26
64	2.68	2.27	2.30	2.47	2.68	2.52	2.71	1.40	3.57	2.47	4.47	3.64	2.38	3.14	2.96	2.89	4.16	4.16
128	3.27	3.00	3.50	2.51	2.09	2.09	4.61	4.50	3.94	4.76	4.80	5.19	2.24	4.11	5.01	4.24	4.68	5.51
256	4.52	3.03	3.43	3.57	3.83	3.29	8.89	8.31	8.31	9.89	7.89	7.89	3.46	4.21	6.16	5.21	6.06	6.16

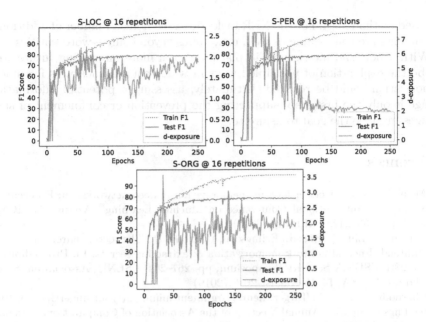

Fig. 2. d-exposure vs. overfitting for S-LOC, S-PER, and S-ORG on CoNLL-2003.

5 Conclusion and Future Work

In this work, we presented a measure of unintended memorization in discriminative neural models. It is inspired by previous work on generative sequence models but offers an approach for tasks where measuring perplexity is not feasible. The core idea is to identify the exposure of potentially private data with confidence assessments of model predictions. We show how ambiguous sentences can be employed towards that goal in a named entity recognition task. One limitation of this methodology is that it can only be applied to NER classes that share some linguistic materials with at least one other class.

We performed a number of in-depth experiments to illustrate the effectiveness of our new metric for assessing model memorization. While we focus on one task here, with a reduced number of NE labels, we are nevertheless able to confirm the findings of the previous work on exposure for generative sequence models. In particular, these are 1) higher d-exposure values for repeated insertions of a test phrase into the training data; and 2) independence of d-exposure from model overfitting. The first finding confirms that the number of occurrence of a phrase in the training data, the expected memorization of that phrase in the model, and the proposed metric all correlate positively. The second finding sets our approach apart from methods such as membership inference attacks which are prone to significant performance drops for overfitted models.

In the future, we plan to perform similar validation experiments for other natural language processing tasks as well. The definition of what constitutes an "ambiguous phrase" for each task poses a challenge but is a necessary step in the proposed methodology. For the NER task addressed here, a number of additional experiments are conceivable as well, e.g., going beyond single-word entities.

With a powerful metric now in place, an even more interesting future step will be the exploration of principled ways in which counter-measures for model memorization could be realized. Ultimately, assessing a potential information leakage is only the first step, supporting the prevention or confinement of such leakages must be the goal to aspire to.

References

1. Arpit, D., et al.: A closer look at memorization in deep networks. In: Proceedings of the 34th International Conference on Machine Learning - Volume 70, ICML 2017, pp. 233–242. JMLR.org (2017)
2. Carlini, N., Liu, C., Kos, J., Erlingsson, Ú., Song, D.: The secret sharer: measuring unintended neural network memorization & extracting secrets. In: Proceedings of the 28th USENIX Security Symposium, pp. 267–284. USENIX Association, Santa Clara, CA, USA, 14–16 August 2019 (2019)
3. Chernodub, A., et al.: Targer: neural argument mining at your fingertips. In: Proceedings of the 57th Annual Meeting of the Association of Computational Linguistics (ACL'2019). Florence, Italy (2019)
4. Hesamifard, E., Takabi, H., Ghasemi, M., Wright, R.: Privacy-preserving machine learning as a service. Proc. Privacy Enhancing Technol. **3**, 123–142 (2018). https://doi.org/10.1515/popets-2018-0024
5. Konečný, J., McMahan, H.B., Yu, F.X., Richtárik, P., Suresh, A.T., Bacon, D.: Federated learning: strategies for improving communication efficiency. In: NIPS Workshop on Private Multi-Party Machine Learning (2016)
6. Long, Y., Bindschaedler, V., Gunter, C.A.: Towards measuring membership privacy (2017). http://arxiv.org/abs/1712.09136
7. Song, C., Ristenpart, T., Shmatikov, V.: Machine learning models that remember too much. In: Proceedings of the 2017 ACM SIGSAC Conference on Computer and Communications Security, CCS 2017, pp. 587–601. Association for Computing Machinery, New York (2017)
8. Tjong Kim Sang, E.F., De Meulder, F.: Introduction to the CoNLL-2003 shared task: language-independent named entity recognition. In: Proceedings of the Seventh Conference on Natural Language Learning at HLT-NAACL 2003, pp. 142–147 (2003)
9. Truex, S., Liu, L., Gursoy, M.E., Yu, L., Wei, W.: Demystifying membership inference attacks in machine learning as a service. IEEE Trans. Serv. Comput. (Early Access), 05 February 2019
10. Zhang, C., Bengio, S., Hardt, M., Recht, B., Vinyals, O.: Understanding deep learning requires rethinking generalization. In: 5th International Conference on Learning Representations, ICLR 2017, Toulon, France, 24–26 April, 2017, Conference Track Proceedings. OpenReview.net (2017)

Investigating the Impact of Pre-trained Word Embeddings on Memorization in Neural Networks

Aleena Thomas[(⊠)] [iD], David Ifeoluwa Adelani, Ali Davody, Aditya Mogadala, and Dietrich Klakow

Spoken Language Systems Group, Saarland Informatics Campus, Saarland University, Saarbrücken, Germany
{athomas,didelani,adavody,amogadala,dietrich.klakow}@lsv.uni-saarland.de

Abstract. The sensitive information present in the training data, poses a privacy concern for applications as their unintended memorization during training can make models susceptible to membership inference and attribute inference attacks. In this paper, we investigate this problem in various pre-trained word embeddings (GloVe, ELMo and BERT) with the help of language models built on top of it. In particular, firstly sequences containing sensitive information like *a single-word disease* and *4-digit PIN* are randomly inserted into the training data, then a language model is trained using word vectors as input features, and memorization is measured with a metric termed as *exposure*. The embedding dimension, the number of training epochs, and the length of the secret information were observed to affect memorization in pre-trained embeddings. Finally, to address the problem, differentially private language models were trained to reduce the exposure of sensitive information.

Keywords: Differential privacy · Word representations · Unintended memorization

1 Introduction

Several advances were made in machine learning for addressing numerous tasks of Computer Vision and Natural Language Processing (NLP). However, there exist some practical hurdles when applying them in the industry, particularly when it involves training the models from data containing sensitive information such as users' attributes, financial information, and health records. It has been recently shown that an adversary can recover sensitive information (as a result of memorization [3]) or observations used for training (a.k.a membership inference attack [11–14]) from a publicly available pre-trained model in a black-box attack, i.e., without access to the training data.

Word embeddings [4,8] are often used as primary features for obtaining state-of-the-art results in NLP tasks as they incorporate both syntactic and semantic relationships between the words. However, when they are trained on

© Springer Nature Switzerland AG 2020
P. Sojka et al. (Eds.): TSD 2020, LNAI 12284, pp. 273–281, 2020.
https://doi.org/10.1007/978-3-030-58323-1_30

user-generated content like social media posts or clinical notes (containing consultation notes, patient discharge summaries, and history notes), the relationship between users and their attributes e.g., interests, disease, and health history can be learned and re-identified using membership inference attack methods. Models trained on sensitive information are publicly available like Twitter-Glove[1] and Clinical-BERT [2] as they help to improve the performance of downstream NLP tasks in the domain of interest. Although, the extent to which these models leak users' information has not been quantified.

In this paper, we aim to quantify the leakage of sensitive information in pre-trained word embeddings, namely GloVe, ELMo, and BERT when they are used for downstream NLP tasks. Recently, the leakage of sensitive information has been studied for text generation tasks [14] like machine translation, dialogue generation and language modeling. This leakage can also be viewed as neural networks memorizing secret information which was proven to be true [3]. A simple attack on a language model is predicting sensitive information like credit card number when given the context in which the secret information appears, this is even more probable when we limit the space of most likely words, say from all words in the vocabulary to only numbers. If indeed word embeddings leads to better performance on many NLP tasks including language model, does it also make this attack easier?

It is not straightforward how to compute sensitive information captured by word embeddings without using them to train an NLP task. So, we have made use of a simple language model with these word vectors as input features. We address the problem of quantifying the leakage of sensitive information in pre-trained embeddings by investigating if they exacerbate the problem of memorization in a language model when used as input features. We quantify the amount of information memorized by neural networks or exposed at inference using the *exposure* metric proposed by [3]. Specifically, we compare the exposure of sensitive information on using different kinds of embeddings: distributed embeddings obtained by GloVe [8] and contextualized embeddings i.e., ELMo [9] and BERT [4]. In our experiments, we observe that leakage in higher dimensional word vectors is greater than or equal to the leakage observed in lower-dimensional vectors of the word representations. This is particularly concerning because oftentimes, the higher dimensional embeddings have better performance when used as features for downstream NLP tasks [4,10]. Training differentially private language models [7] helps to drastically reduce the exposure of private information, thus providing better privacy [3].

2   Memorization in Deep Learning Models

Recently, Carlini et al. [3] introduced the *exposure* metric to measure unintended memorization in neural networks. Given a model f_θ, a secret format s, e.g., $s =$ "My PIN number is ####", and secret $s[r]$ with a randomness $r \in R$

---

[1] Glove trained on 2 billion tweets: https://nlp.stanford.edu/projects/glove/.

Algorithm 1. Precise Exposure

1: **procedure** CALCULATEPRECISEEXPOSURE($\mathcal{D}$, $s[r]$, $EMBEDDING\_TYPE$, R, K)
2:     Additional Inputs: $\{s[r_2], s[r_3], ..., s[r_K]\}$ for multiple insertions
3:     $s[r_1] = s[r]$
4:     **for** k from 1 to K **do**
5:         $\mathcal{D} \leftarrow \mathcal{D} \cup s[r_k]$
6:     **end for**
7:     $Z \leftarrow$ getEmbeddings($\mathcal{D}$, $embedding\_type$)
8:     $\theta \leftarrow$ trainedLSTM(Z)
9:     $\tau \leftarrow \{\}$
10:    **for** $\hat{r} \in$ R **do**
11:        $\tau_{\hat{r}} \leftarrow$ log-perplexity$_\theta(s[\hat{r}])$
12:    **end for**
13:    $\tau' \leftarrow$ sort(τ)
14:    $\rho_r \leftarrow$ getRank($s[r]$, τ')
15:    $exposure(s[r]) \leftarrow \log_2|R| - \log_2\rho_r$
16: **end procedure**

(randomness space), e.g., "My PIN number is 2467"; $r = 2467$, the exposure of the secret $s[r]$ is defined as:

$$\text{exposure}_\theta(s[r]) = \log_2 |R| - \log_2 rank_\theta(s[r]) \tag{1}$$

where, the $rank_\theta(s[r])$ is the rank of $s[r]$ in the sorted list of log-perplexities of $s[\hat{r}]$ for all possible $\hat{r} \in R$. The sorting is in ascending order.

The exposure metric depends on the space of R and the implication is that the maximum value of the metric for longer sequences such as credit card number or 4-digit PIN is higher than exposure for a single word prediction like a disease. Carlini et al [3] measured memorization by (1) adding a sequence (e.g., *John's PIN number is 2467*) containing secret information to the training data (2) training a language model on the augmented dataset (3) computing the exposure based on the rank of the log-perplexity of the inserted secret, say 2467 from the other $R = 10^4$ available combinations when the model is given a context *"John's PIN number is"*. If the rank is very high especially if the domain of the training dataset is very different from the inserted sequence, this is an indication of memorization.

3 Measuring and Preventing Unintended Memorization

3.1 Measuring Memorization of Secrets

Following the approach introduced by Carlini et al. [3], we analyze the effect of different word representations on memorization. We make use of an LSTM language model to compare the levels of exposure while using different pre-trained embeddings as input features.

First, we augment the training data with an additional sequence with a secret such as "my PIN number is 2467" i.e $\mathcal{D} \leftarrow \mathcal{D} \cup s[r]$ in Algorithm 1. For multiple insertion of secrets, we insert multiple sequences, $s[r_k]$ with K different PIN numbers, where $s[r_1] = s[r]$. Next, we obtain pre-trained embeddings for all the training sequences. We represent all the input embeddings with Z which is passed into the LSTM model. The trained weights, θ of the LSTM model are learned after training and used to compute the log-perplexity $\tau_{\hat{r}}$ for all the possible secret values, $\hat{r} \in R$.

Exposure is computed using the rank of the log-perplexity of the inserted sequence containing secret $s[r]$ from the list of all log-perplexities of different secret values ($r \in R$). The step-by-step procedure for computing the exposure of a secret sentence $s[r]$ given a corpus $\mathcal{D}$, R, the number of sentences to be added, K and the word embedding *embedding_type* is in Algorithm 1.

3.2   Preventing Memorization with Differential Privacy

Differential privacy is a strong approach to resist attacks aiming to extract sensitive information from a dataset $\mathcal{D}$. The main idea is that releasing an aggregated result should not disclose too much information about any individual record in the dataset. More specifically, if we define a dataset $\mathcal{D}'$ that differs with $\mathcal{D}$ in only one record, x_n, when the attacker makes a query on both datasets, he/she should get almost the same results.

Definition 1. *(Differential Privacy [5]). A randomized algorithm $\mathcal{M}$ is (ε, δ) differential private if for all sets of outputs S and for all neighboring datasets D_1 and D_2 differing on at most one data point*

$$\Pr[\mathcal{M}(D_1) \in S] \leq \exp(\varepsilon) \Pr[\mathcal{M}(D_2) \in S] + \delta \qquad (2)$$

Intuitively a (ε, δ) differential private algorithm guarantees that the absolute value of information leakage will be bounded by ε with probability at least $1 - \delta$. Therefore ε controls the level of privacy protection and so is called privacy loss.

Differential privacy can be integrated with deep learning to protects models from different kinds of attacks. However, directly applying random noise within a deep learning model yields inferior performance because of the high sensitivity of the network's output to the parameters. A solution to this challenge has been proposed in [1]. The core idea is adding random noise to the stochastic gradient descent (SGD) updates and make it private, leading to differentially private SGD (DPSGD). Differentially private training can be used to prevent unintended memorization and membership inference in deep neural models. In particular, a variant of DPSGD [1] has been used in [3] to train recurrent neural networks. It has been shown there that differential privacy fully eliminates the memorization effects and reduces exposure of secrets.

4   Experimental Setup

In this section, we present the experimental setups of two sets of experiments on the Penn Treebank (PTB) dataset for different word representations: GloVe,

ELMo and BERT embeddings. We train a 1-layer LSTM language model with 256 hidden units on 2,000 sentences from the PTB text data that consists of 35,000 sequences (assuming a minimum context size of one) and 12,921 vocabulary words. The first set of experiments is trained on the dataset augmented with secret sequence(s) using Adam optimizer [6], while the second set of experiments helps to reduce memorization using the DPSGD training. We consider pre-trained embeddings with various vector dimensions, $d = 100, 300, 768, 1024$ i.e GloVe-{100d, 300d}, ELMo-1024d, BERT-{768d, 1024d}.

To study how the length of the secret affects its memorization, we use two types of secrets; namely *single word - disease* and *four digit - PIN*. *Disease* type of secret is inserted as follows - $<$ *name* $>$ *is suffering from* $<$ *disease* $>$. For all the experiments with this type of secret augmented, we compute the exposure value of the sequence, $s[r]$: *john is suffering from alzheimers* after training the model on a dataset including this sentence. Since the number of diseases is too small to be considered as sample space, we assume the vocabulary as the sample space from which the diseases are drawn from. In the PIN type of secret, the inserted secret is of the form - $<$ *name* $>$ *atm PIN number is* $<$ $\#\#\#\#$ $>$. Here, the sample space size for computing the exposure is 10^4.

The memorization could also be affected by the presence of multiple secrets in the dataset, which may confuse the model. In order to analyze the effect of having multiple secrets, we use two types of insertion of secrets:

- **Single insertion** with a pair of secrets: in this case, we augment the dataset with a single sentence that contains either *disease* or *PIN* type secret.
- **Multiple insertions** with unique pairs of secrets: in this case, we augment the dataset with multiple sentences all of which contains either *disease* types or *PIN* types. For example, we test the exposure of the sequence $s[r]$ after augmenting the dataset with M additional secrets like: {*oliver is suffering from influenza, laura is suffering from cholera, ...* }. In the experiments, $M = 16$ for *disease* type and $M = 10$ for the *PIN* type secret.

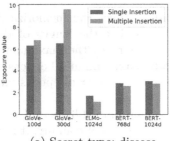
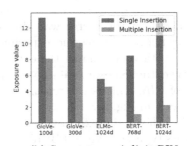

(a) Secret-type: disease   (b) Secret-type: 4-digit PIN

Fig. 1. Exposure values for single insertion of a sequence with a pair of secrets and multiple insertion of sequences with unique pairs of secrets. The number of epochs for the disease and the PIN type secrets are 5 and 40 respectively.

5   Results

In this section, we present the results of the experiments to analyze memorization in word representations. Figure 1 shows the exposure values for different kinds of embedding types for single and multiple insertions of secrets. From the plots, we observe a pattern between the exposure value and embedding dimension regardless of the secret type, or insertion type for GloVe and BERT embeddings. Higher exposure levels are observed for higher dimensions except when the exposure values were already maximum. This indicates that for the same embedding type, representations with higher dimensions may memorize more. This is particularly concerning as a higher performance is generally observed when the higher dimensions of an embedding type are used.

We also observe that multiple type of insertion of secrets decreases the exposure values except for GloVe embeddings with the *disease* secret type. This suggests that the presence of multiple instances of the same type of secret could confuse the model and helps in lowering the exposure levels.

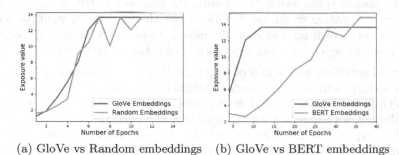

(a) GloVe vs Random embeddings   (b) GloVe vs BERT embeddings

Fig. 2. Exposure values for random, GloVe and BERT embeddings at different stages of training for the disease secret type with single insertion type of secrets

The length of the secret was also found to affect the memorization. One interesting finding during the experiments was that the length of the secret affected the stage of training the exposure values reach the maximum. For the *disease* type, the exposure values were already maximum at 40 epochs unlike in the case of *PIN*. This is the reason for the lower number of epochs for *disease* type of secret in Fig. 1a.

Figure 2 shows the exposure levels of random embeddings and pre-trained embeddings types; GloVe and BERT at different stages of training. It is observed that the memorization in the case of GloVe saturates much earlier in training compared to BERT as shown in Fig. 2b. The memorization in BERT representations is seen to happen later in training, reaching the maximum exposure only after the 36th epoch as compared to the 12th epoch in the case of GloVe. The exposure values in the case of GloVe embeddings were observed to reach its maximum value earlier than that of random embeddings. This shows that

Table 1. Exposure values of *disease-type* of secret for different embedding-types with differential privacy(DP) training vs non-DP training. The number of epochs for both versions is 40.

Embedding type	Single insertion		Multiple insertion	
	Non-DP	DP	Non-DP	DP
GloVe-100d	5.87	1.61	7.9	1.72
GloVe-300d	6.03	1.17	13.65	2.19
ELMo-1024d	13.39	2.04	9.33	0.65
BERT-768d	14.85	0.12	14.85	1.62
BERT-1024d	14.85	0.27	14.85	2.20

although pre-trained embeddings give an improvement in performance over random embeddings, the former are at a higher risk of exposing sensitive information in the training dataset.

Lastly, we performed experiments by training the LSTM models with DPSGD (with parameters $\varepsilon = 10$, $\delta = 2e{-}5$, resulting noise level $\sigma = 0.44$), we observe a drastic reduction in exposure values as shown in Table 1 especially for models with maximum exposure (BERT-768d and BERT-1024d) from 14.85 to less than 2.21 for both single insertion and multiple insertions of *disease-type* of secrets. Our observation confirms what Carlini et al. [3] observed that differential privacy helps in reducing memorization. But the DP versions run considerably slower than non-DP versions, e.g., training the non-DP and DP version using GloVe embeddings take on average, 12 min and 14 hours respectively on GPU (Nvidia Titan X). All the reported exposure values have a maximal standard deviation of 1.09.

6 Conclusion

In this paper, we investigated memorization in word representations commonly used as features for training the state-of-the-art natural language understanding tasks. We compare the degree of memorization of three different word embedding types (GloVe, ELMo and BERT). All the embedding types were found to expose sensitive information up to a certain extent. This observation implies a possible privacy threat when they are used in applications with private and sensitive data. We observed an increase in the exposure levels (except when the exposure value is already maximum) with the embedding dimension for GloVe and BERT, and multiple instances of the sensitive information in the training dataset is seen to lower memorization. Further, we observed that different embedding types start memorizing at different stages of training. The GloVe embeddings were found to reach maximum exposure level earlier in training compared to random embeddings of the same dimension.

As future work, we plan to investigate membership inference attack on the pre-trained embeddings and train differentially private variants of the embeddings to prevent leakage of sensitive information in practical applications. Recently, Vu [15] proposed dpUGC – a differentially private Word2Vec model but the utility of the model was not investigated on NLU tasks. We hope to investigate the utility of the differentially private variants of the word embeddings on standard NLU tasks like named entity recognition and text classification.

Acknowledgments. The presented research has been funded by the European Union's Horizon 2020 research and innovation programme project COMPRISE (http:// www.compriseh2020.eu/) under grant agreement No. 3081705. We thank Emmanuel Vincent and Thomas Kleinbauer for their feedback on the paper.

References

1. Abadi, M., et al.: Deep learning with differential privacy. In: Proceedings of the 2016 ACM SIGSAC Conference on Computer and Communications Security, pp. 308–318. ACM (2016)
2. Alsentzer, E., et al.: Publicly available clinical BERT embeddings. In: Proceedings of the 2nd Clinical NLP Workshop, NAACL, pp. 72–78 (2019)
3. Carlini, N., Liu, C., Erlingsson, Ú., Kos, J., Song, D.X.: The secret sharer: evaluating and testing unintended memorization in neural networks. In: USENIX Security Symposium, pp. 267–284 (2018)
4. Devlin, J., Chang, M.W., Lee, K., Toutanova, K.: BERT: pre-training of deep bidirectional transformers for language understanding. In: Proceedings of NAACL, pp. 4171–4186 (2019)
5. Dwork, C., Kenthapadi, K., McSherry, F., Mironov, I., Naor, M.: Our data, ourselves: privacy via distributed noise generation. In: Vaudenay, S. (ed.) EUROCRYPT 2006. LNCS, vol. 4004, pp. 486–503. Springer, Heidelberg (2006). https:// doi.org/10.1007/11761679_29
6. Kingma, D.P., Ba, J.: Adam: a method for stochastic optimization. In: Bengio, Y., LeCun, Y. (eds.) 3rd International Conference on Learning Representations, ICLR 2015, San Diego, CA, USA, 7–9 May, 2015, Conference Track Proceedings (2015). http://arxiv.org/abs/1412.6980
7. McMahan, B., Ramage, D., Talwar, K., Zhang, L.: Learning differentially private recurrent language models. In: ICLR (2018)
8. Pennington, J., Socher, R., Manning, C.: Glove: global vectors for word representation. In: Proceedings of EMNLP (2014)
9. Peters, M., et al.: Deep contextualized word representations. In: Proceedings of NAACL, Volume 1 (Long Papers), pp. 2227–2237. Association for Computational Linguistics, June 2018
10. Radford, A., Wu, J., Child, R., Luan, D., Amodei, D., Sutskever, I.: Language models are unsupervised multitask learners (2018). https://d4mucfpksywv.cloudfront. net/better-language-models/language-models.pdf
11. Shokri, R., Stronati, M., Song, C., Shmatikov, V.: Membership inference attacks against machine learning models. In: 2017 IEEE Symposium on SP, pp. 3–18 (2017)
12. Shokri, R., Shmatikov, V.: Privacy-preserving deep learning. In: Proceedings of the 22nd ACM Conference on CCS, pp. 1310–1321 (2015)
13. Song, C., Ristenpart, T., Shmatikov, V.: Machine learning models that remember too much. In: Proceedings of the ACM SIGSAC Conference on CCS, pp. 587–601 (2017)

14. Song, C., Shmatikov, V.: Auditing data provenance in text-generation models. In: Proceedings of KDD, pp. 196–206. ACM, New York (2019)
15. Vu, X.-S., Tran, S.N., Jiang, L.: dpUGC: learn differentially private representation for user generated contents. In: Proceedings of CICLing. La Rochelle, France (2019)

Speech

Investigating the Corpus Independence of the Bag-of-Audio-Words Approach

Mercedes Vetráb[1,2](✉) [ID] and Gábor Gosztolya[1,2]

[1] Institute of Informatics, University of Szeged, Árpád tér 2, Szeged, Hungary
{vetrabm,ggabor}@inf.u-szeged.hu
[2] MTA-SZTE Research Group on Artificial Intelligence, Tisza Lajos körút 103, Szeged, Hungary

Abstract. In this paper, we analyze the general use of the Bag-of-Audio-Words (BoAW) feature extraction method. This technique allows us to handle the problem of varying length recordings. The first step of the BoAW method is to define cluster centers (called codewords) over our feature set with an unsupervised training method (such as k-means clustering or even random sampling). This step is normally performed on the training set of the actual database, but this approach has its own drawbacks: we have to create new codewords for each data set and this increases the computing time and it can lead to over-fitting. Here, we analyse how much the codebook depends on the given corpus. In our experiments, we work with three databases: a Hungarian emotion database, a German emotion database and a general Hungarian speech database. We experiment with constructing a set of codewords on each of these databases, and examine how the classification accuracy scores vary on the Hungarian emotion database. According to our results, the classification performance was similar in each case, which suggests that the Bag-of-Audio-Words codebook is practically corpus-independent. This corpus-independence allows us to reuse codebooks created on different datasets, which can make it easier to use the BoAW method in practice.

Keywords: Emotion detection · Bag-of-Audio-words · Human voice · Sound processing

1 Introduction

Human speech is not only used for encoding the words uttered, but it also includes some information about the speakers physical and mental state. One of the latter attributes is the emotional state of the speaker. Nowadays emotion detection from audio data (speech emotion recognition, SER) is an active area of research with a wide range of possible applications, including human-computer interfaces (monitoring human communication) [6], dialog systems [1] and call centers [12]. In the future with good emotion recognition systems, we will be able to create more human-oriented and friendlier systems.

© Springer Nature Switzerland AG 2020
P. Sojka et al. (Eds.): TSD 2020, LNAI 12284, pp. 285–293, 2020.
https://doi.org/10.1007/978-3-030-58323-1_31

Since the beginning of research in this area, many feature extraction and classification techniques have been used along with different datasets to get the best results. The basis of our study is a previous paper [11], where we investigated the Bag-of-Audio-Words (BoAW [7]) technique and its efficiency. One of the major problem using the BoAW technique was the time required to generate a codebook, which could be solved if we utilize a predefined codebook instead of generating a new one for each data set. In this paper, we discuss the consequences of using a predefined codebook. We address the question of whether a codebook from another database can produce similar or better results than by using a codebook from the original database. We perform our experiments on a Hungarian emotion speech database; previous classification accuracy scores on this database were around 66–70%. We measured Unweighted Average Recall (UAR, [9]) scores in the range 66–71%, so our view is that the BoAW method with a predefined codebook is a competitive technique for emotion recognition.

2   The Bag-of-Audio-Words Method

With the representation of emotional speech data, there are many open questions and problems. One of them is feature extraction from recordings. Often the utterances we have to handle are of different lengths, but most classification techniques require fixed-sized feature vectors. The Bag-of-Audio-words is a feature extraction method similar to the Bag-of-Words [7] technique. With the BoAW feature representation, we can resolve the problem of varying length.

In the BoAW procedure, first we have to extract the frame-level feature vectors per recording; unfortunately, the number of vectors created depends on the original length of the evaluated recording and the frame's windowing size. In the next step, we collect all the feature vectors from all the recordings of the training set, put them into one big "bag" and perform clustering on it. Cluster size (N) is one of the parameters of the BoAW method. The result of the clustering step, the center vector of each calculated cluster, is called a "codeword". The group of codewords is then called the "codebook".

After, in the vector quantization step, we again work with individual recordings and create a histogram for each recording (both for the training and test sets). We calculate the closest codeword for each feature vector in the actual recording and replace the original feature vectors by the index of the closest codeword. We can also specify how many closest vectors we examine (this is also a parameter of the BoAW method). As a result, the same sized (i.e. N) histogram is produced for each recording. All of the codeword indices appear on the histogram's x axis. On the y axis, there are quantities which represent the set of recording feature vectors that were mapped to a particular codeword.

In the last step, we normalize the histogram, so the given frequencies are divided by the number of frames of the speech recording. These normalized histograms will be our new feature vectors, that have an independent length from the recording sizes (i.e. they will consist of N values) We will call this set of histograms "Bag-of-Audio-Words" and use it as features for our classifier.

3   Data and Methods

3.1   Data Sets

In each experiment, we created and evaluated our classification model on the Hungarian emotion database training and test sets. The other two databases were used to construct the codebook.

Hungarian Emotion Database. This database contains speech from 97 native Hungarian speakers [10]. Most of the segments were recorded from a continuous, spontaneous speaking television program with actors, while the other part came from an improvisation show. In the first case, the samples are vivid, and the emotions are more clear because of the actors. The samples from the second case, however, are closer to real-life emotions. The database contains 1111 sentences, separated into an 831 sample training set (cca. 20 min long) and a 280 sample test set (cca. 7 min long). We had four emotions: neutral, joy, anger and sad.

German Emotion Database. This database (also known as *EmoDB*) contains speech from 10 native German speakers [2]. The recordings were made with actors aged between 25 and 35. Each participant produced 10 German utterances (5 short and 5 longer sentences), all of them with a different emotion. The classification labels were: neutral, anger, boredom, disgust, fear, happiness and sadness. The whole database contains approximately 25 min of recordings.

Hungarian Speech Database. This database contains Hungarian television news recordings taken from 8 different TV channels [5]. The whole data set consists of 28 h of recordings. In terms of emotion detection, all of the labels can be treated as neutral because newsreaders are not allowed to show any emotion.

3.2   Feature Set

Our frame-level feature set is based on the Interspeech ComParE Challenge [9]. This set contains 65 frame-level features (4 energy-related, 55 spectral and 6 voicing related). We used the open-source openSMILE feature extractor [4] with the `IS13 ComParE` config file. For each frame we calculated the derivatives (i.e. Δ values) as well; these hold information about the dynamics of the samples.

3.3   Evaluation

Classification is performed by the LIBSVM library [3]. We optimized the SVM C complexity parameter in the range 10^{-5}, 10^{-4} to 10^{0}. We applied standardization on the BoAW feature vectors before each model was trained. In the optimization part of our experiments, we worked with the training set, based on speaker-independent 10-fold cross-validation. In the test scenario, we trained one SVM model on the whole training set with the optimal C parameter found above and evaluated it on the test set.

Table 1. *Baseline*: best results got with normalization and standardization, when we evaluate our technique with cross-validation and do it on the test set.

Feature-transformation		UAR		Codebook size
	a	CV	Test	
Normalization	5	58.08%	48.13%	512
	10	57.48%	50.27%	512
Standardization	5	55.43%	53.54%	512
	10	56.57%	64.32%	256

3.4   Parameters of the BoAW Method

The BoAW method has many adjustable parameters. In our study, we tested the effect of the preprocessing method, the codebook size N, and the quantization neighbour number parameters on the learning algorithm performance. For the codebook building we used an open-source program called openXBOW [8].

Codebook size: In each experiment we tested the effect of the following lengths: 32, 64, 128, 256, 512, 1 024, 2 048.

Histogram neighbour number: Instead of looking for just the closest codeword, each vector may also be assigned to a certain number of the closest codewords. Previously [11] we found that using more neighbours leads to a more precise description of the recordings besides the same feature vector size. This is why we experimented with two different settings (5 and 10).

Preprocessing techniques: If some of the features have an extremely high or low value compared to the others, it may dominate the Euclidean distance during the BoAW vector quantization step. Previously [11] we found that preprocessing the frame-level vectors by standardizing or normalizing them can improve the performance, so we tried both solutions.

Derivatives: In a previous study [11] we found that using the derivatives of the frame-level attributes can improve the performance, so we also used them in our experiments. The openXBOW tool also gives the opportunity to create separate codebooks for the original frame-level values and another for the Δs; because we opted for this technique, the codebook sizes provided have to be multiplied by 2 to get the actual number of features.

4   Tests and Results

As the baseline, we create the codebook from the Hungarian emotion database training set. Our results are shown on Table 1. The best result of cross-validation (i.e. 58.08%) came with normalization, 5 neighbours, and a 512-sized codebook. The best result of the test (i.e. 64.32%) came with standardization, 10 neighbours and $N = 512$. In addition, it is clear that in 3 out of 4 cases the results obtained on the test database were lower than the results of cross-validation, which may be due to overfitting to the training set during codebook creation.

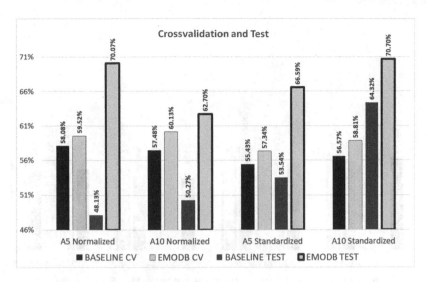

Fig. 1. Results of the *Baseline* and *EmoDB* generated codebooks with cross-validation and evaluation on the test set.

Table 2. *EMODB*: best results with normalization and standardization, when we evaluate our technique with cross-validation and do it on the test set.

Feature-transformation		UAR		Codebook size
	a	CV	Test	
Normalization	5	59.52%	70.07%	1 024
	10	60.13%	62.70%	256
Standardization	5	57.34%	66.59%	128
	10	58.81%	70.70%	256

4.1 Codebook from the *EmoDB* Database

Next, we wanted to know whether working with a codebook from other databases could produce similar or better results than a codebook created from the original database. In this part, the codebooks were created from *EmoDB*; then we built the BoAW representation for the Hungarian emotion database and performed classification using these features.

Examining the results (see Fig. 1 and Table 2) we can see that there was a significant improvement over the baseline in all four test cases. In 2 cases out of 4, we also see a reduction in the size of the required codebook, which can also reduce the time needed to produce a BoAW representation.

This improvement and the fact that all *EmoDB* test cases have more accurate scores than all the *EmoDB* cross-validation scores, in our opinion, might indicate that a codebook made from the original database tends to lead to overfitting,

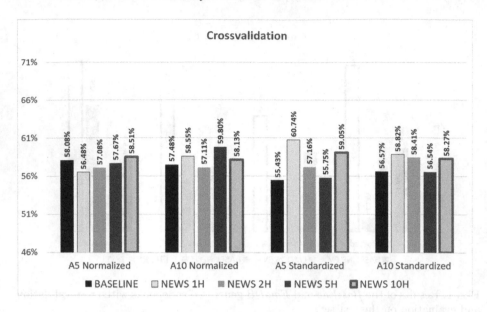

Fig. 2. Cross-validation results got from the Baseline and from the *News* database

and a predefined codebook (which is generated independently from the actual training samples) can eliminate this problem.

4.2   Codebook from the *News* Database

Based on the previous tests, it is apparent that a codebook created from a different database led to significant improvements. On the other hand, it is still not clear whether the type of speech (e.g. rich of emotions or completely neutral) present in the database used for codebook creation affects the emotion classification performance. To examine this, next the codebooks were prepared from subsets of the (non-emotion) Hungarian television recordings database [5]. Otherwise, all classification steps were done similarly as before. To investigate whether the length of the database also affects this performance, we used an 1-h, 2-h, 5-h, and 10-h long subset for codebook creation.

Based on the results of the cross-validation (see Fig. 2), we could not correlate the length of the database with the success of the classification. The same can be said about the type of preprocessing method and the number of closest neighbors: all the scores ranged from 55.75% to 60.74%. Most of the best-performing codebook sizes were 1 024 and 2 048, which are relatively large feature sets. The best result of cross-validation came from a 1-h length database, with standardization, taking 5 neighbors, using 1 024 sized codebook, giving the score of 60.74%. The results did not reveal significant differences depending on the length of the database, hence no general relationship could be found. In addition, we did not get significantly better or worse scores than using a codebook specifically designed for emotion detection from a *EmoDB* database.

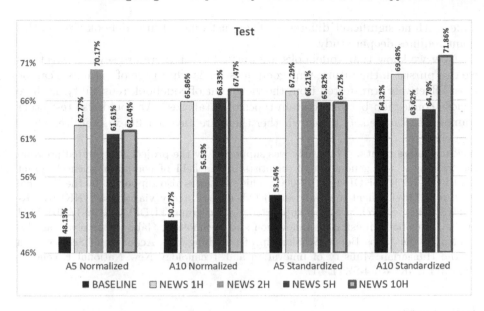

Fig. 3. Test result got from the Baseline and from the Hungarian speech database

The best score of the test was 71.86%, with the 10-h dataset, standardization, with 10 neighbours and a 1 024-sized codebook. However, besides the required increase in the codebook size, no obvious inferences could be made here (Fig. 3).

5   Conclusions

In this paper, the BoAW *(Bag-of-Audio-Words)* feature representation method was simultaneously applied on multiple databases for emotion recognition. We were interested in the possibility of creating BoAW codebooks from other datasets; this would allow the re-using of codebooks for several corpora, therefore allowing to cut execution times significantly. From this viewpoint, building a codebook from other, similar purpose databases gives better scores than those got using purpose-built database codebooks.

Based on our tests, it can be clearly stated that each predefined codebook can be successfully used to extract BoAW feature representations of any other databases. The best score of the tests with the Hungarian emotion database own codebook was 64.32%. Compared to this, when we used other database codebooks we got better results. The best score of the tests with the Hungarian speech database codebook was 66–71.86%. The best score of the tests with the German emotion database codebook was 66–70.70%. With these results, we could not find a clear answer to whether it is advisable to use a codebook between any two databases created for similar purposes but a different language or for a similar language but different purpose. In both cases, our results varied on a similar scale, with no significant difference. They just differed in codebook size, so this point requires deeper study.

Now we know that codebooks are portable, but there are several directions we can pursue in the future. One good question is what type of databases can be most effectively transferred from the viewpoint of codebook reusability. Is there a close connection between certain types of databases? We could also test other frame-level feature sets to see whether there are any benefits in practice.

Acknowledgements. This study was supported by the project "Integrated program for training a new generation of scientists in the field of computer science", grant no. EFOP-3.6.3-VEKOP-16-2017-0002. This study was also supported by the National Research, Development and Innovation Office of Hungary via contract NKFIH FK-124413. This research was also supported by the grant TUDFO/47138-1/2019-ITM of the Hungarian Ministry for Innovation and Technology. Gábor Gosztolya was also funded by the János Bolyai Scholarship of the Hungarian Academy of Sciences and by the Hungarian Ministry of Innovation and Technology New National Excellence Program ÚNKP-19-4-SZTE-51.

References

1. Burkhardt, F., van Ballegooy, M., Engelbrecht, K.P., Polzehl, T., Stegmann, J.: Emotion detection in dialog systems: applications, strategies and challenges. In: Proceedings of ACII, Amsterdam, Netherlands, pp. 985–989 (2009)
2. Burkhardt, F., Paeschke, A., Rolfes, M., Sendlmeier, W., Weiss, B.: A database of German emotional speech. In: Proceedings of Interspeech, pp. 1517–1520 (2005)
3. Chang, C.C., Lin, C.J.: LIBSVM: a library for support vector machines. ACM Trans. Intell. Syst. Technol. **2**, 1–27 (2011)
4. Eyben, F., Wöllmer, M., Schuller, B.: Opensmile: the Munich versatile and fast open-source audio feature extractor. In: Proceedings of ACM Multimedia, New York, NY, USA, pp. 1459–1462 (2010)
5. Tóth, L., Grósz, T.: A comparison of deep neural network training methods for large vocabulary speech recognition. In: Habernal, I., Matoušek, V. (eds.) TSD 2013. LNCS (LNAI), vol. 8082, pp. 36–43. Springer, Heidelberg (2013). https://doi.org/10.1007/978-3-642-40585-3_6
6. James, J., Tian, L., Inez Watson, C.: An open source emotional speech corpus for human robot interaction applications. In: Proceedings of Interspeech, Hyderabad, India, pp. 2768–2772 (2018)
7. Pancoast, S., Akbacak, M.: Bag-of-Audio-Words approach for multimedia event classification. In: Proceedings of Interspeech, Portland, USA, pp. 2105–2108 (2012)
8. Schmitt, M., Schuller, B.: openXBOW - Introducing the Passau open-source cross-modal Bag-of-Words toolkit. J. Mach. Learn. Res. **18**(96), 1–5 (2017). http://jmlr.org/papers/v18/17-113.html
9. Schuller, B., et al.: The Interspeech 2013 computational paralinguistics challenge: social signals, conflict, emotion, autism. In: Proceedings of Interspeech, pp. 148–152 (2013)

10. Sztahó, D., Imre, V., Vicsi, K.: Automatic classification of emotions in spontaneous speech. In: Esposito, A., Vinciarelli, A., Vicsi, K., Pelachaud, C., Nijholt, A. (eds.) Analysis of Verbal and Nonverbal Communication and Enactment. The Processing Issues. LNCS, vol. 6800, pp. 229–239. Springer, Heidelberg (2011). https://doi.org/10.1007/978-3-642-25775-9_23

11. Vetráb, M., Gosztolya, G.: érzelmek felismerése magyar nyelvű hangfelvételekből akusztikus szózsák jellemzőreprezentáció alkalmazásával. In: Proceedings of MSZNY, Szeged, Hungary, pp. 265–274 (2019)

12. Vidrascu, L., Devillers, L.: Detection of real-life emotions in call centers. In: Proceedings of Interspeech, Lisbon, Portugal, pp. 1841–1844 (2005)

Developing Resources for Te Reo Māori Text To Speech Synthesis System

Jesin James[1]([✉]), Isabella Shields (Ngāti Porou)[1],
Rebekah Berriman (Ngāi Tahu)[1],
Peter J. Keegan (Waikato-Maniapoto, Ngāti Porou)[2], and Catherine I. Watson[1]

[1] Department of Electrical, Computer, and Software Engineering,
University of Auckland, Auckland, New Zealand
{jesin.james,c.watson}@auckland.ac.nz
{ishi836,rber798}@aucklanduni.ac.nz
[2] Te Puna Wānanga, University of Auckland, Auckland, New Zealand
p.keegan@auckland.ac.nz

Abstract. Te reo Māori (the Māori language of New Zealand) is an under-resourced language in terms of availability of speech corpora and resources needed to develop robust speech technology. Māori is an endangered indigenous language which has been subject to revitalisation efforts since the late 1970s, which are well known internationally. The Māori community recognises the need for developing speech technology tools for the language, which will improve its study and usage in wider and more digital contexts. This paper describes the development of speech resources in Māori to build one of the first Text To Speech synthesis system for the language. A speech corpus, extended dictionary and a parametric speech synthesiser are the main contributions of the study. To develop these resources, text processing, segmentation and alignment, letter to sound rules creation were also done with existing resources that were modified to be used for Māori. The acoustic similarity of synthesised speech vs natural speech was measured to evaluate the speech synthesis system statistically. Future work required is described.

Keywords: Under-resourced language · Tts system · Te reo Māori

1 Introduction

Speech technology is a dominant research field and technology that talks is becoming the new norm. However, a majority of these studies are happening only in a few privileged languages (1.4% of world languages) [10]. Languages that do not have the technical support to develop speech processing technologies are termed as under-resourced languages. Te reo (means *language*) Māori[1] is the indigenous language of New Zealand and has official language status. However,

---

[1] We thank Te Hiku Media for their generous support in funding this project (https://tehiku.nz/). We thank the MAONZE research group [1] for their encouragement.

P. Sojka et al. (Eds.): TSD 2020, LNAI 12284, pp. 294–302, 2020.
https://doi.org/10.1007/978-3-030-58323-1_32

New Zealand English is the dominant language in the country. The 2018 New Zealand census reports[2] that there are 185955 Māori speakers, which accounts for only 4% of the total population (4.58 million). There is a lack of speech and language resources in Māori, making it under-resourced. In 1998, Laws [12] developed a diphone-based synthetic Māori voice. A Festival-based TTS system was planned [13], but its development was stopped in 2003. The lexicon resources developed by Laws are sadly lost, although a copy of the recorded diphones remains. Since Laws' pioneering work, a lot more tools have become available to developing speech and language resources. But, no more work was done on Māori. In this paper, we present the development of speech resources for Māori (preliminary work reported in [18]), with the larger aim of developing a Text To Speech synthesis (TTS) system.

2 Motivation : Te Reo Māori Revitalisation

Māori language spoken in New Zealand derives from the languages/dialects spoken by arrivals from Eastern Polynesian region of the South Pacific, 800 years ago. It was heavily influenced by English speakers who began arriving in the early 1800s. Since the early 1900s, most Māori were taught in English and were discouraged from speaking Māori in schools. Between 1950–1980 there was a sharp decline in the number of fluent Māori speakers [9,20]. From the 1980s there have been strong Māori revitalisation efforts (known internationally [2]) involving both Māori community initiatives, support from New Zealand Government in education, the media, official contexts and other organisations. Te Hiku Media is an example, who in addition to providing media services to the local Māori, are involved in developing digital tools (like speech tools) for the wider community. The Māori community is aware of sound change over time. It is regarded as a result of the break in intergenerational transmission; thus, this sound change has been regretted [20]. The MAONZE research group [1] has been doing extensive research into sound change in Māori [14,21]. A Māori pronunciation aid (MPAi) is being developed [20], and research is focused on the ways to provide feedback to people from the aid. In this context, a module that can produce synthesised Māori speech can provide speech feedback to MPAi users. Also, a TTS system can be used by people not so proficient in Māori to listen to how words/sentences are spoken. This has potential applications like e-readers, human-computer interaction systems where the technology used in New Zealand currently is English-based. The new generation of Māori users are all exposed to the latest technology. If Māori-based interfaces are available to them, te reo Māori use can be boosted. Given all these applications, and the larger aim to revitalise the language, speech resource development in Māori is essential.

Māori Phonology: (Details in [11,14]) Māori, as with other Polynesian languages did not have an indigenous writing system. The Roman script was used to write Māori since the early 1800s. Māori uses macrons to differentiate

---

[2] https://www.stats.govt.nz/information-releases/2018-census-totals-by-topic-national-highlights-updated.

between long and short vowels. The language has ten consonants <p, t, k, m, n, ŋ, f, w, ɾ, h> and five short vowels <i, e, a, o, u>. Vowel length is phonemic, i.e., there are five contrasting long vowels < ī, ē, ā, ō, ū >. Research points out that the timing unit in Māori as the mora, a unit consisting of a short vowel plus any preceding consonant. There are no consonant clusters.

3   Te Reo Māori Resources Development

As Māori is under-resourced, many resources needed for the TTS system had to be developed. Knowledge of Māori language is essential to build these resources.

Māori Speech Corpus: To build a parametric speech model for Māori, an appropriate speech corpus was developed. The transcript for the corpus was sourced from a collection of Māori myths and legends called Ngā Mahi a Ngā tūpuna [7]. These source files were processed, and text cues for recording were produced. Lines were split according to the presence of [. ? ! ; :]. The source files use old Māori alphabet, where long vowels were represented without macrons (e.g. old alphabet 'aa', new alphabet 'ā'). Conversion to the current Māori alphabet was made by replacing long vowels. Some occurrences of double vowels should not be replaced with macros as the sequence occurs across a morpheme boundary (e.g. whakaaro) and they were hand-corrected. A basic phonetic transcription was created via Python-based coding. This produced a new file which replaced macron symbols (e.g. 'ā') with a symbol and a colon to indicate length (e.g. 'a:'), and 'r' with 'ɾ', and digrams 'ng' and 'wh' with'ŋ' and 'f', respectively. Each line of the transcript was split into separate prompt files for recording.

Lexicon: An existing dictionary from the MAONZE project was used as the starting point. All words which appeared in the transcript but not in the original dictionary were added using Python scripts that performed comparison. The created lexicon contains over 10000 words and 18000 names, along with a phonetic transcription of words, syllable boundaries and stress mark up. The latter two are determined using Bigg's stress rules [3] and the division of words into morae. The automated rules were checked on 959 hand-transcribed rules, and the accuracy was 95%.

Corpus Recording: Recordings took place in a WhisperRoom Sound Isolation chamber. The speaker was recorded using a Rode Lavalier Lapel microphone kept 15 cm from their mouth. The microphone was connected to a Roland OCTA-CAPTURE. Audacity®[3] was used for audio capture at 44.1 kHz sampling frequency. A computer monitor displaying the prompts was set up on a desk inside the recording enclosure. The pre-amplifier gain was set to 37.5 dB. A middle-aged male Māori speaker was used to record the corpus. The speaker was given time to read over each phrase and familiarise with it before recording. Long sentences were read as phrases by speaker, using his own judgement to determine 'natural' phrase boundaries within sentences. The audio playthrough was enabled so that audio quality and correctness of the utterance could be assessed during recording. While the recording was trimmed and saved by the recorder,

---

[3] Audacity® software is copyright ©1999–2019 Audacity Team.

the speaker read the following sentence to be recorded. Each recording was saved in stereo WAV format. Recording sessions were limited to approximately 200 sentences to ensure speaker comfort. Each session took about 2–2.5 h, accounting for a break in between the session. In total, 1030 sentences were recorded. The first 800 of these correspond to the first 800 lines of the transcript. The final 230 were selected from the remaining transcript after a basic analysis of phone and diphone coverage.

Diphone Coverage: A basic analysis of diphone coverage was undertaken after the first 800 sentences were recorded. 30 occurrences were arbitrarily chosen as the goal for each insufficiently covered diphone. Sentences from the remaining unrecorded transcript that had instances of these were selected. Comparison of the frequency of occurrence of long and short vowels largely reflects rates reported in [16]. Figure 1 gives the diphone coverage of the corpus developed. Diphone pairs such as /wu/ and /wo/ only appear in loanwords. Diphones /fu/ and /fo/, although not well covered in the corpus, are very rare. There are few instances where the corpus insufficiently covers a diphone pair, such as 'nge' (/ŋe/).

Alignment: Montreal Forced Aligner (MFA Version 1.0.0) [15] was used to align text with the recordings. Recordings in WAV format, phonetic transcriptions in TextGrid format and dictionary are needed for the alignment. Manual checking of alignment and hand corrections were done. For converting TextGrid to .lab format (needed for MaryTTS voice creation), the phone tier is extracted, and each symbol and its corresponding end time are stored in the .lab format.

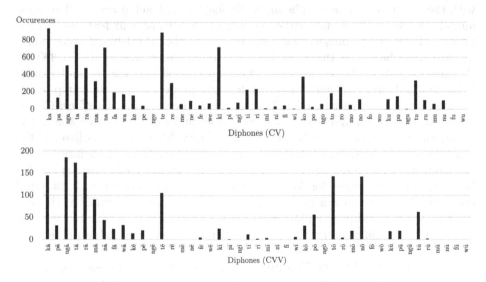

Fig. 1. Occurrences of diphones in the Māori corpus

4   Te Reo Māori TTS System Development and Analysis

This project used MaryTTS [17] (Java-based) to generate a Hidden Markov Model (HMM) - based (parametric speech synthesis) Māori voice. A deep-learning approach was not taken as a sufficiently large corpus is unavailable. An open-source speech synthesiser with good speech quality and support for new languages was needed for this project; which lead to the choice of MaryTTS.

Adding a New Language to MaryTTS: MaryTTS New Language Support was used to develop the Māori TTS system. The locale name used for Māori was 'mi' following Windows locale codes. Requirements for new language addition are the allophone list, lexicon, letter to sound rules and language corpus. The lexicon and language corpus were built, as described previously. An allophone list was added specifying the features: vowel length, vowel height, vowel frontness, lip rounding, consonant type, place of articulation, consonant voicing. 39 allophones (28 for vowels, 10 for consonants, one for silence) are identified for Māori.

Creation of Letter to Sound Rules: MaryTTS transcription tool was used to create letter to sound (LTS) rules using the dictionary and allophone set. First, a manual specification of all letters and corresponding phones that can be used to render them are created. The complete lexicon that is used for training is then aligned to the corresponding phones based on the mapping table. Then a classification and regression tree was built using the training data for LTS rules.

Voice Building: The voice building process in MaryTTS was followed with the language resources. The linguistic features extracted are ToBI accents; quinphones for each phone; part-of-speech of each word and features of each phone. This is *Text analysis and Linguistic analysis*. HMM-based voice building was done based on these features. The pitch range was set to 50–300 Hz (for male speaker). Mel-generalised cepstrum coefficients, log of fundamental frequency and strength were the speech features modelled. The final step builds the language-based speech model. This model will be used for *Waveform Generation*. An end-to-end Māori TTS system was set up as in Fig. 2, with Māori text input, and the output is synthesised speech. Native Māori speakers listened the synthesised speech produced, and they commented that the pronunciations were in alignment with those expected from Māori speakers. A client-server model-based speech synthesiser for Māori was set up in the University of Auckland robotspeech server and is available for the various research activities at the university. We are working on making the online TTS system accessible to the wider public. The lexicon and speech corpora will not be made available publicly, as we are guided by Te Hiku media's data sovereignty stance[4].

Signal-Based Quality Diagnosis: To evaluate the synthesised speech, a simplified version of the signal-based quality diagnosis (mel-cepstral distortion - MCD) described in [5] was implemented. MCD measures the difference between

---

[4] https://tehiku.nz/te-hiku-radio/te-putahi/12707/dr-tahu-kukutai-keoni-mahelona-data-sovereignty.

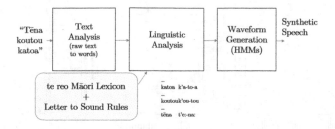

Fig. 2. The end-to-end Māori Text To Speech synthesis system

two sequences of mel cepstra as shown in Fig. 3. Segmentation is done at the word level (using MFA), for the original and synthesised speech. MFCCs are extracted using [4]. Difference in timing of the two sequences is aligned by Dynamic Time Warping (DTW) (based on [6]). Consider the synthesised speech and reference original speech MFCCs as a time series $X = (x_1, x_2...x_N)$ and $Y = (y_1, y_2...y_M)$ respectively. A correspondence between their elements is established by a warping curve $\Phi = (\phi_t, \psi_t); t = 1, ...T$. ($T$ depends on the lengths M and N). The optimal warping curve is the one that minimises the distance between the two time series, represented by: $\hat{\Phi} = (\hat{\phi}_t, \hat{\psi}_t) = \underset{(\phi_t, \psi_t)}{\arg\max} = \sum_{t=1}^{T} \frac{d(x_{\phi_t}, y_{\psi_t}) m_{t,\Phi}}{M_\Phi}$ [19]. Here $m_{t,\phi}$: *local weighting coefficient*, M_ϕ: *path-dependent normalisation* $= \sum_{t=1}^{T} m_{t,\Phi}$, d: *local distance*. The minimum cumulative distance is obtained as: $D(X, Y) = \sum_{t=1}^{T} \frac{d(x_{\hat{\phi}_t}, y_{\hat{\psi}_t}) m_{t,\hat{\Phi}}}{M_{\hat{\Phi}}}$. The distance measure obtained is the *average per-step distance* along the warping curve.

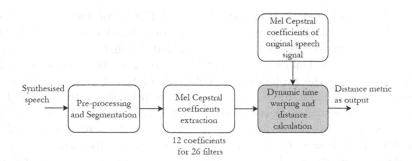

Fig. 3. Acoustic similarity measure for synthesised speech

432 words from 30 sentences in the Māori corpus were tested. Example of time series alignment obtained after warping is shown in Fig. 4. The alignment is perfect when it is between the same words (a), and the alignment is poor when the original and synthesised versions are from different words (c). The alignment is good for the original and synthesised version of the same word (b), which is an indication of the performance of the TTS system. Normalised distance

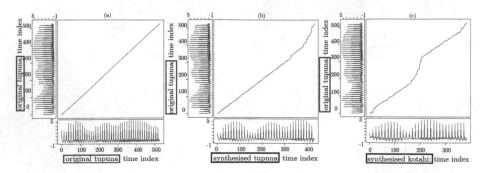

Fig. 4. Time series alignment using DTW of MFCCs. (a) Same words (b) natural vs synthesised version of same word, (c) natural vs synthesised version of two words [6].

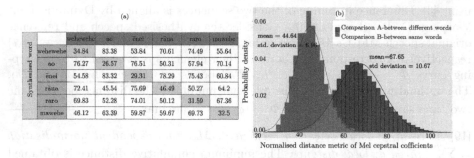

Fig. 5. (a) Confusion matrix of distance between original and synthetised MFCCs. (b) The probability distribution of distance between original and synthesised MFCCs.

measure between the original and synthesised MFCC time series is then taken as described in Fig. 3 [8]. Figure 5 (a) shows the confusion matrix of distance measures for 6 example words. It can be seen that the distance is comparatively lower when the original and synthesised MFCCs are of the *same word* (see Fig. 4). Figure 5 (b) shows the probability distribution of the distance measures for: *Comparison A:* Between MFCCs of original and synthesised versions of *different words* and *Comparison B:* Between MFCCs of original and synthesised versions of *same words* for all words tested. It is clear that *Comparison A* results in larger distance compared to *Comparison B*. This statistically shows the acoustic similarity between the words in the original and synthesised speech signals.

5   Conclusion and Future Work

This paper describes the development of te reo Māori TTS system. Māori is under-resourced, and development of speech technology resources is critical for its revitalisation. A speech corpus was developed containing 1030 sentences. The Māori lexicon was built with 10000 words and 18000 names. Existing tools (like Montreal Forced Aligner) were customised to segment and align the text and speech signals in the corpus. These resources were then used to develop an end-to-end Māori TTS system, where Māori text is entered, and the output is synthesised speech. Acoustic similarity analysis of the synthesised speech was done. Perceptual testing of the synthesised speech will be conducted. Future work will focus on expanding the Māori lexicon and checking entries, especially where orthography does not align with the current Māori phonetics. There is also a need to incorporate modern Māori pronunciations (like the occurrence of affrication and semi-vowels not present in traditional Māori) into the lexicon. Also, the effect of phraseology on the assignment of stress/syllable structure needs to be added to the linguistic analysis. In the real world, code-switching is common in spoken Māori; therefore, any useful Māori TTS system will need to accommodate New Zealand English. We hope to implement this by 2021 [18].

References

1. http://homepages.engineering.auckland.ac.nz/~cwat057/MAONZE/index.html2.
2. http://www.maoriMay12020language.info/mao_lang_abib.html
3. Biggs, B.: Let's Learn Māori: A Guide to the Study of the Māori Language. A.H. & A.W. Reed, Wellington (1969)
4. Ellis, D.P.W.: PLP and RASTA (and MFCC), and inversion) in Matlab. Online web resource (2005). www.ee.columbia.edu/dpwe/resources/matlab/rastamat
5. Falk, T., Moller, S.: Towards signal-based instrumental quality diagnosis for text-to-speech systems, vol. 15, pp. 781–784. IEEE (2008)
6. Giorgino, T.: Computing & visualizing dynamic time warping alignments in R: the dtw package. J. Stat. Softw. **31**(7), 1–24 (2009). Open Access Statistics
7. Grey, S.G.: Ngā Mahi a Ngā tūpuna. New Plymouth, 3rd edition (1928)
8. Hall, K.C., et al.: Phonological corpustools, version 1.3. [computer program] (2017)
9. Harlow, R.: Māori: A Linguistic Introduction. Cambridge University Press, Cambridge (2007)
10. James, J., Watson, C.I., Gopinath, D.P.: Exploring text to speech synthesis in non-standard languages. In: International Conference on Speech Science Technology, Australia, pp. 213–216 (2016)
11. Keegan, P., Watson, C., Maclagan, M., King, J., Harlow, R.: The role of technology in measuring changes in the pronunciation of Māori over generations. In: Language Endangerment in the 21st Century: Globalisation, Technology & New Media, NZ, pp. 65–71 (2012)
12. Laws, M.R.: A bilingual speech interface for New Zealand English to Māori. Ph.D. thesis, Doctoral dissertation, University of Otago, New Zealand (1998)
13. Laws, M.R.: Speech data analysis for diphone construction of a Māori online Text-to-speech Synthesizer. In: IASTED International Conference, USA, pp. 103–108 (2003)
14. Maclagan, M., Harlow, R., King, J., Keegan, P., Watson, C.: Acoustic analysis of Māori: historical data. In: Conference: Australian Linguistic Society, p. 104 (2005)
15. McAuliffe, M., Socolof, M., Mihuc, S., Wagner, M., Sonderegger, M.: Montreal forced aligner: trainable text-speech alignment using Kaldi. In: Interspeech, USA, pp. 498–502 (2017)
16. Rácz, P., Hay, J., Needle, J., King, J., Pierrehumbert, J.B.: Gradient Māori phonotactics. In: Te Reo, vol. 59, pp. 3–21 (2016)

17. Schroder, M., Trouvain, J.: The German text-to-speech synthesis system MARY: a tool for research, development and teaching. Int. J. of Speech Tech. **6**, 365–77 (2003). https://doi.org/10.1023/A:1025708916924

18. Shields, I., Watson, C., Keegan, P., Berriman, R., James, J.: Creating a synthetic te reo mōri voice. In: International Conference on Language Technology for All, Paris (2019). https://lt4all.org/media/papers/P1/136.pdf

19. Tormene, P., Giorgino, T., Quaglini, S., Stefanelli, M.: Matching incomplete time series with dynamic time warping: an algorithm and an application to post-stroke rehabilitation. In: Artificial Intelligence in Medicine, vol. 45, pp. 11–34. Elseivier (2008)

20. Watson, C., Keegan, P., Maclagan, M., Harlow, R., King, J.: The motivation and development of MPAi, a Māori pronunciation aid. In: Annual Conference of the International Speech Communication Association, Stockholm, pp. 2063–2067 (2017)

21. Watson, C., Maclagan, M., King, J., Harlow, R., Keegan, P.: Sound change in Māori and the influence of New Zealand English. J. Int. Phonetic Assoc. **46**(2), 185–218 (2016). Cambridge University Press

Acoustic Characteristics of VOT in Plosive Consonants Produced by Parkinson's Patients

Patricia Argüello-Vélez[1,5], Tomas Arias-Vergara[2,3,4(✉)], María Claudia González-Rátiva[1], Juan Rafael Orozco-Arroyave[2,3], Elmar Nöth[3], and Maria Elke Schuster[4]

[1] Faculty of Communications, Universidad de Antioquia UdeA, Calle 70 N, 52-21 Medellín, Colombia
[2] Faculty of Engineering, Universidad de Antioquia UdeA, Calle 70 N, 52-21 Medellín, Colombia
tomas.arias@udea.edu.co
[3] Pattern Recognition Lab., Friedrich-Alexander University, Erlangen-Nürnberg, Germany
[4] Department of Otorhinolaryngology, Head and Neck Surgery, Ludwig-Maximilians University, Munich, Germany
[5] Facultad de Salud, Universidad Santiago de Cali, Cali, Colombia

Abstract. Voice Onset Time (VOT) has been used as an acoustic measure for a better understanding of the impact of different motor speech disorders in speech production. The purpose of our paper is to present a methodology for the manual measuring of VOT in voiceless plosive sounds and to analyze its suitability to detect specific articulation problems in Parkinson's disease (PD) patients. The experiments are performed with recordings of the diadochokinetic evaluation which consists in the rapid repetition of the syllables /pa-ta-ka/. A total of 50 PD patients and 50 healthy speakers (HC) participated in this study. Manual measurements include VOT values and also duration of the closure phase, duration of the consonant, and the maximum spectral energy during the burst phase. Results indicate that the methodology is consistent and allows the automatic classification between PD patients and healthy speakers with accuracies of up to 77 %.

Keywords: Voice onset time · Acoustic analysis · Speech processing · Diadochokinesis

1 Introduction

Parkinson's disease (PD) is a neurodegenerative disorder characterized by the progressive loss of neurons in the mid-brain [6]. Primary motor symptoms include

Supported by Antioquia University.

ⓒ Springer Nature Switzerland AG 2020
P. Sojka et al. (Eds.): TSD 2020, LNAI 12284, pp. 303–311, 2020.
https://doi.org/10.1007/978-3-030-58323-1_33

tremor, rigidity, freezing of gait, and postural instability. PD also affects muscles involved in the speech production process, resulting in hypokinectic dysarthria, which is a set of motor speech disorders including bradylalia, lack of articulation accuracy, and dysphonia [4]. Many of the symptoms are controlled with medication, however there is no clear evidence indicating the positive effects of those treatments to reduce motor speech disorders. Proper speech therapy combined with the pharmacological treatment improve the communication ability of PD patients [16]. Thus, it makes sense to develop methodologies based on acoustic analysis to evaluate speech impairments in PD patients. The resources of instrumental phonetics allow acoustic analysis of segmental and supra-segmental characteristics ranging from isolated sounds to spontaneous speech analysis. These tools allow a linguistic and physiological understanding of atypical phenomena in speech and their relationship with the presence of symptoms related with subglottic, glottic or supra-glottic nature. In the case of PD, the diadochokinetic exercises (DDK) are used to study the production of voiceless plosive consonants (VPC) and vocal segments, which allows the analysis of coordination in supra-glottic and glottic components [2].

The pronunciation of the VPCs /p/,/t/, and /k/ involves the production of VOT which is defined as the time between the burst and the beginning of the emission of the next vowel [9]. In hypokinetic dysarthria VOT is useful to assess speech impairments by identifying the increase or decrease in duration. These patterns may be related to glottal adduction, degree of vocal cord tension, and quality of intra-oral pressures [5]. Preliminary results describe a significant VOT reduction in some VPCs, which can be explained by the loss of neuromuscular control during speech production. There is also another hypothesis where increase in VOT is related with loss of laryngeal and supra-laryngeal coordination [10].

VOT is measured by manual syllable-by-syllable labeling. The wide-band spectrogram shows the frequency and its relation with the duration of the signal. Abrupt changes associated to physiological phenomena can also be captured. The burst is visually identified as a short explosion bar with energy distributed over the entire frequency spectrum. The onset of the vowel is identified as the high energy values with the corresponding formant structure in the spectrogram [8]. Manual labeling requires to consider the relationship among these results and the signal represented in the oscillogram to have a better view of the signal's disturbances including abnormal changes in the consonant to vowel segment [1]. There are other measurement parameters to define acoustic integrity of VPCs such as the duration of the closure and the point of maximum spectral energy in the burst. These characteristics are considered in this paper through manual labeling and represent physiological correlations with supra-glottic pressure and articulatory accuracy of the sound.

From the automation/engineering point of view, VOT has been considered in DDK exercises to extract relevant information such as VOT duration and VOT ratio between VOT and vowel length (CV ratio). These parameters were used in [11] to classify between PD patients and healthy speakers. The authors reported accuracies of 92.2%. In [12] the authors measured VOT and obtained articulatory characteristics in relation to physiological correlates of vocal quality, articulatory accuracy, occlusion quality, and glottal and supra-glottal coordination. In general, automated methods help in reducing costs and time of clinical screenings including those that required to evaluate and monitor motor speech disorder in PD patients [14]. The automatic computational methods should consider the existence of approximate or incomplete productions in DDK tasks. Note that the alternating and rapid repetition of the plosives /p/, /t/, and /k/ generate variations that reveal patterns like debilitation of the burst, presence of voicing and loss of the articulatory tension. Fusion of automatic and manual labeling methods may improve the accuracy in detecting the aforementioned variations and allow the description of the acoustic "correctness" of each consonant segment. The purpose of our paper is to present a methodology for measuring VOT of VPCs in /pa-ta-ka/ using phonetic-acoustic manual methods and the automatic measurement method to evaluate and analyze the accuracy of the detection of speech disorders in PD patients.

2 Methodology

Details of the proposed methodology are provided below. It includes the description of the database and the steps followed in the manual labeling process along with its automatic evaluation.

2.1 Data

Speech recordings of the PC-GITA database are considered [13]. This corpus includes 50 PD patients and 50 healthy speakers. The participants were asked to perform the rapid repetition of /pa-ta-ka/ for at least 3 seconds. The speech signals were captured in a sound-proof booth using a professional audio setting. All of the patients were evaluated by a neurologist expert following the MDS-UPDRS-III scale [7]. Table 1 summarizes demographic and clinical information of the speakers.

Table 1. Clinical and demographic information of the speakers. Values in terms of (Mean ± Standard deviation).

	PD patients		HC speakers	
	Male	Female	Male	Female
Number of speakers	25	25	25	25
Age [Years]	61 ± 11	60 ± 7	60 ± 11	61 ± 7
Years diagnosed	13 ± 11	9 ± 5	–	–
MDS-UPDRS-III	37.4 ± 21.7	37.6 ± 14.0	–	–

2.2   Acoustic Phonetic Analysis of VPCs

Voiceless plosive consonants are characterized by three stages in Spanish: approach, closure, and release. During the approach phase, the articulators move towards each other, creating an obstruction of airflow during the closure phase. Finally, the articulators move away from each other during the release phase producing an explosive burst of air with energy spread across the audible spectrum. Figure 1 shows time and spectral representation of the VPC /p/, followed by the vowel /a/. The shaded regions represent the closure and the release phases. The closure phase is characterized by the absence of speech, which can be observed in the time signal (Fig. 1A) and in the spectrogram (Fig. 1B). The release stage is typically observed by looking at the spectral representation. Precision to produce voiceless plosive sounds can be reduced due to the presence of a motor problem. Loss of pressure in the lips changes /p/ sounds; impaired movement of the tongue affects /t/ sounds, and loss of contact with the soft palate and no burst deviates /k/ sounds. Altered versions of these sounds are perceived as /β/, /δ/, and /γ/, instead of /p/, /t/, and /k/, respectively. These weakened consonants are characterized by the loss of tension, increased voicing and incomplete contact of the articulators. As a result, there is no silence nor burst during the closure and release phases, respectively. Figure 2 shows an example of a weak consonant /β/ (/p/), produced in the transition from one utterance of /pa-ta-ka/ to another.

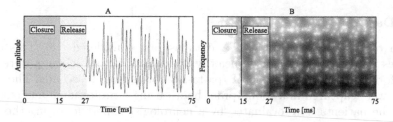

Fig. 1. Time (Figure A) and spectral (Figure B) representations of the voiceless plosive sound /p/. The shaded regions represent the closure and release phases.

2.3   Manual Labeling

Manual labels are found using the software Praat [3], as follows:

1. Determine the start and total duration of the consonant in a syllable by syllable fashion. The total duration of the VPC is measured as the total duration of the approach, closure, and release phases.
2. Identify the closure phase as the time prior to the burst indicated by the point of minimum intensity relative to the surrounding sounds, i.e., tension phase with increased supra-glottic pressure.

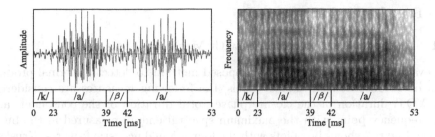

Fig. 2. Weak consonant /β/ (/p/) produced in the syllables /pa-ta-ka/.

3. Measure the maximum spectral energy during the release stage. A spectral slice is extracted in the first energy burst produced in a VPC sound. Then, the point with highest spectral energy is extracted.
4. Measure the VOT by placing labels at the initial burst of the consonant and vowel onset. The time of the initial burst is detected by computing the zero crossing points. The vowel onset is set at the beginning of a periodic-like signal. Formant frequencies and the presence of pitch are used to mark the beginning of voicing in a stop-vowel transition.
5. Identify weak consonants /β/, /δ/, and /γ/, in order to measure negative VOT. In this case, VOT is measured as the time between the end of the previous vowel and the beginning of the next one. The energy between syllables, e.g. /ka/ to /βa/, /pa/ to /δa/, and /ta/ to /γa/, is computed to detect the beginning of the weakened consonant.

These steps are followed to extract the acoustic measures: VOT value, duration of the closure phase, total duration of the consonant, and the frequency point with the maximum spectral energy measured in the burst phase. Mean value, standard deviation, kurtosis, and skewness are computed from the acoustic measures to create 48-dimensional feature vectors (4 measurements * 3 plosives * 4 functionals) per speaker.

2.4 Automatic Classification Between PD Patients and HC Speakers

A radial basis function – Support Vector Machine (rbf–SVM) with margin parameter C and kernel bandwidth γ is considered. Parameters are optimized through a grid search with $10^{-4} < C < 10^4$ and $10^{-6} < \gamma < 10^3$. The selection criterion is based on the performance obtained in the training set following a 10-fold cross validation strategy. The performance of the system is evaluated by means of accuracy (Acc), sensitivity (Sen), specificity (Spe), and the F1-score. Additionally, the Area Under the ROC Curve (AUC) is considered to present results more compactly. The values of the AUC range from 0.0 to 1.0, were 1.0 means perfect classification.

3   Results and Discussion

3.1   Preliminary Observations with Manual Labels

To evaluate the suitability of the proposed method to detect abnormal production of VPCs based on manual labels, the following measures are considered: the VOT, duration of the closure phase, total duration of the consonant, and the frequency point with the maximum spectral energy measured in the burst phase. Figure 3 shows box plots with the four manual acoustic features. Kruskal-Wallis tests were applied and significant differences are found in almost all of the acoustic features except for the duration of the consonants /p/ and /t/ and the frequency of burst in /t/ and /k/. Figure 4A shows the number of positive and negative VOTs measured for the PD and HC groups. In general, the number of positive VOT values is higher than the negative ones. Also, the number of negative VOTs is higher in PD compared with respect to the HC group. Figures 4B and 4C show the number of negative VOT per consonant measured in the HC and PD groups, respectively. The presence of the weak consonants indicates loss of acoustic integrity of VPC, this phenomenon was observed in both HC and PD speakers. As shown in Figs. 4B and 4C, /p/ is more sensible to turn into its voiced version /β/. Finally, it is relatively common to observe an increase in the approximations in /β/ and /γ/ within the HC group. This is because in Spanish the DDK /pa-ta-ka/ has the energy of the accent in /tá/, which maintains the closure and the explosion in this dental sound.

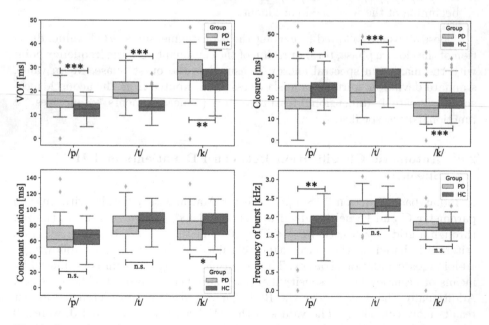

Fig. 3. Box-plots of acoustic measures extracted from each group. Kruskal-Wallis tests were applied with the following significance criteria: p-values: ***$p < 0.001$; **$p < 0.01$; *$p < 0.05$ and n.s. (non-significant). Light grey diamonds represent outliers.

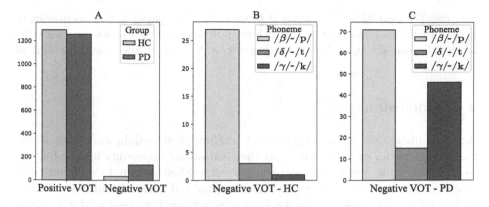

Fig. 4. Number of positive and negative VOT measurements found in our data. Figure 4A shows the number of positive and negative VOTs measured for the PD and HC groups. Figure 4B shows the number of negative VOTs measured in the HC group for each consonant. Figure 4C shows the number of negative VOTs measured in the PD group for each consonant.

3.2 Automatic Classification of PD vs. HC Subjects

Table 2 shows the performance of the rbf–SVM classifier. Four scenarios were considered: feature vectors from consonants /p/, /t/, /k/, and the combination of all. The highest accuracies were obtained with the SVMs trained with features from the consonant /p/ and with features from the three consonants (Acc = 77 %). Furthermore, the lowest accuracy was obtained when the rbf–SVM is trained only with features of the consonant /k/ (Acc = 68 %).

Table 2. Classification results (PD vs. HC) using manually extracted acoustic measures. **Acc:** Accuracy. **Sen:** Sensitivity. **Spe:** Specificity. **AUC:** Area under the ROC curve

Feature set	Acc (%)	Sen (%)	Spe (%)	F1-score	AUC
Consonant /p/	77	80	74	0.77	0.82
Consonant /t/	71	70	72	0.71	0.76
Consonant /k/	68	84	52	0.67	0.74
All consonants	77	76	78	0.77	0.83

The results obtained here confirm that articulatory imprecision is a common characteristic in PD speech and it is exhibited as a slowing down in the transition towards the beginning of the vowel. The decrease in supra-glottic tension, which debilitates the frequency burst in the consonants, is also confirmed by experiments. VOT allows accurate classification of PD vs. HC people. As indicated in [17] there is an increas in VOT of PD patients which is associated with voicing and aspiration. The method proposed in this paper shows accuracies of up to 77% in the consonant /p/, which is approximated as β in several cases due to the absence of tension before the burst as a decrease in the closure in bilabial sounds [15].

4 Conclusions

Acoustic phonetic analysis with manual labeling allows validation of the acoustic characteristics of consonants and their variations depending on the linguistic context while automatic methods are established as rapid detection tools that together determine the accuracy, sensitivity and specificity of cases. In this way, the fusion of both methodologies makes possible the classification between healthy people and people with PD from the measurement of VOT and closure. In the future, we plan to speed up the labeling process and to automatize the feature extraction.

Acknowledgments. The authors acknowledge to the Training Network on Automatic Processing of PAthological Speech (TAPAS) funded by the Horizon 2020 programme of the European Commission. Tomás Arias-Vergara is under grants of Convocatoria Doctorado Nacional-785 financed by COLCIENCIAS. The authors also thanks to CODI from University of Antioquia (grant Numbers 2018-23541 and 2017-15530).

References

1. Abramson, A.S., Whalen, D.H.: Voice Onset Time (VOT) at 50: theoretical and practical issues in measuring voicing distinctions. J. Phonetics **63**, 75–86 (2017)
2. Ackermann, H., Hertrich, I., Hehr, T.: Oral Diadochokinesis in Neurological Dysarthrias. Folia Phoniatrica et Logopaedica **47**(1), 15–23 (1995). https://doi.org/10.1159/000266338
3. Boersma, P., et al.: Praat, a system for doing phonetics by computer. Glot. Int. **5**, 341–345 (2002)
4. Darley, F., Aronson, A., Brown, J.: Clusters of deviant speech dimensions inthe dysarthrias. J. Speech Hear. Res. **12**(3), 462–496 (1969). https://doi.org/10.1044/jshr.1203.462
5. Forrest, K., et al.: Kinematic, acoustic, and perceptual analyses of connected speech produced by Parkinsonian and normal geriatric adults. J. Acoust. Soc. Am. **85**(6), 2608–2622 (1989). https://doi.org/10.1121/1.397755
6. Gelb, D.J., Oliver, E., Gilman, S.: Diagnostic criteria for Parkinson disease. Arch. Neurol. **56**(1), 33–39 (1999)
7. Goetz, C.G., et al.: Movement Disorder Society-sponsored revision of the Unified Parkinson's Disease Rating Scale (MDS-UPDRS): scale presentation and clinimetric testing results. Move. Disord. **23**(15), 2129–2170 (2008). https://doi.org/10.1002/mds.22340
8. Klatt, D.H.: Voice onset time, frication, and aspiration in word-initial consonant clusters. J. Speech Hear. Res. **18**(4), 686–706 (1975), http://www.ncbi.nlm.nih.gov/pubmed/1207100

9. Lisker, L., Abramsson, A.: A cross-language study of voicing in initial stops: acoustical measurements. WORD **20**(3), 384–422 (1964). https://doi.org/10.1080/00437956.1964.11659830

10. Martínez-Fernández, R., Gasca-Salas, C., Sanchéz -Ferro, A., Ángel Obeso, J.: Actualización en la enfermedad de Parkinson. Parkinson's disease: a review. Revista Médica Clínica Las Condes **27**(3), 364–376 (2016). https://doi.org/10.1016/j.rmclc.2016.06.010

11. Montaña, D., Campos-Roca, Y., Pérez, C.J.: A Diadochokinesis-based expert system considering articulatory features of plosive consonants for early detection of Parkinson's disease. Comput. Methods Programs Biomed. **154**, 89–97 (2018). https://doi.org/10.1016/J.CMPB.2017.11.010

12. Novotny, M., Rusz, J., Cmejla, R., Ruzicka, E.: Automatic evaluation of articulatory disorders in Parkinson's Disease. IEEE/ACM Trans. Audio Speech Lang. Process. **22**(9), 1366–1378 (2014). https://doi.org/10.1109/TASLP.2014.2329734, http://ieeexplore.ieee.org/document/6827910/

13. Orozco-Arroyave, J.R., et al.: New Spanish speech corpus database for the analysis of people suffering from Parkinson's disease. In: Language Resources and Evaluation Conference, (LREC), pp. 342–347 (2014)

14. Orozco-Arroyave, J.R., et al.: NeuroSpeech: an open-source software for Parkinson's speech analysis. Dig. Signal Process. **77**, 207–221 (2018)

15. Parveen, S., Goberman, A.M.: Presence of stop bursts and multiple bursts in individuals with Parkinson disease. Int. J. Speech-Lang. Pathol. **16**(5), 456–63 (2014). https://doi.org/10.3109/17549507.2013.808702

16. Schulz, G.M., Grant, M.K.: Effects of speech therapy and pharmacologic and surgical treatments on voice and speech in Parkinson's disease: a review of the literature. J. Commun. Disord. **33**(1), 59–88 (2000). https://doi.org/10.1016/s0021-9924(99)00025-8

17. Tykalova, T., et al.: Distinct patterns of imprecise consonant articulation among Parkinson's disease, progressive supranuclear palsy and multiple system atrophy. Brain Lang. **165**, 1–9 (2017). https://doi.org/10.1016/J.BANDL.2016.11.005

A Systematic Study of Open Source and Commercial Text-to-Speech (TTS) Engines

Jordan Hosier[1], Jordan Kalfen[2], Nikhita Sharma[1], and Vijay K. Gurbani[1,2(✉)]

[1] Vail Systems, Inc., Chicago, USA
{jhosier,nsharma,vkg}@vailsys.com
[2] Illinois Institute of Technology, Chicago, USA
jkalfen@hawk.iit.edu, vkg@iit.edu

Abstract. The widespread availability of open source and commercial text-to-speech (TTS) engines allows for the rapid creation of telephony services that require a TTS component. However, there exists neither a standard corpus nor common metrics to objectively evaluate TTS engines. Listening tests are a prominent method of evaluation in the domain where the primary goal is to produce speech targeted at human listeners. Nonetheless, subjective evaluation can be problematic and expensive. Objective evaluation metrics, such as word accuracy and contextual disambiguation (is "Dr." rendered as Doctor or Drive?), have the benefit of being both inexpensive and unbiased. In this paper, we study seven TTS engines, four open source engines and three commercial ones. We systematically evaluate each TTS engine on two axes: (1) contextual word accuracy (includes support for numbers, homographs, foreign words, acronyms, and directional abbreviations); and (2) naturalness (how natural the TTS sounds to human listeners). Our results indicate that commercial engines may have an edge over open source TTS engines.

1 Introduction

As voice enabled devices gain prominence in our daily lives, it is increasingly important that such technologies possess human-like speech capabilities. The perceptual quality of TTS speech synthesis technology impacts the acceptability of such systems. For this reason, there is a push among TTS researchers to make synthetic speech more naturalistic. The applications for such technologies are vast, including solutions for the visually impaired, hands-free technology, customer-service centers, etc. In the market today, there are many TTS engines with varied capabilities. The goal of this study is to propose a set of evaluation metrics which can be used to evaluate TTS engines. The proposed evaluation is based on a measure we call *contextual word accuracy* (formally defined in Sect. 3), and the necessary, though subjective measure of *naturalness*, i.e., how do human listeners rank the TTS engines?

Seven TTS engines were considered: four open source engines and three commercial engines. The open source engines were:

© Springer Nature Switzerland AG 2020
P. Sojka et al. (Eds.): TSD 2020, LNAI 12284, pp. 312–320, 2020.
https://doi.org/10.1007/978-3-030-58323-1_34

- Mimic[1]: Mimic is the light-weight TTS component based on Carnegie Mellon's FLITE software (see below).
- CMU FLITE[2]: FLITE is a small TTS synthesis engine developed at Carnegie Mellon University (CMU) and is designed for small, embedded machines as well as large servers.
- MaryTTS [3]: MaryTTS is a Java-based multilingual TTS synthesis platform using a Hidden Markov Model (HMM-) model.
- DeepVoice3[4] [2]: DeepVoice3 is a fully convolutional attention-based neural TTS system.

The following commercial engines were evaluated using their respective cloud-based interfaces:

- Voicery[5]: Voicery is a commercial start-up offering a deep neural network.
- Acapela[6]: Acapela is a European company specializing in personalized digitized voices.
- Selvy[7]: Selvy a TTS synthesis engine from a South Korean company.

There are additional commercial engines such as Amazon Polly[8], Google Tacotron [3], and IBM Watson Text to Speech[9]. While we are not aware of any scientific study comparing these engines in a formal manner, it is widely assumed by practitioners that these engines are the state-of-art in TTS. Given this assumption, we use Amazon Polly as a control variable and benchmark on which to evaluate the seven TTS engines under consideration.

The remainder of the paper is organized as follows: Sect. 2 motivates the work, Sect. 3 presents our evaluation corpus of 21 test utterances, Sect. 4 details the evaluation methodology, and Sect. 5 presents results and discusses findings. Beyond Sect. 6 are several appendices that provide the raw data to elaborate on results.

2 Related Work and Contribution

Despite recent advancement in speech synthesis, the evaluation of such technology has seen little advancement and lacks an established gold standard of evaluation metrics. The classic approach for TTS evaluation is to synthesize a set of samples, present the samples to listeners, and to draw conclusions about the systems based on listener evaluation.

---

[1] https://mycroft.ai/documentation/mimic (last visit: April 23, 2020).

[2] http://www.festvox.org/flite/ (last visit: April 23, 2020).

[3] http://mary.dfki.de (last visit: April 23, 2020).

[4] https://github.com/r9y9/deepvoice3_pytorch (last visit: April 23, 2020).

[5] https://www.voicery.com (last visit: March 2020).

[6] https://www.acapela-group.com/ (last visit: April 23, 2020).

[7] http://speech.diotek.com/en/text-to-speech-demonstration.php (last visit: April 23, 2020).

[8] https://aws.amazon.com/polly/ (last visit: February 2020).

[9] https://www.ibm.com/Watson/services/text-to-speech/ (last visit: May 2019).

Objective measures have been developed for speech quality evaluation in telecommunication systems, such as measuring mel cepstral distortion [4,5]. While these serve as a proxy for how well the TTS model represents natural speech, automating this process is challenging and often requires a benchmark natural speech signal [6]. While some measures do not require a reference speech signal [8], subjective listening tests remain the gold standard in the literature. The most common listening tests are Mean Opinion Score tests (MOS, ITU-T Rec. P.10, 2006), MUltiple Stimuli with Hidden Reference and Anchor (MUSHRA, ITU-T Rec. BS.1543, 2015), preference tests, and transcription tasks. The attributes measured by such tests include measures of naturalness, intelligibility, similarity, etc.

The Blizzard Challenge was developed to better understand and compare research techniques in building corpus-based speech synthesizers on the same data [7]. Competitors present the results from a standard listening test and describe their systems. These tests included listening to a fixed number of utterances and subsequently assigning a domain-specific MOS score based on the test set. While this challenge has a well developed listening test, it is also subjective.

Primary Contributions: TTS engines are used in a variety of applications and it is important that such technologies are flexible enough to adapt to the properties of novel environments. However TTS systems can be fragile, and often break down with minor changes in the lexicon. This work proposes a corpus (Sect. 3) of diverse set of English phonological and morphological artifacts (homographs, foreign loan words, acronyms, directional abbreviations, etc.) that present potential challenges to TTS engines. We seek to establish this corpus as a canonical corpus for evaluating TTS engines. Furthermore, we propose two evaluation methodologies (Sect. 4): an objective metric that allows for impartial evaluation of TTS response to complex input, and while the second metric is a subjective listening test, we attempt to control for subjectivity in evaluating it through using multiple advanced voting techniques.

3   Evaluation Corpus

The set of 21 vectors used to evaluate the TTS engines is shown in Table 1. These sentences represent a diverse set of English phonological and morphological grammatical constructs that present potential challenges to TTS engines. While these sentences would be easily produced and understood by humans, they include ambiguities and homographs that could present challenges to a TTS system - challenges which potentially indicate inadequate training of the system. Thus, we test if the system can render these vectors with the accuracy that a human reader could easily achieve.

These stimuli included sentences with homographs (Test cases 10–12) and foreign words (Test cases 18 and 21). We also evaluate forms of abbreviations, including context dependent abbreviations (i.e. "Dr." as a prefix to a name will be expanded as "Doctor", while "Dr." as a suffix to an address is expected to be expanded as "Drive"), abbreviations in addresses (i.e. "Apt.", "Pl.", "Pkwy."), and abbreviations of names (i.e. "Chas." for "Charles"). Finally, we evaluate numbers (i.e. roman numerals, numbers in street addresses, and numbers occurring in a string denoting times or dates) and symbols ("&").

Table 1. Corpus for evaluating the TTS engines

Test case	Sentence
1	American Communications & Engineering, Inc. is located at 123 NW. Main St., Apt. 1A, St. Paul, MN 60655
2	Natoma Professional Ctr. 555 Oakdale Pkwy., is located at 123 S 2nd Pkwy., Ste. 700, Ft. Lauderdale, FL.
3	Valor Telecom Ltd. 1910 E. Kimberly Pl. P.O.B 93425, Old Village Sq., CA
4	Sec. of State Hillary Clinton and Sen. Lisa Murkowski spoke with Pres. Mahmaud Abbas to discuss FASB
5	Ex-Gov. Sarah Palin and Ex-HP CEO Carly Fiorina met with Israeli Ex-Prime Minister Ariel Sharon to discuss RBOC
6	Treasury Sec. Timothy F. Geithner used to be the COO at JPMorgan and earned $4.5-million-a-year and earned an MBA from Harvard
7	Rep. Chas. Rangel Ph.D was censured by PETA
8	Mr. John Smith Sr. and Mrs. Jane Smith worked at Levi Strauss & Co. with their son, John Smith Jr., and daughter Ms. Judy Smith
9	Gen. Douglas MacArther was tired of receiving SPAM from the NYSE
10	They were too close to the door to close it
11	The dove dove into the water
12	The team lead had lead us to victory
13	After I read a book I add it to my list of books that I've read.
14	The farm was used to produce produce
15	People who use are of no use
16	Prof. Robt. B. Reich is a bona fide rocket scientist
17	Dr. Albert Einstein, Phd had a lot of chutzpah turning down the presidency.
18	Jas. A. Barone III said bon voyage to Capt. Wm. O. Barnett before the coup d'etat
19	I was born Mon., Sept. 25, 1989 at 12:30 AM
20	Lt. Cmd. Jas. W. Marks was born Wed. the 3rd. Of Mar. at 2:30 p.m
21	I live in La Crosse county, Wisconsin. This is close to Eau Claire and Prarie du Chien

In summary, these 21 cases present non-trivial challenges to TTS engines to unambiguously pronounce the sentence in a manner consistent with expectations.

4   Evaluation Methodology

We present two metrics of evaluation. The first of these metrics is ϕ, or *contextual word accuracy*. To evaluate ϕ, a sentence is considered as a bag of words. With that assumption, ϕ is defined as:

$$\phi = \frac{1}{n} \sum_{i=1}^{n} I(x_i), \tag{1}$$

where n is the total number of words in the bag, x_i enumerates over all the words in the bag, and $I(x_i)$ is the word pronunciation identity function defined as:

$$I(x) = \begin{cases} 1 : x \text{ is pronounced as expected} \\ 0 : \qquad\qquad \text{otherwise} \end{cases} \tag{2}$$

The range of ϕ is $[0,1]$, and we seek to maximize ϕ. If all of the words in the bag are rendered in the expected manner, ϕ will be 1.0. Thus, contextual word accuracy measures both the phonological and morphological effects of a TTS engine producing all words in the sentence. Scoring word-level accuracy was done manually, and was a rather straighforward process. When determing accuracy, we were tracking word stress and phonetic realization to determine whether a word was rendered correctly or not.

The second metric is *naturalness*. We evaluated the TTS engines on naturalness by synthesizing the 21 sentences and presenting them to listeners. The listening test asked participants to rate engines by placing them in ranked order from most to least human-like.

We recruited 14 participants, each of whom ranked, in descending order of preference, the seven TTS engines according to how natural they deemed the rendering to be. The participants ranged in age from 16 years to 64 years, with a median age of 28. They were asked to listen to a portion of a passage called "The Rainbow Passage" rather than the 21 test vectors used in the previous evaluations in an effort to make the grammatical artifacts that were the target of the accuracy evaluation less salient to participants. "The Rainbow Passage" is a standard reading passage, commonly used in speech evaluations, reading comprehension tests, and for testing language recognition software[10]. The result was an audio file rendered by each TTS engine. (Appendix C contains a link to these files.) In addition, the participants were asked an open-ended question: "What cues in the speech made you find it more (or less) robotic?" (Results in Appendix B.) To minimize selection bias, we explicitly chose individuals who are not in the field of linguistics, and excluded colleagues at our respective academic or industrial institutions. Instead, we chose participants who were not involved in any area related to speech technologies. To eliminate confirmation bias, each subject was presented the recordings in isolation from other participants.

We score the resulting TTS engine rankings in two ways; Condorcet voting and the Borda Count method [1]. These methods are preferred over others (e.g., averaging the votes across all participants) as they are robust and less influenced by presence of outliers. The Condorcet method selects the best candidate (i.e. TTS engine) by considering pairwise head-to-head elections among the candidates, and selects the candidate that would win the majority of the votes in all such pairwise contests. Under certain circumstances (presence of cycles in voting, e.g., A is preferred over B, B is preferred over C, C is preferred over

---

[10] "When the sunlight strikes raindrops in the air, they act like a prism and form a rainbow. The rainbow is a division of white light into many beautiful colors. These take the shape of a long round arch, with its path high above, and its two ends apparently beyond the horizon".

A), the Condorcet method may not elect an authoritative winner, however, this turned out not to be the case with our voting. The Borda Count method asks participants to rank candidates in order of preference. Then, each engine, for each ballot, is given a certain number of points corresponding to the number of engines ranked lower. After counting all the votes, the candidate with the most points is the winner. The advantage of this method is that it selects a broadly acceptable candidate instead of those preferred by a majority.

5   Results and Discussion

5.1   Contextual Word Accuracy (ϕ)

The results for contextual word accuracy are presented in Fig. 1. In tabulating these results, we included Amazon Polly as our control variable as we discussed in Sect. 1. Appendix A shows in detail how each TTS engine fared against each test case, resulting the specific value of ϕ.

Results demonstrate that ϕ is high among commercial TTS engines, with Acapela reaching a word accuracy rate of 0.975 with minimal variance across the accuracy rate for each of the 21 sentences. Amazon Polly is a close second with an average word accuracy rate of 0.967, with some dispersion around the 1st and 3rd quartiles with respect to the median.

The open source engines are less accurate; the best accuracy is seen by FLITE (0.844) and the lowest accuracy by Deep-Voice3 (0.761). This is surprising given that DeepVoice3 uses convolutional sequence learning and is considered a state-of-art neural speech synthesis system.

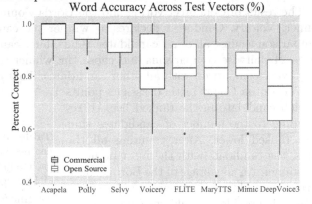

Fig. 1. Contextual word accuracy (%) across the evaluation corpus.

5.2   Naturalness

A method of ranked comparison was used to evaluate naturalness. As mentioned in Sect. 4, we produced an audio file containing the rendering of "The Rainbow Passage" from each engine. (Appendix C contains a link to a ZIP archive of these files; DeepVoice3 only rendered 9s with what appears to be an abrupt, premature termination, and Acapela also terminates prematurely after 12s.) The participants were asked to rank the audio files and answer an open ended question, i.e., "What cues in the speech made you find it more (or less) robotic?" (Answers to the question provided by the participants are in the link in Appendix B).

The identity of each TTS engine was hidden from the participants. Instead, an opaque name ("Engine 1", ..., "Engine 7") was provided for ranking. Participants were told to rank each engine from 1 (most natural sounding) to 7 (least natural sounding), and were permitted to rank more than one TTS engine at the same level. Results of the ranking are in the table in Table 2.

Table 2. Raw rankings of 14 participants (**En** implies TTS Engine N; a - implies that the participant did not vote for any TTS engine at that rank.)

Rank	Participants													
	1	2	3	4	5	6	7	8	9	10	11	12	13	14
1	E7	E6, E7	E7	E7	E7	E7	E6, E7	E6	E2	E7	E7	E7	E6	E7
2	E6	E1	E4	E1, E6	E2	E2	E2	E2, E7	E7	E1	E6	E6	E2	E6
3	E1	E4	E3	E2, E4	E4	E3	E3, E5	E5	E6	E6	E1	E1	E1	E2
4	E2	E5	E2	E3, E5	E6, E3, E5	E6	E4	E1	E1	E4	E4	E5	E7	E1
5	E4	E3	E5	–	E1	E5	E1	E4	E4, E5	E2	E5	E2	E4	E4
6	E3	E2	E6	–	–	E4	–	E3	E3	E5	E3	E4	E5	E5
7	E5	–	E1	–	–	E1				E3	E2	E3	E3	E3

The result of Condorcet voting and the Borda Count indicated a unanimous winner, Voicery. Condorcet declares as winner the candidate that wins every comparison against all other candidates. Thus, for 7 candidates, Condorcet performs 21 pairwise comparisons and chose the winner to be the candidate who wins every comparison with all other candidates. That candidate is Voicery.

The Borda Count method assigns points to each candidate in the ranked lists corresponding to the number of candidates that were ranked lower. After counting all the votes, the candidate with the most points is the winner. An advantage of the Borda Count is that, in addition to declaring an absolute winner, it provides a ranking of the remaining candidates. As Table 3 shows, Voicery received the highest score with Selvy receiving the second highest. The contrast between Fig. 1 and Table 3 is instructive. The ϕ value for Voicery is not the strongest as is evident from Fig. 1, however, it is deemed the most naturalistic. DeepVoice3 did not receive

Table 3. Borda Count of TTS engines based on votes received by each engine

TTS engine	Points
Engine 7 (Voicery)	53
Engine 6 (Selvy)	42
Engine 1 (Acapela)	32
Engine 2 (DeepVoice3)	32
Engine 4 (MaryTTS)	27
Engine 5 (Mimic)	20
Engine 3 (FLITE)	18

a high score in the ϕ metric, but tied for third place in the naturalness metric. This discrepancy demonstrates a need for further research in new metrics for evaluating TTS engines.

6   Conclusion

In this paper, we study evaluating open source and commercial TTS engines on both subjective and objective measures. The two metrics used—aggregate accuracy (objective), and naturalness (subjective)—demonstrate their viability for use in business and academic contexts. We have attempted to control for the subjectivity in naturalness by using robust voting techniques such as Condorcet and Borda Count that have advantages over simple techniques like majority vote.

Our results indicate that the commercial TTS engines are superior to their open source counterparts. While some open source engines receive high marks for aggregate accuracy, they fall short on measures of naturalness. From the seven TTS engines evaluated, none emerge as a clear winner across both metrics. Acapela is the winner among commercial TTS engines with respect to ϕ (c.f., Fig. 1), while FLITE gets the nod in the open source category. The naturalness metric clearly points to Voicery as the winner, but Voicery is not the preferred engine with respect to ϕ. Assuming each metric is weighed evenly, Acapela would be declared the winner, but clearly, naturalness is an important metric where Acapela does not perform as expected.

In summary, although open source TTS engines do not reach the level of naturalness of the commercial engines, they demonstrate aggregate accuracy that show promise for deployment in business and academic settings. Future work should explore ranking TTS engines with weighted contributions of subjective and objective metrics. It could also prove interesting to evaluate the TTS engines using an automated speech recognition (ASR) system, however such a method would only evaluate accuracy as it would not be able to evaluate naturalness. Finally, future work should consider expanding the corpus we propose in Sect. 3, perhaps including non-English langauges, and explore evaluating the naturalness of TTS renderings through more objective measures, including feature extraction for similarity comparisions to human speech.

A   Appendix A: Evaluation of TTS Engines on Our Corpus

URL: http://www.cs.iit.edu/~vgurbani/tsd2020/appendix-a.pdf
SHA-1 Hash: b14f7632306c2c9aa4154882d97c1c829ee48224

B   Appendix B: Survey Answers by Participants

URL: http://www.cs.iit.edu/~vgurbani/tsd2020/appendix-b.pdf
SHA-1 Hash: f92c24fd84c35ee0be210801122dcccf17ab0818

C   Appendix C: Rendering of "The Rainbow Passage"

URL: http://www.cs.iit.edu/~vgurbani/tsd2020/tsd-paper1023.zip
SHA-1 Hash: 8ef25f33b2f95300abb1e3200d0d7cc9ead856e8

References

1. Eric, P.: Voting methods. The Stanford Encyclopedia of Philosophy (2012). http:// plato.stanford.edu/entries/voting-methods/
2. Wei, P., et al.: Deep voice 3: 2000-speaker neural text-to-speech (2017). arXiv preprint arXiv:1710.07654
3. Wang, Y., et al.: Tacotron: a fully end-to-end text-to-speech synthesis model (2017). arXiv preprint arXiv:1703.10135
4. Yamagishi, J., et al.: Analysis of speaker adaptation algorithms for HMM-based speech synthesis and a constrained SMAPLR adaptation algorithm. IEEE Trans. Audio Speech Lang. Process. **17**(1), 66–83 (2009)
5. Tribolet, J. M., et al.: A study of complexity and quality of speech waveform coders. In: IEEE International Conference on Acoustics, Speech, and Signal Processing, ICASSP 1978, vol. 3. IEEE (1978)
6. Möller, S., Falk, T.H.: Quality prediction for synthesized speech: comparison of approaches. In: International Conference on Acoustics (2009)
7. Black, A.W., Tokuda, K.: The blizzard challenge-2005: evaluating corpus-based speech synthesis on common datasets. In: Ninth European Conference on Speech Communication and Technology (2005)
8. Stoll, G., Kozamernik, F.: A method for subjective listening tests of intermediate audio quality. ITU Working Party (2001)

Automatic Correction of i/y Spelling in Czech ASR Output

Jan Švec[1](✉) ⓘD, Jan Lehečka[1] ⓘD, Luboš Šmídl[2] ⓘD, and Pavel Ircing[2] ⓘD

[1] NTIS, University of West Bohemia Pilsen, Pilsen, Czech Republic
{honzas,jlehecka}@ntis.zcu.cz
[2] Department of Cybernetics, University of West Bohemia Pilsen,
Pilsen, Czech Republic
{smidl,ircing}@kky.zcu.cz

Abstract. This paper concentrates on the design and evaluation of the method that would be able to automatically correct the spelling of i/y in the Czech words at the output of the ASR decoder. After analysis of both the Czech grammar rules and the data, we have decided to deal only with the endings consisting of consonants b/f/l/m/p/s/v/z followed by i/y in both short and long forms. The correction is framed as the classification task where the word could belong to the "i" class, the "y" class or the "empty" class. Using the state-of-the-art Bidirectional Encoder Representations from Transformers (BERT) architecture, we were able to substantially improve the correctness of the i/y spelling both on the simulated and the real ASR output. Since the misspelling of i/y in the Czech texts is seen by the majority of native Czech speakers as a blatant error, the corrected output greatly improves the perceived quality of the ASR system.

Keywords: Grammatical error correction · ASR · BERT

1 Introduction

The correct spelling of the homophones y/i is being taught already in primary school and therefore any misspelling of those letters is perceived as a blatant error. There is a range of situations (see Sec. 2) where this spelling depends on the context of the surrounding words. Those words guiding the spelling could appear both before and after the word in question and could be rather distant from it. It means that the n-gram language models that are still prevalent in real-time ASR engines are not able to capture the necessary word dependencies and often select the incorrect variant.

We propose a method that post-processes the ASR output using techniques that are mostly employed in the task called Grammatical Error Correction (GEC)[1]. This task has recently received a significant attention [1,8] and is usu-

---

[1] We are aware of the fact that the phenomenon that we are dealing with falls linguistically into the domain of orthography, not grammar. However, the context dependency described above simply makes GEC methods more suitable.

ⓒ Springer Nature Switzerland AG 2020
P. Sojka et al. (Eds.): TSD 2020, LNAI 12284, pp. 321–330, 2020.
https://doi.org/10.1007/978-3-030-58323-1_35

ally addressed by the cutting-edge NLP techniques. In fact, two-thirds of the participants of the BEA-2019 Shared Task on Grammatical Error Correction, employed an approach based on the Transformer architecture [11], including its recent variant called BERT [4]. We based our solution on the same architecture.

The paper is structured as follows: Sect. 2 offers a brief sketch of the linguistic phenomena that we are trying to address. Section 3 explains the details of our models, Sect. 4 introduces data set for training and evaluation, Sect. 5 describes the experimental setup including a non-trivial baseline model used for comparison and finally Sect. 5.3 discusses the achieved results.

2   Description of Czech y/i Related Grammar

In Czech, the phoneme i could be written both as i and y. The actual spelling depends on the context. The context could be very short, most often it is just the preceding consonant – i is written after consonants ž/š/č/ř/c/j/ď/ť/ň (although the bigrams di/ti/ni are very rare and used in some exceptional cases), and y after consonants h/ch/k/r/d/t/n. This rule has an exception if the word is a foreign word, in which case the spelling depends on the original word. After consonants b/f/l/m/p/s/v/z both i and y could be written. The same rules apply for long vowel í which could be written both as í and ý. The choice of i or y depends on many factors:

1. If the word is or is derived from a so-called *listed word* (a word belonging to a specified set that is mentioned in Czech language reference books), it is usually written with y (*mlýn*, lit. a mill, *mlynář*, lit. a miller).
2. If the word ends with a vowel i preceded by consonant b/f/l/m/p/s/v/z, the choice of i/í or y/ý depends on the intra- or inter-sentence context, e.g.:
   (a) If the word in question is a past tense or conditional, then the choice depends on the *grammatical gender* of the subject (*Chlapci jedli.*, lit. *The boys ate.*/*díky jedly.*, lit. *The girls ate.*). This is complicated by the fact that the subject in Czech could be unexpressed and its gender must be "transferred" from the previous sentence or sentences. Also, if there is multiple subject in the sentence composed of words with different grammatical gender (*The boy and the girl ate.*), the masculine gender "dominates" the feminine and the i is used (*Chlapec a dívka jedli*).
   (b) If the word in question is an adjective, the choice depends on the *grammatical number* of the corresponding noun (*hloupý chlapec*, lit. *stupid boy*/*hloupí chlapci*, lit. *stupid boys*).
   (c) If the word in question is a noun, the choice depends on the morphology of the corresponding *inflectional paradigm* (*chlupy*, lit. *hair* is written with y because its pattern *hrady*, lit. *castles* is written with y since it follows consonant d).
   (d) There is also an exception, for example word *brzy* (lit. *soon*) is a listed word and the grammar of i/y does not depend on the context.

This simplified description is only to illustrate the relative complicated orthography of **i/y** in Czech. These rules have many exceptions and the children are learning the rules through almost the whole time they are attending elementary schools. The knowledge where to write **i/y** is supposed to be an elementary knowledge and it is not tolerated if there is an error in writing of **i/y** in written materials (e.g. newspapers, school works, subtitles, personal letters).

2.1 The Role of Grammar Errors in ASR Output

As we stated in the previous section, the errors in writing **i/y** in Czech are not tolerated. At the same time, the rules are very complicated and there is a necessity to understand not only the meaning of the given word but also the meaning of the whole sentence (more sentences). If the ASR output is used to automatically generate subtitles for the audio or to produce a transcript, the errors in **i/y** are usually flagrant. As stated above, some word forms are not ambiguous because they are always written with **i** or **y** regardless of context. In this cases, the **i/y** occur usually in the middle of the word. The most ambiguities occur in the word endings due to reasons described in Sect. 2.

The speech recognizer usually uses the correct form if the context needed to disambiguate **i/y** fits into the n-gram history of the language model. Otherwise, the recognizer selects the more probable variant. The errors are most frequent in the past tense of verbs. This motivates the work described in this paper - to design, train and evaluate a model which automatically corrects the word form of the ambiguous words.

3 Proposed Solution

In this section, we will describe a novel method for i/y spelling disambiguation based on the surrounding word context. The method is not based on a classical NLP approach using syntactic parsing, it employs machine learning with much simpler features instead. We have observed that the majority of i/y errors is caused by wrong word endings consisting of consonant **b/f/l/m/p/s/v/z** followed with **i/í/y/ý** (see Table 1 and related comments for concrete numbers). We therefore focus only on correcting such cases. Then the task could be simplified to a *classification task*, where for each word we assign the following classes: **i** (the word should end with *i/í*), **y** (the word should end with *y/ý*) and ∅ (the word is not ending with *i/í/y/ý*).

The training data for this classification task could be easily obtained by mining web text data, for example from news portals etc. We use the state-of-the-art approach based on the Transformer architecture and BERT pre-training [4] to be able to generate context-dependent vector representations of input tokens. Although the input to BERT could be the whole word tokens, more common is the use of sub-word tokens. The pre-trained models supplied by Google[2] use

---

[2] Avaialable for download from https://github.com/google-research/bert.

WordPiece tokenization. Unfortunately, the code for generating WordPieces is Google's internal C++ code and only the resulting WordPiece vocabulary is supplied together with pre-trained models. Therefore we decided to use a similar method SentencePiece authored also by Google [6] which allows to estimate the sub-word lexicon and tokenization model from unlabeled textual data[3].

3.1 SentencePiece Model

The SentencePiece method provides a *lossless tokenization*, i.e. the tokenized text could be transformed into a sequence of tokens and back without any loss of characters or punctuation and spacing. The only parameter needed to train the SentencePiece model is the size of the vocabulary. In our experiments we use 100k SentencePieces as we have a huge amount of textual data for Czech language, so the higher number of tokens is outweighed by the precise modelling of the words (higher number of words is directly included into the vocabulary instead of being composed from sub-word tokens). A great advantage of SentencePiece models is the production of self-contained models, which are easily usable in subsequent tasks and provide reproducible results. We can use the SentencePiece algorithm for processing the raw input text, but in the context of ASR (which already produces word-level tokens) we use it to split word tokens into a sequence of sub-word units. This way the model is able to process the words not seen during training.

3.2 BERT Pre-training

For pre-training the BERT Transformer, we used the collection of web data processed in our web mining tool [9]. Our motivation was to train an ASR-friendly BERT Transformer for Czech, so we removed all punctuation marks and casing information from the BERT training data. The architecture of the BERT Transformer is the same as for the Google's BERT-base model.

Our text corpus for pre-training consists of more than 8 million documents harvested during the last decade from Czech news servers. With a total word count exceeding 2.75 billion words and vocabulary size 6.4 million words, this corpus provides rich data source for pre-training Czech BERT models.

From the text corpus, we prepared two variants of datasets: (1) sequences with maximum length of 128 tokens and 20 predictions per sequence, and (2) sequences with maximum length of 512 tokens and 80 predictions per sequence. Since pre-training with longer sequences is disproportionately expensive, dataset (1) was used most of the time during the pre-training, while dataset (2) was used only at the final stage to tune positional embeddings. For both datasets, we used whole word masking and duplication factor of 2. The total counts of training examples were 82.6 million and 38.4 million respectively.

We pre-trained BERT model in two phases. In the first phase, we trained for 2 million gradient steps with dataset (1), batch size 256 and the learning rate

---

[3] SentencePiece code available from https://github.com/google/sentencepiece.

warmed up over the first 10 000 steps to a peak value at $1 \cdot 10^{-4}$, followed by 250 thousand steps with dataset (2) and batch size 64. After that we evaluated the model and decided to train more steps as the performance was still improving. In the second phase, we decreased the learning rate to $2 \cdot 10^{-5}$ and trained for 2.55 million more steps with dataset (1) followed by 200 thousand steps with dataset (2). After the total of 5 million steps, we evaluated the model again and stopped the pre-training as the model had already converged to masked LM accuracy equal to 0.5 and next sentence accuracy 0.98. The whole pre-training took approximately 4 weeks on one 8-core TPU with 128 GB of memory.

3.3   Prediction Model and Fine-Tuning

The pre-trained BERT model could be used to build a task-specific classifier. In this case, the BERT model is embedded into the classification neural network and subsequently optimized with most of the BERT parameters fixed. This transfer learning is called a *fine-tuning* of the Transformer. We used the `keras-bert` library[4] together with the Keras [3] framework.

The classification layers are stacked on the top of the BERT pre-trained Transformer. Those layers are time-distributed dense layers, i.e. the layers output the prediction for each input token (SentencePiece) based on the feature vector generated by BERT Transformer without taking any contextual feature vectors in account. In other words, the classification output for a given token is dependent only on the current BERT feature vector. The contextual dependency is fully modelled using the multi-head self-attention mechanism included in the BERT Transformer. The classification layers consist of two dense ReLU layers (256 and 64 units) and one softmax layer (output probabilities of classes ∅, i, y).

The training data for predicting i/y classes are automatically generated from the mined web text mainly from the news portals (only the texts of articles without discussion). We suppose that the news are written by journalists who are able to write grammatically correct sentences with i/y used correctly. For training we use the sequence length of 128 SentencePiece tokens and the input text is processed as a single stream without any overlaps. For each word ending with consonant **b/f/l/m/p/s/v/z** followed with **i/í/y/ý**, the respective target class is set for the last SentencePiece of the word, all other SentencePieces have an ∅ class assigned. To prevent the transformer from learning an identity map, we randomly flip (with equal probability) the **i/y** at the end of the input word, so that the classifier could not rely on the correctness of the input assignment and is forced to classify based on the word root and the word's context.

During fine-tuning we update the parameters of the following Transformer layers: self-attention normalization layers, feed forward normalization layers, multi-headed self-attention of the last layer and the adapter layers [5]. The classification layers are initialized and fully trained.

In the prediction phase, the target classes are assigned not to the words but to the input SentencePieces. Some kind of decision strategy must be employed

---

[4] Available from https://github.com/CyberZHG/keras-bert.

to create a word-level predictions from the SentencePiece predictions. We experimented with many schemas like average pooling or voting but the best results were achieved with the following schema: if the model predicts **y** class for at least one SentencePiece, then the predicted class for the word is **y**, otherwise if the model predicts **i** class for at least one SentencePiece, the predicted class is **i**. Otherwise the ∅ class is used. Having the word-level predictions, the ending of the word is changed according to the predicted class. If the word does not end with **i/í/y/ý** or the predicted class is ∅, the word is kept untouched.

4   Data Description

We used the large corpus of web text mined from news portals [9]. The downloaded web pages were automatically cleaned into the form of plain-text, the metadata were extracted. The tokenization was performed so that the text consists of a sequence of space separated tokens. The availability of the metadata (esp. the date of publication) allow us to easily split the data into different partitions (See Table 1). We pre-trained the BERT model in Feb 2020, so we used the data that we have never seen (month 02/2020) as the test data (further denoted as *web data*). While the pre-training process was running, we developed the proposed method and we used the year 2018 as development data.

Table 1. Train/development/test partitions.

Training phase	Train data	Dev. data	Test data
BERT pre-training	Years 2000–01/2020	–	–
	2.75 billion tokens	–	–
BERT fine-tuning	Years 2011–2017, 2019	Year 2018	Month 02/2020
	2.1 billion tokens	213 million tokens	15.7 million tokens
Baseline model	Years 2016, 2017, 2019	Year 2018	Month 02/2020
	717 million tokens	213 million tokens	15.7 million tokens

For evaluating the proposed model on an ASR output, we used two different tasks. In the first task, we used 10k paragraphs not containing numerals written as digits[5] from the BERT fine-tuning test data and we synthesized them using our in-house high-quality TTS system [7,10]. The synthetic voice was randomly chosen from the set of 6 voices. The resulting audio was recognized using the UWebASR ASR service [12]. We denote such data as *synth. ASR*. The second task is a real data from the Czech *MALACH* archive [13] containing natural spontaneous interviews with Holocaust survivors.

The Table 2 shows the number of ambiguous cases of i/y at the end of the word. The column *i/y incorr.* shows the number of cases which are incorrectly

---

[5] Numerals such 1000 are synthesized and recognized as *one thousand* and are causing errors during ASR evaluation, since the reference is normalised this way.

assigned using the most probable variant (row Web data) or using the ASR (Synth. ASR / MALACH data). The automatic correction method should focus especially on such cases. The *Clsf. acc.* column shows the classification accuracy when considering the most probable variant or ASR output only, i.e. without using any correction method. The last column *ASR acc.* displays the recognition accuracy when ASR is in use. The values impose a lower bound on the respective metrics. Note that the most probable/ASR output variant have by definition the value of F1-metric equal to 0% (see Sect. 5.2 for description of these metrics).

Table 2. Table summarizing the number of ambiguous cases (more in the text). *Just for the comparison - the number of ambiguous tokens with i/y in the middle is only 6856 for the web data.*

Test data	Tokens	Ambig. endings i/y	i/y incorr	Clsf. acc.%	ASR acc%
Web data	15.7 M	239 k	62 k	74.0	–
Synth. ASR	401 k	6246	910	85.1	91.9
MALACH data	63 k	495	115	83.3	80.9

5 Experiments and Results

5.1 Baseline Method

We compare the results achieved by the proposed method with a strong baseline. The baseline is designed as a logistic regression with TF-IDF feature vectors computed from left- and right- context of the word for which the target class ($\emptyset$, **i**, **y**) is predicted. The TF-IDF features were computed as L2-normalized n-gram (unigram, bigram and trigram) features and maximum number of features was limited to 500 k. The feature vector has a doubled dimensionality, i.e. 1 M features (500 k features for left context and 500 k for right context. We used `sklearn` implementation of logistics regression with the SAGA solver [2]. In the experiments we determined the optimum length of left context to be 10 words and for the right context 5 words.

5.2 Evaluation Metrics

To evaluate the performance of i/y disambiguation we use at first the *classification accuracy* evaluated on the words ending with consonant **b/f/l/m/p/s/v/z** followed by **i/í/y/ý**. Because not all words with such endings are ambiguous (one of such example is the pronoun *si* which is an invalid word with the **y** ending), we extract the set of ambiguous pairs of words from the training, development and test data and we evaluate only on such words.

The classification accuracy is easily understandable since it express the portion of words correctly classified using the automatic grammar error correction. The drawback of this method is that many of the words forms could be correctly guessed only by assigning the most probable label for a given ambiguous pair. We therefore use the input tokens which were replaced with the most probable word-form as a reference point and we compute the *F1* metric using the following numbers:

- TP – number of *true positives*, i.e. the number of cases, where the word form was successfully predicted and the most probable word-form is different from the correct word form.
- FP – number of *false positives* denotes the number of words, which were changed from the correct most probable form into an incorrect one.
- FN – number of *false negatives* counting the number of cases, where the most probable word form is incorrect and it wasn't corrected by the model.

Then the F1-metric is computed using a formula $F1 = \frac{2 \cdot TP}{(2*TP+FP+FN)}$. Such definition of metric allows us to compensate the effect of the prior distribution of the classes **i** and **y** for different words. Together with F1-metric, we are also able to compute precision $P = \frac{TP}{TP+FP}$ and recall $R = \frac{TP}{TP+FN}$.

For an experiment with the ASR result, we use the classical recognition accuracy defined as $Acc = \frac{H-I}{N}$ where H is the number of correctly recognized words, I is the number of insertions and N is the number of words in the reference.

5.3 Results

In the experimental evaluation, we evaluated the baseline method and the fine-tuned BERT model on the textual web data and the ASR outputs on two different datasets. The results are shown in Table 3. The classification accuracy (*Clsf. acc.*) and ASR accuracy (*ASR acc.*) could be directly compared with the lower-bounds presented in Table 2. The fine-tuned BERT model clearly outperforms the baseline and also the lower-bound on all three tasks in both the classification accuracy and the F1-metric. The performance is degrading when the ASR errors are introduced. It is interesting that the Recall is deteriorating more rapidly with lowering ASR accuracy than the Precision for both the baseline and BERT-based models. The effect of i/y spelling disambiguation on the ASR accuracy is not significant due to the low number of i/y incorrectly predicted by an ASR (910 and 115 words, see Table 2), but the i/y disambiguation greatly improves the grammatical correctness and readability of the ASR output.

Table 3. Experimental results

Dataset	Model	Clsf. acc.%	Precision%	Recall%	F1-metric%	ASR acc.%
Web data	Baseline	83.1	73.9	53.8	62.3	–
	BERT fine-tuning	96.7	93.6	93.4	93.5	–
Synth. ASR	Baseline	86.9	58.2	44.6	50.5	91.9
	BERT fine-tuning	96.2	90.5	84.9	87.6	92.0
MALACH	Baseline	81.3	39.6	25.2	30.8	80.8
	BERT fine-tuning	88.8	77.2	50.3	60.9	81.1

6 Conclusion

We presented a simple and powerful method for correcting the ASR output. The method was designed and evaluated on i/y spelling disambiguation task for Czech language, but it could be easily modified to other languages and similar grammatical phenomenons. The method uses the Transformer pre-trained using the BERT approach with training data specially designed to be compatible with ASR output. In the future work we would like to use the same Transformer in other tasks improving the readability of ASR output.

Acknowledgments. This research was supported by the Technology Agency of the Czech Republic, project No. TN01000024. Computational resources were supplied by the project "e-Infrastruktura CZ" (e-INFRA LM2018140) provided within the program Projects of Large Research, Development and Innovations Infrastructures.

References

1. Bryant, C., Felice, M., Andersen, Ø.E., Briscoe, T.: The BEA-2019 shared task on grammatical error correction. In: Proceedings of the Fourteenth Workshop on Innovative Use of NLP for Building Educational Applications, pp. 52–75. Association for Computational Linguistics, Florence (2019)
2. Buitinck, L., et al.: API design for machine learning software: experiences from the scikit-learn project. In: ECML PKDD Workshop: Languages for Data Mining and Machine Learning, pp. 108–122 (2013)
3. Chollet, F., et al.: Keras (2015). https://keras.io
4. Devlin, J., Chang, M.W., Lee, K., Toutanova, K.: BERT: pre-training of deep bidirectional transformers for language understanding. In: Proceedings of the 2019 Conference of the North American Chapter of the Association for Computational Linguistics: Human Language Technologies, vol. 1 (Long and Short Papers), pp. 4171–4186. Association for Computational Linguistics, Minneapolis (2019)
5. Houlsby, N., et al.: Parameter-efficient transfer learning for NLP. In: Chaudhuri, K., Salakhutdinov, R. (eds.) Proceedings of the 36th International Conference on Machine Learning. Proceedings of Machine Learning Research, PMLR, Long Beach, California, USA, 09–15 June 2019, vol. 97, pp. 2790–2799 (2019)
6. Kudo, T., Richardson, J.: SentencePiece: A simple and language independent subword tokenizer and detokenizer for neural text processing. In: Proceedings of the 2018 Conference on Empirical Methods in Natural Language Processing: System Demonstrations. pp. 66–71. Association for Computational Linguistics, Brussels (2018)
7. Matoušek, J., Tihelka, D.: Annotation errors detection in TTS corpora. In: INTERSPEECH, Lyon, France, pp. 1511–1515 (2013)
8. Ng, H.T., Wu, S.M., Briscoe, T., Hadiwinoto, C., Susanto, R.H., Bryant, C.: The CoNLL-2014 shared task on grammatical error correction. In: Proceedings of the Eighteenth Conference on Computational Natural Language Learning: Shared Task, pp. 1–14. Association for Computational Linguistics, Baltimore (2014)
9. Švec, J., Lehečka, J., Ircing, P., Skorkovská, L., Pražák, A., Vavruška, J., Stanislav, P., Hoidekr, J.: General framework for mining, processing and storing large amounts of electronic texts for language modeling purposes. Lang. Res. Eval. **48**(2), 227–248 (2013). https://doi.org/10.1007/s10579-013-9246-z

10. Tihelka, D., Hanzlíček, Z., Jůzová, M., Vít, J., Matoušek, J., Grůber, M.: Current state of text-to-speech system ARTIC: a decade of research on the field of speech technologies. In: Sojka, P., Horák, A., Kopeček, I., Pala, K. (eds.) TSD 2018. LNCS (LNAI), vol. 11107, pp. 369–378. Springer, Cham (2018). https://doi.org/10.1007/978-3-030-00794-2_40
11. Vaswani, A., et al.: Attention is all you need. In: Guyon, I., et al. (eds.) Advances in Neural Information Processing Systems 30, pp. 5998–6008. Curran Associates, Inc. (2017)
12. Švec, J., Bulín, M., Pražák, A., Ircing, P.: UWebASR - web-based ASR engine for Czech and Slovak (2018)
13. Švec, J., Psutka, J.V., Trmal, J., Šmídl, L., Ircing, P., Sedmidubsky, J.: On the use of grapheme models for searching in large spoken archives. In: 2018 IEEE International Conference on Acoustics, Speech and Signal Processing (ICASSP), pp. 6259–6263 (2018)

Transfer Learning to Detect Parkinson's Disease from Speech In Different Languages Using Convolutional Neural Networks with Layer Freezing

Cristian David Rios-Urrego[1]([⊠]) [iD], Juan Camilo Vásquez-Correa[1,2] [iD],
Juan Rafael Orozco-Arroyave[1,2] [iD], and Elmar Nöth[2] [iD]

[1] Faculty of Engineering, University of Antioquia UdeA, Medellín, Colombia
cdavid.rios@udea.edu.co
[2] Pattern Recognition Lab, Friedrich-Alexander-Universität Erlangen-Nürnberg,
Erlangen, Germany

Abstract. Parkinson's Disease is a neurodegenerative disorder characterized by motor symptoms such as resting tremor, bradykinesia, rigidity and freezing of gait. The most common symptom in speech is called
hypokinetic dysarthria, where speech is characterized by monotone intensity, low pitch variability and poor prosody that tends to fade at the end
of the utterance. This study proposes the classification of patients with
Parkinson's Disease and healthy controls in three different languages
(Spanish, German, and Czech) using a transfer learning strategy. The
process is further improved by freezing consecutive different layers of the
architecture. We hypothesize that some convolutional layers characterize the disease and others the language. Therefore, when a fine-tuning
in the transfer learning is performed, it is possible to find the topology
that best adapts to the target language and allows an accurate detection
of Parkinson's Disease. The proposed methodology uses Convolutional
Neural Networks trained with Mel-scale spectrograms. Results indicate
that the fine-tuning of the neural network does not provide good performance in all languages while fine-tuning of individual layers improves
the accuracy by up to 7%. In addition, the results show that Transfer
Learning among languages improves the performance in up to 18% when
compared to a base model used to initialize the weights of the network.

Keywords: Parkinson's disease · Speech processing · Transfer
Learning · Convolutional neural networks

1 Introduction

Parkinson's Disease (PD) is a neurological disorder characterized by progressive
loss of dopaminergic neurons in the substantia nigra of the midbrain [3]. PD produces motor and non-motor deficits in patients such as resting tremor, bradykinesia, rigidity and freezing of gait, which contribute significantly to decrease the

© Springer Nature Switzerland AG 2020
P. Sojka et al. (Eds.): TSD 2020, LNAI 12284, pp. 331–339, 2020.
https://doi.org/10.1007/978-3-030-58323-1_36

quality of life of the patients [6,7]. Most PD patients develop several speech deficits, which are grouped and called hypokinetic dysarthria [18]. This type of dysarthria is characterized by a low voice volume, reduced voice quality, reduction of prosodic pitch, imprecise pronunciation of consonants and vowels, lack of fluency, voice tremor, and others. These symptoms often have adverse effects in the speech intelligibility and the quality of life [20].

Different studies in the literature about the automatic evaluation of PD speech are based on deep learning techniques, especially in Convolutional Neural Networks (CNN). For instance, in [4], the authors implemented different CNNs to discriminate 41 PD patients and 40 healthy controls (HC) using utterances of the sustained vowel /ah/. Each audio was transformed into spectrograms. The authors implemented data augmentation techniques. The best performing network was composed of 2 convolutional layers, 2 max pooling layers and a fully connected layer. This achieved accuracies of up to 75.7%. The authors from [14] modeled the articulatory deficits in PD patients with CNNs. Initially, the transitions between voiced and unvoiced segments were detected to model difficulties of patients to start/stop the vibration of the vocal folds. Then, a time-frequency representation for each transition was computed to train the CNNs. The authors considered speech recordings to classify PD patients and HC subjects in 3 different languages (Spanish, German, and Czech). They obtained accuracies ranging from 70% to 89%, depending on the language. The authors in [17] presented an approach to PD detection using a ResNet architecture dedicated originally to image classification. Initially, the authors trained a base model using the ImageNet and Saarbruecken Voice Database (SVD) databases. Then, the model was re-trained and evaluated using spectrograms calculated on the sustained vowel /ah/ of 50 PD patients and 50 HC subjects from the PC-GITA database. The authors used a 10-fold speaker independent stratified cross-validation strategy. The accuracy obtained in the validation set was 91%. A similar work was performed in [9] where 2 transfer learning strategies were implemented (layer freezing and fine-tuning) for the classification of the PD patients using handwriting signals. The authors showed that the proposed strategies improved the accuracy up to 92.3%. Finally, in [15], the authors proposed to use a transfer learning strategy among languages to discriminate between PD patients and HC subjects. The authors considered recordings in 3 different languages (Spanish, German and Czech). Base models were created for each language and afterwards the parameters were transferred to the other languages. According to their results, the transfer learning strategy improves the accuracy by up to 8%.

The main objective of the present study is to discriminate between PD patients and HC speakers in different languages using a layer freezing strategy in a transfer learning scenario. The aim is to have robust models designed for each language based on previous knowledge from a different corpus. In [5], the efficiency of partial layer freezing was demonstrated for image recognition using CNNs when transfer learning is applied to a small target database. Therefore, we believe that by performing a fine-tuning in the transfer learning, only the layers that perform the disease characterization are transferred from the base language to the target one. We show the effect of copying all layers and fine-tune a sequential number of layers, by freezing some layers of the base models. CNNs were trained with utterances in Spanish, German and Czech using Mel-scale spectrograms. The results indicate that layer freezing improves the performance of the models in up to 7% of accuracy with respect to the models using a transfer learning of all parameters (without layer freezing).

2   Materials and Methods

2.1   Data

Three databases in different languages are considered: Spanish, German and Czech, each database containing PD patients and HC subjects. All recordings were recorded in controlled acoustic conditions and down-sampled to 16 kHz. Demographic information of the participants is shown in Table 1. Labels of the neurological state of the patients, according to the Movement Disorder Society - Unified Parkinson's Disease Rating Scale (MDS-UPDRS-III) are included [2].

Table 1. Clinical and demographic information of the speakers in the three datasets. **G.**: gender (**M.** male or **F.** female). Values are reported in terms of mean $\pm$ standard deviation.

	G	Spanish		German		Czech	
		PD	HC	PD	HC	PD	HC
# of Subjects	M	25	25	47	44	30	30
	F	25	25	41	44	20	19
Age [years]	M	61.3 ± 11.4	60.5 ± 11.6	66.7 ± 8.7	63.8 ± 12.7	65.3 ± 9.6	60.3 ± 11.5
	F	$60.7 \pm \ 7.3$	$61.4 \pm \ 7.0$	66.2 ± 9.7	62.6 ± 15.2	60.1 ± 8.7	63.5 ± 11.1
Years diagnosed	M	8.7 ± 5.9	–	7.0 ± 5.5	–	6.7 ± 4.5	–
	F	12.6 ± 11.6	–	7.1 ± 6.2	–	6.8 ± 5.2	–
MDS-UPDRS-III	M	37.8 ± 22.1	–	22.1 ± 9.9	–	21.4 ± 11.5	–
	F	37.6 ± 14.1	–	23.3 ± 12.0	–	18.1 ± 9.7	–

Subjects from the three corpora were requested to perform different speech tasks including the rapid repetition of /pa-ta-ka/, reading isolated sentences, reading a text, and a monologue. Additional information about the speech tasks for each database is available in [12] for Spanish, [1] for German, and [13] for Czech.

2.2   Segmentation

We consider the onset and offset segments to model the capability of the patients to start/stop the vocal fold vibration [11]. The change between a voiced and unvoiced segment is detected based on the presence of fundamental frequency values. Once the borders are detected, we take 80 ms of the signal to the left and to the right, forming segments with 160 ms length. The segmented transitions are transformed into a Mel-scale spectrogram with 80 Mel filters and a time shift of 4 ms to get a 80×41 time-frequency representation to feed the CNN.

2.3   CNN Model

The CNN implemented here consists of four convolutional layers of size 4, 8, 16, and 32 respectively, each one followed by a max-pooling layer of size 2×2. In addition, 3 fully connected layers of size 128, 64, and 2. ReLu activations are considered in the hidden layers, and a softmax activation function is considered in the output to make the final decision. For the training of the network we used Pytorch with a cross-entropy loss function and an Adam optimizer. Dropout and L2-regularization techniques are also used [15].

2.4   Transfer Learning

The main objective of transfer learning is to take the knowledge (weights, and biases) of previously trained models to improve the performance of a target model [16]. We perform transfer learning among languages for the classification of PD patients and HC subjects. Therefore, we take a base model, that is, a model in a specific language, and we use this model to re-train the network with the remaining two languages.

Frozen Layers. Layer freezing means that the parameters of some layers in a model are not updated when performing transfer learning. In this work, in addition to performing a total transfer of parameters among languages, we also perform a freezing of the 4 convolutional layers in a sequential way. This allows the system to perform a high level characterization from the base model and adjust to the target model with the remaining layers (without layer freezing) [10].

3   Experiments and Results

The experiments are divided as follows: (1) CNNs are trained to classify PD vs. HC speakers in each language individually. Thus they can be used as a base model in the transfer learning. For this case, we use a random parameter initialization. The results are the same as those obtained in [15] and are used as the baseline of this work. (2) CNNs from each language are retrained with data from the remaining two languages using a transfer learning strategy with layer freezing, i.e., we sequentially freeze the convolutional layers in order to keep a constant part of the learned weights from the base models, Fig. 1 summarizes this procedure. All experiments were performed through a 10-fold speaker independent stratified cross-validation strategy. In addition, the McNemar's test was performed between the baseline and the best performing model after transfer learning with layer freezing. This test checks if the disagreements between two cases match. In terms of comparing two binary classification algorithms, the test evaluates whether the two models make errors in the same proportion [8].

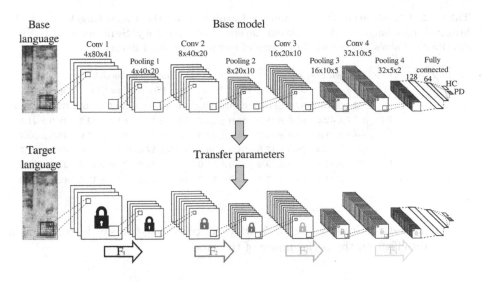

Fig. 1. Transfer learning strategy proposed in this study to classify PD patients vs. HC subjects from speech with utterances from different languages. F_x, $x \in \{1, 2, 3, 4\}$ indicates the number of sequentially frozen convolutional layers.

3.1 Transfer Learning with Layer Freezing

CNNs were trained for each language using a transfer learning strategy with layer freezing, denoted as F_x, where x indicates the number of sequentially frozen convolutional layers. For example, F_3 means a freezing of the first 3 convolutional layers. Table 2 shows results when base models in Spanish and German are re-trained to classify Czech speakers. In this case, the best results are obtained in F_0 for both base models, i.e., transfer learning without layer freezing. The results improve by 4% with respect to the baseline when the Spanish base model is re-trained (from 68.5% to 72.5%). The McNemar's test was performed to compare these two models ($p > 0.05$). This results implies that both models make errors in the same proportion, i.e., transfer learning had no significant effect on the results. This is because the layer freezing increases the sensitivity of the models, but reducing the specificity, similar to the baseline (94% sensitivity). This behavior generates over-fitting in the system and also low accuracy.

The results to test the German data are shown in Table 3. On the one hand, when we used the Spanish base model, the best result is obtained with F_2 with an accuracy of 78.3%, mainly because the sensitivity improves with respect to F_0. This is because the Spanish base model has higher sensitivity (74.0%) than specificity (68.0%) (see Table 4). On the other hand, when we used the Czech base model, CNN with F_4 improved the accuracy by 5.3% compared to F_0 (without layer freezing). In addition, this result improves the accuracy by 18.9% compared to the German base model (without using transfer learning). For this case, the

Table 2. Classification for the transfer learning using the Czech target model. **T. lang.:** Target language. **F. l.:** Frozen layers. **Acc:** Accuracy. **Sen:** Sensitivity. **Spe:** Specificity. Values are reported in terms of mean ± standard deviation.

T. lang.	L. F.	Spanish base model			German base model		
		Acc (%)	Sen (%)	Spe (%)	Acc (%)	Sen (%)	Spe (%)
Czech	F_0	**72.5 ± 13.9**	**82.0 ± 14.7**	**62.0 ± 28.9**	**70.6 ± 14.6**	**80.0 ± 16.3**	**62.5 ± 26.4**
	F_1	65.7 ± 12.6	86.0 ± 18.9	45.0 ± 22.7	65.9 ± 11.5	84.0 ± 12.6	48.0 ± 31.5
	F_2	60.4 ± 17.1	76.0 ± 30.9	44.0 ± 30.9	65.4 ± 16.5	86.0 ± 25.0	45.5 ± 30.7
	F_3	65.9 ± 19.4	78.0 ± 17.5	54.0 ± 35.3	66.5 ± 17.3	92.0 ± 13.9	40.0 ± 32.7
	F_4	60.6 ± 15.1	94.0 ± 9.6	27.0 ± 34.6	58.5 ± 14.5	92.0 ± 13.9	25.0 ± 34.4
Czech baseline		68.5 ± 14.1	94.0 ± 13.5	42.0 ± 33.2	68.5 ± 14.1	94.0 ± 13.5	42.0 ± 33.2

statistical test produced a $p \ll 0.05$, which implies that transfer learning has a significant effect on the performance of the model.

Table 3. Classification for the transfer learning using the German target model. **T. lang.:** Target language. **F. l.:** Frozen layers. **Acc:** Accuracy. **Sen:** Sensitivity. **Spe:** Specificity. Values are reported in terms of mean ± standard deviation.

T. lang.	L. F.	Spanish base model			Czech base model		
		Acc (%)	Sen (%)	Spe (%)	Acc (%)	Sen (%)	Spe (%)
German	F_0	77.3 ± 11.3	86.3 ± 13.8	68.3 ± 14.2	76.7 ± 7.9	87.5 ± 11.0	66.0 ± 15.6
	F_1	75.5 ± 6.7	86.0 ± 13.6	65.0 ± 14.1	77.9 ± 11.9	82.1 ± 18.1	73.8 ± 19.8
	F_2	**78.3±11.3**	**90.0±11.0**	**68.6±13.5**	75.0 ± 12.6	78.4 ± 21.8	71.5 ± 13.2
	F_3	75.7 ± 8.5	78.8 ± 21.8	72.6 ± 17.7	74.7 ± 10.6	80.7 ± 14.4	68.8 ± 17.0
	F_4	75.0 ± 9.8	71.4 ± 18.7	78.6 ± 16.7	**82.0±11.0**	**93.3±7.7**	**70.7±18.4**
German baseline		63.1 ± 11.7	43.1 ± 38.0	83.1 ± 17.7	63.1 ± 11.7	43.1 ± 38.0	83.1 ± 17.7

Finally, Table 4 shows the results of classifying the speakers of the Spanish corpus using base models in German and Czech. For this case, we obtained the best result when the first layer was frozen (F_1), improving the accuracy in up to 7% compared to the CNN without layer freezing. This improvement is supported by McNemar's test with a $p \ll 0.05$ which implies a significant change in model performance because of layer freezing. These results confirm that the transfer learning strategy with layer freezing can improve the classification accuracy of systems when fine-tuning some layers from the base model.

Table 4. Classification for the transfer learning using the Spanish target model. **T. lang.**: Target language. **F. l.**: Frozen layers. **Acc**: Accuracy. **Sen**: Sensitivity. **Spe**: Specificity. Values are reported in terms of mean ± standard deviation.

T. lang.	L. F.	Czech base model			German base model		
		Acc (%)	Sen (%)	Spe (%)	Acc (%)	Sen (%)	Spe (%)
Spanish	F_0	72.0 ± 13.1	67.0 ± 11.6	78.0 ± 23.9	70.0 ± 12.5	62.0 ± 19.9	78.0 ± 29.0
	F_1	**78.0±16.8**	**76.0±20.6**	**80.0±18.8**	**77.0±11.6**	**64.0±18.4**	**90.0±14.1**
	F_2	74.0 ± 10.7	72.0 ± 14.0	76.0 ± 24.6	71.0 ± 20.8	54.0 ± 26.7	88.0 ± 19.3
	F_3	74.0 ± 18.4	66.0 ± 25.0	82.0 ± 17.5	76.0 ± 13.5	60.0 ± 23.1	92.0 ± 14.0
	F_4	73.0 ± 6.7	60.0 ± 13.3	86.0 ± 9.7	68.0 ± 14.7	48.0 ± 30.1	88.0 ± 10.3
Spanish baseline		71.0 ± 15.9	74.0 ± 25.0	68.0 ± 28.6	71.0 ± 15.9	74.0 ± 25.0	68.0 ± 28.6

4   Conclusion

We proposed a methodology based on transfer learning with layer freezing to classify between PD patients and HC subjects from speech in three different languages: Spanish, German, and Czech. The objective is to improve the performance of the network with respect to a random initialization or a full transfer of the parameters. Firstly, we obtained the base models for each language (without transfer learning) using CNNs trained with Mel-scale spectrograms extracted from the transitions between voiced and unvoiced segments. Secondly, the proposed methodology was implemented using 1 language as a target model and the remaining 2 languages as base models.

The results show that the proposed strategy improves the accuracy of CNNs in up to 7% compared to a full fine-tune of the CNN (F_0). These result open a gap to investigate the hypothesis that some layers of the base model are focused on the characterization of the disease, therefore, these layers should be frozen in the transfer learning. While the remaining layers (unfrozen) were in charge of characterizing and adjusting the neural network to the target language. In addition, it was observed that with the proposed method the accuracy of the models improves in a range from 4% to 18% compared to the base models without any transfer learning. In future research, it is necessary to create more robust base models to identify which layers are responsible for characterizing the pathology and the language. A first approach for such understanding could be the use of saliency maps and class-specific image generation [19].

In further experiments, we will train the CNNs with data from other diseases in the same language and with data from different languages, with the aim to accurately identify the layers focused on characterizing the presence of the disease and to observe the level of abstraction of each layer. In addition, we will also address experiments for the detection of PD using transfer learning with CNNs trained for emotion recognition. We hypothesize that as the disease progresses, patients suffer disorders that can affect their emotional life, which can be reflected in changes of emotions that are perceived from the speech.

Acknowledgments. The work reported here was financed by CODI from University of Antioquia by grant Number 2017–15530. This project has received funding from the European Unions Horizon 2020 research and innovation programme under the Marie Sklodowska-Curie Grant Agreement No. 766287.

References

1. Bocklet, T., et al.: Automatic evaluation of parkinson's speech-acoustic, prosodic and voice related cues. In: Proceedings of INTERSPEECH, pp. 1149–1153 (2013)
2. Goetz, C., et al.: Movement disorder society-sponsored revision of the unified parkinson's disease rating scale (mds-updrs): scale presentation and clinimetric testing results. Mov. Disord. Official J. Mov. Disord. Soc. **23**(15), 2129–2170 (2008)
3. Hornykiewicz, O.: Biochemical aspects of parkinson's disease. Neurology **51**(2 Suppl 2), S2–S9 (1998)
4. Khojasteh, P., et al.: Parkinson's disease diagnosis based on multivariate deep features of speech signal. In: Proceedings of LSC, pp. 187–190. IEEE (2018)
5. Kruithof, M., et al.: Object recognition using deep convolutional neural networks with complete transfer and partial frozen layers. In: Proceedings of SPIE, vol. 9995, p. 99950K. International Society for Optics and Photonics (2016)
6. Logemann, J.A., et al.: Frequency and cooccurrence of vocal tract dysfunctions in the speech of a large sample of parkinson patients. J. Speech Lang. Hear. Res. **43**(1), 47–57 (1978)
7. McKinlay, A., et al.: A profile of neuropsychiatric problems and their relationship to quality of life for parkinson's disease patients without dementia. Parkinsonism Relat. Disord. **14**(1), 37–42 (2008)
8. McNemar, Q.: Note on the sampling error of the difference between correlated proportions or percentages. Psychometrika **12**(2), 153–157 (1947)
9. Naseer, A., et al.: Refining parkinson's neurological disorder identification through deep transfer learning. Neural Comput. Appl. **32**(3), 839–854 (2020)
10. Oquab, M., et al.: Learning and transferring mid-level image representations using convolutional neural networks. In: Proceedings of CVPR, pp. 1717–1724 (2014)
11. Orozco-Arroyave, J.R.: Analysis of speech of people with Parkinson's disease, vol. 41. Logos Verlag Berlin GmbH (2016)
12. Orozco-Arroyave, J.R., et al.: New Spanish speech corpus database for the analysis of people suffering from Parkinson's disease. In: Proceedings of LREC, pp. 342–347 (2014)
13. Rusz, J.: Detecting speech disorders in early Parkinson's disease by acoustic analysis (2018)
14. Vásquez-Correa, et al.: Convolutional neural network to model articulation impairments in patients with Parkinson's disease. In: Proceedings of INTERSPEECH, pp. 314–318 (2017)
15. Vásquez-Correa, J.C., et al.: Convolutional neural networks and a transfer learning strategy to classify parkinson's disease from speech in three different languages. In: Nyström, I., Hernández Heredia, Y., Milián Núñez, V. (eds.) CIARP 2019. LNCS, vol. 11896, pp. 697–706. Springer, Cham (2019). https://doi.org/10.1007/978-3-030-33904-3_66
16. Wang, D., Zheng, T.F.: Transfer learning for speech and language processing. In: Proceedings of APSIPA, pp. 1225–1237. IEEE (2015)

17. Wodzinski, M., et al.: Deep learning approach to Parkinson's disease detection using voice recordings and convolutional neural network dedicated to image classification. In: Proceedings of EMBC, pp. 717–720. IEEE (2019)
18. Yorkston, K.M., et al.: The effect of rate control on the intelligibility and naturalness of dysarthric speech. J. Speech Hear. Disord. **55**(3), 550–560 (1990)
19. Yosinski, J., et al.: Understanding neural networks through deep visualization (2015). ArXiv Preprint arXiv:1506.06579
20. Yunusova, Y., Weismer, G.G., Lindstrom, M.J.: Classifications of vocalic segments from articulatory kinematics: healthy controls and speakers with dysarthria. J. Speech Lang. Hear. Res. (2011)

Speaker-Dependent BiLSTM-Based Phrasing

Markéta Jůzová[1,2(✉)] [ID] and Daniel Tihelka[2] [ID]

[1] Department of Cybernetics, Faculty of Applied Sciences,
University of West Bohemia, Pilsen, Czech Republic
[2] New Technology for Information Society, Faculty of Applied Sciences,
University of West Bohemia, Pilsen, Czech Republic
juzova@kky.zcu.cz

Abstract. Phrase boundary detection is an important part of text-to-speech systems since it ensures more natural speech synthesis outputs. However, the problem of phrasing is ambiguous, especially per speaker and per style. This is the reason why this paper focuses on speaker-dependent phrasing for the purposes of speech synthesis, using a neural network model with a speaker code. We also describe results of a listening test focused on incorrectly detected breaks because it turned out that some mistakes could be actually fine, not wrong.

Keywords: Phrase boundary detection · Text-to-speech system · Neural network · Speaker-dependent phrasing

1 Introduction

A phrase is a group of words carrying a special meaning. For humans, it is natural to split sentences into phrases which makes the speech more comprehensible and easy to follow by listeners. And it also has one very important physiological reason – a man needs pauses in speech to breathe. Although text-to-speech (TTS) systems do not need to take a breath, the phrase breaks detection is an important part of the text processing before synthesizing the prompt [15]. Appropriate phrasing makes the TTS outputs more natural and understandable.

More technically, the phrasing problem could be defined as a sequence-to-sequence problem. The author of [15] uses the following: The phrasing is a looking for a sequence of juncture types $j_0, j_1, \ldots j_n$ for an input sequence of tokens $t_0, t_1, \ldots t_n$, where $j_i = 1$ if a phrase break follows a token t_i, and $j_i = 0$ otherwise.

There are many different approaches to this task. One of the most used is also the simplest one – phrase boundaries are put in the input sentence according to punctuation, mostly commas. This approach has also been used in our TTS system [17] for years. However, modern stochastic methods, supporting sequence-to-sequence training, proved to be a good tools for the phrase boundary detection problem [2, 16], outperforming the "classical" classification-based techniques with the decision-making about each juncture type separately [4, 7, 12, 14]. This paper presents a neural network (NN) phrasing model.

© Springer Nature Switzerland AG 2020
P. Sojka et al. (Eds.): TSD 2020, LNAI 12284, pp. 340–347, 2020.
https://doi.org/10.1007/978-3-030-58323-1_37

The main problem of the task of dividing an input sentence with phrase breaks in smaller units is that there are usually more correct phrase boundary positioning – which very complicate the evaluation. Contrary to many natural language processing (NLP) tasks with clear correct and wrong predictions, in the phrasing issue some of *false positives* and *false negatives* are not wrong, in fact. Nevertheless, for this paper, we decided to evaluate the proposed phrasing model on the labeled data in a common way in Sect. 3, i.e. using default measures *accuracy, precision, recall* and *F1-score*. But we also inspected some of the "faults" and prepared a small listening test to estimate the percentage of really wrong predicted phrase breaks and no-breaks (see Sect. 3.1).

2   Training NN-based Phrasing Model with Speaker Code

In general, the phrasing problem is very vague since there are usually more possible (correct) sentence splittings into phrases. And it depends on many aspects (a speaker, situation, audience, etc.) which exact representation is used by humans. Therefore, it seems to be a good idea to focus more on training a speaker-dependent model (as e.g. [8,9,13]) since the speech synthesis should sound more natural when adopting various characteristic of the speaker who had recorded the speech corpus used. So we decided to train one model for phrase boundary detection using data from more speakers and just mark each input sentence with a specific code to allow the network to distinguish one speaker from the others – the similar approach is sometimes used for the speech synthesis itself to improve the performance of the conventional speaker-dependent neural network method [6].

2.1   Training Data

As our training data for this issue, we used our proprietary large-scale speech corpora recorded for the purposes of speech synthesis, 6 Czech voices (both male and female) and 2 English ones; all of them were recorded in neutral, "newspaper" style, and they are used as commercial voices in our TTS system *ARTIC*[17]. These corpora were automatically segmented [3,10,11] and the prosodic breaks and breaths were labeled. Afterwards, this information about the breaks/breaths positions in the signal were "copied" to the text representation of the particular sentences. The corpora were also labelled with part-of-speech (POS) tags – we used our proprietary NN-based tagger for Czech and default *NLTK* tagger for English [1].

Due to that, we obtained text corpora with the information of correct phrase boundaries – specific for each speaker. Naturally, we got some sentences with different phrasing (depending on the speaker), see the example below (EN: *There is nothing worse than having a sports watch under a good suit*):

- speaker1:
  Není nic horšího | než mít pod dobrým oblekem | sportovní hodinky.

- speaker2:
  Není nic horšího | než mít pod dobrým oblekem sportovní hodinky.

The Table 1 contains the basic statistics of all corpora used. 90% of all the data were used for the training phase and 10% for the evaluation in the Sect. 3. The table shows that some corpora have significant number of breaks (pauses in speech) not corresponding any comma in the sentence text representation.

Table 1. Text corpora statistics.

Language	Speaker	No. of sentences	No. of junctures	No. of breaks	No-comma breaks
Czech	Speaker1	9,619	104,387	16,202	4,060
	Speaker2	8,189	91,065	12,487	443
	Speaker3	12,151	119,115	12,851	776
	Speaker4	9,484	102,106	15,133	2,969
	Speaker5	7,662	85,595	12,590	2,451
	Speaker6	9,288	93,542	20,137	10,025
English	Speaker1	19,909	132,556	9,856	2,241
	Speaker2	19,909	133,035	10,229	2,612

2.2 Neural Network Architecture

For the experiment, we designed a NN-based model shown in Fig. 1. As the input of the network, we used POS tags t_i (corresponding to the words w_i in the input sentence which are not used in the model) with the punctuation marks p_i and the speaker code s. The first layer of our model is the *embedding* layer which transforms each POS tag to a vector representation. These are, altogether with the punctuation of the sentence and the speaker code, put to the bidirectional Long-Short-Term-Memory [5] (biLSTM) layer. The output of biLSTM layer is then put to the *Dense* layer, which outputs the sequence of *breaks/no-breaks* for the given sentence (or more precisely for the frame of words at the input).

The proposed model was trained independently for 2 different languages, Czech and English, however, together for all voices per language presented in Sect. 2.1. The Table 2 shows the best settings for the NN architecture.

Table 2. Best settings for the BiLSTM phrasing model.

Language	Best accuracy	Best loss	Frame count	Tags embeddings	Units in biLSTM
Czech	97.7%	0.066	10	64	64
English	98.4%	0.073	10	32	64

3   Results

For the evaluation we used the usual measures: *Accuracy (Acc), Precision (P),*
Recall (R) and *F1-score (F1)*, defined as below:

$$Acc = \frac{tp + tn}{tp + tn + fp + fn} \tag{1}$$

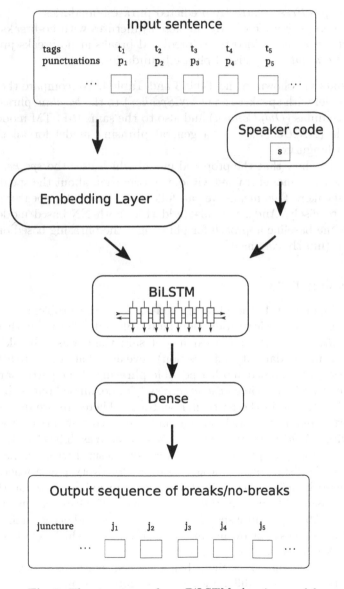

Fig. 1. The structure of our BiLSTM phrasing model

$$P = \frac{tp}{tp + fp} \tag{2}$$

$$R = \frac{tp}{tp + fn} \tag{3}$$

$$F1 = 2 \cdot \frac{P \cdot R}{P + R} \tag{4}$$

where

- $tp = $ *true positives* – correctly predicted phrase boundaries
- $tn = $ *true negatives* – correctly predicted junctures with no-breaks
- $fp = $ *false positives* – incorrectly predicted breaks at no-breaks junctures
- $fn = $ *false negatives* – missed phrase boundaries.

The results are shown in the Table 3 and Table 4. We compare the proposed BiLSTM model with speaker-code (*NN_Speaker*) to the *baseline* phrasing model using only commas (*OnlyComma*) and also to the same BiLSTM model without speaker-code (*NN_General*), i.e. a general phrasing model for all the voices, training per language.

The results show that the proposed model which uses the *spcaker code* outperforms the same model trained without information about the speaker if evaluated per speaker. This means we can follow the particular speaker's phrasing style more precisely. And let us also add that both NN-based models mostly outperform the baseline approach for phrasing – the phrasing based on sentence punctuation (mostly commas).

3.1 Listening Tests

As mentioned in Sect. 1, the phrasing suffers from the problem of ambiguous results which makes a clear evaluation more difficult. The in-depth inspecting of *false positives* (*fp*; the proposed model said there was a break but there was no break in the data at that position) revealed that some of them are not wrong – these just matched another possible phrasing of the particular sentence. And, on the other hand, some *false negatives* (*fn*; i.e. missed phrase boundaries) seemed to be strange in the particular sentence. Therefore, we decided to prepare a short listening test with 30 randomly selected sentences across (Czech) speakers with 25 *false positives* and 25 *false negatives*. These sentences (with predicted and "correct" phrase breaks) were synthesized with our LSTM-based TTS[18] and the listeners were asked to mark for every pause whether it was fine or strange/disturbing, regarding the sentence meaning. Note that the LSTM-based TTS was used to prevent the situation when the listener's evaluation was affect by a possible unnatural speech artefact which could occasionally appear in unit selection synthesis, or by an unnatural intonation which could occasionally appear in DNN-based synthesis.

We had 15 listeners, 7 of them being speech synthesis experts. For some phrase breaks the answers differ a lot, so we counted the answers for each phrase break and divide the breaks into 3 groups:

- "break is OK" – if more than 70% of listeners vote for that
- "break is strange" – if more than 70% of listeners vote for that
- "tie" – otherwise (the answers were almost balanced)

The listening test clearly proved that the results of BiLSTM-based model are, in fact, higher than the results shown in the Table 3 and Table 4 – see Table 5. More than a half of randomly selected *false positives* are considered to be correct by most of the listeners and, similarly, about a half of missed phrase breaks (*false negatives*) were marked as strange by the majority.

Table 3. The comparison of results for Czech voices

Speaker	Phrasing model	Acc	P	R	F1
Speaker1	NN_Speaker	**97.4%**	**100.0%**	**88.9%**	**94.1%**
	NN_General	97.0%	**100.0%**	87.3%	93.2%
	OnlyComma	96.7%	99.8%	86.2%	92.5%
Speaker2	NN_Speaker	**99.6%**	99.8%	**98.5%**	**99.1%**
	NN_General	99.5%	**100.0%**	97.8%	98.9%
	OnlyComma	99.4%	99.8%	97.6%	98.7%
Speaker3	NN_Speaker	**99.3%**	99.5%	**97.0%**	**98.2%**
	NN_General	**99.3%**	99.7%	96.8%	**98.2%**
	OnlyComma	**99.3%**	**100.0%**	96.5%	**98.2%**
Speaker4	NN_Speaker	**97.5%**	**100.0%**	**89.4%**	**94.4%**
	NN_General	97.2%	**100.0%**	88.1%	93.6%
	OnlyComma	96.9%	**100.0%**	87.1%	93.1%
Speaker5	NN_Speaker	**97.4%**	99.5%	**89.1%**	**94.0%**
	NN_General	97.2%	**99.8%**	88.2%	93.6%
	OnlyComma	97.1%	**99.8%**	87.4%	93.8%
Speaker6	NN_Speaker	**91.8%**	98.8%	**72.6%**	**83.7%**
	NN_General	91.1%	**100.0%**	70.3%	82.6%
	OnlyComma	89.6%	**100.0%**	66.5%	79.9%

Table 4. The comparison of results for English voices

Speaker	Phrasing model	Acc	P	R	F1
Speaker1	NN_Speaker	**98.8%**	**100.0%**	**94.6%**	**97.2%**
	NN_General	98.6%	**100.0%**	93.6%	96.7%
	OnlyComma	98.5%	99.3%	93.8%	96.4%
Speaker2	NN_Speaker	**98.5%**	99.8%	**93.6%**	**96.6%**
	NN_General	98.3%	**100.0%**	92.8%	96.3%
	OnlyComma	97.6%	96.4%	93.0%	94.7%

Table 5. Listening test results.

	Break is OK	Tie	Break is strange
fp	14	5	6
fn	5	7	13

4   Conclusion

The paper focused on training a speaker-dependent neural-network model for phrase boundary detection and compared the results to the outputs of a general phrasing model (trained on data from several speakers) and to the results of the baseline system. The results presented in Sect. 3 show the advantages of speaker-dependent phrasing.

The *false positives* and *false negatives* were further examined during the listening test. The answers proved that not all of them are real mistakes so the ability of the proposed model to correctly detect appropriate phrase boundaries is very high.

The future work includes the training on different languages and testing the general and speaker-dependent models on a new, unseen speaker.

Acknowledgements. This research was supported by the Czech Science Foundation (GACR), project No. GA19-19324S, and by the grant of the University of West Bohemia, project No. SGS-2019-027.

References

1. Bird, S., Klein, E., Loper, E.: Natural Language Processing with Python: Analyzing Text with the Natural Language Toolkit. O'Reilly Media Inc., Newton (2009)
2. Fernandez, R., Rendel, A., Ramabhadran, B., Hoory, R.: Prosody contour prediction with long short-term memory, bi-directional, deep recurrent neural networks. In: INTERSPEECH 2014, pp. 2268–2272. ISCA (2014)
3. Hanzlíček, Z., Vít, J., Tihelka, D.: LSTM-based speech segmentation for TTS synthesis. In: Ekštein, K. (ed.) TSD 2019. LNCS (LNAI), vol. 11697, pp. 361–372. Springer, Cham (2019). https://doi.org/10.1007/978-3-030-27947-9_31
4. Hirschberg, J., Prieto, P.: Training intonational phrasing rules automatically for English and Spanish text-to-speech. Speech Commun. **18**(3), 281–290 (1996)
5. Hochreiter, S., Schmidhuber, J.: Long short-term memory. Neural comput. **9**(8), 1735–1780 (1997)
6. Hojo, N., Ijima, Y., Mizuno, H.: DNN-based speech synthesis using speaker codes. IEICE Trans. Inf. Syst. **101**(2), 462–472 (2018)
7. Jůzová, M.: Prosodic phrase boundary classification based on Czech speech corpora. In: Ekštein, K., Matoušek, V. (eds.) TSD 2017. LNCS (LNAI), vol. 10415, pp. 165–173. Springer, Cham (2017). https://doi.org/10.1007/978-3-319-64206-2_19
8. Jůzová, M.: On the comparison of different phrase boundary detection approaches trained on Czech TTS speech corpora. In: Karpov, A., Jokisch, O., Potapova, R. (eds.) SPECOM 2018. LNCS (LNAI), vol. 11096, pp. 255–263. Springer, Cham (2018). https://doi.org/10.1007/978-3-319-99579-3_27

9. Louw, J.A., Moodley, A.: Speaker specific phrase break modeling with conditional random fields for text-to-speech. In: 2016 Pattern Recognition Association of South Africa and Robotics and Mechatronics International Conference, pp. 1–6 (2016)
10. Matoušek, J., Romportl, J.: Automatic pitch-synchronous phonetic segmentation. In: INTERSPEECH 2008, pp. 1626–1629. ISCA, Brisbane, Australia (2008)
11. Matoušek, J., Tihelka, D., Psutka, J.: Experiments with automatic segmentation for Czech speech synthesis. In: Matoušek, V., Mautner, P. (eds.) TSD 2003. LNCS (LNAI), vol. 2807, pp. 287–294. Springer, Heidelberg (2003). https://doi.org/10.1007/978-3-540-39398-6_41
12. Mishra, T., Kim, Y.J., Bangalore, S.: Intonational phrase break prediction for text-to-speech synthesis using dependency relations. In: ICASSP 2015, pp. 4919–4923 (2015)
13. Prahallad, K., Raghavendra, E.V., Black, A.W.: Learning speaker-specific phrase breaks for text-to-speech systems. In: SSW (2010)
14. Read, I., Cox, S.: Stochastic and syntactic techniques for predicting phrase breaks. Comput. Speech Lang. **21**, 3233–3236 (2005)
15. Taylor, P.: Text-to-Speech Synthesis, 1st edn. Cambridge University Press, New York (2009)
16. Taylor, P., Black, A.: Assigning phrase breaks from part-of-speech sequences. Comput. Speech Lang. **12**, 99–117 (1998)
17. Tihelka, D., Hanzlíček, Z., Jůzová, M., Vít, J., Matoušek, J., Grůber, M.: Current state of text-to-speech system ARTIC: a decade of research on the field of speech technologies. In: Sojka, P., Horák, A., Kopeček, I., Pala, K. (eds.) TSD 2018. LNCS (LNAI), vol. 11107, pp. 369–378. Springer, Cham (2018). https://doi.org/10.1007/978-3-030-00794-2_40
18. Vít, J., Hanzlíček, Z., Matoušek, J.: Czech speech synthesis with generative neural vocoder. In: Ekštein, K. (ed.) TSD 2019. LNCS (LNAI), vol. 11697, pp. 307–315. Springer, Cham (2019). https://doi.org/10.1007/978-3-030-27947-9_26

Phonetic Attrition in Vowels' Quality in L1 Speech of Late Czech-French Bilinguals

Marie Hévrová[1,2]([✉]), Tomáš Bořil[1]([iD]), and Barbara Köpke[2]

[1] Faculty of Arts, Institute of Phonetics, Charles University,
Náměstí Jana Palacha 2, 116 38 Praha 1, Czech Republic
marie.hevrova@univ-tlse2.com
[2] URI Octogone-Lordat, Université Toulouse II – Jean-Jaurès,
5 allée Antonio Machado, 31058 Toulouse, France

Abstract. This study examines phonetic attrition of the first language (L1) affected by second language (L2) in Czech speakers living in Toulouse (late Czech-French bilinguals – CF). We compared the production of vowels by 13 CF and 13 Czech monolinguals living in the Central Bohemian Region (C). CF had been living in France for at least one year and started to learn French when they were more than 6 years old. Both C and CF were speakers of Common Czech. We recorded their production in reading task and semi-spontaneous speech and performed measurements of vowel formants. Results show a statistically significant difference between F1 of CF [aː] and F1 of C [aː], and between F3 of CF [iː] and F3 of C [iː]. These findings are discussed in relation to the perceptual approach suggesting that several vowels can be perceived as different in C and CF production.

Keywords: Phonetic attrition · Vowels' quality · Late Czech-French bilinguals

1 Introduction

Intensive use of an L2 can influence the speaker's L1 at the phonetic level [14], a phenomenon often branded as first language phonetic attrition or phonetic cross-linguistic influence. The former, first language attrition, refers to the non-pathological decline of previous L1 language skills [13], which happens as a "natural consequence of decrease in the [L1] use" [12] and consists of long-term changes due to extensive, and not necessarily recent, L2 contact [6]. The latter, cross-linguistic influence (CLI), introduced by [24], refers to any kind of effect that

Supported by a doctoral grant of the French Research Ministry, a Charles University PhD scholarship, the Charles University project SVV – 2019, *Jazyk a nástroje pro jeho zkoumání*, and by the Charles University project Progres Q10 *Language in the shiftings of time, space, and culture.*

© Springer Nature Switzerland AG 2020
P. Sojka et al. (Eds.): TSD 2020, LNAI 12284, pp. 348–355, 2020.
https://doi.org/10.1007/978-3-030-58323-1_38

one language may have on another. For [21], L1 attrition is one among these possible kinds of effect, a position we will adopt here.

For now, only a small part of studies in the area of phonetic attrition and CLI examined vowels by acoustic measurement (see, *e.g.,* [4,17]). In addition, there is no study on the influence of L2 French on L1 Czech at the phonetic level, although several interesting differences exist in the vowel systems of both languages (see [16]). The present paper proposes to fill this gap with a study investigating phonetic attrition in vowels' quality in the L1 speech of Czechs who have been living in France for more than one year and started to learn French after the age of six (henceforth CF, late Czech-French bilinguals).

1.1 Comparison of Czech and French Vowels

Without [ə], Czech comprises 10 monophthongal not nasalized vowels [25] and French 11 monophthongal not nasalized vowels [18]. Czech distinguishes short and long vowels contrary to French, where vowel's length is not a phonological feature. The articulatory features of these Czech and French vowels are described in Table 1 showing that these languages do not attribute the same articulatory properties to [ɛ], [a] and [o]. Some inconsistencies exist among authors in the IPA symbols used for certain vowels (see [16]). We use the symbol [u], and not [ʊ], for Czech /u/ for the reason of simplicity and the symbol [ɛ] for Czech /e/ because this sound is acoustically slightly nearer to French [ɛ] than to French [e].

Table 1. Articulatory properties of Czech and French not nasalized monophthongal vowels, (white column = Czech vowels, gray column = French vowels). Vowels with the same IPA symbol, but different articulatory properties are in bold. Source [16,18]

	Anteriority	Front		Central	Back	
	Lip shape	unrounded	rounded	unrounded	rounded	
Degree of aperture	Close	ɪ, iː	i	y		u, uː	u
	Close-mid		e	ø			o
	Mid	ɛ, ɛː				o, oː	
	Open-mid		**ɛ**	œ			ɔ
	Open		**a**		**a, aː**		ɑ

Regarding the link between articulatory and acoustic properties of vowels, the F1 is traditionally determined by degree of aperture and F2 by anteriority and lip articulation [18,25]. The F3 can also be determined by lip shape [18]. [29] also suggests to include F3 and F4 in acoustic studies of French vowels because F4 with F3 makes a prominent energy packet in the high frequencies (F3/F4). Therefore, in our study, we will analyse F1, F2, F3 and F4.

Based on the results of [10,20,26,27], Table 2 compares F1 and F2 means of Czech and French not nasalized vowels. In the present study, we focus on the production of CF, all female speakers, in a reading task (hereafter RT) and semi-spontaneous speech (hereafter SS). Therefore, the formants obtained from the production of only female speakers in RTs and SSs are compared in Table 2. [26] studied Czech vowels of 48 women aged from 20 to 30 years reading a continuous text. [27] analysed the production of 9 French women reading the monosyllables formed by either /pV1/, where V1 was /e/, /o/, /u/, /y/, or /ø/, or /pV2R/ where V2 was /i/, /ɛ/, /a/, /ɔ/, or /œ/. In [20], 10 Czech women aged 25–34 years commented spontaneously on 20 objects. [10] analysed a speech of 15 French women mainly extracted from broadcast news. We are conscious that the F1 and F2 means in Table 2 cannot be considered as reference values for any female speaker because each study used for the creation of Table 2 has its limitations. For example, [28] reproaches [27] that the /R/ used in coda position could lengthen the previous vowel and consequently increase the F1 value and decrease the F2 value.

The frequency difference limen (DLF) refers to the difference in the frequency values perceptible by the human ear [16]. The DLF for F1 is 10–30 Hz and 20–100 Hz for F2 according to [9]. In Table 2, the F1 values of vowels that differ in Czech and French from 30–60 Hz are in slight gray, and in dark gray when the difference is higher than 60 Hz. F2 values are in slight gray when the difference between Czech and French is 100–200 Hz, and in dark gray when the difference is more than 200 Hz. Table 2 does not contain the values of Czech [oː], as this vowel, infrequent in Czech speech, will not be analyzed in our study. Regarding F3 and F4, to the best of our knowledge, there is no study comparing these formants of Czech and French vowels produced in RTs and SSs. Only studies of formant values of vowels in isolation in Czech and French give means of F3 and F4 for certain vowels [16, 19].

In our study, all CF were living in the Toulouse area. [8] supports that French spoken in Toulouse differs from standard French although more than one variety of Toulouse French exists [7, 8]. For a majority of speakers from Toulouse, the phonological differences between French [e] and [ɛ], [œ] and [ø], [a] and [ɑ], and [ɔ] and [o] are absent in minimal pairs [8], while other speakers from Toulouse may respect these differences according to the position rule [7, 8]. Thus, from a phonological point of view, vowels in Toulouse French can differ from vowels of standard French. However, as far as we know, no study focused entirely on acoustic properties of Toulouse French vowels. Hence, we can only suppose that the Czech vowels of CF may be more influenced by vowels of Toulouse French than standard French. However, no prediction about this can be made as an acoustic study of Toulouse French vowels is lacking.

Taking into account all these considerations, we made the hypothesis that the phonetic CLI is more likely to occur in vowels which are acoustically slightly dissimilar in French and in Czech and in vowels which exist only in one of both languages.

Table 2. F1 and F2 of Czech and French vowels for female speakers in RTs and SSs according to [10, 20, 26, 27]. (CZ = Czech, FR = French).

Formant	Reading task				Semi-spontaneous speech			
	F1		F2		F1		F2	
Language	CZ	FR	CZ	FR	CZ	FR	CZ	FR
i	NA	350	NA	2400	NA	348	NA	2365
i:	328.5	NA	2603	NA	287	NA	2504	NA
ɪ	492.1	NA	2251.2	NA	411	NA	2177	NA
y	NA	350	2050	NA	NA	371	2063	NA
e	NA	450	NA	2300	NA	423	NA	2176
ɛ	686.3	650	1823	2000	650	526	1726	2016
ɛ:	709.5	NA	1904.3	NA	671	NA	1825	NA
a	780.9	750	1480.2	1550	733	685	1322	1677
a:	801.2	NA	1417.6	NA	784	NA	1436	NA
ø	NA	450	NA	1650	NA	420	NA	1693
œ	NA	550	NA	1650	NA	436	NA	1643
u	415.3	350	1003.6	850	330	404	1221	1153
u:	343.6	NA	757	NA	341	NA	851	NA
o	528	450	1166.2	950	474	438	1161	1140
ɔ	NA	600	NA	1200	NA	528	NA	1347

2 Method

We recorded the Czech production in RT and in SS of 13 female native Common Czech speakers (mean = 35.1 years) living in the Central Bohemian region of the Czech Republic (hereafter C) and 13 CF speakers of Common Czech (mean = 34.2 years). All CF have not never lived in any region where some variety of Czech different from Common Czech is spoken. They all declared not to think to speak Czech with some specific accent as for example Moravian accent in socio-linguistic form filled after recording. The average of their length of residence in France was 9.9 years (min = 1.42 year, max = 28.25 years). All C and CF speakers were aged 20–50 years, hence the stability of their f_0 was assured [11].

In the RT, the speakers read a short text chosen from [5]. In the SS, they talked for one minute and a half about one or more proposed topics such as plans for holidays or the next weekend, describing a typical day, job, studies, family, hobbies, etc. CF were recorded in a quiet recording studio (PETRA) at University of Toulouse using a Neumann TLM 49 microphone and sound card MOTU ULmk3. They received a small reward for participation. C were recorded in a quiet, comfortably furnished office with a low level of ambient noise and short natural reverberation in Prague. A head-mounted condenser microphone (Bayerdynamic Opus 55) was plugged directly into a pocket recorder set to uncompressed 48 kHz 16-bit mode.

All recordings were orthographically transcribed. Their semi-automatical segmentation and labeling in Praat [2] were corrected manually. Vowels' boundary placement was guided by the presence of full formant structure. Initial glottal stops and final voice decay time were not considered to be part of the vowel. Vowels ending by the schwa of hesitation, vowels in foreign words such as English names of movies or names of French cities, unpronounced and semi-pronounced vowels in the recordings of SS were excluded from the analysis. Vowels preceded or followed by nasal consonants in RT and in SS were excluded from the analysis too, since nasal context coarticulation may lead to uncontrolled extra formants. The Czech conjunction /a/, meaning "and" in English, longer than 150 ms was considered as a hesitation and excluded from analysis (cf. [23]). The conjunction /a/ with duration lower than 150 ms was labelled as a short Czech [a] and included in analysis. Formants were measured automatically using Praat script computing the mean of formant value from the second third of the vowel duration. This way, we resolved the issue of the effect of coarticulation on the formant value. In total, the analysis involved 10 147 vowels.

The data were analyzed in RStudio [22] using the packages lme4 [1], dplyr [31], rPraat [3], and ggplot2 [30]. We computed the mean value of each formant of each vowel for each task and each group separately. The significance level was set at $\alpha = 0.05$. In order to examine differences between C and CF vowels' formant values, we performed linear mixed-effects models for each formant of each vowel. We analyzed the relationship between group and formants' values. We had intercepts for speakers and words of the vowel's occurrence as random effects. As fixed effects, we entered group and task. Visual inspection of residual plots did not reveal any obvious deviations from homoscedasticity or normality. P-values were obtained by likelihood ratio tests of the full model with the effect in question against the model without the effect in question.

3   Results

The analysis showed that the group affected F1 of [aː] ($\chi^2(1) = 5.6428, p = 0.01753$) increasing the F1 value of CF by 51.17 Hz $\pm$ 21.18 (standard errors). This result is also visible on the Fig. 1 showing F1 and F2 fields with values in Hertz of C and CF obtained in RT and in SS. The group affected also F3 of [iː] ($\chi^2(1) = 7.5502, p = 0.006$) increasing the F3 value of CF by 114.41 Hz $\pm$ 40.13 (standard errors). There were no other significant results.

4   Discussion and Conclusions

Our study showed a significant difference between the groups in F1 value of [aː] and in F3 value of [iː]. By comparison of [aː] F1 value of our C in Table 3 with its values in Table 2, we suppose that the C [aː] F1 corresponds to the standard pronunciation of this vowel in Common Czech. Similarly, comparing the [iː] F3 value of our C with [20] results, we assume that the [iː] F3 of C corresponds to the standard pronunciation of this vowel in Common Czech.

As shown by [14], studies of phonetic L1 attrition and CLI support two possible explanations for sound changes: 'assimilation' and 'dissimilation'. In the former case, L1 sounds shift towards L2 sound's norms. In the latter case,

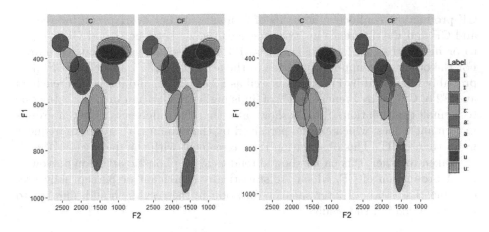

Fig. 1. Czech vowels in RT (left) and in SS (right) plotted in the F1-F2 plane. The ellipses indicate 50% of the formant values, shown in Hz

Table 3. Formant values of C and CF vowels which are supposed to be perceived as different. (v = vowel, m = mean, CI = confidence interval, light gray = C, dark gray = CF, RT = reading task, SS = semi-spontaneous speech)

v	F1m	F1_CI	v	F2m	F2_CI	v	F2m	F2_CI	v	F3m	F3_CI
	RT			SS			SS			RT	
aː	791	767, 815	iː	2421	2377, 2465	ɛː	1746	1701, 1792	iː	3236	3189, 3282
aː	881	855, 907	iː	2515	2490, 2541	ɛː	1912	1838, 1986	iː	3368	3313, 3424
	SS		ɪ	2023	2000, 2046	a	1481	1465, 1496		SS	
ɪ	439	434, 444	ɪ	2140	2115, 2166	a	1589	1570, 1608	iː	3115	3075, 3154
ɪ	417	411, 423	ɛ	1831	1814, 1848				iː	3320	3278, 3361
aː	778	765, 791	ɛ	1943	1924, 1962						
aː	861	844, 879									

the speaker tries to maintain a difference between L1 and L2 sound, which leads to deepening of the acoustic distance between these two sounds. In the light of this suggestion, the significant difference in [aː] F1 value between groups may be considered as the result of dissimilation: the acoustic distance between CF [aː] F1 and French [a] F1 is bigger than the difference between C [aː] F1 and French [a] F1 (see Table 2 and 3). For the CF [iː] F3 value, we can speak about assimilation. According to the study of vowels in isolation [16], the F3 of French [i] is significantly higher than the F3 of Czech [iː]. Therefore, the F3 of CF [iː] is probably influenced by French [i].

Using a perceptual approach, we suppose that DLF can predict if two sounds will be perceived as the same or different. Hence, Table 3 presents formants' mean values for vowels which are expected to be perceived differently in C and

CF production: confidence intervals of formants are not overlapping between C and CF and the difference in formants' mean value between C and CF is equal to or higher than DLF. [aː] F1 and [iː] F3 have been already discussed above. For the others, we suppose that, due to the assimilation, F1 and F2 of CF' [ɪ] is probably influenced by French [i] as well as F2 of CF' [ɛ] and [ɛː] is by French [ɛ] and F2 of CF' [a] by French [a]. F2 of [iː] is higher in CF than in C probably due to a small dissimilation. Table 3 shows also that the differences between groups in formant values, which can be perceived by the human ear, are more frequent in SS than in RT. This observation is in agreement with the findings of [15].

Taken together, this paper showed tendencies of phonetic attrition on vowels in L1 production of CF, which are statistically significant or perceptually predictable. The study of inter-speaker variation in the results should allow us to better understand the results.

References

1. Bates, D., Mächler, M., Bolker, B., Walker, S.: Fitting linear mixed-effects models using lme4. J. Stat. Softw. **67**(1) (2015)
2. Boersma, P., Weenink, D.: PRAAT: doing phonetics by computer (2019)
3. Bořil, T., Skarnitzl, R.: Tools rPraat and mPraat. In: Sojka, P., Horák, A., Kopeček, I., Pala, K. (eds.) TSD 2016. LNCS (LNAI), vol. 9924, pp. 367–374. Springer, Cham (2016). https://doi.org/10.1007/978-3-319-45510-5_42
4. Bullock, B.E., Dalola, A., Gerfen, C.: Mapping the patterns of maintenance versus merger in bilingual phonology: the preservation of [a] vs. [a] in Frenchville French. In: Montreuil, J.P.Y. (ed.) New Perspectives on Romance Linguistics: Phonetics, Phonology and Dialectology, pp. 15–30. John Benjamins, Amsterdam/Philadelphia (2006)
5. Čapek, K.: Jak se co dělá. O lidech. Československý spisovatel, Praha (1960)
6. Chang, C.: Phonetic drift. In: Schmid, M.S., Köpke, B. (eds.) The Oxford Handbook of Language Attrition, pp. 191–203. Oxford University Press, Oxford (2019)
7. Courdès-Murphy, L.: Nivellement et sociophonologie de deux grands centres urbains: Le système vocalique de Toulouse et de Marseille. Ph.D. thesis, Toulouse 2 (2018)
8. Durand, J.: Essai de panorama phonologique: Les accents du midi. In: Baronian, L., Martineau, F. (eds.) Le français d'un continent à l'autre. Mélanges offerts à Yves-Charles Morin, pp. 123–170. Presse de l'Université Laval, Québec (2009)
9. Flanagan, J.: Speech Analysis; Synthesis and Perception. Springer-Verlag, Berlin, New York (1972). https://doi.org/10.1007/978-3-662-01562-9
10. Gendrot, C., Adda-Decker, M.: Impact of duration on F1/F2 formant values of oral vowels: an automatic analysis of large broadcast news corpora in French and German. In: Interspeech 2005, pp. 2453–2456. Lisbon, Portugal (2005)
11. Hollien, H., Shipp, T.: Speaking fundamental frequency and chronologic age in males. J. Speech Hear. Res. **15**(1), 155–159 (1972)
12. Köpke, B.: First language attrition: from bilingual to monolingual proficiency? In: De Houwer, A., Ortega, L. (eds.) The Cambridge Handbook of Bilingualism. CUP, Cambridge (2019)
13. Köpke, B., Schmid, M.: Language attrition: the next phase. In: First Language Attrition: Interdisciplinary Perspectives on Methodological Issues, pp. 1–43. John Benjamins, Amsterdam (2004)

14. de Leeuw, E.: Phonetic attrition. In: Schmid, M.S., Köpke, B. (eds.) The Oxford Handbook of Language Attrition, pp. 204–217. Oxford University Press, Oxford (2019)
15. Major, R.C.: Losing English as a first language. Mod. Lang. J. **76**(2), 190–208 (1992)
16. Maurová Paillereau, N.: Perception et production des voyelles orales du français par des futures enseignantes tchèques de Français Langue Etrangère (FLE). Ph.D. thesis, Sorbonne Paris Cité (2015)
17. Mayr, R., Price, S., Mennen, I.: First language attrition in the speech of Dutch-English bilinguals: the case of monozygotic twin sisters. Bilingualism Lan. Cogn. **15**(4), 687–700 (2012)
18. Meunier, C.: Phonétique acoustique. In: Auzou, P. (ed.) Les dysarthries, pp. 164–173. Solal (2007)
19. Paillereau, N., Skarnitzl, R.: An acoustic-perceptual study on Czech monophthongs. In: Radeva-Bork, T., Kosta, P. (eds.) Current Developments in Slavic Linguistics. Twenty Years After, pp. 453–465. Peter Lang, Berlin (2020)
20. Paillereau, N., Chládková, K.: Spectral and temporal characteristics of Czech vowels in spontaneous speech. AUC PHILOLOGICA **2019**(2), 77–95 (2019)
21. Pavlenko, A.: L2 influence on L1 in late bilingualism. Issues Appl. Linguist. **11**(2) (2000)
22. R Core Team: R: A Language and Environment for Statistical Computing. R Foundation for Statistical Computing, Vienna, Austria (2019)
23. Rubovičová, C.: Tempo řeči a realizace pauz při konsekutivním tlumočení do češtiny ve srovnání s původními českými projevy. Magisterská práce. Univerzita Karlova, Filozofická fakulta, Fonetický ústav, Praha (2014)
24. Sharwood Smith, M.: Cross-linguistic aspects of second language acquisition. Appl. Linguist. **4**(3), 192–199 (1983)
25. Skarnitzl, R., Šturm, P., Volín, J.: Zvuková báze řečové komunikace: Fonetický a fonologický popis řeči. Karolinum, Praha (2016)
26. Skarnitzl, R., Volín, J.: Referenční hodnoty vokalických formantů pro mladé dospělé mluvčí standardní češtiny. Akustické listy **18**, 7–11 (2012)
27. Tubach, J.P.: La Parole et son traitement automatique. Paris Milan Barcelone, Masson (1989)
28. Vaissière, J.: Area functions and articulatory modeling as a tool for investigating the articulatory, acoustic and perceptual properties of sounds across languages. In: Solé, M., Beddor, P.S., Ohala, M. (eds.) Experimental Approaches Phonology, pp. 54–71. OUP, Oxford (2007)
29. Vaissière, J.: On the acoustic and perceptual characterization of reference vowels in a cross-language perspective. In: The 17th International Congress of Phonetic Sciences (ICPhS XVII), pp. 52–59, China (2011)
30. Wickham, II.: ggplot2: Elegant Graphics for Data Analysis. Springer-Verlag, New York (2016). https://doi.org/10.1007/978-0-387-98141-3
31. Wickham, H., François, R., Henry, L., Müller, K.: dplyr: A grammar of data manipulation, R package version 0.8.4 (2020)

Assessing the Dysarthria Level of Parkinson's Disease Patients with GMM-UBM Supervectors Using Phonological Posteriors and Diadochokinetic Exercises

Gabriel F. Miller[1]([✉])(iD), Juan Camilo Vásquez-Correa[2,3](iD), and Elmar Nöth[2](iD)

[1] Multimedia and Signal Processing Lab, Friedrich-Alexander-Universität, Erlangen-Nürnberg, Causerstr. 7, 91058 Erlangen, Germany
gabriel.f.miller@fau.de

[2] Pattern Recognition Lab, Friedrich-Alexander-Universität, Erlangen-Nürnberg, Martensstr 3, 91058 Erlangen, Germany
{juan.vasquez,elmar.noth}@fau.de

[3] Faculty of Engineering, University of Antioquia UdeA, Medellín, Colombia

Abstract. Parkinson's disease (PD) is a neuro-degenerative disorder that produces symptoms such as tremor, slowed movement, and a lack of coordination. One of the earliest indicators is a combination of different speech impairments called hypokinetic dysarthria. Some indicators that are prevalent in the speech of Parkinson's patients include, imprecise production of stop consonants, vowel articulation impairment and reduced loudness. In this paper, we examine those features using phonological posterior probabilities obtained via parallel bidirectional recurrent neural networks. We also utilize information such as the velocity and acceleration curve of the signal envelope, and the peak amplitude slope and variance to model the quality of pronunciation for a given speaker. With our feature set, we train Gaussian Mixture Model based Universal Background Models for a set of training speakers and adapt a model for each individual speaker using a form of Bayesian adaptation. With the parameters describing each speaker model, we train SVM and Random Forest classifiers to discriminate PD patients and Healthy Controls (HC), and to determine the severity of dysarthria for each speaker compared with ratings assessed by expert phoneticians.

1 Introduction

Parkinson's disease (PD) is a neuro-degenerative disorder that produces symptoms such as tremor, slowed movement, and lack of coordination. It is believed that the underlying cause for these physical symptoms is due to the immoderate spread of the protein α-synuclein throughout the peripheral and central nervous systems (PNS, CNS). The general function of α-synuclein is to help regulate the release of dopamine, a type of neurotransmitter that is critical for

© Springer Nature Switzerland AG 2020
P. Sojka et al. (Eds.): TSD 2020, LNAI 12284, pp. 356–365, 2020.
https://doi.org/10.1007/978-3-030-58323-1_39

controlling the start and stop of voluntary and involuntary movements [8]. In the case of PD patients, excessive α-synuclein begins to accumulate along the PNS and CNS, and is toxic to affected cells. This ultimately leads to a loss of neuronal populations, in particular, dopaminergic neurons in the substantia nigra and contralateral striatum, both being structures in the basal ganglia largely responsible for regulating both our reward network and motor systems [15,18]. Currently, there is no treatment to halt or slow the progression of PD, though there are several pharmacotherapeutic and neurosurgical options available that offer an alleviation of certain symptoms. A large contributing factor for there not being any stronger intervening methods, stems from the fact that the disease is often diagnosed after roughly 50% of neurons in the substantia nigra have been irrevocably damaged and over 80% of striatal dopamine has been depleted [17]. This highlights the importance of being able to identify the earliest symptoms of PD in order to be proactive in addressing the disease in the prodromal phase. This of course requires the ability to discern how severe symptoms of a given patient are, and quantify it accurately and consistently.

Speech is well known to be one of the more complex motor skills that we perform requiring precision from over 100 different muscles. This in turn makes our vocal system one of the more sensitive motor related systems to the effects of PD [4]. One of the earliest indicators of PD is a combination of different speech impairments called hypokinetic dysarthria that affects roughly 90% of all those diagnosed with PD [3,9,10,17]. Many studies have focused on identifying speech specific bio-markers that characterize these impairments and distinguish PD patients from healthy controls (HC). Some of the more prevalent speech symptoms include: a hoarse sounding voice, imprecise production of stop consonants (e.g. 'p', 't', 'k'), vowel articulation impairments, and reduced loudness [3,5].

With the aim to reduce the subjectivity of the clinical evaluation process when diagnosing potential PD patients, researchers have pushed to develop many different signal processing and machine learning techniques to identify PD. In [19], the authors considered phonological posterior features (a set of vectors that are used to express the pronunciation of a given speaker), recurrent neural networks based on gated recurrent units, as well as Mel frequency cepstrum coefficients (MFCCs) to assess speech impairments of PD patients. Results for assessing the different levels of dysarthria were best when all features were used. In [21], the authors proposed a series of different features that were used to predict the dysarthria level of both PDs and HCs, most notably articulation features (i.e. formant frequencies, MFCCs and their derivatives) and i-vectors. The scores were correlated with modified Frenchay-Dysarthria-Assessment (m-FDA) scores (a modified version of the common rating system used to evaluate dysarthria which is detailed in Sect 2.1), and Spearman-correlation results of up to 0.63 were achieved when using articulation features and 0.69 with the i-vector approach.

In this paper, we consider several novel ways of characterizing PD, the first one being with phonological posterior features. We believe these features are intuitive in nature; more so than features such as MFCCs or embeddings from neural networks as they are much more interpretable for clinicians [19]. The use of phonological posteriors has been considered for several applications related to pathological speech. In [20], the authors developed a tool to extract phonological posteriors directly from speech signals utilizing a bank of parallel bidirectional recurrent neural networks. These networks estimate the posterior probabilities of the occurrence of different phonological classes, with a reported accuracy over 90%. Another set of features we consider are statistics derived from the amplitude envelope of speech signals and modeled as a kinematic system. Such systems are said to capture the smoothed amplitude fluctuation pattern over time, illustrating how energy is distributed across a given signal [7]. These statistics have been shown to hold a correspondence to the kinematic statistics of the lower lip (i.e. lip velocity and acceleration), which in turn has been noted to be greater in speakers with PD relative to normal geriatrics [5].

The rest of the paper is organized as follows: in Sect. 2.1, we consider the materials and methods used in the evaluation process such as the data set and evaluation methods. In Sect. 2.2, we go more in-depth into the features that were considered. In Sect. 2.3, we discuss the classification method used to evaluate the aforementioned features; in particular their ability to classify PD and HC patients. We also detail how our classifier was used to identify the severity of the dysarthria of all patients. In short, this was done by training Gaussian Mixture Model based Universal Background Models (GMM-UBMs) for a set of training speakers, GMM-UBMs being one of the more dominant techniques for text-independent speaker recognition [14]. We then adapt a model for each individual speaker using a maximum a-posterior adaption process [14], and build GMM-UBM Mean Interval (GUMI) supervectors. We then use these supervectors to derive a kernel that measures the statistical dissimilarity between the UBM and a given adapted speaker distribution based on the Bhattacharyya distance [23]. Finally, we train SVM and Random Forest Classifiers based on the GUMI supervectors, to classify both PD and HC patients and to assess their respective severity of dysarthria. In Sect. 3 we look at the correlation between m-FDA scores and the different features considered, as well as discuss the results of our classifier in making the binary distinction between PD and HC patients, as well as predicting the dysarthria level via the m-FDA. It was found that the best Spearman correlation score when correlating the predicted m-FDA scores with the actual scores was roughly 0.6. These results are competitive to what has been achieved in studies that used more complex features.

2   Procedural Overview

2.1   Dataset and Evaluation Methods

The speech quality of patients is commonly addressed using diadochokinetic (DDK) exercises, which consist of the rapid repetition of syllables like /pa-ta-ka/ [22]. The exercise is particularly helpful in evaluating PD speakers, as it requires the continuous movement of different articulators such as the lips, tongue and velum. The performance of DDK tasks are variable with the timing in which patients perform the exercises, e.g. if a patient has just taken their medication, they generally tend to perform better. Though this was in a sense controlled for, it still is worth mentioning.

In this paper we consider a set of 100 speakers from the PC-GITA corpus [12] (50 PD patients and 50 HC subjects), all of them Colombian Spanish native speakers. All participants were recorded pronouncing the phrase /pa-ta-ka/ repeatedly and were evaluated remotely by clinicians with the m-FDA scale to measure their dysarthria severity [19]. Though the Movement Disorder Society–Unified Parkinson's Disease Rating Scale (MDS-UPDRS-III) is the commonly used scale to evaluate potential PD patients, it only utilizes one item out of 33 to evaluate speech. The FDA scale on the other hand covers a wide range of speech-related motor actions including reflex, respiration, lip movement, palate movement, laryngeal capacity, tongue posture/movement, intelligibility, and swallowing. However, in many cases travelling from home to a clinic is not possible, e.g. for those who live in more rural areas, or for many PD patients in intermediate or advanced stages who typically have a reduced mobility. To overcome some of these issues, the m-FDA scale was introduced. The scale was designed specifically such that it could be administered remotely and thus only considers speech recordings of a given patient and ignores tests such as swallowing which requires a clinician to be present in order to make an evaluation. Some of the different categories evaluated include respiration, lip movement, palate/velum movement, laryngeal movement, intelligibility, and monotonicity. In total, the scale considers 13 items, each of which are assigned scores from 0 (completely healthy) to 4 (very impaired). Thus the scale ranges from 0 to 52 [21].

It's worth noting that the evaluation of HC patients we considered included smokers, who exhibit some speech qualities commonly found in PD patients (e.g. hoarseness, or shortness of breath).

2.2   Features

Phonological Features. For pathological speech processing, only a small subset of basic features are commonly used, e.g. fundamental frequency, jitter, shimmer, or formant frequencies. More complex feature sets like MFCCs, Perceptual Linear Predictors, or embeddings from neural networks are sometimes avoided in this context due to their lack of interpretability [21]. Phonological features are believed to be a viable feature candidate when it comes to speech pathology, as they are commonly understood by clinicians as features describing the movements of the articulators in the vocal tract and also are robust in terms of relaying information about the dysarthria level of a patient. Phonological features are generally represented by phonological posteriors, the probabilities of phonological classes inferred from a given speech signal [1].

In our study, we consider classes that correspond to both plosive and voiced segments of speech. In particular we consider the following phonological classes: 'stop' and 'consonantal' (classes that include phonemes /p/, /t/, and /k/), 'back', and 'open' classes (classes that include /a/), and also the 'anterior' and 'close' classes (classes containing vowels /e/ and /i/ and /i/ and /u/ respectively). The 'stop', 'consonantal', 'back' and 'open' phoneme classes were all chosen as they contain phonemes that makeup the utterance, /pa-ta-ka/. Thus, the expectation for the class posteriors was that they would be higher for less dysarthric patients who are able to fully articulate each syllable. The 'close', and 'anterior' classes on the other hand were used to identify speakers that have difficulty in fully articulating the voiced segments of /pa-ta-ka/. Impairment of vowel articulation, is said to occur as a consequence of a reduced articulatory range of motion, i.e. "undershooting" of articulatory gestures, which is said to be a consequence of PD [9]. The phonological features were extracted using the Phonet toolkit [20], which is freely available and based on recurrent neural networks with gated recurrent units.

Kinematic Features. One of the more important aspects for qualitatively assessing dysarthria is rhythm [3,9,10]. It is well known that the pulmonic air pressure is the primary energy source of speech, and the amplitude modulation describing the pressure and rhythm for a given speaker is largely determined by articulatory behaviors, especially mandible and lip movements [7]. Furthermore, it is noted in [7] that the kinematic parameters of the amplitude envelope capture the smooth amplitude fluctuation pattern over time and indicate how energy is distributed across a given signal.

In practice, the kinematic parameters of the amplitude envelope are obtained by applying the Hilbert transform to the signal, taking the complex-modulus, applying a low pass filter, and then normalizing to consider any potential gain factor [7]. The result is known as a displacement curve. We then take the first and second order difference to obtain the envelope velocity and acceleration.

It was shown in [2,7] how these parameters correspond to articulatory movements during speech. Both papers assert that speaker-specific articulatory kinematics, including velocity, acceleration and spatial displacement reflect speaker individuality because of anatomical idiosyncrasies of the articulators and the way speakers acquired control over them. In particular, the authors in [2] noted that the amplitude envelope co-varied with the area of a speaker's mouth opening (i.e. larger mouth opening areas correlated with peaks in the amplitude envelope displacement curve), and the authors in [7] noted a correspondence between the amplitude envelope and lower lip kinematics. This was done by comparing the peaks and troughs of the displacement curve to the signal measurements of a speaker's lip and mandible movement measured by x-ray microbeams. It was shown that the two signals displayed a strong inverse correspondence, meaning peaks in the first and second order differences of the amplitude envelope typically matched with troughs in the lower lip displacement curve and vice-versa. Though the authors here did not consider speakers with dysarthria in particular, it has been shown in prior research that the lower lip closing velocities expressed as a function of movement amplitude are greater for PD speakers than for normal geriatrics [5]. It was also noted in this study that the increased velocity of lower lip movement may reflect a difference in control of lip elevation for PD speakers, an effect that increases with the severity of dysarthria.

Spectrogram Slope and Peak Standard Deviation. One characteristic common in Parkinson's disease speakers is an inconsistency of speech pattern in the subject speaker [3]. In order to model this, we apply a peak detection algorithm to the spectrogram of each speaker, and take the slope of a fitted line through these peaks. We also utilize the standard deviation of the peak amplitudes in order to evaluate the stability in the energy distribution for the different syllables in the DDK task. As noted in [3], previous findings of acoustic and kinematic studies report a reduced amplitude and velocity of articulators (lips, tongue, jaw) for PD patients, suggesting that articulation deficits reflect hypokinesia and rigidity of the vocal tract. We hypothesized the slope and peak amplitude information would convey this, with speech output volume decreasing over time (corresponding to a more negative slope), and a higher variation in peak amplitudes (corresponding to a higher variability in speech energy output).

2.3   Classification Method

GMM-GUMI Supervectors. One of the most common and effective tools used for text-independent speaker recognition, has been GMM-UBMs [13]. These models are well known for their effectiveness and scalability in modeling the spectral distribution of speech [23]. In this approach, speaker models are obtained from the adaptation of a GMM-UBM through the maximum a-posteriori (MAP) criterion. The GMM-UBM is usually trained by means of the expectation-maximization (EM) algorithm from a background data set, which includes a range of different speakers, and produces a set of parameters, namely mean vectors, covariance matrices and mixture weights, that characterize a speaker set.

For our considerations, we build three different types of UBMs, one consisting of only PD patients, one with HC, and one using a combination of both. We train each UBM based on the aforementioned features, with an optimal number of Gaussian components chosen via 10 fold cross validation. From the UBMs, we adapt speaker models for all patients in a leave two out manner (one PD and one HC patient left out per iteration), and build a GUMI supervector (stacked mean intervals output from the Bayesian adaptation process as detailed in [23]). We then classify PD patients and HC subjects using the GUMI supervectors and two different classification strategies: an SVM with a Bhattacharyya based kernel, and a random forest. We also consider a support vector regression (SVR) approach and a random forest-based regression to predict the m-FDA score assigned to the speakers by expert phoneticians.

3   Results

All extracted features were assigned a Spearman correlation score (with respect to the m-FDAs of all patients). The mean and standard deviation for all features

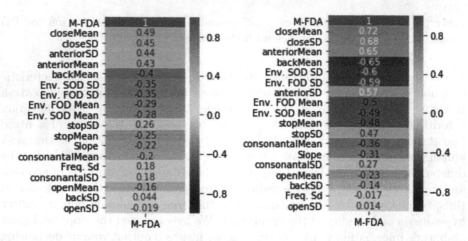

Fig. 1. Correlation between all features considered and m-FDA scores for the total set of speakers (left), and of the 90th percentile of extreme cases (m-FDA scores less than or equal to 2 or greater than or equal to 40) (right).

were estimated over consecutive utterances of the phrase /pa-ta-ka/. Results can be seen in Fig. 1. The average and standard deviation of the posterior probability output for the 'close' class (containing vowels /e/ and /i/) were among the highest absolute correlative scores with the m-FDA (0.49 for the mean and 0.45 for the standard deviation). The positive correlation is a result of the fact that patients that had a higher average posterior probability of uttering vowels /e/ or /i/ rather than /a/ are likely more dysarthric, meaning they would hypothetically have had a higher m-FDA score assigned to them. When we zoom in and look at the more extreme cases, (i.e. speakers with m-FDA scores less than or equal to 2 and greater than or equal to 40 which represents 10% of the overall set), correlative scores are higher. The 'anterior' class, which is said to be characterized by an obstruction located in front of the palato-alveolar region of the mouth [19] which also characterizes a speaker's inability to formulate the /a/ sound consistently, similarly performed well (correlation of 0.44, 0.43 for the mean, and standard deviation respectively for all cases and 0.57 and 0.65 in the more extreme cases). Kinematic features also exhibited high absolute correlative scores (-0.6 in the most extreme cases). This can be attributed to the link noted in [7] that the first and second order differences in the amplitude envelope for a given speaker inversely correspond to the velocity and acceleration of lower lip movement which as noted are typically higher in PD patients [5].

The results for binary classification (PD vs. HC) and for predicting the m-FDA scores of all speakers are shown in Table 1. Results are observed for each type of UBM, and for each classifier. The most accurate predictor with respect to binary classification was achieved with an HC based UBM and an SVM classifier (accuracy of 89%). This same model and classifier achieved the highest correlation predicting the m-FDA score (0.6). The performance of the HC based UBM can likely be attributed to the fact that range of m-FDA scores for PD patients was much more variable compared to HC patients. Thus, when training on only HC patients, there is a much clearer distinction for the classifier to recognize.

Table 1. Results of PD, HC and PD+HC based UBMs to classify patients using SVM and Random Forest (RF) classifiers. Results include the accuracy (ACC) classifying PD and HC subjects, and the Spearman's correlation coefficient ρ predicting the m-FDA score of the participants.

	ACC.	ρ	ACC.	ρ
	RF	RF	SVM	SVM
PD-based UBM	78.0	0.43	75.0	0.33
HC-based UBM	63.0	0.42	89.0	0.60
PD+HC-based UBM	63.0	0.26	72.0	0.24

4 Conclusions

In this paper we considered a set of different features that are useful in distinguishing PD and HC patients, and in assessing the severity of a given patient's speech dysarthria. The features were chosen such that they were both comprehensive and easily interpretable. It was found that the average back, open, anterior and close phoneme class posterior probabilities, as well as the average and standard deviation of the first and second order envelope kinematic parameters were among the strongest indicators, as seen by the correlation with patient m-FDA scores. Those features were also shown to be strongly correlated when considering the most extreme cases (i.e. patients with m-FDA scores above and below certain thresholds). Different methods for classification were also discussed and used to show that the considered features were in fact useful for classification purposes, as well as dysarthria assessment. The best results were found to be competitive with those obtained in studies that utilized more complex features.

The results obtained with our proposed method are similar and comparable to others reported in the literature when the same data was used, and which considered different sets of features. For instance, features based on phonation, articulation, and prosody [12], features based on Gaussian mixture model representations [11], features based on nonlinear dynamics [6], and empirical mode decomposition [16], among others.

Moving forward, studies considering hybrid models that utilize features such as MFCCs, or neural network embeddings as well as more easily interpretable features, such as those we considered in this paper, should be done. In addition, it would be of use to consider a wider variety of languages to ensure the results obtained are consistent in different contexts.

References

1. Cernak, M., Orozco-Arroyave, J., Rudzicz, F., Christensen, H., Vásquez-Correa, J., Nöth, E.: Characterisation of voice quality of Parkinson's disease using differential phonological posterior features. Comput. Speech Lang. **46**, 196–208 (2017)
2. Chandrasekaran, C., Trubabnova, A., Sébastien, S., Caplier, A., Ghazanfar, A.: The natural statistics of audiovisual speech. PLoS Comput. Biol. **5**, e1000436 (2009)
3. Chenausky, K., MacAuslan, J., Goldhor, R.: Acoustic analysis of PD speech. Parkinson's Dis. (2011)
4. Duffy, J.: Motor Speech Disorders: Substrates, Differential Diagnosis, and Management. Elsevier Health Sciences, Amsterdam (2013)
5. Forrest, K., Weismer, G., Turner, G.: Kinematic, acoustic, and perceptual analyses of connected speech produced by Parkinsonian and normal geriatric adults. J. Acoust. Soc. Am. **85**, 2608 (1989)
6. Godino-Llorente, J., Shattuck-Hufnagel, S., Choi, S., Moro-Velazquez, L., Gomez-Garcia, J.: Towards the identification of idiopathic Parkinson's disease from the speech. New articulatory kinetic biomarkers. PloS one **12**, e0189583 (2017)
7. He, L., Dellwo, V.: Amplitude envelope kinematics of speech signal: parameter extraction and applications. In: 28. Konferenz Elektronische Sprachsignalverarbeitung 2017, Saarbrücken (2017)
8. Hornykiewicz, O.: Biochemical aspects of Parkinson's disease. Neurology **51**, S2–S9 (1998)
9. Lai, B., Joseph, K.: Epidemiology of Parkinson's disease. BC Med. J. **43**, 133–137 (2001)
10. Lansford, K., Liss, J., Caviness, J., Utianski, R.: A cognitive-perceptual approach to conceptualizing speech intelligibility deficits and remediation practice in hypokinetic dysarthria. In: Communication Impairments in Parkinson's Disease, vol. 2011 (2011)
11. Moro-Velazquez, L., et al.: A forced gaussians based methodology for the differential evaluation of Parkinson's disease by means of speech processing. Biomed. Signal Process. Control **48**, 205–220 (2019)
12. Orozco-Arroyave, J.R., Arias-Londoño, J.D., Vargas-Bonilla, J.F., Gonzalez-Rátiva, M.C., Nöth, E.: New spanish speech corpus database for the analysis of people suffering from Parkinson's disease. In: Proceedings of the Ninth International Conference on Language Resources and Evaluation (LREC 2014), pp. 342–347 (2014)
13. Reynolds, D.: Comparison of background normalization methods for text-independent speaker verification. In: Proceedings of the European Conference on Speech Communication and Technology, pp. 963–966 (1997)
14. Reynolds, D., Quatieri, T., Dunn, R.: Gaussian Mixture Models, pp. 659–663. Springer, Boston (2009). https://doi.org/10.1007/978-0-387-73003-5
15. Rodriguez-Oroz, M., et al.: Initial clinical manifestations of Parkinson's disease: features and pathophysiological mechanisms. In: The Lancet Neurology, vol. 8, pp. 1128–1139. Lippincott-Raven (2009)
16. Rueda, A., Vásquez-Correa, J., Rios-Urrego, C., Orozco-Arroyave, J., Krishnan, S., Nöth, E.: Feature representation of pathophysiology of parkinsonian dysarthria. In: Proceedings of INTERSPEECH, pp. 3048–3052 (2019)
17. Rusz, J.: Detecting speech disorders in early Parkinson's disease by acoustic analysis. J. Acoust. Soc. Am. (2018)

18. Südhof, T.: Basic neurochemistry: molecular, cellular and medical aspects. In: Neurology 1998. Lippincott-Raven (1999)
19. Vásquez-Correa, J.C., Garcia-Ospina, N., Orozco-Arroyave, J.R., Cernak, M., Nöth, E.: Phonological posteriors and GRU recurrent units to assess speech impairments of patients with Parkinson's disease. In: Sojka, P., Horák, A., Kopeček, I., Pala, K. (eds.) TSD 2018. LNCS (LNAI), vol. 11107, pp. 453–461. Springer, Cham (2018). https://doi.org/10.1007/978-3-030-00794-2_49
20. Vásquez-Correa, J., Klumpp, P., Orozco-Arroyave, J., Nöth, E.: Phonet: a tool based on gated recurrent neural networks to extract phonological posteriors from speech. Proc. Interspeech **2019**, 549–553 (2019)
21. Vásquez-Correa, J., Orozco-Arroyave, J., Bocklet, T., Nöth, E.: Towards an automatic evaluation of the dysarthria level of patients with Parkinson's disease. J. Commun. Disord. **76**, 21–36 (2018)
22. Vásquez-Correa, J.C., Rios-Urrego, C.D., Rueda, A., Orozco-Arroyave, J.R., Krishnan, S., Nöth, E.: Articulation and empirical mode decomposition features in diadochokinetic exercises for the speech assessment of Parkinson's disease patients. In: Nyström, I., Hernández Heredia, Y., Milián Núñez, V. (eds.) CIARP 2019. LNCS, vol. 11896, pp. 688–696. Springer, Cham (2019). https://doi.org/10.1007/978-3-030-33904-3_65
23. You, C., Lee, K.A., Li, H.: GMM-SVM kernel with a Bhattacharyya-based distance for speaker recognition. IEEE Trans. Audio Speech Lang. Process. **18**, 1300–1312 (2010)

Voice-Activity and Overlapped Speech Detection Using x-Vectors

Jiří Málek[✉][iD] and Jindřich Ždánský

Institute of Information Technologies and Electronics,
Technical University of Liberec, Studentská 2, 46010 Liberec, Czech Republic
{jiri.malek,jindrich.zdansky}@tul.cz

Abstract. The x-vectors are features extracted from speech signals using pretrained deep neural networks, such that they discriminate well among different speakers. Their main application lies in speaker identification and verification. This manuscript studies, which other properties are encoded in x-vectors. The focus lies on distinguishing between speech signals/noise and utterances of a single speaker versus overlapped-speech.

We attempt to show that the x-vector network is capable to extract multi-purpose features, which can be used by several simple back-end classifiers. This means a common feature extracting front-end for the tasks of voice-activity/overlapped speech detection and speaker identification. Compared to the alternative strategy, that is training of independent classifiers including feature extracting layers for each of the tasks, the common front-end saves computational time during both training and test phase.

Keywords: Voice activity detection · Overlapped speech detection · x-vectors · Time-delayed deep neural networks

1 Introduction

The goal of speaker embeddings is to map utterances to fixed-dimensional vectors which encode characteristics of the given speaker. The concept of speaker embeddings has been introduced for tasks such as speaker recognition [23] and diarization [7]. Several embedding variants exist such as i-vectors [4] stemming from Gaussian-Mixture-Model-based Universal-Background-Model (GMM-UBM, [20]) or embeddings derived from Deep Neural Networks (DNN). The DNN-based features differ mostly by topology of the network used to extract them. The embeddings derived from fully-connected DNN (sometimes abbreviated as d-vectors) were proposed in [24], whereas utterance-based embeddings for analysis of sequences via long-short term memory (LSTM) networks were presented in [2,11]. The x-vectors studied in this work were introduced in [7,23]. These attempt to alleviate complicated training of sequence-based approaches and yet utilize the context contained in the utterance. The x-vectors are extracted using the time-delayed DNN (TDNN) topology proposed in [18].

© Springer Nature Switzerland AG 2020
P. Sojka et al. (Eds.): TSD 2020, LNAI 12284, pp. 366–376, 2020.
https://doi.org/10.1007/978-3-030-58323-1_40

Although the embeddings/x-vectors are primarily trained to contain information about the speakers, other properties are encoded within as well and are subject of studies. The authors in [26] study i-vectors and d-vectors from [2,24] to find suitability of the embeddings to classify qualities like utterance length, channel information, speaker gender or speaking rate. Recent work in [19] analyzes directly the x-vectors and next to to the already mentioned properties studies also environmental effects. This includes session identification (different instances of single speaker occurrence) and classification of background noise used for augmentation.

The speaker characteristics encoded in the embedding can be utilized to solve several problems besides already mentioned speaker identification and diarization. Fully supervised extraction of target speaker via pretrained DNN-based beamformer was presented in [30,31]. Blind source separation-based extraction of the desired speaker using x-vectors was proposed in [13]. In the context of speech recognition and voice assistant design, the adaptation of general multi-condition acoustic model for specific speaker using embeddings was presented in [29]. Application to speaker adaptive speech synthesis was presented using i-vectors, d-vectors and LSTM-based embeddings in [5,6,27], respectively.

This manuscript investigates, whether the x-vectors encode information about other speech-related properties, specifically absence of speech (non-speech) and presence of multiple active speakers (overlapped speech/cross-talk). Conventional approach to detection of these phenomenons lies in training of Gaussian mixture model (GMM,[15]) using pre-designed features. To this end, kurtosis, spectral flatness measure and mel frequency cepstral coefficients (MFCC) were utilized in [22,28]. Recently, DNN-based approaches were introduced in [14,21].

Our motivation for utilization of x-vectors for these tasks compared to training of a dedicated classifier lies in possibility of sharing common feature extracting front-end for several classification tasks, such as speaker identification and cross-talk/non-speech detection. This configuration lowers the computational demands of classification during both training and test phase. The extensive feature extractor is trained once and the rather undemanding back-end is retrained for multiple purposes. Such joint classifier is beneficial for speaker diarization [7] or when utilizing blind extraction methods for speech enhancement [13]. Without additional information, blind methods extract arbitrary speech source. It is thus beneficial to have prior information, whether to apply the extraction (i.e., detect speech segments with background noise and cross-talk segments) and whether the target speaker is active at all (i.e., perform identification of an active speaker).

We investigate an utterance-wise classification, where the whole utterance is assigned to one of three classes (non-speech, speech, cross-talk) and frame-wise classification, where each frame of the audio-signal is assigned independently. We compare several variants of augmentation for the training datasets of x-vector DNN and investigate functionality of the resulting networks with respect to presence of distortions (reverberation and background noise) in the test utterances.

Moreover, several configurations of the back-end classifiers are discussed, with respect to accuracy and complexity of the classifier.

2 Datasets and Methods

2.1 The x-Vector DNN

Our implementation of the x-vector DNN, described in Table 1, comes from [23]. Its input consists of a single-channel audio signal, i.e., no spatial information is used. The input features are 40 filter bank coefficients computed from frames of length of 25 ms and frame-shift of 12.5 ms. The TDNN (time-delayed DNN) layers introduced in [18] operate on frames with a temporal context centered on the current frame ℓ. The TDNN layers build on top of the context of the earlier layers, thus the final context is a sum of the partial ones.

In contrast to [23], we introduced four differences in the DNN: 1) We use all the frames in the context (and usually longer context) without any sub-sampling in order to exploit the time-dependencies in the signal. 2) To reduce the number of trainable parameters arising from the longer context, we weight all the frames in the context by a trainable matrix at the input of each TDNN layer and perform mean time-pooling. 3) We replaced the rectified linear units at the output of TDNN and fully-connected layers by exponential linear units (ELU), which speeds up convergence in our case. 4) The pooling layer computes only means of frames (variances are omitted) in the context, which is during the training phase set to $L_c = 101$.

The DNN was trained to classify N speakers and possibly non-speech class. The training examples consisted of 201 frames of features and the speaker label.

Table 1. Description of the DNN producing the x-vectors. The input size for the TDNN layers is stated after the mean pooling operation.

Layer	Layer context	Total context	Input × output
TDNN 1	$\ell \pm 80$	161	40×1024
TDNN 2	$\ell \pm 4$	169	1024×768
TDNN 3	$\ell \pm 4$	177	768×512
TDNN 4	$\ell \pm 4$	185	512×384
TDNN 5	$\ell \pm 4$	193	384×256
TDNN 6	$\ell \pm 4$	201	256×128
Fully-conn. 1	ℓ	201	128×128
Pooling	$\ell \pm \frac{L_c - 1}{2}$	$\max(201, L_c)$	$(L_c \cdot 128) \times 128$
Fully-conn. 2	ℓ	$\max(201, L_c)$	128×128
Softmax	$-$	$\max(201, L_c)$	$128 \times N$

2.2   Back-End Classifiers

To process the x-vector embeddings, we utilize three classifiers, which were previously used either directly for cross-talk detection or speaker identification; namely GMM [15], probabilistic linear discriminant analysis (PLDA, [12]) and fully-connected DNN [9]. We assign into three classes: 1) non-speech, which includes silence and noise-only audio, 2) speech, corresponding to utterances of a single person and 3) overlapped speech/cross-talk, for simultaneous talking of two people. The x-vectors are length-normalized prior back-end classifier training. For specific information on training dataset, see Sect. 2.3.

We train the GMM via the maximum-likelihood approach using the expectation-maximization algorithm. The models employ full covariance matrix. The number of components for each class is selected in interval $1 - 25$, via minimization of the Akaike information criterion (AIC). The GMM classifier trained in this manner is rather large, featuring from $490k - 655k$ of free parameters. The precise number varies for each of the x-vector variants. In order to reduce the number of model parameters, we employ optional feature-vector dimensionality reduction via Linear Discriminant Analysis (LDA, efficient implementation from [3]). Since three classes are classified, the reduced feature-vector dimension is 2 and the classifier consists of 15 free parameters.

We utilize the PLDA classifier in a similar form, which is widely applied in speaker identification and diarization scenarios. Here, a hypothesis is tested whether the embedding of an unknown test example is produced by any of known classes (speakers). The known speakers are represented by embeddings computed from short clean utterances called enrollments. In this form, the PLDA has advantage that it allows classification of a class (speaker) unseen in the training phase (open class-set). This advantage is not exploited for the given task, since here we work with known classes/closed class-set. We do not perform any feature dimensionality reduction prior the PLDA modeling, which results into models with about 65k parameters. The selection of the enrollment signals is discussed in Sect. 2.3.

Our DNN classifier has fully-connected topology. The input layer of size 128 accepts one x-vector without any context, in order to be comparable to the other back-end classifiers. Based on best results in preliminary experiments, we selected the hyper-parameters such that the DNN contains one hidden layer of size 128 and ReLU nonlinearity. Training proceeds through minimization of cross-entropy loss via Adam optimizer. The classifier contains about 17k trainable parameters.

2.3   Training Datasets and Their Augmentations

The training data for the x-vector DNN originate from the development part of the Voxceleb database [16] and the training part of the LibriSpeech corpus [17]. The data from training part of the TIMIT dataset [8] are used to train the back-end classifiers. VoxCeleb is an audio-visual dataset consisting of short clips of human speech, extracted from interview videos uploaded to YouTube.

The provided utterances are recorded in various environments and may contain reverberation and background noise. The part of the Librispeech dataset designated "train-360-clean" is utilized in our training. It contains excerpts of read audio-books with total duration 360 hours. The data should be rather free of distortions thus we subject it to additional augmentations. The TIMIT corpus for automatic speech recognition consists of 6300 English phonetically rich sentences read by 630 speakers. The dataset is recorded in anechoic and practically noiseless environment, thus we apply additional augmentations to it as well.

The train set of the x-vector network, as summarized in Table 2, is compiled in three variants, in order to study the influence of various augmentations on the classification. Each training set contains one instance of Voxceleb dataset without any additional augmentation. Further, one or more instances of Librispeech dataset are added, each with one of the following augmentations:

1. *None:* The original Librispeech dataset.
2. *Reverberation:* The utterances are convolved with artificial impulse responses generated by [10]. The artificial RIRs originate from a shoe-box room of size $8 \times 7 \times 3$. We generate RIRs corresponding to four different rooms with T_{60} ranging from $175 - 650$ ms. The source-microphone distance is $1 - 2$ m.
3. *Noise:* The background noise with was added to the original Librispeech dataset.
4. *Reverberation+noise:* The background noise with was added to the reverberated Librispeech dataset.

Noises for augmentations by background noise are taken from the training part of the CHiME-4 simulated dataset ([25], we use channel 1 of six-channel recordings) and the development dataset available in the Task 1 of the DCASE2018 challenge [1]. This data were also added to the training set without speech, creating a *non-speech class* besides the speakers classified by the network.

The noise in the background is amplified, such that the signal-to-noise ratio (SNR) measured in intervals with active speech is 10 dB. This means that the noise is louder compared to global SNR case, when the whole signals are considered without respect to speech activity.

The Training Set of the Back-End Classifiers requires smaller amounts of data, since the classifiers contain smaller number of free parameters. It is derived from the training part of the TIMIT corpus [8]. The original training data consist of 4620 sentences uttered by 462 speakers. A subset of 4400 utterances is used to train the classifiers, 220 sentences are reserved for the enrollment of PLDA.

Since the TIMIT dataset does not contain any cross-talk or environmental distortions, we introduce the overlap and signal augmentations artificially. This is done in a manner similar to [21], in order to make the results approximately comparable to this work. We leave one instance of a sentence as it is (speech class). Another instance containing cross-talk is created, such that an utterance of a different speaker is selected and summed together. A random shift is introduced at the beginning of the summed utterance, such that a minimum length of overlap is one second. The frame-wise true class-labels are created using energy thresholding of the original TIMIT files. Reverberation and noise are added in combinations as described for the x-vector DNN training set. The noise data originate from the train part of the CHiME-4 dataset [25]. Because the x-vector network requires context of frames, the classification of short sentences is burdened with higher error rate. To mitigate, we add 100 frames of non-speech to the beginning and end of the augmented signals.

The described procedure results in 4400 (utterances) × 2 (speech classes) × 5 (reverberation conditions including anechoic) × 2 (background noise presence) + 6900 (noise-only signals) = 94900 training signals and 220 × 2 × 5 × 2 + 238 = 4638 enrollment sentences for PLDA. From each such signal one feature vector for training of back-end classifiers is created. It is an average of all vectors corresponding to the most represented class in the signal.

Table 2. X-vector network variants

X-vector variant	Augmentations
X-vec:Rev	None, reverberation
X-vec:NoiBg	None, reverberation, noise
X-vec:NoiComp	None, reverberation, noise, reverberation+noise, non-speech class

2.4 Test Dataset

Out test dataset is derived from the test part of the TIMIT corpus [8]. The cross-talk is introduced in a same manner as described in Sect. 2.3 for the training set of the back-end classifiers. The original test data consist of 1680 sentences uttered by 168 speakers, sampled at 16 kHz. The noise data originate from the test part of the CHiME-4 dataset [25]. This results in 1680 (utterances) × 2 (speech classes) × 5 (reverberation conditions including anechoic) × 2 (background noise presence) + 2960 (noise-only signals) = 36560 test signals. In other words, there is 16800 signals of both speech and cross-talk in various acoustic conditions and 2960 examples of noise-only signals.

Considering the frame-wise occurrence of classes, about 58% of frames corresponds to speech, 21% to cross-talk and 21% to non-speech. Non-speech frames are located in the noise-only signals and also at the boundaries of speech in all other files.

3 Experiments

We report results of two types of experiments in this section.

1. *The utterance-wise experiments* are designed to assign a single class label to each of the test files. These are meant to verify, whether the x-vectors encode

the information about non-speech/cross-talk. The reference for each file is selected such that: 1) Non-speech is assigned to files with no speech, 2) Speech is assigned to files with speech and without cross-talk and 3) Cross-talk is assigned to files with overlapping utterances. The classification proceeds only on frames, which correspond to the true file reference. An average feature vector is computed using these frames and assigned to the class using one of the back-end classifiers. The utterance-wise experiments tend to be overly optimistic, because the decision of the classifier is supported by information obtained from multiple frames.

2. *The frame-wise experiments* correspond to practical utilization of the classifiers in the real-world, classifying each of the frames within a signal separately. The result for each test file is a set of time-aligned estimated class-labels.

The results are reported separately for each of the acoustic conditions within the test set. There are 3360 anechoic noiseless signals, 16800 noiseless signals (both reverberated and anechoic), 2960 noise-only signals and 16800 noisy signals. The experiments are evaluated using accuracy [%], either per-file for utterance-wise experiments or per-frame for frame-wise scenarios.

The comparison of x-vector network configurations is performed with the GMM classifier without any dimensionality reduction in Sects. 3.1 and 3.2. Using the best configuration, we compare the various discussed back-end classifiers in Sect. 3.3.

3.1   Utterance-Wise Experiments

The results summarized in Table 3 indicate that the x-vectors encode the non-speech/cross-talk information. The classification is highly accurate (more than 95%) for both anechoic and reverberant noiseless conditions. The features also well discriminate the non-speech class (more than 99%).

The classification seems to be significantly less accurate in the presence of background noise. The accuracy drops to 65.9% for X-vec:Rev, which does not have any noisy data within its training set. The augmentations applied to the training data of the x-vector network compensate partly for this deterioration. The best accuracy for the noisy data rises to 80.6%, achieved by the X-vec:NoiComp network.

Table 3. Accuracy [%] achieved in the utterance-wise experiments using GMM back-end classifier.

X-vector variant	Anechoic	Noiseless	Noise-only	Noisy	Total
X-vec:Rev	99.38	95.30	99.93	65.93	82.18
X-vec:NoiBg	98.69	95.96	99.90	73.98	86.18
X-vec:NoiComp	98.78	96.07	99.90	80.61	89.27

3.2   Frame-Wise Experiments

The accuracy is lower compared to the utterance-wise case; the best total accuracy is 76.7% achieved by the X-vec:NoiComp variant. We conjecture that this is caused: 1) by the fact that the back-end classifiers analyze each frame independently (compared to frame-average over the whole signal) and 2) by the design of the back-end training, which corresponds to utterance-wise classification. The training examples are averages of x-vectors in training signals, which may be too approximate for the frame-wise scenario.

The effect of augmentation is also much less significant for the frame-wise experiment. The X-vec:NoiComp network outperforms the X-vec:Rev variant by 1.2% in total results, compared to more than 7% for utterance-wise classification (Table 4).

Table 4. Accuracy [%] achieved in the frame-wise experiments using GMM back-end classifier.

X-vector variant	Anechoic	Noiseless	Noise-only	Noisy	Total
X-vec:Rev	82.70	76.18	99.73	67.30	75.48
X-vec:NoiBg	81.56	75.98	99.51	68.11	75.72
X-vec:NoiComp	82.49	77.82	99.55	68.48	76.68

3.3   Comparison of Back-End Classifiers

The comparison of the back-end classifiers is presented in Table 5. The highest accuracy (76.7%) is achieved using the GMM classifier without any dimensionality reduction. The DNN classifier yields total accuracy lower by 1.6%, however, it has the advantage of significantly lower number of free parameters ($528k$ for the GMM and $17k$ for the DNN). Compared to GMM, the GMM:LDA and PLDA achieve total accuracy lower by about 3%. PLDA achieves the lowest accuracy for the non-speech class. We conjecture, this is partly due to sub-optimal enrollment set, which is difficult to compile for the heterogeneous non-speech class. All classifiers (i.e., x-vectors in general) are highly accurate for detection of long intervals of non-speech (column Noise-only in Table 5), however encounter errors at the boundaries of speech.

This experiment can be partially compared to investigation performed in [21], where similar (but not identical) test set was created by adding augmentation via reverberation and background noise to TIMIT. In [21], the baseline classifier (GMM model trained on MFCC, spectral-flatness measure and kurtosis) achieved 64.5% accuracy on the noisy data. Thus, the x-vectors appear to be better suited to the discussed classification then the conventional pre-designed features. However, the DNN-based feature extractors/classifiers dedicated to classification of cross-talk achieved accuracy 71.8 − 79.9% on the noisy data, thus outperforming the x-vectors.

Table 5. Comparison of back-end classifiers via accuracy [%] obtained in the frame-wise experiments using x-vector setting X-vec:NoiComp. Last three columns state accuracy for each class achieved on the whole test dataset.

Classifier	Anechoic	Noiseless	Noise-only	Noisy	Total	Total speech	Total cross-talk	Total non-speech
GMM (no reduction)	82.49	77.82	99.55	68.48	76.68	77.78	77.64	73.77
GMM:LDA	80.16	76.81	99.80	62.99	73.90	65.75	86.91	83.19
PLDA	80.13	76.35	92.46	65.22	73.68	73.33	83.59	64.51
DNN	82.23	75.55	99.42	67.12	75.09	71.29	86.48	73.97

4 Conclusions

This manuscript investigated to what extend the speech presence and cross-talk are encoded within the x-vector features. The following conclusions were drawn: 1) The x-vectors can be used for detection of cross-talk and non-speech in a frame-wise manner, especially for environments with low activity of background noise. 2) The detection using x-vectors outperforms the conventional pre-designed features, such as kurtosis or MFCC, but it achieves lower accuracy compared to DNN-based feature extractors/classifiers specialized for this task. 3) The negative effects of reverberation can be mitigated to high degree using the augmentation of training data for the x-vector network. 4) Significant accuracy deterioration is observed on data with background noise; the augmentation does have limited effect here. 5) The GMM classifier without any dimensionality reduction achieves the highest accuracy from the back-end classifiers. The accuracy of DNN classifier is slightly lower, but it consists of considerably less trainable parameters.

For the future work: 1) In the current form, the frame-wise classification suffers from short spurious changes between classes, especially for noisy environments. This behavior can be mitigated by inclusion of smoothing of the output results, e.g., in the form of weighted finite-state transducers. 2) Frame-wise classification can be improved by training a back-end classifier, which takes frame context into consideration, such as TDNN or convolutional neural network. 3) The classification may be improved by inclusion of the cross-talk directly in the training of the x-vector network. However, direct addition of a cross-talk class to the training dataset violates the idea behind the current targets of the x-vector network, i.e., one speaker is active in one training utterance at the most. More plausible variant lies in a change of the x-vector network cost-function/targets. One variant is to allow multi-label classification, i.e., the training utterance can contain more than one speaker.

Acknowledgments. This work was supported by the Technology Agency of the Czech Republic (Project No. TH03010018).

References

1. DCASE 2018 challenge. http://dcase.community/challenge2018/index. Accessed 27 Mar 2020
2. Bhattacharya, G., Alam, J., Stafylakis, T., Kenny, P.: Deep neural network based text-dependent speaker recognition: preliminary results. In: Proceedings of the Odyssey, pp. 2–15 (2016)
3. Cai, D., He, X., Han, J.: SRDA: an efficient algorithm for large-scale discriminant analysis. IEEE Trans. Knowl. Data Eng. **20**(1), 1–12 (2007)
4. Dehak, N., Kenny, P.J., Dehak, R., Dumouchel, P., Ouellet, P.: Front-end factor analysis for speaker verification. IEEE Trans. Audio Speech Lang. Process. **19**(4), 788–798 (2010)
5. Doddipatla, R., Braunschweiler, N., Maia, R.: Speaker adaptation in DNN-based speech synthesis using d-vectors. In: INTERSPEECH, pp. 3404–3408 (2017)
6. Fu, R., Tao, J., Wen, Z., Zheng, Y.: Phoneme dependent speaker embedding and model factorization for multi-speaker speech synthesis and adaptation. In: ICASSP 2019–2019 IEEE International Conference on Acoustics, Speech and Signal Processing (ICASSP), pp. 6930–6934. IEEE (2019)
7. Garcia-Romero, D., Snyder, D., Sell, G., Povey, D., McCree, A.: Speaker diarization using deep neural network embeddings. In: 2017 IEEE International Conference on Acoustics, Speech and Signal Processing (ICASSP), pp. 4930–4934. IEEE (2017)
8. Garofolo, J.S., et al.: TIMIT acoustic-phonetic continuous speech corpus. Linguist. Data Consortium **10**(5) (1993)
9. Goodfellow, I., Bengio, Y., Courville, A.: Deep Learning. MIT Press, Cambridge (2016). http://www.deeplearningbook.org
10. Habets, E.A.: Room impulse response generator. Technische Universiteit Eindhoven, Technical report, vol. 2(2.4), p. 1 (2006)
11. Heigold, G., Moreno, I., Bengio, S., Shazeer, N.: End-to-end text-dependent speaker verification. In: 2016 IEEE International Conference on Acoustics, Speech and Signal Processing (ICASSP), pp. 5115–5119. IEEE (2016)
12. Ioffe, S.: Probabilistic linear discriminant analysis. In: Leonardis, A., Bischof, H., Pinz, A. (eds.) ECCV 2006. LNCS, vol. 3954, pp. 531–542. Springer, Heidelberg (2006). https://doi.org/10.1007/11744085_41
13. Janský, J., Málek, J., Čmejla, J., Kounovský, T., Koldovský, Z., Žd'ánský, J.: Adaptive blind audio source extraction supervised by dominant speaker identification using x-vectors. In: ICASSP 2020–2020 IEEE International Conference on Acoustics, Speech and Signal Processing (ICASSP), pp. 676–680 (2020)
14. Kunešová, M., Hrúz, M., Zajíc, Z., Radová, V.: Detection of overlapping speech for the purposes of speaker diarization. In: Salah, A.A., Karpov, A., Potapova, R. (eds.) SPECOM 2019. LNCS (LNAI), vol. 11658, pp. 247–257. Springer, Cham (2019). https://doi.org/10.1007/978-3-030-26061-3_26
15. McLachlan, G.J., Peel, D.: Finite Mixture Models. Wiley, Hoboken (2004)
16. Nagrani, A., Chung, J.S., Zisserman, A.: Voxceleb: a large-scale speaker identification dataset. arXiv preprint arXiv:1706.08612 (2017)
17. Panayotov, V., Chen, G., Povey, D., Khudanpur, S.: Librispeech: an ASR corpus based on public domain audio books. In: 2015 IEEE International Conference on Acoustics, Speech and Signal Processing (ICASSP), pp. 5206–5210. IEEE (2015)
18. Peddinti, V., Povey, D., Khudanpur, S.: A time delay neural network architecture for efficient modeling of long temporal contexts. In: Sixteenth Annual Conference of the ISCA (2015)

19. Raj, D., Snyder, D., Povey, D., Khudanpur, S.: Probing the information encoded in x-vectors. arXiv preprint arXiv:1909.06351 (2019)
20. Reynolds, D.A., Quatieri, T.F., Dunn, R.B.: Speaker verification using adapted gaussian mixture models. Digit. Signal Process. **10**(1–3), 19–41 (2000)
21. Sajjan, N., Ganesh, S., Sharma, N., Ganapathy, S., Ryant, N.: Leveraging LSTM models for overlap detection in multi-party meetings. In: 2018 IEEE International Conference on Acoustics, Speech and Signal Processing (ICASSP), pp. 5249–5253. IEEE (2018)
22. Shokouhi, N., Sathyanarayana, A., Sadjadi, S.O., Hansen, J.H.: Overlapped-speech detection with applications to driver assessment for in-vehicle active safety systems. In: 2013 IEEE International Conference on Acoustics, Speech and Signal Processing, pp. 2834–2838. IEEE (2013)
23. Snyder, D., Garcia-Romero, D., Sell, G., Povey, D., Khudanpur, S.: X-vectors: robust DNN embeddings for speaker recognition. In: 2018 IEEE International Conference on Acoustics, Speech and Signal Processing (ICASSP), pp. 5329–5333. IEEE (2018)
24. Variani, E., Lei, X., McDermott, E., Moreno, I.L., Gonzalez-Dominguez, J.: Deep neural networks for small footprint text-dependent speaker verification. In: 2014 IEEE International Conference on Acoustics, Speech and Signal Processing (ICASSP), pp. 4052–4056. IEEE (2014)
25. Vincent, E., Watanabe, S., Nugraha, A.A., Barker, J., Marxer, R.: The 4th CHiME speech separation and recognition challenge. http://spandh.dcs.shef.ac.uk/chime_challenge/chime2016/. Accessed 27 Mar 2020
26. Wang, S., Qian, Y., Yu, K.: What does the speaker embedding encode? In: Interspeech, pp. 1497–1501 (2017)
27. Wu, Z., Swietojanski, P., Veaux, C., Renals, S., King, S.: A study of speaker adaptation for DNN-based speech synthesis. In: Sixteenth Annual Conference of the International Speech Communication Association (2015)
28. Yella, S.H., Bourlard, H.: Overlapping speech detection using long-term conversational features for speaker diarization in meeting room conversations. IEEE/ACM Trans. Audio Speech Lang. Process. **22**(12), 1688–1700 (2014)
29. Zhao, Y., Li, J., Zhang, S., Chen, L., Gong, Y.: Domain and speaker adaptation for cortana speech recognition. In: 2018 IEEE International Conference on Acoustics, Speech and Signal Processing (ICASSP), pp. 5984–5988. IEEE (2018)
30. Zmolikova, K., Delcroix, M., Kinoshita, K., Higuchi, T., Ogawa, A., Nakatani, T.: Speaker-aware neural network based beamformer for speaker extraction in speech mixtures. In: Interspeech, pp. 2655–2659 (2017)
31. Zmolikova, K., et al.: Speakerbeam: speaker aware neural network for target speaker extraction in speech mixtures. IEEE J. Sel. Topics Signal Process. **13**(4), 800–814 (2019)

Introduction of Semantic Model to Help Speech Recognition

Stephane Level, Irina Illina[⊠][iD], and Dominique Fohr

Université de Lorraine, CNRS, Inria, 54000 Nancy, France
{irina.illina,dominique.fohr}@loria.fr

Abstract. Current Automatic Speech Recognition (ASR) systems mainly take into account acoustic, lexical and local syntactic information. Long term semantic relations are not used. ASR systems significantly decrease performance when the training conditions and the testing conditions differ due to the noise, etc.. In this case the acoustic information can be less reliable. To help noisy ASR system, we propose to supplement ASR system with a semantic module. This module re-evaluates the N-best speech recognition hypothesis list and can be seen as a form of *adaptation in the context of noise*. For the words in the processed sentence that could have been poorly recognized, this module chooses words that correspond better to the semantic context of the sentence. To achieve this, we introduced the notions of a *context part* and *possibility zones* that measure the similarity between the semantic context of the document and the corresponding possible hypothesis. The proposed methodology uses two continuous representations of words: *word2vec* and *FastText*. We conduct experiments on the publicly available TED conferences dataset (TED-LIUM) mixed with real noise. The proposed method achieves a significant improvement of the word error rate (WER) over the ASR system without semantic information.

Keywords: Automatic Speech Recognition · Semantic context · Embeddings

1 Introduction

Despite constant efforts and some spectacular advances, the ability of a computer to recognize speech is still far from equaling that of humans. Current ASR systems significantly deteriorate performance when the conditions in which they are trained and those in which they are used differ. The causes of variability between these conditions can be the acoustic environment and/or the acquisition of the signal. Even if many approaches to compensate this variability have been proposed [18], the performance of an ASR system on a given word always depends on the distortion at the precise moment when this word was spoken.

Current ASR systems mainly take into account only acoustic (acoustic model), lexical and syntactic information (local n-gram language models). We

© Springer Nature Switzerland AG 2020
P. Sojka et al. (Eds.): TSD 2020, LNAI 12284, pp. 377–385, 2020.
https://doi.org/10.1007/978-3-030-58323-1_41

suggest moving towards a *contextualization* of the ASR system. Indeed, lexical and semantic information is important for an ASR system to be efficient. Recently, several researchers have proposed to use semantic information to improve the ASR performance. For example, exploring the topic and semantic context to enable the recovery of proper names [14], using a semantic language model based on the theory of frame semantics [2], assigning semantic category labels to entire utterances and re-ranking the N-best list of ASR [11]. [7] learns semantic grammar for the ASR system. In [5] authors combine information from the semantic parser and ASR's language model for re-ranking. In [4], a method for re-ranking black-box ASR hypotheses using an in-domain language model and semantic parser trained for a particular task is investigated.

In this article, we propose to complete the noisy ASR step by adding the semantic information in order to detect the words in the processed sentence that could have been poorly recognized and to investigate words of similar pronunciations that correspond better to the context. This semantic analysis re-evaluates (rescores) the N-best transcription hypotheses (N-best) and can be seen as a form of *dynamic adaptation in the specific context of noisy data*. Reevaluation is performed through a definition of context part and possibility zones. Semantic information is introduced using predictive continuous representations [3,9]. These representations have proven to be effective for a series of natural language processing tasks [1]. The efficiency and the semantic properties of these representations motivate us to explore them for our task of ASR in mismatched conditions. We hope that in very noisy parts, the language model and the semantic model could remove the acoustic ambiguities in order to find the words spoken by the speaker. All our models are based on high-performance DNN technologies. Compared to the previous works using the rescoring of N-best list [12,15,16], we don't use several features, and we only rely on semantic information. Furthermore, the specificity of our approach is the use of the context part and the possibility zones of N-hypotheses list: semantic part represents the semantic information of the topic context of the document to recognize and possibility zone corresponds to the area where we want to find the words to be corrected. This allows us to give less importance to the words in the possibility zone which do not correspond to the context of the document, and to give low semantic score to the corresponding hypothesis.

2 Proposed Methodology

2.1 Semantic Model

An effective way to take into account semantic information is to re-evaluate (rescore) the best hypotheses of the ASR system. This system provides an acoustic score $P_{ac}(w)$ and a linguistic score $P_{lm}(w)$ for each word of the hypothesis sentence. The best sentence is the one that maximizes the probability of the word sequence:

$$\hat{W} = \arg \max_{h_i \in H} \prod_{w \in h_i} P_{ac}(w)^{\alpha} \cdot P_{lm}(w)^{\beta} \tag{1}$$

$\hat{W}$ is the recognized sentence (the end result); H is the set of N-best sentence hypotheses; h_i is the i-th sentence hypothesis; w is a hypothetical word. α and β represent the weights of the acoustic and the language models. These weights are essential because acoustic scores and linguistic scores are not always normalized (they are often likelihoods and not probabilities).

We want to add semantic information to guide the recognition process. The most natural approach to integrating this information is to modify the calculation of the probability of the sequence of words in the following way:

$$\hat{W} = \arg \max_{h_i \in H} \prod_{w \in h_i} P_{ac}(w)^{\alpha} \cdot P_{lm}(w)^{\beta} \cdot P_{sem}(w)^{\gamma} \tag{2}$$

We added the semantic probability of each word: $P_{sem}(w)$. To have a good balance between the different models, we introduce a third weight γ to weigh the semantic information. It will be adjusted on a development corpus.

2.2 Definition of Context Part and Possibility Zones

To estimate the semantic probability, we propose to introduce the concepts of *context part* and *possibility zone*. A *context part* consists of words which are common to all the N-best hypotheses generated by the ASR. We assume that they are correct. This context part allows to extract semantic information of the topic context of the document or of the current part of the document to be recognized. The context part can contain several parts. A *zone of possibilities* is an area between the context parts. It is in this area that we want to find the words to be corrected. From the N-best hypotheses of a sentence, we extract *only one* context part and *one or more* possibility zones. Each zone can contain several words. Figure 1 illustrates these concepts on an example. Here, the 2-best hypotheses list is the following:

H1: *the cat eats the big fat mouse*
H2: *the cat bits the bigfoot mouse*

In this example, the context part Z_{cont} is composed of four words: $Z_{cont} = \{the, cat, the, mouse\}$. These are the words which are common to all the hypotheses and we assume that they are correct. Between these words, we define two possibility zones: the first is made up of two alternatives, eats and bits: $Z_{pos,1} = \{eats, bits\}$. The second is also made up of two alternatives: $Z_{pos,2} = \{bigfat, bigfoot\}$. One alternative corresponds to a choice in the possibility zone. We assume that the possibility zones correspond to the zones where the ASR hesitates between different solutions.

To obtain the context part, we use a dynamic programming algorithm which allows us to pair the hypotheses two by two in order to determine the words common to all the hypotheses. If the context part is empty, we don't study this sentence.

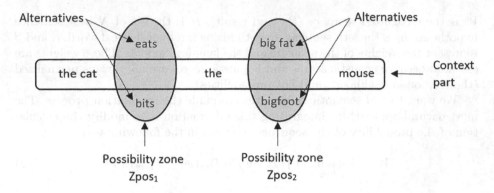

Fig. 1. Illustration of the context part and the possibility zones, as an example.

2.3 Semantic Representation of the Context Part and the Possibility Zones

To take into account the semantics of the document, we propose to represent *each word of the N-best hypotheses by an embedding vector*. In our approach, we used *word2vec* [9] and *FastText* [3]. We compute an average embedding E_{cont} for the context part which is equal to the average of the embedding vectors of all the words in the context part. In the same way, we calculate an average embedding $E_{pos}(i, a_h)$ for i-th possibility zone of alternative a_h of hypothesis h as the average of the embedding vectors of all the words in this alternative of possibility zone. We use the angular similarity to estimate a semantic score between each possibility zone and the context part:

$$S_{sem}(E_{cont}, E_{pos}(i, a_h)) = 1 - \frac{\cos^{-1}\cos(E_{cont}, E_{pos}(i, a_h))}{\pi} \tag{3}$$

From the semantic representations of the context part and the possibility zones, we compute a semantic probability of a hypothesis h. **A semantic probability of a hypothesis** h $P_{sem}(h)$ is computed as follows:

$$P_{sem}(h) = \prod_{i=1}^{N_p} S_{sem}(E_{cont}, E_{pos}(i, a_h)) \tag{4}$$

where N_p is the number of possibility zones. We assume that the Eq. (2) can be approximated as follow:

$$\hat{H} = \arg\max_{h \in H} P_{ac}(h)^\alpha \cdot P_{lm}(h)^\beta \cdot P_{sem}(h)^\gamma \tag{5}$$

where $\hat{H}$ is the N-best list. The Eq. (5) is used to re-rank the N-best hypothesis list. For each hypothesis we compute the semantic score and associate it with acoustic and linguistic scores according to (5). The hypothesis obtaining the best score is considered as the recognized sentence.

3 Experiments

3.1 Corpus Description

We used the publicly available TED-LIUM corpus [6], containing the recordings of the TED conferences. This corpus is well suited to our study because each conference is focused on a particular subject. We want to add the semantic module to improve the performance of our recognition system.

We used the partition of the TED corpus into a train, a development and a test corpus proposed in the TED-LIUM distribution: 452 h for training, 8 conferences (496 sentences, 17926 words) for development and 11 conferences (1091 sentences, 27021 words) for testing.

3.2 Recognition System

Our recognition system is based on the *Kaldi* voice recognition toolbox [13]. We used TDNN triphone acoustic models, trained on the training part of TED-LIUM. The lexicon and language model was provided in the TED-LIUM distribution. The lexicon contains 150k words and the language model has 2 million 4-g, learned from a textual corpus of 250 million words. We also performed the recognition using the RNNLM model [10]. We want to see if using more powerful language model (LM), the proposed semantic module can improve the ASR. As usual, we used the development set to choose the best parameter configuration and the test set to evaluate the proposed methods with this best configuration. We used the word error rate (WER) to measure the ASR performance.

The performance of our ASR system on TED-LIUM using n-gram LM is around 8% of WER. We are not interested in noise-free conditions because in this case the acoustics allow to properly guide the recognition. This research work was carried out as part of an industrial project. This project concerns the recognition of speech in noisy condition, more precisely, in a fighter aircraft. To get closer to actual conditions, we added noise to the development and test sets: additive noise at 10 dB and 5 dB SNR (noise of F16 from the NOISEX-92 corpus [17]).

3.3 Embeddings

We trained *word2vec* model on a text corpus of a billion words extracted from the *OpenWebText* corpus. The generated models have the size of 300 and model 700K words. As *FastText* model, we used the same embedding dimension. The advantage of *FastText* compared to *word2vec* is the taking into account of all possible words.

4 Experimental Results

4.1 Overall Results

Before performing the speech recognition evaluation, we wanted to investigate the impact of the semantic module alone on the search for the best sentence, without using the acoustic and linguistic scores. For this, for a reference sentence text, we simulated the recognition errors by replacing a random word (or two successive words) of the reference sentence by one (or two) acoustically close word(s). This can be easily performed using a phonetic dictionary. In this way, we generated N-best hypotheses for the given sentence ($N = 10$). We performed this generation for every 496 sentences of the development set.

After N-best hypotheses generation, we used our semantic module to rank the 11 hypotheses (the 10 generated sentences plus the correct sentence) and we evaluated the number of errors corrected on the top hypothesis. Here, we did not use the acoustic and the language scores. For 496 sentences of the development set, the word2vec-based semantic module corrects about 67% of simulated errors and the FastText semantic module corrects about 61% of errors. We see that the long context embeddings alone succeed to correct the large number of errors. This shows that the proposed semantic module captures well the semantic information of a sentence.

Table 1 presents the WER for the development and the test sets for two noise condition (10 dB and 5 dB) and two language models (n-gram and RNNLM). The first line of results (method *Random*), corresponds to the random selection of the recognition result from the N-best hypotheses without using the semantic module. The second line, *Baseline*, corresponds to the speech recognition system without using the semantic module (standard ASR). The last line, *Oracle*, represents the maximum performance that can be obtained by searching in the N-best hypotheses: selection of the hypothesis which minimizes the WER for each sentence. The other lines of the table give the performance of the proposed approaches. At each case of the table, value between the parentheses corresponds to the recognition result using the RNNLM. From this table we can make the following observations.

Table 1. Recognition results in terms of WER (%). N-best hypotheses list of 50 hypotheses. TED-LIUM development and test sets, SNR of 10 dB and of 5 dB. n-gram LM and RNNLM (between the parentheses).

Method	SNR 10 dB		SNR 5 dB	
	Dev	Test	Dev	Test
Random	17.9 (14.8)	24.1 (21.5)	34.2 (29.8)	42.1 (39.3)
Baseline system	15.7 (12.3)	21.1 (17.7)	32.7 (28.2)	40.3 (37.1)
word2vec embedding	15.3 (12.0)	20.7 (17.6)	31.9 (**27.4**)	39.4 (36.4)
FastText	**15.2 (11.8)**	**20.5 (17.5)**	**31.8 (27.4)**	**39.2 (36.1)**
Oracle	9.6 (6.9)	12.8 (10.3)	25.4 (21.1)	30.5 (27.6)

The proposed semantic module outperforms the baseline system for all conditions and all evaluated embeddings. For example, on the test set, the semantic module with the *FastText* obtained an absolute improvement of 0.6% for 10 dB and n-gram LM (21.1% WER versus 20.5% WER) and 1.1% for 5 dB and n-gram LM (40.3% versus 39.2%) compared to the baseline system. This represents 8% of relative improvement for 10 dB and about 11% for 5 dB in the reduction of the gap between the baseline and the oracle systems. For all datasets, noise levels and two language models the obtained improvements are significant (confidence interval is computed according to matched-pairs test [8]). This shows that the proposed semantic module is able to capture a significant proportion of the semantic information in the data.

The proposed embeddings give similar performances with a slight superiority of the *FastText* embedding. All these observation are valid for two experimented language models: n-gram and RNNLM.

4.2 Impact of Hyperparameters

Figure 2 (left) shows the evolution of the WER according to the parameter γ (cf. Eq. (2)) for the development set, SNR of 5 dB and n-gram LM. We observe that this parameter plays an important role. For too large values of γ (bigger than 300), the semantic information becomes dominant compared to the acoustic and linguistic information and the WER begins to increase. Therefore, the value of γ between 100 and 300 seems to be optimal. Figure 2 (right) reports the WER as a function of the N-best list size. We can see that 5 or 10 hypotheses are not enough. Using more than 25 hypotheses shows no further improvement.

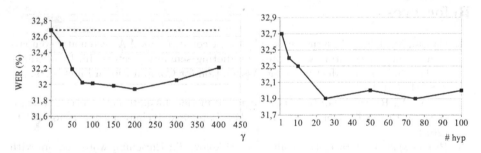

Fig. 2. Semantic module with word2vec embedding, TED-LIUM development set, SNR of 5 dB. WER as a function of the semantic weight γ (left figure) and the N-best hypothesis number (right figure). The dotted line corresponds to the baseline result. n-gram LM.

5   Conclusion and Discussion

In this article, we proposed a new approach of introducing semantic information for the performance improvement of a noisy ASR system. We investigated a new methodology for taking into account semantics through predictive representations that capture the semantic characteristics of words and their context.

The efficiency and the semantic properties of these representations motivate us to explore these representations for our task of speech recognition. We used *word2vec* and *FastText* embeddings. The semantic information is taken into account through the rescoring module of the N-best hypotheses of the recognition system. Semantic representations are applied to the context part and possibility zones. We evaluated our methodology on the corpus of TED-LIUM conferences with added real noise. The proposed methodology shows a better WER compared to the baseline system. This represents 8% of relative im-provement for 10 dB and about 10% for 5 dB in the reduction of the gap between the baseline and the oracle systems. These improvements are statistically significant. This observation is valid for the ASR with n-gram and with RNNLM.

It is important to note that in *word2vec* and *FastText* the word embedding is static and the words with multiple meanings are conflated into a single representation. In future work, we would like to investigate the dynamic BERT embedding. We will conduct a deep analysis of the performance of semantic module as a function of the noise characteristics (e.g., nonstationarity) and the uncertainty propagation in noisy environment to guide the rescoring.

Acknowledgments. The authors thank the DGA (Direction Générale de l'Armement, part of the French Ministry of Defence), Thales AVS and Dassault Aviation who are supporting the funding of this study and the "Man-Machine Teaming" scientific program in which this research project is taking place.

References

1. Baroni, M., Dinu, G., Kruszewski, G.: Don't count, predict! A systematic comparison of context-counting vs. context-predicting semantic vectors. In: Proceedings of the 52nd Annual Meeting of the Association for Computational Linguistics, pp. 238–247 (2014)
2. Bayer, A., Riccardi, G.: Semantic language models for automatic speech recognition. In: Proceedings of the IEEE Spoken Language Technology Workshop (SLT) (2014)
3. Bojanowski, P., Grave, E., Joulin, A., Mikolov, T.: Enriching word vectors with subword information. In: Transactions of the Association for Computational Linguistics, pp. 135–146 (2017)
4. Corona, R., Thomason, J., Mooney, R.: Improving black-box speech recognition using semantic parsing. In: Proceedings of the The 8th International Joint Conference on Natural Language Processing, pp. 122–127 (2017)
5. Erdogan, H., Sarikaya, R., Chen, S., Gao, Y., Picheny, M.: Using semantic analysis to improve speech recognition performance. Comput. Speech Lang. **19**, 321–343 (2005)
6. Hernandez, F., Nguyen, V., Ghannay, S., Tomashenko, N., Estève, Y.: TED-LIUM 3: twice as much data and corpus repartition for experiments on speaker adaptation. In: Karpov, A., Jokisch, O., Potapova, R. (eds.) SPECOM 2018. LNCS (LNAI), vol. 11096, pp. 198–208. Springer, Cham (2018). https://doi.org/10.1007/978-3-319-99579-3_21

7. Gaspers, J., Cimiano, P., Wrede, B.: Semantic parsing of speech using grammars learned with weak supervision. In: Proceedings of the HLT-NAACL, pp. 872–881 (2015)
8. Gillick, L., Cox, S.: Some statistical issues in the comparison of speech recognition algorithms. In: Proceedings of ICASSP, vol. 1, pp. 532–535 (1989)
9. Mikolov, T., Sutskever, I., Chen, K., Corrado, G.S., Dean, J.: Distributed representations of words and phrases and their compositionality. In: Advances in Neural Information Processing Systems, vol. 26, pp. 3111–3119 (2013)
10. Mikolov T., Kombrink S., Burget L., Cernocky J.-H., Khudanpur S.: Extensions of recurrent neural network language model. In: Proceedings of the ICASSP, pp. 5528–5531 (2011)
11. Morbini, F., et al.: A reranking approach for recognition and classification of speech input in conversational dialogue systems. In: Proceedings of the Spoken Language Technology Workshop (SLT), pp. 49–54. IEEE (2012)
12. Ogawa, A., Delcroix, M., Karita, S., Nakatani, T.: Rescoring N-best speech recognition list based on one-on-one hypothesis comparaison using encoder-classifier model. In: Proceedings of the ICASSP (2018)
13. Povey, D., et al.: The Kaldi speech recognition toolkit. In: Proceedings of IEEE Workshop on Automatic Speech Recognition and Understanding (2011)
14. Sheikh, I., Fohr, D., Illina, I., Linarès, G.: Modelling semantic context of OOV words in large vocabulary continuous speech recognition. IEEE/ACM Trans. Audio Speech Lang. Process. **25**(3), 598–610 (2017)
15. Shin, J., Lee, Y., Jung, K.: Effective sentence scoring method using BERT for speech recognition. In: Proceedings of Machine Learning Research, vol. 101, pp. 1081–1093 (2019)
16. Song, Y., et al.: L2RS: a learning-to-rescore mechanism for automatic speech recognition. arXiv:1910.11496v1 (2019)
17. Varga, A., Steeneken, H.: Assessment for automatic speech recognition: II. NOISEX-92: a database and an experiment to study the effect of additive noise on speech recognition systems. Speech Commun. **12**(3), 247–251 (1993)
18. Zhang, Z., Geiger, J., Pohjalainen, J., Mousa, A., Jin, W., Schuller, B.: Deep learning for environmentally robust speech recognition: an overview of recent developments. ACM Trans. Intell. Syst. Technol. **9**(5), 1–28 (2018)

Towards Automated Assessment of Stuttering and Stuttering Therapy

Sebastian P. Bayerl[1]([⊠]) [iD], Florian Hönig[2] [iD], Joëlle Reister[2], and Korbinian Riedhammer[1] [iD]

[1] Technische Hochschule Nürnberg Georg Simon Ohm, Nuremberg, Germany
{sebastian.bayerl,korbinian}@ieee.org
[2] Institut der Kasseler Stottertherapie, Bad Emstal, Germany

Abstract. Stuttering is a complex speech disorder that can be identified by repetitions, prolongations of sounds, syllables or words and blocks while speaking. Severity assessment is usually done by a speech therapist. While attempts at automated assessment were made, it is rarely used in therapy. Common methods for the assessment of stuttering severity include percent stuttered syllables (%SS), the average of the three longest stuttering symptoms during a speech task or the recently introduced Speech Efficiency Score (SES). This paper introduces the Speech Control Index (SCI), a new method to evaluate the severity of stuttering. Unlike SES, it can also be used to assess therapy success for fluency shaping. We evaluate both SES and SCI on a new comprehensively labeled dataset containing stuttered German speech of clients prior to, during and after undergoing stuttering therapy. Phone alignments of an automatic speech recognition system are statistically evaluated in relation to their relative position to labeled stuttering events. The results indicate that phone length distributions differ in respect to their position in and around labeled stuttering events.

Keywords: Speech and voice disorders · Pathological speech · Language

1 Introduction

Stuttering is a speech disorder with a prevalence of 1% of the population [4]. It is a complex disorder of nerve coordination between both brain hemispheres. It can be identified by repetitions, prolongations of sounds, syllables or words, and blocks while speaking.

In addition to these so-called core symptoms, a wide variety of linguistic, physical, behavioral and emotional accompanying symptoms can occur, some of them overlapping the core symptoms. Stuttered disfluencies are usually accompanied by physical tension [12]. The frequency of occurrence and the duration of the symptoms vary considerably depending on individual severity and can seriously impair the communication of the person who stutters (PWS) [3].

© Springer Nature Switzerland AG 2020
P. Sojka et al. (Eds.): TSD 2020, LNAI 12284, pp. 386–396, 2020.
https://doi.org/10.1007/978-3-030-58323-1_42

The individual appearance of the symptoms of each PWS also depends on the respective communication situation, the linguistic complexity of the utterance and the typical phased progress of the speech disorder [6,19]. Since PWS know exactly what they want to say, the cause of the stuttered disfluency does not lie in planning or formulating speech, but in executing the plan of articulation [12]. The condition is treatable but not curable.

One possible technique to overcome stuttering is a technique called fluency shaping [9,26]. Good results could be achieved by adapting it to stuttering therapy [13]. PWS learn a method to overcome blocks which is characterized by "easy" voice onset [10]. A German adaption of this technique is the *Kasseler Stottertherapie* which has also been proven to work well [7,8]. To assess the severity of stuttering and stuttering therapy success in some way, it is important to measure stuttering in a reliable way. This is important both for therapeutic practice and research. A stuttering diagnosis consists of the objective and subjective evaluation of the stuttering symptoms as well as the evaluation of the impairment of everyday life caused by the disorder. It should provide a reliable picture of the individual severity of stuttering.

The objective evaluation of linguistic symptoms typically measures the frequency of stuttering events in percent of stuttered syllables (%SS), whereby the number of stuttered syllables is related to overall spoken syllables. However, this measure has only little agreement among different observers [6] and does not take into account the type of stuttering symptom, e.g. one-time syllable repetition vs. several-second tense block, nor its duration, which significantly reduces the significance of %SS regarding the severity of stuttering [6,24]. Additionally to %SS, the duration of stuttering events can be determined in order to increase the reliability of the results. However, commonly only a small part of the duration of stuttering events is taken into account, e.g.; in SSI-4 only the average of the three longest stuttering symptoms is used [23]. These methods also do not record atypical stuttering disfluencies, which however can occur as accompanying linguistic symptoms and can significantly influence the impression of the severity of stuttering. Subjective stuttering severity rating scales are a widely used measure for assessing the severity of stuttering. These are commonly used both in speech therapy [18] and in clinical research [27]. For clinical purpose, severity rating scales are more reliable than %SS, to provide a statement about individual stuttering severity [11].

Methods for the automated assessment of stuttering and stuttering severity have been proposed in the past. Nöth, Niemann, Haderlein, et al. use a standard speech recognition system and evaluated vowel and fricative durations on a standardized reading task to discriminate between PWS and normal speakers [16]. To classify prolongations and repetitions, Chee et al. extracted Mel Frequency Cepstral Coefficients (MFCC) and used them to train k-NN and LDA classifiers on a very small sample taken from the University College London Archive of Stuttered Speech [5][1]. Mundada et al. use the K-Means clustering algorithm to separate normal speakers from PWS. They also use MFCC feature

---

[1] Available at https://www.uclass.psychol.ucl.ac.uk/uclassfsf.htm.

extraction and Dynamic Time Warping (DTW) for classification [15]. Świetlicka et al. use artificial neural networks to discriminate between syllable repetitions, blocks before words that start with a plosive, and phone prolongations [25]. Alharbi et al. recognize the need to develop customized ASR that can produce full verbatim transcripts including pseudo words and word parts without meaning. Their approach is mainly focused on the detection of repetitions [1]. Ochi et al. investigated the automatic evaluation of soft articulatory contact, as it is taught in stuttering therapy. Detecting modified speech is necessary to account for it in automatic evaluation of PWS that went through speech therapy [17].

Our Contributions. In this work, we introduce the Speech Control Index (SCI), a new method to evaluate the severity of stuttering which can also be used to assess therapy success for fluency shaping. We evaluate both SES and SCI on a new comprehensively labeled dataset acquired at the Institut der Kasseler Stottertherapie(KST) containing stuttered German speech of clients prior to, during and after undergoing stuttering therapy. Based on phone alignments of an automatic speech recognition system, we perform a statistical evaluation of phone length distributions in relation to stuttering events.

2   Data

The data used in this paper was specifically created and labeled with stuttering and stuttering therapy in mind. In the future, data gathered for this work will be used to create means to provide unobstrusive monitoring of stuttering. Thus, the dataset was created to represent reality as good as possible. No special recording equipment was used and the dataset was recorded with consumer hardware. All recordings were created before, during and after therapy at the KST. The therapy contains a number of different tasks such as reading, calling unacquainted people for inquiry purposes or talking to strangers in the street.

The labeling was done by two clinical linguists familiar with stuttering therapy at the KST. The data is labeled in great detail differentiating twelve states of fluent or disfluent speech as well as prosodic pauses and blocks. The focus is to comprehensively label stuttering behavior such as interrupted or repeated words or sentences in whole or parts. The dataset also labels interjections, which can be a typical stuttering related behavior, even though it is also common in regular speakers. Another unique feature of the dataset is the labeling of modified speech: speech as it is produced when applying the fluency shaping technique taught and trained at the KST. Additionally to the labeling of stuttering behavior, a transcript is provided in which word abortions are marked and transcribed in a verbatim way. During preprocessing, the recordings were resampled to 16 kHz where necessary and in case of stereo recordings only one channel is used. The dataset contains 214 recordings by 37 speakers of which 28 were male and 9 were female. The dataset amounts to about 207 min of labeled speech.

To the best of our knowledge, these features make it one of the largest and most comprehensively labeled datasets containing stuttered speech. One of its most important features is the existence of stuttered and modified speech prior to, during and after therapy, enabling extensive research and the creation of practical applications that can be used in a therapeutic context.

3 Method

To assess the severity of stuttering or disfluency of speakers using fluency shaping, common evaluation methods such as %SS or SSI-4 are insufficient, as these methods do not account for therapy artefacts and accompanying linguistic symptoms. Since a purely subjective measure of stuttering severity has many drawbacks in clinical practice, we chose to calculate the SES based on classifying speech as either *efficient, inefficient* or *silence*.

3.1 Speech Efficiency Score

The Speech Efficiency Score (SES) is a recent method for the evaluation of (dis)fluent speech that was proposed by Amir et al. [2]. This method puts the fraction of fluent speech in relation to the fraction of disfluent speech. Thus, SES determines the communicative efficiency of a speaker by focusing on the time domain.

$$SES = \frac{\text{Efficient time}}{\text{Total time} - \text{Silence}} \cdot 100\% \tag{1}$$

With this method, all kinds of disfluencies, both typical and atypical to stuttering, are taken into account, as well as the duration of the fluent and disfluent speech components, which makes it superior to previous methods. Amir et al. concluded that, due to the high correlation they found between SES and subjective severity rating scales, SES also provides reliable information about the severity of stuttering. Since SES considers prolongations, which are perceived as abnormal, to be inefficient, it must be assumed that the SES fails to take adapted speaking behaviors into account. This in turn implies that for the calculation of SES, speech fractions that contain modified speech, such as fluency shaping, are counted as *inefficient*.

Fluency shaping focuses on restructuring the way of speaking, aiming at modifying speech in a way that little or no stuttering symptoms occur. The technique includes gentle voice onsets as well as syllable and word bindings, in which the vibration of the vocal cords is not supposed to stop. It allows PWS to regain a high degree of control over their own speech and speak much more fluently. However, applying this technique, especially at the beginning of the therapy, sounds quite unnatural due to the prolongations that are not present in a normal flow of speech [20]. Since calculating SES includes speech fractions that have been modified by fluency shaping as *inefficient*, the measure does not give a reliable picture of the severity of stuttering in PWS who apply this technique.

3.2   Speech Control Index

To address the shortcomings of SES in the context of speech therapy using fluency shaping, we propose a new method that can be used to assess the severity of stuttering but still is able to account for and measure therapeutic success. The Speech Control Index (SCI) was developed at the KST and accounts for speech modifications which relate to fluency shaping. By adding modified speech to the controlled speech, the SCI not only provides a measure for the individual severity of stuttering, but also whether or not PWS are able to control their speech by using the speaking technique. The SCI quantifies the proportion of time between *controlled* speech components, which means fluent and modified speech, and *uncontrolled* speech components such as disfluencies and blocks. Thus SCI, similar to SES, considers speaking over time.

To achieve this, speech fractions are grouped in one of three categories:

1. **Controlled time** - all parts of speech produced that can be considered fluent or modified, which means a PWS uses a speaking technique to overcome stuttering. Additionally prosodic pauses are added to this category.
2. **Disfluent time** - all parts of a sample that can be identified as stuttered disfluencies are being counted to disfluent speech, i.e. repetitions of sounds, syllables, words, prolongations, blocks and silent blocks. In addition, speech fractions containing atypical stuttering disfluencies such as the repetition of phrases, interjections, revisions including incomplete words and phrases are being added to disfluent time.
3. **Silence** - long pauses in which the PWS is not speaking and not trying to speak as well as interruptions by the dialogue partner, etc.

Accordingly, "Total time" in Eq. 2 is the sum of the three aforementioned categories.

Based on the correlation between subjective severity rating scales and the SES, Amir et al. concluded that SES also provides reliable information about the severity of stuttering [2]. As calculation of SCI is similar to SES beside the attribution of modified speech fractions, the same is expected to hold for the SCI. In cases where PWS do not use the speaking technique, which can be assumed for recordings done prior to therapy, both measures are equal. The same is true for cases in which only little speaking technique is applied, which is confirmed by Fig. 1.

$$SCI = \frac{\text{Controlled time}}{\text{Total time} - \text{Silence}} \cdot 100\% \qquad (2)$$

3.3   Phone Durations

One of the core symptoms of stuttering is the prolongation of sounds. This should be directly observable in the time alignment outputs produced by an automatic speech recognition (ASR) system. Such information can be used to differentiate between a PWS and a normal speaking person. A major difficulty is that phone lengths are unique speech properties characteristic of every speaker and may vary depending on various factors. To generalize such an assessment, a sample of multiple speakers is necessary. It can be assumed that especially close to and during a stuttering event, phone durations should on average be longer than during fluent speech portions. To verify these assumptions, phone alignments were produced and categorized with respect to their relative position to stuttering events: Phones inside labeled disfluencies, phones within 0.25 s before a disfluency, 0.25 s before and after a disfluency, 0.25 s before, after and inside a disfluency. To have a set that is free from modifications, which also prolong phone lengths, a set of phones was chosen which where within speech fractions labeled as fluent. The sets were then refined by the phone classes vowels, fricatives, sonorants and plosives. Altogether, 44 sets of phone duration distributions were created, but the individual sets became to small to make generalizable conclusions.

To obtain the alignments for calculating phone lengths, an ASR system trained based on the system described in [14] was used. For training, the German part of the Spoken Wikipedia Corpora, the German subset of the m-ailabs read speech corpus as well as the Tuda-De corpus were used[2]. Only minor modifications to the training recipe were made to reduce the number of training targets in acoustic model training from 732 to 260. The model was trained using the Kaldi toolkit [21], using speaker adaptive training on top of LDA and MLLT features [22]. Prior to computing the forced alignments, the lexicon transducer of the ASR system was modified to be able to align incomplete words. The transcripts created for the files were checked against the lexicon and pronunciations for missing and incomplete words were generated by using a grapheme-to-phoneme (g2p) model trained on the original lexicon[3].

4   Experiments

SCI and SES were computed for each of the 214 files in the dataset. Pearson's correlation between the SCI and SES over all 214 files is at 0.142 and only shows a very weak linear relationship between the two indices. This is confirmed by the distribution plots in Fig. 2, and the irregular plot for SES values over higher SCI values in Fig. 1. Comparing the SCI and SES directly, the absolute difference is less than 0.1% points for 114 recordings, which is indicated by the plot in Fig. 1. This is exactly the part of the data that has no labeled modifications in it, which is supported by a correlation of 1 between SCI and SES for this part of the data. This shows that SCI and SES are identical for samples without speech modifications.

---

[2] Kaldi recipe available at https://github.com/uhh-lt/kaldi-tuda-de.

[3] G2P tool available online at https://www-i6.informatik.rwth-aachen.de/web/Software/g2p.html.

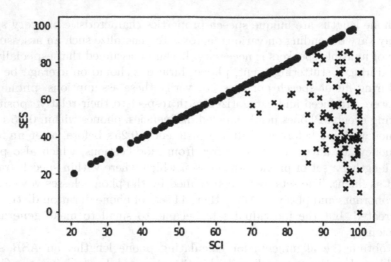

Fig. 1. Plot of SES over SCI values computed from labels for every file in the dataset. Crosses representing samples that contain modified speech, dots representing samples without.

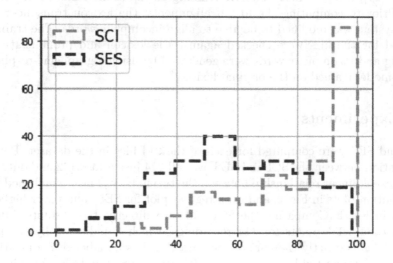

Fig. 2. Value distribution of SCI and SES scores in the dataset ($N = 214$).

Table 1. Phone duration (in seconds) distributions descriptive statistics.

Dataset	N	Mean phone dur.	Phone dur. at 90th P	Phone dur. at 95th P	Percent outlier
Inside disfluency	9818	0.230	0.570	0.850	3.14
Before disfluency	7898	0.199	0.460	0.670	2.12
Before to after disfluency	23227	0.192	0.480	0.730	2.58
All phones	73410	0.150	0.330	0.520	1.99
Fluent	41195	0.109	0.200	0.310	0.84

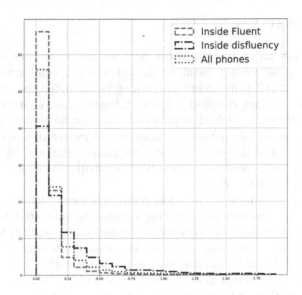

Fig. 3. Fluent, All, and inside disfluency phone length distributions plotted as relative portions of phone durations. Area under step function represents percentage of values inside a 0.1 s wide phone length interval.

Table 1 shows the descriptive statistics about the created phone subsets. In this context, outliers were defined as phones of which the duration is at least three times the standard deviation σ greater than the mean phone duration in the overall set. The set containing all phones has about 2% outliers, which is higher than the expected value for this definition of outliers. The difference to the set containing only fluent speech as well as the set inside labeled disfluencies is most striking. Fluent speech only contains 0.84% outliers and the average phone duration relative to the set containing all phones is 27% shorter. Phones inside a disfluency compared to the set containing all phones are on average 53% longer. Relative difference between average duration of phones inside fluently labeled speech compared to speech inside disfluencies is 111%. These numbers show a clear relationship between phone duration and stuttering related disfluencies.

It can be concluded that especially phone durations starting from the 90th percentile within a sample can be very useful in differentiating stuttered speech from normal speech. The plot in Fig. 3 supports this observation. It contains histogram plots of the relative portion of phone durations in 0.1 s wide intervals. This shows that apart from the phones with a duration below 0.2 s, the relative number of phones inside these 0.1 second wide intervals is greatest for phones inside disfluencies. Looking at the relative fraction of phones above or below a duration of 0.2 s, might be enough to differentiate between fluent and disfluent speech.

5   Conclusion

The SCI provides an accurate measure with similar properties as the SES for speakers who speak mostly fluent or do not use a special speech technique. The advantage of SCI is its ability to account for modified speech of PWS who underwent therapy and regained a level of fluency and control that is more effective than stuttering, even though speech may not be classified as natural or normal. An extensive comparison between the objective measures SSI-4 (%SS and mean duration of the three longest symptoms), SES and SCI, as well as a comparison of these procedures with subjective stuttering severity rating scales will be a part of future work.

The data showed that there is a clear relation between the duration of phones and their relative position to stuttering events. As indicated here, a normal speech recognition system can be easily modified to distinguish fluent and disfluent speech in utterances based on heuristic measures as long as it can produce alignments. For this the recognition system needs to be able to recognize incomplete words and syllable repetitions. This insight will be used to build automatic stuttering recognition systems that can differentiate different levels of fluency. The comprehensively labeled dataset enables future exploration of different kinds of disfluencies and the use of statistical learning methods such as support vector machines or neural networks. By classifying the amount of fluent, disfluent and modified speech in a speech sample, the automated and continuous calculation of the SCI can provide a reliable measure for stuttering severity and therapy success. This will provide valuable feedback to the client as well as the therapist.

Acknowledgements. The authors thank the Institut der Kasseler Stottertherapie for their support and excellent collaboration. This work is supported by a research grant of the Bayerisches Staatsministerium für Bildung und Kultus, Wissenschaft und Kunst as well as the BAYWiss (Bayerisches Wissenschaftsforum).

References

1. Alharbi, S., Hasan, M., Simons, A.J., Brumfitt, S., Green, P.: A lightly supervised approach to detect stuttering in children's speech. In: Proceedings of Interspeech 2018, pp. 3433–3437. ISCA (2018)

2. Amir, O., Shapira, Y., Mick, L., Yaruss, J.S.: The speech efficiency score (SES): a time-domain measure of speech fluency. J. Fluency Disord. (2018). https://doi.org/10.1016/j.jfludis.2018.08.001

3. Anders, K., Rudorf, E.: Kompendium der Akademischen Sprachtherapie und Logopädie: Bd.3, chap. In: Kohlhammer, W. (ed.) Stottern bei Jugendlichen und Erwachsenen, pp. 225–241 (2017)

4. Carlson, N.R.: Physiology of Behavior, 11th edn. Pearson, London (2012)

5. Chee, L.S., Ai, O.C., Hariharan, M., Yaacob, S.: MFCC based recognition of repetitions and prolongations in stuttered speech using k-NN and LDA. In: 2009 IEEE Student Conference on Research and Development (SCOReD), pp. 146–149. IEEE (2009)

6. Ellis, J.B., Ramig, P.R.: J. Fluency Disord. 34(4), 295–299 (2008). https://doi.org/10.1016/j.jfludis.2009.10.004

7. Euler, H.A., Gudenberg, A.W.V., Jung, K., Neumann, K.: Computergestützte Therapie bei Redeflussstörungen: Die langfristige Wirksamkeit der Kasseler Stottertherapie (KST). Sprache · Stimme · Gehör 33(04), 193–202 (2009). https://doi.org/10.1055/s-0029-1242747

8. Euler, H., Gudenberg, A.W.V.: Die Kasseler Stottertherapie (KST). Ergebnisse einer computer-gestützten Biofeedbacktherapie för Erwachsene1. Sprache-stimme-gehor 24, 71–79 (2000). https://doi.org/10.1055/s-2000-11084

9. Ingham, R.J., Kilgo, M., Ingham, J.C., Moglia, R., Belknap, H., Sanchez, T.: Evaluation of a stuttering treatment based on reduction of short phonation intervals. J. Speech Lang. Hear. Res. 44(6), 1229–1244 (2001)

10. Borden, G.J., Baer, T., Kenney, M.K.: Onset of voicing in stuttered and fluent utterances. J. Speech Hear. Res. 28, 363–72 (1985). https://doi.org/10.1044/jshr.2803.363

11. Karimi, H., O'Brian, S., Onslow, M., Jones, M.: Absolute and relative reliability of percentage of syllables stuttered and severity rating scales. J. Speech Lang. Hear. Res. 57(4), 1284–1295 (2014)

12. Lickley, R.: Disfluency in typical and stuttered speech. In: Fattori sociali e biologici nella variazione fonetica-Social and Biological Factors in Speech Variation (2017)

13. Mallard, A., Kelley, J.: The precision fluency shaping program: replication and evaluation. J. Fluency Disord. 7(2), 287–294 (1982)

14. Milde, B., Köhn, A.: Open source automatic speech recognition for German. In: Proceedings of ITG 2018 (2018)

15. Mundada, M., Gawali, B., Kayte, S.: Recognition and classification of speech and its related fluency disorders. Int. J. Comput. Sci. Inf. Technol. (IJCSIT) 5(5), 6764–6767 (2014)

16. Nöth, E., et al.: Automatic stuttering recognition using hidden markov models. In: Sixth International Conference on Spoken Language Processing (2000)

17. Ochi, K., Mori, K., Sakai, N.: Automatic evaluation of soft articulatory contact for stuttering treatment. Proc. Interspeech 2018, 1546–1550 (2018)

18. Onslow, M., Packman, A., Harrison, E., et al.: The Lidcombe Program of Early Stuttering Intervention: A Clinician's Guide. Pro-ed, Austin (2003)

19. Packman, A., Attanasio, J.S.: Theoretical Issues in Stuttering (2004)

20. Packman, A., Onslow, M., Doorn, J.V.: Prolonged speech and modification of stuttering: perceptual, acoustic, and electroglottographic data. J. Speech Lang. Hear. Res. 37(4), 724–737 (1994)

21. Povey, D., et al.: The Kaldi speech recognition toolkit. In: IEEE 2011 Workshop (2011)

22. Povey, D., Kuo, H.K.J., Soltau, H.: Fast speaker adaptive training for speech recognition. In: Ninth Annual Conference of the International Speech Communication Association (2008)
23. Riley, G.: SSI-4 Stuttering Severity Instrument, 4th edn. (2009)
24. Starkweather, C.W.: Fluency and Stuttering. Prentice-Hall, Inc., Upper Saddle River (1987)
25. Świetlicka, I., Kuniszyk-Jóźkowiak, W., Smołka, E.: Hierarchical ANN system for stuttering identification. Comput. Speech Lang. **27**(1), 228–242 (2013)
26. Webster, R.L.: An operant response shaping program for the establishment of fluency in stutterers. Final report (1972)
27. Yairi, E., Ambrose, N.G.: Early childhood stuttering I: persistency and recovery rates. J. Speech Lang. Hear. Res. **42**(5), 1097–1112 (1999)

Synthesising Expressive Speech – Which Synthesiser for VOCAs?

Jan-Oliver Wülfing, Chi Tai Dang, and Elisabeth André[✉]

Human-Centred Multimedia, University of Augsburg, Universitätsstrasse 6a,
86159 Augsburg, Germany
{wuelfing,dang,andre}@hcm-lab.de
http://www.hcm-lab.de

Abstract. In the context of people with complex communication needs who depend on Voice Output Communication Aids, the ability of speech synthesisers to convey not only sentences, but also emotions would be a great enrichment. The latter is essential and very natural in interpersonal speech communication. Hence, we are interested in the expressiveness of speech synthesisers and their perception. We present the results of a study in which 82 participants listened to different synthesised sentences with different emotional contours from three synthesisers. We found that participants' ratings on expressiveness and naturalness indicate that the synthesiser CereVoice performs better than the other synthesisers.

Keywords: Complex Communication Needs · Voice Output Communication Aid · Expressive Speech Synthesis · Online survey

1 Introduction

How often do we vocally speaking people use our tone of voice to communicate our intentions, wishes, or desires to a communication partner throughout the day? Depending on the emotions to be conveyed, the tone of voice is portrayed by a variation of prosodic features (rhythm, speed and pitch, etc.) and voice quality [5]. For instance, a sad person has different tone of voice than a happy one. The first one typically speaks slower and lower pitched than the latter one.

As Hoffmann and Wülfing pointed out in a survey [11] with 129 participants, people who cannot or almost not articulate themselves vocally would like to do the same with the help of their VOCA (*Voice Output Communication Aid*). These VOCAs fall into the group of technologies in the domain of AAC (*Alternative and Augmentative Communication*). VOCAs take text input and synthesise the input as auditory output. Yet, the possibilities and potentials of synthesisers have not been used extensively. In the past, industry has mainly focused on naturalness neglecting variability in expressive style. However, as text-to-speech synthesisers continue to improve, the question arises of whether synthesisers may help people use VOCAs to express their feelings, wishes, and intentions as well.

© Springer Nature Switzerland AG 2020
P. Sojka et al. (Eds.): TSD 2020, LNAI 12284, pp. 397–408, 2020.
https://doi.org/10.1007/978-3-030-58323-1_43

As a first step to answer this question, we investigate the expressiveness of three freely available synthesisers in terms of recognised emotions and their naturalness in terms of perceived pronunciation quality. For this purpose, we conducted a survey with 82 participants in order to investigate which of these synthesisers shows the highest expressiveness and naturalness for sentences generated for the German language. We decided to evaluate MaryTTS v5.2[1] developed collaboratively by the German Research Center for Artificial Intelligence and Saarland University and eSpeak[2] v1.48.04 developed by Jonathan Duddington and maintained by Reece Dunn. Both are open source synthesisers. eSpeak provides voices created by using formant synthesis. MaryTTS provides both unit selection and voices based on Hidden-Markov Models (HMM) [13]. As a third synthesiser, we chose the commercial CereVoice unit selection speech system[3] v4.0.6 developed by CereProc's Ltd. CereVoice is a commercial-grade real-time ESS (*Expressive Speech Synthesis*) system [2]. For our study, we used an academic licence provided by CereProc Ltd.

All three synthesisers have capabilities to manipulate prosodic features and make use of a markup language that more or less follows the industry standard SSML (*Speech Synthesis Markup Language*) v1.1[4]. eSpeak uses SSML, however, with fewer options to manipulate. For MaryTTS, MaryXML[5] serves as its own data representation format which facilitates the synthesis of prosodic utterances - the syntax is similar to SSML. In addition to SSML support, CereVoice offers CereVoice XML extensions[6] for emotional synthesis control. In our previous work [16], we evaluated how a VOCA that enables the specification of certain emotional states via Emojis would be perceived by users with CCN. To this end, we presented them with a first prototype VOCA 'EmotionTalker' (ET) in their daily environment. Here, we focus on which speech synthesiser to use for enhancing a VOCA with expressive speech. To this end, we compared three publicly available speech synthesisers (eSpeak, MaryTTS, CereVoice) in a perception study with 82 participants. Our long-term objective is to pave the way towards a new generation of VOCAs that convey emotions and personality.

2   Related Work

Recently, the naturalness of synthesised speech has significantly improved. In some cases, it has become hard to distinguish artificially created voices from human voices. This is in particular true for commercial speech synthesisers, such as CereVoice. In the area of speech synthesis, basically two approaches have been used: unit selection approaches and statistical parametric synthesis approaches (see [3] for a recent survey). Unit selection approaches make use

---

[1] http://mary.dfki.de (accessed 02/06/20).
[2] http://espeak.sourceforge.net (accessed 02/06/20).
[3] https://www.cereproc.com/en/products/academic (accessed 11/06/20).
[4] https://www.w3.org/TR/speech-synthesis11/ (accessed 02/06/20).
[5] http://mary.dfki.de/documentation/maryxml/ (accessed 12/06/20).
[6] https://www.cereproc.com/de/products/sdk (accessed 12/06/20).

of a large inventory of human speech units that are subsequently selected and combined based on the sentence to be synthesised. Statistical parametric synthesis approaches create acoustic models from recorded speech (for example, using Hidden Markov Models or Deep Neural Networks) that are used to reconstruct synthesised speech from the generated parameters. Usually, more natural synthesis results are obtained by unit selection approaches. However, unit selection approaches offer little flexibility to manipulate speech parameters in a way that different emotional styles are conveyed. To give users more control over the synthesised speech, specific extensions for the industry standard SSML have been developed, such as CereProc XML extensions or MaryXML, that enable users to create different styles of expressive speech.

To evaluate the quality of the produced speech, a variety of perceptual quality dimensions of synthetic speech, such as intelligibility and naturalness, have been defined (see [10] for an overview) that are also employed in the annual 'Blizzard' challenge[7] on advancing speech synthesis. Also, the emotional atmosphere of a scene and the moods of the characters have been included as a quality dimension in audiobook synthesis tasks. Wagner et al. [15] point out that the evaluation of TTS is still using criteria from the early days of speech synthesis research and argue for a user-centered approach that considers a larger diversity of users including gender and age. A user-centered approach is in particular recommended for AAC users who would like to communicate with expressive voices as shown in our previous research [16]. When developing VOCAs with expressive speech, the question arises of how to enable AAC users to control the quality of speech in an easy manner. Recent work on expressive VOCAs (see [16] and [8]) makes use of expressive keyboards that include Emojis to specify the emotions to be conveyed. While such interfaces enable an easy specification of the emotional content, they provide the AAC user only with a limited amount of control over the synthesised speech. However, when being engaged in a conversation, the fine-grained control of a large number of parameters that would ensure a high quality of expressive speech is no option. For this reason, we decided to focus in our study on a few set of parameters that can be easily mapped on emotions to be conveyed without requiring extensive fine-tuning.

3 Study

In order to evaluate the expressive capabilities of the three synthesisers to be considered for integration into a VOCA, we performed an online survey. Participants were acquired through a mailing list at the first author's home university, the news-site of the department to which the authors are affiliated, and a forum entry especially for AAC users and their personal assistants.

3.1 Online Survey

The online survey consisted of 27 WAV-files (3 sentences * 3 emotions * 3 synthesisers) which were prepared in advance. For the study, we relied on German voices. In particular, we used the following voices: eSpeak (Formant, male,

---

[7] http://www.festvox.org/blizzard (accessed 02/06/20).

de), MaryTTS (HMM, female, bits1-hsmm), CereVoice (Unit Selection, female, Gudrun). Following Murray et al. [12], we selected three emotionally neutral sentences. 'Emotionally neutral' means that the semantics of a sentence does not provide any clue on the speaker 's emotion. For example, one of the sentences was "Ich kann da drüben Leute sehen" (engl. "I can see people over there"). In order to convey the emotions (happy, sad, angry), we used SSML-markups to manipulate pitch, volume, rate and contour. In light of later integration into an easy-to-use VOCA GUI, we did not exploit the full potential of XML extensions to enable more sophisticated emotional control. The online survey and sentences were reviewed by several researchers in terms of wording and conveyed emotions.

Structure. The survey had three parts. First of all, participants had to agree to a DPA (Data Processing Agreement) in order to continue. Then, they had to provide demographic data including age, sex, and cultural background (in order to exclude any disposition). Next, participants had to listen to the 27 sentences. After each audio clip, they were asked in the online survey to type the sentence heard, to indicate the emotion perceived, and how satisfied they were with their choice of the selected emotion. After evaluating all 27 sentences, the participants were presented again with three sentences explicitly indicated as happy, sad, or angry. This time, participants had to mark how satisfied they were with the naturalness and expressivity of the corresponding speech synthesiser. This third part was designed as a double check of the second part.

Questions. In the second part of the survey, we presented the participants with a forced response choice. Following the approach of Murray et al. [12], we included two additional emotions (fear and disgust) and a neutral state as distractors. That is, we disguised the number and the category of the emotions actually being tested. The participants had to listen to short sentences played back through WAV-files in a randomised order of the speech synthesisers. The first question in part two "Please, write the heard sentence into the box" (transl.) was asked in order to identify any acoustic issues. The second question "Which emotion do you link to the sentence" provided us with the perceived emotion. The last question "How satisfied are you with the choice of the perceived emotion" served as a confidence measure for the previous answer. The third part of the online survey served to get information on the participants' subjective impression of the speech synthesiser. Participants were asked "Please, evaluate the synthesiser XX in respect ...", "... to its articulation", and "... to its expressivity".

4   Results

The online survey was conducted between February and May 2019 with 82 German-speaking participants, who filled in the survey completely. We had 32 male/50 female participants aged between 18 and 65 years ($M = 28.78, SD =$

10.61). In addition, the participants had the opportunity to state their origin. The large majority came from Germany. In addition, Austria, Poland, Russia, Asia, Latin, and Turkey were stated. Participants needed on average 798 s ($SD = 151.41$) to complete the survey.

In total, participants had to evaluate three sentences for three synthesisers for each of the three emotions, i.e., for each synthesiser, they had to correctly assign emotions to nine sentences. The highest number of correctly assessed emotions were: Seven correct for CereVoice by one participant, six correct for MaryTTS by one participant, and four correct for eSpeak by nine participants. Regarding the emotions, the highest number of correctly assessed emotions was achieved for Sadness (eight hits by 16 participants), followed by Angry (five hits by six participants) and Happiness (four hits by three participants).

4.1 Average Number of Recognised Emotions

Which of the synthesisers expresses which of the emotions best? In order to answer this question, we look at the correctly assessed emotions. Table 1 gives an overview of the mean values and the corresponding standard deviations for the number of correctly assessed emotions from the synthesised sentences across all three synthesisers and separately for each of the three emotion classes. If we consider only the correctly assessed emotions independent of the synthesisers (aggregated over all synthesisers), then the class *Sad* was recognised best with 3.68 sentences ($SD = 1.92$), followed by the class *Angry* with $M = 2.22, SD = 1.60$. The class *Happy* was expressed the worst of all ($M = 1.28, SD = 1.11$). When all emotion classes are considered together for each of the synthesisers, CereVoice scores best with an average of 2.78 ($SD = 1.42$) correctly assessed emotions, closely followed by MaryTTS with 2.62 ($SD = 1.54$) correctly assessed emotions. The synthesiser eSpeak has the worst average score of 1.78 ($SD = 1.31$) correctly assessed emotions.

Table 1. Means and standard deviations for the number of correctly assessed emotions. "Assessed" is abbreviated with A.

#A. emotions per synthesiser (0..9)		#A. emotions overall (0..9)	
E - eSpeak	$M = 1.78, SD = 1.31$	a - Angry	$M = 2.22, SD = 1.60$
M - MaryTTS	$M = 2.62, SD = 1.54$	h - Happy	$M = 1.28, SD = 1.11$
C - CereVoice	$M = 2.78, SD = 1.42$	s - Sad	$M = 3.68, SD = 1.92$

#A. emotions per synthesiser and emotion class (0..3)			
Emotion	E - eSpeak	M - MaryTTS	C - CereVoice
a - Angry	$M = .94, SD = .85$	$M = .67, SD = .74$	$M = .61, SD = .64$
h - Happy	$M = .29, SD = .48$	$M = .62, SD = .60$	$M = .37, SD = .53$
s - Sad	$M = .55, SD = .63$	$M = 1.33, SD = .99$	$M = 1.8, SD = .99$

4.2   Performance Between Synthesisers

Which of the synthesisers has the best/worst numbers of correctly assessed instances across all emotion classes? The answer to this question is provided by a comparison of the mean values for assessed emotion instances of all three synthesisers (see Table 1, "#Assessed emotions per synthesiser").

Here, a repeated measurement ANOVA [9] showed highly significant differences between the synthesisers ($F(2, 162) = 18.05, p < .001$). The post-hoc pairwise comparisons (with Bonferroni corrections) for each measured synthesiser revealed that there are significant differences between the synthesiser eSpeak (denoted by E) and MaryTTS (denoted by M) (E-M: $p < .001$, $-.84, 95\% - CI[-1.27, -.42]$) as well as eSpeak and CereVoice (denoted by C) (E-C: $p < .001$, $-1.00, 95\% - CI[-1.40, -.60]$), meaning that emotions were in general recognised significantly better with MaryTTS and CereVoice than with eSpeak. Figure 1 shows all mean values and standard deviations of Table 1, whereby the blue bars indicate an unequal distribution of the correctly assessed emotion classes within the synthesisers, which we discuss further in the following.

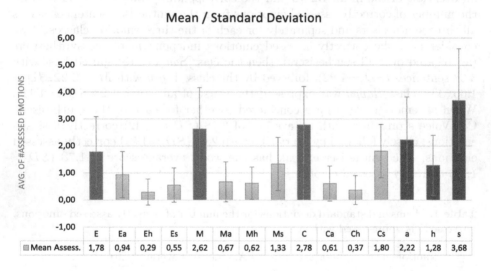

Fig. 1. Means and standard deviations of correctly assessed emotions from sentences. (Color figure online)

Performance Within Individual Synthesisers. *If we consider the mean values within individual synthesisers, which of the emotion classes is expressed better/worse than the other classes?* To answer this question, we have a more detailed look at the individual emotion classes across the three synthesisers.

Repeated measurement ANOVAs for each of the emotion classes and synthesisers revealed further differences of the correctly assessed emotions for each of the synthesisers as indicated by the blue bars in Fig. 1. We found highly significant differences in the recognition of synthesised emotions within the synthesiser eSpeak ($F(2, 162) = 22.00, p < .001$). Post-hoc pairwise comparisons showed that the recognition of the emotions *Angry, Sad, Happy* (in that order) differ significantly from well to badly recognisable. With the synthesiser CereVoice, the highly significant differences between all three emotion classes ($F(2, 162) = 97.59, p < .001$), i.e., post-hoc comparisons, showed that *Sad* was recognised best and *Happy* worst. Smaller amount of differences were found with MaryTTS ($F(2, 162) = 23.63, p < .001$). The significant differences with MaryTTS from post-hoc pairwise comparisons showed that *Sad* could be better distinguished from the other emotion classes.

4.3 Performance Between Emotion Classes

Considering the recognition of emotion classes aggregated over all synthesisers, which emotion class is recognised best? And which synthesiser performs best on which emotion class? For the answer to these questions, we combine the assessed rates of the different emotion classes across all synthesisers (c.f., Table 1). For the analysis within an emotion class we take a more detailed view on the individual synthesisers (c.f., green bars in Fig. 1).

A repeated measurement ANOVA comparing the correctly assessed emotions for each emotion class showed a highly significant difference ($F(2, 162) = 59.80, p < .001$) in correctly assessed emotions between the emotion classes. Post-hoc pairwise comparisons revealed that the class *Sad* was most frequently and thus significantly more often correctly identified by participants (a-s: $p < .001$, $-1.46, 95\% - CI[-2.04, -.88]$; h-s: $p < .001, -2.40, 95\% - CI[-2.97, -1.84]$) than for the other classes. Furthermore, the class *Angry* was significantly more often identified than the class *Happy* (a - h: $p < .001, .94, 95\% - CI[.47, 1.41]$), meaning that the class *Happy* was the worst recognisable.

Performance Within Individual Emotion Classes. *If we consider the mean values within individual emotion classes, which of the synthesisers expresses the emotions better/worse than the other synthesisers?* To answer this question, we have a more detailed look at the means across the three synthesisers for each of the emotion classes (c.f., blue bars in Fig. 1).

For the emotion class *Angry*, we found significant differences ($F(2, 162) = 6.03, p < .005$) between the synthesisers, where post-hoc analysis identified eSpeak as significantly better recognisable than the other synthesisers. For the emotion class *Happy*, there was a significant difference ($F(2, 162) = 10.52, p < .005$) between the synthesisers in favour of MaryTTS revealed by post-hoc pairwise comparisons. Finally, for the emotion class *Sad*, the statistics showed highly significant differences ($F(2, 162) = 59.78, p < .001$), where the post-hoc analysis identified that each of the synthesisers significantly differed from each other in the order *CereVoice, MaryTTS, and eSpeak* from best to worst.

4.4   Satisfaction with the Choice of Assessed Emotions

For each of the assessed emotions, participants were asked to rate on a Likert scale (*"not satisfied at all - 1"*, *"undecided - 3"*, *"very satisfied - 5"*), how satisfied they were with the choice of the assessed emotion class. Table 2 contains all mean values and standard deviations. Participants seemed to have different degrees of satisfaction with their choice between the synthesisers. While participants rated on average with less than *"undecided-3"* for eSpeak, the ratings for MaryTTS and CereVoice tended to be higher towards *"satisfied - 4"*. However, the mean values for satisfaction hardly differed between the emotion classes (a, h, s), with mean values slightly above *"undecided - 3"*.

Table 2. Overview of the means and standard deviations for the satisfaction ratings (on a scale of 1 ... 5) for a chosen emotion (and emotion class).

For chosen emotions per synthesiser		For chosen emotions	
eSpeak	$M = 2.81, SD = 0.94$	a - Angry	$M = 3.12, SD = 0.67$
MaryTTS	$M = 3.26, SD = 0.63$	h - Happy	$M = 3.12, SD = 0.71$
CereVoice	$M = 3.27, SD = 0.63$	s - Sad	$M = 3.11, SD = 0.74$
Satisfaction ratings for chosen emotions per synthesiser and emotion			
Emotion	E - eSpeak	M - MaryTTS	C - CereVoice
a - Angry	$M = 2.91, SD = 1.10$	$M = 3.27, SD = 0.70$	$M = 3.12, SD = 0.68$
h - Happy	$M = 2.76, SD = 1.03$	$M = 3.34, SD = 0.75$	$M = 3.26, SD = 0.79$
s - Sad	$M = 2.76, SD = 1.00$	$M = 3.17, SD = 0.64$	$M = 3.38, SD = 0.78$

4.5   Satisfaction Between Synthesisers

Which synthesiser showed the highest satisfaction with the choice on average when all emotion classes were included? To address this question, we compared the given satisfaction ratings between each of the synthesisers. As already indicated by Table 2, the repeated measurement ANOVA showed highly significant differences between the synthesisers ($F(2, 162) = 27.33, p < .001$). Overall, the participants were significantly more satisfied with their choice of an emotion class while listening to sentences synthesised by MaryTTS (E-M: $p < .001$, $-.45, 95\% - CI[-.65, -.26]$) and CereVoice (E-C: $p < .001$, $-.47, 95\% - CI[-.67, -.26]$) than by eSpeak.

Satisfaction Within Individual Synthesisers. *With which of the conveyed emotion classes were the participants most satisfied measured by the mean values within the synthesisers?* For answering this question, we compared the values within the individual emotion classes across the three synthesisers.

Only CereVoice showed a measurable significant effect ($F(2, 162) = 3.43, p <$ .05), meaning that participants were more satisfied with the choice of the class *Sad* than with the class *Angry* (a-s: $p = .037, -.20, 95\% - CI[-.39, -.01]$).

4.6   Satisfaction Between Emotion Classes

We also analysed the aggregated satisfaction ratings (all synthesisers together) for the emotions to investigate whether satisfaction with the choice for one of the emotions was rated distinctly better. However, no significant effects were found.

Satisfaction Within Individual Emotion Classes. *Which synthesiser elicits the highest satisfaction ratings for individual emotion classes?* To answer this question, we conducted ANOVAs for each of the emotion classes and synthesisers.

For all emotion classes, we found significant differences (*Angry*: $F(2, 162) =$ $7.56, p < .01$; *Happy*: $F(2, 162) = 22.199, p < .001$; *Sad*: $F(2, 162) = 24.459, p <$ .001) between the synthesisers, where post-hoc analysis identified eSpeak as significantly less satisfactory when choosing the emotion class than both of the other synthesisers. In addition, for the emotion class *Sad*, the post-hoc pairwise comparisons also revealed that satisfaction with emotions generated by CereVoice resulted in significantly higher ratings than with MaryTTS.

4.7   Pronunciation/Emotion

In the final part of the online survey, participants had to rate both the pronunciation and the synthesised emotions on a Likert scale from very poor (1) to very good (5). The synthesisers were presented one after the other, and for each synthesiser sentences with all three emotion classes were generated, which could be listened to by the participant as often as desired before both ratings were given. Table 3 contains the mean values and standard deviations for both ratings. The mean values indicate that eSpeak was rated worst and CereVoice was rated best for pronunciation as well as synthesised emotions.

Table 3. Means and standard deviations for the ratings of pronunciation and synthesised emotions on a scale of 1 ... 5.

Rating of Pronunciation/Emotion (1 .. 5)			
Emotion	E - eSpeak	M - MaryTTS	C - CereVoice
Pronunciation	$M = 1.74, SD = .93$	$M = 2.77, SD = .99$	$M = 3.27, SD = .89$
Emotion	$M = 1.60, SD = .65$	$M = 3.88, SD = .95$	$M = 4.06, SD = .78$

Rating of Pronunciation/Synthesised Emotion. A repeated measurement ANOVA on the ratings for pronunciation showed significant differences between the synthesisers ($F(2, 162) = 88.83, p < .001$). Post-hoc pairwise comparisons revealed that pronunciation of the generated sentences were rated from best to worse in the order CereVoice, MaryTTS, and eSpeak (E-M: $p < .001$, $-1.02, 95\% - CI[-1.32, -.72]$; E-C: $p < .001$, $-1.52, 95\% - CI[-1.81, -1.24]$; M-C: $p < .001$, $-.50, 95\% - CI[-.72, -.23]$).

A similar picture could be found for the ratings of the synthesised emotions. A repeated measurement ANOVA on the ratings for synthesised emotions showed significant differences between the synthesisers ($F(2, 162) = 345.47, p < .001$). The post-hoc pairwise comparisons identified the synthesiser eSpeak as worse than MaryTTS and CereVoice (E-M: $p < .001$, $-2.28, 95\% - CI[-2.56, -2.0]$; E-C: $p < .001$, $-2.46, 95\% - CI[-2.70, -2.23]$) in terms of the synthesised emotions.

5   Discussion

As Aylett et al. [1] mentioned, the time to only mimicry the naturalness of human voice is over. People especially those with CCN (*Complex Communication Needs*) have a great need for speech synthesisers that are able to convey a variety of expressive styles in a natural manner. This aspect is also important in light of the rapidly increasing speech interaction and its acceptance in smarthomes [6], to respond appropriately to the emotions of residents [7].

Researchers spent decades in developing natural sounding TTS (*Text-to-Speech*) incorporating prosodic elements with different approaches. As shown in Table 1, there are differences in correctly assessing emotions per synthesiser (in decreasing order: CereVoice [M = 2.78, SD = 1.42], MaryTTS [M = 2.62, SD = 1.54], eSpeak [M = 1.78, SD = 1.31]). These results are confirmed in the final part of the online survey (see Table 3). It comes as no surprise that the quality of the single synthesisers provided different, but consistent subjective assessments as they are based on different underlying techniques: formant synthesis (eSpeak), HMM-based synthesis (MaryTTS) and unit selection (CereVoice).

Our results are in line with previous studies investigating the quality of different types of speech synthesisers (see, for example, the chapter on Perceptual Quality Dimension by [10]). Formant synthesis tends to sound mechanical and artificial while the greatest amount of naturalness is typically achieved with unit selection. Even though we did not exploit the full potential of MaryXML and CereProc XML to control the quality of the expressive speech, MaryTTS and CereVoice performed better in terms of expressivity than eSpeak. CereProc showed the best results both in terms of satisfaction with the pronunciation, i.e. naturalness, and ability to convey emotional states as a whole, i.e. expressiveness. While it can be argued that we only used simple markups, we have to take into account that CCN users need to be able to control their voices in an easy and quick manner. The next step would be to integrate capabilities for expressive speech into EmotionTalker by enabling AAC users to specify emotions at a higher level of abstraction, but still communicate the intended expressive style in a believable manner.

The current research complements our previous research on the evaluation of EmotionTalker, a first prototype of a VOCA interface that included Emojis to enable people specify the intended emotion. For this experiment, we relied on a small number CCN users who tested EmotionTalker in their daily environment. Even though we aimed to include AAC users in our current evaluation by contacting an AAC forum, the current evaluation was not specifically addressed to AAC users. This was due to our focus on a perceptive study with a large number of users. For the online survey, it could be objected that we could not control the participants' surroundings and their equipment for listening to the sentences. However, to complete the survey, participants had to listen to all sentences with all synthesisers. So, they had a direct comparison.

6 Conclusion

Our objective was to identify a natural speech synthesiser with variability in expressive style for integration into a VOCA. To this end, we evaluated the ability of three synthesisers (eSpeak/MaryTTS/CereVoice) to convey emotionally neutral utterances in a happy, sad, or angry manner. Our assumption that CereVoice has the best capabilities was confirmed. In our online survey most of the 82 participants rated CereVoice better than MaryTTS - eSpeak was rated worst. As outlined by [4], people with CCN may have deficits in building emotional competencies during childhood. In order to improve their capabilities, it would have potential to equip VOCAs with ESS and usable input methods. CereVoice seems to be an adequate candidate, as our findings show.

The next step will be to extend our tests with EmotionTalker. We plan to have people with CCN test EmotionTalker in their own environment in specified situations over one week. It has to be shown if they can socialise more easily with a VOCA capable of ESS. Furthermore, novel synthesis paradigms should be taken into account, see the recent developments on the MaryTTS architecture to enable synthesis based on Deep Neural Networks [14] or the recently announced neural speech synthesis system CereWave AI by CereProc Ltd.[8]

Acknowledgements. The work presented here is partially supported by 'PROMI - Promotion inklusive' and the employment centre. We thank the students, Lena Tikovsky and Ewald Heinz, for their contribution to this work.

References

1. Aylett, M.P., Cowan, B.R., Clark, L.: Siri, echo and performance: you have to suffer darling. In: Conference on Human Factors in Computing Systems, Extended Abstracts, Glasgow, Scotland, UK. ACM, New York (2019). https://doi.org/10.1145/3290607.3310422
2. Aylett, M.P., Pidcock, C.J.: Adding and controlling emotion in synthesised speech. Tech. Rep. UK patent GB2447263A (2008)

---

[8] https://www.cereproc.com/en/v6 (accessed 11/06/2020).

3. Aylett, M.P., Vinciarelli, A., Wester, M.: Speech synthesis for the generation of artificial personality. IEEE Trans. Affect. Comput. **11**(2), 361–372 (2020). https://doi.org/10.1109/TAFFC.2017.2763134
4. Blackstone, S.W., Wilkins, D.P.: Exploring the importance of emotional competence in children with complex communication needs. Perspect. Augmentative Altern. Commun. **18**(3), 78–87 (2009). https://doi.org/10.1044/aac18.3.78
5. Chafe, W.: Prosody: the music of language. In: Genetti, C., Adelman, A. (eds.) How Languages Work - An Introduction to Language and Linguistics, 2nd edn, pp. 236–256. Cambridge University Press, Cambridge (2019)
6. Dang, C.T., Andre, E.: Acceptance of autonomy and cloud in the smart home and concerns. In: Dachselt, R., Weber, G. (eds.) Mensch und Computer 2018 (MuC 2018) - Tagungsband (2018)
7. Dang, C.T., Aslan, I., Lingenfelser, F., Baur, T., André, E.: Towards somaesthetic smarthome designs: exploring potentials and limitations of an affective mirror. In: Proceedings of the 9th International Conference on the Internet of Things. IoT 2019. Association for Computing Machinery, New York (2019). https://doi.org/10.1145/3365871.3365893
8. Fiannaca, A.J., Paradiso, A., Campbell, J., Morris, M.R.: Voicesetting: voice authoring UIs for improved expressivity in augmentative communication. In: Mandryk, R.L., Hancock, M., Perry, M., Cox, A.L. (eds.) Proceedings of the 2018 CHI Conference on Human Factors in Computing Systems, CHI 2018, Montreal, QC, Canada, 21–26 April 2018, p. 283. ACM (2018). https://doi.org/10.1145/3173574.3173857
9. Girden, E.R.: ANOVA: Repeated Measures. Sage, Newbury Park (1992)
10. Hinterleitner, F.: Quality of Synthetic Speech. TSTS. Springer, Singapore (2017). https://doi.org/10.1007/978-981-10-3734-4
11. Hoffmann, L., Wülfing, J.O.: Usability of electronic communication aids in the light of daily use. In: Proceedings 14th Biennial Conference of the International Society for Augmentative and Alternative Communication, p. 259 (2010)
12. Murray, I.R., Arnott, J.L.: Applying an analysis of acted vocal emotions to improve the simulation of synthetic speech. Comput. Speech Lang. **22**(2), 107–129 (2008). https://doi.org/10.1016/j.csl.2007.06.001
13. Schröder, M., Charfuelan, M., Pammi, S., Steiner, I.: Open source voice creation toolkit for the MARY TTS platform. In: INTERSPEECH 2011, 12th Annual Conference of the International Speech Communication Association, Florence, Italy, 27–31 August 2011, pp. 3253–3256. ISCA (2011)
14. Steiner, I., Maguer, S.L.: Creating new language and voice components for the updated marytts text-to-speech synthesis platform. In: Calzolari, N., et al. (eds.) Proceedings of the Eleventh International Conference on Language Resources and Evaluation, LREC 2018, Miyazaki, Japan, 7–12 May 2018. European Language Resources Association (ELRA) (2018)
15. Wagner, P., et al.: Speech synthesis evaluation - state-of-the-art assessment and suggestion for a novel research program. In: Proceedings of the 10th ISCA Speech Synthesis Workshop, pp. 105–110 (2019). https://doi.org/10.21437/SSW.2019-19
16. Wülfing, J.-O., André, E.: Progress to a VOCA with prosodic synthesised speech. In: Miesenberger, K., Kouroupetroglou, G. (eds.) ICCHP 2018. LNCS, vol. 10896, pp. 539–546. Springer, Cham (2018). https://doi.org/10.1007/978-3-319-94277-3_84

Perceived Length of Czech High Vowels in Relation to Formant Frequencies Evaluated by Automatic Speech Recognition

Tomáš Bořil[✉] and Jitka Veroňková

Faculty of Arts, Institute of Phonetics, Charles University, Nám. Jana Palacha 2, Praha 1, Czech Republic
{tomas.boril,jitka.veronkova}@ff.cuni.cz

Abstract. Recent studies measured significant differences in formant values in the production of short and long high vowel pairs in the Czech language. Perceptual impacts of such findings were confirmed employing listening tests proving that a perceived vowel length is influenced by formant values related to a tongue position. Non-native speakers of Czech may experience difficulties in communication when they interchange the vowel length in words, which may lead to a completely different meaning of the message. This paper analyses perception of two-syllable words with manipulated duration and formant frequencies of high vowels i/iː or u/uː in the first syllable using automatic speech recognition (ASR) system. Such a procedure makes it possible to set a fine resolution in the range of examined factors. Our study confirms the formant values have a substantial impact on the perception of high vowels' length by ASR, comparable to mean values obtained from listening tests performed on a group of human participants.

Keywords: High Czech vowels · Vowel length · Vowel quality · Automatic speech recognition · Perception

1 Introduction

The acquisition of a vowel system is one of the key aspects of learning a second language (L2). Czech vowel system consists of five pairs of short and long monophthongs and three diphthongs [8,12,13]. Since the vowel length is phonologically distinctive, its improper interchange in L2 speakers' production may lead to a misunderstanding (e.g.., /kruːciː farmaːr̝i/ vs /kruci farmaːr̝i/ (meaning *turkey farmers* vs *cruel farmers*).

This research was supported by the Czech Science Foundation project No. 18-18300S "Phonetic properties of Czech in non-native and native speakers' communication".

P. Sojka et al. (Eds.): TSD 2020, LNAI 12284, pp. 409–417, 2020.
https://doi.org/10.1007/978-3-030-58323-1_44

Differences between formant values (i.e., vowel quality correlating with a tongue setting in a vocal tract) of a short and a long vowel in a pair are traditionally described as insignificant (both in production and perception perspective) except for /i/ and /iː/ [5]. Later, a differentiation of short [ɪ] and long [iː] symbols in the international phonetic alphabet (IPA) was proposed [4].

In addition to statistical evaluation of production data of [ɪ] and [iː], [10] performed a perception analysis of manipulated items with a stimulus array covering the spectral and the durational span between both vowels in one syllable where both lengths create meaningful words with a comparable probability frequency. The study also found a significant difference in the perception of Bohemian (the western part of the Czech Republic) and Moravian (the eastern region of the Czech Republic) where Bohemians relied more on the spectrum, whereas Moravians relied more on the duration. Later, [14] found differences in pronunciation of [ɪ] and [iː] in the speech of Czech Radio newsreaders.

[12] focuses on the production of Czech in Bohemian and Moravian regions, and there is a clear trend of the [u] vs [uː] formant shift in the Bohemian subgroup in addition to the previously observed [ɪ] and [iː] relation. Spontaneous Czech speech was analysed in [7], the formant shifts between [ɪ] – [iː] and [u] – [uː] were measured, and also a promising difference between the [o] and [oː] formant positions appeared. [9] conducted a listening test with artificial one-syllable pseudowords containing manipulations of [ɪ] – [iː] and [u] – [uː] vowels analogous to [10] experiment. In both Czech high vowels, the quality (formant values) played a crucial role in a vowel length discrimination in the subgroup of listeners from the Bohemian region.

The main purpose of this paper is to compare the automatic speech recognition (ASR) of Czech high vowels' length with human perception in 3 experiments.

To emphasize the difference of qualities, we decided to use the [ʊ] IPA symbol for the short vowel and [uː] for the long vowel in the following text.

Experiment 1 examines perception of quantity (phonological length) of vowels [ɪ] and [iː] based on their quality (formant values in the spectrum). ASR evaluates items manipulated with a fine resolution in both duration and formant dimensions. A subset of this data set with a less detailed formant scale is also evaluated perceptually by human participants (Bohemian region) in a listening test. The question is whether ASR perceives the boundary between short and long vowels in a comparable manner and whether these results correspond to [10].

Experiments 2 and 3 analyse ASR behaviour on vowels [ʊ] and [uː] manipulated similarly. Experiment 3 focuses on the fine detail of the transition part found in experiment 2. The question is, whether the effect of formant values has an impact on the perceived length in compliance with the novel findings in [9], where artificial one-syllable pseudowords were tested by human participants in a listening test.

The ASR approach applied in this study may bring several advantages. The number of items in a listening test is naturally limited due to the requirement of keeping human participants entirely focused. For this reason, the number of tested factors and the resolution of coverage of their span have to be notably decreased in many experiments. The purpose of such experiments is to map a subjective perception of random individuals and then to estimate the mean value of the population. ASR systems are trained on a large sample of the population, and hence they also may provide evaluation similar to an average representative of the population. Such a procedure can be repeated many times with different settings and a large number of items, which would be impossible with human participants of listening tests.

2   Method

2.1   Experiment 1

For the first experiment, we created 147 manipulated items (21 formant steps and 7 duration steps) using Praat [2] and rPraat [3] as follows. A minimal pair consisting of two words [vɪrɪ] (meaning *viruses*) and [viːrɪ] (meaning *vortices*) was chosen to serve as boundaries lying on a diagonal of a two-dimensional duration–formant space to be explored. The advantage of the analysis of vowel in the first syllable is that it is not prone to phrase-final lengthening [15].

We recorded both words in a slow speech rate by an adult female speaker in a quiet low-reverb room (PCM uncompressed, the sample rate of 32 kHz, 16-bit depth). Estimated median values of formant frequencies F1–F4 of the target (first syllable) short [ɪ] were 405, 2295, 2866, and 4099 Hz and of the long [iː] were 305, 2700, 3000, and 4099 Hz (we rounded the fourth formant values in both vowels to the same number because instantaneous values reached a large variability around roughly the same values in both short and long vowels). For the manipulation purposes, we chose the record of [viːrɪ] as a basis because stimuli with shorter durations of the target vowel can be easily created by truncating the original long vowel.

The upper-part spectrum of the basis stimulus obtained by a high-pass Hann filter with a cut-off frequency of 4500 Hz was stored as a separate signal to be returned to manipulated signals at the final step of stimuli creation to obtain a more natural sound with a full range of the spectrum.

To obtain the source (excitation) signal and formant object, the basis stimulus was resampled to 16000 Hz and processed using the Burg method of linear predictive coding (LPC) with a prediction order of 15 (leading to max. 7 formant frequencies detected), 25 ms segmentation window length with 5 ms time step and pre-emphasis frequency of 50 Hz. Note: preliminary, prediction orders of 16 and 15 were examined in all experiments, the order of 16 in experiment 1 lead to an unnatural, artificial distortion at high frequencies; the order of 16 was necessary for experiments 2 and 3. To avoid random jumps in the formant object, formant trajectories were subsequently smoothed by a formant-tracking algorithm with 4 formant tracks.

In the next step, formant frequencies in the time interval of the first vowel duration were manipulated between the values of [ɪ] and [iː] in 21 linear steps. For each step, the manipulated sound was created by filtering the source (excitation) signal with the formant filter.

Finally, to create the whole set of target stimuli, each sound file was obtained by a concatenation of the first part of the original basis stimulus (until the first vowel), the shortened vowel from formant-manipulated signals with the upper-part spectra signal superposed, and the remaining part of the basis stimulus. The target vowel was shortened to durations in the range from 90 ms to 300 ms in 7 linear steps.

Automatic Speech Recognition. To evaluate manipulated stimuli by an automatic speech recognition system (ASR), we concatenated all stimuli in a random order into one long sound file. Each item was separated by a short pause and a neutral nonmanipulated word [vlakɪ] (meaning *trains*) by the same speaker to reduce possible interferences of two successive manipulated stimuli and also to clearly distinguish the boundaries of tested items in case the item was not recognized properly, e.g.., as two separate one-syllable words.

In total, we prepared five replications of the experiment, i.e., five different permutations of all manipulated items with different random order to avoid a possible effect of the order of stimuli.

To evaluate the concatenated sound file, we employed a commercial state-of-the-art ASR system Beey by NEWTON Technologies [6] set to the Czech language recognition and with additional text postprocessing switched off.

Although all nonmanipulated filler-words [vlakɪ] were recognized correctly, the ASR occasionally had problems with the recognition of manipulated items (probably due to their overall lower quality) and recognized them as a different word or a couple of two one-syllable words, e.g., [viːlɪ] (*fairies*), [bɪlɪ] (*they were*), [ɪ vɪ] (*also you*) or [bɪ jɪ] (*would her*). Not surprisingly, the consonants were affected, and the vowels remained either [ɪ] or [iː]. For this reason, we focused on the length of the first-syllable vowel [ɪ] or [iː] in such cases, ignoring mismatches in consonants.

For each item, the resulting score was calculated as a mean value of all five replications of the experiment.

Listening Test. To compare the results of ASR with human perception, we performed a listening test with 20 participants (native speakers of Czech, both male and female students, median age $= 23$ years) using comfortable headphones in a quiet room. To keep them focused throughout the test, we decided to select a subset of items only. The resolution of the vowel duration scale was kept the same, i.e., 7 linear steps between 90 ms and 300 ms. The resolution of formant transition was reduced to 5 discrete steps, resulting to 35 items. In addition to these "items-of-interest", other 15 two-syllable words with different vowels were included as distractors. Each of the total of 50 items in the test was initiated with a short desensitization beep sound.

The listening test was administrated using Praat multiple forced-choice (ExperimentMFC) environment [2]. After a short training set (6 items) to resolve possible problems and questions, the main test with 50 items in a random order for each listener was performed. Each item could be played three times at the most. The task was to click on a button with the word closest to the sound (both words with a short and a long vowel in the first syllable were offered). After the first 25 items, the participants were instructed to take a short break and listen to a song included in the test folder.

2.2 Experiment 2

In the second experiment, we created a set of stimuli focused on short [ʊ] and long [uː]. We recorded an adult male voice saying [kruʊiː] (meaning *cruel* in plural) and [kruːciː] (meaning *turkey* adjective).

Estimated median values of formant frequencies F1 – F4 of the target (first syllable) short [ʊ] were 360, 906, 2774, and 3994 Hz, and of the long [uː] were 288, 567, 2774, and 3994 Hz (we rounded the third and the fourth formant values in both vowels to the same number because instantaneous values reached a large variability around roughly same values in both short and long vowels).

The process of manipulation was conducted in the same manner as in the experiment 1; the LPC prediction order was set to 16. The transition between two formant boundaries was divided into 19 linear steps. The duration of the vowel in the first syllable ranged from 90 ms to 300 ms in 7 linear steps.

This time, only the ASR task was performed with five random permutations of stimuli. Each item was concatenated with a nonmanipulated word [farmaːrɪ] (meaning *farmers*), both variants creating a meaningful phrase with a similar probability frequency, i.e., the ASR should not prefer one variant at the expense of the other.

2.3 Experiment 3

The third experiment continued with the same original records of experiment 2, but we aimed at the middle transient area. The formant axes were focused on the lower two thirds (as compared to experiment 2) with detailed 21 steps, and the duration focused on the middle part ranging from 125 ms to 230 ms in 9 detailed steps.

3 Results

We are aware of the fact our findings depend on a speech rate, a prosody, and an individual speaker's vocal space area; therefore we do not want to interpret our results as absolute values of boundaries between short and long vowel perception. Since this dependence can be a result of a complex combination of many factors, we do not even normalise duration and formant values because it could imply a universal rule. Rather than that, we focus on the shape of boundaries in the duration – formants relation which reflects the fact the vowel length perception is influenced by formant values, i.e., vowel quality.

414   T. Bořil and J. Veroňková

3.1   Experiment 1

The results of ASR are depicted in Fig. 1a; a grey value of each rectangle represents a mean value of five replications of the experiment. Due to the statistic approach of ASR, some items were classified differently in some of the replications, which is mostly the case of items near the visible edge between short and long area.

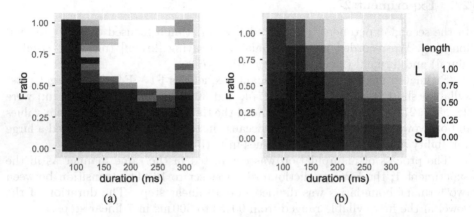

(a)   (b)

Fig. 1. Evaluation of [ɪ] and [iː] vowels in experiment 1. The vowel is manipulated both in duration and formant values, Fratio stands for ratio on the range between formant values of natural [ɪ] and [iː]. Shades of grey represent mean values of evaluated vowel lengths from (a) 5 realisations of ASR, (b) 20 participants of the listening test (white = long, black = short).

The shortest items (duration of 90 ms) were identically identified as short vowel [ɪ]. All other items above the 90 ms duration were split into short [ɪ] and long [iː] with an almost horizontal boundary implying ASR used the vowel quality (i.e., spectrum) as the main cue to differentiate these two variants. This result complies with Bohemian Czech listeners in [9] (analysing artificial one-syllable words), although the ASR boundary seems slightly more horizontal.

We tested a statistic significance of duration and Fratio (a ratio on the span between typical formant values of the short and the long vowel) effects using mixed-effects models with logistic regression (binomial family for binary outcome) [1] in [11]. Both fixed effects (duration and Fratio) were centred and standardised, replication was a random effect. The model formula (including random slopes) is $length \sim duration + Fratio + (1 + duration + Fratio|replication)$, p-values were obtained by likelihood ratio tests of the full model with the effect against the model without the effect.

For both Fratio and duration effects, $p < 0.001$. We also passed a subset of data with a duration equal or larger than 160 ms, and for the Fratio, p-value remained <0.001; however, for the duration, $p = 0.2554$. This finding corresponds with 1a very well because vowel quality seems to be the main cue for longer durations.

Figure 1b represents the mean values of 20 participants of our listening test. These results are similar to ASR decision in Fig. 1a, although the Fratio scale is sampled in much fewer steps. However, for durations equal to or larger than 230 ms, some listeners evaluated items with Fratio = 0 (i.e., [ɪ]) as long. Statistical evaluation of both fixed effects was conducted analogously to the one with the ASR, subject (human participant) being a random effect. For both Fratio and duration, p < 0.001.

3.2 Experiment 2

Figure 2a represents results of ASR evaluating records with manipulated [ʊ]/[uː] vowels. For durations lower than or equal to 125 ms, all vowels were recognized as short despite the Fratio. For longer durations, the effect of the Fratio is visible. For both Fratio and duration, p < 0.001.

These ASR results are closely comparable to the relations observed in the listening tests of one-syllable pseudo-words in [9].

3.3 Experiment 3

The results of experiment 3 (i.e., detail zoom of the transition area of experiment 2) are depicted in Fig. 2b. The impact of vowel quality on recognized length is apparent and compatible with observations in [9]. For both Fratio and duration factors, p < 0.001.

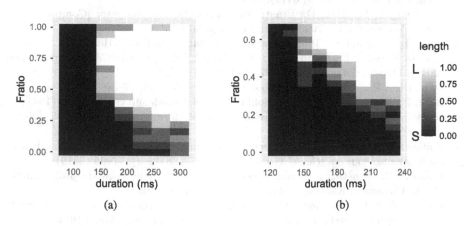

(a)   (b)

Fig. 2. Evaluation of [ʊ] and [uː] vowels. Fratio stands for ratio of the range between formant values of natural [ʊ] and [uː]. Shades of grey represent mean values of 5 evaluated vowel lengths by ASR in (a) experiment 2, (b) experiment 3 (white = long, black = short).

4   Conclusions

In the task of the evaluation of perceived phonological vowel length, ASR trained on an extensive sample of population reached results comparable with listening tests conducted on human subjects. The recent findings of the impact of vowel quality on perceived length of Czech high vowels in one-syllable pseudo-words [9] were confirmed on real two-syllable words in this paper.

Due to its phonological status in Czech, a mismatch in the vowel length could lead to misunderstandings and generally difficult communication, which is typical of foreign learners of the Czech language. Interestingly, based on our informal observation, we can say the vast majority of naïve L1 users of Czech language is not aware of these differences in quality of short and long pairs of high vowels. Teachers of L2 Czech learners, especially during the pronunciation training, should be aware of the fact that their perception of the phonological vowel length could be influenced not only by the vowel duration but also by the quality of short and long high vowel pairs.

The ASR technique may bring advantages in the process of evaluation in such a way that the count of items is not limited and the range of examined parameters can be covered in much more detail than in listening tests. On the other hand, a combination with these perception experiments is recommended as they may uncover additional effects such as region, sex or age of the listener.

References

1. Bates, D., Mächler, M., Bolker, B., Walker, S.: Fitting linear mixed-effects models using lme4. J. Stat. Softw. **67**(1), 1–48 (2015)
2. Boersma, P., Weenink, D.: Praat: doing phonetics by computer [Computer program]. Version 6.1.10 (2020). http://www.praat.org/
3. Bořil, T., Skarnitzl, R.: Tools rPraat and mPraat. In: Sojka, P., Horák, A., Kopeček, I., Pala, K. (eds.) TSD 2016. LNCS (LNAI), vol. 9924, pp. 367–374. Springer, Cham (2016). https://doi.org/10.1007/978-3-319-45510-5_42
4. Dankovičová, J.: Czech. J. Int. Phonetic Assoc. **27**(1–2), 77–80 (1997)
5. Hála, B.: Akustická podstata samohlásek. Česká akademie věd a umění (1941)
6. NEWTON Technologies: Beey [web-based platform]. Version 0.7.16.5 (2020). https://editor.beey.io
7. Paillereau, N., Chládková, K.: Spectral and temporal characteristics of Czech vowels in spontaneous speech. AUC PHILOLOGICA **2019**(2), 77–95 (2019)
8. Palková, Z.: Fonetika a fonologie češtiny: s obecným úvodem do problematiky oboru. Univerzita Karlova, vydavatelství Karolinum (1994)
9. Podlipský, V.J., Chládková, K., Šimáčková, Š.: Spectrum as a perceptual cue to vowel length in Czech, a quantity language. J. Acoust. Soc. Am. **146**(4), EL352–EL357 (2019). Acoustical Society of America
10. Podlipský, V.J., Skarnitzl, R., Volín, J.: High front vowels in Czech: a contrast in quantity or quality? In: Proceedings of Interspeech, vol. 2009, pp. 132–135 (2009)
11. R Core Team: R: A Language and Environment for Statistical Computing. R Foundation for Statistical Computing, Vienna, Austria (2020). https://www.R-project.org/

12. Šimáčková, Š., Podlipský, V.J., Chládková, K.: Czech spoken in Bohemia and Moravia. J. Int. Phonetic Assoc. **42**(2), 225–232 (2012)
13. Skarnitzl, R., Šturm, P., Volín, J.: Zvuková báze řečové komunikace: Fonetický a fonologický popis řeči. Univerzita Karlova v Praze, Nakladatelství Karolinum (2016)
14. Skarnitzl, R.: Dvojí i v české výslovnosti. Naše řeč **95**(3), 141–153 (2012)
15. Volín, J., Skarnitzl, R.: Temporal downtrends in Czech read speech. In: Proceedings of Interspeech, vol. 2007, pp. 442–445 (2007)

Inserting Punctuation to ASR Output in a Real-Time Production Environment

Pavel Hlubík[1,2], Martin Španěl[1], Marek Boháč[1],
and Lenka Weingartová[1(✉)]

[1] NEWTON Technologies, Na Pankráci 1683/127, 140 00 Prague, Czech Republic
{pavel.hlubik,martin.spanel,marek.bohac,lenka.weingartova}@newtontech.cz
[2] Faculty of Information Technology, Czech Technical University in Prague,
Prague, Czech Republic

Abstract. The output of a speech recognition system is a continuous stream of words that has to be post-processed in various ways, out of which punctuation insertion is an essential step. Punctuated text is far more comprehensible to the reader, can be used for subtitling, and is necessary for further NLP processing, such as machine translation. In this article, we describe how state-of-the-art results in the field of punctuation restoration can be utilized in a production-ready business environment in the Czech language. A recurrent neural network based on long short-term memory is employed, making use of various features: textual based on pre-trained word embeddings, prosodic (mainly temporal), morphological, noise information, and speaker diarization. All the features except morphological tags were found to improve our baseline system. As we work in a real-time setup, it is not possible to employ information from the future of the word stream, yet we achieve significant improvements using LSTM. The usage of RNN also allows the model to learn longer dependencies than any n-gram-based language model can, which we find essential for the insertion of question marks. The deployment of an RNN-based model thus leads to a relative 22.6% decrease in punctuation errors and improvement in all metrics but one.

Keywords: Automatic speech recognition · Czech language · Punctuation insertion

1 Introduction

In our everyday business practice we employ automatic speech recognition (ASR) for different purposes, from meeting transcriptions to subtitling or media monitoring. We have long keenly felt the absence of a reliable punctuation adding system in our target languages, in this case Czech. The usefulness of punctuation marks (full stops, commas, question marks, etc.) is twofold - it significantly improves the comprehensibility of a text for a human reader, but also it is necessary for further natural language processing (NLP) of the recognized text, which

Supported by the Technology Agency of the Czech Republic (No. FW01010468).

© Springer Nature Switzerland AG 2020
P. Sojka et al. (Eds.): TSD 2020, LNAI 12284, pp. 418–425, 2020.
https://doi.org/10.1007/978-3-030-58323-1_45

requires reliable sentence boundaries. Morphosyntactic tagging, machine translation, dialogue analysis and other advanced algorithms all display significantly worsened performance without - or with incorrect - sentence boundaries. There is ample anecdotal evidence for ambiguity caused by incorrectly placed commas, such as "stop clubbing, baby seals" or "let's eat kids", but the truth is that in real-world speech technology applications, these errors may well render the ASR output unusable without manual corrections by human editors.

While our company does employ human editors to create 100% transcripts for specific purposes, adding punctuation to recognized text was by our internal review evaluated as one of the priorities to shorten editing time and speed up the process (the other being emergent content out-of-vocabulary tokens).

Our previous approach to punctuation adding was rule-based. Regarding commas, contexts with high-probability of a comma were mined from text corpora and refined by linguists. The Czech language has quite a rigid system of comma placement based on syntax, therefore these rules were able to add commas with high precision around subordinate clauses. Other contexts, such as parentheses, vocatives, or enumerating items in lists, could not be captured.

Full stops were added based on length of non-speech events (mainly pauses), which also is not without specific disadvantages. Both systems were complemented with a set of black lists, stating contexts where punctuation marks should not occur. No attempt was made to create rules for question mark placement.

Due to the aforementioned limitations of our baseline system, a neural network-based approach was developed, the results of which are presented here.

Working in a production environment comes with its own set of advantages and limitations. One of the main advantages is access to data - our company transcribes approximately 920 TV, radio and internet broadcasts a week, which are then corrected by human annotators. Our chief limitation lies in the fact that punctuation needs to be inserted into streamed data in real-time. The nature of our workflow does not allow for processing finished ASR outputs, but needs to run in parallel. This brings up the challenge of inserting punctuation into unfinished sentences or phrases.

Within this experiment, we considered adding full stops, commas and question marks only, since other punctuation symbols were too rare in our datasets.

1.1   Related Works

Many previous works about punctuation restoration have been published. Usually n-grams are used in multiple ways: they can be directly used to train a language model [15], or they can serve as a basis for a set of rules (as in our case) [1,2]. N-gram models unfortunately suffer from sparsity issue [18], which hurts their ability of generalization. In recent years, recurrent neural networks (RNN), namely their type - long short-term memory (LSTM), [5] - proved to be able to generalize much better with regard to unseen sequences, partially due to their ability to work with larger contexts than any n-gram. This also leads us to believe that a model based on LSTM could be suitable for predicting question marks, as these usually depend on the beginning of a sentence.

We base our approach on the work of Tilk and Alumäe [18], where a two-stage model is proposed. First, a purely textual model is trained on the Wikipedia dataset, subsequently the output of its last hidden layer is utilized as high-level input features for a second stage, which also takes pause duration into account. This is followed by a bidirectional RNN with attention mechanism [19], which unfortunately does not fit the constraints of our setup.

Worth mentioning is also the use of convolutional neural networks (CNN). As CNNs prove to be effective in various tasks regarding sequences – sentence classification or sentiment analysis [6,7], it might be useful to employ them for punctuation insertion as well [3]. A proposed approach is to consider a sliding window of m words, a sample matrix formed with embedding of these words by convolutional filters of various sizes and then predict punctuation after word $w_{m/2}$.

2   Method

As mentioned above, our approach is constrained by our production workflow. Our system incorporates many technological submodules and its back-end is complex. In this paper we focus our attention solely on the submodule adding punctuation to recognized words. For a diagram of the whole system see Fig. 1.

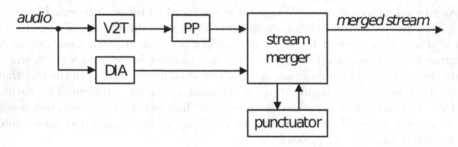

Fig. 1. Diagram of our ASR workflow. Voice-to-text (V2T) and diarization (DIA) modules take audio input and produce slightly delayed real-time streams of timed events. Post-processing module (PP) provides formatting of numbers, abbreviations, titles, etc. The delay between V2T and DIA event streams is variable, the stream merger module compensates for this variability between event streams.

The stream merger is the connection point between the whole processing chain and the punctuation submodule. The voice-to-text (V2T) module [11–13] produces two types of events: words and non-speech events. At the end time of every V2T event there is a slot that can contain document events (e.g. speaker or language change). Slots after word events may also contain punctuation marks. Some slots are disabled by the post-processing (PP) module that binds specific words together. The stream merger also implements several heuristic overrides (e.g. changing comma after the last word of the utterance into a full stop).

2.1 Baseline Punctuation Module

The main motivation for our work is to improve our current punctuation module by incorporating machine learning algorithms. The baseline module is a hierarchic chain of partial tasks starting with those with highest precision (in order to limit excess punctuation): i) rule-based adding of commas, ii) black-list blocking of slots, iii) utilization of diarization and iv) tempo-based addition of full stops.

Comma addition is based on large text corpora analysis employed to extract a set of n-gram rules (up to 2 words before and after punctuation position). These rules are implemented via weighted finite-state transducers as shown in [1,2]. These rules were optimized towards high precision and cannot process language phenomena such as enumerations or parentheses. Black-list slot blocking is a set of rules that prevent the punctuation module from placing full stops in certain slots, such as after prepositions or inside frequent collocations.

Full stop placing is triggered in free slots followed by longer non-speech events. The length threshold of non-speech is adapted via a flowing window that logs the duration of last 20 observed non-speech events (hesitations, breaths, silences, etc.). Moreover, full stops are automatically placed into slots where speaker change occurs. This rule can also override an already placed comma.

2.2 Dataset

The dataset used for this task consists of machine transcriptions of various broadcasts from the Czech TV and radio collected over several months. These machine transcriptions do not contain any punctuation. We also possess manual corrections of these transcriptions, in which mistakes of the ASR system are corrected by human editors and punctuation is added. To mimic the conditions of the model's future deployment, we did not wish to train it on these corrected transcripts, therefore a sequence alignment of machine and manually corrected transcripts is performed, and punctuation is projected into original machine transcriptions, which can be then used as labelled data.

As is the usual practice, we split the dataset into training, validation and test parts.[1] For number of files and tokens in each part, see Table 1.

Table 1. Dataset size. Tokens are speech events provided by the ASR system.

Split	Files	Tokens
Train	11204	12.5M
Validation	467	480k
Test	448	421k

---

[1] The test set is publicly available on: http://newtontech.net/punctuator/tsd2020_testdata.zip.

2.3 Features

In an attempt to utilize all the information we posses about the text, we tried to employ various feature types from previous works. With regard to information related to prosody of speech, we decided to incorporate temporal features only. The reasons were twofold: other prosodic features, such as F0 contours or energy features, were not shown to add much to the accuracy of punctuation insertion [4,14], their extraction from the speech signal is more difficult and requires longer computing time, thereby forbidding their application in our real-time use case.

Consequently, we opted to include 4 types of features that could be reliably acquired directly from the raw ASR output:

Textual features consisted of 300-dimensional word embeddings, obtained by a pre-trained fasttext embedder [10]. They were based on n-grams of characters rather than single words to more effectively deal with unknown words. Information about morphology is also to some extent contained in the embeddings and it saves us the need to lemmatize words.

Prosodic features (primarily temporal) were related to both words and non-speech segments. We extracted word duration, word tempo, type of non-speech segment (pause, breath, hesitation or other noise) and its duration. Word tempo indicates relative increase or decrease of word duration, thereby capturing phrase-final lengthening and other changes. It was computed as the ratio of real word duration to its predicted duration based on phonemes contained in the word and word length. Reference phoneme durations were taken from [20].

Morphological features were extracted using the MorphoDiTa tagger [16].

Diarization features were employed in a 3-dimensional vector. The first position (0 or 1) indicates whether a speaker change point occurred during the word or preceding noise events. The second position represents the time offset of the change point from the beginning of the word, the third position being the offset value if the change point occurred within a preceding noise.

2.4 Model

The model we use is an LSTM-based RNN with 2 hidden layers. The first one is a dense layer of size 100 with softmax activations acting as an input filter, the second one an LSTM layer with 200 units. The output layer is a softmax layer of size 4, which corresponds to the number of classes we use.

In training, the first three predicted labels are omitted and the others are shifted to the left, so that the network predicts punctuation with delay of three words, utilizing the features of three words after predicted punctuation.

The input vectors for the model have the dimension of 396 and consist of concatenated feature vectors of all types described above.

We employed Tensorflow 2.0 to create and train our models. In all experiments, we trained the model with the Adam optimizer [8] and learning rate $\alpha = 10^{-4}$. One GPU was utilized for training, which we have found to bring sufficient speedup. Dropout rate of 0.2 is applied to all hidden layers, which seems to be enough to prevent overfitting. Convergence of the model usually occurs after 300 epochs, which corresponds to several hours in our training setup.

3   Experiments and Results

One of our goals during the experiments was to evaluate the contribution of different types of features. As expected with regard to findings of Tilk and Alumäe [18], temporal prosodic features (which include pause duration) are useful for inserting full stops. A model trained on prosodic features only outperformed our baseline in inserting full stops, however failed terribly when it came to commas, with recall <1%. This corroborates the findings of [4] and [9], and is in agreement with our knowledge about non-final prosodic boundaries, which can be marked by means of different prosodic events (see e.g. [17]), since prosodic features work in synergy and can to some extent substitute one another.

Morphological features were employed in a hope they would be beneficial in certain situations, such as inserting commas into enumerations. This assumption did not hold. Excluding these features from training vectors did not worsen performance of our model and a model trained exclusively on them performed very poorly overall.

The most significant finding about feature importance is the model's sensitivity to diarization features. In the training data, speaker change points co-occur with full stops and question marks, as speakers usually finish their sentence before another speaker takes the floor. But this accounts directly only for approximately a third of full stops/question marks present in the data set. We found out that if we omit these features - replace them with zeros - to mimic a situation when the diarization system is temporarily unavailable, performance drops significantly. This drop cannot be explained by errors around speaker change points only, as there are not enough of these. We hypothesize that a decision to insert a full stop greatly changes the model's hidden state, which in turn affects many future predictions.

3.1   Performance Comparison and Discussion

One of our main concerns regarding evaluation of the model is the comparison with our baseline system. We measure the performance of both models in a setup that simulates conditions under which the model is going to be used in production. The model is deployed on server and receives one word at a time, which will be the case in production. Our neural network-based model outperforms the baseline in all metrics except one: The baseline system shows higher precision in inserting commas. Full results can be found in Table 2.

From the comparison of the results it can be seen that the new model reduces number of errors in punctuation by 22.6%, which should bring a valuable improvement in our workflow. On the other hand, the neural network seems to struggle with precision when inserting commas. The baseline, rule-based model is very precise in this regard, with precision of 80.7%. Neural network trades some of this precision for recall, which might not necessarily be a desired result in a production case. We have concluded from pilot testing that excess commas are perceived by human readers as more noticeable errors than missing ones.

Table 2. Comparison of performance: precision and recall for full stops (.), commas (,) and question marks (?), plus a total error rate. Precision is a rate of true positives (TP) over the number of TP plus false positives (FP). Recall means the number of TP over the number of TP+FP. Total error rate is the fraction of misclassified samples.

	Prec(.)	Rec(.)	Prec(,)	Rec(,)	Prec(?)	Rec(?)	Err.
Baseline	0.587	0.421	**0.807**	0.572	–	–	0.0903
Neural network	**0.720**	**0.660**	0.739	**0.641**	0.611	0.172	**0.0699**
Relative improvement	22.7%	56.7%	−8.4%	12.0%	–	–	22.6%

Furthermore, we hypothesize that the use of RNN allows the model to learn longer dependencies, which is essential for the insertion of question marks, which are usually coded at the beginning of the sentence.

It should be noted that classes in our data set are not evenly distributed. There is one majority class of "blank" symbol (i.e. no punctuation). Generally, training algorithms are known to suffer due to nonuniform prior distribution of classes. However, due to satisfying results and a higher desirability of precision at the expense of recall, we were not forced to tackle the issue.

4   Conclusion and Future Work

We presented a RNN-LSTM-based approach to inserting punctuation into ASR output utilizing pre-trained word embeddings, prosodic features consisting of temporal information about words and non-speech events (e.g. pause duration, word tempo, noise type), morphological and diarization features. This approach was tested in a production-ready environment, where the data stream is processed word by word, without the possibility to look into the future.

This new model achieved a total error rate of 6.99% and outperformed our baseline (a rule-based model) in all metrics but one. The relative decrease of punctuation errors is 22.6%. Our results imply that the least useful feature in our experiment were morphological tags, which did not add much to overall performance. On the other hand, word embeddings, prosodic and diarization features all contributed to performance improvement. The diarization features especially seem to add a significant value.

In the future we would like to explore some other possibilities. As the baseline model performs well on commas, we would like to utilize its potential. One way could be including its predictions into feature vectors used by the network. Another way might be training an ensemble model per se.

Input text preprocessing is also an area where many more experiments can be done. When manually evaluating punctuated text, we noticed a lot of mistakes around numbers. While our evidence for this claim remains speculative, we would like to explore the contribution of substituting all numbers with a single number token. We also decided not to lemmatize words in a hope that more meaning would be preserved in word sequences, yet lemmatization remains a standard step in an NLP pipeline and should be at least evaluated in our case.

References

1. Boháč, M., Blavka, K.: Using suprasegmental information in recognized speech punctuation completion. In: TSD (2014)
2. Boháč, M., Rott, M., Kovář, V.: Text punctuation: an inter-annotator agreement study. In: TSD (2017)
3. Che, X., Wang, C., Yang, H., Meinel, C.: Punctuation prediction for unsegmented transcript based on word vector. In: LREC (2016)
4. Christensen, H., Gotoh, Y., Renals, S.: Punctuation annotation using statistical prosody models. In: ITRW on Prosody in Speech Recognition and Understanding, pp. 35–40 (2001)
5. Hochreiter, S., Schmidhuber, J.: Long short-term memory. Neural Comput. **9**(8), 1735–80 (1997)
6. Kalchbrenner, N., Grefenstette, E., Blunsom, P.: A convolutional neural network for modelling sentences. In: Proceedings of the 52nd Annual Meeting of the ACL (Volume 1: Long Papers), pp. 655–665 (2014)
7. Kim, Y.: Convolutional neural networks for sentence classification. In: EMNLP, pp. 1746–1751 (2014)
8. Kingma, D.P., Ba, J.: Adam: a method for stochastic optimization. In: International Conference on Learning Representations (2014)
9. Levy, T., Silber-Varod, V., Moyal, A.: The effect of pitch, intensity and pause duration in punctuation detection. In: 2012 IEEE 27th Convention of Electrical and Electronics Engineers in Israel, pp. 1–4 (2012)
10. Mikolov, T., Grave, E., Bojanowski, P., Puhrsch, C., Joulin, A.: Advances in pre-training distributed word representations. In: LREC (2018)
11. Nouza, J., et al.: Making Czech historical radio archive accessible and searchable for wide public. J. Multimedia **7**, 159–169 (2012)
12. Nouza, J., et al.: Speech-to-text technology to transcribe and disclose 100,000+ hours of bilingual documents from historical Czech and Czechoslovak radio archive. In: Interspeech (2014)
13. Nouza, J., Šafařík, R., Červa, P.: ASR for South Slavic languages developed in almost automated way. In: Interspeech, pp. 3868–3872 (2016)
14. Öktem, A., Farrús, M., Wanner, L.: Attentional parallel RNNs for generating punctuation in transcribed speech. In: SLSP, pp. 131–142 (2017)
15. Stolcke, A., et al.: Automatic detection of sentence boundaries and disfluencies based on recognized words. In: ICSLP (1998)
16. Straková, J., Straka, M., Hajič, J.: Open-source tools for morphology, lemmatization, POS tagging and named entity recognition. In: Proceedings of 52nd Annual Meeting of the ACL: System Demonstrations, pp. 13–18 (2014)
17. Swerts, M.: Prosodic features at discourse boundaries of different strength. J. Acoust. Soc. Am. **101**, 514–21 (1997)
18. Tilk, O., Alumäe, T.: LSTM for punctuation restoration in speech transcripts. In: Interspeech (2015)
19. Tilk, O., Alumäe, T.: Bidirectional recurrent neural network with attention mechanism for punctuation restoration. In: Interspeech (2016)
20. Weingartovà, L.: Identifikace mluvčího v temporální doméně řeči [Speaker identification in the temporal domain of speech]. Ph.D. thesis, Charles University in Prague (2015)

Very Fast Keyword Spotting System with Real Time Factor Below 0.01

Jan Nouza[✉][iD], Petr Červa[iD], and Jindřich Žďánský

Institute of Information Technologies and Electronics,
Technical University of Liberec, Studentska 2, 46117 Liberec, Czech Republic
{jan.nouza,petr.cerva,jindrich.zdansky}@tul.cz

Abstract. In the paper we present an architecture of a keyword spotting (KWS) system that is based on modern neural networks, yields good performance on various types of speech data and can run very fast. We focus mainly on the last aspect and propose optimizations for all the steps required in a KWS design: signal processing and likelihood computation, Viterbi decoding, spot candidate detection and confidence calculation. We present time and memory efficient modelling by bidirectional feedforward sequential memory networks (an alternative to recurrent nets) either by standard triphones or so called quasi-monophones, and an entirely forward decoding of speech frames (with minimal need for look back). Several variants of the proposed scheme are evaluated on 3 large Czech datasets (broadcast, internet and telephone, 17 h in total) and their performance is compared by Detection Error Tradeoff (DET) diagrams and real-time (RT) factors. We demonstrate that the complete system can run in a single pass with a RT factor close to 0.001 if all optimizations (including a GPU for likelihood computation) are applied.

Keywords: Spoken term detection · Keyword spotting · Deep neural network · Feedforward sequential memory network · Real-time factor

1 Introduction

Keyword spotting (KWS) is a frequently used technique in spoken data processing whose goal is to detect selected words or phrases in speech. It can be applied off-line for fast search in recorded utterances (e.g. telephone calls analysed by police [1]), large spoken corpora (like broadcast archives [2]), or data collected by call-centres [3]. There are also on-line applications, namely for instant alerting, used in media monitoring [4] or in keyword activated mobile services [5].

The performance of a KWS system is evaluated from two viewpoints. The primary one is a detection reliability, which aims at missing as few as possible keywords occurring in the audio signal, i.e. to achieve a low miss detection rate (MD), while keeping the number of false alarms (FA) as low as possible. The second criterion is a speed as most applications require either instant reactions, or they are aimed at huge data (thousands of hours), where it is appreciated

© Springer Nature Switzerland AG 2020
P. Sojka et al. (Eds.): TSD 2020, LNAI 12284, pp. 426–436, 2020.
https://doi.org/10.1007/978-3-030-58323-1_46

if the search takes only a small fraction of their duration. The latter aspect is often referred to as a real-time (RT) factor and should be significantly smaller than 1.

There are several approaches to solve the KWS task [6]. The simplest and often the fastest one, usually denoted as an *acoustic approach*, utilizes a strategy similar to continuous speech recognition but with a limited vocabulary made of the keywords only. The sounds corresponding to other speech and noise are modelled and captured by filler units [7]. An *LVCSR approach* requires a very large continuous speech recognition (LVCSR) system that transcribes the audio first and after that searches for the keywords in its text output or in its internal decoder hypotheses arranged in *word lattices* [8]. This strategy takes into account both words from a large representative lexicon as well as inter-word context captured by a language model (LM). However, it is always slower and fails if the keywords are not in the lexicon and/or in the LM. A *phoneme lattice approach* operates on a similar principle but with phonemes (usually represented by triphones) as the basic units. The keywords are searched within the phoneme lattices [9]. The crucial part of all the 3 major approaches consist in assigning a *confidence score* to keyword candidates and setting thresholds for their acceptance or rejection. The basic strategies can be combined to get the best properties of each, as shown e.g. in [10, 11], and in general, they adopt a two-pass scheme.

The introduction of deep neural networks (DNN) into the speech processing domain has resulted in a significant improvement of acoustic models and therefore also in the accuracy of the LVCSR and phoneme based KWS systems. Various architectures have been proposed and tested, such as feedforward DNNs [12], convolutional (CNN) [13] and recurrent ones (RNN) [14]. A combination of the Long Short-Term Memory (LSTM) version of the latter together with the Connectionist Temporal Classification (CTC) method, which is an alternative to the classic hidden Markov model (HMM) approach, have become popular, too. The CTC provides the location and scoring measure for any arbitrary phone sequence as presented e.g. in [15]. Moreover, modern machine learning strategies, such as training data augmentation or transfer learning have enabled to train KWS also for various signal conditions [16] and languages with low data resources [17].

The KWS system presented here is a combination of several aforementioned approaches and techniques. It allows for searching any arbitrary keyword(s) using an HMM word-and-filler decoder that accepts acoustic models based on various types of DNNs, including feedforward sequential memory networks that are an efficient alternative to RNNs [19]. An audio signal is processed and searched within a single pass in a frame synchronous manner, which means that no intermediate data (such as lattices) need to be precomputed and stored. This allows for very short processing time (under 0.01 RT) in an off-line mode. Moreover, the execution time can be further reduced if the same signal is searched repeatedly with a different keyword list. The system can operate also in an on-line mode, where keyword alerts are produced with a small latency. In the following text, we will focus mainly on the speed optimization of the algorithms, which is the main and original contribution of this paper.

2   Brief Description of Presented Keyword Spotting System

The system models acoustic events in an audio signal by HMMs. Their smallest units are states. Phonemes and noises are modelled as 3-state sequences and the keywords as concatenations of the corresponding phoneme models. All different 3-state models (i.e. physical triphones in a tied-state triphone model) also serve as the fillers. Hence any audio signal can be modelled either as a sequence of the fillers, or - in presence of any of the keywords – as a sequence of the fillers and the keyword models. During data processing, the most probable sequences are continuously built by the Viterbi decoder and if they contain keywords, these are located and further managed. The complete KWS system is composed of three basic modules. All run in a frame synchronous manner. The first one – a *signal processing* module - takes a frame of the signal and computes log-likelihoods for all the HMM states. The second one – a *state processing* module – controls Viterbi recombinations for all active keywords and filler states. The third one – a *spot managing* module – focuses on the last states of the keyword/filler models, computes differences in accumulated scores of the keywords and the best filler sequences, evaluates their confidence scores and those with the scores higher than a threshold are further processed. This scheme assures that the data is processed almost entirely in the forward direction with minimum need for look-back and storage of already processed data.

3   KWS Speed and Memory Optimizations

The presented work extends – in a significant way – the scheme proposed in [18]. Therefore, we will use a similar notation here when explaining optimizations in the three modules. The core of the system is a Viterbi decoder that handles keywords w and fillers v in the same way, i.e. as generalized units u.

3.1   Signal Processing Module

It computes likelihoods for each state (senone) using a trained neural network. This is a standard operation which can be implemented either on a CPU, or on a GPU. In the latter case, the computation may be more than 1000 times faster. Yet, we come with another option for a significant reduction in the KWS execution.

The speed of the decoder depends on the number of units that must be processed in each frame. We cannot change the keyword number but let us see what can be done with the fillers. Usually, their list is made of all different physical triphones, which means a size of several thousands of items. If monophones are used instead, the number of fillers would be equal to their number, i.e. it would be smaller by 2 orders and the decoder would run much faster, but obviously with a worse performance.

We propose an optional alternative solution that takes advantages from both approaches. We model the words and fillers by something we call quasi-monophones, which can be thought as triphone states mapped to a monophone structure. In each frame, every quasi-monophone state gets the highest likelihood of the mapped states. This simple triphone-to-monophone conversion can be easily implemented as an additional layer of the neural network that just takes max values from the mapped nodes in the previous layer. The benefit is that the decoder handles a much smaller number of different states and namely fillers. In the experimental section, we demonstrate the impact of this arrangement on KWS system's speed and performance.

3.2   State Processing Module

The decoder controls a propagation of accumulated scores between adjacent states. At each frame t, new score d is computed for each state s of unit u by adding log likelihood L (provided by the previous module) to the higher of the scores in the predecessor states:

$$d(u, s, t) = L(s, t) + \max_{i=0,1}[d(u, s - i, t - 1)] \tag{1}$$

Let us denote the score in the unit's end state s_E as

$$D(u, t) = d(u, s_E, t) \tag{2}$$

and $T(u, t)$ be the frame where this unit's instance started. Further, we denote two values d_{best} and D_{best}:

$$d_{best}(t) = \max_{u,s}[d(u, s, t)] \tag{3}$$

$$D_{best}(t) = \max_{u}[D(u, t)] \tag{4}$$

The former value serves primarily for pruning, the latter is propagated to initial states s_1 of all units in the next frame:

$$d(u, s_1, t + 1) = L(s_1, t + 1) + \max[D_{best}(t), d(u, s_1, t)] \tag{5}$$

3.3   Spot Managing Module

This module computes acoustic scores S for all words w that reached their last states. This is done by subtracting these two accumulated scores:

$$S(w, t) = D(w, t) - D_{best}(T(w, t) - 1) \tag{6}$$

The word score $S(w,t)$ needs to be compared with score $S(v_{string},t)$ that would be achieved by the best filler string v_{string} starting in frame $T(w,t)$ and ending in frame t.

$$R(w,t) = S(v_{string},t) - S(w,t) \tag{7}$$

In [18], the first term in Eq. 7 is computed by applying the Viterbi algorithm within the given frame span to the fillers only. Here, we propose to approximate its value by this simple difference:

$$S(v_{string},t) \cong D_{best}(t) - D_{best}(T(w,t) - 1) \tag{8}$$

The left side of Eq. 8 equals exactly the right one if the Viterbi backtracking path passes through frame $T(w,t)$, which can be quickly checked. A large experimental evaluation showed that this happens in more than 90% cases. In the remaining ones, the difference is so small that it has a negligible impact on further steps.

Hence, by substituting from Eq. 6 and Eq. 8 into Eq. 7 we get:

$$R(w,t) = D_{best}(t) - D(w,t) \tag{9}$$

The value of $R(w,t)$ is related to the confidence of word w being detected in the given frame span. We just need to normalize it and convert it to a human-understandable scale where number 100 means the highest possible confidence. We do it in the following way:

$$C(w,t) = 100 - k\frac{R(w,t)}{(t - T(w,t))N_S(w)} \tag{10}$$

The R value is divided by the word duration (in frames) and its number of HMM states N_s, which is further multiplied by constant k before subtracting the term from 100. The constant influences the range of the confidence values. We set it so that the values are easily interpretable by KWS system users (see Sect. 5.4).

The previous analysis shows that the spot managing module can be made very simple and fast. In each frame, it just computes Eq. 9 and 10 and the candidates with the confidence scores higher than a set threshold are registered in a time-sliding buffer (10 to 20 frames long). A simple filter running over the buffer content detects the keyword instance with the highest score and sends it to the output.

3.4   Optimized Repeated Run

In many practical applications, the same audio data is searched repeatedly, usually with different keyword lists (e.g. during police investigations). In this case, the KWS system can run significantly faster if we store all likelihoods and two additional values (d_{best} and D_{best}) per frame. In the repeated run, the signal processing part is skipped over and the decoder can process only the keywords because all information needed for optimal pruning and confidence calculation is covered by the 2 above mentioned values.

4 System and Data for Evaluation

4.1 KWS System

The KWS system used in the experiments is written in C language and runs on a PC (Intel Core i7-9700K). In some tasks we employ also a GPU (GeForce RTX 2070 SUPER) for likelihood computation.

We tested 2 types of acoustic models (AM) based on neural networks. Both accept 16 kHz audio signals, segmented into 25 ms long frames and preprocessed to 40 filter bank coefficients. The first uses a 5-layer feedforward DNN trained on some 1000 h of Czech data (a mix of read and broadcast speech). The second AM utilizes a bidirectional feedforward sequential memory network (BFSMN) similar to that described in [19]. We have been using it as an effective alternative of RNNs. In our case, it has 11 layers, each covering 4 left and 4 right temporal contexts. This AM was trained on the same source data augmented by about 400 h of (originally) clean speech that passed through different codecs [20]. For both types of the NNs we have trained triphone AMs, for the second also a monophone and quasi-monophone version.

4.2 Dataset for Evaluation

Three large datasets have been prepared for the evaluation experiments, each covering a different type of speech (see also Table 1). The Interview dataset contains 10 complete Czech TV shows with two-persons talking in a studio. The Stream dataset is made of 30 shows from Internet TV Stream. We selected the shows with heavy background noise, e.g. Hudebni Masakry (Music Masacres in English). The Call dataset covers 53 telephone communications with call-centers (in separated channels) and it is a mix of spontaneous (client) and mainly controlled (operator) speech. All recordings have been carefully annotated with time information (10 ms resolution) added to each word.

Table 1. Datasets for evaluation and their main parameters.

Dataset	Speech type	Signal type	Total duration [min]	# keywords
Interview	Planned	Studio	272	3524
Stream	Informal	Heavy noise	157	1454
Call	Often spontaneous	Telephone	613	2935

5 Experimental Evaluation

5.1 Keyword List

Our goal was to test the system under realistic conditions and, at the same time, to get statistically conclusive results. A keyword list of 156 word lemmas with

555 derived forms was prepared for the experiments. For example, in case of keyword "David" we included its derived forms "David", "Davida", "Davidem", "Davidovi", etc. in order to avoid false alarms caused by words being substrings of others. The list was made by combining 80 most frequent words that occurred in each of the datasets, from which some were common and some appeared only in one set. The searched word forms had to be at least 4 phonemes long. The mean length of the listed word forms was 6.9 phonemes. The phonetic transcriptions were automatically extracted from a 500k-word lexicon used in our LVCSR system.

5.2 Filler Lists

The list of fillers was created automatically for each acoustic model. The triphone DNN model generated 9210 fillers and the triphone BFSMN produced 10455 of them. In contrast to these large numbers, the monophone and quasi-monophone BFSMN model had only 48 fillers (representing 40 phonemes + 8 noises).

5.3 Evaluation Conditions and Metrics

A word was considered correctly detected if the spotted word-form belonged to the same lemma as the word occurring in the transcription at the same instant - with tolerance ±0.5 s. Otherwise it was counted as a false alarm. For each experiment we computed Missed Detection (MD) and False Alarm (FA) rates as a function of acceptance threshold value, and drawn a Detection Error Tradeoff (DET) diagram with a marked Equal Error Rate (EER) point position.

5.4 Evaluation Results

The Interview dataset was used as a development data, on which we experimented with various models, system arrangements and also user preferences. In accord with them, the internal constant k occurring in Eq. 10 was set to locate the confidence score equal to 75 close to the EER point. The first part of the experiments focused on the accuracy of the created acoustic models. We tested the triphone DNN and 3 versions of the BFSMN one. Their performance is illustrated by DET curves in Fig. 1, where also the EER values are displayed. It is evident that the BFSMN-tri model performs significantly better than the DNN one, which is mainly due to its wider context span. This is also a reason why even its monophone version has performance comparable to the DNN-tri one. The proposed quasi-monophone BFSMN model shows the second best performance but the gap between it and the best one is not that crucial, especially if we take into account its additional benefits that will be discussed later.

Similar trends can be seen also in Fig. 2 and Fig. 3 where we compare the same models (excl. the monophone BFSMN) on the Stream and Call datasets. In both cases, the performance of all the models was worse (when compared to that of the Interview set) as it can be seen from the positions of the curves and

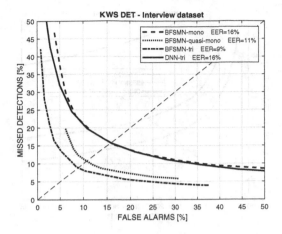

Fig. 1. KWS results for the Interview dataset in form of DET curves drawn for 4 investigated neural network structures.

the EER values. This is due to the character of speech and signal quality as explained is Sect. 4.2. Yet, we can notice the positive effect of the training of the BFSMN models on the augmented data (with various codecs), especially on the Call dataset. Again, the gap between the best triphone and the proposed quasi-monophone version seems to be not that critical.

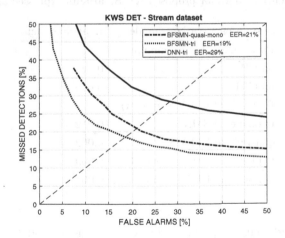

Fig. 2. DET curves compared for 3 models on the Stream dataset

Now, we shall focus on the execution time of the proposed scheme. As explained in Sect. 3, the three modules of the KWS system can be split into 2 parts: the first with the signal processing module, the second with the remaining two. Both can run together on a PC (in a single thread), or if extremely

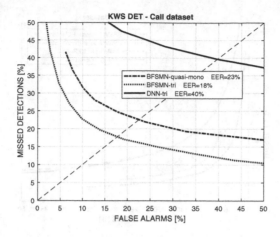

Fig. 3. DET curves compared for 3 models on the Call dataset

fast execution is required, the former can be implemented on a GPU. We tested both approaches and measured their RT factors. Similar measurements (across all the tree datasets) were performed also in the second part for all the proposed variants and operation modes (see Table 2 for results.). The total RT factor is obtained by adding the values for selected options in each of the two parts.

Table 2. Execution times for proposed KWS variants expressed as RT factors.

System part, variant, mode	Real-time factor
Part 1 (signal proc. module)	
on CPU	0.12
on GPU	0.0005
Part 2 (rest of KWS system)	
triphone BFSMN	0.012
quasi-mono BFSMN	0.002
triphone BFSMN, repeated	0.009
quasi-mono BFSMN, repeated	0.001

Let us remind that the proposed quasi-monophone model performs slightly worse but it offers two practical benefits: a) a speed that can get close to 0.001 RT (if a GPU is used for likelihood computation) and b) a small disk memory consumption in case of repeated runs (with different keywords) because only $48 \times 3 + 2 = 146$ float numbers per frame need to be stored. Moreover, the speed of the proposed KWS system is only slightly influenced by the number of keywords. A test made with 10.000 keywords (instead of 555 ones used in the main experiments) showed only twice slower performance.

6   Conclusion

In this contribution we focus mainly on the speed aspect of a modern KWS system, but at the same time we aim at the best performance that is available thanks to the advances in deep neural networks. The used BFSMN architecture has several benefits for practical usage. In contrast to more popular RNNs, it can be efficiently and fast trained on a large amount (several thousands of hours) of audio and at the same time yields performance comparable to more complex RNNs and LSTMs as shown in [19]. Its phoneme accuracy is high (due its large internal context) so that it fits both to acoustic KWS systems as well as to standard speech-to-text LVCSR systems. The latter means that it is well suited for a tandem KWS scheme where a user requires that the sections with detected keywords are immediately transcribed by a LVCSR system. In our arrangement this can be done very effectively by reusing some of the precomputed data. (Let us recall that if we use the quasi-monophones, their values are just max values from the original triphone neural network and hence both acoustic models can be implemented by the same network with an additional layer.)

The results presented in Sect. 5 allow for designing an optimal configuration that takes into account the three main factors: accuracy, speed and cost. If the main priority is accuracy and not the speed, the KWS system can run on a standard PC and process data with a RT factor about 0.1. When very large amounts of records must be processed within very short time then the addition of a GPU and the adoption of the proposed quasi-monophone approach will allow for completing the job in time that can be up to 3 orders shorter than the audio duration.

We evaluated the performance on Czech datasets as these were available with precise human checked transcriptions. Obviously, the proposed architecture is language independent and we plan to utilize it for other languages investigated in our project.

Acknowledgments. This work was supported by the Technology Agency of the Czech Republic (Project No. TH03010018).

References

1. Zheng, N., Li, X.: A robust keyword detection system for criminal scene analysis. In 5th IEEE Conference on Industrial Electronics and Applications, Taichung, pp. 2127–2131 (2010)
2. Cardillo, P.S., Clements, M., Miller, M.S. Phonetic searching vs. LVCSR: how to find what you really want in audio archives. Int. J. Speech Technol. **5**, 9–22 (2002)
3. Zhou, X., Dai, D., Xie, B., Li, X.: Multidimensional evaluation platform for call center speech service quality based on keyword spotting. In: Yang, Y., Ma, M. (eds.) Proceedings 2nd International Conference on Green Communications and Networks 2012. Lecture Notes in Electrical Engineering, vol. 225, pp. 535–544. Springer, Heidelberg (2012). https://doi.org/10.1007/978-3-642-35470-0_66
4. Oh, Y., Park, J.-S., Park, K.-M.: Keyword spotting in broadcast news. In: Global-Network-Oriented Information Electronics, Sendai, Japan, pp. 208–213 (2007)

5. Michaely, A.H., Zhang, X., Simko, G., Parada, C. Aleksic, P.: Keyword spotting for Google assistant using contextual speech recognition. In: IEEE Automatic Speech Recognition and Understanding Workshop (ASRU), Okinawa, pp. 272–278 (2017)
6. Szoke, I., et al.: Comparison of keyword spotting approaches for informal continuous speech. In: INTERSPEECH 2005, Lisbon, pp. 633–636 (2005)
7. Rohlicek, J.R., Russell, W., Roukos S., Gish, H.: Continuous hidden Markov modeling for speaker-independent word spotting. In: ICASSP, Glasgow, UK, vol. 1, pp. 627–630 (1989)
8. Weintraub, M.: LVCSR log-likelihood ratio scoring for keyword spotting. In: ICASSP 1995, Detroit, vol. 1, pp. 297–300 (1995)
9. Foote, J., Young, S., Jones, G., Jones, K.S.: Unconstrained keyword spotting using phone lattices with application to spoken document retrieval. Comput. Speech Lang. **11**, 207–224 (1997)
10. Motlicek, P., Valente, F., Szoke, I.: Improving acoustic based keyword spotting using LVCSR lattices. In ICASSP 2012, Kyoto, pp. 4413–4416 (2012)
11. Akbacak, M., Burget, L., Wang, W., van Hout, J.: Rich system combination for keyword spotting in noisy and acoustically heterogeneous audio streams. In: ICASSP 2013, Vancouver, BC, pp. 8267–8271 (2013)
12. Chen, N.F., Lee, C.-H.: A hybrid HMM/DNN approach to key-word spotting of short words. In: Interspeech 2013, Lyon, pp. 1574–1557 (2013)
13. Palaz, D., Synnaeve, G., Collobert, R.: Jointly learning to locate and classify words using convolutional networks. In: Interspeech 2016, San Francisco, pp. 3660–3664 (2016)
14. Lengerich, C., Hannun, A.: An end-to-end architecture for keyword spotting and voice activity detection. In: NIPS 2016, Barcelona, Spain (2016)
15. Zhuang, Y., Chang, X., Qian, Y., Yu, K.: Unrestricted vocabulary keyword spotting using LSTM-CTC. In: Interspeech 2016, San Francisco, pp. 938–942 (2016)
16. Ko, T., Peddinti, V., Povey, D., Khudanpur, S.: Audio augmentation for speech recognition. In: Proceedings Interspeech 2015, Dresden, pp. 3586–3589 (2015)
17. Gales, M.J.F., Knill, K.M., Ragni, A., Rath, S.P.: Speech recognition and keyword spotting for low-resource languages: babel project research at CUED. In: SLTU-2014, pp. 16–23 (2014)
18. Nouza, J., Silovsky, J.: Fast keyword spotting in telephone speech. Radioengineering **18**(4), 665–670 (2009)
19. Zhang, S., Jiang, H., Xiong, S., Wei, S, Dai, L.: Compact feedforward sequential memory networks for large vocabulary continuous speech recognition. In: Proceedings Interspeech 2016, San Francisco, pp. 3389–3393 (2016)
20. Málek, J., Ždánský, J., Červa, P.: Robust recognition of conversational telephone speech via multi-condition training and data augmentation. In: Sojka, P., Horák, A., Kopeček, I., Pala, K. (eds.) TSD 2018. LNCS (LNAI), vol. 11107, pp. 324–333. Springer, Cham (2018). https://doi.org/10.1007/978-3-030-00794-2_35

On the Effectiveness of Neural Text Generation Based Data Augmentation for Recognition of Morphologically Rich Speech

Balázs Tarján[1,2]([✉]) [iD], György Szaszák[1], Tibor Fegyó[1,2], and Péter Mihajlik[1,3]

[1] Department of Telecommunications and Media Informatics,
Budapest University of Technology and Economics, Budapest, Hungary
{tarjanb,szaszak,mihajlik}@tmit.bme.hu
[2] SpeechTex Ltd., Budapest, Hungary
fegyo@speechtex.com
[3] THINKTech Research Center, Vác, Hungary

Abstract. Advanced neural network models have penetrated Automatic Speech Recognition (ASR) in recent years, however, in language modeling many systems still rely on traditional Back-off N-gram Language Models (BNLM) partly or entirely. The reason for this are the high cost and complexity of training and using neural language models, mostly possible by adding a second decoding pass (rescoring). In our recent work we have significantly improved the online performance of a conversational speech transcription system by transferring knowledge from a Recurrent Neural Network Language Model (RNNLM) to the single pass BNLM with text generation based data augmentation. In the present paper we analyze the amount of transferable knowledge and demonstrate that the neural augmented LM (RNN-BNLM) can help to capture almost 50% of the knowledge of the RNNLM yet by dropping the second decoding pass and making the system real-time capable. We also systematically compare word and subword LMs and show that subword-based neural text augmentation can be especially beneficial in under-resourced conditions. In addition, we show that using the RNN-BNLM in the first pass followed by a neural second pass, offline ASR results can be even significantly improved.

Keywords: Speech recognition · Neural text generation · RNNLM · Data augmentation · Call center speech · Morphologically rich language

1 Introduction

Deep learning has penetrated machine learning in the past years, including speech technology and language modeling in particular [5,12]. Despite the success of this architectural paradigm shift, application of Neural Network Language Models (NNLM) in a single decoding pass is still challenging due to their

© Springer Nature Switzerland AG 2020
P. Sojka et al. (Eds.): TSD 2020, LNAI 12284, pp. 437–445, 2020.
https://doi.org/10.1007/978-3-030-58323-1_47

structure and computational complexity. NNLMs can still be used in ASR, when passing to the 2-pass decoding scheme: in the first pass, a small footprint generic Language Model (LM) is used, and the output of this step is a simplified recognition network with reduced search space. On this reduced lattice, a second decoding pass is applied with the NNLM for rescoring the hypotheses obtained in the first pass. Although by splitting the decoding into two parts we can leverage knowledge of the NNLMs and demonstrate significant Word Error Rate Reduction (WERR), it also introduces considerable processing delay [4,5,12].

Therefore, techniques exploiting the capabilities of NNLMs in a single-pass decoding approach have received particular attention recently [9,13]. A possible technique is to augment the in-domain training data with a large text corpus generated by an NNLM [1,3]. Of course, there is a compromise: the augmented model is no more suitable for capturing long contexts, and lose capability to support continuous space features. So far there has been no throughout evaluation of what NNLM capabilities can be transferred by neural text based data augmentation and how these compare to traditional Back-off N-gram Language Models (BNLM), especially for the morphologically rich languages. The only exception is our earlier study for Hungarian [14] showing that by combining subword lexical modeling with text based approximation of NNLM (referred to as RNN-BNLM) we can greatly improve the performance of an online ASR system.

In this paper we significantly extend our previous work: (1) we quantify the amount of knowledge that can be transferred from the NNLM to single pass decoding with a BNLM augmented with data generated by the NNLM; (2) we show that the performance of offline decoding can also be significantly improved if we apply the augmented model in the first-pass for generating the lattice; (3) we evaluate the impact of training corpus size on the effectiveness of the data augmentation method. Rich morphology, per se, results in extremely large vocabularies, which constitutes a challenge for language modeling. Since data sparsity problems can be often handled by estimating language models on statically derived subword units (such as morphs) [2,6], we will also evaluate morph-based models in our experiments.

In a related work, Suzuki et al. [13] use a domain balanced mixture of the training corpora to train a shallow RNNLM for text generation and improve speech recognition results for Japanese, Korean and English tasks. For Korean subword-based language models are also utilized, but only for text generation, since in the language model of the ASR system subwords are merged. Using subword units for language models and ASR has been mostly considered for Finnish and Estonian, which are morphologically very rich languages [2,6]. In [4], the authors managed to outperform word-based baseline model on Finnish and Estonian conversations by training subword RNNLMs and utilizing them in the second pass to rescore ASR lattices. N-gram based approximation of RNNLM was also investigated in a recent paper [9], where subword and character-based models were trained for Finnish and Arabic OOV keyword search tasks. Although the interpolation of approximated RNNLM and BNLM models improved OOV retrieval the proposed system was not evaluated on in-vocabulary tokens and no Word Error Rate (WER) was presented either.

2   Data and Methods

2.1   Database

Conventional Training Data. Data for modeling word units are taken from the Hungarian Call Center Speech Database (HCCSD). The HCCSD corpus contains real conversations recorded in customer service centers. The conversations are transcribed and validated by human proofreaders. A total of 3.4M word tokens could be used allowing for a dictionary 100K distinct word forms. In order to speed up training, the final vocabulary was limited to the most 50K word forms. The remaining Out-Of-Vocabulary (OOV) words were replaced with ⟨unk⟩ and the sentence endings were mapped to the ⟨eos⟩ symbol. Training corpus statistics are summarized in Table 1.

Table 1. Training and test database statistics

	Training	Validation	Evaluation
Duration [h:m]	290:07	7:31	12:12
# of word tokens	3,401,775	45,773	66,312
# of morph tokens	3,822,335	57,849	84,385

Morph Segmented Training Data. Morphologically rich languages like Hungarian show heavy agglutination and hence vocabulary gets much larger. This also results in higher variability regarding word sequences, and estimation of model parameters becomes less accurate. Segmenting words into smaller units is driven by the idea to both decrease vocabulary size and increase sequential consistency in morph sequences [6]. Morfessor [2] is a popular algorithm for segmenting words into subword units as it iteratively finds the optimal decomposition of vocabulary words into subword units, called *morphs*. In [10] it was shown that Morfessor can outperform the nowadays so popular character-level Byte Pair Encoding (BPE) algorithm.

The training corpus contained 3.8M units after applying Morfessor and decomposing words into morphs (see Table 1). The number of vocabulary entries decreased to around 1/3 of the word vocabulary, that is 32K entries covering the same text corpora as the word based model. The morph vocabulary was finally limited 30K morphs based on frequency, in order to provide enough training samples to ⟨unk⟩. Morphs in non-word-initial position were additionally tagged by the '+' sign to preserve this syntactic information relative to original word boundaries. The following example illustrates a morph-based tokenization (decomposition) of the sentence 'well I will discuss this with my wife':

Conventional tokenization: *hát megbeszélem a nejemmel*
Morph-based tokenization: *hát meg +beszél +em a nejem +mel*

Development and Test Data. For validation and testing, two further disjoint data sets were created using 20 h of conversations, reserved from the HCCSD corpus (see Table 1). The validation set is required for the optimization of the hyperparameters (e.g. Morfessor segmentation, control training of language models), whereas the evaluation set is used for performance evaluation and comparison of the models.

2.2 Language Modeling Methods

Back-Off N-Gram Models. N-gram models are statistical, count-based models estimated on large text corpora. Back-off N-gram Language Models (BNLM) formed the state-of-the-art in language modeling for ASR over several decades, and still today, for a number of tasks they are the primary choice, especially in systems requiring real-time or smaller footprint setups. All BNLMs in this work are estimated with the SRI language modeling toolkit [11] and smoothed with Chen and Goodman's modified Kneser-Ney discounting.

Recurrent Neural Language Model. We implemented[1] a 2-layered LSTM structure according to the scheme presented in [14]. After fine-tuning the hyperparameters on the validation set, we use a batch size of 32 sequences, composed of 35 tokens each (tokens can be either words or morphs). LSTM states are preserved between the batches (stateful LSTM). The 650 dimensional embedding vectors were trained from scratch, as transfer learning from existing Hungarian pretrained embeddings proved to be suboptimal. After trying several optimizers, we decided on the traditional, momentum accelerated Stochastic Gradient Descent (SGD) algorithm. The initial learning rate was set to 1, which is halved after every epoch where the cross entropy loss increases. To prevent overfitting dropout layers are used with keep probabilities of 0.5. Early stopping with a patience of 3 epochs is also applied.

Text Generation Based Data Augmentation. Approximation of a NNLM with a back-off ngram language model can be achieved in several different ways [1,3]. In [1] three such methods are described and evaluated, coming to a conclusion that the so called text generation based data augmentation yields the best results. The main idea of this approach is to estimate the BNLM parameters from a large text corpus generated by a NNLM. In our work, we generated 100 million words/morphs with the corresponding RNNLM (RNN-BNLM 100M) that was formerly trained on the in-domain training set. In order to get an insight

---

[1] https://github.com/btarjan/stateful-LSTM-LM.

how the corpus size influences the language model capabilities, we also generated a larger text corpus with 1 billion morphs (RNN-BNLM 1B). To achieve the best results the models trained on augmented text (RNN-BNLMs) are interpolated with the baseline models (BNLM + RNN-BNLM). Interpolation weights are optimized on the development set.

3   Results and Discussion

3.1   Experimental Setup

40 dimensional MFCC vectors were used as input features for a Factored Time Delay Neural Network (TDNN-F) acoustic model trained applying LF-MMI criterion in a similar manner as in [7] using the Kaldi Toolkit [8]. The matrix size (hidden-layer dimension) was 768 and the linear bottleneck dimension was 80 resulting in a total number of 6M parameters in the twelve hidden layers. Acoustic and language model resources were compiled into weighted finite-state transducers and decoded with our in-house ASR decoder, called VoXerver.

Table 2. WER of the online ASR system using the proposed language models

Token type	Model	# of n-grams [million]	Memory usage [GB]	WER [%]	WERR over Word/Morph BNLM [%]	
Word	BNLM	5.0	1.3	21.9		
	RNN-BNLM 100M	4.8	0.9	22.5	-2.6*	
	BNLM + RNN-BNLM 100M	7.0	1.5	21.3	2.7*	
Morph	BNLM	5.1	1.0	21.1	3.4*	
	RNN-BNLM 100M	8.5	1.1	21.1	3.7*	0.3
	RNN-BNLM 1B	7.2	0.9	20.5	6.4*	3.2*
	BNLM + RNN-BNLM 100M	7.9	1.1	20.4	6.8*	3.5*
	BNLM + RNN-BNLM 1B	7.2	1.1	20.2	7.7*	4.5*
		46.6	5.9	19.9	8.8*	5.6*

* Sign indicates significant difference compared to Word or Morph-based BNLM models and was tested with Wilcoxon signed-rank test ($p < 0.05$).

3.2   Online ASR Results with Data Augmentation

We perform single-pass decoding with 4-gram BNLM and RNN-BNLM models and calculate WER on the evaluation set. In order to ensure the fair comparison among the modeling approaches, we pruned each RNN-BNLM so that they had similar runtime memory footprint as the baseline BNLM models ($\approx$1 GB). The most promising model, where the baseline is augmented with 1 billion token corpus (BNLM + RNN-BNLM 1B) however, is also evaluated in a setup allowing for larger memory consumption to determine the full capability of the model.

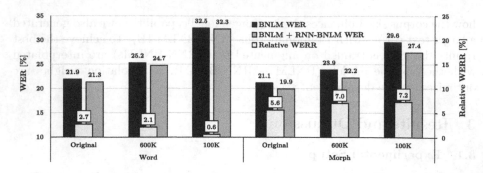

Fig. 1. Impact of training data limitation on the WER of baseline and augmented LMs and the corresponding relative WERRs

Results with Original Training Corpus. First we discuss the online ASR results (see Table 2) obtained with models trained on the original training corpus (3.4M word/3.8M morph tokens). The n-gram model estimated on the corpus that was generated with the word-based RNNLM (RNN-BNLM 100M) has a slightly higher WER than the baseline word-based BNLM (2.6% relative WER increase), but with the interpolated model (BNLM + RNN-BNLM 100M) we are able to significantly outperform both of them (2.7% rel. WERR).

Switching to subword setups we observed the following results: the simple act of replacing words with subwords in the baseline BNLM already yields a significant WER reduction (3.4% rel.). The LM trained on the 100-million-morph generated corpus (RNN-BNLM 100M) has the same WER as the morph-based BNLM (21.1% WER). However using a ten times larger corpus to train the approximative model reverses this trend: morph-based RNN-BNLM 1B model is the first augmentation model that outperforms a baseline BNLM by itself, without taking any benefit from interpolation (20.5% WER). When adding interpolation, we can leverage a further increase in performance. BNLM + RNN-BNLM 1B model can reduce WER of morph-based BNLM by 5% or even 6% if runtime memory consumption is not a restricting factor. All in all, with morph-based neural text generation we managed to reduce the WER of our call center speech transcription system by 9% relative while preserving real-time operation.

Impact of Training Corpus Size. The RNNLM used to generate augmentation data is trained on in-domain training corpus, hence we assume that the amount of available training data is closely related to the effectiveness of this modeling approach. In order to confirm this hypotheses, we repeated the experiments from the previous section, but we limited the size of training database (see Fig. 1). The original corpus containing 3.4M tokens was reduced to two smaller corpora following a log-uniformly spaced scale (600K and 100K). We found that in case of word-based modeling the less training data is used the smaller is the benefit of data augmentation. In contrast, morph-based augmented models even increase their advantage over the baseline for smaller training sets. Based on

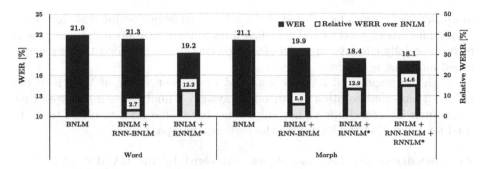

Fig. 2. A comparison of online (baseline LM: BNLM, augmented model: BNLM+RNN-BNLM) and offline (rescoring BNLM with RNNLM: BNLM+RNNLM, rescoring BNLM+RNN-BNLM with RNNLM: BNLM+RNN-BNLM+RNNLM) ASR results with word and morph based lexical modeling. * indicates offline, 2-pass decoding

the above, we conclude that text based augmentation can be indeed effective in under-resourced conditions, if it is paired with subword lexical modeling approach so that the RNNLM has enough samples for learning.

3.3 Comparing Online and Offline ASR Results

In this section we compare the performance of the original RNNLM applied for 2-pass, offline decoding and the RNN-BNLMs in order to assess the amount of knowledge that can be transferred to the online ASR system (see Fig. 2). With offline, 2-pass decoding, the baseline WER can be reduced by ≈12–13% (BNLM + RNNLM). Word-based augmentation can capture 22% of this WERR as it reduces the WER by 2.7% compared to the 12.2% of 2-pass decoding. Using morph-based lexical modeling and a 10 times larger augmentation corpus the relative WERR can be increased to 5.6% (Morph BNLM + RNN-BNLM). On this basis we can conclude that up to 45% of the WERR (5.6% from 12.9%) potential hold by the RNNLM can be transferred to the first pass of the decoding.

Text based data augmentation was introduced to improve online ASR results by transferring knowledge from the neural model to the BNLM. However, we found that even offline speech recognition can benefit from this approach. The last column in Fig. 2 shows that significant (p = 0.01) WERR can be achieved if the lattice used for rescoring is generated with the augmented model (BNLM + RNN-BNLM + RNNLM) instead of the original BNLM (BNLM + RNNLM).

4 Conclusions

In this paper neural LMs were used to transfer their knowledge to traditional back-off LMs by generating samples for probability estimation. The morphological complexity of Hungarian was treated by using morph-based models evaluated on a call center ASR task. We found that by generating a text with 1 billion morphs, the WER can be reduced by 9% relative while preserving real-time operation. The investigated neural text based data augmentation technique proved to be especially effective in under-resourced conditions provided that subword-based modeling is applied.

With the augmented LMs we managed to transfer ≈45% of WERR of the offline, 2-pass configuration to our online system. Finally, we also showed that augmented LMs can improve not only online but offline ASR results if they are used for generating the lattice for the 2nd decoding pass.

Acknowledgements. The research was supported by the CAMEP (2018-2.1.3-EUREKA-2018-00014) and NKFIH FK-124413 projects.

References

1. Adel, H., Kirchhoff, K., Vu, N.T., Telaar, D., Schultz, T.: Comparing approaches to convert recurrent neural networks into backoff language models for efficient decoding. Interspeech **2014**, 651–655 (2014)
2. Creutz, M., Lagus, K.: Unsupervised discovery of morphemes. In: Proceedings ACL-02 Workshop on Morphological and Phonological Learning, vol. 6, Morristown, NJ, USA, pp. 21–30 (2002)
3. Deoras, A., Mikolov, T., Kombrink, S., Karafiat, M., Khudanpur, S.: Variational approximation of long-span language models for LVCSR. In: 2011 IEEE International Conference on Acoustics, Speech, and Signal Processin, pp. 5532–5535. IEEE, May 2011
4. Enarvi, S., Smit, P., Virpioja, S., Kurimo, M.: Automatic speech recognition with very large conversational finnish and estonian vocabularies. IEEE/ACM Trans. Audio Speech Lang. Process. **25**(11), 2085–2097 (2017)
5. Irie, K., Zeyer, A., Schl, R., Ney, H., Gmbh, A.: Language modeling with deep transformers. Interspeech **2019**, 3905–3909 (2019)
6. Kurimo, M., et al.: Unlimited vocabulary speech recognition for agglutinative languages. In: HLT-NAACL 2006, Morristown, NJ, USA, pp. 487–494 (2007)
7. Povey, D., et al.: Semi-orthogonal low-rank matrix factorization for deep neural networks. In: Interspeech 2018, ISCA, ISCA, pp. 3743–3747, September 2018
8. Povey, D., et al.: The kaldi speech recognition toolkit. In: IEEE 2011 Workshop on Automatic Speech Recognition & Understanding. IEEE Signal Processing Society (2011)
9. Singh, M., Virpioja, S., Smit, P., Kurimo, M.: Subword RNNLM approximations for out-of-vocabulary keyword search. Interspeech **2019**, 4235–4239 (2019)
10. Smit, P., Virpioja, S., Kurimo, M.: Improved subword modeling for WFST-based speech recognition. In: Interspeech 2017. ISCA, ISCA, pp. 2551–2555, August 2017
11. Stolcke, A.: SRILM - an extensible language modeling toolkit. In: Proceedings International Conference on Spoken Language Processing, Denver, US, pp. 901–904 (2002)
12. Sundermeyer, M., Schlueter, R., Ney, H.: LSTM neural networks for language modeling. Interspeech **2012**, 194–197 (2012)

13. Suzuki, M., Itoh, N., Nagano, T., Kurata, G., Thomas, S.: Improvements to N-gram language model using text generated from neural language model. In: ICASSP 2019–2019 IEEE International Conference on Acoustics, Speech, and Signal Processing, pp. 7245–7249 (2019)
14. Tarján, B., Szaszák, G., Fegyó, T., Mihajlik, P.: Investigation on N-gram approximated RNNLMs for recognition of morphologically rich speech. In: Martín-Vide, C., Purver, M., Pollak, S. (eds.) SLSP 2019. LNCS (LNAI), vol. 11816, pp. 223–234. Springer, Cham (2019). https://doi.org/10.1007/978-3-030-31372-2_19

Context-Aware XGBoost for Glottal Closure Instant Detection in Speech Signal

Jindřich Matoušek(✉) and Michal Vraštil

Department of Cybernetics, New Technology for the Information Society (NTIS), Faculty of Applied Sciences, University of West Bohemia, Plzeň, Czech Republic
jmatouse@kky.zcu.cz, vrastilm@students.zcu.cz

Abstract. In this paper, we continue to investigate the use of classifiers for the automatic detection of glottal closure instants (GCIs) in the speech signal. We introduce context to extreme gradient boosting (XGBoost) and show that the context-aware XGBoost outperforms its context-free version. The proposed context-aware XGBoost is also shown to outperform traditionally used GCI detection algorithms on publicly available databases.

Keywords: Glottal closure instant (GCI) · Pitch mark · Detection · Classification · Extreme gradient boosting · Context-awareness

1 Introduction

Detection of *glottal closure instants* (GCIs), also called *pitch marks* or *epochs*, in speech signals was shown to be useful in many practical applications, especially in those where *pitch-synchronous* speech processing was required (see e.g. [7,9,23]). GCI detection could be viewed as a task of determining peaks in *voiced parts* of the speech signal that correspond to the moment of glottal closure, a significant excitation of a vocal tract during the speaking.

Many algorithms were proposed to detect GCIs in the speech signal. Traditionally, they exploit some expert knowledge and hand-crafted rules and thresholds to identify GCI candidates from local maxima of various speech representations (e.g. linear predictive coding like in DYPSA [20], YAGA, wavelet components, multi-scale formalism (MMF) [11]), glottal flow (GEFBA) [12], probabilistic source-filter model (PSFM) [19], and/or from discontinuities or changes in signal energy (Hilbert envelope, Frobenius norm, zero-frequency resonator, or

This research was supported by the Czech Science Foundation (GA CR), project No. GA19-19324S, and by the grant of the University of West Bohemia, project No. SGS-2019-027. Computational resources were supplied by the project "e-Infrastruktura CZ" (e-INFRA LM2018140) provided within the program Projects of Large Research, Development and Innovations Infrastructures.

P. Sojka et al. (Eds.): TSD 2020, LNAI 12284, pp. 446–455, 2020.
https://doi.org/10.1007/978-3-030-58323-1_48

SEDREAMS [8]). Dynamic programming is then often used to refine the GCI candidates [19, 20, 22].

Recently, classification-based approaches were re-introduced by Matoušek et al. [16–18]. In this approach, GCI detection could be viewed as a two-class classification problem: whether or not a peak in a speech waveform represents a GCI [3]. The advantage is that once a training dataset is available, classifier parameters are set up automatically without manual tuning. It was shown that classification-based GCI detection, and especially the one based on *extreme gradient boosting* (XGBoost), was able to perform very well and consistently outperformed traditionally used algorithms on several test datasets [18].

In this paper, we continue to investigate the use of XGBoost for GCI detection. More specifically, we introduce context to XGBoost detection and examine whether the presence of neighboring GCI candidates can improve GCI detection.

2 Experimental Data

Experiments were performed on clean 16 kHz-sampled speech recordings (hereafter referred to as UWB). The recordings were primarily intended for speech synthesis. We used 88 utterances ($\approx$11.5 min of speech) for the development of the proposed classifiers, and 20 test utterances ($\approx$2.5 min of speech) were held out for an unbiased comparison with other methods. The set of utterances was the same as in [14] – it comprised various Czech (male and female), Slovak (female), German (male), US English (male), and French (female) voices. Most voices were part of both the development and test datasets. Reference GCIs produced by a human expert using both speech and electroglottograph (EGG) signals were available for each utterance and were synchronized with the corresponding minimum negative sample in the speech signal.

Speech waveforms were processed in the same way as in [18]. They were mastered to have equal loudness, low-pass filtered by a zero-phase Equiripple-designed filter with 0.5 dB ripple in the pass band, 60 dB attenuation in the stop band, and with the cutoff frequency 800 Hz to reduce the high-frequency structure in the speech signal. The signals were then zero-crossed to identify peaks (both of the negative and positive polarity) that are used for feature extraction in further processing. Since the polarity of speech signals was shown to have an important impact on the performance of a GCI detector [15], all speech signals were switched to have the negative polarity, and only the negative peaks were taken as the candidates for the GCI placement. For the purpose of training and testing, the location of each reference GCI was mapped to a corresponding negative peak in the filtered signal. There were 98227 and 20338 candidate peaks in the development and test datasets respectively (marked by both ∘ and • in Fig. 1), 56025 and 10807 of them corresponded to true GCIs (marked by • only).

3 Experiments and Results

In all following experiments, we used *extreme gradient boosting* (XGBoost) [5] as the GCI detection model. It is an efficient implementation of gradient boosted

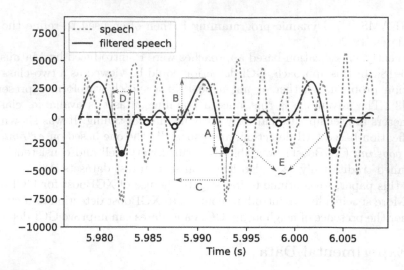

Fig. 1. Illustration of feature extraction: amplitude of a negative peak (A), amplitude of a positive peak (B), difference between two negative peaks (C), width of a negative peak (D), correlation between waveforms of two negative peaks (E). GCI candidates are marked by ○, true GCIs by ●.

decision trees designed for speed and performance that dominated many Kaggle competitions. XGBoost was also shown to outperform other classifiers in the GCI detection problem [18].

To evaluate the performance of the proposed models, standard classification measures like *recall* (R), *precision* (P), $F1$, and *area under the receiver operating characteristic curve* (AUC) were utilized. *Scikit-learn* [21] and *XGBoost* [5] toolkits were employed to train and evaluate the proposed models.

3.1   Baseline Model

The baseline XGBoost system did not use any information about the detection/prediction of neighboring peaks; it trained and predicted each peak independently on the neighboring peaks [18]. Inspired by [3], the input features for classification were associated with negative peaks in the low-pass filtered speech waveforms. Each peak is described by a set of local descriptors reflecting the position and shape of other 3 neighboring peaks [16]: the amplitudes of the given negative peak and 6 neighboring (3 prior and 3 subsequent) negative peaks (7 features, denoted as A in Fig. 1), amplitudes of 6 neighboring positive peaks (6, B), the time difference between the given negative peak and each of the neighboring negative peaks (6, C), the width of the given negative peak (a distance between two zero-crossings) and each of the neighboring negative peaks (7, D), the correlation of the waveform around the given negative peak and the waveforms around each of the neighboring negative peaks (6, E). The baseline 32 features were then extended with other acoustic and spectral features: zero-crossing rate (ZCR), log energy, harmonic-to-noise ratio (HNR), voiced/unvoiced, the 1st (F1) and 2nd (F2) formant frequencies, F1/F2 distance and ratio, peak ratio to 6 neighboring peaks, spectral centroid/bandwidth/roll-off, peak slope, maximum of power spectral density function estimate (PSD) and its corresponding frequency, and mel-frequency cepstral coefficients (MFCCs). All these features were calculated from 10ms-long speech segments extracted around every peak candidate, resulting in a total number of 66 features. *Recursive feature elimination* (RFE) with cross-validation was applied to select important features automatically [17]. Finally, the most correlated features were removed, so that the resulting feature set consisted of 50 features. Extensive XGBoost model hyper-parameter tuning using grid search with repeated 10-fold cross-validation (with 10 repetitions) was conducted on the development dataset [18].

Note that although no knowledge of the prediction of neighboring peaks is available (i.e., 0 neighboring peaks are taken into account at the *prediction level*), the feature set comprises the context of 3 neighboring peaks[1] (GCI candidates) implicitly on the *feature level* (denoted as F3P0 hereafter). To switch off the impact of the context, features related to the neighboring peaks were discarded. The model with no contextual features was denoted as F0P0 and consisted of 20 features.

3.2 Context Modeling

The idea behind *context modeling* is that a classifier can use information about the prediction of n neighboring peaks. We believe that octal halving/doubling errors can be eliminated in this way. Therefore, context modeling can be seen as an alternative to dynamic programming-based GCI post-processing.

To avoid a bias towards the training data and to ensure a generalization performance on unseen data, *out-of-fold* (OOF) predictions were utilized:

1. The baseline context-free classifiers at the prediction level F3P0 and F0P0 were 10-fold cross-validated and out-of-fold *probabilistic predictions* were collected.
2. *Contextual information* at the prediction level (the out-of-fold predictions of n preceding and n succeeding peaks denoting the probability of the previous/current/next peak to be a GCI) together with the original features of a current peak were then used to train a set of contextual classifiers F3Pn and F0Pn (where $n = 1$–10 stands for the context length) on the out-of-fold data.

To evaluate the influence of the context modeling on GCI detection accuracy, the context-free models F3P0 and F0P0 were used to make predictions on the test dataset. The predictions of n neighboring peaks were then combined with the original features of each current peak and inputted to the contextual models F3Pn and F0Pn which in turn yielded unbiased predictions on the test dataset.

It can be clearly seen in Fig. 2 that information about the prediction of neighboring peaks does help, especially in the case of F0Pn which does not

---

[1] 3 preceding and 3 succeeding peaks were found optimal [16].

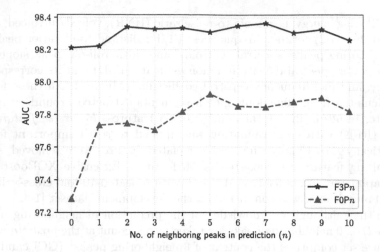

Fig. 2. The impact of neighboring peaks on the prediction of the actual peak for F0Pn and F3Pn systems with respect to AUC score on the test dataset.

contain any other contextual information at the feature level. It is also evident that using context on both feature and prediction levels (the case of F3Pn) yields the best results. The comparison of the best contextual systems F0P5 (for no neighboring peak at the feature level and 5 neighboring peaks at the prediction level) and F3P7 (3 neighboring peaks at the feature level and 7 neighboring peaks at the prediction level), and their baselines F0P0, F3P0 is given in Table 1.

Table 1. Comparison of classifiers' GCI detection performance on the test dataset (left) and the corresponding statistical significance according to McNemar's test [6] (right). The symbols $\gg$ and $>$ mean that the row classifier is significantly better at the significance level $\alpha = 0.01$ and $\alpha = 0.05$ respectively than the column classifier. The symbol $=$ means that the respective classifiers perform the same.

Model	R (%)	P (%)	$F1$ (%)	AUC (%)	Model	F3P7	F3P0	F0P5	F0P0
F3P7	**97.79**	**99.05**	**98.42**	**98.36**	F3P7	$=$	$>$	$\gg$	$\gg$
F3P0	97.50	99.03	98.26	98.21	F3P0	$<$	$=$	$\gg$	$\gg$
F0P5	97.34	98.67	98.00	97.92	F0P5	$\ll$	$\ll$	$=$	$\gg$
F0P0	96.37	98.38	97.36	97.28	F0P0	$\ll$	$\ll$	$\ll$	$=$

4   Comparison with Other Methods

In order to compare the proposed classifiers with different GCI detection algorithms, standard GCI detection measures that concern the *reliability* and *accuracy* of the GCI detection algorithms were used [20]. The former includes the

Table 2. Summary of the performance of the GCI detection algorithms for the four datasets.

Dataset	Method	IDR (%)	MR (%)	FAR (%)	IDA (ms)	A25 (%)	E10 (%)
UWB	F3P7	**96.78**	**2.34**	0.88	0.24	98.73	**95.66**
	F3P0	96.60	2.56	**0.85**	0.23	98.79	95.54
	SEDREAMS	93.12	4.00	2.88	0.28	98.10	91.69
	MMF	85.08	11.43	3.48	0.47	97.85	83.55
	DYPSA	89.64	6.25	4.11	0.37	98.04	88.22
	REAPER	92.81	5.51	1.69	0.27	98.00	91.45
	GEFBA	91.24	7.68	1.08	**0.22**	**98.89**	90.34
	PSFM	88.17	9.71	2.12	0.39	98.27	86.88
BDL	F3P7	**94.19**	**2.80**	3.01	0.37	98.59	**92.90**
	F3P0	94.04	2.93	3.03	**0.36**	98.58	92.74
	SEDREAMS	91.80	3.03	5.16	0.45	97.37	90.02
	MMF	90.42	4.63	4.95	0.56	97.15	87.87
	DYPSA	89.43	4.38	6.19	0.54	97.13	86.89
	REAPER	93.24	4.39	2.37	0.56	98.01	91.47
	GEFBA	87.93	10.05	**2.02**	1.02	**99.11**	87.18
	PSFM	87.05	9.65	3.30	0.71	96.95	84.50
SLT	F3P7	**96.64**	1.34	2.01	**0.17**	99.73	**96.39**
	F3P0	96.49	1.57	**1.95**	0.19	99.71	96.22
	SEDREAMS	94.66	**1.13**	4.21	0.17	99.67	94.36
	MMF	92.44	5.29	2.26	0.40	99.17	91.78
	DYPSA	93.25	2.91	3.84	0.32	99.39	92.75
	REAPER	95.57	1.66	2.77	0.19	99.67	95.27
	GEFBA	94.85	2.62	2.53	0.17	**99.76**	94.63
	PSFM	86.95	10.46	2.60	0.45	99.26	86.42
KED	F3P7	**96.82**	**2.31**	0.87	0.24	98.63	**95.83**
	F3P0	96.60	2.56	0.85	0.22	98.76	95.68
	SEDREAMS	92.30	6.03	1.66	0.29	99.12	91.76
	MMF	90.16	7.16	2.68	0.35	98.99	89.52
	DYPSA	90.27	7.07	2.65	0.30	99.25	89.72
	REAPER	91.05	8.18	**0.78**	0.28	99.47	90.67
	GEFBA	88.51	10.36	1.13	**0.21**	**99.74**	88.30
	PSFM	89.47	9.59	0.94	0.39	99.22	88.85

percentage of glottal closures for which exactly one GCI is detected (*identification rate*, IDR), the percentage of glottal closures for which no GCI is detected (*miss rate*, MR), and the percentage of glottal closures for which more than one GCI is detected (*false alarm rate*, FAR). The latter includes the percentage of detections with the identification error $\zeta \leq 0.25$ ms (*accuracy to* ± 0.25 ms, A25) and standard deviation of the identification error ζ (*identification accuracy*, IDA). In addition, we use a more *dynamic evaluation measure* [13]

$$E10 = \frac{N_R - N_{\zeta > 0.1T_0} - N_M - N_{FA}}{N_R} \tag{1}$$

that combines the reliability and accuracy in a single score and reflects the local *pitch period* T_0 pattern (determined from the reference GCIs). N_R stands for the number of reference GCIs, N_M is the number of missing GCIs (corresponding to MR), N_{FA} is the number of false GCIs (corresponding to FAR), and $N_{\zeta > 0.1T_0}$ is the number of GCIs with the identification error ζ greater than 10% of the local pitch period T_0. For the alignment between the detected and reference GCIs, dynamic programming was employed [13].

We compared the proposed classifiers with six existing state-of-the-art GCI detection methods:

- *Speech Event Detection using the Residual Excitation And a Mean-based Signal* (SEDREAMS) [8], shown in [9] to provide the best of performances compared to other methods;
- fast GCI detection based on *Microcanonical Multiscale Formalism* (MMF) [11];
- *Dynamic Programming Projected Phase-Slope Algorithm* (DYPSA) [20] available in the VOICEBOX toolbox;
- Google's *Robust Epoch And Pitch EstimatoR* (REAPER) [2];
- *Glottal closure/opening instant Estimation Forward-Backward Algorithm* (GEFBA) [12];
- *Probabilistic source-filter model* (PSFM) [19].

We used the implementations available online; no modifications of the algorithms were made. Since all algorithms (except REAPER) estimate GCIs also during unvoiced segments, their authors recommend filtering the detected GCIs by the output of a separate voiced/unvoiced detector. We applied an F_0 contour estimated by the REAPER algorithm for this purpose. There is no need to apply such post-processing on GCIs detected by the proposed classification-based approach since the voiced/unvoiced pattern was included directly in the feature set. To obtain consistent results for all methods, the detected GCIs were shifted towards the neighboring minimum negative sample in the speech signal.

4.1   Test Datasets

Firstly, the evaluation was carried out on the UWB test dataset (≈ 2.5 min of speech) described in Sect. 2. GCIs produced by a human expert were used as reference GCIs.

Secondly, two voices, a US male (BDL) and a US female (SLT) from the CMU ARCTIC databases intended for unit selection speech synthesis [1] were used as a test material. Each voice consists of 1132 phonetically balanced utterances of a total duration of ≈54 min per voice. Additionally, KED TIMIT database [1] comprising 453 phonetically balanced utterances (≈20 min) of a US male speaker was also used for the evaluation. All these datasets comprise clean speech. Since there are no hand-crafted GCIs available for these datasets, GCIs detected from contemporaneous EGG recordings by the Multi-Phase Algorithm (MPA) [13] (again shifted towards the neighboring minimum negative sample in the speech signal) were used as the reference GCIs. Original speech signals were downsampled to 16 kHz. It is important to mention that no voice from these datasets was part of the training dataset used to train the proposed classifiers.

4.2   Results

The results in Table 2 confirm that the proposed context-aware XGBoost model (F3P7) consistently outperforms the standard context-free XGBoost (F3P0). It is also evident that both XGBoost models (and especially the contextual one) generally perform very well for all tested datasets. They excel in terms of *reliability*, especially with respect to the identification (IDR) and miss (MR) rates, and also in terms of the dynamic detection accuracy (E10). As for the *accuracy*, they also performed reasonably well as they often achieved the second-best results (behind the GEFBA algorithm which, however, tends to miss GCIs quite often) in terms of identification accuracy (IDA) and of the smallest number of timing errors higher than 0.25 ms (A25).

5   Conclusions

In this paper, we showed that the introduction of context to XGBoost classifier improved GCI detection. The proposed context-aware XGBoost outperformed its context-free version, improving GCI detection accuracy $F1$ by 0.16% to 98.42% (statistically significant at the significance level $\alpha = 0.05$). From a more practical point of view, the improvement means that, on average, 2.28 peaks would be classified better and 1.45 GCIs would be identified better in a 10s-long utterance. The context-aware XGBoost also yielded very good results when compared to other existing state-of-the-art methods on several test datasets.

In our future work, we plan to investigate whether a deep learning algorithm could further increase the performance of the proposed classification-based GCI detection method [4,10,24]. Robustness of the proposed method to noisy signals and/or to emotional or expressive speech will also be researched.

References

1. FestVox Speech Synthesis Databases. http://festvox.org/dbs/index.html

2. REAPER: Robust Epoch And Pitch EstimatoR. https://github.com/google/REAPER
3. Barnard, E., Cole, R.A., Vea, M.P., Alleva, F.A.: Pitch detection with a neural-net classifier. IEEE Trans. Signal Process. **39**(2), 298–307 (1991). https://doi.org/10.1109/78.80812
4. Bulín, M., Šmídl, L., Švec, J.: On using stateful LSTM networks for key-phrase detection. In: Ekštein, K. (ed.) TSD 2019. LNCS (LNAI), vol. 11697, pp. 287–298. Springer, Cham (2019). https://doi.org/10.1007/978-3-030-27947-9_24
5. Chen, T., Guestrin, C.: XGBoost: reliable large-scale tree boosting system. In: Conference on Knowledge Discovery and Data Mining (2016). https://doi.org/10.1145/2939672.2939785
6. Dietterich, T.: Approximate statistical tests for comparing supervised classification learning algorithms. Neural Comput. **10**, 1895–1923 (1998)
7. Drugman, T., Alku, P., Alwan, A., Yegnanarayana, B.: Glottal source processing: from analysis to applications. Comput. Speech Lang. **28**(5), 1117–1138 (2014). https://doi.org/10.1016/j.csl.2014.03.003
8. Drugman, T., Dutoit, T.: Glottal closure and opening instant detection from speech signals. In: INTERSPEECH, Brighton, Great Britain, pp. 2891–2894 (2009)
9. Drugman, T., Thomas, M., Gudnason, J., Naylor, P., Dutoit, T.: Detection of glottal closure instants from speech signals: a quantitative review. IEEE Trans. Audio Speech Lang. Proces. **20**(3), 994–1006 (2012). https://doi.org/10.1109/TASL.2011.2170835
10. Goyal, M., Srivastava, V., Ap, P.: Detection of glottal closure instants from raw speech using convolutional neural networks. In: INTERSPEECH, Graz, Austria, pp. 1591–1595 (2019). https://doi.org/10.21437/Interspeech.2019-2587
11. Khanagha, V., Daoudi, K., Yahia, H.M.: Detection of glottal closure instants based on the microcanonical multiscale formalism. IEEE/ACM Trans. Audio Speech Lang. Proces. **22**(12), 1941–1950 (2014). https://doi.org/10.1109/TASLP.2014.2352451
12. Koutrouvelis, A.I., Kafentzis, G.P., Gaubitch, N.D., Heusdens, R.: A fast method for high-resolution voiced/unvoiced detection and glottal closure/opening instant estimation of speech. IEEE/ACM Trans. Audio Speech Lang. Proces. **24**(2), 316–328 (2016). https://doi.org/10.1109/TASLP.2015.2506263
13. Legát, M., Matoušek, J., Tihelka, D.: A robust multi-phase pitch-mark detection algorithm. In: INTERSPEECH, Antwerp, Belgium, vol. 1, pp. 1641–1644 (2007)
14. Legát, M., Matoušek, J., Tihelka, D.: On the detection of pitch marks using a robust multi-phase algorithm. Speech Commun. **53**(4), 552–566 (2011). https://doi.org/10.1016/j.specom.2011.01.008
15. Legát, M., Tihelka, D., Matoušek, J.: Pitch marks at peaks or valleys? In: Matoušek, V., Mautner, P. (eds.) TSD 2007. LNCS (LNAI), vol. 4629, pp. 502–507. Springer, Heidelberg (2007). https://doi.org/10.1007/978-3-540-74628-7_65
16. Matoušek, J., Tihelka, D.: Classification-based detection of glottal closure instants from speech signals. In: INTERSPEECH, Stockholm, Sweden, pp. 3053–3057 (2017).https://doi.org/10.21437/Interspeech.2017-213
17. Matoušek, J., Tihelka, D.: Glottal closure instant detection from speech signal using voting classifier and recursive feature elimination. In: INTERSPEECH, Hyderabad, India, pp. 2112–2116 (2018). https://doi.org/10.21437/Interspeech.2018-1147
18. Matoušek, J., Tihelka, D.: Using extreme gradient boosting to detect glottal closure instants in speech signal. In: IEEE International Conference on Acoustics Speech and Signal Processing, Brighton, United Kingdom, pp. 6515–6519 (2019). https://doi.org/10.1109/ICASSP.2019.8683889

19. Mv, A.R., Ghosh, P.K.: PSFM - a probabilistic source filter model for noise robust glottal closure instant detection. IEEE/ACM Trans. Audio Speech Lang. Proces. **26**(9), 1645–1657 (2018). https://doi.org/10.1109/TASLP.2018.2834733
20. Naylor, P.A., Kounoudes, A., Gudnason, J., Brookes, M.: Estimation of glottal closure instants in voiced speech using the DYPSA algorithm. IEEE Trans. Audio Speech Lang. Proces. **15**(1), 34–43 (2007). https://doi.org/10.1109/TASL.2006.876878
21. Pedregosa, F., et al.: Scikit-learn: machine learning in Python. J. Mach. Learn. Res. **12**, 2825–2830 (2011)
22. Sujith, P., Prathosh, A.P., Ramakrishnan, A.G., Ghosh, P.K.: An error correction scheme for GCI detection algorithms using pitch smoothness criterion. In: INTER-SPEECH, Dresden, Germany, pp. 3284–3288 (2015)
23. Tihelka, D., Hanzlíček, Z., Jůzová, M., Vít, J., Matoušek, J., Grůber, M.: Current state of text-to-speech system ARTIC: a decade of research on the field of speech technologies. In: Sojka, P., Horák, A., Kopeček, I., Pala, K. (eds.) TSD 2018. LNCS (LNAI), vol. 11107, pp. 369–378. Springer, Cham (2018). https://doi.org/10.1007/978-3-030-00794-2_40
24. Yang, S., Wu, Z., Shen, B., Meng, H.: Detection of glottal closure instants from speech signals: a convolutional neural network based method. In: INTERSPEECH, Hyderabad, India, pp. 317–321 (2018). https://doi.org/10.21437/Interspeech.2018-1281

LSTM-Based Speech Segmentation Trained on Different Foreign Languages

Zdeněk Hanzlíček(✉) 🆔 and Jakub Vít🆔

NTIS - New Technology for the Information Society, Faculty of Applied Sciences,
University of West Bohemia, Univerzitní 22, 306 14, Plzeň, Czech Republic
{zhanzlic,jvit}@ntis.zcu.cz
http://www.ntis.zcu.cz/en

Abstract. This paper describes experiments on speech segmentation by using bidirectional LSTM neural networks. The networks were trained on various languages (English, German, Russian and Czech), segmentation experiments were performed on 4 Czech professional voices. To be able to use various combinations of foreign languages, we defined a reduced phonetic alphabet based on IPA notation. It consists of 26 phones, all included in all languages. To increase the segmentation accuracy, we applied an iterative procedure based on detection of improperly segmented data and retraining of the network. Experiments confirmed the convergence of the procedure. A comparison with a reference HMM-based segmentation with additional manual corrections was performed.

Keywords: Speech segmentation · Neural networks · LSTM

1 Introduction

The aim of speech segmentation is to determine phone boundaries in a speech recording with a given orthographic transcription. For words with several pronunciation forms, the proper phonetic transcription is selected. The segmentation process could also involve insertion of pauses. An accurate speech segmentation is important for many application in the field of speech processing.

For a long time, HMM-based speech segmentation [1] was a predominant method. Recently, neural networks play an important role in almost all speech processing applications. One of the most employed type is long short-term memory (LSTM) recurrent neural network [2,5].

A common system for speech segmentation is language dependent, i.e. it is trained and run on the same language. The aim of this research is to analyze

This research was supported by the Czech Science Foundation (GA CR), project No. GA19-19324S, and by the grant of the University of West Bohemia, project No. SGS-2019-027. Computational resources were supplied by the project "e-Infrastruktura CZ" (e-INFRA LM2018140) provided within the program Projects of Large Research, Development and Innovations Infrastructures.

P. Sojka et al. (Eds.): TSD 2020, LNAI 12284, pp. 456–464, 2020.
https://doi.org/10.1007/978-3-030-58323-1_49

whether it is feasible to use a LSTM network to segment speech data of another language than it has been trained on. This would make possible to segment data of a new language, for which no reference training data are available.

For our experiments, we utilized Czech, English, German and Russian speech data sets recorded for a unit selection TTS system [10]. Our first segmentation experiments were performed on Czech data because the most accurate reference segmentation was available for these voices; the other languages were used to train segmentation models. We assume that the proposed approach can be applied to other language combinations of training and segmentation data.

This paper is organized as follows: Sect. 2 describes the phonetic alphabet used for our multi-language experiments. Section 3 gives an overview of the neural network architecture and the segmentation process. Experiments and the evaluation are presented in Sect. 4. Conclusions and plans for the future work are given in Sect. 5.

2   Phonetic Alphabet

A common phonetic alphabet used for computer applications is SAMPA [11] which uses a limited set of 7-bit ASCII symbols. However, it is defined for individual languages and different language-specific phones can be assigned to the same symbol. Therefore, SAMPA is not directly applicable for multi-language tasks. Recently, various modifications, extensions or redefinitions of the original SAMPA were introduced, e.g. X-SAMPA, that allow to overcome this limitation.

We decided to use directly the International Phonetic Alphabet (IPA) [7] which generally describes all distinctive speech sounds and allows a straight and naturally consistent combination of different languages. No phonetic transformation between different languages is needed. The complete list of phones included in our data, including diacritic combinations, is presented in Table 1.

The complete set contains 127 phones; some of them are included only in one language, e.g. phones ɾ, r̝̊, ɛʊ, dz, c, ɟ, ɲ, r̝, and ɣ are specific for the Czech language. This could be a significant complication of the segmentation process since those phones would not be included in the training data and the network would not recognize them. To cope with this problem, we have defined a reduced phonetic alphabet based on IPA notation, where all similar phones are joint together and represented by one symbol. As an extra effect, compacting the phonetic alphabet increases the robustness of the segmentation process [3,4,6]. The reduction process consists of the following steps

1. removing all punctuation marks, e.g. for vowel duration (aː, ɔː, ě, etc.), consonant syllabicity (r̝, l̩, m̩, etc.), palatalization (pʲ, bʲ, dʲ, etc.), nasalization (ã, ɛ̃, õː, etc.),
2. splitting all composed (strongly coarticulated) phones to single phones, e.g. diphthongs (ɛɪ, ɛə, aʊ, etc.), affricates (ts, tʃ, dz, dʒ, etc.),
3. unifying acoustically similar phones – see Table 2.

Table 1. The complete list of phones in particular languages.

IPA	Languages	IPA	Languages	IPA	Languages	IPA	Languages
p	cs, de, en, ru, sk	pf	de	pʲ	ru	b	cs, de, en, ru, sk
bʲ	ru	t	cs, de, en, ru, sk	ts	cs, de, ru, sk	tʃ	cs, de, en, sk
tʲ	ru	d	cs, de, en, ru, sk	dz	cs, sk	dʒ	cs, de, en, sk
dʲ	ru	c	cs, sk	ɟ	cs	ɟ̟	sk
k	cs, de, en, ru, sk	kʲ	ru	g	cs, de, en, ru, sk	gʲ	ru
ʔ	cs, de, en, sk	m	cs, de, en, ru, sk	mʲ	ru	m̩	cs, en
ŋ̍	en	n	cs, de, en, ru, sk	n̪	sk	nʲ	ru
ŋː	de	ɲ	cs, sk	ɳ	sk	ŋ	cs, de, en, sk
r̩	cs	r	cs, de, ru, sk	r̝̊	cs	rʲ	ru
fʲ	ru	r̩	cs, sk	r̩ː	sk	f	cs, de, en, ru, sk
ð	en	v	cs, de, en, ru, sk	vʲ	ru	θ	en
zʲ	ru	s	cs, de, en, ru, sk	sʲ	ru	z	cs, de, en, ru, sk
z̨	ru	ʃ	cs, de, en, sk	ʒ	cs, de, en, sk	ʂ	ru
ʐ	ru	ç	de	x	cs, de, ru, sk	xʲ	ru
ɣ	cs, sk	ʁ	de	h	de, en	ɦ	cs, en, sk
ʋ	sk	ɹ	en	j	cs, de, en, ru, sk	ɻ	cs, de, en, sk
lʲ	ru	l̩	cs, en, sk	l̩ː	sk	ʎ	sk
w	en	ɕː	ru	z̩ː	ru	ɫ	ru
tɕ	ru	i	de, ru	iː	cs, de, en, sk	ĭ	ru
e	de, ru	eɪ	en	eː	de	ĕ	ru
ɛ	cs, de, en, ru, sk	ɛʊ	cs	ɛə	en	ɛ̃	de
ɛ̃ː	de	ɛː	cs, de, sk	a	cs, de, ru, sk	aɪ	de, en
aʊ	cs, de, en	ã	de	ãː	de	aː	cs, de, sk
ɑ	en	ɑː	en	ɔ	de, sk	ɔɪ	en
ɔɣ	de	ɔː	en	o	cs, de, ru	oʊ	cs, en
õː	de	oː	cs, de, sk	u	de, ru, sk	uː	cs, de, en, sk
y	de	yː	de	ø	de	øː	de
œ	de	œː	de	ɒ	en	ʌ	en
ɨ	en, ru	ʉ	en, ru	ɪ	cs, de, en, ru, sk	ɪɛ	sk
ɪa	sk	ɪu	sk	ɪə	en	ɪ̯	sk
ʏ	de	ʊ	cs, de, en, ru	ʊɔ	sk	ʊə	en
ʊ̯	sk	ə	cs, de, en, ru	əʊ	en	ɵ	ru
ɐ	de, ru	æ	de, en, ru, sk	ɜ	en	ɜː	en

Table 2. Reduced alphabet – definition of similar phones.

Reduced phone	Assigned phones	Reduced phone	Assigned phones	Reduced phone	Assigned phones	Reduced phone	Assigned phones
t	t c	d	d ɟ	m	m ɱ	n	n ŋ ɲ
r	r ɾ ʁ ɹ	s	s θ	z	z ð	ʃ	ʃ ʂ ɕ
ʒ	ʒ ʑ ʐ	x	ç x h	ɦ	ɦ ɣ	l	l ʎ ɫ
v	v w	i	i ɨ ɪ y ʏ	e	e ɛ ø œ	a	a ɑ ʌ ɐ æ
o	ɔ ɒ ɒ ɵ	u	u ʉ ʊ	ə	ə ɜ		
Remaining (unassigned) phones				p b k g ʔ f j			

The resulting reduced alphabet contains 26 phones. The selection of assigned phones was performed manually with a strict requirement to share all phones by all languages.

3 System Architecture

The network for acoustic modeling consists of 2 bidirectional LSTM layers followed by linear projection and softmax activation. The network inputs vectors of 13 normalized MFCCs and outputs classification scores (that can be considered as posterior probabilities) of particular phones – see Fig. 1. The speech waveform is downsampled to 16 kHz, pre-processed by a preemphasis filter and parameterized with 5 ms frame shift. During training, cross entropy loss is minimized. We did not use any network for duration modeling within this research.

3.1 Segmentation Procedure

For a given utterance the network outputs a classification score matrix, in which rows correspond to phones and columns to speech frames. According to given phonetic transcription, lines of score matrix corresponding to particular phones are selected and composed to a new matrix in which the optimal alignment between frames and phones is found by a simple application of dynamic programming – see Fig. 1. Since each word can have more phonetic transcriptions, the alignment procedure is not performed on a single matrix but on a structure composed of matrices for particular words [3].

3.2 Detection of Incorrectly Segmented Phones

During the segmentation process, the most suitable phonetic transcription of each word is selected and aligned with the speech data. However, the result is not always fully correct. The selected transcription may not exactly correspond to the spoken word due to a mispronunciation, text-speech mismatch or due to an improper phonetic transcription. Problem could be also caused by the acoustic model that can be insufficiently robust to work properly on a given voice.

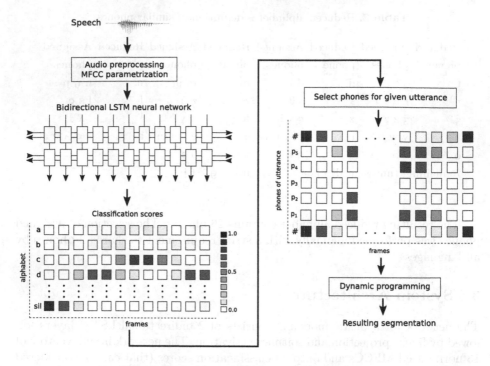

Fig. 1. Neural network for acoustic modeling.

We proposed a simple procedure for detection of such improperly segmented phones, referred to as invalid phones. First, all frames aligned with particular phones are checked whether the highest classification score corresponds to the given phone. When it is not fulfilled for more than 1/3 of frames, the phone is supposed to be invalid.

When the acoustic model fails, the segmentation can contain markedly short or long segments assigned to particular phones, especially when no duration model is used to reduce/mask that problem. Therefore, the mean duration is calculated for particular phones and phone instances with duration out of interval 50–200% of the mean value are also taken as invalid.

3.3 Iterative Segmentation Process

The segmentation performed by models trained on different languages can be inaccurate due to different phone sets in the training and segmentation data. It can contain many invalid phones as defined in the previous paragraph. Retraining of the network by using this initial segmentation (excluding invalid phones) could improve the result. The retraining-segmentation procedure can be repeated until the resulting segmentation is not significantly changing.

Table 3. Training and segmentation data.

	Language	Speaker	#sentences	#words	#phones	Duration
Training data	Czech (CZ)	Male	12,487	107,102	561,878	13:25:27
		Female	12,136	118,875	627,466	16:11:25
	German (DE)	Male	20,096	132,529	625,515	17:30:51
		Female	13,001	95,136	468,585	12:30:35
	English (EN)	Male	19,909	132,872	448,860	10:59:11
		Female	11,482	115,684	442,606	12:27:51
	Russian (RU)	Male	20,829	108,395	539,609	10:55:17
		Female	20,829	108,402	539,509	13:22:08
Segmentation data	Czech (CZ)	Male 1	12,240	119,922	631,698	13:44:02
		Male 2	12,150	119,166	627,525	15:00:54
		Female 1	12,151	119,113	628,081	14:58:42
		Female 2	12,708	108,909	570,100	12:40:33

4   Experiments and Results

4.1   Experimental Data

For our experiments, we used speech data recorded by professional voice talents for the purposes of unit selection speech synthesis [9]; particular voices are described in Table 3. Speech data was supplemented by a phonetic segmentation created by a HMM-based segmentation procedure with various additional correction procedures [8]. Czech voices selected for the segmentation experiments have been utilized for many years in a TTS system [10] and lots of additional manual corrections have been made over time, therefore their phonetic transcription and segmentation can be considered very accurate and applicable for our segmentation experiments.

4.2   Initial Segmentation

We trained individual LSTM networks for all languages by using training data described in Table 3. Besides, we trained one network for all foreign languages (without Czech) together. All networks were applied on the segmentation data and the segmentation accuracy was evaluated by comparison with the reference segmentation using the mean segmentation error. Results are presented in Fig. 2; results for the multi-language network are labeled with XX.

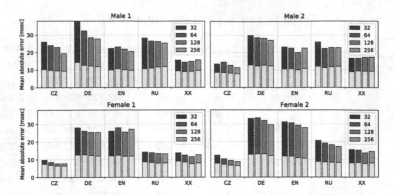

Fig. 2. Mean segmentation error for various training data and the number of units in both LSTM layers. The lower part of each bar corresponds to the error determined for valid phones only. The complete bar corresponds to all phones.

Not surprisingly, the best results were obtained for the Czech network, where the training and segmentation data are phonetically consistent, and also for the multi-language network, which is supposed to be the most robust one. Figure 2 also proves the relevance of invalid phones detection: The mean segmentation error without invalid phones is significantly lower, i.e. the detection procedure successfully revealed the badly segmented data.

4.3   Iterative Segmentation

We performed several steps of the iterative segmentation procedure; the starting points were segmentation results from the previous paragraph (0-th iteration). The evaluation by the mean segmentation error and the number of invalid phones is presented in Fig. 3. The labels in all graphs refer to languages used in the 0-th iteration, although the training/segmentation procedure ran with speech data of particular speakers. In all cases, segmentation error and the number of invalid phones were decreasing during 2–3 iterations. The final values are different for particular languages of initial networks. The resulting accuracy is consistent with results for the initial segmentation, i.e. the best accuracy was obtained with the Czech and multi-language initial networks.

An interesting issue is also the ability of a network with the selected topology to learn a given segmentation. We performed a simple experiment: the network was trained directly using the reference segmentation and used to re-segment the training data. In this manner the mean segmentation error and the number of invalid phones were determined for particular speakers; the values are included as reference lines in Fig. 3.

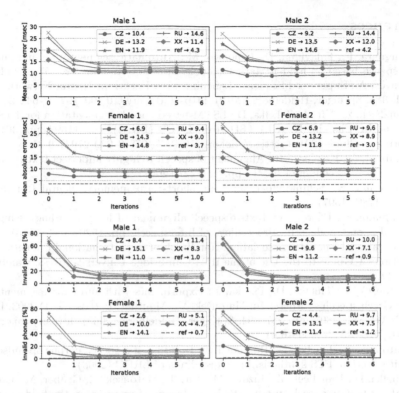

Fig. 3. Mean segmentation error and the number of invalid phones.

5   Conclusion

This paper presented an initial research on LSTM-based speech segmentation used with different language of training and segmentation data. We performed experiments with models trained on Czech, German, English and Russian data and also model trained on all foreign languages together. The segmentation procedure was tested on Czech speech data, however, we assume that this approach is applicable to other language combinations of training/segmentation data. Primary results demonstrate that native (Czech in this study) and multi-language networks can accomplish comparable results.

In our future work, we intend to include other languages, e.g. French, Slovak and Polish. The segmentation accuracy should be analyzed in more detail. The definition of reduced alphabet should be also based on a proper data analysis. Since the speech data were originally recorded for speech synthesis, the segmentation should be evaluated by its application in a TTS-system. We will also focus on the network robustness to be able to segment speech data of worse quality, that was not originally recorded for the purposes of speech synthesis, e.g. audio books, which are more difficult to work with.

References

1. Brugnara, F., Falavigna, D., Omologo, M.: Automatic segmentation and labeling of speech based on hidden Markov models. Speech Commun. **12**, 357–370 (1993)
2. Graves, A.: Supervised Sequence Labelling with Recurrent Neural Networks. SCI, vol. 385. Springer, Heidelberg (2012). https://doi.org/10.1007/978-3-642-24797-2
3. Hanzlíček, Z., Vít, J., Tihelka, D.: LSTM-based speech segmentation for TTS synthesis. In: Ekštein, K. (ed.) TSD 2019. LNCS (LNAI), vol. 11697, pp. 361–372. Springer, Cham (2019). https://doi.org/10.1007/978-3-030-27947-9_31
4. Haubold, A., Kender, J.R.: Alignment of speech to highly imperfect text transcriptions. In: Proceeding of ICME, pp. 224–227 (2007)
5. Hochreiter, S., Schmidhuber, J.: Long short-term memory. Neural Comput. **9**, 1735–1780 (1997)
6. Hoffmann, S., Pfister, B.: Text-to-speech alignment of long recordings using universal phone models. In: Proceedings of Interspeech, pp. 1520–1524 (2013)
7. International Phonetic Association: Handbook of the International Phonetic Association: A Guide to the Use of the IPA. Cambridge University Press, Cambridge (1999)
8. Matoušek, J., Tihelka, D., Psutka, J.: Experiments with automatic segmentation for Czech speech synthesis. In: Matoušek, V., Mautner, P. (eds.) TSD 2003. LNCS (LNAI), vol. 2807, pp. 287–294. Springer, Heidelberg (2003). https://doi.org/10.1007/978-3-540-39398-6_41
9. Matoušek, J., Tihelka, D., Romportl, J.: Building of a speech corpus optimised for unit selection TTS synthesis. In: Proceedings of LREC (2008)
10. Tihelka, D., Hanzlíček, Z., Jůzová, M., Vít, J., Matoušek, J., Grůber, M.: Current state of text-to-speech system ARTIC: a decade of research on the field of speech technologies. In: Sojka, P., Horák, A., Kopeček, I., Pala, K. (eds.) TSD 2018. LNCS (LNAI), vol. 11107, pp. 369–378. Springer, Cham (2018). https://doi.org/10.1007/978-3-030-00794-2_40
11. Wells, J.: SAMPA computer readable phonetic alphabet. In: Gibbon, D., Moore, R., Winski, R. (eds.) Handbook of Standards and Resources for Spoken Language Systems, pp. 684–732. Mouton de Gruyter, Berlin and New York (1997)

Complexity of the TDNN Acoustic Model with Respect to the HMM Topology

Josef V. Psutka[1,2](✉) [iD], Jan Vaněk[2] [iD], and Aleš Pražák[2] [iD]

[1] Department of Cybernetics, University of West Bohemia, Pilsen, Czech Republic
[2] NTIS - New Technologies for the Information Society, UWB, Pilsen, Czech Republic
{psutka_j,vanekyj,aprazak}@kky.zcu.cz

Abstract. In this paper, we discuss some of the properties of training acoustic models using a lattice-free version of the maximum mutual information criterion (LF-MMI). Currently, the LF-MMI method achieves state-of-the-art results on many speech recognition tasks. Some of the key features of the LF-MMI approach are: training DNN without initialization from a cross-entropy system, the use of a 3-fold reduced frame rate and the use of a simpler HMM topology. The conventional 3-state HMM topology was replaced in a typical LF-MMI training procedure with a special 1-stage HMM topology, that has different pdfs on the self-loop and forward transitions. In this paper, we would like to discuss both the different types of HMM topologies (conventional 1-, 2- and 3-state HMM topology) and the advantages of using biphone context modeling over using the original triphone or a simpler monophone context. We would also like to mention the impact of the subsampling factor to WER.

Keywords: Speech recognition · Acoustic modeling · HMM topology · Lattice-free MMI

1 Introduction

Lattice-free maximum mutual information (LF-MMI) HMM-DNN models [9] achieved state-of-the-art word error rates (WER) on different well-known speech databases such as Switchboard and Wall Street Journal (WSJ) in recent years [5,9]. The conventional HMM topology in ASR is a 3-state left-to-right HMM that can be traversed in a minimum of 3 frames. This topology was replaced in the typical LF-MMI training procedure with a topology that can be traversed in one frame. This one-state HMM topology has different pdfs on the self-loop and forward transitions. The observations are associated with the arcs (rather than the states). This topology is based on similarity to Connectionist Temporal Classification (CTC) [3]. In this article, we would like to mention different types of HMM topologies.

In [9], it was also proposed an effective approach using left-biphones to allow context-dependent modeling. We would like to discuss the advantages of using

© Springer Nature Switzerland AG 2020
P. Sojka et al. (Eds.): TSD 2020, LNAI 12284, pp. 465–473, 2020.
https://doi.org/10.1007/978-3-030-58323-1_50

biphone context modeling over the use of the original triphone or a simpler monophone context. We would also like to mention the impact of the subsampling factor to WER.

Table 1. Statistics of train and test data-sets.

	Train	Dev	Test
# of speakers	2670	10	20
# of sentences	581 k	–	–
# of tokens	3.1M	26 k	53 k
Dataset length [hours]	738	3.3	6.7

Last but not least, we also describe the computational and memory requirements of the TDNN LF-MMI acoustic model (AM). Even in the case of transferring the calculation of AM to the GPU, we may be interested in memory demands, especially for low-performance graphics cards, or to answer the question of how many parallel tasks can we run on a single GPU at a time.

The following sections briefly describe the training and testing datasets. In Sect. 3, we describe a typical TDNN LF-MMI setup. The experiments and results are described in Sect. 4. The conclusions are presented in Sect. 5.

2   Training and Testing Data

All experiments were performed using a high-quality Czech speech corpus. This corpus consists of multiple read-speech databases and contains a total of 2670 different speakers. Each speaker read at least 150 sentences. A total of 738 738 h of speech data were available. No speech augmentation was performed. Data were sampled at 16 kHz with a resolution of 16 bits.

The test part contains recordings from 30 people (15 men and 15 women), where each speaker read randomly selected newspaper articles for 20 min. Our test, therefore, includes a total of 10 10 h of speech. We also excluded a development subset from this test set. Details of the training and testing files are summarized in Table 1.

3   Experimental Setup

3.1   Acoustic Feature Extraction

The front-end is based on the Mel-frequency cepstral coefficients (MFCC). These 40-dimensional features were used not only as an input to the DNN but also to the GMM. Only in the case of training basic HMM-GMM model, delta and delta-delta features were added to the original coefficients. No mean and variance normalizations were used. No i-vectors or other speaker adaptation techniques were used in the feature extraction process either. Feature vectors were calculated every 10 ms (100 frames per second) from the 32 ms frames.

3.2   Acoustic Modeling

Structure and parameters of the acoustic models in LVCSR system were tuned using KALDI toolkit [8].

GMM: The first step is building a monophone acoustic model. A monophone AM is trained from the flat start using the MFCCs features (static + delta + delta delta). Secondly, we trained the triphone AM. As the number of triphones is typically too large, decision trees are used to tie their states. We also applied linear discriminant analysis (LDA) and Maximum Likelihood Linear Transform (MLLT) over a central frame spliced across ±3 frames. LDA+MLLT project the concatenated frames into 40 dimensions space. We used the feature-space Maximum Likelihood Linear Regression (fMLLR) and Speaker-adaptive training procedure (SAT) to adapt GMM models. The whole training data were forced aligned using the resulting HMM-GMM model. This alignment is necessary as an input for DNN training [7–9] as opposed to the end-to-end approach (such as [6] and [4]), where this information is not needed.

TDNN_CE: Time Delay Neural Networks (TDNN) have shown to be effective in modeling long-range temporal dependencies [14]. The TDNNs used for cross-entropy (CE) training were slightly modified compared to those presented in [7]. The first splicing was the Linear Discriminant Analysis (LDA) transforms layer $(-2, -1, 0, 1, 2)$. Subsequent layers then had contexts $(-1, 0, 1)$, $(-1, 0, 1)$, $(-3, 0, 3)$ and $(-6, -3, 0)$. The $(-1, 0, 1)$ means that the first layer sees 3 consecutive frames of input thus the $(-3, 0, 3)$ means that the hidden layer sees 3 frames of the previous layer, separated by 3 frames. In total, we have five hidden layers of ReLu activation function with 650 nodes. The softmax output layer computes posteriors for clustered GMM based triphone states (4408 states). The overall context is therefore 13 frames to the left and the 7 to the right. State-level Minimum Bayes Risk (sMBR) [13] has been used to improve previously trained models to achieve state-of-the-art results.

TDNN_LF-MMI: Maximum mutual information (MMI) [1] is a discriminative objective function that aims to maximize the probability of the reference transcription while minimizing the probability of all other transcriptions. The denominator graph has traditionally been estimated using n-best lists or later using lattices.

Povey et al. [9] applied MMI training with HMM-DNN models using a full denominator graph (hence the name lattice-free) by using a phone language model (instead of a word language model). Instead of a frame-level objective, the log-probability of the correct phone sequence as the objective function is used. The LF-MMI (Lattice-Free Maximum Mutual Information) training procedure has a sequence discriminative training criterion without the need for frame-level cross-entropy pre-training. In regular LF-MMI, all utterances are split into fixed-size chunks (usually 150 frames) to make GPU computations efficient [9]. This is done using the alignments from the HMM-GMM system. **Standard setup:** 12 TDNN layers; dimension in the hidden layers is 1024, bottleneck dimension is 128; context is ±28 i.e. context per layer 1 1 1 0 3 3 3 3 3 3 3 3.

3.3 Language Modeling

Our ASR system is using the universal trigram back-off Language Model (LM) with the mixed-case vocabularies with more than 1.2M words. Our training text corpus contains the data from newspapers (520M tokens), web news (350M tokens), subtitles (200M tokens), and transcriptions of some TV programs (175M tokens, details can be found in [11]). The resulting LM has 35M bigrams and almost 30M trigrams. Although we have a comprehensive vocabulary, the percentage of OOV words on the test set is 1.3%.

3.4 Decoding

All recognition experiments were performed using our in-house real-time ASR system. This LVCSR system is optimized for low latency in the real-time (RT) operation with very large vocabularies. To enable recognition with a vocabulary containing more than one million words in RT, we speeded up decoding using a parallel approach (Viterbi search on CPU and DNN segments scores on GPU [12]). The optimal weight/tradeoff between the acoustic model and the language model was set on the development data for each recognition experiment.

4 Experiments

4.1 HMM-topology

Figure 1 shows a simple left-right HMMs with 1-, 2- and 3- emitting states. The conventional HMM topology in ASR is a 3-state left-to-right HMM [15] (*3state*) (shown in Fig. 1(f)). This HMM can be traversed in a minimum of 3 frames. The *3state_skip* (shown in Fig. 1(e)) has additional skip transitions. The skip transitions are used because of frame subsampling (i.e., because the output rate at the end of the network is 33.33 Hz compared to typical setups where it is 100 Hz [9,10]). A similar extension (addition of a skip transition) was performed for the classical 2-state HMM (shown in Fig. 1(c) and (d)).

The conventional HMM 3-state topology was replaced in a typical LF-MMI training procedure with a special 1-stage topology (see Fig. 1(b), that has different pdfs on the self-loop and forward transitions (highlighted in bold in the image). The observations are associated with the arcs (rather than the states). All HMM transitions probabilities are fixed and uniform because adjusting them does not improve the recognition results [9]. In Table 2 we can see the impact of a different HMM topologies on the final WER. In all experiments, a frame subsampling factor of 3 was used. It can be seen that the 1-state models (*arc*-based or *state*-based HMMs) perform slightly better than a 2 or 3-state model.

4.2   Context-Dependent Modeling

As the past studies have shown [2] context-dependent(CD) modeling has been a fundamental part of HMM-based models, not only for HMM-GMM, but also for HMM-DNN. Commonly used CD phones are biphones and triphones. The higher order context is rarely used due to high computational burdens. An alternative to CD modeling, is context-independent (CI) modeling, i.e. monophones. CI models have a significantly smaller number of states and can be simply used without state tying.

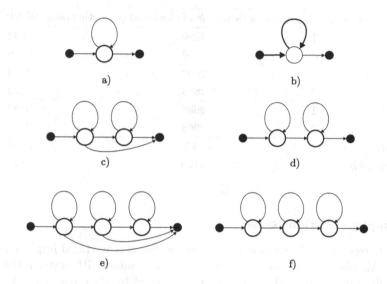

Fig. 1. Different HMM topologies. The circles represents the states and arrows the transitions. Input and output states are non-emitting and are shown in black. a) *1state*, b) *1state_{arc}*, c) *2state_skip*, d) *2state*, e) *3state_skip* and f) *3state*

Table 2. Impact of the HMM-topology on recognition results

	WER %		
	Monophone	Biphone	Triphone
1state	10.58	9.95	10.09
1state_{arc}	10.29	9.86	10.02
2state_skip	10.57	10.07	10.17
3state_skip	10.62	10.09	10.15

A pruned context-dependency left biphone tree is used for regular LF-MMI training. In Table 2, it can be seen the advantages of using biphone context modeling over the use of triphone or a simpler monophone context.

4.3 Subsampling

As in [9], we investigated an impact of frame subsampling factor. Subsampling factor 3 speeds up training by a factor of 2. Subsampling can save a lot of calculations if the implementation supports this. An example of the impact of the subsampling factor on recognition results is depicted on the Table 3.

Table 3. Impact of subsampling factor on recognition results (triphones CD tree was used)

HMM topology	Subsampling factor	# of clustered phonetic states	WER %
1$state$	1	3320	11.42
1$state$	3	3040	10.09
1$state_{arc}$	1	2992	10.86
1$state_{arc}$	3	2888	10.02
2$state$	1	2936	10.80
2$state\_skip$	3	2968	10.17
3$state$	1	4232	11.30
3$state\_skip$	3	4120	10.15

4.4 Implementation Issues

Unfortunately, our LVCSR system is based on the classic HMM implementation [15]. HMMs observations in "HTK-style" are associated with states rather than arcs. This brings the need to transform arc-based to $state$-based HMM (especially for the 1$state_{arc}$ HMM). The Fig. 2 shows an example of such a transformation. However, it can be seen from the figure that after the conversion, the original single-state arc-based model (with the different pdfs associated with the self-loop and forward transitions) changed to two states $state$-based model. Thus both HMMs may emit the same outputs: either a, or ab, or abb, etc.

Fig. 2. An example of arc-based transformation to $state$-based HMM.

4.5 Computational Aspect of DNN Acoustic Models

In this paper, we have evaluated three types of context-dependent acoustic models: triphone, left biphone and monophone. They shared the same structure and differ only in the last layer and number of outputs. In some experiments, a subsampling factor of 3 was used. Subsampling can save a lot of calculations if the implementation supports this and the TDNN context is equal to the subsampling factor and/or its multiples. However, the speed-up is not equal to the subsampling factor because only a part of NN is subsampled. The total number of parameters for the 12 TDNN layers is approximately 6.4 M, and the estimated number of MAD operations (multiply-and-add operations for which the GPU is particularly suitable) required to evaluate the input signal (without downsampling) is 317 M per second. Due to the subsampling and the bottleneck NN structure, the NN inference may be run on a low-end GPU even in multiple parallel copies. Note that this estimate assumes absolute reusing of already computed intermediate results in the TDNN layers. Moreover, we have excluded the last layer with a different number of outputs for a clear comparison.

5   Conclusion

This paper discussed and compared some interesting parameters of acoustic modeling using TDNN LF-MMI in terms of computational complexity. The influence of HMM topology was investigated, 1- 2- and classical 3-states HMM were tested and compared. Various context dependencies (monophone, left biphone and triphone) were also investigated. The effect of subsampling was also analyzed. The most interesting results are summarized in Table 4.

Table 4. Summary of the recognition results

			WER [%]
GMM			19.95
TDNN_CE			12.05
		sMBR	11.51
TDNN_LF-MMI		$3state$ triph.	11.30
		$2state$ triph.	10.80
	subsmpl. = 3	$1state$ biph.	9.95
		$1state_{arc}$ biph.	**9.86**
		$1state$ monoph.	10.58

New methods based on the use of TDNN have yielded more than 10% absolute improvement compared to the solution based on the standard HMM-GMM. The best recognition result (9.86% WER) was achieved using $1state_{arc}$ HMM topology together with left-biphones. TDNN_CE with sMBR also worked very similarly to TDNN_LF-MMI for a $3state$ triphone model (without subsampling).

A very interesting result was also achieved using a monophone model with $1state$ HMM topology. In this case, there were as many outputs of the DNN as there were different phonemes in the task. With an appropriate network structure, we can even evaluate every third frame (using subsampling). Although there was a deterioration of 0.72 % (from the best result), this result was very promising, because using monophones instead of biphones significantly simplified the whole decoding process.

As future work, we would like to analyze the influence of the DNN context. We are mainly interested in its possible minimization with regard to the recognition results and use in real-time. We would also like to perform similar experiments on well-known speech databases and verify the obtained results by a test of statistical significance.

Acknowledgments. This paper was supported by the project LO1506 of the Czech Ministry of Education, Youth and Sports under the program NPU I.

References

1. Bahl, L., Brown, P., de Souza, P., Mercer, R.: Maximum mutual information estimation of hidden Markov model parameters for speech recognition. In: ICASSP 1986, vol. 11, pp. 49–52 (1986)
2. Deng, L., Acero, A., Dahl, G., Yu, D.: Context-dependent pre-trained deep neural networks for large vocabulary speech recognition. IEEE Trans. Audio Speech Lang. Process. **20**, 30–42 (2012)
3. Graves, A., Fernández, S., Gomez, F.: Connectionist temporal classification: labelling unsegmented sequence data with recurrent neural networks. In: Proceedings of the International Conference on Machine Learning, ICML 2006, pp. 369–376 (2006)
4. Hadian, H., Sameti, H., Povey, D., Khudanpur, S.: End-to-end speech recognition using lattice-free MMI. In: Interspeech 2018, pp. 12–16 (2018)
5. Han, K.J., Hahm, S., Kim, B., Kim, J., Lane, I.R.: Deep learning-based telephony speech recognition in the wild. In: Interspeech 2017, pp. 1323–1327 (2017)
6. Hannun, A., et al.: Deep speech: scaling up end-to-end speech recognition. abs/1412.5567 (2014). http://arxiv.org/abs/1412.5567
7. Peddinti, V., Povey, D., Khudanpur, S.: A time delay neural network architecture for efficient modeling of long temporal contexts. In: Interspeech 2015, pp. 3214–3218 (2015)
8. Povey, D., et al.: The Kaldi speech recognition toolkit. In: IEEE 2011 Workshop on Automatic Speech Recognition and Understanding, January 2011
9. Povey, D., et al.: Purely sequence-trained neural networks for ASR based on lattice-free MMI. In: Interspeech 2016, pp. 2751–2755 (2016)
10. Sak, H., Senior, A.W., Rao, K., Beaufays, F.: Fast and accurate recurrent neural network acoustic models for speech recognition. In: Interspeech 2015, pp. 1468–1472 (2015)
11. Švec, J., Hoidekr, J., Soutner, D., Vavruška, J.: Web text data mining for building large scale language modelling corpus. In: Habernal, I., Matoušek, V. (eds.) TSD 2011. LNCS (LNAI), vol. 6836, pp. 356–363. Springer, Heidelberg (2011). https://doi.org/10.1007/978-3-642-23538-2_45
12. Vanek, J., Trmal, J., Psutka, J.V., Psutka, J.: Optimized acoustic likelihoods computation for NVIDIA and ATI/AMD graphics processors. IEEE Trans. Audio Speech Lang. Process. **20**(6), 1818–1828 (2012)

13. Veselý, K., Ghoshal, A., Burget, L., Povey, D.: Sequence-discriminative training of deep neural networks. In: Interspeech 2013, pp. 2345–2349 (2013)
14. Waibel, A., Hanazawa, T., Hinton, G., Shikano, K., Lang, K.J.: Phoneme recognition using time-delay neural networks. IEEE Trans. Acoust. Speech Signal Process. **37**(3), 328–339 (1989)
15. Young, S.: The HTK hidden Markov model toolkit: Design and philosophy. Entropic Cambridge Research Laboratory, Ltd, vol. 2, pp. 2–44 (1994)

Dialogue

Leyzer: A Dataset for Multilingual Virtual Assistants

Marcin Sowański[1,2]([⊠])🆔 and Artur Janicki[2]([⊠])🆔

[1] Samsung R&D Institute Poland, Warsaw, Poland
m.sowanski@samsung.com
[2] Warsaw University of Technology, Warsaw, Poland
a.janicki@tele.pw.edu.pl

Abstract. In this article we present the Leyzer dataset, a multilingual text corpus designed to study multilingual and cross-lingual natural language understanding (NLU) models and the strategies of localization of virtual assistants. The proposed corpus consists of 20 domains across three languages: English, Spanish and Polish, with 186 intents and a wide range of samples, ranging from 1 to 672 sentences per intent. We describe the data generation process, including creation of grammars and forced parallelization. We present a detailed analysis of the created corpus. Finally, we report the results for two localization strategies: train-on-target and zero-shot learning using multilingual BERT models.

Keywords: Virtual assistant · Multilingual natural language understanding · Text corpus · Machine translation

1 Introduction

Virtual assistants (VAs) have been available since 1960s, but the release of their recent generation on smartphones and embedded devices has opened them to a broader audience. The most popular development approach for such systems is to release initial set of languages, usually English as the first, and then the following languages. Although there might be various reasons for choosing such approach, it is clear that adding support for new languages is a time- and cost-consuming process.

There are over 6900 living languages in the world, from which more than 91 have over 10 million users. If we want to build an unfragmented e-society, we have to develop methods that will allow us to create multilingual VAs also for, so called, low-resource languages.

In this work we present Leyzer[1], a dataset containing a large number of utterances created for the purpose of investigation of cross-lingual transfer learning in

---

[1] Named after Ludwik Lejzer Zamenhof, a Polish linguist and the inventor of the international language Esperanto, the most widely used constructed international auxiliary language in the world. https://en.wikipedia.org/wiki/L._L._Zamenhof.

© Springer Nature Switzerland AG 2020
P. Sojka et al. (Eds.): TSD 2020, LNAI 12284, pp. 477–486, 2020.
https://doi.org/10.1007/978-3-030-58323-1_51

natural language understanding (NLU) systems. We believe that Leyzer presents great opportunities to investigate multilingual and cross-lingual NLU models and localization strategies, which allow translating and adapting an NLU system to a specific country or region. While creating our dataset, we focused particularly on testing localization strategies that use machine translation (MT) and multilingual word embeddings. First localization strategy that we tested was the so called *train-on-target*, where the training corpus of a system is translated from one language to another and the model trained from this corpus is tested on a parallel testset that was created manually by language experts (LEs). Second localization strategy tested was *zero-shot learning*, where the system that used multilingual embeddings is supposed to generalize from the language it was trained on to new languages that it will be later tested on. Finally, we report results for two types of baseline models that were trained either on single language data only or on all data available in three languages at once.

To the best of our knowledge, Leyzer is the largest dataset in terms of the number of domains, intents (where *intent* is understood as an utterance-level concept representing system functionality available for the user) and slots (where *slot* is defined as a word-level concept representing the parameters of a given intent) in the area of multilingual datasets focused on problems of the localization of VA datasets. It has been publicly released, with the code to allow reproduction of the experiments and is available at https://github.com/cartesinus/leyzer.

2   Related Datasets

There exist a couple of text corpora which are often used in the context of VAs, which can be divided into two groups.

Table 1. Statistics of existing corpora compared to Leyzer, proposed in this work. First group consists of resources designed to train and test VAs without focusing on multilingual setup. Second group concerns multilingual VAs.

Dataset	Languages	# Utterances	# Domains	# Intents	# Slots
ATIS [11]	en	5871	1	26	83
Larson et al. [8]	en	23,700	10	150	0
Liu et al. [9]	en	25,716	19	64	54
Snips [5]	en, fr	2,943/1,136	–	7	72
Schuster et al. [12]	en, es, th	43,323/8,643/5,083	3	12	11
Leyzer (this work)	en, es, pl	3779/5425/7053	20	186	86

The first group, represented by The Air Travel Information System (ATIS) [11] dataset consists of spoken queries from flight domain in the English language. ATIS has a small number of intents and is heavily unbalanced with most utterances belonging to three intents. Larson et al. [8] created a dataset to study out-of-scope queries that do not fall into any of the system's supported intents. Presented corpus consists of 23,700 queries equally distributed among 150 intents which can be grouped into 10 general domains. Yet another corpus for English is the one created by Liu et al. [9]. Their dataset, created as a use case of a home robot, can be used to train and compare multiple NLU platforms (Rasa, Dialogflow, LUIS and Watson). The dataset consists of 25,716 English sentences from 21 domains that can be divided into 64 intents and 54 slot types.

The Snips [5] dataset represents the second category of VAs datasets that were designed to train and evaluate multilingual VAs. The dataset has a small number of intents; each intent, however, has a large number of sentences. Schuster et al. [12] proposed a multilingual dataset for English, Spanish and Thai to study various cross-lingual transfer scenarios. The dataset consists of 3 domains: Alarm, Reminder and Weather with small number of intents and slots (11 intents and 12 slots in total). Different languages have different number of sentences, with English having 43,323, Spanish 8,643 and Thai having 5,083 ones. It follows that there is a large number of sentences per intent and per slot type.

Table 1 summarizes the existing corpora used to test VAs, and compares them with our dataset, proposed in this article. There are many multi-domain and multi-intent resources for English from which to choose. However, to the best of our knowledge, there exist no multilingual resources with many domains, intents and slot types.

3 Our Dataset

We designed our dataset to be useful mostly in the following two areas related to VAs:

- development and evaluation of VAs, and
- creation and localization of the dataset into other languages in order to have a parallel multilingual dataset.

Commercial VA systems often face multiple challenges:

1. Number of languages and their linguistic phenomena, which represents a challenge of building a multilingual system and handling phenomena such as flexion, which has impact on slot recognition,
2. Number of domains and their distribution, that introduce two major challenges:
   (a) how to train a model to equally represent each domain, even if our trainset is not balanced in terms of number of sentences per domain,
   (b) how to treat sentences that are similar or identical in more than one domain,
3. Number of intents and how they differ. This introduces a problem of having multiple intents that differ only by one parameter or word,
4. Number of slots and their values, that introduces a challenge of how to train a model that will recognize slots not by their values but rather by their syntactic function in the sentence.

We approached these typical problems by creating a dataset (Table 2) that consists of a large number of intent classes (186), yet also contains a wide range of samples per intent class, ranging from 1 to 672 sentences per intent. We selected three languages that represent separate language families (Germanic, Romance, Slavic) to address problems typical for multilingual systems.

There is no easy mapping between the intents in Leyzer and these of Larson et. al. [8], some intents however, overlap. When comparing the intents of Leyzer and the intents in the corpus created by Liu et al. [9] we found out that out of their 18 domains (called scenarios in [9]) we could match seven domains in Leyzer. Similarly to Schuster et al. [12], in our paper we tested train-on-target and one zero-shot scenarios. When compared to Schuster et al., our dataset consists of more intents and slots, which, we believe, may have significant impact on the results, especially for the train-on-target scenario. If an NLU system has hundreds of closely-related intents, MT systems may easily fail to properly distinguish them, which, as a consequence, may lead to a lot of mismatches.

Leyzer differs from corpora such as MultiWoz [1], because our dataset contains isolated utterances instead of dialogues. We wanted to create a resource that is controllable and cheap in terms of the time needed to create or modify it. We also wanted to demonstrate that VAs able to handle hundreds of intents and slots are still a challenging task.

3.1   Creation of Corpus

Generation of Leyzer consisted of four steps: creating base grammars, creating target grammars, applying forced parallelization, slot expansion and splitting data into train-, dev- and testsets. They are briefly characterized below.

In contrast to approaches such as MultiWoz, where utterances are usually gathered with the use of crowdsourcing, we decided to use grammars that are written by qualified LEs. We believe that all concerns on grammar-based generated text, namely on their lack of naturalness, can be eliminated if the procedure of quality control is implemented. We think that grammar-based corpora have two noteworthy advantages: they are cheap in generation and remodeling, and they can cover all possible ways to express a given intent, which crowdsourced approaches can easily miss.

Base Grammars Creation. Starting with English, we created 20 grammars with sentence patterns in the JSpeech Grammar Format (JSGF). Initial set of intents in each domain was inspired by example commands available in Almond Virtual Assistant [2]. Slot values were crawled from the Internet or created manually. Depending on slot type, we gathered from a few to a few hundreds values for each slot.

All sentence patterns in the corpus were generated from grammars. Each of such patterns represents possible way to utter a sentence without explicitly giving the content of the slots. Later on, grammars were filled with the slot values. Since sentences generated in such fashion might contain some unnatural expressions or grammatical errors, we requested verification by LEs. Wherever it was possible, incorrect sentences were fixed, and if that was not possible, sentences were removed.

Target Grammars Creation. The same procedures were used to create target grammars. To have intents and slots with same meaning in all languages, LEs were asked to create grammars with intents which represent the same meaning as in English, but at the same time, represent the most natural way of expressing such an intent in the target language. Slot values were either crawled or created manually.

Forced Parallelization. Although, as discussed in the previous step, the same intents will have the same meaning in all languages, there is no sentence-to-sentence mapping between different languages. It is so because intents can be expressed differently across languages and our creation procedure did not imply parallel translations. To mitigate this problem, we decided to create a parallel subset of our corpus that can be used as a testset for cross-lingual experiments. All English patterns were machine translated into Polish and Spanish with Google Translate and then verified and fixed by the LEs in the OmegaT[2] tool.

Slot Expansion. Patterns for all languages, as presented in Table 3, were expanded with slot values that were previously crawled or manually created. We paid a lot of attention to gathering enough slot values so that during expansion each pattern, if possible, has a different slot value. This way, we were able to avoid the systematic error of the system that memorizes the slots on the basis of their values. Once the patterns were expanded, the LEs verified them and changed them, if needed.

Data Split. The last step of corpus creation was splitting it into three parts: trainset, testset and development set. To create the testset, we first created parallel sentences, as described in Forced Parallelization step, and later expanded the slots. Then, we selected at least one sentence from each intent which at the same time was available in all three languages. This way it will be possible to test cross-lingual scenarios. The training and development parts of the corpus were taken from the target grammar patterns that were expanded with the slots. Up to 10% of such expansion formed the development set, while the remaining part formed the trainset.

3.2   Domain Selection

Following [2] we used 20 domains, which represent popular applications that can be used on mobile devices, computers or embedded devices. We can categorize them into groups with similar functions:

---

[2] A computer-assisted translation tool: https://omegat.org/.

- **Communication** with Email, Facebook, Phone, Slack and Twitter domains in that group. All these domains contain a kind of command to send a message.
- **Internet** with Web Search and Wikipedia. The aim of these domains is to search for information on the web and, therefore, these domains will have a lot of open-title queries.
- **Media and Entertainment** with Spotify and YouTube domains in that group. The root function of these applications is to find content with name entities connected with artists or titles.
- **Devices** with Air Conditioner and Speaker domains. These domains represent simple physical devices that can be controlled by voice.
- **Self-management** with Calendar and Contacts. These domains consist of actions that involve time planning and people.
- **Other** non categorized domains represent functions and language not common to the other categories. In that sense, remaining domains can be represented as intentionally not matching other domains.

Table 2. Statistics of sentences, intents and slots across domains and languages in Leyzer dataset.

Domain	# Intents	# Slots	# English Utt.	# Spanish Utt.	# Polish Utt.
Airconditioner	13	3	48	61	52
Calendar	8	5	69	120	190
Contacts	12	4	306	481	615
Email	11	7	294	315	301
Facebook	7	4	48	581	193
Fitbit	5	3	89	116	263
Google Drive	11	5	55	241	305
Instagram	10	6	144	471	579
News	4	3	31	30	42
Phone	5	4	192	283	130
Slack	13	8	268	268	295
Speaker	7	2	73	72	43
Spotify	18	7	633	827	823
Translate	9	6	462	109	452
Twitter	6	3	147	270	122
Weather	10	5	154	159	123
Websearch	7	2	167	291	1498
Wikipedia	8	1	200	234	162
Yelp	12	5	222	142	326
Youtube	10	3	177	354	539
Total	186	86	3779	5425	7053

As mentioned above, several domains differ in size to better reflect proportions from the real world problems where some applications will only have a few possible ways to express commands, while the other ones will have almost infinite number of valid expressions.

3.3 Intent and Slot Selection

There is a close relationship between intents and slots in our corpus, as the intents represent functions or actions that users want to perform, while the slots are the parameters of these intents. In many cases intents represent the same action, but they have been distinguished on the basis of the number of parameters. During the creation of intents our principle was that intents must differ from each other either by the language (different important keywords) or by the number of slots they have. The reason for that is purely pragmatic because in order to avoid system's unstability we cannot have two identical sentences with different intents. The model input is a sentence and its output is the intent, so if in the training corpus we had two identical sentences pointing to different intents, then the model would not able to learn to which intent this sentence should be assigned.

Table 3. Representative patterns from selected domains of the corpus.

Domain	Intent	Sentence Pattern
Calendar	AddEventWithName	Add an event called **$EVENT_NAME**
Email	ShowEmailWithLabel	Show me my emails with label **$LABEL**
Facebook	ShowAlbumWithName	Show photos in my album **$ALBUM**
Slack	SendMessageToChannel	Send **$MESSAGE** to **$CHANNEL** on slack
Spotify	PlaySongByArtist	Play **$SONG** by **$ARTIST**
Translate	TranslateTextToLanguage	Translate **$TEXT** to **$TRG_LANG**
Weather	OpenWeather	What's the weather like
Websearch	SearchTextOnEngine	Google **$TXT_QUERY**

The slots in our corpus can be categorized into two groups:

- **Open-titled** – where the value of the slot can be treated as infinite and therefore cannot be listed. Open-title slots are challenging for NLU systems because they force them to generalize the unseen data.
- **Close-titled** – where the values of the slots can be listed.

4   Experiments

4.1   Experimental Setup

As an architecture for all of our experiments we used the Joint BERT architecture [4] implemented in the NeMo toolkit [7]. We used the pre-trained multilingual cased BERT model [13] consisting of 12-layers and 110 M parameters. If not stated otherwise, we trained models for 100 epochs and saved checkpoints for each one. All checkpoint were evaluated on test part of corpora. Reported results come from the checkpoint which achieved the highest score in the tests. The batch size was 128. Adam [6] was used for optimization with an initial learning rate of $2e - 5$. The dropout probability was set to 0.1. We trained each model independently with all data available in the training part of corpus. In all of our experiment we used the first version of our corpus (0.1.0).

4.2 Testing Scenarios

We evaluated the proposed corpus using the following four scenarios:

- **Single-language Models** – here we trained each language independently on all sentences available in the trainset and we evaluated the model on a testset.
- **Multi-language Model** – in this experiment we trained one model using all training data available for all three languages and independently evaluated it for each language.
- **Train-on-target** – similar to strategy proposed by Cettolo et al. [3], we used Google Translate to translate English patterns into Polish and Spanish, and expanded them with target slot values.
- **Zero-shot Learning** – to test this scenario we trained English model with multilingual cased BERT from the English part of Leyzer trainset and tested it on Polish and Spanish testsets.

We used the accuracy to evaluate the performance of intent prediction and the standard BIO structure to calculate macro $F1$-score that does not take label imbalance into account. We used the evaluation metric implemented in scikit-learn [10] and provided in the NeMo evaluation script. Using this script, we tested each model epoch, and the results for the ones that scored best on both the intent and the slot level are presented in Table 4.

4.3 Results and Discussion

The Single-BERT models scored relatively low on both the intent and the slot level, yielding 47%, 52% and 69% intent accuracy for English, Polish and Spanish, respectively. We believe that reason for that is a large number of intent classes in our corpus, which, by the way, was a motivation to create such corpus.

In order to give some perspective to our experiments, we trained the model on the training part of the ATIS dataset with the same parameters as in the Single-BERT scenario. When evaluated on the test part of ATIS, we received 97.31% on the intent and 55.23% on the F1-macro slot level (and 97.11% for F1-micro). Those results suggest that easier problems, such as ATIS, can be easily learned by Single-BERT model.

The Multi-BERT experiment scored better than the Single-BERT models on both intent and slot level. We believe that the reason for this is that multilingual

Table 4. Results for NeMo models trained on various configurations of Leyzer corpus

Model type	Language	Intent acc.	Slot F1 macro
Single-BERT	English	46.58	45.07
	Polish	51.66	54.56
	Spanish	68.88	67.79
Multi-BERT	English	62.80	76.48
	Polish	64.17	74.83
	Spanish	72.26	84.66
Train-on-target	Polish	41.67	40.70
	Spanish	46.42	52.38
Zero-shot	Polish	13.82	15.39
	Spanish	30.21	24.13

model had more data to learn how to separate intent classes and eliminate inconsistencies. Presented results suggest that multilingual models might benefit from joint learning on multiple languages, at least for problems that are formulated as in this paper.

The train-on-target models scored low when compared to the Single-BERT models. We think that the MT errors, especially in the most important components of the sentence (usually verbs) led to a drastic performance drop. On the intent classification level the accuracy for Polish and Spanish were respectively 9.9% and 22.5% relative lower than the baseline.

The zero-shot scenario scored very low when compared to the Single-BERT or the train-on-target experiments. Large number of intent classes, combined with different slot values in each language is a non-trivial problem, and, apparently, more sophisticated methods are needed.

The results presented in this article may seem unsatisfactory, especially if we compare them to other VA publications. However, it is noteworthy that a search for the best architecture and parameters was not an intent of this work – we rather wanted to set the baselines and to show complexity of the MT problem for the proposed data. We aimed to create a challenging corpus which can be a subject of future works, such as the localization of VAs with the use of train-on-target and zero-shot learning scenarios.

5   Conclusions and Future Work

In our work we introduced a new dataset, named Leyzer, designed to study multilingual and cross-lingual NLU models and localization strategies in VAs. We also demonstrated the results for the models trained on our corpus that can set the baseline for further work.

In the future we plan to extend our dataset to new languages and increase the number of sentences per intent. Another line of work that we consider is to add follow-up intents, as this would allow to build a fully autonomous VA from our dataset.

The Leyzer dataset, the translation memories and the detailed experiment results presented in this paper are available at https://github.com/cartesinus/leyzer. We hope that this way we will foster further research in machine translation for the virtual assistants.

Acknowledgements. We thank Małgorzata Misiaszek for her help in verifying the quality of our corpus and improving its consistency.

References

1. Budzianowski, P., et al.: MultiWOZ - a large-scale multi-domain wizard-of-Oz dataset for task-oriented dialogue modelling. In: Proceedings of the 2018 Conference on Empirical Methods in Natural Language Processing, Brussels, Belgium, pp. 5016–5026. Association for Computational Linguistics (2018). https://www.aclweb.org/anthology/D18-1547
2. Campagna, G., Ramesh, R., Xu, S., Fischer, M., Lam, M.S.: Almond: the architecture of an open, crowdsourced, privacy-preserving, programmable virtual assistant. In: Proceedings of the 26th International Conference on World Wide Web, pp. 341–350 (2017)
3. Cettolo, M., Corazza, A., De Mori, R.: Language portability of a speech understanding system. Comput. Speech Lang. **12**(1), 1–21 (1998)
4. Chen, Q., Zhuo, Z., Wang, W.: BERT for joint intent classification and slot filling (2019)
5. Coucke, A., et al.: Snips voice platform: an embedded spoken language understanding system for private-by-design voice interfaces. arXiv preprint arXiv:1805.10190 (2018)
6. Kingma, D.P., Ba, J.: Adam: a method for stochastic optimization. In: Proceedings of the 6th International Conference on Learning Representations (ICRL 2015), San Diego, CA (2015)
7. Kuchaiev, O., et al.: NeMo: a toolkit for building AI applications using neural modules (2019)
8. Larson, S., et al.: An evaluation dataset for intent classification and out-of-scope prediction. In: Proceedings of the 2019 Conference on Empirical Methods in Natural Language Processing and the 9th International Joint Conference on Natural Language Processing (EMNLP-IJCNLP 2019), Hong Kong, China (2019)
9. Liu, X., Eshghi, A., Swietojanski, P., Rieser, V.: Benchmarking natural language understanding services for building conversational agents. arXiv preprint arXiv:1903.05566 (2019)
10. Pedregosa, F., et al.: Scikit-learn: machine learning in Python. J. Mach. Learn. Res. **12**, 2825–2830 (2011)
11. Price, P.: Evaluation of spoken language systems: the ATIS domain. In: Proceedings of the Speech and Natural Language Workshop, Hidden Valley, PA (1990)
12. Schuster, S., Gupta, S., Shah, R., Lewis, M.: Cross-lingual transfer learning for multilingual task oriented dialog. In: Proceedings of the 2019 Annual Conference of the North American Chapter of the Association for Computational Linguistics (NAACL-HLT 2019), Minneapolis, MN (2019)
13. Wolf, T., et al.: Huggingface's transformers: State-of-the-art natural language processing. ArXiv abs/1910.03771 (2019)

Registering Historical Context for Question Answering in a Blocks World Dialogue System

Benjamin Kane(✉) ⓘ, Georgiy Platonov, and Lenhart Schubert

University of Rochester, Rochester, NY 14627, USA
{bkane2,gplatono,schubert}@cs.rochester.edu

Abstract. Task-oriented dialogue-based spatial reasoning systems need to maintain history of the world/discourse states in order to convey that the dialogue agent is mentally present and engaged with the task, as well as to be able to refer to earlier states, which may be crucial in collaborative planning (e.g., for diagnosing a past misstep). We approach the problem of spatial memory in a multi-modal spoken dialogue system capable of answering questions about interaction history in a physical blocks world setting. We employ a pipeline consisting of a vision system, speech I/O mediated by an animated avatar, a dialogue system that robustly interprets queries, and a constraint solver that derives answers based on 3D spatial modelling. The contributions of this work include a semantic parser competent in this domain and a symbolic dialogue context allowing for interpreting and answering free-form historical questions using world and discourse history.

Keywords: Question answering · Blocks world · Semantic parsing · Discourse context

1 Introduction

Intelligent, task-oriented dialogue agents that interact with humans in a physical setting are a long-standing AI goal and have received renewed attention in the last 10 or 20 years. However, they have generally lacked the sort of recall of earlier discourse and perceived "world" situations and events—an episodic memory—needed to provide a sense of shared contextual awareness and, ultimately, a basis for diagnosing past errors, planning to re-achieve an earlier situation, repeating a past action sequence, etc.

The blocks world domain is an ideal setting for developing prototypes with such capabilities.

In this work, we present a speech-based question-answering system for a physical blocks world featuring a virtual agent, that not only models and understands

This work was supported by DARPA grant W911NF-15-1-0542, NSF NRT Graduate Training Grant 2019–2020, and NSF EAGER Award IIS-1940981.

© Springer Nature Switzerland AG 2020
P. Sojka et al. (Eds.): TSD 2020, LNAI 12284, pp. 487–494, 2020.
https://doi.org/10.1007/978-3-030-58323-1_52

spatial relations but is able to register historical context and answer questions about the session history, such as *"Which block did I just move?"*, *"Where was the Toyota block before I moved it?"*, *"Did the Target block ever touch the Texaco block?"*, *"Was the Twitter block always between two red blocks?"*, etc. Since explicit storage of detailed successive scene models would be difficult to extend to general complex settings as well as being cognitively implausible (people seem to reconstruct past situations from high-level properties [15]), we maintain a compact symbolic record of changes to the world, allowing reconstruction of past states when combined with current spatial observations.

2   Related Work

Early studies featuring the blocks world include [18] and [3], both of which maintained symbolic memory of blocks-world states. They demonstrated impressive planning capabilities, but their worlds were simulated, interaction was text-based, and they lacked realistic understanding of spatial relations.

Modern efforts in blocks worlds include work by Perera et al. [13], which is focused on learning spatial concepts (staircases, towers, etc.) based on verbally-conveyed structural constraints, e.g., *"The height is at most 3"*, as well as explicit user-given examples and counterexamples.

Bisk et al. [2] use deep learning to transduce verbal instructions into block displacements in a simulated environment.

Some deep learning based studies achieve near-perfect scores on the CLEVR question answering dataset [10,12]. A common limitation of these approaches is reliance on unrealistically simple spatial models and domain-specific language formalisms, and in relation to our work, there is no question answering functionality or episodic memory.

We are not aware of any recent study in a physical blocks world domain that makes use of spatial memory in answering questions about past states and events.

Outside of the blocks world domain, the TRAINS and TRIPS systems [4,5] were noteworthy for their dialogue-based problem solving ability in a virtual map environment and their support of planning through temporal reasoning based on Allen Interval Logic [1]. A system aimed at human-like performance on a virtual reality map recall task [11] was based on the LIDA symbolic cognitive architecture and represented spatial context using a grid representation of the world and hierarchical "place nodes" with progressively updated activations.

Recent deep-learning based approaches to modelling spatial episodic memory include [16] and [6]. The former uses an unsupervised encoder-decoder model to represent episodic memory as latent embeddings, and show that this model can allow a robot to recall previous visual episodes in a physical scene. The latter introduces a neuro-symbolic Structured Event Memory (SEM) model which is capable of segmenting events in video data and reconstructing past memory items. These methods, however, do not readily lend themselves to use for reasoning about historical relations or interactions in a blocks world question answering system.

3   Blocks World System and Eta Dialogue Manager

Figure 1a, b depict our physical blocks world (consisting of a square table with several cubical blocks, two Kinect sensors and a display) and the system's software architecture. The blocks are color-coded as green, red, or blue, and marked with corporate logos which serve as unique identifiers. The system uses audio-visual I/O: the block tracking module periodically updates the block positioning information by reading from the Kinect cameras and an interactive avatar, David, is used for communication. The block arrangement is modeled as a 3D scene in Blender, which acts as system's "mental image" of the state of the world.

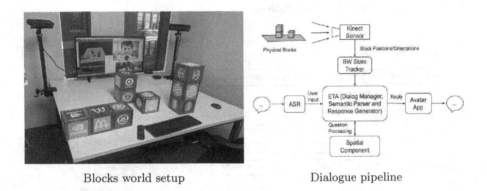

Blocks world setup   Dialogue pipeline

Fig. 1. System overview. (Color figure online)

The Eta dialogue manager (DM) is responsible for semantic parsing and dialogue control. Eta is designed to follow a modifiable dialogue schema, the contents of which are formulas in episodic logic [17] with open variables describing successive steps (events) expected in the course of the interaction. These are either realized directly as instantiated actions, or expanded into sub-schemas[1].

In order to instantiate schema steps and interpret user inputs, the DM uses *hierarchical pattern transduction*, similarly to the mechanism used by the LISSA system [14] to extract context-independent *gist clauses* given the prior utterance. Transduction hierarchies specify patterns at their nodes to be matched to input, with terminal nodes providing result templates, or specifying a subschema. The pattern templates look for particular words or word features (including "wildcards" matching any word sequence of some length). Eta uses gist clause extraction for tidying-up the user's utterance, and then derives an *unscoped logical form* (ULF) [9] (a preliminary form of the episodic logic syntax of the dialogue schema) from the tidied-up input. ULF differs from similar semantic representations, e.g., AMR, in that it is close to the surface form of English, type-consistent, and covers a rich set of phenomena. To derive ULFs, we introduced semantic composition into the transduction trees. The resulting parser is quite

---

[1] Intended actions obviated by earlier events may be deleted.

efficient and accurate for the domain at hand. The input is recursively broken into constituents, such as a VP segment, until a lexical subroutine supplies ULFs for individual words, which are propagated back up and composed into larger expressions by the "calling" node. The efficiency and accuracy of the approach lies in the fact that hierarchical pattern matching can segment utterances into meaningful parts, so that backtracking is rarely necessary.

An example of a transduction tree being used for parsing a historical question into ULF is shown and described in Fig. 2. As can be seen from this example, the resulting ULF retains much of the surface structure, but uses semantic typing and adds operators to indicate plurality, tense, aspect, and other linguistic phenomena. Eta also has a limited coreference module utilizing syntactic constraints, recency, and other heuristics.

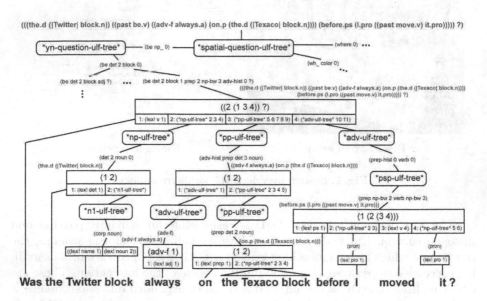

Fig. 2. An example ULF parse, with the input shown in red, and the resulting ULF (at each composition step) shown in green. The nodes with rectangles represent ULF composition nodes, where the numbers in the upper box correspond to the indices of the lower boxes (if no upper boxes, simple concatenation). All unframed nodes are patterns to be matched to the corresponding span of input text. (Color figure online)

4   Historical Question-Answering

To answer historical questions, the DM needs to maintain a dialogue context including some sort of spatial episodic memory, so that the ULF obtained from parsing can be resolved into operations over this episodic memory. Based on the cognitive considerations discussed in [15], we maintain a high-level symbolic memory with which the agent can reconstruct past scenes, rather than a detailed visual or vector-based memory.

The vision system records the centroid coordinates and moves of blocks in real time. On the DM side, a "perceive-world" action in the schema causes the DM to request ULF perceptions from the vision system. We rely on a simple linear, discrete time representation. The temporal entities (|Now0| etc.) are related to each other and to perceived actions propositionally, making use of the episodic operators described in [17]. Based on this context, the DM can efficiently reconstruct a scene at any past time by backtracking from perceived block locations, and evaluate approximate spatial relationships based on centroid coordinates. A simplified example is shown in the top half of Fig. 3.

An example of answering a historical question given a ULF parse is shown in the bottom half of Fig. 3. Phrases with head types "adv-e", "adv-f", and "ps", indicate temporal constraints that are applied during the scene reconstruction algorithm, and their semantic types allow them to be lifted to the sentence level. frequency modifiers) map a set of times to a subset of those times, whereas binary modifiers take two times and map to a truth value. Any constraint may be further modified by a "mod-a" term (e.g. "just.mod-a"), which modifies how that mapping is applied.

Note that the example in Fig. 3 is ambiguous; the answer could be "A, D, C" or "A, C". In fact, we found that many natural historical questions are similarly underspecified, presenting a major source of difficulty. To deal with this issue, the DM's pragmatic module attempts to infer temporal constraints in these ambiguous cases – in this particular example, Eta would infer the constraint "most recently".

The algorithm shown extracts the uninverted base ULF relation, where arguments are represented as entities or variables (possibly with restrictions for noun modifiers). This base ULF, and any temporal constraints, are used to compute a list of times with attached facts through backtracking over past times. In the case of a binary constraint with a complex noun phrase or relative clause, this algorithm is applied recursively (as shown by the red constituents in Fig. 3). The algorithm would likewise be applied recursively in the case of a query where the historical content is embedded in a noun phrase, e.g. "the first block that I moved".

Once a list of final times is obtained, an answer is generated by making the appropriate substitutions in the query ULF, applying syntactic transformations, and converting to surface form. If no relations are obtained, the DM's pragmatics module will attempt to respond to any presuppositions of the query, based on the work in [8]. For instance, if the query is "What block was the Twitter block on?", Eta will respond "The Twitter block wasn't on any block."

5   Evaluation and Discussion

Since the COVID-19 pandemic made testing the physical blocks world system on-site impossible, the authors had to resort to evaluating using a virtual environment that mirrors our setup, sans the physical block tracker and the audio I/O. However, as the crucial components being evaluated (parser, DM, and spatial context) were unchanged, the results should not be affected.

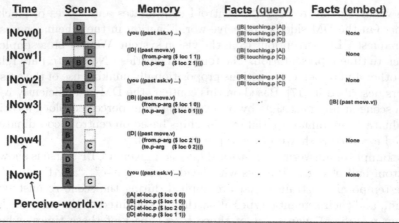

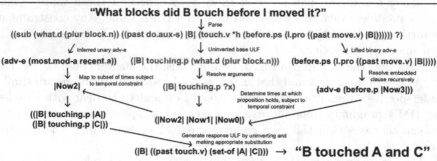

Fig. 3. A simplified example of how the context is represented and how the DM uses the context to compute relations given temporal constraints (top half), and an example of the DM determining an answer from a specific historical query (bottom half). (Color figure online)

We enlisted 4 student volunteers for the user study, both native and non-native English speakers. The participants were instructed to move the blocks around and ask general questions about changes in the world, with no restrictions on wording. After the system displayed its answer, the participants were asked to provide feedback on it's quality by marking it as correct, partially correct or incorrect. Each participant contributed about 100 questions or above (primarily historical questions, but also including some non-historical spatial questions).

Each session started with the blocks positioned in a row at the front of the table. The participants were instructed to move the blocks arbitrarily to test the robustness and consistency of the spatial models. The data is presented in Table 1. Non-historical questions, as well as a few malformed questions, were excluded when computing accuracy.

We find these results encouraging, given the pragmatic richness of the task and the unrestricted form of the questions. About 77% of Eta's answers were judged to be fully correct, with accuracy rising to 80% when including partially correct answers. We find that the semantic parser itself is very reliable, with 94%

Table 1. Evaluation data.

Total number of questions asked	496
Well-formed historical questions	387
Correct answers	297 (77% of 387)
Partially correct answers	13 (3% of 387)
Incorrect answers	77 (20% of 387)
Number of correctly parsed questions	363 (94% of 387)
Accuracy (correct + partially correct)	80%

of grammatical sentences being parsed correctly. Parsing failures accounted for a third of the incorrect answers.

Analyzing the remaining incorrect answers, we find that a major source of error is in the handling of under-specified historical questions, as described in Sect. 4. There are many nuances to how humans naturally interpret these, that are difficult to capture with simple set of pragmatic rules.

For example, Eta will plausibly interpret "What blocks did I move before the Twitter block?" as meaning "What blocks did I *recently* move before I moved the Twitter block?"; however if the user instead asked "How many blocks did I move before the Twitter block?", it seems that the questioner really means "How many blocks did I *ever* move before I moved the Twitter block?". Currently, Eta would add "recently" for the latter case, which would be incorrect. In future work, we aim to investigate this phenomenon further and improve the pragmatic inference module to handle these cases correctly. In addition, the tense structure in some more complex questions violated our simplifying assumption of discrete linear time. In future work, we plan to look into the use of more general temporal reasoning systems such as the tense trees described in [7] to enable more robust handling of different aspectual forms and more complex embedded clauses.

6   Conclusion

We have extended a spatial question answering system in a physical blocks world system with the ability to answer free-form historical questions using a symbolic dialogue context, keeping track of a record of block moves and other actions. A custom semantic parser allows historical questions to be parsed into a logical form, which is interpreted in conjunction with the context to generate an answer. We obtained an accuracy of 80%, which we believe is a strong result in view of the free-form and often underspecified nature of the historical questions that users asked, though it also leaves much room for improvement. Overall, we believe that the pragmatic richness and complexity that we've observed in historical question-answering indicates that further work towards representing episodic memory and enabling dialogue systems to reason about historical context will be fruitful in this sparsely researched area.

References

1. Allen, J.F., Ferguson, G.: Actions and events in interval temporal logic. J. Logic Comput. **4**(5), 531–579 (1994)
2. Bisk, Y., Shih, K.J., Choi, Y., Marcu, D.: Learning interpretable spatial operations in a rich 3D blocks world. In: 32nd AAAI Conference on Artificial Intelligence (2018)
3. Fahlman, S.E.: A planning system for robot construction tasks. Arti. Intell. **5**(1), 1–49 (1974)
4. Ferguson, G., Allen, J.: Trips: an integrated intelligent problem-solving assistant. In: AAAI (1998)
5. Ferguson, G., Allen, J., Miller, B.: Trains-95: towards a mixed-initiative planning assistant. In: Proceedings of 3rd International Conference on Artificial Intelligence Planning Systems, pp. 70–77 (1996)
6. Franklin, N.T., Norman, K.A., Ranganath, C., Zacks, J.M., Gershman, S.J.: Structured event memory: a neuro-symbolic model of event cognition. bioRxiv (2019)
7. Hwang, C.H., Schubert, L.K.: Interpreting tense, aspect and time adverbials: a compositional, unified approach. In: Gabbay, D.M., Ohlbach, H.J. (eds.) ICTL 1994. LNCS, vol. 827, pp. 238–264. Springer, Heidelberg (1994). https://doi.org/10.1007/BFb0013992
8. Kim, G., et al.: Generating discourse inferences from unscoped episodic logical formulas. In: Proceedings of 1st International Workshop on Designing Meaning Representations, pp. 56–65. ACL (2019)
9. Kim, G.L., Schubert, L.: A type-coherent, expressive representation as an initial step to language understanding. In: Proceedings of 13th International Conference on Computational Semantics-Long Papers, pp. 13–30 (2019)
10. Kottur, S., Moura, J.M., Parikh, D., Batra, D., Rohrbach, M.: Clevr-dialog: a diagnostic dataset for multi-round reasoning in visual dialog (2019). arXiv:1903.03166
11. Madl, T., Franklin, S., Chen, K., Trappl, R.: Spatial working memory in the LIDA cognitive architecture. In: Proceedings of International Conference on Cognitive Modelling, pp. 384–390 (2013)
12. Mao, J., Gan, C., Kohli, P., Tenenbaum, J.B., Wu, J.: The neuro-symbolic concept learner: Interpreting scenes, words, and sentences from natural supervision (2019). arXiv:1904.12584
13. Perera, I., Allen, J., Teng, C.M., Galescu, L.: Building and learning structures in a situated blocks world through deep language understanding. In: Proceedings of 1st International Workshop on Spatial Language Understanding. pp. 12–20 (2018)
14. Razavi, S., Schubert, L., Ali, M., Hoque, H.: Managing casual spoken dialogue using flexible schemas, pattern transduction trees, and gist clauses. In: 5th Annual Conference on Advances in Cognitive Systems (2017)
15. Rensink, R.: Scene Perception, pp. 151–155. Oxford University Press, Oxford (2001)
16. Rothfuss, J., Ferreira, F., Aksoy, E., You, Z., Asfour, T.: Deep episodic memory: encoding, recalling, and predicting episodic experiences for robot action execution. IEEE Rob. Autom. Lett. **3**, 4007–4014 (2018)
17. Schubert, L., Hwang, C.: Episodic logic meets little red riding hood: a comprehensive, natural representation for language understanding. In: Natural Language Processing and Knowledge Representation: Language for Knowledge and Knowledge for Language (2000)
18. Winograd, T.: Understanding natural language. Cogn. Psychol. **3**(1), 1–191 (1972)

At Home with Alexa: A Tale of Two Conversational Agents

Jennifer Ureta[ID], Celina Iris Brito, Jilyan Bianca Dy, Kyle-Althea Santos,
Winfred Villaluna, and Ethel Ong[✉][ID]

De La Salle University, Manila, Philippines
{jennifer.ureta,ethel.ong}@dlsu.edu.ph

Abstract. Voice assistants in mobile devices and smart speakers offer
the potential of conversational agents as storytelling peers of children,
especially those who may have limited proficiency in spelling and grammar. Despite their prevalence, however, the built-in automatic speech
recognition features of voice interfaces have been shown to perform
poorly on children's speech, which may affect child-agent interaction.
In this paper, we describe our experiments in deploying a conversational storytelling agent on two popular commercial voice interfaces -
Google Assistant and Amazon Alexa. Through post-validation feedback
from children and analysis of the captured conversation logs, we compare
the challenges encountered by children when sharing their stories with
these voice assistants. We also used the Bilingual Evaluation Understudy
to provide a quantitative assessment of the text-to-speech transcription
quality. We found that voice assistants' short waiting time and the frequent yet misplaced interruptions during pauses disrupt the thinking process of children. Furthermore, disfluencies and grammatical errors that
naturally occur in children's speech affected the transcription quality.

Keywords: Conversational agents · Voice interfaces · Storytelling

1 Introduction

Stories abound in the everyday conversations of children. Through storytelling,
children can gain an understanding of their world and express their experiences
through recollection and sharing with others. This collaborative storytelling
is not limited to human-to-human interaction, but may also be manifested in
human-to-robot interaction [20].

Commercial voice assistants, such as Apple's Siri, Google Assistant and Amazon's Alexa, that are ubiquitously embedded in mobile phones, tablets and smart
speakers [11], such as the Google Home and Amazon Echo, enable users to give
voice commands and queries in natural language. Children who have limited
proficiency in spelling and grammar can utilize these technologies to express
their narrative by talking to the voice assistant. Not only is voice more natural

Supported by DOST-PCIEERD.

for children to carry a conversation; they can also do away with less structure typically required from written text [16].

Despite their prevalence, however, the built-in automatic speech recognition features of voice interfaces have been shown to perform poorly on children's speech. Furthermore, while studies on child-agent interaction through conversational interfaces are surfacing [5,8,10], there are those that reported problems of using voice interfaces by non-native English speakers [6,19]. These two challenges may affect the child-agent interaction.

Our study seeks to investigate the challenges that children encounter during a collaborative storytelling session with voice-based conversational agents. We pay particular focus on two popular voice interfaces, Amazon Alexa running in Echo and Google Assistant in Home, where we deployed our collaborative storytelling agent. In Sect. 2, we give a short review of related work on storytelling and voice interfaces, followed by a description of the design of our collaborative storytelling agent in Sect. 3. In Sect. 4, we present our results from conducting validation with children and analyzing the transcription quality.

2 Related Work

Voice interfaces can be used to engage children in learning activities. However, previous studies have reported the challenges of voice interfaces in understanding the speech of young children, as the built-in automatic speech recognition facility performed poorly on children's speech [5,8]. The problem is mainly attributed to the differences in children's speech from adults' speech not only in content but also in patterns of stress, intonation and prosody [10,13]. This can lead to incorrect transcription of input speech, which causes misunderstanding and the generation of inappropriate responses [16].

Despite the challenges, voice interfaces in robots and digital assistants have found applications as homework tutors [22], diagnostic tools for reading disorders [12] and social assistance [9]. A storytelling system composed of both reader and listener robots was developed by [21] to investigate the effect of a listener robot acting as a side-participant in a storytelling situation with children. They found that children preferred storytelling with the listener robot than without it.

Children employ different repair strategies when they encounter problems with voice-driven interfaces [2]. Instead of giving up, they often showed persistence by repeating themselves, augmenting their speech, adjusting the tone and pronunciation of their words and substituting with a simpler word [2,14].

Unlike task-oriented voice assistants typically found in retail applications, storytelling agents have to engage children in a conversation that is fluent, user-directed and consistent with the context of the shared story [15]. This mimics the spontaneous turn-taking that typically occurs in human-to-human storytelling. The sharing that occurs between storytellers is beneficial in improving children's listening and comprehension skills, enhancing their ability to interact with others [18], and using language to express their thoughts and sense of the world [3,4].

3   Method

The conversational storytelling agent (CSA) was deployed on two voice assistants (VA), namely Google Assistant and Alexa, using the smart speakers Google Home and Amazon Echo, respectively, as the physical interface. An issue we ran into while porting the agent was that Alexa does not allow getting the whole user input due to security issues. For Alexa to process the user's input, specific keywords need to be detected for mapping to the appropriate intent, so we required participants to add the phrase *"my turn"* before their actual input.

10 children between the age of 7 to 11 years old were invited to participate in the study. They were briefed regarding the keywords they could use to start and end the sessions, to seek for help and to take the dialogue turn in the case of Alexa. Each participant was asked to share their own story with each of the VA. While the original intent was to have the child share two different stories, in the course of testing with Alexa, it was observed that the agent exits the application when the participant takes time to craft his/her story, thus exceeding the built-in 7-second wait time of the device. Because of this, 7 out of 10 children used the same story for both devices.

An *observation checklist* was used to monitor the child-agent interaction, with a focus on instances where children enjoy or get frustrated with storytelling. A *post-interview and survey form* asked participants to rate the agent's collaborative features using a 5-point Likert scale and to give qualitative feedback on the interaction. The verbal conversation and the transcription of speech to text were also recorded.

Results were analyzed using three criteria general UX, frustration and enjoyment. The *general UX* criterion assesses the CSA and the participant's capability to understand and follow each other's commands and responses. The *frustration* criterion $[1, 7]$ refers to aspects of the interaction with the CSA that caused the participants to feel bored, irritated or distracted. The *enjoyment* criterion is used to assess the quality of the conversation based on the satisfaction of the participants and includes acknowledgement of the CSA as an actual being that children would talk to again. We also used the Bilingual Evaluation Understudy (BLEU) [17] to analyze and determine the quality of the text-to-speech translation performed by each of the voice assistants.

4   Results

4.1   User Feedback

Table 1 presents the results of user feedback from the survey forms. Requiring the phrase *"my turn"* for Alexa made it difficult and unnatural for the children to carry on a smooth conversation flow which led to a lower general UX score compared to Google Assistant. There were also instances wherein they forget to say the keywords before starting their story. Occurrences of misunderstanding also affected the score, especially when Alexa and Google Assistant misinterpreted the words in the child's input. Examples of these are shown in Table 2. When

Table 1. Average rating from participants' survey forms.

Criteria	Google	Alexa
General UX	3.67	3.61
Frustration	3.93	3.63
Enjoyment	3.73	3.47

misunderstandings occur, participants tend to get thrown off and confused at first. They will then try to make sense of what the agent said. If they are unable to do so, they tend to give up and continue on with their story.

In the conversation with P2, Alexa misheard *"insects"* as *"sex"* (lines 2 and 4), and *"he then"* as *"heathen"* in line 6. At first, P2 tried to correct the mistake by repeating what he said in line 3. But when Alexa repeated the same mistake, P2 just ignored the misunderstanding and continued with his/her story. For P7 and P10, there were clear indications of their confusion, as seen in lines 3 of their respective log. For P7, he/she was initially thrown off by the mistake that the interface made but did not try to correct it at all and just continued with the story. For P10, he/she got really confused with the misunderstanding and was only able to move on with the story when the storytelling agent issued the prompt *"So what happens next?"* in line 6.

Children's frustration and enjoyment in sharing stories with the conversational agent were affected by the latter's ability to understand the utterance in order to generate appropriate responses and the frequent need for children to have to repeat themselves as a repair strategy. These instances of misunderstanding are detailed in the next section.

4.2   Transcription Quality

BLEU is a metric which is primarily used to evaluate the quality of machine-translated text by comparing a candidate translation to one or more reference translations. BLEU scores range from 0 to 1, with values closer to 1 representing a higher similarity with the reference text.

BLEU was used to evaluate how effective the voice interfaces were in transcribing the speech of the children. We used the manually transcribed utterance of the participants from the recorded vouce conversations as the reference and compared the transcriptions of the voice assistants against these. As shown in Table 3, the number of dialogue turns (*input*) the child took as well as the BLEU scores for both interfaces were calculated. Based from the results, Google Assistant has a higher BLEU score than Alexa for all transcribed conversations.

Table 3 also indicates the number of instances when Alexa asked each participant to repeat their utterances because the agent failed to "hear" the input. Every time this happens, a BLEU score of 0 is assigned to the utterance because an empty string is compared with the actual utterance of the participant found in the reference transcription. The higher the number of repetitions, the lower

Table 2. Examples of misunderstanding between the agent and the children.

		Excerpt of conversation of **P2** with Alexa (A)
1	P2:	the fish would go up to the river everyday to see if there were *insects*
2	A:	I need help, please use *sex* in a sentence
3	P2:	the fish would go up to the river everyday to see if there were *insects*
4	A:	I need help, please use *sex* in a sentence
5	P2:	*he then* would go back if there were none
6	A:	Tell something about *heathen*
7	P2:	it would then go to the reef and rest and wait for the next day

		Excerpt of conversation of **P7** with Google Assistant (GA)
1	P7:	after we play *soccer* me and my friend got tired and went back at my house
2	GA:	I need help, please use *software* in a sentence
3	P7:	I don't know what that mean (*misunderstanding*)
4	GA:	The moon is cold
5	P7:	my mom give us drinks . . . my mom give us drinks and towel

		Excerpt of conversation of **P10** with Google Assistant (GA)
1	P10:	when he got there he got the books were interesting
2	GA:	What if the *erica* got get?
3	P10:	Yes? What (*P10 got confused*)
4	GA:	Tell something about erica
5	P10:	What? (*P10 got confused*)
6	GA:	So what happens next?
7	P10:	when he opened the book it wasnt really that big

Table 3. BLEU scores for Alexa and Google assistant.

P	Alexa			Google assistant		
	Inputs	Repeats	BLEU	Inputs	Repeats	BLEU
P1	7	4	0.20	12		0.61
P2	15	2	0.56	23		0.90
P3	34	19	0.35	18		0.91
P4	23	9	0.51	19		0.93
P5	23	10	0.27	8		0.56
P6	13	4	0.42	10		0.76
P7	18	7	0.46	13		0.64
P8	11	4	0.28	5		0.80
P9	13	3	0.56	16		0.94
P10	25	5	0.51	17		0.77

the BLEU score. Those participants who made at least 30% repetitions have BLEU scores that fall below 0.50.

Another factor that affected the BLEU score is the total number of words uttered by a participant. This is illustrated in the plot in Fig. 1. From the plot, we get a correlation coefficient of 0.1334; the more words that participants say and were heard by Alexa, the better the score becomes. The 2 outlying cases in the given plot are from P3 and P5. P3 spoke in a soft voice and would at times mumble. For P5, despite his/her loud and clear voice, Alexa still misinterpreted the words he/she said, as seen in lines 11–13 of the transcribed log in Table 4. This may be due to P5 speaking fast in some parts which resulted in Alexa mishearing the words.

Table 4. Examples of Alexa misinterpreting the participants' utterances.

Line	Transcribed	Alexa
11	*He gone* to the *mall to buy* a new game!	**rigan** to the **multiply** on you game
12	**he** go and buy the *game he wanted*	**hi** go and buy the **give you 1 that**
13	when he played the game he loved it so he *bought* the game from the store and *gone* back to his home	when he played the game he loved it so he the game from the store and **gun** back to his home

The plot for Google Assistant is shown in Fig. 2. It has a correlation coefficient of -0.0359, which means there is no correlation between the number of words and the BLEU score that generally floats above 0.5.

Multiple disfluencies and grammatical errors can be found in natural child speech [8]. Disfluencies like the ones shown in Table 5 for P5 and P9 often led Alexa to mistake them as the end of an utterance. These problems in the participants' speech also affect the BLEU scores negatively.

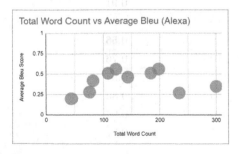

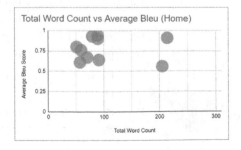

Fig. 1. Correlation between the BLEU score and the number of words per participant with Alexa.

Fig. 2. Correlation between the BLEU score and the number of words per participant with Google Assistant.

Table 5. Examples of disfluencies and grammatical errors in participants' utterances.

Alexa	
P3	then in math class I didn't understand
P3	If I had 5 mistakes, then I will fail
P4	and then I ate recess
P5	He - he go .. gone to the mall to buy a new game
P5	so-so Jacob and his little sister play the played till 12 pm O clock
P7	after we play soccer me and my friend got tired and went back
P9	he was disappoint - ed that but his friend comforted him
Google assistant	
P1	but thay already made an idea they sell drinks
P4	until in december 4 it should be returned
P5	and when he go camping

5   Conclusion

Conversational agents can engage children in collaborative storytelling to develop their language and literacy skills. In this paper, we deployed our conversational storytelling agent in voice interfaces, particularly Amazon Alexa and Google Assistant, to provide access to children with limited proficiency in spelling and grammar. Our results are in line with those reported in previous studies where voice interfaces perform poorly on children's speech. Our findings showed that these problems, combined with the short waiting time, frequent interruptions during pauses and mishearing words affect the child-agent interaction and led to difficulties in carrying out a smooth turn-based storytelling session.

We also used BLEU scores to compare the transcription quality of Alexa and Google Assistant, with an average of 0.34 and 0.65 respectively. Analysis of the conversation logs showed a high incidence of repetitions among participants when conversing with Alexa, leading to BLEU scores that fall below 0.50. Disfluencies that are descriptive in children's speech also affect the BLEU scores negatively. For future work, word error rate (WER) should be considered and a comparison between the two metrics in the area of storytelling can also be done. While children employ repair strategies and do their best to finish their stories, their inability to carry on a smooth conversation flow with the storytelling agent led to frustration and non-enjoyment of the interaction. Future voice interface designers should take into account the spontaneous nature of children's storytelling, their limited vocabulary and pronunciation abilities, and the length of time they need to formulate their stories.

References

1. Blythe, M., Reid, J., Wright, P., Geelhoed, E.: Interdisciplinary criticism: analysing the experience of riot! a location-sensitive digital narrative. J. Behav. Inf. Technol. **25**(2), 127–139 (2006)
2. Cheng, Y., Yen, K., Chen, Y., Chen, S., Hiniker, A.: Why doesn't it work? voice-driven interfaces and young children's communication repair strategies. In: Proceedings of 17th ACM Conference on Interaction Design and Children, pp. 337–348. ACM (2018)
3. Duranti, A., Goodwin, C.: Rethinking Context: Language as an Interactive Phenomenon. Cambridge University Press, Cambridge (1992)
4. Engel, S.: The Stories Children Tell: Making Sense of the Narratives of Childhood. W H Freeman & Co. Ltd., New York (1995)
5. Gerosa, M., Giuliani, D., Narayanan, S., Potamianos, A.: A review of ASR technologies for children's speech. In: Proceedings of the 2nd Workshop on Child, Computer and Interaction, WOCCI 2009, pp. 1–8, November 2009
6. Harwell, D.: The accent gap: how Amazon's and Google's smart speakers leave certain voices behind, July 2018
7. Hone, K.S., Graham, R.: Towards a tool for the subjective assessment of speech system interfaces (SASSI). Natural Lang. Eng. **6**(3–4), 287–303 (2000)
8. Kennedy, J., et al.: Child speech recognition in human-robot interaction: evaluations and recommendations. In: Proceedings of the 2017 ACM/IEEE International Conference on Human-Robot Interaction, pp. 82–90 (2017)
9. Keren, G., Fridin, M.: Kindergarten social assistive robot (kindsar) for children's geometric thinking and metacognitive development in preschool education: a pilot study. Comput. Hum. Behav. **35**, 400–412 (2014)
10. Lovato, S., Piper, A.M.: "Siri, is this you?": understanding young children's interactions with voice input systems. In: Proceedings of the 14th International Conference on Interaction Design and Children, pp. 335–338, June 2015
11. Lovato, S.B., Piper, A.M., Wartela, E.A.: 'hey google, do unicorns exist?': conversational agents as a path to answers to children's questions. In: Proceedings of the 18th ACM International Conference on Interaction Design and Children, pp. 301–313 (2019)
12. Maier, A., et al.: An automatic version of a reading disorder test. ACM Trans. Speech Lang. Process. **7**, 15 (2011)
13. Meinedo, H., Trancoso, I.: Age and gender detection in the I-DASH project. ACM Trans. Speech Lang. Process. **7**, 16 (2011)
14. Most, T.: The use of repair strategies by children with and without hearing impairment. Lang. Speech Hearing Serv. Schools **33**(2), 112–123 (2002)
15. Ong, D.T., De Jesus, C.R., Gilig, L.K., Alburo, J.B., Ong, E.: A dialogue model for collaborative storytelling with children. In: Proceedings of the 26th International Conference on Computers in Education, pp. 205–210. APSCE (2018)
16. Ong, E., Alburo, J.B., De Jesus, C.R., Gilig, L.K., Ong, D.T.: Challenges posed by voice interface to child-agent collaborative storytelling. In: Proceedings of the 22nd Conference of the Oriental COCOSDA, pp. 1–6, October 2019
17. Papineni, K., Roukos, S., Ward, T., Zhu, W.J.: Bleu: A method for automatic evaluation of machine translation. In: Proceedings of the 40th Annual Meeting on Association for Computational Linguistics, pp. 311–318, July 2002
18. Peck, J.: Using storytelling to promote language and literacy development. Reading Teach. **43**(2), 138–141 (1989)

19. Pyae, A., Scifleet, P.: Investigating differences between native English and non-native English speakers in interacting with a voice user interface: A case of google home. In: Proceedings of the 30th Australian Conference on CHI, pp. 548–553, December 2018
20. Sun, M., Leite, I., Lehman, J., Li, B.: Collaborative storytelling between robot and child: a feasibility study. In: Proceedings 2017 Conference on Interaction Design and Children, pp. 205–214, June 2017
21. Tamura, Y., Kimoto, M., Shiomi, M., Iio, T., Shimohara, K., Hagita, N.: Effects of a listener robot with children in storytelling. In: Proceedings of the 5th International. Conference on Human Agent Interaction, pp. 35–43. ACM, NY (2017)
22. Ward, W., Cole, R., Bolaños, D., Buchenroth-Martin, C., Svirsky, E., Weston, T.: My science tutor: a conversational multimedia virtual tutor. J. Educ. Psychol. **105**, 1115 (2013)

ConversIAmo: Improving Italian Question Answering Exploiting IBM Watson Services

Chiara Leoni[✉], Ilaria Torre[iD], and Gianni Vercelli[iD]

DIBRIS, University of Genoa, Viale F. Causa 13, 16145 Genoa, Italy
chiara.leoni@outlook.com, {ilaria.torre,gianni.vercelli}@unige.it

Abstract. Chatbots, conversational interfaces and NLP have achieved considerable improvements and are spreading more and more in everyday applications. Solutions on the market allow their implementation easily in different languages, but the proposals for the Italian language are not so effective as the English ones. This paper introduces ConversIAmo, the prototype of a conversational agent which implements a question answering system in Italian on a closed domain concerning artificial intelligence, taking the answers from online articles. This system integrates IBM services (Watson Assistant, Discovery and Natural Language Understanding) with functions developed within ConversIAmo and Tint, an open-source tool for the analysis of the Italian language. Our QA pipeline turned out to give better results than those obtained from using Watson Discovery service on its own, as for precision, F1-score and correct answer ranking (on average +12%, +21% and +20% respectively). Our main contribution is to address the need for an effective but easy-to-apply method aimed to improve performances of IBM Watson services for the Italian language. In addition, the AI domain is a new one for an Italian conversational agent.

Keywords: Conversational agents · Question answering · IBM Watson · Artificial intelligence · Italian language

1 Introduction

Artificial intelligence has become a trending topic in the last few years and both researchers and companies are striving to improve results in many areas, from medical diagnosis to any kind of business process and products. Meanwhile, Software-as-a-Service (SaaS) solutions offered by the IT corporations on the market are now integrating powerful AI-as-a-Service (AIaaS) products, including conversational and QA (Query Answering) modules. Task-oriented dialog agents, designed for specific goals and set up to have short conversations to reach their purpose, include digital assistants on smartphones or home controllers (Siri, Cortana, Alexa, Google Now/Home, etc.), which can give travel directions, control home appliances, find restaurants, and so forth, and many

© Springer Nature Switzerland AG 2020
P. Sojka et al. (Eds.): TSD 2020, LNAI 12284, pp. 504–512, 2020.
https://doi.org/10.1007/978-3-030-58323-1_54

companies deploy their own task-based conversational agents to support customers. They are usually based on a knowledge structure representing the most common intents expressed by the user and related to the task. This implies a finite number of cases, designed by a dialog designer, each one with many input examples to train the classification, sets of entities for the given domain and preset answers (e.g., Google Dialogflow, Amazon Lex, Microsoft Bot Framework, Oracle Digital Assistant and IBM Watson Assistant as the most famous ones).

However, while several conversational and QA systems exist in English language, few examples are available in Italian (e.g., [4,6,12]), and performances using commercial tools are on average lower.

In this paper we present a QA prototype system, ConversIAmo, which uses unstructured text documents in Italian language in the Artificial Intelligence (AI) domain. Based on Watson services, ConversIAmo integrates new modules that we developed and Tint, an Italian NLP tool, with the goal of improving performances compared to Watson Discovery on Italian questions.

Watson Discovery Service (WDS from now on) showed experimentally good recall but low precision and weak ranking of the correct answers (around 51% of correct answers among the first three), unlike when the English version is used for English texts. Since the relevance of ranking is a well-known principle in interactive IR and QA systems, the main goal, that guided our approach, was to improve this measure, keeping the recall high. Results seem encouraging since we obtained that by questioning our ConversIAmo prototype on a dataset on AI in Italian language, precision, F1-score and accuracy outperform WDS (respectively +12%, +21% and +20%).

Our *contribution* consists not only in the creation of a question-answer dataset in Italian language regarding the topic of AI, which can be used for further research, but mainly in the proposal of an easy-to apply method to integrate IBM NL-related services with new modules to create an Italian speaking agent about AI. This is the first chatbot in Italian on AI domain and, to the best of our knowledge, also in other languages.

The paper is structured as follows: Sect. 2 presents related works, Sect. 3 describes ConversIAmo, Sect. 4 its experimental evaluation, results and discussion.

2   Background and Related Works

With the surge of technologies available, conversational agents are being used in many different fields. Beyond off-the-shelf solutions, different technologies allow to create custom dialog systems that can be trained and specialized on specific application scenarios. IBM Watson, is one of the most widely-adopted QA frameworks [6]. It combines several different techniques for NLP, IR and ML and uses IBM's DeepQA software and the Apache UIMA (Unstructured Information Management Architecture) framework implementation. Its effectiveness increases when it is extensively trained [1,11], but this task is very time consuming, thus other approaches have been proposed, such as using automatically generated question-answer pairs [8]. Several conversational agents have been developed using Watson services. Recently it has been exploited in [13] to build a multilingual student support system regarding exam stress, in [10] to build a parallel programming assistant (PAPA) to support programmers, in [1] to provide answers about programs and other issues in a university.

However, while performances are usually good with dialog agents in English, the effectiveness with other languages is not the same. Italian in particular, is not currently fully supported by Watson services, as reported in [2,6]. Our experience confirms this gap. We found that Watson Discovery did not get the same precision and accuracy that we got with English texts. We had to develop new modules that were used in the answer selection and ranking process to improve these measures on Italian texts. Conversely, recall was very high (around 95%) and not further improvable with ConversIAmo. Recent systems that use Watson services with Italian text are described in [6] and [4]. The former is a virtual assistant that supports students and staff of a smart campus. The authors compare the trained and untrained versions finding improvements after training, even though they notice that there were no improvements with out-of-scope questions, maybe due to the language, which is not fully supported [6]. In [4], the authors describe a pipeline for Italian that uses IBM services and tools for Italian language processing. The same group also developed a query expansion module to improve the retrieval phase [5]. Like to us, they exploit Tint for linguistic analysis.

In addition to the QA systems above, few examples can be further mentioned among Italian-based QA systems [12,14]. Some of the reasons might be difficulties related to the highly variable structures of queries, that may impact the question analysis and interpretation, and shortage of multilingual datasets [14].

3   ConversIAmo Prototype

ConversIAmo is a QA prototype that exploits Watson Assistant (WA), Watson Discovery Service (WDS), and Watson Natural Language Understanding (NLU). Moreover, it includes Tint and ad-hoc modules to increase performances for Italian language. WA is the IBM platform to build and manage chatbots, WDS is the service to retrieve information from unstructured data and NLU to extract metadata from text such as entities, keywords, categories, relations, etc. Tint is an open-source tool for NLP in Italian, based on Stanford CoreNLP (tint.fbk.eu). ConversIAmo Question Answering Pipeline is shown in Fig. 1.

Setup and Training

ConversIAmo dialog flow has been created using the WA graphical interface on IBM Cloud which allows to insert nodes that correspond to different *intents* of the user's question. As typical in conversational agents, intents are associated to *question classes*, which are mapped to corresponding Lexical Answer Types (LAT). As in many other QA systems [4,6,9], question classes are organized in a taxonomy. The main classes are *factoid questions* and *description questions*, each organized into sub-classes. *Factoid* class refers to questions that expect specific entities as answer types, while *Description* class refers to questions that expect as answer descriptive text that concerns the topic(s) of the question, e.g., "what's the difference between supervised learning and unsupervised learning?" The sub-classes we considered for *factoid questions* are: HUMAN (split in: individual and group), NUMERIC (split in: count, date, money, percent, period), LOCATION and ENTITY. Each sub-class is associated to a set of suitable entity types. E.g., HUMAN_group sub-class expects Organization or Company as entity types. *Description questions* are split in GENERIC_DESCRIPTION (DESCRIPTION) and DEFINITION. A further class is ABBREVIATION. For each class, examples are to be provided in order to train WA to classify them. We provided 10 examples for each sub-class on our AI domain in Italian.

Finally, the setup includes document ingestion and information extraction. Once prepared and formatted as required, the documents on the AI subject domain are uploaded on WDS to let it extract *concepts* and *named entities*, which are then imported into WA to be used in the QA flow.

QA Flow
The QA flow is the process performed each time the user submits a question and the system has to find some answers to output (see Fig. 1).

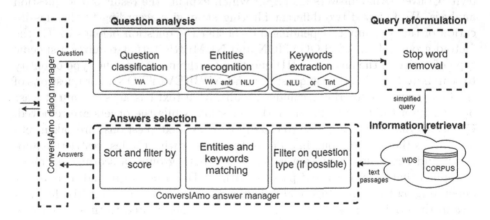

Fig. 1. Question answering scheme.

Question Analysis. This is the first phase of all QA systems and the fundamental one to determine the success of the process since its output will be used in the next steps. We deploy different services (WA, NLU and Tint) to accomplish this task, which includes three processes, other then the morpho-syntactic and syntactic analysis carried out using Tint. (i) *Question classification* is handled by WA, which is in charge of handling directly the user's question. The intent recognized by WA in the user question is one of the question classes specified above, which corresponds to the expected LAT. (ii) *Named entities extraction* is accomplished by combining named entities recognized by WDS, and imported in WA, with those extracted by NLU. Their intersection resulted to be the most effective combination. (iii) As for *keywords extraction* we have developed and tested two different approaches: the simplest, exploiting the keywords extracted by NLU, and a more complex one, developed with the tool Tint, specifically tailored for Italian. Thanks to its linguistic analysis, it allows to identify the linguistic features and select those candidates to become keywords: nouns, adjectives and verbs. Then, looking for *direct dependencies* between these words with any of the others selected, in particular between nouns and their adjectives, we merged related keywords. Overall, this method for keyword identification includes more keywords than those extracted by Watson NLU.

Information Retrieval. As first, we execute stop words removal through a function that enriches the set of Italian question words (e.g., "quali, qual, quale", are three forms of "which") taking into account the context of the word.

Then the flow continues with this reworked query stop words passed to Discovery, which returns the text passages that it retrieves with an associated score.

Answers Selection and Dialog Flow Expansion. Filtering and sorting of text passages is the step where Watson services for Italian mainly failed. Thus, we do not exploit any pre-existing service for this stage, but we implemented our own "ConversIAmo answers manager" which exploits the result of the question analysis. We followed two different filtering strategies according to the classification of the user input, depending on whether the question belongs to: (I) the factoid group (HUMAN, LOCATION and NUMERIC), that requires a specific type of entity in the answer or (II) questions without any specific type of entity to search for (i.e., description questions and ABBREVIATION). For questions of the first group, the filtering technique requires that text passages contain at least one entity of the type required by the question, while the others are removed. Questions that WA is not able to classify (unclassified questions) are taken into account as the second group in order to treat them with the less restrictive approach and not to lose any answer. Then, for both groups, a scoring technique is applied that takes each text passage with its Discovery score and increases it depending on the percentage match between (i) the *keywords* and (ii) the *entities* in the original question and in the text passage, limited to those occurring in the same *role* (as from the morpho-syntactic analysis). Once the scores have been updated, the passages are rearranged in descending order, then the scores are normalized and results below a certain threshold are deleted, to limit them to the most inherent to the question.

At the end, the results are displayed to the user and s(he) is asked to check the correct one. If an answer is selected, it is inserted in a node of WA dialogue flow within its question class branch and with the named entities identified in the question as entry condition for the node. This is aimed to extend the conversational agent knowledge base and improve results over time.

4   Experimental Results

Question Classification. In order to test the approach, we used a question-answer dataset that we built since none was available in Italian nor, as far as we know, in other languages on the subject of AI. Questions respect the principles in [7] about the way people usually interact with machines, and follow the example of popular question-answer datasets such as WikiQA dataset, MS MARCO, the Stanford Question Answering Dataset, and the Italian version of SQuAD. The dataset is composed of 110 questions on basic topics in AI, annotated with their correct question type extracted manually from the corpus of 130 articles each with its correct passages of text as answers. Questions are distributed among classes as follows: *factoid questions* 37.3% (NUMERIC 20%, HUMAN 10.9% and LOCATION 6.4%, further split in sub-classes); *description questions* 60% (DESCRIPTION 48.2%, DEFINITION 11.8%) and ABBREVIATION 2,7%.

To test WA's ability to classify the questions, we passed as input all the 110 questions in our dataset and we obtained the following results: 9 wrong classifications on 110 (8%), of which 8 DESCRIPTION labeled as DEFINITION, and 13 unclassified questions (11%) that Assistant was not able to assign to any intent, all belonging to *description questions*. Since we apply the same method for both DESCRIPTION and DEFINITION, such misclassification has no consequences on the answer selection, but it can impact the final dialog node expansion.

From these data, 10 examples have proved to be enough for factoid questions training, because they usually have in common some question words (e.g., *"Dove"*, "Where" or *"In quale città/stato/paese"*, "In what/which city/state/country" for LOCATION), while they are not enough to cover the variety of question forms that ask for a description, resulting in misclassified or unclassified questions. As explained in Sect. 3, we face unclassified questions by treating them as description questions and not inserting them in new dialog nodes.

QA Results. To evaluate the performance of ConversIAmo compared to WDS, we uploaded the test corpus of 130 articles, and use the widely adopted metrics in QA and IR communities *precision, recall* and *F1 score*. Moreover, we use *accuracy* computed as the ratio of questions that returned at least one correct answer within the first 3 answers of the response [3]. By running WDS, we found that while performance is good as for *recall*, it is not for the other measures. *Accuracy* in particular is below expectations for a QA system, where the correctness of the first answers is of foremost importance for the user experience. The design of ConversIAmo was mostly aimed to keep the recall at that high level (we obtained also a slight improvement of this parameter, though) while improving ranking, and thus *accuracy*, that is the placement of the correct text passages provided as answers. By improving ranking, we were also able to reduce the number of answers to be returned to the user and this led to an increase of *precision* and *F1 score*.

Figure 2 shows the results for factoid (left side) and description type questions (right side). Each side reports the results for WDS compared to ConversIAmo.

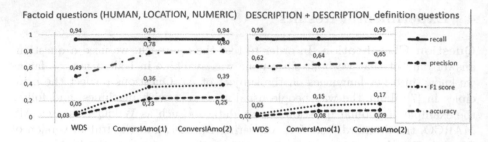

Fig. 2. Results on factoid and description type questions.

Results for the latter are provided with two configurations: ConversIAmo(1) uses Tint for keyword extraction, while ConversIAmo(2) uses NLU. Other than that there are no differences between the two versions as for NLP processing, question analysis, stop word removal and results filtering.

As showed in Fig. 2, for factoid questions we achieved a consistent +30% in *accuracy* (from WDS 49% to our 80%), keeping the *recall* at its max, improving *precision* and *F1 score* by respectively about 20% and 35%, with the two different approaches on keyword extraction that perform almost similarly.

While we achieved very good improvements for factoid questions, only a slight improvement has been accomplished with description questions. In these latter, *recall* is kept at its max, *precision* and *F1 score* have a slight increment (about 7% and 12% respectively), but *accuracy* is not significantly improved (only +2/3%). Again, the two versions of ConversIAmo perform similarly.

The difference in results is mostly related to the fact that factoid questions involve directly an entity type and the filtering technique we designed, combined with the scoring technique, works well, while this is not the case for the broad type of description questions. In the dataset used for the test, the questions that fall in this class are very different from each other and more complex (e.g., "what is the difference between ..."), such that improvements can difficultly be gained using rule-based approaches and without extensive training. However, improvements could come from refining the keyword extraction method used in ConversIAmo(1), which performed worse than expected (we discuss it in Sect. 5).

As a general result of our approach, we got that, despite the inverse relationship between *precision* and *recall* that is typical in IR systems, and that we also found with WDS results, our approach was able to keep *recall* at WDS max level and we achieved a significant improvement in *accuracy*. In detail, the combined results of factoid and description questions, including the abbreviation class, which performed similarly to the latter, are: +20% *accuracy* (from 51% to 71%) and improvements also on *precision* (+12%) and *F1 score* (+21%).

5   Conclusions and Discussion

In this paper we presented ConversIAmo, the prototype of an Italian speaking agent on the AI domain, the first as far as we know. Based upon IBM

Watson framework (Watson Assistant, NLU, Discovery), it exploits custom-made Java functions and Tint, a NLP tool for Italian language, in order to improve performances, compared to IBM Watson service used on its own. The results are encouraging since we gained improvement in accuracy and slightly in precision and F1 score, while recall was already high. In addition, ConversIAmo is designed to dynamically feed the agent with answers, dialog nodes and entities, to improve results over time. About limits, we acknowledge that the approach is effective with factoid questions, while less with description questions. This is true for both question classification and QA results. The method for keyword extraction that we proposed as an alternative to NLU keyword extraction was intended to improve such results, but the two perform similarly. Thus, as future work we plan to improve this method, and also try other approaches for keyword expansion (e.g., as in [5]). Moreover we plan further tests to balance the need of an extensive training with the deployment of an effective easy-to-apply method.

References

1. Asakiewicz, C., Stohr, E.A., Mahajan, S., Pandey, L.: Building a cognitive application using Watson DeepQA. IT Prof. **19**(4), 36–44 (2017)
2. Bellomaria, V., Castellucci, G., Favalli, A., Romagnoli, R.: Almawave-SLU: a new dataset for SLU in Italian. In: Proceedings of the Sixth Italian Conference on CL (2019)
3. Boyer, J.M.: Natural language question answering in the financial domain. In: Proceedings of the 28th Annual International Conference on Computer Science and Software Engineering, pp. 189–200. IBM Corporation (2018)
4. Damiano, E., Spinelli, R., Esposito, M., De Pietro, G.: An effective corpus-based question answering pipeline for Italian. In: De Pietro, G., Gallo, L., Howlett, R.J., Jain, L.C. (eds.) KES-IIMSS 2017. SIST, vol. 76, pp. 80–90. Springer, Cham (2018). https://doi.org/10.1007/978-3-319-59480-4_9
5. Esposito, M., Damiano, E., Minutolo, A., De Pietro, G., Fujita, H.: Hybrid query expansion using lexical resources and word embeddings for sentence retrieval in question answering. Inf. Sci. **514**, 88–105 (2020)
6. Gaglio, S., Re, G.L., Morana, M., Ruocco, C.: Smart assistance for students and people living in a campus. In: 2019 IEEE International Conference on Smart Computing (SMARTCOMP), pp. 132–137. IEEE (2019)
7. Hill, J., Ford, W.R., Farreras, I.G.: Real conversations with artificial intelligence: a comparison between human-human online conversations and human-chatbot conversations. Comput. Hum. Behav. **49**, 245–250 (2015)
8. Lee, J., Kim, G., Yoo, J., Jung, C., Kim, M., Yoon, S.: Training IBM Watson using automatically generated question-answer pairs. In: 50th Hawaii International Conference on System Sciences, HICSS 2017, Hawaii, USA, 4–7 January 2017, pp. 1–9 (2017)
9. Li, X., Roth, D.: Learning question classifiers. In: Proceedings of the International Conference on Computational Linguistics, vol. 1, pp. 1–7 (2002)
10. Memeti, S., Pllana, S.: PAPA: a parallel programming assistant powered by IBM Watson cognitive computing. J. Comput. Sci. **26**, 275–284 (2018)
11. Murtaza, S.S., Lak, P., Bener, A., Pischdotchian, A.: How to effectively train IBM Watson: classroom experience. In: 2016 49th Hawaii International Conference on System Sciences (HICSS), pp. 1663–1670. IEEE (2016)

12. Pipitone, A., Tirone, G., Pirrone, R.: QuASIt: a cognitive inspired approach to question answering for the Italian language. In: Adorni, G., Cagnoni, S., Gori, M., Maratea, M. (eds.) AI*IA 2016. LNCS (LNAI), vol. 10037, pp. 464–476. Springer, Cham (2016). https://doi.org/10.1007/978-3-319-49130-1_34
13. Ralston, K., Chen, Y., Isah, H., Zulkernine, F.: A voice interactive multilingual student support system using IBM Watson. In: 2019 18th IEEE International Conference on Machine Learning and Applications (ICMLA), pp. 1924–1929 (2019)
14. Siciliani, L., Basile, P., Semeraro, G., Mennitti, M.: An Italian question answering system for structured data based on controlled natural languages. In: Proceedings of the Sixth Italian Conference on Computational Linguistics (2019)

Modification of Pitch Parameters in Speech Coding for Information Hiding

Adrian Radej and Artur Janicki[(⊠)] [iD]

Institute of Telecommunications, Warsaw University of Technology,
ul. Nowowiejska 15/19, 00-665 Warsaw, Poland
261187@pw.edu.pl, ajanicki@tele.pw.edu.pl

Abstract. The article presents a method of using F0 parameter in speech coding to transmit hidden information. It is an improved approach, which uses interpolation of pitch parameters instead of transmitting exact original values. Using an example of the Speex codec, we describe six variants of this method, named originally as HideF0, and we compare them by analyzing the capacity of the hidden channels, their detectability and the decrease in quality introduced by pitch manipulation. In particular, we perform listening tests using 20 participants to verify how perceptible the pitch manipulations are. The results are presented and discussed. We prove that minor modifications of pitch parameters are hardly perceptible, what can be used to create hidden transmission channels. One of the best proposed variants, called HideF0-FM, is shown to enable hidden transmission at the bitrate of over 120 bps at no speech quality degradation at all. Higher bitrates are also possible, only with minor quality degradation and limited detectability.

Keywords: Speech coding · Information hiding · Pitch · Listening tests · Speex

1 Introduction

Large volume of encoded voice streams transmitted over the Internet has attracted those trying to use them as a carrier of hidden information. Numerous researchers have proposed various steganographic methods to be used with IP telephony voice streams [12]. Some of these methods are based on exploiting unused fields in protocol headers, other manipulate the encoded speech data, yet another group modifies time relationship between packets.

Existence of hidden channel can result in a major security breach. They can be used to allow leakage of sensitive data out of, for example, a governmental institution, or they can be used to control behavior of malicious software, which can be used to attack a host or a network. Therefore it is very important to be aware of various information hiding techniques and research on their countermeasures.

A relatively small group of algorithms use pitch parameters to hide information. One of such methods, called HideF0, was proposed in [7]. In this paper

© Springer Nature Switzerland AG 2020
P. Sojka et al. (Eds.): TSD 2020, LNAI 12284, pp. 513–523, 2020.
https://doi.org/10.1007/978-3-030-58323-1_55

an improved version of this method is presented. In particular, we will try to find out if changes in pitch parameters are noticeable by listeners, therefore an auditory assessment of perceptibility of pitch manipulation will be shown.

The article is organized as follows: we will start with a brief overview of main information hiding techniques used in speech coding. Next, in Sect. 3, we will present our algorithm with particular focus on the new variants. In Sect. 4 we will describe the experiments and their results. This section will be followed by discussion in Sect. 5 and conclusions in Sect. 6.

2   Hiding Information Using Speech Coding

Speech coding has been used for information hiding already for several years [5]. A large group of data hiding methods used with encoded speech is based on a very popular steganographic method: it uses least significant bits (LSB) to transmit hidden data. For example, in [2] the author proposed applying the LSB method directly to G.711 speech samples, in order to transmit the side information to extend the conveyed acoustic bandwidth.

The LSB method can be also used for encoded speech parameters. In [15] the authors used it with the G.723.1 codec by embedding a secret message into various bitstream parameters (VQ index, codebook lags, pulse positions etc.), achieving bitrates up to 133.33 bps. It is noteworthy that the LSB methods are easily prone to removing the hidden content by applying the so called content threat removal (CTR).

Another group of algorithms replaces completely the voice payload encoded by one codec, using another, more efficient speech codec. Such a method was called transcoding steganography [11]. The payload type in the RTP header remains unchanged, i.e., it indicates that the original, less efficient codec is used. The saved bits are used to hide own data.

So far, only a few steganographic methods used pitch or pitch-related parameters to hide information. In [6] the LSB technique was used for $F0$ parameter in G.729 codec. The authors achieved the steganographic bandwidth of 200 bps. In [14] a similar technique was proposed for the AMR codec.

The authors in [10] described a method dedicated to the ACELP codec, which was based on embedding secret information into the fractional pitch delay parameters, while at the same time keeping the integer pitch delay parameters unchanged. A variant of LSB was used for information hiding in the so called random LSB of pitch and Fourier magnitude steganography (RLPFS) [9]. The authors claimed that they were able to create a covert channel with maximum capacity of 266.64 bps at the cost of a steganographic noise between 0.031 and 0.62 MOS, but the method was detection-resistant only when the bitrate was ca. 44 bps.

The method discussed in this article, originally proposed in [7], was based on interpolation of the pitch contour. In its first version it offered the hidden channel of ca. 200 bps of capacity, at the steganographic cost of 0.5–0.7 MOS. In this paper several new variants of this algorithm are proposed and evaluated.

3   Proposed Algorithm

The proposed method takes advantage of the fact that parameters describing the pitch value, used in speech coding, for voiced speech change relatively slowly in time. This is why one can try to use approximated pitch values instead of the original ones and use the save bits to hide information.

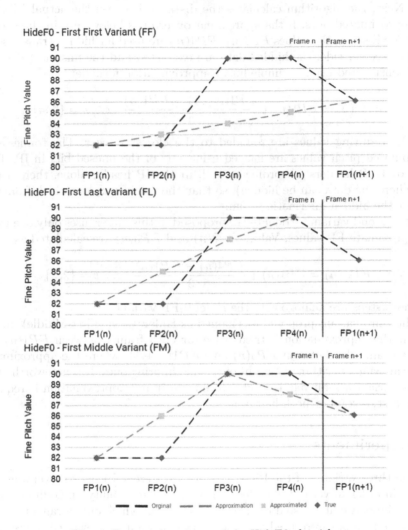

Fig. 1. Proposed variants of the HideF0 algorithm.

In this paper we will analyze three main variants of this method (see Fig. 1):

- HideF0-FF (First-First);
- HideF0-FL (First-Last);
- HideF0-FM (First-Middle).

We will explain them using an example of the Speex codec, where the pitch values are represented using four Fine Pitch parameters (FP1–FP4) per 20 ms frame, each occupying seven bits.

The first variant (HideF0-FF) is used as a reference method [8]. It uses the first FP value from the current frame ($FP1(n)$) and the first FP value from the next frame ($FP1(n+1)$) and uses these values to approximate the remaining ones. Next, the algorithm calculates the distance between the actual FPs and the approximated ones. If the approximation error is below certain threshold θ in the MSE sense, the values $FP2(n)..FP4(n)$ are used for hidden transmission. On the receiver side, the hidden data are extracted and the missing FP values are reconstructed using a simple linear approximation formula:

$$FPx(n) = FP1(n) + \frac{FP1(n+1) - FP1(n)}{4} \cdot x, \quad x = \{2..4\} \qquad (1)$$

and the resulting values are rounded to the closest integer. The frames with manipulated pitch values are flagged using any of the unused bits in IP, TCP, UDP or RTP headers (according to [13], in the IP header alone, there are 64 bits where the data can be hidden), so that the receiver knows which frames to extract the hidden information from.

The second variant – HideF0-FL, proposed in this paper, uses only one frame to approximate FP values. Values $FP2(n)$ and $FP3(n)$ are calculated as:

$$FPx(n) = FP1(n) + \frac{FP4(n) - FP1(n)}{3} \cdot x, \quad x = \{2,3\} \qquad (2)$$

The next steps are analogous to the HideF0-FF variant.

The third variant proposed was named as HideF0-FM (First-Middle). In this variant the approximation is tried twice for each frame: between $FP1(n)$ and $FP3(n)$, and also between $FP3(n)$ and $FP1(n+1)$, where the approximated values are simply arithmetic means of the neighboring ones. It is noteworthy that in this variant a 2-bit flag is needed to inform if any approximation is required in the first, second or both half-frames.

4   Experiments

The three variants of the HideF0 algorithm were subjects to several experiments, in order to verify their effectiveness and detectability. In addition to the base variants, we also tested their modifications, in which only a random subset of qualified frames were used for hidden transmission – we wanted to see what impact it would have on the detectability of hidden transmission. In this paper we denote them as "Rnd" variants, in contrast to "All" variants, using every frame meeting the MSE condition for data hiding. In total, for all six variants of the HideF0 algorithm we ran the following experiments:

- Measurement of quality loss against the capacity of the hidden channel;
- Perceptibility tests for various capacities of the hidden channel;

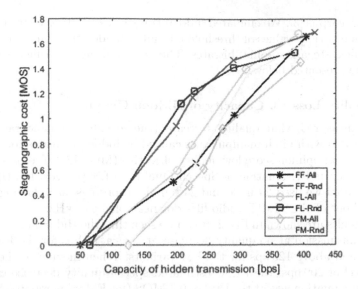

Fig. 2. Quality decrease (steganographic cost) in the function of capacity of hidden channel (steganographic bandwidth).

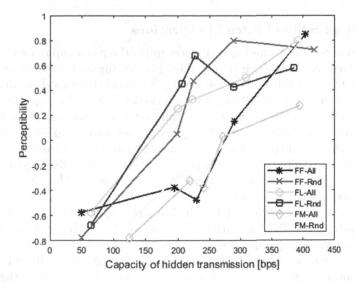

Fig. 3. Results of perceptibility tests for various variants of the HideF0 algorithm. Value "−1" denotes "speech modifications imperceptible", value "1" denotes "speech modifications clearly perceptible."

– Detectability tests for various capacities of the hidden channel.

All experiments were run for the narrowband Speex codec mode 5 (quality 8), working with bitrate 15 kbps, using the US English recordings taken from the TIMIT corpus [3]. We emulated hidden transmission with six various HideF0 variants and various values of threshold θ to allow hidden transmission at various (the so called steganographic) bitrates. The details of the experiments and their output are presented below.

4.1 Quality Loss vs. Capacity of Hidden Channel

First we measured what quality decrease (the so called steganographic cost) was associated with pitch manipulation caused by hidden transmission. We analyzed the mean opinion score low quality objective (MOS-LQO) results returned by the Perceptual Evaluation of Speech Quality (PESQ) algorithm [1]. As the audio material we used 24 male and 24 female recordings, each lasting ca. 30 s, composed out of the TIMIT audio files downsampled to 8 kHz.

The results are shown in Fig. 2. It can be seen that the HideF0 method allows hidden transmission at no quality decrease at the ca. 50 bps for the FF and FL variants, and above 120 bps for the FM variants. When moving to the bitrates at the level of 200 bps, the PESQ-estimated speech quality decrease caused by pitch approximation was at the level of 0.4 MOS (for FM variants), 0.5 MOS (for the FM-All and FL-All variants) and 1.2 MOS for random variants of FM and FL. For bitrates over 350 bps the quality loss for all variants exceeded 1.4 MOS.

4.2 Perceptibility of Pitch Modifications

In the second test we wanted to verify how much the pitch approximation caused by the hidden transmission is perceptible. The testing methodology applied was similar to the preference tests used, e.g., for synthetic speech evaluation [4]. Twenty listeners, aged 19–30 yrs, were exposed to 60 random, gender-balanced TIMIT speech recordings, which were transcoded with various share of manipulated frames. The listeners were in a quiet environment and used headphones. For each audio file the participants were asked to answer the question: "Has this recording been manipulated?". The possible answers were "No" (scored as -1), "Difficult to say" (scored as 0) and "Yes" (scored as 1). The scores were then averaged across the participants.

The results are displayed in Fig. 3. It shows that for the bitrates below 200 bps the perceptibility of the FM variants was clearly lower than for the remaining HideF0 variants and yielded values below -0.4. For bitrates 200–270 bps the perceptibility was similar to that of the FF-All variant and oscillated around 0, which denotes "Difficult to say". For bitrates over 300 bps most of the listeners noticed that the audio was manipulated, with the score for FM-All being the lowest (ca. 0.2). Interestingly, even if no pitch approximation was used at all (left bottom end of each line in the plot), a few participants pointed them also as suspicious.

4.3 Detectability of Hidden Transmission

In the third test we wanted to test if the use of HideF0 can be easily detected by analysis of the bitstream of encoded speech. Following the state-of-the-art

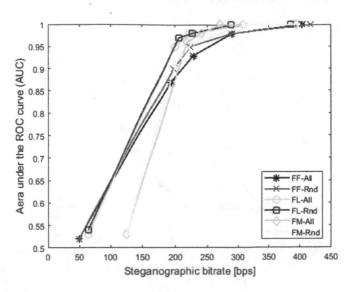

Fig. 4. Area under the ROC curve (AUC) for detection of hidden transmission assuming method-aware detection system.

techniques we used the machine learning approach. We tried several algorithms, such as support vector machines (SVM) or Naïve Bayes (NB), but we achieved the best results for the Random Forest (RF) classifier, therefore the below results are presented for this algorithm only.

First we tried a naïve approach, i.e., we assumed that we have no prior knowledge of a technique used to hide data, which is usually the case. We tried to train the RF classifier based on 2/3 of the encoded speech data (with and without pitch manipulation), using the remaining data as a testing set. As a feature vector we used histograms of byte values of the voice payload. Depending on hidden channel capacity, the RF classifier yielded the area under the ROC curve (AUC) in the range of 0.50–0.52, what indicated a random classification.

To consider an opposite case, we assumed the worst-case detection scenario: the full knowledge of the data hiding technique, so that the detection algorithm was aware that HideF0 was used and in which variant. In this case the feature vector consisted of difference values (deltas) between the actual FP values and the approximated ones, using the approximation formulae for the respective HideF0 variant, calculated for a window spanning over 2.5 s. The RF algorithm was tested using the data, where 3/4 of encoded speech was benign and 1/4 of encoded speech was manipulated using HideF0.

We analyzed AUC and precision of the hidden transmission detection for various HideF0 variants. The results are depicted in Figs. 4 and 5, respectively. They show that for lower bitrates (i.e., when the steganographic cost equals 0) the detection was hardly possible, despite being aware of the data hiding method - the AUC was below 0.55. For bitrates over 200 bps the AUC exceeded 0.9 for

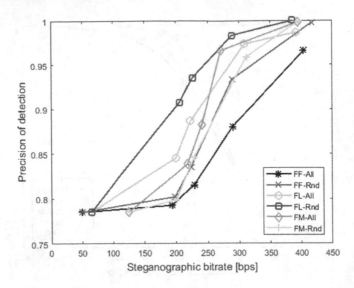

Fig. 5. Precision of detection of hidden transmission assuming method-aware detection system.

all variants, what meant that the detection became easier. But even for bitrates exceeding 300 bps the precision of detection for some of the HideF0 variants (FF, FM-Rnd) was below 96%, what would result in a relatively high false alarm rate.

5   Discussion

Approximation of pitch-related parameters is mostly effective when these parameters change slowly and monotonously. This is the case when the speech is voiced. When the speech is unvoiced, the $F0$ is undetermined and pitch-related parameters (such as FP in Speex) take unpredictable values, therefore their approximation results in high differences and is easily noticeable. Only the frames for which the approximation error is below certain threshold θ take part in hiding data. The presented capacity values of the hidden channel were averaged across the analyzed recordings, but it must be remembered that the actual capacity depends on the voice activity of the speaker and the amount of voiced speech within the transmitted signal.

In several tests the variant HideF0-FM yielded the best results. This can be easily explained by the fact that it is easier to interpolate a single pitch value between two neighbors than two or three values in a row. Therefore such an interpolation can happen more often, so that this variant can lead to higher bitrates of hidden transmission at lower quality cost. It is noteworthy, however, that since such an interpolation can happen twice per frame, it requires another bit flag hidden in the TCP, UDP or RTP header, what increases the side channel capacity by 50 bps and may also have impact on increased detectability of the method as a whole.

The HideF0 "Rnd" variants which involved random use of the frames for hidden transmission, did not turn out to be very successful in terms of quality, when comparing them with "All" methods for the same size of the hidden channel. This can be explained by the fact that creating a hidden channel of the same capacity as for the "All" variant, required random selection of frames out of a larger set of frames, among which there might be frames with much higher approximation error. This could lower the quality and increase the perceptibility of such a manipulation. However, the "Rnd" variants may turn out to be quite difficult to detect for lower steganographic bitrates using statistical detection methods, but this would need to be verified in additional experiments.

The applied perceptibility test requires some comments. The listeners were informed that the recordings might have been manipulated, therefore they paid special attention to any distortions in the perceived speech. This is probably the reason why some of the listeners found files with no modifications also as manipulated. We think that in real environment speech transmitted with such quality would raise no suspicions at all. Therefore we suspect that the perceptibility test was biased toward increased perceptibility of HideF0.

The listeners turned out to be moderately sensitive to pitch manipulation: for the PESQ-estimated quality degradation of 1.0 MOS (which is relatively high) the perceptibility oscillated around 0, what meant that on average the listeners were not sure if any manipulation took place.

6   Conclusions

In this paper we discussed the idea of using interpolation of pitch parameters in encoded speech bitstream for the purpose of hidden transmission. The main objective was to verify experimentally how efficient such hidden channels would be and if they are easy to perceive and detect. These elements were novel in this article:

- New variants of the HideF0 method, named First-Last (FL) and First-Middle (FM), were proposed and tested.
- Versions "Rnd" with random subset of frames used to hide data were proposed and evaluated.
- Perceptual listening tests with 20 participants were conducted and they results were analyzed.
- Experiments with detection of all six variants were run and their outcomes were analyzed.

We can conclude that the discussed methods, especially the newly proposed HideF0-FM variant, can pose a security risk, as they allow to create a relatively highly efficient hidden channel (with the steganographic bitrate over 120 bps) at no quality decrease, with lack of perceptibility and detectability, while the original version of this algorithm (named here as HideF0-FF) offered the costless variant at the bitrate of ca. 50 bps only. The HideF0-FM methods can also provide higher steganographic bitrates (around 200 bps), while still not being well noticed by listeners nor efficiently detected by a trained classifier, even if it is method-aware.

Acknowledgements. This work has been partially funded under the SIMARGL project, which has received funding from the European Union's Horizon 2020 research and innovation programme under grant agreement No. 833042.

References

1. Recommendation P.862: Perceptual evaluation of speech quality (PESQ): An objective method for end-to-end speech quality assessment of narrow-band telephone networks and speech codecs (2001)
2. Aoki, N.: A band extension technique for G. 711 speech using steganography. IEICE Trans. Commun. **89**(6), 1896–1898 (2006)
3. Garofolo, J., Lamel, L., Fisher, W., Fiscus, J., Pallett, D., Dahlgren, N.: TIMIT acoustic-phonetic continuous speech corpus. Linguistic Data Consortium, Philadelphia, US (1993)
4. Gu, Y., Kang, Y.: Multi-task WaveNet: a multi-task generative model for statistical parametric speech synthesis without fundamental frequency conditions. In: Proceedings of the Interspeech 2018, Hyderabad, India, pp. 2007–2011 (2018). https://doi.org/10.21437/Interspeech.2018-1506
5. Huang, Y., Liu, C., Tang, S., Bai, S.: Steganography integration into a low-bit rate speech codec. IEEE Trans. Inf. Forensics Secur. **7**(6), 1865–1875 (2012)
6. Iwakiri, M., Matsui, K.: Embedding a text into conjugate structure algebraic code excited linear prediction audio codecs. Inf. Process. Soc. Jpn. **39**(9), 2623–2630 (1998)
7. Janicki, A.: Novel method of hiding information in IP telephony using pitch approximation. In: Proceedings of the International Workshop on Cyber Crime (IWCC 2015), Toulouse, France, pp. 429–435, August 2015
8. Janicki, A.: Pitch-based steganography for Speex voice codec. Secur. Commun. Netw. **9**(15), 2923–2933 (2016). https://doi.org/10.1002/sec.1428
9. Kheddar, H., Bouzid, M., Megias, D.: Pitch and Fourier magnitude based steganography for hiding 2.4 kbps MELP bitstream. IET Signal Proc. **13**(3), 396–407 (2019). https://doi.org/10.1049/iet-spr.2018.5339
10. Liu, X., Tian, H., Huang, Y., Lu, J.: A novel steganographic method for algebraic-code-excited-linear-prediction speech streams based on fractional pitch delay search. Multimed. Tools Appl. **78**(7), 8447–8461 (2018). https://doi.org/10.1007/s11042-018-6867-7
11. Mazurczyk, W., Szaga, P., Szczypiorski, K.: Using transcoding for hidden communication in IP telephony. Multimed. Tools Appl. **70**(3), 2139–2165 (2012). https://doi.org/10.1007/s11042-012-1224-8
12. Mazurczyk, W., Szczypiorski, K.: Steganography of VoIP streams. In: Meersman, R., Tari, Z. (eds.) OTM 2008. LNCS, vol. 5332, pp. 1001–1018. Springer, Heidelberg (2008). https://doi.org/10.1007/978-3-540-88873-4_6
13. Murdoch, S.J., Lewis, S.: Embedding covert channels into TCP/IP. In: Barni, M., Herrera-Joancomartí, J., Katzenbeisser, S., Pérez-González, F. (eds.) IH 2005. LNCS, vol. 3727, pp. 247–261. Springer, Heidelberg (2005). https://doi.org/10.1007/11558859_19

14. Nishimura, A.: Data hiding in pitch delay data of the adaptive multi-rate narrow-band speech codec. In: Fifth International Conference on Intelligent Information Hiding and Multimedia Signal Processing (IIH-MSP 2009), Kyoto, Japan, pp. 483–486, September 2009. https://doi.org/10.1109/IIH-MSP.2009.83
15. Xu, T., Yang, Z.: Simple and effective speech steganography in G.723.1 low-rate codes. In: International Conference on Wireless Communications Signal Processing (WCSP 2009), Nanjing, China, pp. 1–4, November 2009. https://doi.org/10.1109/WCSP.2009.5371745

ConfNet2Seq
Full Length Answer Generation from Spoken Questions

Vaishali Pal[1(✉)] , Manish Shrivastava[1] , and Laurent Besacier[2]

[1] LTRC, International Institute of Information Technology - Hyderabad,
Hyderabad, India
`vaishali.pal@research.iiit.ac.in`, `m.shrivastava@iiit.ac.in`
[2] LIG - Université Grenoble Alpes, Grenoble, France
`laurent.besacier@univ-grenoble-alpes.fr`

Abstract. Conversational and task-oriented dialogue systems aim to interact with the user using natural responses through multi-modal interfaces, such as text or speech. These desired responses are in the form of full-length natural answers generated over facts retrieved from a knowledge source. While the task of generating natural answers to questions from an answer span has been widely studied, there has been little research on natural sentence generation over spoken content. We propose a novel system to generate full length natural language answers from spoken questions and factoid answers. The spoken sequence is compactly represented as a confusion network extracted from a pre-trained Automatic Speech Recognizer. This is the first attempt towards generating full-length natural answers from a graph input (confusion network) to the best of our knowledge. We release a large-scale dataset of 259,788 samples of spoken questions, their factoid answers and corresponding full-length textual answers. Following our proposed approach, we achieve comparable performance with best ASR hypothesis.

Keywords: Confusion network · Pointer-generator · Copy attention · Natural answer generation · Question answering

1 Introduction

Full-length answer generation is the task of generating natural answers over a question and an answer span, usually a fact-based phrase (factoid answer), extracted from relevant knowledge sources such as knowledge-bases (KB) or context passages. Such functionality is desired in conversational agents and dialogue systems to interact naturally with the user over multi-modal interfaces, such as speech and text. Typical task-oriented dialogue systems and chatbots formulate coherent responses from conversation context with a natural language generation (NLG) module. These modules copy relevant facts from context while generating new words, maintaining factual accuracy in a coherent fact-based natural response. Recent research [7,10] utilizes a pointer-network to copy words from relevant knowledge sources. While the task of generating natural response

P. Sojka et al. (Eds.): TSD 2020, LNAI 12284, pp. 524–531, 2020.
https://doi.org/10.1007/978-3-030-58323-1_56

to text-based questions have been extensively studied, there is little research on natural answer generation from spoken content. Recent research on Spoken Question Answering and listening comprehension tasks [6] extracts an answer-span and does not generate a natural answer. This motivates us to propose the task of generating full length answer from spoken question and textual factoid answer. However, such a task poses significant challenges as the performance of the system is highly dependent on Automatic Speech Recognizer (ASR) error. To mitigate the effect of Word Error Rate (WER) on ASR predictions, a list of top-N hypothesis, ASR lattices or confusion networks has been used in various tasks such as Dialogue-state-tracking [2,16], Dialogue-Act detection [8] and named-entity recognition. These tasks show that models trained using multiple ASR hypotheses outperforms those trained top-1 ASR hypothesis. While classification and labeling tasks benefit from multiple hypothesis by aggregating the predictions over a list of ASR hypothesis, it is non-trivial to apply the same for NLG using pointer-networks. Our proposed system aims to take advantage of multiple time-aligned ASR hypotheses represented as a confusion network using a pointer-network to generate full-length answers. To the best of our knowledge, there is no prior work for full length answer generation from spoken questions. Our overall research contributions are as follows:

- We propose a novel task of full-length answer generation from spoken question. To achieve this, we develop a ConfNet2Seq model which encodes a confusion network and adapts it over a pointer-generator architecture.
- We compare the effects of using multiple hypothesis encoded with a confusion network encoder and the best hypothesis encoded with a text encoder.
- We publicly release the dataset, comprising of spoken question audio file, the corresponding confusion network, the factoid answer and full-length answer.

2   Related Work

Spoken Language Usage Understanding (SLU) has the additional challenge of disambiguation of ASR errors which drastically affect performance. Several methods have been proposed to curb the effects of the WER. Word lattices from ASR were first used by [1] over ASR top-1 hypothesis for tasks such as named-entity extraction and call classification. Word confusion networks have been recently used by [4] for intent classification in dialogue systems and by [2,9] for dialogue state tracking (DST). [2] show that confusion network gives comparable performance to top-N hypotheses of ASR while [9] show that using confusion network improves performance in both in time and accuracy. Another related task in SLU is that of Spoken Question Answering. Recent work [6] on SQuAD dataset introduces the task for machine listening comprehension where the context passages are in audio form. [5] released Open-Domain Spoken Question Answering Dataset (ODSQA) with more than three thousand questions in Chinese and used an enhanced word embedding comprising of word embedding and pingyin-token embedding. [15] developed a QA system for spoken lectures and generates an answer span from the video transcription.

3   Models

Our system generates full length answer from a textual factoid answer and spoken question. We use a pointer generator architecture over two sequences, i.e., over the textual factoid answer sequence and the encoded question sequence produced by the confusion network encoder. In this section, we describe the 1) Confusion network encoder, 2) Final model over spoken question and factoid answer. The full architecture is shown in Fig. 1.

3.1   Confusion Network Encoder

A Confusion Network is a weighted directed acyclic graph with one or more parallel arcs between consecutive nodes where each path goes through all the nodes. Each set of parallel arcs represents time-aligned alternative words or hypothesis of the ASR weighed by probability. The total probability of all parallel arcs between two consecutive nodes sums up to 1. A confusion network C can be defined formally as a sequence of sets of parallel weighted arcs as:

$$C = [(< w_1^1, \pi_1^1 >, < w_1^2, \pi_1^2 >, ..., < w_1^{n_1}, \pi_1^{n_1} >), ...,$$
$$(< w_m^1, \pi_m^1 >, < w_m^2, \pi_m^2 >, ..., < w_m^{n_m}, \pi_m^{n_m} >)] \tag{1}$$

where w_i^j is the jth ASR hypothesis at position i, and π_i^j its associated probability. We use a confusion network encoder to transform a 2-dimensional confusion network into an 1-dimensional sequence of embeddings as described in [8]. Each word w_i^j of the confusion network can be encoded by weighing the word embedding by the ASR probability followed by a non-linear transformation as:

$$q_i^j = \tanh(W_1 \pi_i^j Embedding(w_i^j)) \tag{2}$$

where W_1 is a trainable parameter. Each set of parallel arcs can be encoded into a vector by a weighted sum over the words of the parallel arc set. The weights measure the relevance of each word among the alternate time-aligned hypothesis. The learnt weight distribution for each parallel-arc set is:

$$\alpha_i^j = \frac{\exp(W_2 q_i^j)}{\sum_j \exp(W_2 q_i^j)} \tag{3}$$

where W_2 is a trainable parameter. The final encoding of each set of parallel arcs is:

$$\beta_i = \sum_i \alpha_i^j q_i^j \tag{4}$$

3.2   Full Length Answer Generation from Spoken Questions

We have followed a Seq2Seq with pointer generator architecture as [10] to generate full-length answers from a question and factoid answer. However, we query with spoken questions instead of textual questions. The confusion network is extracted from spoken questions using a standard ASR. The question is encoded

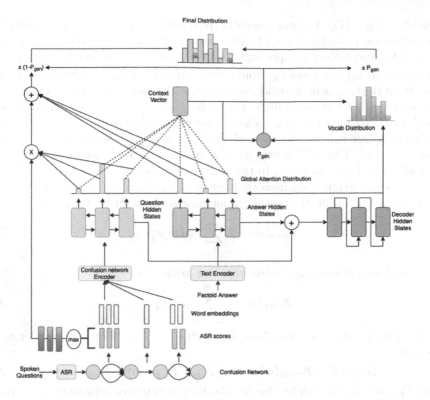

Fig. 1. Full length answer generation from spoken question and textual factoid answer: The confusion-network encoder generates a sequence of 1D-encodings of the sequence of parallel arcs (2D graph). The ASR scores are multiplied with the global-attention weights of the encodings to generate the copy-attention distribution of the question.

as $Q = \{q_1, q_2, ..., q_n\}$ where q_t is the encoding from the confusion network encoder explained in Sect. 3.1.

The factoid answer is represented as $A = \{a_1, a_2, a_3, \dots, a_m\}$ where a_t is the GloVe embedding [11] of a word. We encode the sequences using two 3-layered bi-LSTMs which share weights as:

$$h_Q^t = BILSTM(h_Q^{t-1}, q_t)$$
$$h_A^t = BILSTM(h_A^{t-1}, a_t)$$

(5)

The encoded hidden states of the 2 encoders are stacked together to produce a single list of source hidden states, $h_S = [h_Q; h_A]$. The decoder is initialized with the combined final states of the two encoders as $h_T^0 = h_Q^n + h_A^m$.

The global attention weights $attn_i^t$ are computed on the n hidden states of the question and m hidden states of the answer, stacked to produce a total of $m + n$ global attention weights. For each source state, h_i, and decoder state, s_t:

$$attn_i^t = softmax(v^T tanh(W_h h_i + W_s s_t + b_{attn}))$$

(6)

where b_{attn}, v , W_h, W_s are learnable parameters. The copy mechanism for summarization introduced in [13] takes advantage of a word distribution over an extended vocabulary comprising of source words and vocabulary words. The probability of copying a word w from a text sequence is $\sum_{k:w_k=w}^{m} attn_k^t$. To copy words from the confusion network, we compute the global attention weights over each set of parallel-arc encodings. Here, the global attention weights denote a probability distribution over parallel-arc sets instead of words. These attention weights $attn_i^t$ are sampled to select the hidden state representation, β_i, of a set of parallel arcs. The ASR scores π_i is a probability distribution over the set of parallel words at position j in the confusion network. These are sampled to select the most likely word from that set of parallel arcs. The final probability of copying a word from the confusion network is the joint-probability:

$$\widetilde{P}_{copy}(w) = \sum_{i:w_i^j=w}^{n} attn_i^t \pi_i^j \tag{7}$$

The probability of copying a word from the answer is:

$$P_{copy}(w) = \sum_{k:w_k=w}^{m} attn_k^t \tag{8}$$

The final probability of a word output at $P(w)$ at time t by the decoder is as shown in

$$P(w) = P_{gen} P_{vocab}(w) + (1 - P_{gen})(\widetilde{P}_{copy}(w) + P_{copy}(w)) \tag{9}$$

where P_{gen} is a soft switch for the decoder to generate words or copy words from the source. $P_{vocab}(w)$ is the probability of generating a word from the vocabulary. These parameters are computed as described in [13].

4   Dataset

To generate data for our task, we use $258,478$ samples from the full-length answer generation dataset introduced in [10] where each sample consists of a question, factoid answer and full-length answer. The samples in the dataset were chosen from SQuAD and HarvestingQA. Each sample in our dataset is also a 3-tuple (q, f, a) in which q is a spoken-form question, f is a text-form factoid answer and a is the text-form full-length natural answer. $256,478$ samples were randomly selected as the training set, 1000 as the development set and 1000 as the test set. We also extracted 470 samples from NewsQA dataset and 840 samples from Freebase to evaluate our system on cross-domain datasets.[1]

We used Google text-to-speech to generate the spoken utterances of the questions. Google Voice *en-US-Standard-B* was used to generate $239,746$ spoken questions in male voice and Google Voice *en-US-Wavenet-C* was used to generate $16,730$ spoken questions in female voice. All samples are in US accented English. The ASR lattice was extracted using Kaldi ASR [12] and converted to a confusion network for compact representation using SRILM [14]. We used

---

[1] Code and dataset at: https://github.com/kolk/ConfnetPointerGenBaseline.

the pre-trained ASpIRE Chain Model which has been trained on Fisher English to transcribe the spoken question and extract the ASR lattices. The training dataset has a WER of 22.94% and test set has a WER of 37.57% on the best hypothesis of the ASR, while the cross-dataset evaluation test sets- NewsQA has a WER of 34.60% and Freebase has a WER of 43.80%.

5   Experiments and Results

We built our system over OpenNMT-Py [3]. We used a batch size of 32, dropout rate of 0.5, RNN size of 512 and decay steps 10000. The maximum number of parallel arcs in the confusion network and maximum sentence length are set to 20 and 50 respectively. The confusion network contains noise and interjections such as *DELETE* and [noise], [laughter], uh, oh which leads to degradation in system performance. To mitigate the effect of such noise, we remove the whole set of parallel arcs if all the arcs are noise and interjection words. As shown in Table 1, the pruned confusion network, named clean confnet, outperforms the system marginally for the SQuAD/HarvestingQA dataset. We also compare the system with a model trained on the best hypothesis of the extracted from the ASR lattice using Kaldi. Here, the confusion network encoder is replaced with a text encoder which shares weights with the factoid answer encoder.

As shown in Table 1, we observe for SQuAD/HarvestingQA dataset that the Best-ASR-hypothesis outperforms the clean confusion network model with a 5% margin in BLEU score and 2% margin in ROGUE-L score. To asses the cross-domain generalizability, we also perform cross-dataset evaluation by evaluating our models on 840 samples of a KB based dataset (Freebase) and 470 samples of a machine comprehension dataset (NewsQA). The clean confusion network marginally outperforms the best-hypothesis model in ROGUE scores for cross-dataset evaluation and gives comparable results on BLEU scores. This shows that the confusion network system generalizes better on cross-domain noisy data and is less sensitive to noise introduced by new domains and noisy input signal, when compared with the Best-ASR-Hypothesis model. A plausible reason to this could be that the confusion network model is itself trained on a closed set of hypothesis, as compared to the Best-ASR-Hypothesis model which makes simplifying assumptions about the input signal. A compelling extension to the confusion network model is to adapt the copy attention over all the time-aligned hypotheses of the confusion network input. This would allow the confusion network model to copy among top-N words at any given time-step of the confusion network, instead of an erroneous word with the highest ASR score.

An example of results on a SQuAD/HarvestingQA test sample is in Table 1.

- **Gold Question:** what was the title of the sequel to conan the barbarian?
- **Top-Hypothesis:** what was the title of the sequels are counting the barbarian
- **Factoid Answer:** conan the destroyer
- **Full-length Answer:** the title of the sequel to conan the barbarian was conan the destroyer

Table 1. Top section shows the scores on 1000 SQuAD/HarvestingQA test samples. Bottom 2 section shows the scores for cross-dataset evaluation on a Knowledge-Base (Freebase) dataset and a machine comprehension (NewsQA) dataset. For each section, the top row displays the score on the best hypothesis of the confusion network, the middle row displays the scores on the confusion network, while the bottom row displays the results on the pruned clean confusion network

Test dataset	Input	BLEU	ROGUE-1	ROGUE-2	ROGUE-L
SQuAD/HarvestingQA	Best hypothesis	**60.26**	**82.43**	**70.61**	**78.21**
	Confnet	55.38	81.60	68.02	76.68
	Clean confnet	55.92	81.39	67.79	76.78
Freebase	Best hypothesis	**43.21**	71.37	51.72	64.98
	Confnet	41.86	72.42	51.84	**65.78**
	Clean confnet	42.89	**72.54**	**52.77**	66.39
NewsQA	Best hypothesis	49.98	75.82	59.59	72.65
	Confnet	53.45	**76.45**	60.32	72.78
	Clean confnet	**56.86**	76.07	**61.18**	**73.12**

- **Clean Confnet Model prediction:** the title of the sequels to the barbarian was conan the destroyer
- **Best-Hypothesis Model prediction:** the title of the sequels are counting the barbarian

6   Conclusion

We propose the task of generating full-length natural answers from spoken questions and factoid answer. We generated a dataset consisting of triples (spoken question, factoid answer, full length answer) and extracted confusion network from the questions. We have used the pointer-network over ASR graphs (confusion network) and show that it gives comparable results to the model trained on the best hypothesis. Our system achieves a BLEU score of 55.92% and ROGUE-L score of 76.78% on SQuAD/HarvestingQA dataset. We perform cross-dataset evaluation to obtain a BLEU score of 42.89% and ROGUE-L score of 66.39% on Freebase, and a BLEU score of 56.86% and ROGUE-L score of 73.12% on NewsQA dataset.

References

1. Hakkani-Tür, D., Béchet, F., Riccardi, G., Tür, G.: Beyond ASR 1-best: using word confusion networks in spoken language understanding. Comput. Speech Lang. **20**(4), 495–514 (2006). https://doi.org/10.1016/j.csl.2005.07.005
2. Jagfeld, G., Vu, N.T.: Encoding word confusion networks with recurrent neural networks for dialog state tracking. CoRR abs/1707.05853 (2017). http://arxiv.org/abs/1707.05853

3. Klein, G., Kim, Y., Deng, Y., Senellart, J., Rush, A.M.: OpenNMT: open-source toolkit for neural machine translation. In: Proceedings of the ACL (2017). https://doi.org/10.18653/v1/P17-4012

4. Ladhak, F., Gandhe, A., Dreyer, M., Mathias, L., Rastrow, A., Hoffmeister, B.: LatticeRnn: recurrent neural networks over lattices. In: INTERSPEECH (2016)

5. Lee, C., Wang, S., Chang, H., Lee, H.: ODSQA: open-domain spoken question answering dataset. CoRR abs/1808.02280 (2018). http://arxiv.org/abs/1808.02280

6. Li, C., Wu, S., Liu, C., Lee, H.: Spoken squad: a study of mitigating the impact of speech recognition errors on listening comprehension. CoRR abs/1804.00320 (2018). http://arxiv.org/abs/1804.00320

7. Liu, C., He, S., Liu, K., Zhao, J.: Curriculum learning for natural answer generation. In: IJCAI, pp. 4223–4229. ijcai.org (2018)

8. Masumura, R., Ijima, Y., Asami, T., Masataki, H., Higashinaka, R.: Neural ConfNet classification: fully neural network based spoken utterance classification using word confusion networks. In: 2018 IEEE International Conference on Acoustics, Speech and Signal Processing, ICASSP 2018, pp. 6039–6043, April 2018. https://doi.org/10.1109/ICASSP.2018.8462030

9. Pal, V., Guillot, F., Shrivastava, M., Renders, J.M., Besacier, L.: Modeling ASR ambiguity for dialogue state tracking using word confusion networks. In: INTERSPEECH 2020, Shanghai, China (2020, in press). https://arxiv.org/abs/2002.00768

10. Pal, V., Shrivastava, M., Bhat, I.: Answering naturally: factoid to full length answer generation. In: Proceedings of the 2nd Workshop on New Frontiers in Summarization, Hong Kong, China, pp. 1–9. Association for Computational Linguistics, November 2019. https://doi.org/10.18653/v1/D19-5401. https://www.aclweb.org/anthology/D19-5401

11. Pennington, J., Socher, R., Manning, C.D.: Glove: global vectors for word representation. In: EMNLP (2014)

12. Povey, D., et al.: The Kaldi speech recognition toolkit. In: IEEE 2011 Workshop on Automatic Speech Recognition and Understanding. IEEE Signal Processing Society, December 2011. IEEE Catalog No.: CFP11SRW-USB

13. See, A., Liu, P.J., Manning, C.D.: Get to the point: summarization with pointer-generator networks. CoRR abs/1704.04368 (2017). http://arxiv.org/abs/1704.04368

14. Stolcke, A.: SRILM-an extensible language modeling toolkit. In: Proceedings of the 7th International Conference on Spoken Language Processing (ICSLP 2002), pp. 901–904 (2002)

15. Unlu, M., Arisoy, E., Saraclar, M.: Question answering for spoken lecture processing, pp. 7365–7369, May 2019. https://doi.org/10.1109/ICASSP.2019.8682580

16. Zhong, V., Xiong, C., Socher, R.: Global-locally self-attentive encoder for dialogue state tracking. In: ACL (2018)

Graph Convolutional Networks
for Student Answers Assessment

Nisrine Ait Khayi$^{(\boxtimes)}$ and Vasile Rus

Institute for Intelligent Systems, University of Memphis, Memphis, TN, USA
{ntkhynyn,vrus}@memphis.edu

Abstract. Graph Convolutional Networks have achieved impressive results in multiple NLP tasks such as text classification. However, this approach has not been explored yet for the student answer assessment task. In this work, we propose to use Graph Convolutional Networks to automatically assess freely generated student answers within the context of dialogue-based intelligent tutoring systems. We convert this task to a node classification task. First, we build a DTGrade graph where each node represents the concatenation of the student answer and its corresponding reference answer whereas the edges represent the relatedness between nodes. Second, the DTGrade graph is fed to two layers of Graph Convolutional Networks. Finally, the output of the second layer is fed to a softmax layer. The empirical results showed that our model reached the state-of-the-art results by obtaining an accuracy of 73%.

Keywords: Graph Convolutional Networks · Student answers assessment · Intelligent tutoring systems

1 Introduction

Student answers assessment or short text grading is a well-defined problem in Natural Language Processing (NLP). It is a an extremely challenging task as students can express the same answer in multiple ways owing to different individual styles and varied cognitive abilities and knowledge levels. Table 1 shows four answers, articulated by four different college students, to a question asked by the state-of-the-art intelligent tutoring system (ITS) DeepTutor [13]. It should be noted that all four student answers in Table 1 are correct answers to the tutor question. As can be seen from the table, some students write full sentences (student answer A4), some others write very short answers (A3), and yet other students write elaborate answers that include additional concepts relative to the reference answer (A1).

Assessing the freely generated student answers in conversational tutoring can be achieved using various approaches. Semantic similarity is a widely adopted and scalable approach in which the student answer is compared to a reference answer produced by an expert. Typically, a normalized semantic similarity score, from 0 to 1 (or from 0 to 5), between the student answer and the expert answer

© Springer Nature Switzerland AG 2020
P. Sojka et al. (Eds.): TSD 2020, LNAI 12284, pp. 532–540, 2020.
https://doi.org/10.1007/978-3-030-58323-1_57

Table 1. Examples of student answers showing the diversity of responses from Deep-Tutor

Problem description:
While speeding up, a large truck pushes a small compact car
Tutor question:
How do the magnitudes of forces they exert on each other compare?
Reference answer:
The forces from the truck and car are equal and opposite
Student answers:
A1. The magnitudes of the forces are equal and opposite to each other Due to Newton's third law of motion
A2. they are equal and opposite in direction
A3. equal and opposite
A4. the truck applies an equal and opposite force to the car

is generated. A high score implies that the student answer is correct, and a low score implies the student answer is incorrect.

More recently deep learning has shown its effectiveness in solving the students answers assessment task [1,2,9,11]. These deep learning models have the advantage of capturing semantic and syntactic information for the text input. Graph Convolutional Networks, in particular, have received a growing attention recently [4,6]. Graph neural networks have been effective at tasks that have rich relational structure and can preserve global structure information of a graph in graph embeddings.

In this paper, we propose a novel approach based on Graph Convolutional Networks [15], for the students answers assessment task. We construct a DTGrade graph where each node consists of the concatenation of a student answer and its corresponding reference answer. We model the graph with a Graph Convolutional Network (GCN) that encodes relevant information about its neighborhood as a real-valued feature vector. The edge between two nodes is built using word frequency and word's document frequency method and an embedding based method. Then, we turn the assessment task into a node classification task.

The rest of the paper is organized as follows: Sect. 2 presents a review of several prior research works that used Graph Convolutional Networks for different NLP tasks. Section 3 explains the proposed approach. Section 4 summarizes the conducted experiments to evaluate the performance of our approach and the results obtained on the DT-Grade dataset. Finally, we discuss conclusions and highlight future research directions to improve results and overcome the limitations.

2   Related Work

Graph Convolutional Networks (GCN) have yielded great results in multiple NLP tasks. For instance, Sahu and colleagues [14] proposed a novel inter-sentence relation extraction model that builds a labelled edge Graph Convolutional Network on a document-level graph. The experimental results showed that the model has achieved a comparable performance to state-of-the-art neural models on the inter-sentence relation extraction task. Working on the same task, Zhang and colleagues [17] proposed a novel model for the relation extraction task. Their model consists of the following components: 1) an instance encoder based on convolutional neural networks (CNN) to encode the instance semantics into a vector, 2) a relational knowledge learning component that employs graph convolutional networks to learn explicit relational knowledge, and 3) a knowledge-aware attention component to select the most informative instance that matches the relevant relation. The experimental results showed that this model outperforms several baselines such as CNN. GCNs have been applied successfully as well for the semantic role labeling task that can be described as the task of discovering in texts who did what to whom. To this end, Marcheggiani and colleagues [12] have proposed a model that consists of the following components: 1) word embeddings, 2) a BiLSTM encoder that takes as input the embedding representation of each word, 3) a syntax-based GCN encoder that re-encodes the BiLSTM representation based on the predicted syntactic structure of the sentence, and 4) a classifier to predict the role associated with each word. The empirical results showed that this based GCN model has achieved the state-of-the-art results. GCNs have been explored successfully in text classification. For this purpose, Yao and colleagues [16] proposed to use Graph Convolutional Networks for text classification. They built a single text graph for the whole corpus based on word co-occurrence and document word relations then learnt a Text Graph Convolutional Network for the corpus. The proposed model has been evaluated using multiple benchmarks. The experimental results showed that GCN outperforms several baselines such as Bi-Directional LSTM and LSTM. In this work, we don't consider a heterogenous graph where nodes present words and documents. The nodes represent documents only as a concatenation between student answers and reference answers. Based on these successes of Graph Convolutional Networks on NLP related tasks, we have explored their potential for assessing student answers. To the best of our knowledge, this is the first attempt at using GCNs for assessing student generated answers in conversational intelligent tutoring systems.

3   Proposed Method

Our proposed method consists of building first a graph from the DTGrade. The built graph is fed into two GCN layers. Finally, we apply a classifier to predict the class of each text node (Fig. 1).

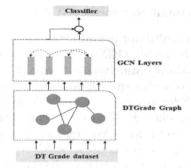

Fig. 1. The model architecture consists of: 1) building a DTGraph, 2) feeding it to two GCN layers, and finally 3) applying a classifier

3.1 DT-Grade Graph

We build a text graph from the DT-Grade dataset based on the citation relation approach [15]. We consider each document, whose content is the combination of the student answer and its corresponding reference answer, as a node. Thus, the classification of a pair of student answer and reference answer turns to a node classification task. The number of the nodes in the text graph is 900 which is the number of instances in the DT-Grade dataset. Formally given a graph G = (V,E) where V and E are sets of nodes and edges. The weight of the edge between two nodes is calculated using two methods: a TF-IDF method and an embedding based method. In the first one, we compute the term frequency-inverse document frequency (TF-IDF) between two text nodes. We add an edge between two nodes if the weight is above a threshold of 0.9. The second method is based on word2vec embeddings. First, word2vec is used to learn a vector representation for each word in the text representing each node. Then, we compute the Word Mover's Distance (WMD) to measure the similarity between two texts representing two nodes in the graph. Texts that share many words should have smaller distances than texts with very dissimilar words. WMD has been introduced to measure the distance between two text documents that takes into account the alignments between words. In this paper, we consider the text associated with each node as a short document. The WMD algorithm finds the values of an auxiliary 'transport' matrix T, such that Tij describes how much d_i^a should be transported to. The WMD learns T to minimize:

$$D(x_i, x_j) = \min_{T>=0} \sum_{i,j=1}^{n} T_{ij}||x_i - x_j||_2^p \qquad (1)$$

Subject to: $\sum_{i,j=1}^{n} T_{ij} = d_i^a, \sum_{i,j=1}^{n} T_{ij} = d_i^b$
where: d_i^a and d_i^b are the n-dimensional normalized bag-of-vectors for the two nodes' texts, $x_i \in R^d$ is the embedding vector of the ith word and p is usually set to 1 or 2. The resulted graph is fed afterwards into a two-layers GCN, as explained next.

3.2   Graph Convolutional Networks (GCN)

GCN is a recent class of multilayer neural networks that operate on graphs [8, 15]. For every node in the graph, GCN encodes relevant information about its neighborhood as a real-valued feature vector. Formally given a graph $G = (V, E)$ where V and E are sets of nodes and edges. Every node is assumed to connect with itself, i.e., $(v, v) \in E$ for any v. Let $X \in R^{n \times m}$ be a matrix containing all n nodes with their features, where m is the dimension of the feature vectors, each row $x_i \in R$ is the feature vector for v. We consider A an adjacency matrix of the graph G and its degree matrix D where $D_{ii} = \sum_j A_{ij}$. When using GCN with multiple layers, the information about larger neighbors is captured. Following the recommendation of Kipf et al. [15] that multiple layers yield better performance, we consider multiple layers of GCN. The new k-dimensional node feature matrix of layer $L^{(j+1)}$ is computed as following:

$$L^{(j+1)} = p(\tilde{A}L^{(j)}W_j) \tag{2}$$

where $\tilde{A} = D^{-1/2}AD^{-1/2}$ is the normalized symmetric adjacency matrix and W_j is a weight matrix and p is an activation matrix and $L^{(0)} = X$.

3.3   The Classifier

The output of the second GCN layer is fed into a softmax layer as following:

$$Z = softmax(\tilde{A}ReLU(\tilde{A}XW_0)W_j) \tag{3}$$

where $\tilde{A} = D^{-1/2}AD^{-1/2}$ is the normalized symmetric adjacency matrix, W_j, W_0 are weight parameters and $softmax(x_i) = \exp(x_i) \div \sum_i \exp(x_i)$. $\tilde{A}XW_0$ contains the first layer document embeddings and $(\tilde{A}ReLU(\tilde{A}XW_0)W_j)$ contains the second layer document embeddings.

4   Experiments

Our experiments were conducted in the context of student generated answers in response to hints (in the form of questions) in conversational intelligent tutoring systems. To this end, we have used a previously annotated dataset as described next.

4.1   DT-Grade Dataset

The DT-Grade dataset [3] was created by extracting student responses from logged tutorials interactions between 36 junior level college students and a state of the art ITS. During the interactions, each student solved 9 conceptual physics problems – they had to provide the correct answer and a full justification based on Physics principles. Their answer was evaluated and if the answer was incorrect or incomplete, e.g., a full justification was not provided, a dialogue followed in which the ITS helped the student discover the solution through personalized scaffolding in the form of hints that varied in their degree of information/help provided. Each annotation instance in the DT-Grade dataset consists of the following attributes: (1) problem description (describes the scenario or context), (2) tutor question, (3) student answer (as typed by the students, i.e., without correcting spelling and grammatical errors) and (4) reference answers. In addition, the data includes the correctness class of each student answer. Each student response was categorized by human experts into one of the following four classes: (1) Correct: Answer is correct; (2) Correct-but- incomplete: The response provided by the student is correct, but something is missing; (3) Incorrect: Student answer is incorrect; and (4) Contradictory: The student answer is contradicting with the answer.

In this work, we consider only two classes: correct and incorrect. The correct answers are those labeled as "correct" in the DT-Grade dataset. All the other instances are considered "incorrect". As a result, we obtained the following class distribution shown in Table 2.

Table 2. The distribution of classes in training (800 instances) and testing data (100 instances)

Dataset	Correct(%)	Incorrect(%)
Training	41	59
Testing	41.59	58.41

4.2 Experimental Setting

Several experiments have been conducted with different parameters settings to evaluate the performance of our proposed method. To this end, we trained and evaluated a two-layer GCN using the DTGrade dataset. In all experiments, we trained our model for a maximum of 1000 epochs (training iterations) using the Categorical Cross Entropy loss function and Adam optimizer [10] with a learning rate of 0.01. We stopped the training when the validation loss does not decrease for 100 consecutive epochs, as suggested in prior works [15]. To avoid overfitting, we applied a dropout rate = 0.5. For the graph convolution layer, we used a hidden layer size of 16 units with L2 regularization and ReLU activation. We selected randomly 600 instances for training, 100 instances for validation, and 200 instances as an independent test set.

In the first set of experiments, we have used the TF-IDF approach to compute the weight of the DTGrade graph edges. Then, we repeated the experiment with the following filters: 1) local pool filter [15] which is considered as a baseline filter for Graph Convolutional Networks, 2) Chebyshev polynomial filter [7] and 3) ARMA filter [5].

In a second set of experiments, we have used the word2vec embedding with 300 dimension and WMD distance (see Sect. 3.1) to compute the weight of the edges. We report the accuracy of the model using the three filters.

4.3   Results and Analysis

Table 3 summarizes the results of using GCN with different parameters settings. Several observations can be made. First, the use of the TF-IDF method to compute the weights between the edges outperform the word2vec based method in all experiments. The highest accuracy obtained with TF-IDF was 73% versus 70% of the word2vec method. The performance degradation when using the embedding based approach may due to adding some edges between nodes that are not very related closes. This explains the incorrect assessment of many short students' responses. Added to this, the word2vec embedding based approach may not propagate label information to the whole graph well in comparison with the TF-IDF approach. Second, the empirical results show that ARMA filter outperforms the other polynomial filters regardless the method used for weighting the edges in the DTGraph. This is attributed to the implementation strategy of the ARMA filter that allows better handling of the graph variations.

The results depicted in Table 3 show also that Graph Convolutional Networks outperform the previous deep learning models: Transformer [2], Bi-GRU Capsnet [1], LSTM and Bi-GRU by obtaining the state of the-art results on the DTGrade dataset. Graph neural networks have been effective at tasks thought to have rich relational structure and can preserve global structure information of a graph in graph embeddings.

Table 3. Performance of GCN using binary encoding with different filters

Model	Accuracy
GCN (TF-IDF+localpool filter)	68
GCN (TF-IDF+ Chebyshev filter)	72
GCN (TF-IDF+ARMA filter)	**73(+0.5)**
GCN (word2vec+WMD+ localpool filter)	62.5
GCN ((word2vec+WMD+chebyshev filter)	70
GCN ((word2vec+WMD+ARMA filter)	70
Transformer Encoder+Elmo	71
Bi-GRU+Glove	56.25
LSTM + Glove	60
Bi-GRU Capsnet+ Elmo	72.5

5 Conclusion

Motivated by good results of applying the Graph Convolutional Networks (GCN) in the NLP, we propose to use a GCN based model to assess the correctness of student answers in conversational intelligent tutoring systems. This is the first time such model is applied for this task. The results demonstrated the effectiveness of the proposed model by yielding state of the-art results on the DT-Grade dataset. A highest accuracy of 73% has been achieved when using the TF-IDF and the ARMA filter. As a future direction, we are planning to explore more novel deep learning models that perform well on a small size of dataset such as ours.

References

1. Ait Khayi, N., Rus, V.: Bi-GRU Capsnet for student answers assessment. In: The 2019 KDD Workshop on Deep Learning for Education (DL4Ed) in Conjunction With the 25th ACM SIGKDD Conference on Knowledge Discovery and Data Mining (KDD 2019), Anchorage, Alaska, USA (2019)
2. Ait Khayi, N., Rus, V.: Attention based transformer for student answers assessment. In: The Flairs-33rd International Conference (2020)
3. Banjade, R., Maharjan, N., Niraula, N.B., Gautam, D., Samei, B., Rus, V.: Evaluation dataset (DT-Grade) and word weighting approach towards constructed short answers assessment in tutorial dialogue context. In: The 11th Workshop on Innovative Use of NLP for Building Educational Applications, pp. 182–187 (2016)
4. Battaglia, P.W., et al: Relational inductive biases, deep learning, and graph network. arXiv preprint arXiv:1806.01261 (2018)
5. Bianchi, F.M., Grattarola, D., Alippi, C., Livi, L.: Graph neural networks with convolutional ARMA filters. arXiv preprint arXiv:1901.01343 (2019)
6. Cai, H., Zheng, V.W., Chang, K.: A comprehensive survey of graph embedding problems, techniques and applications. IEEE Trans. Knowl. Data Eng. **30**(9), 1616–1637 (2018)
7. Defferrard, M., Bresson, X., Vandergheynst, P.: Convolutional neural networks on graphs with fast localized spectral filtering. In: Advances in Neural Information Processing Systems, pp. 3844–3852 (2016)
8. Duvenaud, D., et al.: Convolutional networks on graphs for learning molecular fingerprints. In: NIPS (2015)
9. Gong, T., Yao, X.: An attention-based deep model for automatic short answer score. Int. J. Comput. Sci. Softw. Eng. **8**(6), 127–132 (2019)
10. Kingma, D.P., Ba, J.: Adam: a method for stochastic optimization. arXiv preprint arXiv:1412.6980 (2014)
11. Maharjan, N., Gautam, D., Rus, V.: Assessing free student answers in tutorial dialogues using LSTM models. In: Penstein Rosé, C., Martínez-Maldonado, R., Hoppe, H.U., Luckin, R., Mavrikis, M., Porayska-Pomsta, K., McLaren, B., du Boulay, B. (eds.) AIED 2018. LNCS (LNAI), vol. 10948, pp. 193–198. Springer, Cham (2018). https://doi.org/10.1007/978-3-319-93846-2_35
12. Marcheggiani, D., Titov, I.: Encoding sentences with graph convolutional networks for semantic role labeling. In: EMNLP (2017)
13. Rus, V., D'Mello, S.K., Hu, X., Graesser, A.C.: Recent advances in intelligent tutoring systems with conversational dialogue. AI Mag. **34**(3), 42–54 (2013)

14. Sahu, S.K., Christopoulou, F., Miwa, M., Ananiadou, S.: Inter-sentence relation extraction with document-level graph convolutional neural network. In: ACL (2019)
15. Kipf, T., Welling, M.: Semi supervised classification with graph convolutional networks. In: ICLR (2017)
16. Yao, L., Mao, C., Luo, Y.: Graph convolutional networks for text classification. In: The AAAI Conference on Artificial Intelligence, vol. 33, pp. 7370–7377 (2019)
17. Zhang, N., et al.: Long-tail relation extraction via knowledge graph embeddings and graph convolution networks. In: NAACL-HLT (2019)

Author Index

Adelani, David Ifeoluwa 273
Ait Khayi, Nisrine 532
Alekseev, Anton 222
André, Elisabeth 397
Aragón, Mario Ezra 231
Argüello-Vélez, Patricia 303
Arias-Vergara, Tomas 303
Azarova, Irina 122

Barančíková, Petra 135
Bayerl, Sebastian P. 386
Berend, Gábor 197
Berriman, Rebekah 294
Besacier, Laurent 524
Bodnár, Jan 189
Boháč, Marek 418
Bojar, Ondřej 135
Bořil, Tomáš 348, 409
Brito, Celina Iris 495

Červa, Petr 426
Cook, Paul 153, 248

Dahiya, Anirudh 240
Dang, Chi Tai 397
Davody, Ali 273
Dy, Jilyan Bianca 495

Fegyó, Tibor 437
Ficsor, Tamás 197
Fidalgo, Robson 257
Fohr, Dominique 377
Franco, Natália 257
Funk, Adam 3

George, Elizabeth Jasmi 206
Giachanou, Anastasia 30
González, Luis C. 231
González-Rátiva, María Claudia 303
Gosztolya, Gábor 285
Gurbani, Vijay K. 312

Hanzlíček, Zdeněk 456
Helali, Mossad 265

Hévrová, Marie 348
Hlubík, Pavel 418
Hönig, Florian 386
Horák, Aleš 112
Hosier, Jordan 312

Illina, Irina 377
Ircing, Pavel 214, 321

James, Jesin 294
Janicki, Artur 477, 513
Jayan, A. R. 71
Jónsson, Haukur Páll 95
Jůzová, Markéta 340

Kabiri, Arman 153
Kalfen, Jordan 312
Kane, Benjamin 487
Keegan, Peter J. 294
King, Milton 248
Klakow, Dietrich 265, 273
Kleinbauer, Thomas 265
Köpke, Barbara 348
Kurfalı, Murathan 79

Lehečka, Jan 214, 321
Leoni, Chiara 504
Level, Stephane 377
Loftsson, Hrafn 95
López-Monroy, A. Pastor 231

Macková, Kateřina 171
Málek, Jiří 366
Manohar, Kavya 71
Mareček, David 180
Marjanović, Saša 61
Matoušek, Jindřich 446
Maynard, Diana 3
Medveď, Marek 112
Mihajlik, Péter 437
Miletic, Aleksandra 61
Miller, Gabriel F. 356
Mírovský, Jiří 50

Mogadala, Aditya   273
Montes-y-Gómez, Manuel   231
Musil, Tomáš   180

Nikolenko, Sergey   222
Nivre, Joakim   11
Nöth, Elmar   303, 331, 356
Nouza, Jan   426

Ong, Ethel   495
Orozco-Arroyave, Juan Rafael   303, 331

Pal, Vaishali   240, 524
Paul, Soma   87
Pereira, Jayr   257
Pikuliak, Matúš   162
Platonov, Georgiy   487
Poláková, Lucie   50
Ponzetto, Simone Paolo   41
Pražák, Aleš   465
Psutka, Josef V.   465

Radej, Adrian   513
Rajan, Rajeev   71
Reister, Joëlle   386
Riedhammer, Korbinian   386
Rios-Urrego, Cristian David   331
Robnik-Šikonja, Marko   104
Rosa, Rudolf   180
Rosso, Paolo   30, 41
Rus, Vasile   532

Sabol, Radoslav   112
Sánchez-Junquera, Javier   41
Santos, Kyle-Althea   495
Saxena, Prateek   87
Schubert, Lenhart   487
Schuster, Maria Elke   303
Ševčíková, Magda   189
Sharma, Dipti Misra   240
Sharma, Nikhita   312

Shields, Isabella   294
Shrivastava, Manish   240, 524
Šimko, Marián   162
Símonarson, Haukur Barri   95
Šmídl, Luboš   214, 321
Snæbjarnarson, Vésteinn   95
Sowański, Marcin   477
Španěl, Martin   418
Steingrímsson, Steinþór   95
Stosic, Dejan   61
Straka, Milan   171
Švec, Jan   214, 321
Szaszák, György   437

Tarján, Balázs   437
Terzić, Dušica   61
Thomas, Aleena   273
Tihelka, Daniel   340
Torre, Ilaria   504

Ulčar, Matej   104
Ureta, Jennifer   495

Vaněk, Jan   465
Vásquez-Correa, Juan Camilo   331, 356
Vercelli, Gianni   504
Veroňková, Jitka   409
Vetráb, Mercedes   285
Vidra, Jonáš   144
Villaluna, Winfred   495
Vít, Jakub   456
Vraštil, Michal   446

Watson, Catherine I.   294
Weingartová, Lenka   418
Wülfing, Jan-Oliver   397

Žabokrtský, Zdeněk   144, 189
Zakharov, Victor   122
Žďánský, Jindřich   366, 426
Zhang, Guobiao   30

Printed in the United States
By Bookmasters